CW00417855

THE OXFORD HANDBOOK OF

PROJECT
MANAGEMENT

THE OXFORD HANDBOOK OF

PROJECT MANAGEMENT

Edited by

PETER W. G. MORRIS

JEFFREY K. PINTO

and

JONAS SÖDERLUND

OXFORD

UNIVERSITY PRESS

OXFORD
UNIVERSITY PRESS

Great Clarendon Street, Oxford OX2 6DP

Oxford University Press is a department of the University of Oxford.
It furthers the University's objective of excellence in research, scholarship,
and education by publishing worldwide in

Oxford New York

Auckland Cape Town Dar es Salaam Hong Kong Karachi
Kuala Lumpur Madrid Melbourne Mexico City Nairobi
New Delhi Shanghai Taipei Toronto

With offices in

Argentina Austria Brazil Chile Czech Republic France Greece
Guatemala Hungary Italy Japan Poland Portugal Singapore
South Korea Switzerland Thailand Turkey Ukraine Vietnam

Oxford is a registered trade mark of Oxford University Press
in the UK and in certain other countries

Published in the United States
by Oxford University Press Inc., New York

British Library Cataloguing in Publication Data
Data available

Library of Congress Cataloging in Publication Data
Data available

Typeset by SPI Publisher Services, Pondicherry, India
Printed in Great Britain
on acid-free paper by
MPG Books Group, Bodmin and King's Lynn

ISBN 978–0–19–956314–2

1 3 5 7 9 10 8 6 4 2

PREFACE

PROJECTS are a ubiquitous part of our social and commercial life; their contributions serve as milestones in mankind's development, cultural achievements, and technical advances. But while "projects" have a long and honored history, "project management" has been, at best, an informal discipline, at least until the 1950s. Since then, however, its formal development has recast it as increasingly popular, and necessary, so much so that it is now a mainstream subject of general management.

Its growth over this past half-century has been heavily practitioner-led. Initially characterized by the tools and techniques it used, it was, and to a large extent still is, heavily execution-oriented (to complete an undertaking "on time, in budget, to scope"). Only towards the end of the twentieth century did a broader perspective begin to enter: one concerned with the front-end development period as much as the downstream delivery; one interested in the institutional conditions surrounding and enabling projects; one recognizing that projects are produced by, with, and for people who work together in unique organizational and commercial contexts based on the need to grapple with time-bound, budget-constrained, largely technical issues. Working with this broader, bigger canvas, a far richer landscape has emerged, and as the relevance of managing projects effectively within the modern economy has become more evident, so academic interest in the area has grown. No longer is project management a branch of production management, it is now— well, what?

Project management is many things to many people. Its vibrancy is obvious—as testified by the astonishing number of conferences held on it around the world every year. It continues to develop at a rapid pace, both conceptually and in its practical influence. As this book shows, it is still open to many different interpretations, at several different levels.

Academic scholarship has an important role in shaping this development: in sense-making and path-building; in bringing rigor, improving understanding, and teaching good practice. Yet to date there are very few books which address the subject comprehensively from a solid academic research perspective (or perspectives). That's what we've begun to do with this book.

The book is not the definitive compendium on the complete intellectual base to the management of projects. The field is too large for that, and frankly, as a rapidly emerging discipline, it would not be possible for any one book to find the perfect moment to capture and bottle it—not yet at any rate. But it does present and discuss many of the leading ideas in the domain, doing so by drawing on the contributions of over forty of the world's foremost academics in the area.

We'd like to begin this book therefore by acknowledging our thanks to all our contributors, most of whom have had to put up with a fairly extended critiquing and editing process: thanks then for their patience; thanks above all for the quality of their contributions. For us, the book's editors, this has been quite an extraordinary process: we are amazed at how positively everyone responded to the many challenges that were thrown up.

In acknowledging the contributors we'd also like to thank all the institutions and people who, whether directly or indirectly, made possible our work in putting this book together: to our employers and colleagues, to our families (bless them all).

Thanks finally to OUP for taking the initiative to suggest this book, and for publishing it.

We believe passionately in this field. We hope the book reflects this, and the commitment all have brought to bear in writing it. We hope therefore, above all, that you, our readers, will find it stimulating and useful.

Peter Morris
Jeffrey Pinto
Jonas Söderlund

Contents

PART I: HISTORY AND FOUNDATIONS

PART II: INDUSTRY AND CONTEXT

PART III: STRATEGY AND DECISION-MAKING

PART IV: GOVERNANCE AND CONTROL

List of Figures

LIST OF TABLES

LIST OF CONTRIBUTORS

Karlos Artto is a Professor of Project Business at Aalto University, Finland, where he leads the Project Business research group. His publications include more than 100 academic papers, book chapters, and books on project business and on the management of project-based firms. He belongs to several editorial boards of academic journals. He has supervised more than 100 master's theses and several doctoral dissertations.

Kjesti Bjørkeng is Senior Researcher at SINTEF Technology and Society and a core member of Centre for Management and Organization Studies Research at the University of Technology, Sydney. She has published her research in books and handbooks and in journals such as *Management Learning* and *Society and Business Review*. Her primary interest areas are organizational knowing and learning viewed from a practice-based perspective.

Tim Brady has been researching innovation and innovation management since 1980, joining CENTRIM (Centre for Research in Innovation Management) at the University of Brighton in 1994. He was Deputy Director of the ESRC-funded CoPS Innovation Centre. A member of the EPSRC's "Rethinking Project Management" Network, he organized the 2007 IRNOP research conference. Current research interests include learning and capability development in project-based business.

Christophe Bredillet is Dean and Provost at SKEMA Business School, Lille, France. He is Professor of Strategy, Programme, and Project Management and Director of Postgraduate Studies. He is editor of the *Project Management Journal*. His interests and research activities cover principles and theories of project management and business dynamics.

Mike Bresnen is Professor of Organisation Studies at Manchester Business School, University of Manchester. He is Associate Editor of *Organisation* and a founding member of the Innovation, Knowledge, and Organisational Networking (IKON) research center based at Warwick Business School. He has researched and published widely on the organization and management of the construction process, as well as on inter-organizational relations, project management, and innovation in the biomedical field.

Stewart Clegg is Research Professor and Director of the Centre for Management and Organization Studies Research at the University of Technology, Sydney. He is also a Visiting Professor at Copenhagen Business School and EM-Lyon. A prolific publisher in leading academic journals in social science, management, and organization theory, he is also the author and editor of many books, including *Handbook of Power*, *Handbook of Macro-Organization Behaviour*, and *Handbook of Organization Studies*.

Bernard Cova is Professor of Marketing at Euromed Management, Marseilles, France, and Visiting Professor at Bocconi University, Milan, Italy. For twenty-five years he has worked on the development of a specific marketing approach to assist companies selling projects and solutions. He is also known for his research on communal consumption and collaborative marketing approaches.

Andrew Davies is Reader in the Innovation and Entrepreneurship Group and Co-Director of the EPSRC Innovation Studies Centre, at Imperial College Business School, Imperial College, London. His research focuses on innovation in projects and project-based firms. He is author of *The Business of Projects: Managing Innovation in Complex Products and Systems*, Cambridge University Press (2005), co-authored with Michael Hobday.

Bent Flyvbjerg is Professor and Founding Chair of Major Programme Management at Oxford University and Founding Director of Oxford's BT Centre for Major Programme Management. He was twice a Visiting Fulbright Scholar to the USA, where he did research at UCLA, UC Berkeley, and Harvard. His books include *Megaprojects and Risk* and *Decision-Making on Mega-Projects*. His publications have been translated into eighteen languages.

Hans Georg Gemuenden is a Professor at Berlin University of Technology (TU Berlin), where he holds the Chair for Technology and Innovation Management. He has written several books and many articles in the fields of innovation and technology management, entrepreneurship, project management, strategy, marketing, and accounting, published in *Organization Science, Research Policy, Management International Review, International Journal of Project Management*, and other journals.

Joana Geraldi is a Lecturer in the School of Construction and Project Management at UCL. Her research involves the management of change and complexity in projects and programs and how organizations create a context for project and program work. She has authored and co-authored several articles, published mainly in the *International Journal of Project Management* and the *Project Management Journal*. She was awarded the 2008 IPMA and APM research awards.

Nuno A. Gil earned a Ph.D. in Engineering from UC Berkeley, after professional practice stints in structural engineering and project management. He joined the

Manchester Business School in 2004. He focuses his research on the delivery of large engineering projects/programmes, investigating development processes, design architectures, contracting strategies, and governance structures. A key element that ties his research together is a focus on new infrastructure development.

Gernot Grabher is Professor of Urban and Regional Economic Studies at the Hafen City University, Hamburg. He has held Visiting positions at the Center for Advanced Study in the Behavioral Sciences, Columbia University and at Stanford University, Cornell University, Santa Fe Institute, and Copenhagen Business School. He is co-editor of *Economic Geography* and the *Regions and Cities* book series of the Regional Studies Association, and is an editorial board member of six international geography journals.

Markus Hällgren is an Assistant Professor at the Umeå School of Business, Sweden. His primary research interest is projects-as-practice and organization theory applied to projects. He is currently studying the practice of managing deviations in construction projects and of managing innovation in distributed systems, as well as group dynamics in mountain climbing expeditions.

Mike Hobday is Professor of Innovation Management at CENTRIM (Centre for Research in Innovation Management), Brighton University. His research includes innovation in complex products and systems. As well as many journal publications, he is the author of various books including *The Business of Projects: Managing Innovation in Complex Products and Systems*, with Andrew Davies, Cambridge University Press, 2005.

Damian Hodgson is Senior Lecturer in Organisational Analysis and a member of the Centre for Research in the Management of Projects at the Manchester Business School. His research focuses on the professionalization of project management and contemporary processes of organizational and societal projectification. He is co-convenor of a series of workshops entitled "Making Projects Critical".

Martin Hoegl is a Professor at WHU–Otto Beisheim School of Management (Germany), where he holds the Chair of Leadership and Human Resource Management. His main research interests include leadership and collaboration in project-based organizations. He has published in leading international journals, including the *Academy of Management Journal, Journal of International Business Studies, Journal of Management, MIT Sloan Management Review, Organization Science*, and others.

Oliver Ibert is Professor of Economic Geography at the Free University of Berlin and head of the research unit "Regionalization and Economic Spaces" at the

Leibniz-Institute for Regional Development and Structural Planning (IRS) in Erkner. In 2002 he received his Ph.D. in social sciences from the University of Oldenburg. His research focuses on temporary organizations, knowledge practices, user-induced innovation, and planning theory.

Stylianos Kavadias is the Edward J. Brown Jr. Associate Professor of Technology and Operations Management at the College of Management of Georgia Tech. His research focuses on the strategic, organizational, and process determinants of resource allocation in project portfolios, and has published frequently in *Management Science*. He teaches project management and product development in MBA and executive programs at Georgia Tech.

Jaakko Kujala is a Professor of Project and Quality Management at the University of Oulu, Finland. He has over ten years' experience in the automation system industry and has initiated several large research projects with the participation of leading project-based firms, such as Nokia Siemens Networks, Kone, Wärtsilä, and Metso. His research interests include contextual variables and business models in project-based firms.

Raymond Levitt is Professor of Civil and Environmental Engineering at Stanford University where he directs the Collaboratory for Research on Global Projects and the Stanford Advanced Project Management executive program. His research group developed SimVision® to predict and mitigate schedule and quality risks on fast-track projects. Dr Levitt co-founded and is a Director of Design Power, Vité, and Visual Network Design.

Lars Lindkvist is Professor of Business Administration at the Department of Management and Engineering, Linköping University, where he is a member of the KITE Research Group. His work within the area of project organization and knowledge processes is published in *Journal of Management Studies*, *Organization Studies*, *Management Learning*, *Journal of Management and Governance*, and *International Journal of Project Management*.

Christoph Loch is Chaired Professor of Technology Management at INSEAD. His research interests revolve around R&D management, project management, strategy deployment, and motivating professionals. He has published four books and fifty articles in leading journals, of which twenty are co-authored with practicing managers. He holds a Wirtschaftsingenieur degree from the Darmstadt Institute of Technology, an MBA from the University of Tennessee, and a Ph.D. from Stanford University.

Nick Marshall is a Senior Research Fellow in the Centre for Research in Innovation Management at the University of Brighton. His research and publications are primarily in the area of organizational knowledge, learning, and innovation, especially in project-based and other temporary settings. Before joining CENTRIM in 1999 Nick was a Research Fellow at Warwick Business School. He holds a Ph.D. from King's College London.

Eunice Maytorena is a Lecturer in Construction Project Management at the Manchester Business School. An architect by training, her work includes architectural design and consultancy, research in various aspects of the built environment, and project management. Eunice has worked on several research projects investigating risk perceptions on projects. Her research interests include project management, risk management, and managerial and organizational cognition.

Peter W. G. Morris is Professor and Head of the School of Construction and Project Management at University College London (UCL). He is the author of over 110 papers and several books on the management of projects. A previous Chairman of the Association for Project Management, he was awarded the Project Management Institute's 2005 Research Achievement Award, APM's 2008 Sir Monty Finniston Life-Time Achievement Award, and IPMA's 2009 Research Award.

Miriam Muethel is Assistant Professor at the Chair of Leadership and Human Resource Management at WHU–Otto Beisheim School of Management (Germany). Her research interests comprise organizational behavior and innovation management. She has published in the *Journal of International Management, Academy of Management Proceedings*, and edited several books. Before joining WHU, Dr Muethel worked as an international project management consultant at Volkswagen.

Ralf Müller is Associate Professor at Umeå University in Sweden and Adjunct Professor at the Norwegian School of Management BI and at SKEMA Business School in France. He lectures and researches in project leadership, project governance, and research methodologies. Prior to his academic career he was worldwide Director of Project Management at NCR Corporation's Teradata Business Unit.

Daniel Muzio is a Senior Lecturer in Employment Relations at the University of Leeds. His research interests include organizational theory, the sociology of the professions, and the interface between professional organizations and professional occupations. He has published widely in a range of leading academic journals. He has also edited *Redirections in the Study of Expertise* (Palgrave, 2007) on the transformation of medicine, law, and management consultancy.

David Partington is a chartered mechanical engineer whose career spans four decades as a designer, manager, teacher, researcher, writer, and consultant. He gained his Ph.D. from Cranfield School of Management, where he has worked since 1995. He is author of the Proaction suite of project management training simulations.

Sergio Pellegrinelli is Director of SP Associates and Visiting Fellow at Cranfield School of Management. He is an experienced strategy consultant and management development professional and works for numerous international clients. He has conducted research, published papers, and presented at international conferences on programme management competence and practices, strategy development and implementation, and the role of management consultants.

Jeffrey K. Pinto holds the Andrew Morrow and Elizabeth Lee Black Chair in the Management of Technology at Penn State University. He is the author or editor of 23 books and over 120 scientific papers. Dr Pinto is a two-time recipient of the Distinguished Contribution Award from the Project Management Institute (1997, 2001) for outstanding service to the project management profession. He received PMI's Research Achievement Award in 2009.

Tyrone S. Pitsis is Reader at the Faculty of Business, University Technology, Sydney, and co-director of the Centre for Management and Organization Studies. His research interest is positive psychology of organizational innovation through project-based organizing. He has several Australian Research Council grants, and has published papers in leading journals and books. His latest publication is *Handbook of Organizational & Managerial Innovation* (Elgar-Allen, 2008).

Andrea Prencipe is Professor of Innovation at the University G. d'Annunzio and Honorary Professor at SPRU (University of Sussex). His research interests encompass learning in project-based organizations, modularity, social capital, and innovation processes. Andrea sits on the editorial boards of *Long Range Planning* and *Organization Science*.

Robert Salle is Professor of Business Marketing at the EM Lyon Business School, France. His research activities focus on project marketing and solution selling. He also lectures and consults on B2B for industrial companies; one of his favorite topics being relationship portfolio management. He participated in the creation of the Industrial Marketing and Purchasing Group in the early 1980s.

Hedley Smyth is a Senior Lecturer in the School of Construction and Project Management at UCL. His teaching responsibilities are for Enterprise Management and his research particularly focuses upon relationship marketing and management, and on trust at the interface between clients and contractors and between the project and corporate body.

Anders Söderholm is a Professor of Management at the Mid Sweden University, Sweden, and is also serving as the Vice Chancellor of the university. His research interests are primarily project-based organizations and project management based on organizational theory approaches. He is the co-author of *Neo-Industrial Organising* (Routledge, 1999) and *A New Grammar of Organizing* (Edward Elgar, 2007).

Jonas Söderlund is Professor at BI Norwegian School of Management. He is a founding member of the KITE Research Group (Knowledge Integration and Innovation in Transnational Enterprise) based at Linköping University. He has published widely on the management and organization of projects, project-based firms, and project competence, including papers in *Organization Studies, Human Resource Management, International Journal of Innovation Management,* and *International Business Review.*

Fredrik Tell is Professor of Management at the Department of Management and Engineering, Linköping University, and is Deputy Director of the KITE Research Group. His research includes management of complex technologies and standards, organizational knowledge, innovation and industry dynamics, and business history. He has been a visiting researcher at the London School of Economics, University of Sussex, and Stanford University.

Rodney Turner is Professor of Project Management at the SKEMA Business School, Lille, France. He is Visiting Professor at Henley Business School, the Kemmy Business School, Limerick, and the University of Technology Sydney. Rodney is the author or editor of sixteen books, and is editor of *The International Journal of Project Management.* He is Vice President, Honorary Fellow, and former chairman of the UK's Association for Project Management.

Jennifer Whyte is Reader in Innovation and Design in the School of Construction Management and Engineering at the University of Reading. As an Advanced Institute of Management (AIM) Fellow, she has been studying management practices in project-based design environments. She is a member of the Innovative Construction Research Centre (ICRC); and leads a Challenging Engineering exploration group.

Graham Winch is Professor of Project Management and Director of the Centre for Research in the Management of Projects at the Manchester Business School. He is the author of *Managing Production: Engineering Change and Stability* (OUP, 1994), and *Managing Construction Projects: An Information Processing Approach* (2nd edn. Wiley, 2010). He has published over forty refereed journal articles and numerous other papers

INTRODUCTION

TOWARDS THE THIRD WAVE OF PROJECT MANAGEMENT

PETER MORRIS, JEFFREY PINTO,
JONAS SÖDERLUND

PROJECTS AND PROJECT MANAGEMENT

PROJECTS have been with us since the coming of man (arguably even before but in different languages), certainly since the beginnings of organized hunting and farming. Mankind's earliest buildings, military campaigns, and religious festivals attest to our ability to conceive goals, develop plans for achieving them, and deliver the desired outcomes successfully. In the past we did this almost instinctively—like so many branches of management—without necessarily articulating or consciously reflecting on our way of doing so. Slowly, however, as Chapter 1 of this book outlines, tools emerged (the bar chart in the eighteenth to early twentieth centuries for example), project organization structures became formalized (project coordinators in the 1920s and the matrix organization, first proposed in the 1930s), and ultimately, in the early to mid 1950s, a fully blown discipline—project management—was articulated and mandated by the US Air Force to integrate the engineering and production of its technically complex, urgent missile development programs.

In fact, projects, in one form or another, have played a central role in delivering the innovation that drives our society today; their management, even if not always fully acknowledged, has played a decisive role in ensuring the "collective creative endeavors that...produced the communications, information, transportation and defense systems that structure our world and shape the way we live our lives" (Hughes 1998: 4).

Project management's growth since its formal articulation in the 1950s has been relentless and impressive. There are now professional project management societies in more than seventy countries with a combined membership of over half a million people (see http://www.PMI.org and http://www.IPMA.ch and Chapter 4). Over a hundred higher education institutions around the world offer university degrees in project management. Yet despite this "professional" base and the emphasis on learning and knowledge, the intellectual underpinnings of the subject have generally been at best variable, and if we are to be frank, fairly thin. Much of this is perhaps due to the tools and techniques bias of the early years of the discipline—critical path network scheduling, work breakdown structures, earned value, configuration management, and so on (many of which were conceived and applied in an environment—defense/aerospace—that was heavily shielded from external disruption). Hence project management was for many years seen as a branch of a subset of general management (production and operations), one which reflects a highly technocratic and rationalistic perspective (Packendorff 1995). A discipline divorced from what Parsons called the institutional levels of enterprise management (Parsons 1960). Indeed, this is the tradition that still dominates many of the textbooks to this day and whose positivist, normative character arguably underlies the dominant professional model of the discipline—its "body of knowledge" (PMI 2008). As such, it frames, and in our view limits and diverts, much of the public debate about the core of project management (Cicmil and Hodgson 2006).

But against this narrow view, in the 1970s and 1980s, stimulated in large part by studies of the apparent poor track record of many projects and much project management (as it was then framed)—see for example Jugdev and Müller (2005)—scholars began to think more widely about projects, what characterized successful projects and what managing them "successfully" really entails (Morris and Hough 1987) and in doing so began developing a broader view of the theoretical underpinnings of the subject. A bigger, and in many ways a more ambitious paradigm began to emerge, covering not just planning and control but technological and commercial issues, organization and people, and external matters—what Morris termed "the management of projects" (Morris 1994).

PROJECTS AS ORGANIZATIONS

The principal shift in moving to this new paradigm was the focus on the project: on what must be done to develop and deliver it successfully: the project in its context; the project as the entity that sponsors are investing in or stakeholders are reacting to; the project as it is shaped, developed, defined, and delivered. The project as the unit of analysis rather than project management processes (such as risk management, planning and scheduling, etc.) *per se*. This focus has been reinforced by subsequent studies of major projects, notably those of Miller and Lessard (2000) and Flyvbjerg, Bruzelius, and Rothengatter (2003), and has been reiterated under a variety of rubrics such as "rethinking project management" (Winter et al. 2006) and "reinventing project management" (Shenhar and Dvir 2007).

Projects in this view then are primarily organizational entities used to integrate activities and people across different organizational and disciplinary domains: organizational constructs (Lundin and Söderholm 1995) "inventing the future" in which the dynamics of management need to be addressed (Davies and Hobday 2005); "temporary organizations" requiring strategic processes, human and physical investments, and often political actions reflecting power struggles and, in some cases, public resistance.

This organizational and contextual perspective shapes the foundation for the kind of analysis that we believe is central to the domain today and which, accordingly, underlies this Handbook. This focus clearly positions project management within the realm of management and organization studies as a critical capability often needed across a range of organizations; a vital part in the practice of general management.

THE RISING ROLE OF THEORY

As the scope of the discipline has broadened, so the subject has risen progressively in its academic standing, as seen in its rising position in the literature (see Chapters 2 and 3) and in its adoption and treatment in the curricula of many business and engineering schools. Meanwhile, in parallel, project management research has risen in profile. Spurred by a number of reviews of the growing literature (see for example Packendorff 1995; Söderlund 2004a, 2004b; Pinto 2002), there has been pressure to better shape the theoretical basis of the subject and to make project management research more relevant to managers, sponsors, policy-makers, and others concerned with the management of projects, doing so without diminishing standards of academic rigor. Progress has been slow and patchy, however, though there are signs that this is now changing, both in the topics being investigated, in the way they are addressed, and in the manner in which they come together holistically as a coherent domain (Chapter 2).

Yet despite this, at this broad level of analysis and discourse there are still very few books explicitly concerned with the theoretical base of the domain, or the relevance of research. Addressing this gap is thus an explicit aim of this Handbook. Indeed, we hope this book will be an early contributor to a number of works that will address and gradually correct this lacuna. One book alone cannot do justice to the domain: it is too big and complex: this book does not answer, by a long way, all the research issues in the subject. But it does address many of the most important ones, and it suggests, both directly and through its omissions, potential avenues for future work.

GUIDING PRINCIPLES OF THE BOOK

The primary audience for this Handbook is thus intended to be the academic research community: faculty and doctoral students and those on master's degree programmes on project management and project-based organizations all over the world. It is also a book meant for practitioners wanting to know more about the kind of research agenda being pursued within project management. As such the book is intended to offer rigorous, research-oriented, and up-to-date academic views of the discipline. This subject we take to be that which is concerned with the management of projects as organizational entities in their own right, covering their context and front-end development and definition as well as their realization; and concerned with doing this effectively so that value is built and benefit realization is optimized, not just delivered efficiently "on time, in budget, to specification."

The book thus aims to:

- offer a theory-based treatment of projects and their management;
- cover more than project management *qua* implementation or execution management but instead, as we've just said, takes as its locus projects, their place in business and society, and what is involved in developing and delivering them successfully;
- address the conceptual and theoretical, as well as some of the practical, issues associated with such a broad and ambitious view of the subject area.

What the book is not is a "how to" textbook. It will not appeal to the practitioner who simply wants an authoritative guide on how to manage projects. It does not address the mechanics of how to schedule the critical path, how to derive an appropriate contracting strategy, how to estimate and track costs, how to form teams and lead people, or similar such important things. These, and many other practical matters, are ably covered elsewhere by literally dozens and dozens of books and thousands of articles—and it is frankly not really what the project management research community is much about anymore, although some of it can be important for the basic training in the skills of project management. Instead it addresses the phenomenon of projects and issues about our understanding of projects from different perspectives, and of how to manage them—particularly in different forms and in different contextual settings. It is reflective and conceptual. For as Chapter 1 concludes, the challenges now shaping the future of the domain are less about tools and techniques than about interpretive matters: about leadership as much as management; about strategy and governance, risk and uncertainty; about programs and learning, people and relationships; about information and knowledge; technology and innovation; context and philosophy.

All these are important topics—not just for postgraduate students and teachers but for researchers, managers, legislators, and other stakeholders. They should help them better understand projects: their theoretical reality: what they are and how they—and their management—differ; what kind of management and organization it takes to shape and deliver them successfully. Understanding them more fully should help us improve our language (and conceptualization) of the subject so we can better grasp and communicate the wide spectrum of knowledge and experience called upon in exploring and shaping the domain.

RESEARCHING THE THIRD WAVE

A handbook of this sort, which has engaged the contributions of some of the foremost researchers in the field across the world today, is both a reflection of the interests of the editors and an instant snapshot of the collective mindset of the scholars who participated in developing its chapters. As editors, we sought to enlist the contributions of some of the most noted project management theoreticians actively at work today, while offering some broad guidelines for the organization of the book and their proposed contributions. Not everyone, it is important to say, felt able to contribute within the timeframes we were working to. Nevertheless, the topics which the book addresses represent areas in project management research that we felt were most current and critical for building and elaborating theory. In this way, we, as editors, proposed an agenda. And yet, by the same token, this Handbook has also been a vehicle for discovery: we may have proposed, but the contributors disposed, justly accepting or modifying our suggestions within their own special experiences and current interests. Thus, producing this book led to a number of insights, some deliberately sought, some which only emerged as we edited and wrote it.

What struck us was the manner in which the major themes of the Handbook arose, not always mirroring our *a priori* suggestions but deriving and developing from a willingness on the part of editors and authors alike to explore together critical project management themes and shape them within this current work. The amount of editorial–authorial dialogue that lies behind these chapters has been quite extraordinary and well beyond our previous experience. The result is thus a collection of chapters that is neither intended nor claims to cover every critical topic or thematic element in the project management field but rather, one which reflects some of the most critical and *au courant* topics within the discipline.

The "management of projects" paradigm has been critical in pointing to a whole swathe of important, under-researched areas bearing directly on project performance, and to a great extent has moved project management on from its first wave of formalization, with its prime focus on normative tools and techniques. It provided a springboard into a new dimension for project management as an academic field—a "second-wave" paradigm, including such developments as "temporary organizations," "contingency models," and models for "rethinking project management." But what has emerged in writing this book has expanded and is taking forward this second-wave paradigm, moving it in several new directions to a putative "third wave," as judged not just by ourselves but through the persuasiveness of our leading scholars, the chapter authors—one that is more engaged with the outside looking in: with projects and their management in their institutional contexts.

Characteristics of this third wave are: (1) an interest in the theoretical foundations and history of project management; (2) an awareness of the importance of context—societal, sectoral, enterprise (the firm), business unit, project; (3) an acknowledgement of the linkages between firms (enterprises) and projects; and hence (4) an interest in the linkage between strategy and projects, and the role of projects for innovation, in inventing the "future perfect" (5) an appreciation of the role of governance and control to foster and assure effective use of resources within and across organizations; (6) an increased recognition of the role of leadership and the challenges of creating trust and building competence when operating at this level in shaping projects ("invented not found") and creating appropriate contexts for the project; and (7) seeing projects as often complex organizations involving cross-firm relationships engaged in addressing uncertainty and novelty, and facing special challenges of learning and knowledge integration.

These features have emerged as centrally important when summarizing the entire scope of the present Handbook. Hence we have grouped the chapters into six overall parts: Part I: History and Foundations, Part II: Industry and Context, Part III: Strategy and Decision-making, Part IV: Governance and Control, Part V: Contracting and Relationships, and Part VI: Organizing and Learning.

At the same time, we wanted the chapters to cross boundaries and simple distinctions and to explore common themes of importance to project management at the present stage of its development. These topics relate to the seven features identified above but they also show that many are not easily divided along traditional lines. Instead they illustrate themes that are critical to this third wave of project management: themes to do with:

- Context: Grabher and Ibert on their truly original idea of project ecologies (Chapter 7); Bresnen and Marshall on the influence of institutional theory on the shaping of practice (Chapter 6); Lindkvist on how industry types affect project learning and knowledge integration (Chapter 19).

- The two-way interaction between corporate enterprises and projects: Artto, Davies, Kujala, and Prencipe (Chapter 5) on projects as forms of business activity; Söderlund and Tell on the nature of the project-based firm (Chapter 8); Loch and Kavadias (Chapter 9) on the linkages between projects and strategy; and Cova and Salle on the role of project shaping (Chapter 16).
- The way we organize projects to deliver complex outcomes: Pellegrinelli, Partington, and Geraldi on programme management (Chapter 10); Brady and Hobday on projects and innovation (Chapter 11); Müller on project governance (Chapter 12).
- Relationships and contracting as a core dimension of organizing projects, and one which has seen major change in recent years: Bresnen and Marshall and the importance of institutional context in introducing partnering (Chapter 6); Clegg, Bjørkeng, and Pitsis on how alliancing is changing the institution of contracting and contract administration (Chapter 17); and Gil, Smyth, and Pinto on trust and partnering (Chapter 18); Cova and Salle again on networks (Chapter 16).
- New demands on people: Hoegl, Muethel, and Gemünden on teamwork and leadership in dispersed projects (Chapter 20); Hällgren and Söderholm on "projects-as-practice" (Chapter 21); and Hodgson and Muzio on project managers as professionals (Chapter 4).
- Technology and the way we work: Whyte and Levitt on the influence of information and communication technologies on the way we have managed and organized (Chapter 15); Hoegl et al. again on virtual environments (Chapter 20).
- Failure and risks (potential and perceived) and what to do about it: Winch and Maytorena on limits of classical risk and uncertainty practice (Chapter 14); Flyvbjerg on optimism bias and reference forecasting (Chapter 13); and Lindkvist again on the role of deviations to trigger learning (Chapter 19); Brady and Hobday again on innovation (Chapter 11).
- A reflective stance about the role of theory and reflective researchers and practitioners: Hällgren and Söderholm on focusing on practice as a research method (Chapter 21); Hodgson and Muzio again on the "peculiar" position of project management as a professional discipline (Chapter 4).

In moving forward we have been necessarily evaluative and critical. This is a deliberate characteristic of the book and a core theme for the first part of the book: History and Foundations. Hence Morris in Chapter 1 portrays the evolution of the subject showing how it has evolved from its initial holistic project focus, bifurcating in the late 1970s and 1980s into a normative "execution" paradigm on the one hand, and the broader project-focused one on the other. Söderlund in Chapter 2 reviews the literature and suggests a framework to arrange for unified pluralism in project management theory and discusses the need to explicate perspectives, address specific types of projects and problems, and take process into account. Turner, Pinto, and Bredillet in Chapter 3 examine the academic growth and the emerging themes within the leading project management journals over the past twenty years and document the growing awareness of research approaches, methodologies, and extant literature. Hodgson and Muzio analyze the tactics of professionalization employed within the field of project management thereby enhancing our understanding of project management as a practice and professional field of a particular kind and critically examining the prospects for a project management profession.

Being critical of course, as any researcher knows, can suggest new opportunities, and there is one such opportunity which has struck us forcibly from the emerging text. Most project management, we posit, largely relates to technical issues (analysis, design, execution, testing, etc.), performed on a commercial platform, addressed by and through people, with all the challenges this presents. Truly a modern form of socio-technical work (Burns and Stalker 1961; Emery and Trist 1960)! Yet few researchers seem to be interested in or capable of approaching the subject from this dual perspective. Partly this may reflect the formation and interests of the current research-active community. Somehow we seem unable, to date, to conceptualize as a valid field of research and teach the ménge of technical, commercial, organizational, and human issues that the real world of project management involves. Maybe this is the real challenge of the third wave, one we have only glimpsed by reflecting on what we have and have not achieved.

Positive signs

There is clearly then still a way to go and much research to be done. Which, actually, is exciting: it would be boring if we had all the answers. This Handbook offers lots of ideas for future research, and in doing so will, we are sure, position the domain of project management as an important one in management studies. Indeed, a goal of this Handbook has been to identify new challenges and new vistas for research. Hence, all chapters end with suggestions for future research and an account of unresolved issues. The fact that research works to identify new questions and new research issues is an important positive sign about the contemporary project landscape.

Projects and their management will, we believe, continue to grow as an area of interest within the broader field of general management for the foreseeable future. This is particularly true if we look at the practice of project management—a field that is highly vivid, with new applications and innovations being introduced constantly. These developments make use of, integrate, test, and challenge the theories that exist. In that sense, practice is an important source for inspiration to the project management researcher: simultaneously a test-bed for managerial innovations and theoretical ideas. So far, the practice side of project management has given the theorists plenty to think about and plenty of new ideas. But the research community too has contributed notably to practice. Precedence diagramming was invented at Berkeley; resource scheduling was the result of academic work; the MIT and Harvard auto studies of the late 1980s and early 1990s have had a huge influence on product development processes; knowledge management and organizational learning have a very strong research background; most of our "people" knowledge is research based; and the studies of major projects and of project success and failure have had a major impact on practice (see Morris 2010). This strong theory–practice interrelationship is thus a second important and positive sign for the health of the subject.

As with any research-led piece of work, an explicit aim of the book has been to strengthen the theoretical base of the domain, to draw attention to dangers, identify alternatives, and test assumptions. In that respect, the book is theory-rich. Theory builds knowledge and tries to make sense of practice. It seeks to offer new ideas to trigger improvements in practice. By explicating theoretical bases underlying the domain, communication between the academic and the practitioner communities should be strengthened. Project management scholarship not only has a critical role in shaping and critiquing theoretical perspectives, it has a duty to do so: to emphasize the importance of evidence and insist on rigor of argument. In performing this role it will shape the thinking of the people who will lead the projects of the future. It is therefore a very positive sign that the teaching and learning of project management are being addressed in an increasingly serious way through more research-focused conferences, special journal issues, wider general management publication, and better books. It is not only the topics and theories that we teach that are important but how we teach them. The development of the pedagogy of the subject is accordingly another positive sign for research in shaping project management.

It is also positive that research may sometimes give different views to similar problems and in doing so raise debate and challenge. Accordingly, there have been some pleasant inter-chapter dialogues in the book, and there are still some contrasts between the main arguments presented in the various chapters. For example, if Flyvbjerg in Chapter 13 rests his case on data, Winch and Maytorena, in Chapter 14, on risk and uncertainty, question its utility with regard to assessing future performance. At the heart of current risk management practices is the "expected utility" paradigm. This is based on the assumption, amongst several, that the distributions around the probabilities of the occurrence of a risk event, and the size of the impact should that event occur, are measurable. In fact it is often difficult to do this due to the poverty of the dataset (and hence the utility of the probabilities); the future may not be like the past; it is often difficult to quantify the impact of the event; there is the effect of time lags. The fact that we have multiple theories and multiple explanations opens up possibilities for problematizing common assumptions and conventional practice—this is a key step in knowledge development and a step that is impossible to be omitted.

In sum

What this Handbook has to offer then is much that is of contemporary interest and plenty also of future research opportunities. Indeed, it offers the beginnings of a new research agenda: a reorientation of much of the traditional focus on management "within" the project, so to speak, largely removed from context but now, here, paying more attention to the enabling institutional conditions and to the embedded, socio-technical, and processual nature of project management which, we suspect, is so distinctive about managing projects and that creates so many of its challenges.

Whether you agree or not, researchers, we are arguing, would seem—do need—to engage more widely with the full range of issues and topics that face those who are engaged practically in the management of projects. The academic community has to be able to formulate and meld conceptual frameworks that are integrative and multi-disciplinary, reflecting the mix of issues that project and program managers and their sponsors face on a daily basis; doing so from a theoretically sound position; turning theory, via data, and data via theory, efficiently into outputs which are of value to all who are interested in projects and their management.

If this Handbook helps the communities involved to do this then we will not have labored in vain, and we shall look forward to future scholarly commentaries on how best to study projects and their management in the ever-changing context of tomorrow.

References

Burns, T., and Stalker, G. M. (1961). *The Management of Innovation*. London: Tavistock.

Cicmil, S., and Hodgson, D. (2006). *Making Projects Critical*. Basingstoke: Palgrave Macmillan.

Davies, A., and Hobday, M. (2005). *The Business of Projects*. Cambridge: Cambridge University Press.

Emery, F. E., and Trist, E. L. (1960). "Socio-technical systems," in C. W. Churchman and M. Verhulst (eds.), *Management Science, Models and Techniques*, vol. ii. London: Pergamon, 83–7.

Flyvbjerg, B., Bruzelius, N., and Rothengatter, W. (2003). *Megaprojects and Risk: An Anatomy of Ambition*. Cambridge: Cambridge University Press.

Hughes, T. P. (1998). *Rescuing Prometheus*. New York: Vintage.

Jugdev, K., and Müller, R. (2005). "A retrospective look at our evolving understanding of project success," *Project Management Journal*, 36/4: 19–31.

Lundin, R. A., and Söderholm, A. (1995). "A theory of the temporary organization," *Scandinavian Journal of Management*, 11/4: 437–55.

MILLER, R., and LESSARD, D. R. (eds.) (2000). *The Strategic Management of Large Engineering Projects*. Cambridge, MA: MIT Press.

MORRIS, P. W. G. (1994). *The Management of Projects*. London: Thomas Telford.

——(2010). "Research and the future of project management," *International Journal of Managing Projects in Business*, 3/1: 138–46.

——and HOUGH, G. H. (1987). *The Anatomy of Major Projects: A Study of the Reality of Project Management*. Chichester: John Wiley & Sons Ltd.

PACKENDORFF, J. (1995). "Inquiring into the temporary organization: new directions for project management research," *Scandinavian Journal of Management*, 11/4: 319–34.

PARSONS, T. (1960). *Structure and Process in Modern Societies*. Glencoe, IL: Free Press.

PINTO, J. K. (2002). "Project Management 2002," *Research Technology Management*, 45/2: 22–37.

PROJECT MANAGEMENT INSTITUTE (2008). *A Guide to the Project Management Body of Knowledge*, 4th edn. Newton Square, PA: Project Management Institute.

SHENHAR, A., and DVIR, D. (2007). *Reinventing Project Management: The Diamond Approach to Successful Growth and Innovation*. Boston: Harvard Business School Press.

SÖDERLUND, J. (2004a). "Building theories of project management: past research, questions for the future," *International Journal of Project Management*, 22: 183–91.

——(2004b). "On the broadening scope of the research on projects: a review and a model for analysis," *International Journal of Project Management*, 22: 655–67.

WINTER, M., SMITH, C., MORRIS, P. W. G., and CICMIL, S. (2006). "Directions for future research in project management: the main findings of a UK government-funded research network," *International Journal of Project Management*, 24/8: 638–49.

PART I

HISTORY AND FOUNDATIONS

CHAPTER 1

A BRIEF HISTORY OF PROJECT MANAGEMENT

PETER W. G. MORRIS

INTRODUCTION

Project Management is a social construct. Our understanding of what it entails has evolved over the years, and is continuing to do so. This chapter traces the history of this evolution. It does so from the perspective of the professional project management community. It argues that although there are several hundred thousand members of project management professional associations around the world, and many more who deploy tools, techniques, and concepts which they, and others, perceive to be "project management," there are differing views of the scope of the subject, of its ontology and epistemologies. Maybe this is true of many subjects which are socially constructed, but in the real world of projects, where people are charged with spending significant resources, misapprehension can be serious.

Later chapters in this book reflect aspects of this uncertainty and some indeed question whether project management is or should be a distinct domain or a profession—having a body of knowledge of its own—at all. Many certainly note the strains between its normative character as a professional discipline and the importance of understanding context when applying it. Nevertheless, despite this uncertainty the fact remains that many thousand people around the world see themselves as competent project professionals having shared "mental models" of what is meant by the discipline. But are these models fit-for-purpose? The chapter argues that in part at least some are, or were, too limited in scope to address the task of delivering projects successfully.

The account unavoidably draws on my personal engagement with, and reflection on, the field. (History is always seen through the eye of the historian.) It is an account of a "reflective practitioner." Some commentators would doubtless tell the story differently, with different emphases. Hence, referring to the models again, a major theme running through the chapter is the danger of positioning project management with too narrow a focus—as an execution-only oriented discipline: "the application of knowledge, skills, tools and techniques...to meet project requirements" (PMI 2008: 8). (So, who sets the requirements? Isn't that part of the project?) Instead, the chapter argues the benefits of focusing on the management of the project as a whole, from its early stages of conception—to include the elicitation and definition of requirements—to its post-commissioning phases, emphasizing context, the front-end, stakeholders, the various measures of project success, technology and commercial issues, people, and the importance of value and of delivering benefit: what I have termed elsewhere "the management of projects" (Morris and Hough 1987; Morris 1994; Morris and Pinto 2004)—as well of course as being master of the traditional core execution skills.

EARLY HISTORY

The word "project" means something thrown forth or out; an idea or conception (*Oxford English Dictionary*); "management" is "the art of arranging physical and human resources towards purposeful ends" (Wren 2005: 12). "Project Management" means...? The term as such appears not to have been in much if any use before the early 1950s, though of course projects had been managed since the dawn of civilization: the ancient cities of Mesopotamia, the pyramids of Egypt, Stonehenge; history is full of examples of outstanding engineering feats, military campaigns, and other singular undertakings, all attesting to man's ability to accomplish complex, demanding projects. But, barring a few exceptions, it is not until the early 1950s that the language of contemporary project management begins to be invented.

There are several important precursors to this emergence, however. Adamiecki published his harmonogram (effectively a vertical bar chart) in 1903 (Marsh 1975). (Following Priestley's idea of putting lines to a horizontal timescale published in 1765 in his *Chart of Biography*.) Gantt's bar chart followed in 1917. Formal project coordinator roles appear in the US Army Air Corps in the 1920s (Morris 1994), project engineers and project officers (Johnson 2002), and project engineers in Exxon and other process engineering companies in the 1930s. And in 1936 Gulick, in a theoretical paper, proposed the idea of the matrix organization (Gulick 1937).

There is surprisingly little evidence of the contemporary language and tools of project management to be seen in the Second World War, despite the emergence of

Operations Research (OR). The Manhattan Project—the US program to develop the Atom Bomb—is often quoted as one of the earliest examples of modern project management. This may be over-cooking the case: we see in the project—the program—none of the tools or language of today's world of project management.

THE 1950S AND 1960S: SYSTEMS DEVELOPMENT

Project management as a term seems to first appear in 1953, arising in the US defense-aerospace sector (Johnson 2002). The emerging advent of thermonuclear-armed ICBMs (InterContinental Ballistic Missiles), and in particular the threat from Russian ICBMs, became an increasingly severe US preoccupation from the early 1950s prompting the US Air Force (and Navy and Army) to look very seriously at how the development of their missiles could be accelerated. Under procurement processes developed by Brigadier Bernard Schriever for the US Air Force (USAF) in 1951, the USAF Air Research and Development and Air Material Commands were required to work together in "special project offices" under a "project manager" who would have full responsibility for the project, and contractors were required to consider the entire "weapons system" on a project basis (Johnson 2002: 29–31). The Martin (Marietta) company is credited with having created "the first recognizable project management organization" in 1953—in effect a matrix (Johnson 1997).

The management of major systems programs

In 1954 Schriever was appointed to head the Atlas ICBM development where he continued his push for integration and urgency, proposing a more holistic approach involving greater use of contractors as system integrators to create the system's specifications and to oversee its development (Hughes 1998; Johnson 2002). As with Manhattan, Schriever concentrated on building an excellent team. To shorten development times, Schriever also aggressively promoted the practice of concurrency—the parallel planning of all system elements with many normally serial activities being run concurrently (lampooned as "design-as-you-go!"). Unfortunately, concurrency amplified technical problems, as was discovered when missile testing began in late 1956. As a result, Schriever developed rigorous "systems engineering" testing, tracking, and configuration management techniques on the next missile program, Minuteman, which were soon to be applied on the Apollo moon program.

Meanwhile the US Navy was developing its own project and program management practices. Following Teller's 1956 insight that the rate of missile technology development would enable ICBMs to fit in submarines by the early to mid 1960s, when the submarines would be ready (Sapolsky 1972: 30), the Navy began work on Polaris. Admiral Raborn was appointed as head of the Polaris SPO (Special Projects Office) in 1955. Like Schriever, Raborn emphasized quality of people and team morale. Polaris's SPO exerted more hands-on management than the Air Force, one result of which was the development in 1957 of PERT as a planning and monitoring tool. PERT, the Planning and Evaluation Review Technique, never quite fulfilled its promise but, like Critical Path Method (CPM), invented by DuPont in 1957–9, became iconic as a symbol of the new discipline of project management. Raborn, cleverly and presciently, used PERT as a tool in stakeholder management (though the term was not used), publicizing it to Congress and the Press as the first management tool of the nuclear and computer age.

In 1960 the Air Force implemented Schriever's methods throughout its R&D organizations, documenting them as the "375-series" regulations: a phased life-cycle approach; planning for the entire system up front; project offices with the authority to manage the full development, assisted by systems support contractors (Morrison 1967). Essentially project and program management had become the fundamental means to organize complex systems development, and system engineering the engineering mechanism to coordinate them (Johnson 1997).

These principles were then given added weight, and thrust, first by the arrival of Robert McNamara as US Secretary of Defense in 1960 and second by NASA (specifically Apollo); from there they spread throughout the USA, and then NATO's, aerospace and electronics industries.

McNamara was an OR enthusiast and a great centralizer. The Program Planning and Budgeting System (PPBS) was his main centralizing tool but he introduced in addition several OR-based practices such as Life-Cycle Costing, Integrated Logistics Support, Quality Assurance, Value Engineering, Configuration Management, and the Work Breakdown Structure, the latter being promoted in 1962 in a joint Department of Defense (DoD)/NASA guide: "PERT/Cost Systems Design." This "guide" generated a proliferation of systems and much attendant complaining from industry, so instead Earned Value (as an element of DoD's C/SCSC—Cost/Schedule Control Systems Criteria—requirements) was introduced in 1964 as a performance management approach (Morris 1994).

Meanwhile Sam Philips, recently a USAF brigadier managing Minuteman, was heading NASA's Apollo program "of landing a man on the moon and returning him safely to earth," in President Kennedy's historic words of 1961. Apollo brought systems (project) management squarely into the public gaze. Philips imposed configuration management as his core control discipline with rigorous design reviews and work package management—"the devil is in the interface" (Johnson 2002). Matrix structures were deployed to harness specialist resources while task forces addressed specific problems. Quality, reliability, and ("all-up") testing became hugely important as phased testing became too time consuming and costly.

Back on earth, Precedence scheduling had been invented in 1962, by IBM; and in the late 1960s resource allocation scheduling techniques were developed (Morris 1994).

Organization and people management

Project management came to be seen, for many years, as epitomized by tools such as PERT and CPM, Work Breakdown Structures, and Earned Value. In reality, however, a more fundamental feature is integration around a clear objective: whether as "single point of integrative responsibility," in Archibald's pithy phrase (Archibald 1976), project "task forces," or the matrix. This integration should ideally, as per Schriever, be across the whole project life cycle. (Regarding which, it is salutary to note that in the "execution" delivery view of project (see below pp. 20–2), the project manager is generally not the single point of integrative responsibility for the overall project but only for the execution phase.) People skills are also important. As we have seen, Schriever, Raborn, and Philips all emphasized high-level leadership, teamwork, and task performance. Apollo sponsored several studies on team and individual skills (Baker and Wilemon 1974; Wilemon and Thamhain 1977).

In 1959 the *Harvard Business Review* published an article on the new integrator role, "the project manager" (Gaddis 1959), and by the late 1960s and early 1970s these ideas on organizational integration had begun to attract serious academic attention, for example Lawrence and Lorsch's 1967 study on integration and differentiation, Galbraith's on forms of integration (1973), and Davis and Lawrence's work on the matrix (1977). The intellectual environment meanwhile became increasingly attuned to "the systems approach" (Cleland and King 1968; Johnson, Kast, and Rosenzweig 1973).

As NASA reached (metaphorically and literally) its apogee, project management began now to be seen as a management approach which had potentially very widespread application and benefit. Society could address its major social challenges, NASA claimed, using the same systems approaches that had got man to the moon—employing "adaptive, problem-solving, temporary systems of diverse specialists, linked together by coordinating executives" (Webb 1969: 23). But it was not going to be so easy, either in NASA, DoD, or the wider world. For, as Sayles and Chandler, two leading academics, pointed out in 1971, "NASA was a closed loop—it set its own schedule, designed its own hardware...As one moves into the (more political) socio-technical area, this luxury disappears" (Sayles and Chandler 1971: 160).

The birth of the professional project management associations

Simultaneously, with the spread of the matrix and DoD project management techniques, many executives suddenly found themselves pitched into managing projects for the first time. Conferences and seminars on how to do so proliferated. The US

Project Management Institute (PMI) was founded in 1969; the International Management Systems Association (also called INTERNET, now the International Project Management Association—IPMA) in 1972, with various European project management associations being formed contemporaneously. Crucially, however, the perspective was essentially a middle management, project execution one centered around the challenges of accomplishing the project goals that had been given, and on the tools and techniques for doing this; it was rarely the successful accomplishment of the project *per se*, which is after all what really matters. Worse, the performance of projects, already too often bad, was now beginning to deteriorate sharply.

THE 1970S TO THE 1990S: WIDER APPLICATION, NEW STRANDS, AND ONTOLOGICAL DIVERGENCE

In some cases, projects were failing precisely because they lacked project management—Concorde for example: an immense concatenation of technological challenges with no effective project management (Morris and Hough 1987). But in others, although "best practice" was being earnestly applied, the paradigm was wrong. Concorde's American rival for example was managed by two ex-USAF senior officers according to DoD principles but with no effective program for addressing stakeholder opposition (remember Raborn!)—which in fact led in 1970 to Congress refusing to fund the program and its cancellation (Horwitch 1982). The whole nuclear power industry throughout the 1970s and 1980s exhibited similar problems of massive stakeholder (environmentalist) opposition coupled with the challenges of introducing major technological developments during construction (concurrency again, with the concomitant challenge of "regulatory ratcheting" as authorities sought to codify and apply changing technical requirements on power plants already well under construction.) Exceptionally high cost inflation worldwide blew project estimates. The oil and gas industry faced additional costs as it moved into difficult new environments such as Alaska and the North Sea. Even the US weapons programs were not performing well, with problems of technology selection and proving, project definition, supplier selection, and above all concurrency, which DoD at times proscribed as costs grew and at others, chafing at the lack of speed, reluctantly allowed (Morris 1994).

Success and failure studies

The causes of project success and failure now began to receive serious attention. DoD had commissioned a number of studies on project performance concluding that technological uncertainty, scope changes, concurrency, and contractor engagement were major issues (Marshall and Meckling 1959; Peck and Scherer 1962; Summers 1965; Perry et al. 1969; Large 1971). Developing world aid projects were analyzed (Hirschman 1967), the World Bank in a major review of project lending between 1945 and 1985 concluding that more attention was needed to technological adequacy, project design, and institution-building (Baum and Tolbert 1985). The US General Accounting Office and the UK National Audit Office conducted several highly critical reviews of publicly funded projects. Various academic and other research bodies reported on energy and power plants, systems projects, R&D projects, autos, and airports (Morris 1994).

In fact, Morris and Hough in their 1987 study of project success and failure, *The Anatomy of Major Projects*, listed 34 studies covering 1,536 projects and programs of the 1960s and 1970s (and added a further 8 of their own). Typical sources of difficulty were: unclear success criteria, changing sponsor strategy, poor project definition, technology (fascination with; uncertainty of; design management), concurrency, poor quality assurance, poor linkage with sales and marketing, inappropriate contracting strategy, unsupportive political environment, lack of top management support, inflation, funding difficulties, poor control, inadequate manpower, and geophysical conditions. Most of these factors fell outside the standard project management rubric of the time, as expressed in the textbooks and conference hall floors and as would soon be formalized by PMI in its Body of Knowledge (PMI 2008).

Later studies of project success and failure, such as those by Miller and Lessard (2000) on very large engineering projects, Flyvbjerg, Bruzelius, and Rothengatter (2003) on road and rail projects, and Meier (2008) on US defense and intelligence projects, as well as the notorious CHAOS Reports by Standish (1994 and later) on software development projects, emphasized similar factors, namely:

- the importance of managing the front-end project definition stages of a project.[1] (DoD had come to the same conclusion, following the US 1972 Commission on Government Procurement, with its creation of the front-end Milestone o);
- the pivotal role of the owner (or sponsor);
- the need to manage in some way project "externalities".

Miller and Lessard further made the critical distinction between projects' efficiency (on time, in budget, to scope) and effectiveness (achieving the sponsor's objectives) measures, showing that their projects generally did much worse on the latter (around 45 percent) than the former (around 75 percent). (Is it reasonable that effectiveness should be so much worse than efficiency?) But by the time of their report, the early 2000s, the project management community was becoming much more aware of the importance of business value, as we shall see.

These studies signposted a growing bifurcation in the way project management is perceived, with many taking the predominantly middle management, execution, delivery-oriented perspective, others taking a broader, more holistic view where the focus is on managing projects. The difference may at first seem slight but the latter involves managing the front-end development period; the former is focused on activity once requirements have been set. The unit of analysis moves from delivery management to the project as an organizational entity which has to be managed successfully. Both paradigms involve managing multiple elements but the "management of projects" is an immensely richer, more complex domain than execution management. This intellectual contrast was marked clearly in the publication of PMI's "Guide to the Project Management Body of Knowledge" (BoK) in 1983/7.

Project management Bodies of Knowledge

The drive behind the development of a project management Body of Knowledge (BoK) was the idea then gaining ground that if project management was to be a profession surely there should be some form of certification of competence (Cook 1977). This would then require some definition of the distinctive knowledge area that the professional is competent in. The initial 1983 PMI BoK (PMBoK®) identified six knowledge elements: scope, time, cost, quality, human resources, and communications management; the 1987 edition added risk and contract/procurement; the 1996 edition added integration. (There have since been several further updates.)

The UK's Association for Project Management (APM) followed a similar path a few years later but considered the PMI BoK too narrow in its definition of the subject. APM's model was strongly influenced by the "management of projects" paradigm: that managing scope, time, cost, resources, quality, risk, procurement, etc. alone is not enough to assure successful project outcomes. In 1991 APM thus produced a broader document which gave recognition to matters such as objectives, strategy, technology, environment, people, business and commercial issues, and so on. The APM BoK has gone to five revisions, Versions 3 and 5 being based on special research (Morris, Jamieson, and Shepherd 2006). In 1998 the IPMA (which today comprises 45 national project management associations representing more than 40,000 members) published its Competence Baseline to support its certification programme (Pannenbacker et al. 1998). In doing so it adopted the APM BoK almost wholly as its model of project management. In 2002 the Japanese project management associations, ENAA and EPMF, also produced a broadly based BoK: *P2M* (Project and Program Management) (ENAA 2002).

New product development

Meanwhile during the 1980s a stream of insights began appearing from the product development industries. Their influence was to prove significant. Again the initial impetus was studies of success and failure, notably by Kleinschmidt, Edgett, and Cooper, the result of which was to emphasize a staged approach to development, with strong scrutiny at stage gates where there is a predisposition not to proceed unless assured of the investment and management health of the development process (Cooper 1986).

These ideas were taken further in two research programs which were to have a strong influence on practice across project-based sectors—pharmaceuticals and other R&D industries, manufacturing, oil and gas, utilities, systems development: one based at Harvard (Clark and Fujimoto 1990; Wheelwright and Clark 1992); the other centered at MIT, the International Motor Vehicle Program (IMVP) (Womack, Jones, and Roos 1990). Both drew heavily on Japanese auto manufacturers' practices, particularly Toyota's. Clark et al. articulated many of the principles now underlying good project development practice: portfolio selection (in relation to market demands and technology strategy and the pace of scheme development); stage reviews; the "Shusa"—the "large project leader"; project teams representing all the functions critical to overall project success; and the importance of the sponsor. Critically, the Shusa—the "heavyweight project manager"—has as his first role "to provide for the direct interpretation of the market and customer needs" (Wheelwright and Clark 1992: 33). The (heavyweight) project core team exists throughout the project duration but—reflecting the domain's dual paradigms—project management is positioned in project execution following approval of the project plan!

Supply chain management

Both programs dealt extensively with supply chain issues. The IMVP addressed "lean management"; Clark et al. introduced "alliance or partnered" projects. Lean emphasizes productivity improvements through reduced waste, shorter supply lines, lower inventory, and similar; partnering is about gaining productivity improvements through alignment of supply chain members. Partnering became extremely significant as a supply chain practice in the 1990s and beyond.

Traditional forms of contract had long frustrated project management's goal of achieving project-wide integration. The scope is supposed to be fixed by the tender documents but when changes occur, as they often do, the contractor may be highly motivated to claim for contract variations, particularly since the contract had been awarded to the cheapest bidder. This creates a disposition towards conflict. Further, the contractor only enters the project once the design is substantially complete; this meant that "buildability" inputs are often missed. The 1980s and 1990s saw substantial efforts across many sectors but particularly the whole construction spectrum to address these issues and improve project performance. Partnering, with its move from an essentially transactional to a relationship form of engagement of contractors, with the focus on alignment and performance improvement, was an important element of this move for change.

Concurrent engineering

Simultaneous development, or concurrent engineering, was a major theme of both the IMVP and Harvard auto programs. The new practice of concurrent engineering was a more successful, sophisticated version of concurrency, avoiding the problems which had so encumbered project management since the days of Schriever. Concurrent engineering comprises parallel working where possible (simultaneous engineering); integrated teams drawing on all the functional skills needed to develop and deliver the total product (marketing, design, production—hence design-for-manufacturability, design-to-cost, etc.); integrated data modeling; and a propensity to delay decision-taking for as long as possible (Gerwin and Susman 1996).

Concurrency was often really part of the broader issue of how to manage technical innovation in a project environment. Various solutions began to emerge in the 1980s: prototyping off-line so that only proven technology is used in commercially sensitive projects (compare the nuclear power story with its 330 mW prototype plants!); rapid prototyping where quick impressions could be gained by quasi-mock-ups; use of pre-planned product improvements (P³I), particularly on shared platforms—a form of program management (Wheelwright and Clark 1992).

Technology management

Slowly the projects world got better at managing technical uncertainty—but not always. Defense, and intelligence, continues as an exception: the case for technology push and urgency may simply be so great for national security that the rules have to be disregarded—with predictable consequences. Hence Meier in 2008 reporting on a CIA/DoD study: "most unsuccessful programs (studied) fail at the beginning. The principal causes of (cost and schedule) growth...can be traced to...immature technology, lack of corporate technology roadmaps, requirements instability, ineffective acquisition strategy, unrealistic program baselines, inadequate systems engineering" (Meier 2008).

At the heart of many project difficulties lies the crucial issue of requirements. For if one isn't clear on what is required, it shouldn't be a surprise if one doesn't get it. The only trouble is, it's often very hard to do this. In building, architects take "the brief" from their clients—usually followed by scheme designs, specifications, and detailed design. In software (and many systems) projects the product is less physically obvious and harder to visualize and articulate. Requirements management (engineering) rose into prominence in the late 1980s (Davis, Hickey, and Zweig 2004). Several systems development models were published in the 1980s and 1990s—the Waterfall, Spiral, and Vee (Forsberg, Mooz, and Cotterman 1996)—all emphasizing a move from user, system, and business requirements (requirements being solution free), through specifications, systems design, and build, and then back through mirrored levels of testing (verification and validation).

The extent to which project management should be responsible for ensuring that requirements are adequately defined is typical of the conceptual problem of the discipline: should project management cover the management of the front-end, including development of the requirements; or just the realization of these requirements, once these are fixed? (The latter being the view of PMBoK® and many systems engineers, but not of the more holistic "management of projects" approach.)

Quality management

Quality is seen by many as a technology measure. The "House of Quality"/QFD (Quality Function Deployment), for example, which links critical customer attributes to design parameters, is of this school. But, as the Quality gurus—Deming, Crosby, Juran, Ishikawa—of the 1970s and 1980s insisted, quality relates to the total work effort. It is about more than just technical performance.

The 1980s and 1990s saw a marked impact of quality thinking on project management. Quality Assurance became a standard management practice in many project industries. More fundamental was the increasing popularity of Total Quality Management with its emphasis on performance metrics, stable supplier relationships, and putting the customer first. The former trickled into enterprise-wide project management and benchmarking in the late 1990s; the latter strengthened the philosophy of aligned supply chains (partnering). (Another influence was Deming's contention that improvement isn't possible without statistical stability, which led to the maturity model idea—see below.) An International Standard on *Quality Management in Projects* (ISO 10006) was even published, in 1997 (ISO 1997/2003).

Health, safety, and environment

A series of high-profile accidents, mostly in transport (shipping, rail) and energy (oil and gas, building construction), in the 1980s propelled Health and Safety to be seen as central project criteria not just as important as the traditional iron triangle trio but much more so. Legislation in the early 2000s strengthened this further.

"Environment," which of course had become increasingly recognized in the 1980s and 1990s as an important dimension of project management responsibility, partly due to environmental opposition (the nuclear, oil, and transport sectors), sustainability (the Bruntland Commission of 1987), and legislation (such as Environmental Impact Assessments), became widely tagged to Health and Safety. HSE (Health, Safety, and Environment) became inescapably supremely important across a large swathe of project-based industries.

Risks and opportunities

Curiously, although most of the standard project management techniques had been identified by the mid 1960s, risk management does not appear to have been one of them. Probabilistic estimating was of course present in PERT from the outset (and was officially abandoned by 1963) but this is not the same as the formal project risk management process (of identification, assessment, mitigation strategy, and reporting) that was articulated in the 1987 edition of PMBoK®. By the mid 1980s, however, formal procedures of risk management had become a commonly used practice, with software packages available to model the cumulative effect of different probabilities. (Almost always this was assessed on predicted cost or schedule completion, rarely on business benefit).

In the late 1990s/early 2000s an important risk management conceptual development occurred: risk was now defined—for example in APM's *PRAM Guide* (Simon, Hillson, and Newland 1997)—as uncertainty, rather than as the possibility of a negative event occurring, thereby bringing consideration of "opportunity" into the process (ICE 1998). The result was to reinforce a growing interest in looking at how project upsides—the positives: value, benefits, opportunities—could be better managed. This was to be a growing dimension of the subject in the early 2000s.

Value and benefits

Value is one of the richer, less explored, and promising topics in project management. Value Analysis (VA) had been developed by General Electric in the late 1940s and was one of the techniques ushered in to DoD by McNamara in 1960. Simply put, value can be defined as the quotient of function/cost or quality/cost, performance/ resources or similar. The aim of VA, VE, and VM is to analyze, in a structured manner using a wide selection of different stakeholders, the project's requirements and ways of addressing these. Value Engineering (VE) focuses on the proposed engineering solution. Value Management (VM) looks at the more strategic questions of whether the project should be being done at all, and whether a scheme or its development strategy could be improved. "Optioneering" is a similar idea though it lacks the workshop basis. Common in construction, it is often still rare in IT projects.

Closely allied to opportunities and value is benefits, which too became an area of strong interest in the early 2000s. Arising out of the development of program(me) management in the mid 1990s (see below), benefits are "the measurable improvement resulting from an outcome" (OGC 2003). The focus is entirely right: a shifting from the preoccupation with efficiency (the iron triangle) to effectiveness (achieving business benefit).

New funding models

Another paradigm change was meanwhile at work moving project management towards a more holistic perspective: the funding of public sector projects by the private sector. The so-called BOT/BOOT (Build-Own-(Operate)-Transfer) method of project development was originally introduced in the Turkish power sector in

1984 (Morris 1994). The intent was—is—for private sector groupings to be given operational responsibility for the facility, generally only for a defined period, for which they receive an income. The cost of building the facility is borne by the private sector group on the basis of its future operating earnings. Following some early UK trial projects, the Channel Tunnel was financed and built on this basis in 1987–94.

The method is superficially attractive since it relieves governments from the pressures of capital expenditure (but at the expense of an enlarged operating budget). It requires very careful legal drafting however and often proved to be chronically slow and expensive to define and bid. Nevertheless, the prospect of getting benefits today and have someone else pay for them tomorrow proved irresistible to many governments and the idea soon morphed into PFI and PPP (Private Finance Initiative/Public–Private Partnership) projects for areas such as health, schools, and prisons.

There were two putative conceptual benefits to project management from this set of developments. One, a greater emphasis on Whole Life Costs, on operating efficiency, and on benefits and effectiveness; two, the development of project companies as deliverers of services as opposed simply to products. Similarly in IT services and Facilities Management; and in aero-engines the emphasis moved from capital cost to "power-by-the-hour."

THE 1990S AND EARLY TWENTY-FIRST CENTURY: ENTERPRISE-WIDE PROJECT MANAGEMENT

As we turn the century we see project management become increasingly popular, better enabled technologically, sometimes dangerously commodified, and more reflective. It becomes for many enterprises a core competence.

Information technology

Information and Communications Technology (ICT) has had a huge influence in promoting project management, particularly from the 1990s. Microsoft made an enormous contribution to the domain with its releases of *MS Project* during the 1990s. Personal computing brought project management tools directly to the user. Ten years previously, planners were only beginning to move away from punched cards and big main frames. Artificial Intelligence may not have fulfilled all that was hyped of it in the 1970s but mobile telecommunications, broadband, and the internet significantly increased project communications capabilities and project productivity. Modeling power too had improved greatly, whether through the humble potential of Excel or the broader efforts of CAD (CAM and CAE) and 4D simulation or asset configuration models.

The early 2000s saw the major project management software suppliers beginning to provide enterprise-level platforms for use on multiple projects by multiple users; meanwhile the major ERP (Enterprise Resource Planning) suppliers (HP, Oracle, SAP) included project management modules and interfaces to specialist project management packages (Microsoft, PlanView, Primavera, etc.). Latterly there has been a move towards web-based project collaboration, communication, planning, and management tools offered as "software-as-a-service" resources.

Critical Chain

One genuinely new and original development in scheduling was Critical Chain, promoted by Goldratt from his "Theory of Constraints" around 1996–7 (Leach 2004). Key ideas include considering resource availability when deciding which is the real critical path; stripping contingencies from the activity level and managing them, as buffers, at the project level; and only working on one activity at a time, and doing so as fast as possible. (Ideas which require care in understanding: sometimes for example multi-tasking is unavoidable.) Implementation of these ideas generally requires behavioral changes and the motivational energy created can be real and substantial.

Agility

By the early 2000s another conceptual challenge was being put forward, again at quite a micro level of operations: Agile. Agile project management addresses the distinctive challenges of software development (Leffingwell 2007). In Agile, software project estimating is considered (by Agile proponents) as inherently unreliable. The Agile theory is therefore that cost may have to be sacrificed to ensure that some functionality at least can be developed within a given time; the iron triangle is abandoned! Requirements are elicited by close customer–programmer pairing with development then being over a very short time (e.g. ninety days maximum). Project management becomes in effect task management!

Enterprise-wide project management

The expansion of project management software from single project to enterprise-level applications paralleled a growing awareness that project management worked differently (a) for different types of projects and/or in different contexts, (b) at different levels in an organization. The former reflects the fundamental thesis of contingency theory: that organization and management will vary depending on context (environment) and technology (Burns and Stalker 1961; Shenhar and Dvir 2007) and is seen in the early 2000s with growing discussion of the special characteristics of different classes of projects—mega or complex for example—and even PMI sector-based qualifications. It is a major theme of this book. The latter, so-called "enterprise-wide project management," has opened a large field of development ranging across program management, governance, training and career development, to organizational learning.

Program and portfolio management

Around the turn of the century program(me) management began receiving increased attention (Artto et al. 2009), but as a more "business-driven" discipline than project management—an emphasis different from the product development base of a decade earlier, as we saw above, where technology was the underlying issue (technology platforms in Wheelwright and Clark (1992: 49), and from that of DoD in the 1950s and 1960s where it was more heavyweight project management (Baumgartner 1979; Sapolsky 1972). This conception, as promoted by PMI, APM, the UK Office of Government and Commerce (OGC), and others, reconfirms the view of project management as execution management: "the application of knowledge, skills, tools and techniques…to meet project requirements" and proposing that "programmes deal with outcomes, projects deal with outputs" (OGC 2003), a conception echoed in PMI's standard on Program Management (PMI 2006). But this is dangerous. Projects also produce outcomes and benefits. Is it not the job of project management to achieve benefits too? Once again we have the fundamental question lying at the heart of the subject: if project management is only about execution, what is the overall discipline?

Strategy and governance

The early 2000s saw a parallel growing interest in strategy in which the same issue arises (Artto et al. 2008). Does responsibility for aligning project strategy with the sponsor's strategy rest with project management, program management, or portfolio management, or all three? On projects, clearly it must be with those managing the project front end. But the implication of the OGC and PMI model is that project management doesn't operate at the front end but is, as we've seen, an execution-oriented, output-focused discipline. Why shouldn't project management also manage the front-end development stages? Who is responsible for the management of the project if not the project manager (or some version thereof, such as a Project Director)? The domain remained, and remains, confused, the strategy–development–definition stages—the project front-end—being balkanized amongst elements which are indeed different but which together represent the overall practice of managing projects within the enterprise. A view of the discipline "as a whole" had yet really to engage.

The role of the sponsor is generally key (Morris and Hough 1987; Miller and Lessard 2000). Often it can go wrong—gate reviews rushed, risks ignored—and affect project performance significantly. The early 2000s saw a growing recognition of the importance of project governance, not least as a result of instances of high-profile corporate malfeasance—the collapse of Enron and WorldCom in 2001–2—and the legislation and corporate action which followed (Sarbanes–Oxley etc.). APM explored the implications for project management in 2004 listing such principles as proper alignment between business strategy and the project plan; transparent reporting of status and risk; and periodic third party "assurance" reviews (APM 2004). The late 1990s and early 2000s in fact saw rising application of stage gate reviews, peer reviews, and peer assists as governance mechanisms. In many cases this was also combined with efforts to implement organizational learning.

Project-based learning, PMOs, and maturity

The 1990s saw a huge rise in interest in knowledge management and organizational learning. Projects were seen both as attractive vehicles for generating new knowledge, and simultaneously, given their unique, temporary nature, as especially difficult challenges for organizational learning. While tools and techniques might help, the consensus was that the real opportunity, and challenge, lies in leveraging tacit knowledge. Communities of Practice, peer assists and peer reviews, and project-based learning reviews became more common.

PMOs—Project/Program Management Offices—began to be seen in the late 1990s/early 2000s as important organizational mechanisms for addressing these issues: holders of best practice, organizers of training and support, recorders of project portfolio status, and initiators of project reviewers—the linchpin in building enterprise-wide project/program management capability (Hobbs and Aubry 2008). Maturity models, methodologies, and training, learning, and development became increasingly visible as means to assist in this endeavor.

The concept of project management maturity gained considerable traction in the early 2000s. Drawing on Carnegie-Mellon's Software Engineering Institute's Capability Maturity Model, first PMI with its OPM3® product and later OGC with its PMMM and P3M3 frameworks attempted to categorize levels of project management capability. OPM3® proved extremely complicated; PMMM and P3M3 unrealistically simple, missing completely several topics present in the APM BoK, not least nearly all the human skills such as leadership and teamwork as well as such important items as Quality Management, Information Management, and nearly everything to do with Procurement and Contracting (OGC 2008). No project management maturity model seems yet quite able to reflect the range and subtlety of topics and skills that organizations need in order to manage projects efficiently and effectively, however. The management of projects is, as a discipline, or a domain, much more complicated than software engineering.

OGC's guidance manuals (methodologies)—*PRINCE2*, *Managing Successful Programmes*, and the *Management of Risk* (OGC 2002a, 2002b, 2003)—published across the turn of the century proved highly influential. These are excellent documents but, as thousands became certificated as "PRINCE2 Practitioners," the danger grew of people believing that passing a test after a four-day course meant being qualified as a competent project manager. The net results were indeed to "spread the word" but also perhaps to commodify the discipline. The same criticism could be made of PMI's immensely popular, and influential, PMP (Project Management Professional) certification. Competency implies more than just knowledge. Skills and behaviors are also important. Experience develops competency. (Of the professional bodies' certification programmes, only IPMA's competency framework certificates more than knowledge.)

All these attempts to provide guidance through "one size fits all" normative standards perforce avoid the crucial point that a project management "best practice" standard model just may not fit or be appropriate in all circumstances. This insight, though obvious from contingency theory, means that care must be taken when benchmarking performance (another trend of the 2000s): in short, it demands a more sophisticated interpretation of application. Perhaps training and development could help?

Training, career development, and professionalism

From the 1990s there was an unprecedented rise in demand for project managers, particularly in construction and IT. Project management became increasingly seen as a core competency, recognized within, and across, institutions as a career track in its own right. Demand outstripped supply. Recruitment, career development, and competency uprating became more important. National vocational qualification programs were introduced in Australia and the UK in the mid 1990s. University degrees in project management sprang up in their dozens. Several companies and government agencies created university-based "Academy" programs. (DoD had established its Defense Systems Management College in 1971.)

Meanwhile PMI's membership continued to grow and grow (it had half a million members and credential holders in 185 countries by 2010), driven by good events, very professional communications and marketing, and the PMP certification program. In the UK, APM was the fastest growing of all the UK's professional institutions throughout the 1990s and 2000s and in 2008–9 applied for "chartered professional association" status to put it alongside such professions as engineering and medicine.

Academic research

Long seen as a subset of production scheduling, at the university level, teaching and research in project management grew strongly in the 1990s and early twenty-first century as its broader applicability became more recognized, and as academics became more aware of projects as special, and interesting, organizational phenomena. In 2000 PMI launched the first of its biannual Research Conferences; IRNOP—the International Research Network on Organizing by Projects—had been holding biannual conferences since 1994; EURAM (the European Academy of Management) found project management to be its most popular track at its annual conferences. By 2008 there were four or five academic journals in the area. Project management began, as a result, to get seriously self-reflective. The locus became increasingly the business schools, or in some instances technology departments, approached either from a social science or a technology perspective.

A major program, *Rethinking Project Management*, was conducted in 2004–6 representing leading academics and practitioners in Europe and North America to reflect on the project management research agenda. Themes arising out of the study (and suitably "problematizing" it) emphasized:

- the complexity of projects and project management;
- the importance of social interaction among people;
- value creation (but noting that "value" and "benefit" have multiple meanings linked to different purposes);
- seeing projects as "multidisciplinary, having multiple purposes, not always pre-defined";
- the development of "reflective practitioners who can learn, operate and adapt effectively in complex project environments, through experience, intuition and the pragmatic application of theory in practice" (Winter et al. 2006).

CONCLUDING PERSPECTIVES

And perhaps this is as good a point as any at which to draw to a close this history of the development, till now, of the domain—the discipline—of managing projects and programs. An account which acknowledges that everyone's experience of doing so is different and that all projects are indeed unique. A rendering which, while championing the existence and utility of good practices and sound principles for the management of projects and programs, recognizes that multiple agendas, the complexities and contingencies of context, and the sometime fuzziness of benefits can nevertheless distort the normative models proffered by many popular guides and texts. A telling which has shown that projects are "created not found"; whose realization therefore requires social skills as well as technical competencies. An account which, perhaps above all, has highlighted the distinction between the more straightforward world of project management seen as execution management, and the more complex but important one of managing projects as whole entities. This surely is what the domain—the discipline—should be about.

NOTE

1. Aristotle noted 2,370 or so years ago that defining the question is half the answer (*Ethics*: Book 1.C.4: literally: "For the beginning is thought to be more than half the whole").

REFERENCES

ARCHIBALD, R. (1976, 1997). *Managing High-Technology Programs and Projects.* New York: Wiley.

ARTTO, K., MARTINSUO, M., DIETRICH, P., and KUJALA, J. (2008). "Project strategy: strategy types and their contents in innovation projects," *International Journal of Managing Projects in Business,* 1/1: 49–70.

——— GEMÜNDEN, H. G., and MURTOROA, J. (2009). "Foundations of program management: a bibliometric view," *International Journal of Project Management,* 27/1: 1–18.

ASSOCIATION FOR PROJECT MANAGEMENT (2004). *Directing Change: A Guide to Governance of Project Management.* High Wycombe: APM.

——— (2005). *Body of Knowledge for Managing Projects and Programmes,* 5th edn. High Wycombe: APM.

BAKER, B. N., and WILEMON, D. L. (1974). "A summary of major research findings regarding the human element in project management," *Project Management Journal,* 5/2: 227–30.

BAKER, N. R., MURPHY, D. C., and FISHER, D. (1974). *Determinants of Project Success.* National Technical Information Services N-74-30392; see also "Factors affecting project success," in Cleland and King 1988.

BAUM, W. C., and TOLBERT, S. M. (1985). *Investing in Development.* Oxford: Oxford University Press.

BAUMGARTNER, J. S. (1979). *Systems Management.* Washington, DC: Bureau of National Affairs.

BURNS, T., and STALKER, G. M. (1961). *The Management of Innovation.* London: Tavistock.

CLARK, K. B., and FUJIMOTO, T. (1990). *Product Development Performance.* Boston: Harvard Business School Press:

CLELAND, D. I., and KING, W. R. (1968). *Systems Analysis and Project Management.* New York: McGraw-Hill.

CLELAND, D. I., and KING, W. R. (eds.) (1988). *Project Management Handbook*. New York: Van Nostrand Reinhold.

COOK, D. L. (1977) "Certification of project managers—fantasy or reality?" *Project Management Quarterly*, 8/3.

COOPER, R. G. (1986). *Winning at New Products*. Reading, MA: Addison-Wesley.

DAVIS, A. M., HICKEY, A. M., and ZWEIG, A. S. (2004). "Requirements management in a project management context," in P. W. G. Morris and J. K. Pinto (eds.), *The Wiley Guide to Managing Projects*. Hoboken, NJ: Wiley, chapter 17.

DAVIS, S. M., and LAWRENCE, P. R. (1977). *Matrix Organizations*. Reading, MA: Addison Wesley.

ENAA (2002). *P2M: A Guidebook of Project & Program Management for Enterprise Innovation: Summary Translation*. Tokyo: Project Management Professionals Certification Center (PMCC).

FLYVBJERG, B., BRUZELIUS, N., and ROTHENGATTER, W. (2003). *Megaprojects and Risk: An Anatomy of Ambition*. Cambridge: Cambridge University Press.

FORSBERG, K., MOOZ, H., and COTTERMAN, H. (1996). *Visualizing Project Management*. New York: John Wiley and Sons.

GADDIS, P. O. (1959). "The project manager," *Harvard Business Review*, May–June: 89–97.

GALBRAITH, J. (1973). *Designing Complex Organisations*. Reading, MA: Addison-Wesley.

GERWIN, D., and SUSMAN, G. (1996). "Special Issue on Concurrent Engineering," *IEEE Transactions in Engineering Management*, 43/2: 118–23.

GULICK, L. (1937). "Notes on the theory of organization," in L. Urwick (ed.), *Papers on the Science of Administration*. New York: Columbia University Press, 1–46.

HIRSCHMAN, A. O. (1967). *Development Projects Observed*. Washington, DC: The Brookings Institute.

HOBBS, B., and AUBRY, M. (2008). "An empirically grounded search for a typology of project management offices," *Project Management Journal*, 39 Supplement: S69–S82.

HORWITCH, M. (1982). *Clipped Wings: The American SST Conflict*. Cambridge, MA: MIT Press.

HUGHES, T. P. (1998). *Rescuing Prometheus*. New York: Vintage.

INSTITUTION OF CIVIL ENGINEERS (1998). *RAMP: Risk Analysis and Management for Projects*. London: Institution of Civil Engineers and Institute of Actuaries.

ISO 10006 (2003), *Quality management systems: guidelines for quality management in projects*. British Standards Institute, London.

JOHNSON, R. A., KAST, F. E., and ROSENZWEIG, J. E. (1973). *The Theory and Management of Systems*. New York: McGraw-Hill.

JOHNSON, S. B. (1997). "Three approaches to big technology: operations research, systems engineering, and project management," *Technology and Culture*, 38/4: 891–919.

——(2002). *The Secret of Apollo: Systems Management in American and European Space Programs*. Baltimore: The Johns Hopkins University Press.

LARGE, J. P. (1971). *Bias in Initial Cost Estimates: How Low Estimates can Increase the Cost of Acquiring Weapons Systems*. Rand, R-1467-PA&E, Santa Monica, CA.

LAWRENCE, P., and LORSCH, J. (1967). *Organisation and Environment: Managing Integration and Differentiation*. Cambridge, MA: Harvard University Press.

LEACH, L. P. (2004). "Critical chain project management," in P. W. G. Morris and J. K. Pinto (eds.), *The Wiley Guide to Managing Projects*. Hoboken, NJ: Wiley, chapter 33.

LEFFINGWELL, D. (2007). *Scaling Software Agility*. Upper Saddle River, NJ: Addison Wesley.

MARSH, E. R. (1975). "The harmonogram of Karol Adamiecki", *Academy of Management Journal*, 18/2: 358–64.

MARSHALL, A. W., and MECKLING, W. H. (1959). *Predictability of the Costs, Time and Success of Development*. Rand Corporation, P-1821, Santa Monica, CA.

MEIER, S. R. (2008). "Best project management and systems engineering practices in pre-acquisition practices in the federal intelligence and defense agencies," *Project Management Journal*, 39/1: 59–71.

MILLER, R., and LESSARD, D. R. (2000). *The Strategic Management of Large Engineering Projects*. Cambridge, MA: MIT Press.

MORRIS, P. W. G. (1994). *The Management of Projects*. London: Thomas Telford.

——and HOUGH, G. H. (1987). *The Anatomy of Major Projects*. Chichester: Wiley and Sons.

——and PINTO, J. K. (eds.) (2004). *The Wiley Guide to Managing Projects*. Hoboken, NJ: Wiley.

——JAMIESON, H. A. J., and SHEPHERD, M. M. (2006). "Research updating the APM Body of Knowledge 4th edition," *International Journal of Project Management*, 24: 461–73.

MORRISON, E. J. (1967). "Defense systems management: the 375 series," *California Management Review*, 9/4.

OFFICE OF GOVERNMENT COMMERCE (2002a). *Managing Successful Projects with PRINCE 2*. Norwich: The Stationery Office.

——(2002b). *Management of Risk: Guidance for Practitioners*. Norwich: The Stationery Office.

——(2003). *Managing Successful Programmes*. Norwich: The Stationery Office.

——(2008). *Portfolio, Programme and Project Management Maturity Model*. Norwich: The Stationery Office.

PANNENBACKER, K., KNOPFEL, H., MORRIS, P. W. G., and CAUPIN, G. (1998). *IPMA and its Validated Four-Level Certification Programmes: Version 1.00*. Zurich: International Project Management Association.

PECK, M. J., and SCHERER, F. M. (1962). *The Weapons Acquisition Process: An Economic Analysis*. Cambridge, MA: Harvard University Press.

PERRY, R. L., DiSALVO, D., HALL, G. R., HARMAN, A. L., LEVENSON, G. S., SMITH, G. K., and STUCKER, J. P. (1969). *System Acquisition Experience*. Rand Corporation, RM-6072-PR, Santa Monica, CA.

PINTO, J. K., and SLEVIN, D. P. (1988). "Critical success factors across the project life cycle," *Project Management Journal*, 19/3: 67–75.

PROJECT MANAGEMENT INSTITUTE (2006). *The Standard for Program Management*. Newton Square, PA: Project Management Institute.

——(2008). *A Guide to the Project Management Body of Knowledge*, 4th edn. Newton Square, PA: Project Management Institute.

SAPOLSKY, H. (1972). *The Polaris System Development: Bureaucratic and Programmatic Success in Government*. Cambridge, MA: Harvard University Press.

SAYLES, L. R., and CHANDLER, M. K. (1971). *Managing Large Systems: Organizations for the Future*. New York: Harper and Row.

SHENHAR, A., and DVIR, D. (2007). *Reinventing Project Management: The Diamond Approach to Successful Growth and Innovation*. Boston: Harvard Business School Press.

SIMON, P., HILLSON, D., and NEWLAND, K. (1997). *Project Risk Analysis and Management (PRAM)*. High Wycombe: Association for Project Management.

STANDISH GROUP (1994). *The CHAOS Report*, http://www.standishgroup.com.

SUMMERS, R. (1965). *Cost Estimates as Predictors of Actual Weapons Costs*. Rand Corporation, RM-3061-PR, Santa Monica, CA.

WEBB, J. E. (1969). *Space Age Management: The Large-Scale Approach*. New York: McGraw-Hill.

WHEELWRIGHT, S. C., and CLARK, K. B. (1992). *Revolutionizing Product Development*. Boston: Harvard Business School Press.

WILEMON, D. L., and THAMHAIN, H. J. (1977). "Leadership effectiveness in program manage-
    ment," *Project Management Quarterly*, 8/2.
WINTER, M., SMITH, C., MORRIS, P. W. G., and CICMIL, S. (2006). "Directions for future
    research in project management: the main findings of a UK government-funded research
    network," *International Journal of Project Management*, 24/8: 638–49.
WOMACK, J. R., JONES, D. T., and ROOS, D. (1990). *The Machine that Changed the World.* New
    York: Macmillan International.
WREN, D. A. (2005). *The History of Management Thought.* Hoboken, NJ: Wiley.

CHAPTER 2

THEORETICAL FOUNDATIONS OF PROJECT MANAGEMENT

SUGGESTIONS FOR A PLURALISTIC UNDERSTANDING

JONAS SÖDERLUND

THEORETICAL FOUNDATIONS AND FRAGMENTATION

Project management can be seen as a specific "scientific field." A scientific field may be defined as "all work being done on a particular cognitive problem" (Cole 1983: 130) that shares a common focus and accumulated knowledge that researchers in the field build on and which serves to differentiate it from other scientific fields (Fagerberg and Verspagen 2009). Theoretical foundations—the theme for the present chapter—constitute the common heritages of the theories discussed, refuted, and corroborated to make predictions about the focal phenomenon, to highlight dangers, disclose alternatives, and examine assumptions. Project management, like many other sub-disciplines in management, is perhaps best described as a "fragmented adhocracy" (Whitley 1984), i.e. a scientific field that draws upon several different theoretical traditions without a strong set of common core principles and ideas (Engwall 1995). This has also been documented in literature reviews in which authors refer to distinctive traditions with regard to project management research[1] within the "rationalistic, tool-oriented tradition" and the "organization theory tradition" (e.g. Packendorff 1995) and extended further to the identification of an even broader set of traditions and a number of so-called "schools of thought" (Söderlund 2002).

The present chapter is a story and analysis of project management as a scientific field, its theoretical foundations, and some avenues for the future. It is a story about fragmentation, progress, and pluralism, i.e. the acknowledgement of a diversity of views and perspectives. The chapter is structured in the following way. First, we present a summary of the present state of theorizing within the area, arguing that a number of different schools of thought and *perspectives* can be identified that give a better account of the developments made in the past ten to fifteen years compared to the common distinction into either rationalistic or organization theory traditions. Second, we discuss the importance of types and typologies in project management and that there is a need to frame the specific phenomenon under study to seek commonalities and explore the differences among *projects*. Third, we discuss the importance of "complementarities" to understand the role and existence of projects and concomitantly two separate organizational *problems* (referred to as the cooperation and coordination problem), which are important to contrast and compare present theories within the field. Fourth, and finally, we analyze project management research in terms of features tied to their *process* dynamics—projects are evolving, time limited, and intentionally designed to disappear. Accordingly, project management research has focused on the different processes in and phases of the life cycle of projects where each phase is to be associated with quite specific organizational and managerial dynamics and challenges. These challenges would then also have implications on the type of theorizing and analysis we need to consider to increase our understanding of the formation, implementation, and termination of projects.

Using these four initial statements as a basis, this chapter analyzes past and present theorizing and future research avenues in terms of:

1. Perspectives. Research has developed considerably, introducing new perspectives and approaches to the study of projects and project management.
2. Projects: types and typologies. Research has been broadened to cover different classes of projects in different contexts, introducing a new set of types and typologies.
3. Problems: cooperation and coordination. Research is occupied with a range of different managerial and organizational problems; somewhat simplified, two distinct problems, that of cooperation and that of coordination, may be identified that have attracted considerable scholarly attention and continue to attract it.

4. Processes. Research focuses on different phases in the project life cycle and different processes of projects; the different phases and processes may call for particular analytical foci and approaches.

It will be argued that these distinctions are useful to provide an overview of the current state of knowledge within the project management domain and to classify and compare different scholarly contributions. Combined, they also highlight the need for further explorations and the identification of areas previously not addressed by research.

Perspectives and pluralism

Project management grew out of the practical problems raised by coordinating activities in complex undertakings. Initially, Gantt charts, work breakdown structures, and planning techniques played key roles which rooted project management in an operations management tradition that was principally developed by and for practitioners who needed tools and techniques to improve the efficiency of project implementation. Management researchers also played an important part in advancing knowledge about project management with a series of influential articles and textbooks. The prestigious journal *Management Science* published articles in the 1960s on topics exploring PERT (Program Evaluation and Review Technique) and critical paths in project management and network planning. Since these early contributions on project activity networks (PERT and critical-path planning methods), more advanced methods and analyses have followed. In the late 1960s and early 1970s, papers examined parallel strategies in development projects, project cost control, and different planning and programming solutions to the problem of optimal resource use and cost–time trade-offs (e.g. Abernathy and Rosenbloom 1969; Cooper 1976). Subsequent articles in the 1970s and 1980s increased the understanding of yet more complex problems by introducing dynamic situations involving multi-pass, heuristic decomposition procedures for project scheduling and project scheduling with continuously divisible constrained resources (e.g. Holloway, Nelson, and Suraphongschai 1979; Weglarz, 1981).

Two streams of empirical investigations run parallel to this development of the "management science" or "Optimization School" in project management. One stream focused on the success and failure of projects with the objective of identifying the best practice of project management, sometimes referred to as the "critical success factor" research (see Chapter 1, and Factor School). This came out of studies financed by governments to investigate the poor success of publicly funded projects. The RAND Corporation and the World Bank played an important part during the 1960s to push the research agenda forward in terms of a better conceptualization of what project success is and how to achieve it. Academic journals, such as *California Management Review*, published critical analyses of the use and misuse of project management (Avots 1969). More elaborate investigations began in the 1970s and had their breakthrough in the 1980s with a series of publications in the top-tier management journals (e.g. Thamhain and Gemmill 1974; Pinto and Prescott 1988).

In addition to studies of critical success factors, research centered on understanding projects as organizational forms and processes. The first publications appeared in the late 1960s and early 1970s. First, we find the emergence of the contingency tradition in project management with analyses of different kinds of matrix organizations for successful project implementation (see Contingency School). Secondly, a series of papers in the *Academy of Management Journal* analyzed more "processual" and "behavioral" concerns of projects as organizational forms (see Behavior School), including the ambiguities of project management, organizational conflicts, and power in project management (e.g. Wilemon and Cicero 1970). In the 1970s, we observe the analyses of projects as temporary organizational systems and a series of related human and behavioral inquiries, including individual motivation and professional development in projects (Goodman and Goodman 1972, 1976).

These streams of project management research are still important today—with their focus on the rationalistic approaches to project management and the operations research of project management, the broad-scale investigations of the criteria and factors of project success, and investigations of projects as organizational forms. However, the field has further explored similar issues to those investigated in papers from the 1960s and 1970s. To some extent, literature has also moved beyond these three streams of research to address other kinds of problems and processes.

Söderlund (2010) summarizes the evolution of project management research and identifies seven distinctive traditions or schools in project management research published in the leading management and organization journals.[2] He argues that there has been a considerable development and a growing pluralism since the early publications on operations research in the 1950s, through the investigations of success factors, to a number of different organization and management theory interpretations of projects and project management. These are important developments because they enhance the multidimensional investigation of projects and highlight how research has evolved the last couple of decades.

Table 2.1 summarizes the identified schools of thought in project management research, starting with the three more or less conventional ones mentioned earlier, followed by the ones that have emerged more recently. Each school is preoccupied with a particular view of projects, a main focus, and a set of related research questions. They also portray different ideas of project management, i.e. what project management is about or should be about. The following seven schools are summarized:[3] (1) Optimization School (logic-based, prescriptive research drawing on management science, optimization techniques, and systems analysis); (2) Factor School (empirical research relying on descriptive statistics of the criteria and factors

Table 2.1 Schools of project management research: an overview

	Main focus of analysis	Key question investigated	Project management idea	Key influence	Emergence[a]
Optimization School	Planning, breakdown techniques, and scheduling of complex tasks	How to manage/plan a project?	"Optimizing project implementation by planning"	Applied mathematics	1950s
Factor School	Success factors and project outcomes/ project performance	What determines project success?	"Targeting project management by factors"	Diverse	1960s
Contingency School	Project organization design/ structure	Why do projects differ?	"Adapting project organization to contingencies"	Organization theory	1970s
Behavior School	Project organization processes	How do projects evolve/ behave?	"Shaping processes of project organization"	Organization theory, Organizational behavior	1970s
Governance School	Governance of project organizations/transactions	How are projects (transactions) governed?	"Governing project organization/transactions"	Economics	1980s
Relationship School	Formation of project networks and relationships	How are the early stages of projects managed and how are project networks formed?	"Forming and developing projects in the early stages"	Marketing, Economic geography	1990s
Decision School	The interplay among decision-makers in projects	Why are projects instigated, why do they continue to live?	"Politicking and influencing decision-making processes"	Psychology, Political science	1970s/2000s

[a] It is always difficult to exactly determine a date for the emergence of a particular tradition or school. For the Optimization School the first "scientific" publications appeared in *Management Science* in the 1950s. The first scholarly publications in the Factor School appeared in the 1960s, but it was not until the 1980s that the more elaborate publications appeared in journals such as *Journal of Management* and *Administrative Science Quarterly*. The Contingency School developed in two waves—the first one already in the 1970s and the more focused one emerging in the beginning of the 1990s with publications in *Research Policy and Organization Studies*. The Behavior School goes, as indicated earlier, back to the 1970s. However, the resurrection of this tradition came in the 1990s with a series of papers on projects as temporary organizations. The Governance School emerged in parallel with other works on transaction costs and governance problems. The focused publications appeared in project management journals and mainstream management journals in the 1980s. The Relationship School grew out of several different disciplines and research traditions. In particular, a set of studies on project marketing in the 1990s triggered further explorations about project networks and stakeholder management. Finally, research within the Decision School dates back to the 1970s with studies on escalated commitment and planning disasters and regained momentum in the 2000s through work on mega-projects, optimism bias, and reference class forecasting.

for project success and failure); (3) Contingency School (empirical research, case-study-based, and survey-based research on the difference between projects, characteristics of projects, and contextual dimensions); (4) Behavior School (interpretive and descriptive research on organizational processes, behavior, and learning in projects); (5) Governance School (prescriptive research on governance and contract problems in projects); (6) Relationship School (descriptive case-study research on relations between actors in projects); and (7) Decision School (descriptive and interpretive research on politics and decision-making in projects).

A few things stand out from the above overview: (1) project definitions differ, (2) project management is many things at the same time, (3) research addresses distinctly different key questions, (4) pluralism is growing within project management research, (5) and project management research draws from a wide range of disciplines and influences.

Based on this school categorization, one might say that we have several theories of project management and that these theories draw upon quite different theoretical foundations ranging from applied mathematics to psychology and political science. These theories would then give different explanations as to why projects exist, why and how they differ, and how they behave (cf. Söderlund 2004a). Ultimately, they would, of course, give us quite different perspectives on what determines their success and failure. In this respect, project management has begun to develop multiple theories and multiple perspectives on projects (what are they) and project management (what is the role and focus of project management).

The existence of many theories provides the theorist and the practitioner with a "conceptual toolbox" (Weick 1992) that is needed to deal with non-trivial management and organizational problems, since there is no one single best answer or one single best approach—neither to manage a project nor to study it. On the contrary, many different viewpoints and approaches are applicable at different times and in different places. The conceptual toolbox helps in understanding and explaining a particular and limited range of observations. This limitation is true for management studies in general and equally true for project management. We might therefore say that different theories offer different explanations to different parts of the problem, and as stressed by Anderson (2007: 762): "Managers with a richer set of tools will be more likely to find appropriate tools to help them solve whatever problems they are currently facing." This statement is similarly true for the theorist: the one with a richer set of tools will be more likely to apply accurate perspectives and come up with novel and creative interpretations of the focal phenomenon and its behavior.

However, pluralism and growth of a scientific field are not without challenges—a scientific field might evolve into too much fragmentation with little possibility of fruitful debates and sharing of experiences and ideas. To avoid the "fragmentation trap" (Knudsen 2003), some kind of "unification" is desirable in terms of a common "cognitive problem" and connected sub-problems. An important part of such unification is the ongoing discussion about the nature and characteristics of projects—how are they similar and how are they different? Classifications, types, and typologies are helpful in answering such questions.

Projects: types and typologies

Classification is perhaps one of the "most central and generic of all our conceptual exercises." Without it "there could be no advanced conceptualization, reasoning, language, data analysis or, for that matter, social science research" (Bailey 1994: 1). Classifications in types and typologies are important instruments if we are comparing the similarities and differences across projects. They are also important if we are going to develop, in the spirit of Merton (1968), so-called "middle range theories," i.e. theories that "lie between the minor but necessary working hypotheses...and the all-inclusive systematic efforts to develop a unified theory" (1968: 39). Hence, they play an important part when comparing research findings across datasets and empirical contexts. For practice, agreement on how to determine project type is a "necessary step in developing new methods and tools for project management that are effective on different types of projects" (Crawford, Hobbs, and Turner 2005: 13).

Research has taken an interest in specific types of projects and their associated characteristics. For many, the type as such is an important driver for the research inquiries pursued—to investigate a particular kind of project with explicit attributes. For others, the development of typologies has been part of the entire research agenda. The latter is particularly common among scholars in the aforementioned Contingency School and its various developments of comparative schemes and "typological theories" of project management (for instance Shenhar and Dvir 1996). In the following overview, we will discuss classification into types and the development of typologies according to four logics, namely size, institutional/industry context, organizational condition, and task features.

First, with regard to size common themes include major projects, mega-projects, grand-scale projects, large engineering projects and programs (see for instance Morris and Hough 1987; Hobday 1998; Flyvbjerg, Bruzelius, and Rothengatter 2003; Miller and Lessard 2000). Second, as to institutional context, studies have documented the special nature of public projects (compared to private projects) and the differences among projects with regards to industry or sector properties, such as transportation, infrastructure, biotechnology, telecom, power plant, film-making, and construction projects (e.g. Faulkner and Anderson 1987; Morris 1973). Third, projects have been classified in terms of their "organizational condition." This includes such distinctions as inter-organizational projects (Jones and Lichtenstein 2008), global projects (Berggren 2004), dispersed projects, virtual, and co-located projects (e.g. Jarvenpaa and Leidner 1999). It also includes such comparisons as the "relationship continuity" of projects, repeat collaboration, and "embedded projects," although the latter analyses tend to integrate the institutional context with the organizational conditions (e.g. Cacciatori, Grabher, and Prencipe 2007; Skilton and Dooley 2010). Fourth, researchers have analyzed the specific "task features" associated with the output and nature of the task, typically complexity and uncertainty, or combinations or variations of these features. Söderlund (2005) suggested the distinction of projects into three primary types: business projects (projects for clients, delivery projects, complex systems projects), development projects (internal projects for the development of new technology, products, services, and knowledge), and change projects (expansions of organizational capacity, production facilities, new market development, change of organizational structure and processes, implementation of new IT systems). Similar typologies have been used in publications on the "value of project management" (Thomas and Mullaly 2007) and in comparative studies of critical success factors (Blindenbach-Driessen and van den Ende 2006).

Focusing more on the technological characteristics of the task, Morris identified three prime factors in the organizational analysis of project management: complexity, uncertainty, and pace (Morris 1973); which were further studied by Shenhar and Dvir (2007). Some studies concentrate on one of these features, such as complexity in so-called CoPS (Complex Products and Systems) projects (Hobday 1998). Others give attention to the technological uncertainty, most importantly the work of uncertainty by De Meyer, Loch, and Pich (2002), or even completely on one specific category associated with extreme sorts of uncertainty, such as "renewal projects" (Ekstedt et al. 1999) and "vanguard projects" (Brady and Davies 2004, see also Wheelwright and Clark 1992). Related to the latter is the typology of exploration and exploitation projects (cf. Brady and Davies 2004) and unique versus repetitive projects (Lundin and Söderholm 1995).

The above overview reflects the vital point that projects differ on important counts and that specific types of projects might require specific theories and success measurements. Table 2.2 summarizes some of the literature and the different attempts to make distinctions among projects. The list presented is far from complete but gives an idea of some of the attempts made to draw attention to particular categories and characteristics of projects (see also Crawford, Hobbs, and Turner 2005, for an extensive analysis).

The attempts at classification that have been made so far are important since they highlight the specific characteristics and challenges of different types of project and allow for comparisons across projects. Consequently, they improve the analysis of why and how projects differ—which is an important issue for theory development. To understand further the existence of projects, we need to examine the "complementarities" and the distinct organizational problems associated with the organization and management of projects.

Table 2.2 Projects: types and typologies

	Types/typologies	Authors (examples)
Size	Major projects	Morris and Hough (1987)
	Large engineering projects	Miller and Lessard (2000)
	Mega-projects	Flyvbjerg, Bruzelius, and Rothengatter (2003)
	Grand-scale projects	Shapira and Berndt (1997)
Institutional and industry context	Public projects	Hellgren and Stjernberg (1995)
	Industry-type projects	Crawford, Hobbs, and Turner (2005)
Organizational condition	Global projects	Berggren (2004)
	Inter-organizational projects	Jones and Lichtenstein (2008)
	Cross-functional projects	Blindenbach-Driessen and van den Ende (2006)
	Embedded projects	Cacciatori, Grabher, and Prencipe (2007)
Task features	Business, development, and change projects	Söderlund (2005), Thomas and Mullaly (2007), Blindenbach-Driessen and van den Ende (2006)
	Complexity, uncertainty (technological, novelty), pace	Shenhar and Dvir (2007)
	CoPS projects (Complex Products and Systems)	Hobday (1998), Davies and Brady (2000)
	Uncertainty (variation, foreseen uncertainty, unforeseen uncertainty, chaos)	De Meyer, Loch, and Pich (2002), Pich, Loch, and De Meyer (2002)
	Renewal projects	Ekstedt and Wirdenius (1995)
	Exploration and exploitation projects (vanguard projects)	Brady and Davies (2004)
	Repetitive and unique projects	Lundin and Söderholm (1995)
	Derivative, platform, breakthrough	Wheelwright and Clark (1992)

Problems: cooperation and coordination

Projects exist for various reasons, but they share one overall intent, namely to realize complementarities, which create a fundamental integration challenge. Such complementarities may be, to draw from Roberts (2004: 34), technological, social, or economic and involve "the interactions among changes in different variables in affecting performance." Complementarity, in general, thus exists when performing more of one variable/task increases the returns of doing more of the other. To be able to benefit from complementarities, two chief organizational problems need to be resolved: cooperation and coordination (Grant 1996). A great number of difficulties abound: sub-system managers have different priorities; managers from different organizations might give priority to different activities; and decision-making might be halted since neither hierarchical nor market solutions work to establish cooperation. Hence, to be able to sort out complementarities, the "cooperation problem" must be resolved. Dealing with the cooperation problem, however, does not perforce mean that the "coordination problem" has been solved. People might still have very different views on what to do, when to do it, and how to do it, despite sharing the same goal or having aligned incentive systems. The problem of coordination thus points out the importance of synchronized adjustments and actions.

The problem of cooperation originates from the fact that individuals and actors have conflicting goals and behave opportunistically, whereas the problem of coordination stems from the complexity of the task and the necessity to communicate and synchronize activities to achieve action efficiencies. The focus on these two problems might seem limited and not to grasp the entire spectrum of managerial problems that research on project management has explored. The argument is, however, that this spectrum of investigated problems could more or less be grouped as belonging to either one of these sorts, be it risks, rewards, relational contracting, or trust (which are here associated with the cooperation problem), or communication, knowledge integration, boundary objects, and errors (which belong to the category of coordination problems). Below we deal with these problems separately and in more detail to give an overview of extant literatures and theories.

The cooperation problem in project management

Cooperation is primarily a matter of achieving some kind of joint effort or operation through the association of a number of people/actors for mutual benefit. In that respect, we are dealing with the problem of achieving common goals, which occurs because people are somewhat selfish or give priority to local concerns. This is, according to Roberts (2004: 75), not to deny elements of altruism, but merely to "assert that pure altruism is unlikely" and that interests and preferences among individuals differ (March and Simon 1958). This might be particularly important in the presence of interdependencies, which proliferate if complementarities are to be achieved. The pressing matter is then to motivate and reward people so they choose a behavior and make prioritizations in a manner that is advantageous to achieve common action and thereby realize the common purpose.

A range of studies within project management has addressed the cooperation problem. Studies have focused on contractual arrangements, transaction costs in complex projects, opportunistic behavior and incentive systems, and the virtues of partnering and alliancing. Although there are, of course, important differences between these studies and many of them draw on rather different assumptions about rationality and the interest of human beings, they all deal in one way or another with the cooperation problem of project management. Recent topics include partnering (Bresnen and Marshall 2002), alliancing (Miller and Lessard 2000), formation of project networks (Cova, Ghauri, and Salle 2002), trust in projects (Meyerson, Weick, and Kramer 1996), risks and rewards in large-scale projects, and private–public partnerships (Kwak and Anbari 2009). It also involves the nature of safeguards and the consequences of hold-up problems in large-scale projects (Gil 2007).

Studies have addressed projects as a cooperation structure similar to a form of contract designed to achieve cooperation and economic exchange, which otherwise either would be handled within the boundaries of the firm or, given the cooperation difficulties, paired with task complexities and uncertainties, perhaps not at all. The project as a way out from the cooperation problem thus makes complex transactions achievable. This view of projects leads into a closer examination of various cooperation measures and mechanisms including contract forms, authority systems, goal formulation, incentive structures, motivation, and alignment. For obvious reasons, this stream of research typically also makes use of specific lines of theorization, including transaction cost theory (Reve and Levitt 1984), agency theory (Turner and Müller 2004), and authority (Stinchcombe and Heimer 1985). A salient feature of projects as "temporary cooperation" lends special interest in cooperation terms, namely the inherent logic of temporary transactions or interaction processes, which creates unique challenges. Actors may decide to behave opportunistically due to the lack of long-term relationships and "ongoing games of interaction" (Axelrod 1984). Actors may also, due to the lack of common history and diverse backgrounds, have difficulties in reaching consensus and trust, which may reduce the possibility of forming working relationships. For instance, Meyerson, Weick, and Kramer (1996) discuss the importance of establishing "swift trust" in project cooperation, and show that an important way of doing this is to rely on outside mechanisms, such as work roles, professions, and personal networks. According to these authors, project participants tend to trust one another because they represent a particular profession, such as chemists, engineers, or lawyers, or because they are part of the same social network without necessarily knowing each other personally. Building further on some of these ideas, Grabher (2002) analyzes the importance of stable and permanent networks to facilitate the formation of partnerships and thereby make project cooperation possible. In his studies, the "project ecology" is singled out as having a critical role in facilitating project cooperation, which generally emphasizes the embedded nature of projects—projects are temporary but they are created and carried out surrounded by a permanent network of professions, relations, and contacts. In some project contexts, it seems difficult, if not impossible, to rely on these long-term safeguard mechanisms and prospects for repeated interactions. For instance, Havila and Salmi (2009) discuss the problem of "project ending" as a built-in part of the successful outcomes of one-off projects in the capital goods and construction industries. The fact that cooperation is temporary and intended for termination opens up a whole cadre of risks that actors behave in a short-sighted and, in some situations, even an opportunistic way. The failure of the project then becomes a failure of cooperation.

The coordination problem in project management

The problem of coordination draws attention to a different set of challenges. This organizational problem may be severe despite common goals and cooperation routines, i.e. coordination might still be problematic despite the cooperation problem being solved. Typically, these challenges are dealt with by the use of classic coordination mechanisms such as standardization, planning, mutual adjustments, and team coordination (Thompson 1967; Van de Ven, Delbecq, and Koenig 1976). In Thompson's analysis, the need for coordination is largely dependent upon the nature of the task—principally uncertainty and interdependence. In the project management context, this was discussed already in Galbraith (1973) and elaborated further by Allen (1995). The latter pointed out three variables for deciding the appropriate structure required to solve the coordination problem: degree of sub-system interdependence, degree of disciplinary knowledge change, and project duration. In Allen's terms, a high degree of sub-system interdependence calls for tight project coordination, such as co-location and frequent team interactions. A high degree of disciplinary knowledge development, on the other hand, would reduce the economies of integration and speak in favor of a functional structure while limiting the merits of tight project coordination. Third, he adds, project duration is important since members can be tightly coordinated during a limited period of time without losing disciplinary knowledge depth. Shenhar and Dvir (2007) build on some of these observations in their analysis of the distinctive problems of project coordination. To analyze different types of projects and different solutions to the coordination problem at hand, they center on principally three "contingency factors": uncertainty (technological and market), complexity, and pace. Similar attempts to understand coordination in projects have been presented by Pich, Loch, and De Meyer (2002) in their treatise of unforeseeable uncertainty and complexity, and Lindkvist, Söderlund, and Tell (1998) in their distinction between analyzable and systemic complexity on the one hand, and error detection and error diagnostics, on the other. The key messages in these contributions are similar: Project organization is a matter of coordination that deals with task interdependence and task uncertainty—if there are no task interdependencies and task uncertainty, then there is only a limited coordination problem and no fundamental need for a project.

Projects as cooperation and coordination

The above discussion has highlighted two primary and rather different origins of the project as a solution to organizational problems. Based on these two origins we argue that projects exist for two specific and often separate reasons: either to sort out a problem of cooperation, or to sort out a problem of coordination. In real life, however, they are frequently intertwined, although to understand the theoretical foundations of project management it is helpful to separate them analytically. Looking at the literature, a set of terms, processes, and phenomena would be associated with these two rather different organizational problems. Cooperation studies typically involve the analysis of motivation, authority, contracts, and opportunism, whereas coordination studies relate to plans, schedules, and communication. The above account also presents some of the published work within these two areas and the typical research questions investigated. Table 2.3 summarizes our observations and tries to extend the analysis by outlining the differences between these two problems in terms of behavioral assumptions, project management topics, and theoretical constructs.

PROCESS: DYNAMICS AND PHASES

One of the most salient features of projects is their inherent organizational dynamics. Projects are born—they are created by man and they are designed to dissolve. The matter of birth and death of projects has accordingly been a core element of project management since the introduction of the project life cycle. This distinction is seen in the conventional descriptions of the project life cycle according to conceptualization, planning, implementation, and termination. It is also seen in studies of the critical success factors and how these factors vary over the phases of the project life cycle (Pinto and Prescott 1988). Generally, this focus on process signals an interest in the actions of individuals and the sequence of events that describes how things change over time (cf. Van de Ven 1992). In that respect, a project is treated not as a state but as a process, or perhaps rather as different processes operating at different levels of analysis.

Table 2.3 Projects as cooperation and coordination

	Cooperation	Coordination
Project management definition	Project management is the act of ensuring governance of complex transactions between separate parties involved in a project	Project management is the act of ensuring communication and information-sharing among involved actors in a project
Project differences	Relationship continuity (transaction frequency), asset specificity	Task characteristics (uncertainty and complexity, interdependence)
Managerial problems	Motivation and incentives	Interdependence and communication
Project management topics investigated	Partnering, alliances, networks, contracts, risks and rewards	Communication, learning, knowledge integration, planning
Typical theoretical constructs and lenses	Trust, authority, power, control, transaction costs	Learning, communication, problem-solving, coordination costs

In recent years, more elaborate forms of descriptions of the process dynamics involved in projects have been suggested, including contributions within the Behavior School where an acknowledged theme of analysis is the behavior and evolution of projects as temporary organizations. Examples include Gersick's (1988) work on punctuated equilibrium in project teams, the turnaround process in complex projects discussed by Engwall and Westling (2004), the evolutionary model of problem-solving in development projects presented in Lindkvist and Söderlund (2002), and the four sequencing concepts introduced in Lundin and Söderholm (1995): action-based entrepreneurialism, fragmentation for commitment-building, planned isolation, and institutionalized termination. The common theme in these process-oriented studies is the alternative view on processes and that there are different processes involved, be they technical, social, or a combination thereof.

The study of processes also typically highlights the importance of context and the nested nature of process and context (Kreiner 1995). To improve the analysis of the context of projects, a number of writers have suggested that research and practice need to address projects with a longer time perspective to fully acknowledge their institutional context (Engwall 2003). This extended view has profound implications for the study of project management. In a somewhat simplified way, one may therefore say that research must look at what happens before, during, and after a project to be able to understand its life history and journey from its embryonic start to its afterlife. This also has a bearing on the theories we need and for the type of research questions we raise.

In terms of the birth of projects, Morris (1994) was among the first to stress the importance of a holistic view of early phases of projects to fully understand the "management of projects." This leads us to questions, such as where projects come from, where ideas for projects emerge, what networks are built to shape projects, and how the demands for a project are framed and formulated. This insight has later on been followed by researchers who investigate the formation phase of projects (Miller and Floricel 2000), the marketing of projects (Cova, Ghauri, and Salle 2002), and the design of project networks (Hellgren and Stjernberg 1995). Some of the problems with the early stages of projects relate to decision-making—whether a particular project should be funded, how dominant stakeholders evaluate the project proposal, and matters associated with optimism and aspirations in decision-making (see Shapira and Berndt 1997; Flyvbjerg, Bruzelius, and Rothengatter 2003). The Relationship and the Decision Schools from our overview take particular interest in the early stages of projects, including work on "escalation of commitment" (Staw and Ross 1978), "network design" (Hellgren and Stjernberg 1995), and "optimism bias" (Lovallo and Kahneman 2003). Besides these investigations of the early phase of projects, a set of studies have investigated the capabilities necessary to create and shape projects.

Davies and Brady (2000) speak of "project capabilities" associated with repeatable solutions in the bid phase of projects. Miller and Olleros (2000) argue that "project-shaping" is fundamental to competitive advantage in project-based industries. Lampel (2001) extends some of these ideas and shows the importance of "entrepreneurial competencies" for successful project execution. These contributions indicate the significance of understanding how projects are created and shaped for both theory and practice.

The implementation of projects and the life of projects are the typical focus for a great deal of research and covered more or less by all schools discussed earlier. Investigations include a broad set of issues embracing the optimization of project implementation, the critical success factors, the design parameters for effective coordination, and the risks in projects. We here touch upon a range of elements that are found in standard textbooks, such as division of labor, work breakdown structures, planning and scheduling, organizing, teamwork, control, and communication. The bulk of papers in the leading journals devote their attention to this set of issues. In the school overview presented earlier, the Optimization School and the Contingency School are especially focused on this phase.

The death and afterlife of projects are somewhat more complicated matters, since many would say these are not the prime focus for projects and project management, but rather the prime focus of the owner of the project or the owner of the end-result. Despite this concern, we would like to mention it, since many projects continue to live and are reinterpreted through the history of time, due to the emergence of new knowledge and problems in projects that were not discovered either originally or during its implementation. In that respect, the life of a project should be filled with errors and problems, since it is during its life that errors should be detected, not when the end-results have been taken over by the maintenance organization, production units, clients, or end-users. In addition, to be able to learn, continue to develop, and evaluate accurately the outcome of a project, life after its death becomes important. This topic is addressed in project evaluations that span longer time horizons to secure client satisfaction, value creation, learning, and capability-building (see for instance Brady and Davies 2004 and Shenhar and Dvir 2007). Along these lines, inquiries would also embrace questions with regards to when a project is completed, when it ceases to exist, whether a project can be reincarnated, and whether it really is over when everybody thinks it is over (see for instance Brady and Davies 2009). The latter emphasizes the fact that the success of a project is not only dependent on who is evaluating, and how it is evaluated, but equally important is when it is evaluated. If one expands the analysis to include the death of projects, "project ending" and various psychological processes become important, such as separation, mourning, and detachment.

Perspectives, projects, problems, and processes

The above account has a set of implications for theory development in project management. The chief idea has been to offer a guide to and overview of the literature and current theoretical considerations in project management. This is not a complete view—more can and needs to be said. Still, the intent to identify a set of schools in project management research and from these schools discuss different perspectives is an important beginning to further the refinements, corroborations, and refutations of theories. The recommendations are summarized in four points.

First, we need to explicate the perspective applied and understand that there are different ideas about projects and project management, since there is a danger, Argyris (1977) reminds us, of leaving underlying assumptions hidden. Second, we need to better understand the phenomenon under study. One way of doing this is to offer more elaborate typologies. As mentioned earlier, this is important for the development of middle-range theories that are suited for specific types of projects. The obvious danger, though, is the overemphasis on alternative categories which gives rise to distinct literatures with the only determinable difference being the actual setting.

Third, projects are created for a variety of reasons and, to accurately address the specific organizational problems of projects, one is forced to attack the complicated inquiry of project existence, i.e. why do projects exist and what organizational problem is solved with the project solution? The answer to these questions has significant implications on the answers to another set of questions, including why projects differ, how they behave, and what determines their success or failure. This chapter has addressed these questions primarily through the ideas of complementarities and two corresponding organizational problems—cooperation and coordination. As a consequence, what is critical to develop is a better conceptualization of cooperation and coordination in projects and awareness that extant theories address different organizational problems. However, the problems dealt with in practice may often be intertwined and highly correlated. Theories of cooperation are different from theories of coordination and the theoretical foundations tend to draw on different assumptions about the motivation of individuals, their rationality, and the underlying explanations of project failure. To understand society's complex projects, we must acknowledge that these projects struggle with problems of cooperation and coordination, and in some cases, the chief difficulty lies in the specific combination of solutions to sort them out. For instance, solutions to a cooperation problem may create severe coordination problems.

Fourth, projects are inherently dynamic entities: projects are created, shaped, and designed to die. They differ considerably from conventional ideas about organizations as following the principle of "going concern." The management and development of such organizations are accordingly associated with a number of challenges and problems. To address these challenges, support from neighboring disciplines is needed. However, depending on the phase and process, different theories might be called for.

These four distinctions can be discussed in light of a "neo-conventional view" and compared with an "extended view." The latter is principally intended to shed some light on the main developments made within project management research in the past decade. It takes into account how perspectives have been added, how the views of different types of projects have been made more sophisticated, and how research has addressed separate organizational problems focusing on different processes and phases in the life of the project. These views are compared in Table 2.4 together with a few comments about the implications for research and managerial practice.

These distinctions are helpful in the comparison of project management studies with a particular focus on the perspectives applied, the type of project under study, the problem addressed, and the processes involved. The applied perspective makes the research frame the focal project in a particular way, as well as observe specific problems and processes. For instance, the decision-making theorist (Decision School, *Perspective*) would often explore major public investment projects (*Projects*), the cooperation problems (*Problem*) involved, and the political processes (*Process*) unfolding in the early phases of the project (*Process*). The contingency theorist (Contingency School, *Perspective*) normally analyzes complex R&D projects or engineering projects (*Project*) to examine the coordination problem (*Problem*) during project implementation (*Process*). Figure 2.1 schematically shows the interrelationships among these four distinctions.

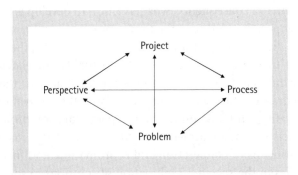

Fig. 2.1 A framework for understanding the theoretical foundations of project management research

Table 2.4 Theoretical foundations of project management: distinctions and implications

	Neo-conventional view	Extended view	Research implications	Managerial implications
Perspective	Project management dominated by rationalistic approaches, but an alternative organization theory perspective has been added (Packendorff 1995).	A considerable number of perspectives, schools and theories abound. These perspectives differ in terms of their project definition, key questions raised, primary focus of analysis, and linkages to base discipline.	Research should specify more clearly what perspectives are applied, how the research is building on existing research, and in what sense the research adds to existing knowledge within that particular perspective.	A project is many things at the same time: different actors perceive the same project in different ways.
Project	Projects are similar versus one size does not fit all (Shenhar 2001).	There are more elaborate attempts to identify types and construct typologies, primarily according to size, institutional context, organizational condition, and task features.	Research should specify clearly what type of project is under study, what the characteristics of that type are, and in what way the research contributes to existing research about the focal project type.	Projects differ and should be analyzed, managed, and organized differently, although there may be important similarities across projects and particularly across projects within projects of the same type.
Problem	Project management is the planning and organizing of resources to take the project to completion.	Project management is associated with two distinct organizational problems: the cooperation problem and the coordination problem.	Research should specify what organizational problem is dealt with and what sub-problem the study is emphasizing.	Projects are solutions to problems of particular kinds. Principally these problems relate to either the cooperation problem or the coordination problem. Each of these problems requires specific solutions—what might solve one problem could easily accentuate the other.

(continued)

Table 2.4 Continued

	Neo-conventional view	Extended view	Research implications	Managerial implications
Process	Project management varies according to the project life cycle; different tasks are carried out in different phases.	Projects are created, born, and designed to die. Project management involves the creative act of shaping projects, the implementation activities needed to reach set goals, and the decisions required to push progress forward or halt the entire project.	Research should pay more attention to process and acknowledge the fact that projects are evolving processes of organizing. It should also be more specific about what kind of process is centered in the particular study (political, social, technical, learning, sense-making, etc.).	Projects are dynamic, evolving entities and should be analyzed, managed, and organized differently depending on phase and focal process.

FRAGMENTATION WITH PROGRESS

What has been suggested in the present chapter is the need for a pluralistic under-standing of projects and project management, and that there is an opportunity for further development and refinements of theoretical ideas and perspectives. This underscores the fact that theories need to be questioned, debated, and replaced, and, equally important, need to be refined, tested, and improved.

Pluralism can also be viewed in light of Popper's (1945) claim that the more open a scientific field is towards new research ideas and approaches, the tougher the com-petition and, consequently, the better the chances for scientific breakthrough. At the same time, scientific fields struggle with the balance between exploration and exploitation, unification and pluralism, the search for new topics, methods, and the capitalization and improvement of existing knowledge (March 1996). Hence, there is a need for some kind of "unification" since too much fragmentation could easily hinder communication among scholars, which ultimately leads to a failure of knowledge-sharing and knowledge accumulation. The downside of too much uni-fication is the risk of getting caught in the specialization trap where the researcher is too involved with very narrow definitions of projects and occupied with protect-ing one's "home turf," building increasingly stronger internal consistency, but becoming increasingly distanced from the outside world and more and more irrel-evant to practice. The desire is, of course, that project management, as a scientific field, will be able to strike a fruitful balance between specialization and fragmenta-tion and between rigor and relevance.

The following claims are made: (1) there are multiple perspectives that illumi-nate different aspects, problems, and phases of projects, (2) there is some kind of unification within research in the sense that contributions tend to draw on simi-lar base disciplines and engage in similar kinds of questions and problems, (3) consciousness is growing of the distinctive managerial and organizational prob-lems involved in project management and that these problems relate to specific theoretical traditions, (4) acknowledgement is rising of the process dynamics involved in projects, from the early stages to their implementation and closure and the fact that these phases and processes relate to specific managerial prob-lems, and (5) elaborations are emerging on the phenomenon as such and the dis-cussion about clarifications of characteristics, similarities, and differences across project populations.

Conclusions

In line with the distinctions discussed earlier, we would call for research into broadening the set of perspectives, including critical and practice perspectives (Cicmil and Hogdson 2006) and analyses that seek to transcend conventional single project foci with the objective of enhancing the multi-level understanding of projects (cf. Sydow, Lindkvist, and DeFillippi 2004). Important here would, of course, be the ongoing debate on what schools are most relevant, what are the theories within each school that should be supported, and what theories should be refuted. In this respect, the different schools discussed earlier identify for the researcher what to build on and what to criticize. Besides the introduction of new perspectives and the refinements of existing ones, the ongoing elaboration of better conceptualizations of projects, types, and typologies is needed to improve the language that we use to speak about our common cognitive problem. This seems pressing since projects are used in a wider spectrum of sectors far beyond the traditional engineering and construction areas in which much of modern project management techniques were molded. Mega-projects, programs, grand-scale projects, etc. are of course just labels, but they are labels that attempt to differentiate them from other phenomena within the same group. Important here, it seems, is the ongoing debate of what labels to use, what categories to cherish, and what typologies to abandon. Each project type may very well be associated with quite unique organizational problems.

This chapter has analyzed two fundamental organizational problems: cooperation and coordination. For the theorist it seems critical to know the nature of the problem under study—if it is a problem of cooperation or a problem of coordination—but at the same time acknowledge that, in some situations, the pressing and interesting issues emerge in the amalgamation of them—that solutions to a particular cooperation problem might create intricate coordination problems.

Lastly, projects are not only static phenomena, organizational structures, investments, networks—they are perhaps foremost processes, and, as such, are different kinds of processes. This creates a whole cadre of opportunities for the theorist—projects are shaped and abandoned continuously, which implies that there are series of entrepreneurial and political actions occurring to create projects and kill projects. Accordingly, projects cease to exist and what specific processes are involved in such processes are still very much open questions.

NOTES

1. As highlighted in a series of recent reports, project management has expanded to cover other levels of analysis beyond the single project level. For instance, research focuses on the nature of project-based firms and some of their managerial challenges, such as project portfolio management, project capabilities, innovation, and human resource management (cf. Söderlund 2004b). The focus in the present review is on the project level and particularly the research that has taken interest in the shaping, creation, management, organization, and implementation of the single project.

2. The school categorization is based on a literature review of 305 articles published in the leading organization and management journals over more than 50 years. Similar categorizations are presented in Söderlund (2002). Alternatives have been offered to include more schools and somewhat different schools (for instance Turner, Anbari, and Bredillet 2008). The main point here is not to give a complete overview of the field, simply to illustrate some of the main development trajectories. Missing, although partly touched upon by research in the Behavior School, are projects-as-practice, gender issues, critical perspectives, and institutional analysis, to name but a few. The review is based on literature until 2008 on journal articles. Hence, it does not cover the most recent journal articles and the work published in reports and monographs.

3. The schools are summarized in greater depth in Söderlund (2002, 2010) and some of them are further elaborated and analyzed in Turner, Anbari, and Bredillet (2008). For details about the Optimization School, see Tavares (2002). For details about the Factor School, see Jugdev and Müller (2005). For details about the Contingency School, see Sauser, Reilly, and Shenhar (2009).

REFERENCES

ABERNATHY, W. J., and ROSENBLOOM, R. (1969). "Parallel strategies in development projects," *Management Science*, 15/10: 486–505.

ALLEN, T. J. (1995). "Organization and architecture for product development," Working Paper, MIT Sloan School of Management.

ANDERSON, M. C. (2007). "Why are there so many theories? A classroom exercise to help students appreciate the need for multiple theories of a management domain," *Journal of Management Education*, 31/6: 757–76.

ARGYRIS, C. (1977). "Double loop learning in organizations," *Harvard Business Review*, September–October: 115–25.

AVOTS, I. (1969). "Why does project management fail?" *California Management Review*, 12/1: 77–82.

AXELROD, R. (1984). *The Evolution of Cooperation*. New York: Basic Books.

BAILEY, K. (1994). *Typologies and Taxonomies: An Introduction to Classification Techniques*. Thousand Oaks, CA: Sage.

BERGGREN, C. (2004). "Global dreams—local teams: rhetoric and realities of transnational innovation," *International Journal of Innovation Management*, 8/2: 115–45.

BLINDENBACH-DRIESSEN, F., and VAN DEN ENDE, J. (2006). "Innovation in project-based firms: the context dependency of success factors," *Research Policy*, 35/4: 545–61.

BRADY, T., and DAVIES, A. (2004). "Building project capabilities: from exploratory to exploitative learning," *Organization Studies*, 25/9: 1601–21.

————(2009). "They think it's all over, it is now: Heathrow Terminal 5," paper presented at the EURAM Conference, Liverpool.

BRESNEN, M., and MARSHALL, N. (2002). "The engineering or evolution of co-operation? A tale of two partnering projects," *International Journal of Project Management*, 20/7: 497–505.

CACCIATORI, E., GRABHER, G., and PRENCIPE, A. (2007). "Continuity in project-based organizing: antecedents, artifacts, and adaptiveness," paper presented at the VII. IRNOP Conference, September 19–21, 2007, Brighton.

CICMIL, S., and HODGSON, D. (2006). "New possibilities for project management theory: a critical engagement," *Project Management Journal*, 37/3: 111–22.

COLE, S. (1983). "The hierarchy of the sciences?" *American Journal of Sociology*, 89/1: 111–39.

COOPER, D. F. (1976). "Heuristics for scheduling resource-constrained projects: an experimental investigation," *Management Science*, 22/11: 1186–94.

COVA, B., GHAURI, P., and SALLE, R. (2002). *Project Marketing: Beyond Competitive Bidding.* London: Wiley.

CRAWFORD, L., HOBBS, B., and TURNER, R. (2005). *Project Categorization Systems: Aligning Capability with Strategy for Better Results.* Newton Square, PA: Project Management Institute.

DAVIES, A., and BRADY, T. (2000). "Organisational capabilities and learning in complex product systems: towards repeatable solutions," *Research Policy*, 29: 931–53.

————and HOBDAY, M. (2005). *The Business of Projects.* Cambridge: Cambridge University Press.

DE MEYER, A., LOCH, C., and PICH, M. (2002). "Managing project uncertainty: from variation to chaos," *Sloan Management Review*, 43/2: 60–7.

EKSTEDT, E., and WIRDENIUS, H. (1995). "Renewal projects: sender target and receiver competence in ABB 'T50' and Skanska '3T'," *Scandinavian Journal of Management*, 11/4: 409–21.

————LUNDIN, R. A., SÖDERHOLM, A., and WIRDENIUS, H. (1999). *Neo-industrial Organising: Renewal by Action and Knowledge Formation in a Project-Intensive Economy.* London: Routledge.

ENGWALL, L. (1995). "Management research: a fragmented adhocracy?" *Scandinavian Journal of Management*, 11/3: 225–35.

ENGWALL, M. (2003). "No project is an island: linking projects to history and context," *Research Policy*, 32: 789–808.

————and WESTLING, G. (2004). "Peripety in an R&D drama: capturing a turnaround in project dynamics," *Organization Studies*, 25: 1557–78.

FAGERBERG, J., and VERSPAGEN, B. (2009). "Innovation studies: the emerging structure of a new scientific field," *Research Policy*, 38: 218–33.

FAULKNER, R. R., and ANDERSON, A. B. (1987). "Short-term projects and emergent careers: evidence from Hollywood," *American Journal of Sociology*, 92: 879–909.

FLYVBJERG, B., BRUZELIUS, N., and ROTHENGATTER, W. (2003). *Megaprojects and Risk: An Anatomy of Ambition.* Cambridge: Cambridge University Press.

FREDRICKSON, J. (1990). "Introduction: the need for perspectives," in J. Fredrickson (ed.), *Perspectives on Strategic Management.* New York: Harper.

GALBRAITH, J. R. (1973). *Designing Complex Organizations*. Reading, MA: Addison-Wesley.

GEMMILL, G., and WILEMON, D. L. (1970). "The power spectrum in project management," *Sloan Management Review*, 12/1: 15–25.

GERSICK, C. (1988). "Time and transition in work teams: toward a new model of group development," *Academy of Management Journal*, 31/1: 9–41.

GIL, N. (2007). "On the value of project safeguards: embedding real options in complex products and systems," *Research Policy*, 36/7: 980–99.

GOODMAN, L. P., and GOODMAN, R. A. (1972). "Theater as a temporary system," *California Management Review*, 15/2: 103–8.

GOODMAN, R. A., and GOODMAN, L. P. (1976). "Some management issues in temporary systems: a study of professional development and manpower: the theater case," *Administrative Science Quarterly*, 21/3: 494–501.

GRABHER, G. (2002). "Cool projects, boring institutions: temporary collaboration in social context," *Regional Studies*, 36/3: 205–14.

——(2004). "Temporary architectures of learning: knowledge governance in project ecologies," *Organization Studies*, 25: 1491–514.

GRANT, R. M. (1996). "Toward a knowledge-based theory of the firm," *Strategic Management Journal*, 17, Special Issue: 109–22.

HAVILA, V., and SALMI, A. (2009). *Managing Project Ending*. New York: Routledge.

HELLGREN, B., and STJERNBERG, T. (1995). "Design and implementation in major investments: a project network approach," *Scandinavian Journal of Management*, 11/4: 377–94.

HOBDAY, M. (1998). "Product complexity, innovation and industrial organisation," *Research Policy*, 26: 689–710.

——(2000). "The project-based organization: an ideal form for management of complex products and systems?" *Research Policy*, 29: 871–93.

HOLLOWAY, C. A., NELSON, R., and SURAPHONGSCHAI, V. (1979). "Comparison of a multipass heuristic decomposition procedure with other resource-constrained project scheduling procedures," *Management Science*, 25/9: 862–72.

JARVENPAA, S. L., and LEIDNER, D. E. (1999). "Communication and trust in global virtual teams," *Organization Science*, 10/6: 791–815.

JOHNSON S. B. (1997). "Three approaches to big technology: operations research, systems engineering and project management," *Technology and Culture*, 38/4: 891–919.

JONES, C., and LICHTENSTEIN, B. (2008). "Temporary inter-organizational projects: how temporal and social embeddedness enhance coordination and manage uncertainty," in S. Cropper, M. Ebers, C. Huxham, and P. S. Ring (eds.), *Oxford Handbook of Interorganizational Relations*. Oxford: Oxford University Press.

JUGDEV, K., and MÜLLER, R. (2005). "A retrospective look at our evolving understanding of project success," *Project Management Journal*, 36/4: 19–31.

KNUDSEN, K. (2003). "Pluralism, scientific progress, and the structure of organization theory," in H. Tsoukas and C. Knudsen (eds.), *Oxford University Press Handbook on Organization Theory*. Oxford: Oxford University Press. ·

KREINER, K. (1995). "In search of relevance: project management in drifting environments," *Scandinavian Journal of Management*, 11/4: 335–46.

KWAK, Y. H., and ANBARI, F. T. (2009). "Analyzing project management research: perspectives from top management journals," *International Journal of Project Management*, 27: 435–46.

LAMPEL, J. (2001). "The core competencies of effective project execution: the challenge of diversity," *International Journal of Project Management*, 19/8: 471–83.

LINDKVIST, L., and SÖDERLUND, J. (2002). "What goes on in projects? On goal-directed learning processes," in K. Sahlin-Andersson and A. Söderholm (eds.), *Beyond Project Management*. Malmö: Liber Abstrakt.

——— and TELL, F. (1998). "Managing product development projects: on the significance of fountains and deadlines," *Organization Studies*, 19/6: 931–51.

LOVALLO, D., and KAHNEMAN, D. (2003). "Delusions of success: how optimism undermines executives' decisions," *Harvard Business Review*, July: 56–63.

LUNDIN, R. A., and SÖDERHOLM, A. (1995). "A theory of the temporary organization," *Scandinavian Journal of Management*, 11/4: 437–55.

MARCH, J. G. (1996). "The future, disposable organizations and the rigidities of imagination," *Organization*, 2/3–4: 427–40.

—— and SIMON, H. (1958). *Organizations*. New York: Wiley.

MERTON, R. K. (1968). *Social Theory and Social Structure*. New York: Free Press.

MEYERSON, D., WEICK, K. E., and KRAMER, R. M. (1996). "Swift trust and temporary groups," in R. H. Kramer and T. R. Tyler (eds.), *Trust in Organizations*. Thousand Oaks, CA: Sage.

MILLER, R., and FLORICEL, S. (2000). "Transformations in arrangements for shaping and delivering engineering projects," in R. Miller and D. Lessard (eds.), *The Strategic Management of Large Engineering Projects*. Cambridge, MA: MIT Press.

—— and LESSARD, D. (2000). *The Strategic Management of Large Engineering Projects*. Cambridge, MA: MIT Press.

—— and OLLEROS, X. (2000). "Project shaping as a competitive advantage," in R. Miller and D. Lessard (eds.), *The Strategic Management of Large Engineering Projects*. Cambridge, MA: MIT Press.

MORRIS, P. W. G. (1973). "An organizational analysis of project management in the building industry," *Build International*, 6/6: 595–616.

—— (1994). *The Management of Projects*. London: Thomas Telford.

—— and HOUGH, G. H. (1987). *The Anatomy of Major Projects: A Study of the Reality of Project Management*. Chichester: John Wiley.

PACKENDORFF, J. (1995). "Inquiring into the temporary organization: new directions for project management research," *Scandinavian Journal of Management*, 11/4: 319–34.

PICH, M. T., LOCH, C. H., and DE MEYER, A. (2002). "On uncertainty, ambiguity, and complexity in project management," *Management Science*, 48/8: 1008–23.

PINTO, J. K., and PRESCOTT, J. E. (1988). "Variations in critical success over the stages of the project life cycle," *Journal of Management*, 14: 5–18.

——— (1990). "Planning and tactical factors in the project implementation process," *Journal of Management Studies*, 27/3: 305–27.

POPPER, K. R. (1945). *The Open Society and its Enemies*. London: Routledge and Kegan Paul.

REVE, T., and LEVITT, R. (1984). "Organization and governance in construction," *International Journal of Project Management*, 2: 17–25.

ROBERTS, J. (2004). *The Modern Firm*. Oxford: Oxford University Press.

ROSS, J., and STAW, B. M. (1986). "Expo 86: an escalation prototype," *Administrative Science Quarterly*, 31: 274–97.

SAUSER, B. J., REILLY, R. R., and SHENHAR, A. J. (2009). "Why projects fail? How contingency theory can provide new insights: a comparative analysis of NASA's Mars Climate Orbiter loss," *International Journal of Project Management*, 27/7: 665–79.

SHAPIRA, Z., and BERNDT, D. J. (1997). "Managing grand-scale construction projects: a risk-taking perspective," *Research in Organizational Behavior*, 19: 303–60.

SHENHAR, A. (2001). "One size does not fit all projects: exploring classical contingency domains," *Management Science*, 47/3: 394–414.

——and DVIR, D. (1996). "Toward a typological theory of project management," *Research Policy*, 25: 607–32.

————(2007). *Reinventing Project Management: The Diamond Approach to Successful Growth and Innovation*. Boston: Harvard Business School Press.

SKILTON P., and DOOLEY, K. (2010). "The effects of repeat collaboration on creative abrasion," *Academy of Management Review*, 35/1: 118–34.

SÖDERLUND, J. (2002). "On the development of project management research: schools of thought and critique," *International Project Management Journal*, 6/1: 20–31.

——(2004a). "Building theories of project management: past research, questions for the future," *International Journal of Project Management*, 22: 183–91.

——(2004b). "On the broadening scope of the research on projects: a review and a model for analysis," *International Journal of Project Management*, 22: 655–67.

——(2005). "Developing project competence: empirical regularities in competitive project operations," *International Journal of Innovation Management*, 9/4: 451–80.

——(2010). "Pluralism in project management research: navigating the crossroads of specialisation and fragmentation," *International Journal of Management Reviews*, forthcoming.

STAW, B. M., and ROSS, J. (1978). "Commitment to a policy decision: a multi-theoretical perspective," *Administrative Science Quarterly*, 23/1: 40–64.

STINCHCOMBE, A., and HEIMER, C. (eds.) (1985). *Organization Theory and Project Management*. Oslo: Norwegian University Press.

SYDOW, J., LINDKVIST, L., and DEFILIPPI, R. (2004). "Project-based organizations, embeddedness and repositories of knowledge: editorial special issue," *Organization Studies*, 25/9: 1475–89.

TAVARES, L. V. (2002). "A review of the contribution of operational research to project management," *European Journal of Operational Research*, 136: 1–18.

THAMHAIN, H. J., and GEMMILL, G. R. (1974). "Influence styles of project managers: some project performance correlates," *Academy of Management Journal*, 17/2: 216–24.

THOMAS, J., and MULLALY, M. (2007). "Understanding the value of project management: first steps on an international investigation in search of value," *Project Management Journal*, 38/3: 74–89.

THOMPSON, J. D. (1967). *Organizations in Action*. New York: McGraw Hill.

TURNER, J., ANBARI, F., and BREDILLET, C. (2008). "Perspectives on research in project management," paper presented at the Academy of Management Meeting, Anaheim.

TURNER, J. R., and MÜLLER, R. (2004). "Communication and co-operation on projects between the project owner as principal and the project manager as agent," *European Management Journal*, 22/3: 327–36.

VAN DE VEN, A. H. (1992). "Suggestions for studying strategy process: a research note," *Strategic Management Journal*, 13: 169–88.

——DELBECQ, A. L., and KOENIG, R. (1976). "Determinants of coordination modes within organizations," *American Sociological Review*, 41/2: 322–38.

WEGLARZ, J. (1981). "Project scheduling with continuously divisible, doubly constrained resources," *Management Science*, 27/9: 1040–53.

WEICK, K. E. (1992). "Agenda setting in organizational behavior: a theory-focused approach," *Journal of Management Inquiry*, 1: 171–82.

WHEELWRIGHT, S. C., and CLARK, K. B. (1992). *Revolutionizing Product Development*. Boston: Harvard Business School Press.

WHITLEY, R. (1984). "The fragmented state of management studies: reasons and consequences," *Journal of Management Studies*, 21/3: 331–48.

WILEMON, D. L., and CICERO, J. P. (1970). "Project manager: anomalies and ambiguities," *Academy of Management Journal*, 13/3: 269–82.

CHAPTER 3

THE EVOLUTION OF PROJECT MANAGEMENT RESEARCH

THE EVIDENCE FROM THE JOURNALS

RODNEY TURNER

JEFFREY PINTO

CHRISTOPHE BREDILLET

INTRODUCTION

This chapter seeks to address the question of the current state of project management research through an analysis of the domain's advance over time, as evidenced in the pages of its principal academic research outlets. While there are many ways in which theoreticians and researchers have sought to examine the evolving nature of the project management research field, our attempt here involves a more forensic approach, based on a critical review of some of the published literature. Over the past twenty years there has been a substantial improvement in the quality and rigor of project management research, as evidenced by the standard of papers being published in three leading academic research journals that focus on project management research:

- The *International Journal of Project Management*, published by Elsevier (IJPM)
- The *Project Management Journal*, published by Wiley (PMJ)
- The *IEEE Transactions on Engineering Management* (IEEE-TEM), published by the Institute of Electrical and Electronics Engineers Technology Management Council (formerly IEEE Engineering Management Society)

This chapter represents the collective thoughts and reflections of the three journals' editors at the time of writing on the evolution of the project management research field.

In the 1970s, most "research" writing in project management was dominated by practitioners, who set the research agenda and research style (Turner et al. 2010). In the 1980s it became heavily influenced also by the professional associations, the Project Management Institute (PMI®), the International Project Management Association (IPMA), the Association for Project Management (APM), and the Australian Institute of Project Management (AIPM). During this phase, there was a concerted push on the part of these associations to establish the domains' knowledge base through its "body of knowledge," of which several variants appeared (Project Management Institute 1987, 2008; International Project Management Association 2006; Association for Project Management 2006; Australian Institute of Project Management 2004). Ultimately, as in the 1970s, much of the research in Project Management at this time could be characterized as very practitioner oriented. This tended to mean:

- it was narrow in scope, in the worst cases just focusing on improving optimization tools such as critical path analysis;
- it lacked rigor because it typically was not based on sound research methodologies;
- it often employed single case studies, including "war stories," which, while offering practical guidance to practitioners, were often hard to generalize for the wider purpose of developing theory;
- it often did not draw from nor make reference to the literature, often lacking citations.

As a result, project management came to be seen in many academic institutions as something of a "quasi-discipline," with little agreement as to roots or heritage ("Is it decision sciences? Organization Theory? Operations Research?"). Fundamentally, project management research was an outcropping of other fields and many of its early researchers made their academic "homes" in allied but separate disciplines, including construction, engineering, and management science.

However, since the early 1990s there has been a substantial improvement in the quality and rigor of research in project management, as can be seen in the three research journals. Specifically:

- the papers cover a wider range of topics, showing that project management is a richer, more diverse field, and people are recognizing that a much wider range of methods are available for the successful delivery of projects;

- the research on which the papers are based uses more rigorous methodologies, with the result that the research is sounder and can contribute to theory development;
- there are an increasing number of citations to recent journal articles, with the result that the research is soundly based on recent theory development;
- there are citations to a much wider range of journals outside the field, showing that project management is drawing on and contributing to a wider range of other domains, making the research richer, and ensuring it is backed by theory development elsewhere; and
- papers are being cited by articles from a wider range of journals, showing that project management research is making a wider contribution outside the field.

The purpose of our analysis here is to present evidence to support the above contentions, through an evaluation of project management research as it has been published in the three leading academic project management journals.

Our analysis examined three distinct aspects of this published work:

1. Topics—we refer to "topics" as the specific project management issues or subjects addressed in the paper itself. Analyzing topic content allowed us to make some observations about the range of issues these papers addressed. In identifying the range of topics that we classified for this chapter, we relied on the previous work of Morris (2001) and Kwak and Anbari (2009) who developed such classification schemes.

2. Methodologies employed—we also wanted to understand the types of analytic techniques used within the publications. Methodologies ranged from the highly conceptual and qualitative to the more quantitative and statistically rigorous techniques. There were a total of twenty-one possible methodologies that we identified as being used in project management research.

3. Citation patterns—we examined the citations that these papers referred to; that is, we wanted to ascertain the types of journals or other outlets that authors used as references for their published work. We were interested in determining the degree to which these papers made reference to other project management literatures, business, engineering, psychology, or other sources. In short, what were the sources of inspiration for these papers? A total of thirty-six possible outlets can be identified for IJPM for example as citation sources for project management publications (Table 3.1), ranging from academic journals, to conference proceedings, and most recently to web sources. Further, it is interesting to note the trends for these citations. As you will see from the tables, much of the early project management work had, as its key sources, reference to a relatively limited set of disciplinary journals. Over the past twenty years, this set has dramatically broadened. The list of key sources for project management publication citations now includes the fields shown in Table 3.2.

In the next sections we will examine each of the three journals' publication patterns in detail, using the above three criteria.

Table 3.1 Citations by articles published in IJPM

	1987 No.	1987 Ave	1997 No.	1997 Ave	2007 No.	2007 Ave
Number of papers	31		45		85	
Number of papers without citations	18	.58	4	.09	0	0
Project Management Journals						
International Journal of Project Management	6	.19	48	1.07	366	4.31
Project Management Journal	2	.06	10	.22	67	.79
Other	3	.09	1	.02	6	.07
IEEE Transactions	0	.00	17	.38	29	.34
Engineering	2	.06	3	.07	19	.22
Engineering Management	1	.03	11	.24	48	.56
Cost Engineering	1	.03	18	.40	4	.05
Construction	8	.26	21	.47	86	1.01
Construction Management	2	.06	46	1.02	209	2.46
Procurement and Supply Chain					24	.28
ICT			17	.38	37	.44
ICT Management			4	.09	1	.01
Quality			9	.20	77	.91
Research			4	.09	6	.07
General Management	6	.19	16	.36	164	1.93

Business Studies			2	.04	34	.36
Strategy			9	.20	31	.42
Marketing			4	.09	17	.20
Governance					3	.04
Decision Science	6	.19	24	.53	110	1.29
HRM, OB, Education and Learning, Health	3	10	13	.29	182	2.14
Finance, Economics and Politics	5	.16	3	.07	34	.40
Law			4	.09	11	.13
Accounting			9	.20		
Risk and Insurance					12	.14
Environment					8	.09
Ethics and Philosophy					6	.07
Total number of journal articles cited	45	1.45	293	6.51	1593	18.74
Ignoring articles without citations		3.46		7.15		18.74
Conference Papers						
PMI Practitioner Conferences	2	.06	8	.18	14	.16
PMI Research Conference	0		0	.00	20	.24
IPMA Practitioner Conference	6	.19	9	.20	1	.01
IPMA Expert Seminars			1	.02		
IRNOP			1	.02	16	.19

(continued)

Table 3.1 Continued

	1987 No.	1987 Ave	1997 No.	1997 Ave	2007 No.	2007 Ave
EURAM			0	.00	5	.06
Other Project Management Conference			3	.07	6	.07
Other Conferences	7	.23	30	.67	51	.60
Total Conference Paper citations	15	.48	52	1.16	113	1.33
Ignoring articles without citations		1.15		1.27		1.33
Web pages cited					68	.80

Table 3.2 Areas to which project management citations are made

Engineering and Engineering Management

Cost Engineering

Construction and Construction Management (including Facilities Management)

General Management

Decision Sciences, Operations Research, and Management Science

Human Resource Management, Organizational Behavior, Education and Training, and other people issues

Finance, Economics, and Politics

ICT (Information and Communication Technologies) and ICT Management, but only as it applies to computerizing the construction process, not as it applies to the management of ICT projects

Research and Innovation

Quality

Business Studies

Strategy

Law

Marketing

Accounting

Procurement Governance

Risk, Safety, and Insurance

Environment

Ethics and Philosophy

INTERNATIONAL JOURNAL OF PROJECT MANAGEMENT (IJPM)

IJPM was founded in 1983 by the UK's Association for Project Management on behalf of the International Project Management Association (IPMA). In March 2009, IJPM was admitted to the Social Science Citation Index (Thomson World of Science), reinforcing the substantial improvement in the quality and rigor of project management research.

To demonstrate the improvement in the quality and rigor of articles published in IJPM, we compared articles published at ten-year intervals, 1987, 1997, and 2007. We chose those years, rather than a year later, because there will not yet, at the time of writing, be many citations of articles published in 2008. In 1987 IJPM was publishing just four issues per year. The number of issues had grown to six in 1997 and the current eight in 2007. Also the number of papers per issue has grown. In 1987 and 1997 it was about eight papers per issue, giving thirty-one and forty-five papers in each of those two years. By 2007 it was almost eleven papers per issue, eighty-five in total. The increasing number of papers is indicative of the growing interest in the subject.

Topics covered

Table 3.3 shows the topics covered by papers published in the journal in the three years 1987, 1997, and 2007. The classifications used in the table are the ones that the authors used to classify their papers when submitting papers to the journal.

Total number of topics

In 1987, papers covered an average of about one and a half topics each, whereas in 1997 and 2007 they covered an average of about two topics each. In 2007 many papers covered three topics, for instance describing the application of a technique in a given industry (usually construction) in a particularly country (usually a recently developed country in the Far East). However, the increasing number of papers is largely responsible for the larger number of topics, with many topics being mentioned just once in each of the three years. But the increasing number of papers published is in itself an indication of the growing interest in project management.

Range of topics

In 1987, there was at least one paper about a topic from each of the topic areas. So the full breadth of field areas was covered. The most popular setting was within the engineering and construction industry, a quarter of papers being specifically about that industry. We will see this repeated in the number of citations of papers from construction and construction management journals. The next most popular topics were computer support, managing time, execution and control, post-commissioning operation and maintenance, and projects in newly developed countries with three mentions each (10 percent of papers).

In 1997 the most popular topic was still the engineering and construction industry, with now almost a third of papers being about the topic. The second most popular topic was now risk management, which had received only one mention in 1987, with one fifth of papers being about that topic. There was an increase in interest in computer support (13 percent), managing time (11 percent), while interest in execution and control (9 percent) and newly developed countries (7 percent) remained about the same. But in 1997 (and in 2007) there were no papers about post-commissioning operation and maintenance. Other topics being mentioned by around 10 percent of papers in 1997 were managing resources, and research and development projects.

Table 3.3 Topics covered by papers in IJPM

	1987 No.	1987 Ave	1997 No.	1997 Ave	2007 No.	2007 Ave
Number of papers	31		45		85	
Total number of topics covered	45	1.45	91	2.02	168	1.98
General						
Organizational strategy					2	.02
Project management	1	.03	4	.09	5	.06
Program management			3	.07	1	.01
Portfolio management					2	.02
Complexity						
Project office					1	.01
Project-based organizations					5	.06
Project success and strategy	1	.03	1	.02	2	.02
Sponsorship			1	.02		
Systems						
Computer support	3	.10	6	.13	4	.05
Standards						

(continued)

Table 3.3 Continued

	1987 No.	1987 Ave	1997 No.	1997 Ave	2007 No.	2007 Ave
Audits and health checks	1	.03			1	.01
Managing context					1	.01
Project management research					1	.01
Functions						
Managing requirements			2	.04		
Managing configuration			2	.04		
Managing scope			2	.04	2	.02
Managing value					2	.02
Managing organization			1	.02	2	.02
Managing quality			1	.02	2	.02
Managing cost	1	.03	1	.02	3	.04
Managing time	3	.10	5	.11	6	.07
Managing risk	1	.03	9	.20	11	.13
Managing resources	1	.03	4	.09	4	.05
Managing environment	1	.03	1	.02	2	.02

Managing safety					1	.01
Life cycle						
Start-up					1	.01
Feasibility and design	2	.06	3	.07	1	.01
Execution and control	3	.10	4	.09	1	.01
Close-out and commissioning					1	.01
Operation and maintenance	3	.10			1	.01
Finance						
Appraisal	1	.03	1	.02	1	.01
Project finance	2	.06			1	.01
Contracts						
Project contract organization	1	.03				
Contract management	1	.03	1	.02	2	.02
Partnerships and alliances					10	.12
PPP/PFI					3	.04
BOOT			2	.08		
Contract procurement and tendering	1	.03			1	.01

(continued)

Table 3.3 Continued

	1987 No.	1987 Ave	1997 No.	1997 Ave	2007 No.	2007 Ave
Bidding						
Supply chain					3	.04
Contract administration						
Claims						
People						
Individual competence/ learning	2	.06	1	.02	5	.06
Organizational capability					2	.02
Managing teams			2	.04		
Leadership			2	.04	1	.01
Managing culture	1	.03			2	.02
Managing stakeholders					2	.02
Managing conflict and negotiation					1	.01
Managing communication						
Managing ethics						

Managing decisions			1	.02	7	.08
General management						
Managing innovation			1		1	.01
Human resource management					5	.06
Managing information					1	.01
Organizational behavior						
Transaction costs/Agency theory					1	.01
Gender					1	.01
Geography						
Old world	1	.03			2	.02
New developed countries	3	.10	3	.07	6	.07
International projects			1	.02	1	.01
Industry						
Engineering and construction	8	.26	14	.31	31	.36
Manufacturing			2	.04	1	.01
Information, computers, and telecoms			3	.07		
Infrastructure			2	.04	2	.02

(continued)

Table 3.3 Continued

	1987 No.	1987 Ave	1997 No.	1997 Ave	2007 No.	2007 Ave
Government	1	.03	1	.02	1	.01
Research and development			4	.09	4	.05
Services					4	.05
Leisure					2	.02

There were also three papers about program management, though two of these were more about portfolio management.

In 2007 the most popular topic was still projects in the engineering and construction industry, with now over a third of papers being about that topic. However, during the year there was a special issue on that topic, so the growth in papers in that area since 1997 can be explained by that. The second most popular topic was still risk management (13 percent) followed closely by partnering and alliancing (12 percent). However, many of the papers in the special issue were about partnering and alliancing, but even without that issue, partnering and alliancing would still have been the third most popular topic. No other topic now received a mention by more than 10 percent of papers, but several were mentioned by more than 5 percent of papers. There is no loss of interest in a topic since 1997, but the interesting appearance of two new topics is human resource management and the services industry.

Research methodologies used

Table 3.4 lists the research methodologies used by papers in IJPM in the three years taken for this analysis.

Papers with a methodology section

In 1987 there was just one paper having a section describing the research methodology employed. In 1997 there were thirteen, about a quarter; in 2007 about three quarters of papers had a methodology section (sixty-one). This is an indication of a growing concern for rigor.

Total number of methods used

The papers in 1987 used just one method each. In 1997 and 2007 about 20 percent of papers were using mixed methods. It was quite common to combine a literature search with another method, perhaps a survey, case study, or the development of a new technique. But other techniques would also be combined, such as the development of a new technique and a case study to illustrate it, or a survey with semi-structured interviews.

Range of methods used

In 1987 there was a very narrow range of methods used, and they illustrate the then practitioner focus of the journal. The methods used in 1987 were predominantly citing examples of existing techniques or introducing new ideas, comparison of techniques, conceptual papers, literature reviews, and case studies. Many of these were aimed at illustrating the application of project management for practitioners. The greatest number of papers (29 percent) were conceptual papers. These are

Table 3.4 Methodologies used by articles published in IJPM

	1987 No.	1987 Ave	1997 No.	1997 Ave	2007 No.	2007 Ave
Number of papers	31		45		85	
Papers with a methodology section	1	.03	13	.29	61	.72
Total number of methods used	31	1.00	54	1.20	99	1.16
Methods used						
Example of an existing technique	6	.19				
Development of a new technique	3	.10	6	.13	12	.14
Comparison of techniques	2	.06	1	.02		
Conceptual paper	9	.29	15	.33	10	.12
Theoretical development	2	.06	2	.04	1	.01
Literature review	2	.06	5	.11	17	.20
Content analysis					1	.01
Case study	7	.22	5	.11	15	.18
Pilot study			1	.02	1	.01
Survey			11	.24	22	.26
Semi-structured interviews			2	.04	2	.02
Grounded theory			2	.04		
Delphi			2	.04		

ANOVA			1	.01
Field study			5	.06
Action research	1	.02	6	.07
Ethnographic study	2	.04		
Discourse			1	.01
Modeling				
Computer simulation	1	.02	4	.05
Role game			1	.01

papers that give a perspective on an element of theory. In 1997 and 2007, no papers gave an illustration of an existing technique, showing a move away from a practitioner focus. In 1997, there were fifteen conceptual papers (33 percent). However these were often outlining concepts for academic researchers. In 2007, the percentage of conceptual papers fell to 12 percent.

In 1997 and 2007, it was clear that the methods used in the papers had broadened out significantly, as a range of new methods approaches were employed. After conceptual papers, survey is the next most popular technique, 24 percent of papers. By 2007, this was the most popular technique overall, appearing in 26 percent of papers. The percentage for this technique was not much changed from 1997, but conceptual papers were now not so common. Overall, it is clear that the two years (1997 and 2007) showed evidence that: (1) there has been a shift away from practitioner-based techniques and the adoption of more rigorous methods, and (2) a much wider range of research and analytical techniques is being used.

Number of citations by papers published in the journal

Table 3.1 shows the number of citations by papers published in IJPM in each of the three years 1987, 1997, and 2007. These citation patterns are intended to show the source of referencing done by authors published in IJPM to identify the types of journals from which they are drawing their citations.

In 1987, more than half the papers (58 percent) have no citations at all. This was not a once-off. There were a similar number without citations in 1988. In 1997, four papers still had no citations. Papers from 1987 which have citations typically have around ten, though the record was over fifty. Papers from 1997 typically have around 20 citations, and from 2007 around 40 (though the record was over 100). The average number of citations of journal articles from 1987 was 1.5. If we ignore the papers without citations, the average rises to 3.5. By 1997 that had doubled to 7.0; articles are making twice as many citations. By 2007, the average number of citations of journal articles had almost trebled again, to almost nineteen. That is over twelve times more than the average number of citations in 1987.

Over the years, there has been very little change in the number of citations of conference papers, running at just under 1.5 throughout the twenty years. The change is that people are now citing the new research conferences, and whereas citations of the PMI practitioner conferences have remained fairly stable, citations of IPMA's practitioner conference have almost disappeared. However, in 2007 a very large number of the citations of the PMI practitioner conferences were from just two papers and one was self-citations.

The new arrival is the citation of web pages. The average for 2007 was 0.8 citations of a web page per paper. While most papers still cite none, some make web pages the main source of literature.

Sources of papers being cited by papers in IJPM

Table 3.1 shows where the papers being cited by papers in IJPM were themselves published. Over the twenty years, self-citations in IJPM have increased almost twentyfold, compared to the twelvefold overall increase of citations by papers in the journal. Citations of papers in PMJ have increased about twelvefold, in line with the overall increase. Over the years, papers in the journal have been citing papers from an increasing number of fields.

The most significant number of citations is of construction journals, with an average of almost 3.5 citations per paper in 2007. There is also a strong interest in engineering and engineering management, with an average of about 0.8 citations per paper in 2007. Over the years there is a growing interest in management topics. By 2007, general management, business, and strategy receive an average of about 2.7 citations per paper, decisions sciences about 1.3, and Human Resources and Organizational Behavior about 2.1.

Cited articles about ICT are primarily about computers' role in the construction design and execution processes. In 1997 there was only one article cited about managing ICT projects, and none in 2007. Many of the articles are generic and apply to all industries. But if people write about a specific industry it is primarily about construction. There has been increasing interest in research, looking at research projects, research in construction, and the research process itself.

The absence of papers on procurement in 1987 and 1997 is surprising. There was an article on contract management in the very first issue of IJPM. There has recently been a growing interest in forms of contract, particularly BOT and PPP/PFI. Articles on contract management appear in journals on Construction Management, Procurement, Law, or Project Management. Governance and the Environment are popular issues at the moment.

Project Management Journal (**PMJ**)

The *Project Management Journal* (PMJ) was founded in 1970 by the Project Management Institute. Until 2007 it was an in-house journal distributed only to members of PMI. However in 2007 management of the journal transferred to Wiley.

This review has only had access to copies from 1997 and 2007, so we review developments over that ten-year period. (See, however, Morris 2001 for a review of all papers and topics covered between 1990 and 2000.) Also PMJ does not appear in the leading citation indexes, and so it is not possible to determine how many times papers in PMJ have been cited. PMI has wanted to maintain the journal at its original size. So it is still only running to four issues a year, with approximately six papers per issue. In 1997 there were twenty-three papers and in 2007 thirty-one.

Topics covered

Table 3.5 shows the topics covered by papers in PMJ in 1997 and 2007. In 1997, the average number of topics per paper is just under two, whereas in 2007 it is about two and a quarter. Thus there was a slight increase in the number of topics per paper in those years, whereas IJPM was static at two. But the differences may not be very significant. Thus PMJ had roughly the same number of topics per paper as IJPM, but because there are very much fewer papers the total number of topics covered is less.

Range of topics

With many of the topics being mentioned only once per year in each journal, it is difficult to draw comparisons between the two journals. But there are some areas of interest. Whereas in IJPM every topic area was covered in all years, in PMJ in 1997 there were no papers on the project life cycle, or on financial issues. There were papers on life cycle in 2007, but still none on financial issues. As with IJPM, execution and control was one of the most popular topics in PMJ in 2007 (not having been mentioned in 1997). In 1997, the most popular topic in PMJ was projects in the construction industry, with slightly over a third of papers being about that topic, similar to IJPM. However, by 2007 there was only one paper on that topic. Perhaps this reflects a change of focus of PMI itself towards other industries. In 1997 and 2007 there were three papers on research and development projects (13 percent). This was also the only other type of project receiving more than one mention in IJPM. The second most popular type of project in PMJ in 2007 was IT projects with two mentions (6 percent). Unlike IJPM, in PMJ there was quite a change in the topics receiving the most mentions between 1997 and 2007. In 1997 the popular topics (receiving three or more mentions) were: managing quality, managing time, and decision-making. Managing time was popular in IJPM but the other two were not. In 2007 the popular topics in PMJ were: success and strategy, research into project management, project organization, execution and control, organizational capability, teams, leadership, culture, decision-making, and old world countries; almost a complete change on focus. Only decision-making is common to the two years. Two differences from IJPM are interesting. First, in PMJ there is little interest in risk (though this is not the case in the Morris (2001) survey of PMJ). Secondly, whereas in PMJ there were two papers on the topic of systems thinking, there were none in IJPM.

Table 3.5 Topics covered by papers in PMJ

	1997 No.	1997 Ave	2007 No.	2007 Ave
Number of papers	23		31	
Total number of topics covered	43	1.87	69	2.23
General				
Organizational strategy				
Project management	1	.04	5	.16
Program management				
Portfolio management	1	.04	1	.03
Complexity			2	.06
Project office			1	.01
Project-based organizations				
Project success and strategy	2	.09	3	.10
Sponsorship				
Systems			2	.06
Computer support				
Standards	2	.09	1	.03
Audits and health checks				
Managing context				
Project management research			3	.10
Functions				
Managing requirements				
Managing configuration				
Managing scope				
Managing value				
Managing organization	1	.04	3	.01
Managing quality	3	.13		
Managing cost	1	.04		
Managing time	3	.13	1	.03
Managing risk	2	.09	1	.03
Managing resources	2	.09		
Managing environment				

(continued)

Table 3.5 Continued

	1997 No.	1997 Ave	2007 No.	2007 Ave
Managing safety	1	.04		
Life cycle				
Start-up				
Feasibility and design			1	.03
Execution and control			4	.13
Close-out and commissioning				
Operation and maintenance				
Finance				
Appraisal				
Project finance				
Contracts				
Project contract organization				
Contract management				
Partnerships and alliances	1	.04		
PPP/PFI				
BOOT				
Contract procurement and tendering			1	.03
Bidding	2	.09	1	.03
Supply chain				
Contract administration				
Claims	1	.04		
People				
Individual competence/ learning	1	.04	2	.06
Organizational capability			5	.16
Managing teams	2	.09	3	.09
Leadership			4	.13
Managing culture			3	.10
Managing stakeholders			1	.03
Conflict and negotiation			1	.03
Managing communication			1	.03
Managing ethics				
Managing decisions				

General management				
Managing innovation				
Managing information				
Organizational behavior			3	.10
Transaction costs/Agency theory			1	.03
Gender			1	.03
Geography				
Old world			3	.10
New developed countries	2	.09	3	.03
International projects			1	.03
Industry				
Engineering and construction	8	.35	1	.03
Manufacturing		.		
Information, computers, and telecoms			2	.06
Infrastructure				
Government				
Research and development	3	.09	3	.10
Services				
Leisure				

Research methodologies used

Table 3.6 shows the research methodologies used by PMJ. In 1997 about half the papers had a methodology section, about twice the ratio for IJPM for the same year. In 2007 about three quarters of papers had a methods section, almost the same as IJPM.

Total number of methods used

In 1997 the average number of methods per paper was about 1.1, meaning that about 10 percent of papers were using mixed methods. But by 2007 the average number was about 1.5, meaning about half the papers were using mixed methods. This compares to 1.2 in IJPM in both years.

Range of methods used

Because of the smaller number of papers published in PMJ, even though there are more methods on average per paper in 2007, there is a much smaller range of actual

Table 3.6 Methodologies used by articles published in PMJ

	1997 No.	1997 Ave	2007 No.	2007 Ave
Number of papers	23		31	
Papers with a methodology section	12	.52	23	.74
Total number of methods used	25	1.09	47	1.52
Methods used				
Example of an existing technique	1	.04		
Development of a new technique	4	.17	1	.03
Comparison of techniques	1	.04		
Conceptual paper	6	.26	5	.16
Theoretical development				
Literature review	3	.13	12	.39
Content analysis			1	.03
Case study	2	.09	8	.26
Pilot study			2	.06
Survey	8	.35	10	.32
Structured interviews				.03
Grounded theory			2	.06
Delphi				
ANOVA				
Field study				
Action research				
Ethnographic study				
Discourse				
Modeling			4	.13
Computer simulation			1	.03
Role game	1			

methods used when compared to IJPM. In PMJ in 1997, the most popular method is already surveys (35 percent), though conceptual papers is a close second (26 percent). However, there are still several papers developing a new technique (17 percent). By 2007 the most popular method was literature search (39 percent). Survey was a close second (32 percent). In 2007 a quarter of papers used a case-study method and around 16 percent were conceptual papers. These are similar figures to IJPM.

Number and sources of citations by papers published in PMJ

Table 3.7 shows the number of citations by papers published in PMJ in 1997 and 2007. The table shows citations of articles in other journals and of conference

Table 3.7 Citations by articles published in PMJ

	1997 No.	1997 Ave	2007 No.	2007 Ave
Number of papers	23		31	
Number of papers without citations	4	.17	1	.03
Project Management Journals				
International Journal of Project Management	3	.13	112	3.61
Project Management Journal	6	.26	76	2.45
Other	3	.13	14	.45
IEEE Transactions	3	.13	10	.32
Engineering	0		1	.03
Engineering Management	12	.52	22	.71
Cost Engineering	0	.0	1	.03
Construction	0		2	.06
Construction Management	6	.26	5	.16
Procurement and Supply Chain	3	.13	4	.13
ICT	5	.22	25	.81
ICT Management	2	.09	5	.16
Quality	11	.48	9	1.52
Research	8	.35	47	.29
General Management	6	.26	83	2.68
Business Studies	1	.03	11	.35
Strategy	4	.17	34	1.10
Marketing	3	.13	10	.32
Governance				
Decision Science	3	.13	77	2.48
HRM, OB, Education and Learning, Health	1	.04	55	1.77
Finance, Economics, and Politics	1	.04	15	.48
Law	0		0	
Accounting	0	.	6	.19
Risk and Insurance	5	.22	3	.10
Environment			0	.0
Ethics and Philosophy			0	.0

(continued)

Table 3.7 Continued

	1997 No.	1997 Ave	2007 No.	2007 Ave
Total number of journal articles cited	101	4.39	640	20.65
Ignoring articles without citations		5.32		21.33
Conference Papers				
PMI Practitioner Conferences	3	.138	10	.32
PMI Research Conference			27	.87
IPMA Practitioner Conference			4	.13
IPMA Expert Seminars				
IRNOP			14	.45
EURAM			5	.16
Other Project Management Conference			3	.10
Other Conferences	6	.26	17	.55
Total Conference Paper citations	9	.39	80	2.58
Ignoring articles without citations		.47		2.67
Web pages cited			**	**

papers. (We did not collect the data for web pages.) There are several points of interest.

There are five papers with no citations: four from 1997 and one from 2007. These papers did in fact cite books, but no journal articles. There is very little interest in construction and construction management, but there is a similar interest in engineering and engineering management to IJPM. There is a much stronger interest in research and research management than is the case for IJPM. There is a similar interest in general management, strategy, and business, a slightly stronger interest in decision sciences, but a slightly weaker interest in Human Resource Management and Organizational Behavior. Otherwise the spread of citations is very similar to IJPM. There are one or two fields that receive a small number of citations in IJPM but none in PMJ, but this may merely reflect the smaller number of articles published.

In 1997 the citation of conference papers is much smaller than in IJPM, but the conferences cited are only the PMI practitioner conference and conferences outside the field of project management. In 2007, papers in PMI cite about twice as many conference papers as IJPM, with the PMI Research Conference, the PMI practitioner conferences, and IRNOP the most popular.

IEEE Transactions on Engineering Management (IEEE-TEM)

IEEE Transactions on Engineering Management (IEEE-TEM) is a publication of the IEEE Technology Management Council (formerly IEEE Engineering Management Society) and is a research-based, refereed journal in engineering management that has been published quarterly since 1954. Its worldwide subscription base is approximately 10,000. Unlike the *International Journal of Project Management* and the *Project Management Journal*, IEEE-TEM is not exclusively focused on the publication of project management research, but pursues a broader purpose, including the publication of leading-edge research articles and technical notes in engineering, technology, and innovation management. It is thus composed of seven departments, including: People and Organizations, Information Technology, R&D and Engineering Projects, e-Business, Models and Methodologies, Technology and Innovation Management, and Manufacturing Systems. As a result, the number of actual "project management" articles published in each issue of IEEE-TEM varies, depending upon submissions relative to those manuscripts submitted to other departments. IEEE-TEM is listed in the Social Sciences Citation Index.

Following the methodology applied to the analysis of IJPM's citation patterns, we developed a similar table for project management articles published in IEEE-TEM for each of the years 1988, 1997, and 2007. We selected 1988 as it was the earliest year for which IEEE-TEM was listed in full online text format. Of the twenty-eight refereed articles published in 1988, six (21 percent) were project oriented. In 1997, a total of five (14 percent) of the thirty-six articles published in IEEE-TEM focused on project issues. Finally, in 2007, a total of fifty-five articles were published, of which six (11 percent) were project management papers. Using the "citations by articles" classification scheme from Table 3.9, several interesting patterns emerged.

Topics covered

Table 3.8 shows the topics covered in the published articles from the journal for the dates 1988, 1997, and 2007. In 1988 and 1997, the average number of topics per paper is nearly 2.5, increasing in 2007 to 4.3. Thus there was an increase in the number of topics per paper in those years, similar to PMJ and IJPM counts for the earlier years but showing a strong increase in the most recent data.

Because of the smaller number of actual articles, it is important not to "over-read" the data. Nevertheless, there are some interesting changes in topic patterns from the early years of the analysis, when the most popular topics were those of managing time/schedule, managing resources, and project execution and control. These results are consonant with the earlier observations that IEEE-TEM tended to promote

Table 3.8 Topics covered by papers in IEEE–TEM

	1988 No.	1988 Ave	1997 No.	1997 Ave	2007 No.	2007 Ave
Number of papers	6		5		6	
Total number of topics covered	15	2.50	12	2.40	26	4.33
General						
Organizational strategy					1	.17
Project management	1	.17			1	.17
Program management						
Portfolio management						
Complexity						
Project office					1	.17
Project-based organizations						
Project success and strategy			1	.20	1	.17
Sponsorship						
Systems						
Computer support						
Standards						
Audits and health checks						
Managing context						
Project management research			1	.20		

Functions

Managing requirements	1			.20		
Managing configuration		.17	1	.20		
Managing scope			1	.20		
Managing value						
Managing organization						
Managing quality						
Managing cost	3				2	.33
Managing time		.50				
Managing risk		.33			2	.33
Managing resources	2	.33				
Managing environment						
Managing safety						
Life cycle						
Start-up	2	.33	1	.20		
Feasibility and design						
Execution and control	2	.33			1	.17
Close-out and commissioning	1	.17	1	.20		
Operation and maintenance						

(continued)

Table 3.8 Continued

	1988 No.	1988 Ave	1997 No.	1997 Ave	2007 No.	2007 Ave
Finance						
Appraisal						
Project finance						
Contracts						
Project contract organization						
Contract management						
Partnerships and alliances			1	.20		
PPP/PFI						
BOOT						
Contract procurement and tendering						
Bidding						
Supply chain						
Contract administration						
Claims						
People						
Individual competence/learning			1	.20	2	.33
Organizational capability					1	.17
Managing teams	1	.17	1	.20	3	.50

	1	2	3
Leadership			
Managing culture			
Managing stakeholders			
Managing conflict and negotiation	.17		
Managing communication			
Managing ethics			
Managing decisions			
General management			
Managing innovation			
Human resource management			
Managing information		.33	
Organizational behavior			
Transaction costs/Agency theory			
Gender			
Geography			
Old world			
New developed countries			
International projects			
Industry			
Engineering and construction			.50

(continued)

Table 3.8 Continued

	1988 No.	1988 Ave	1997 No.	1997 Ave	2007 No.	2007 Ave
Manufacturing					2	.33
Information, computers, and telecoms	1	.17			2	.33
Infrastructure					1	.17
Government			1	.20		
Research and development	1	.17	1	.20		
Services						
Leisure						

Table 3.9 Methodologies used by articles published in IEEE–TEM

	1997 No.	1997 Ave	2007 No.	2007 Ave
Number of papers	5		6	
Papers with a methodology section	3	.60	5	.80
Total number of methods used				
Methods used				
Example of an existing technique	1	.20		
Development of a new technique	2	.40	2	.33
Comparison of techniques	1	.20		
Conceptual paper				
Theoretical development				
Literature review	2	.40	3	.50
Content analysis				
Case study			1	.17
Pilot study	2	.40		
Survey			4	.67
Structured interviews				
Grounded theory				
Delphi	1	.20	1	.17
ANOVA	2	.40	4	.67
Field study			1	.17
Action research				
Ethnographic study				
Discourse	1	.20		
Modeling			3	.50
Computer simulation	1	.20		
Role game				

more "technical" papers with a background in decision sciences and operations research, aimed at optimization. Most recently, however, issues such as individual competence, managing teams, and organizational behavior point to a broadening of the traditional themes, similar to patterns observed in the other journals.

Research methodologies used

Perhaps the most intriguing finding for research methods used (see Table 3.9) was the movement toward large-scale field survey methods, coupled with more sophisticated data analysis employing ANOVA and multiple regression methods. A technique that was essentially unused in IEEE-TEM in its early days became the most popular research method in project management articles published in 2007. Modeling remains a popular research technique and, given the readership and philosophy of the journal, is likely to continue apace. Nevertheless, the intriguing results here suggest that greater emphasis and acceptance of social science research methods is an emerging theme.

Number and sources of citations by papers published in the journal

Using the "citations by articles" classification scheme from Table 3.10, several interesting patterns emerged.

The total number of papers published in IEEE-TEM has continued to increase at a strong rate, from twenty-eight total papers published in 1988 to fifty-five published in 2007. This trend (a near doubling of the number of published papers in the past twenty years) reflects a significant increase in the popularity of the journal and the breadth of papers it receives as submissions. Papers directly related to project management (that is, those that are assigned to the department editor for R&D and Engineering Projects) continue to remain relatively steady at approximately 14 percent of papers published in each issue. Thus, it is common for one or two papers each issue to deal with project management themes.

The average number of citations per project management article has steadily increased over the past twenty years. In 1988, the average paper had 18.5 citations, though the high was 41. In 1997, the average paper had nearly 37 citations (36.6) with a high of 76. Finally, in 2007, the average paper had over 63 citations, with a high of 88.

Trends in citations showed some interesting patterns. In 1987, the preponderance of cited work came from the decision science journals. In fact, half of the total average citations for this year were either decision science or research journals. Project management journals, including IJPM, PMJ, and IEEE, received a steadily increasing number of average citations across the twenty-year timeframe, reinforcing an

Table 3.10 Citations by articles published in IEEE–TEM

	1988 No.	1988 Ave	1997 No.	1997 Ave	2007 No.	2007 Ave
Number of papers	6		5		6	
Number of papers without citations	0		0		0	
Project Management Journals						
International Journal of Project Management	0	.00	0	.00	11	1.83
Project Management Journal	2	.33	10	2.00	12	2.00
Other	0	.00	11	2.20	2	.33
IEEE Transactions	5	.83	14	2.80	19	3.17
Engineering	4	.67	3	.60	5	.83
Engineering Management	2	.33	6	1.20	7	1.17
Cost Engineering	0	.00	1	.20	0	.00
Construction	0	.00	1	.20	1	.17
Construction Management	0	.00	1	.20	7	1.17
Procurement and Supply Chain	0	.00	1	.20	7	1.17
ICT	4	.67	0	.00	2	.33
ICT Management	0	.00	0	.00	5	.83
Quality	0	.00	0	.00	1	.17

(continued)

Table 3.10 Continued

	1988 No.	1988 Ave	1997 No.	1997 Ave	2007 No.	2007 Ave
Research	8	1.33	30	6.00	8	1.33
General Management	5	.83	26	5.20	43	7.17
Business Studies	1	.17	7	1.40	6	1.00
Strategy	1	.17	15	3.00	21	3.50
Marketing	0	.00	6	1.20	14	2.33
Governance	0	.00	0	.00	2	.33
Decision Science	47	7.83	4	.80	36	6.00
HRM, OB, Education and Learning, Health	0	.00	2	.40	41	6.83
Finance, Economics, and Politics	0	.00	6	1.20	8	1.33
Law	0	.00	0	.00	1	.17
Accounting	0	.00	0	.00	1	.17
Risk and Insurance	0	.00	0	.00	5	.83
Environment	0	.00	2	.40	1	.17
Ethics and Philosophy	0	.00	0	.00	0	.00
Total number of journal articles cited	111	18.50	183	36.60	379	63.17
Ignoring articles without citations		18.50		36.60		63.17

Conference Papers

PMI Practitioner Conferences	0	.00	1	.20	2	.33
PMI Research Conference	0		0	.00	0	.00
IPMA Practitioner Conference	0	.00	0	.00	2	.33
IPMA Expert Seminars	0		0	.00	0	.00
IRNOP	0		0	.00	0	.00
EURAM	0		0	.00	0	.00
Other Project Management Conference	0		0	.00	0	.00
Other Conferences	21	3.50	26	5.20	43	7.17
Total Conference Paper citations	21	3.50	27	5.40	47	7.83
Ignoring articles without citations		3.50		5.40		7.83
Web pages cited						

earlier point that SSCI reappraisal of the standing of IJPM appears to have prompted higher citation patterns in other journals. Other classes of journals that were increasingly cited were those for "General Management," "HRM, OB, Education and Learning, Health," "Marketing," and "Strategy." In all these cases, the average citations per article showed dramatic increases over time—General Management increased from an average of less than one citation per article in 1988 to 5.2 average citations in 1997 and 7.17 citations in 2007. The HRM class increased from zero average citations in 1988 to 6.83 in 2007. Marketing and Strategy showed equally significant increases.

Conference paper citations showed a relatively steady increase from 1988 to 2007, though few were from Project Management-focused conferences (e.g. PMI or IPMA conferences).

The analysis of research methods (Table 3.9) offers some preliminary information on the alternative methods for conducting research and analyzing results. In recent years, there has been a significant increase in the use of survey methods for large-sample research, coupled with regression and ANOVA statistical techniques. Though the actual sample size is limited, the trends point to a stronger inclination to adopt field research, literature reviews, and modeling techniques as primary research methods.

Some Emergent Themes from the Review of the Three Journals

In analyzing, from an editor's perspective, the current state of project management literature, some interesting trends appear to be operating.

The research and literature base is growing

An analysis of the citation patterns demonstrates the strong increase in the numbers of cited works from other journals and disciplinary sources. In 1988, the average number of IEEE citations per article for example was 18.5. That figured doubled by 1997 and nearly doubled again by 2007, to an average of 63.17 citations per article. This increase in citation activity suggests the emergence of a large body of work from which to draw these citations. The fact that the average article could, in 2007, cite over 63 other sources demonstrates the growth of the literature base for project management research. Kwak and Anbari's (2009) recent analysis of publishing patterns of 8 "allied disciplines" across 18 top management journals over the past 50 years found a total of nearly 1,000 articles published on project management with nearly 80 percent appearing in print since 1980.

The literature is becoming increasingly diverse

The data reflects a dramatic ramping-up of research work being conducted in the domain of project management. Early work in project-based subjects within IEEE-TEM, for example, was often centered on the themes of research policy or optimization techniques from operations research/management science. The changing citation patterns suggest a broadening of topics. This trend is mirrored in an analysis by Morris (2001) who undertook an analysis of research trends during the decade of the 1990s, examining the output of the *Project Management Journal, Project Management Network* (PMN), and the *International Journal of Project Management*.

Other work, best characterized by Söderlund (2004a and 2004b), has examined publication patterns of project-based work and noted an important cross-fertilization between work that appears in traditional project management journals and that which is being done within other management domains, noting, "traditional project management researchers become increasingly more interested in issues related to traditional management, organization and inter-firm cooperation. Another trend is that researchers in other disciplines show greater awareness of the importance of projects in understanding the functioning of markets and firms" (2004a: 656). Thus, one aspect of this issue of increasing diversity relates to the authors themselves and the work they conduct, reflecting their acknowledgement that project management research (and the examination of project-based firms) does not represent a "special case" or setting, but concerns the practical realities of modern work environments.

More recent analyses have provided some further evidence of this trend; for example, the huge increase in the average number of citations from general management journals or those relating to Human Resource Management, Organizational Behavior, or Education themes. Indeed, both of these categories have now supplanted Decision Science journals as the top classes for citations in IEEE-TEM, suggesting that not only is the literature becoming increasingly diverse, but the academics and researchers conducting work and publishing in the journal are either themselves from a number of allied disciplines or are able to tap into these journal outlets. Further, the fact that these categories contain the largest average number of citations suggests that the topics in project management have become increasingly diverse and often of a "business-oriented" nature.

Project research methods are diverse and evolving

The various research methodologies employed in conducting project management work are showing increasing sophistication and methodological rigor. As we noted at the beginning of the chapter, many of the original works in the major journals were anecdotal, single-case analyses, or "war stories" aimed at addressing means for improving some specific project management tool or technique. Increasingly, the methods and research approaches have become more varied and grounded in rigorous methods, including field research, surveys, and modeling, with commensurately rigorous evaluation approaches (multivariate statistical techniques). The overall effect of this advance in research methods has been to develop a knowledge base that is more generalizable and valuable to practitioners and researchers alike.

Research themes continue to evolve within the field

Research trend analysis demonstrated that certain themes grew in importance over the twenty-year timeframe, as evidenced both by the topics selected and the citation patterns within those journals. For example, there has been a significant increase in papers related to the themes of risk, HR management, partnering and alliances, and project-based firms. These trends are supported by the work of Crawford, Pollack, and England (2006) and Anbari, Bredillet, and Turner (2010) who noted the emergence of certain themes through a meta-analytic, longitudinal study of project research. Among their findings was the notion that some themes (for example, Strategic Alignment) are growing topics in the field while others, such as Quality Management, appear to be of decreasing significance. The larger question, of course, is whether these trends reflect opportunities for research to "fill in the gaps," as some authors suggest (cf. Morris 2001; Themistocleous and Wearne 2000) or if they in fact reflect a de-emphasis due to the sense of over-saturation or the failure for new dimensions of these themes to be shown as relevant for project-based work.

It is, of course, common for research trends to evolve; in fact, one could cogently argue that such evolution demonstrates the overall vibrancy of the field as more work is done along broader themes or academics from other disciplines seek to understand project-based firms from alternative perspectives. In better understanding the evolving nature of research in project-based firms, future work would be well served to move beyond the analysis of the trends themselves and perhaps attempt a harder, but more intriguing study of the question of "why" such trends evolve; that is, what are the identifiable forces that influence these changing project research themes?

CONCLUSIONS

As we have noted, the field of project management, as a research and academic discipline, has seen a significant increase in trend analysis in recent years. Trends, as they pertain to the evolution of topics, research methods, publication outlets, number of topical papers published, and comparisons in these trends across the top project management outlets, have all been explored with increasing frequency.

Through the subsequent half century, project management research has shown dramatic evidence of expansion, both in breadth of topics covered as well as the sheer volume of papers produced on different aspects of the field. This interest in better understanding and reconceptualizing the field of project management from an output perspective (knowledge creation and dissemination) bespeaks a positive attitude toward the future of project management research.

It is interesting to consider future directions for project management research. This chapter, as well as the recent work of Morris (2001) and Kwak and Anbari (2009), has analyzed publication patterns both as a means to determine how the field has progressed (as evidenced by the topics covered and methods employed) over time as well as to identify obvious "holes" that bear research investigation. This latter theme is illustrated by Morris (2001) who compared his research findings with the current bodies of knowledge to ascertain those topics that were being researched versus those that offered opportunities for investigation.

Alternatively, an intriguing strategy would be to approach the study of project management research from the academics' perspective. Work to date has employed the journals as the means for information regarding research trends; however, a counter-argument could be made for addressing the "source" of project management research. That is, it would be interesting to identify and sample fifty of the leading project management researchers to understand their agendas, perspectives on strong research opportunities, and perceived future opportunities. Comparing their perspectives with an equal sample of mid- to high-level practitioners and executives would allow for some triangulation in pinpointing current needs and subsequent gaps in the literature.

But we should not get carried away too quickly. As Bredillet (2009: 2) has noted, "the evolution of project management models does not necessarily represent the incremental sophistication of project management methods." That is, the manner in which we change our perceptions of project management, including the theoretical models we use to describe it, does not presume that older project management methods were wrong, *per se*. Our work seeks to broaden theory rather than substitute one theory for another. Project research more and more represents this broadening of methods, recognizing the contingency effects of industries and project classes that make the discipline both exciting and unique.

References

ANBARI, F. N., BREDILLET, C. B., and TURNER, J. R. (2010). "Exploring research in project management; nine schools of project management research," *International Journal of Project Management*, 28 (to appear).

ASSOCIATION FOR PROJECT MANAGEMENT (2006). *APM Body of Knowledge*, 5th edn. (1st edn. 1992). Princes Risborough: Association for Project Management.

AUSTRALIAN INSTITUTE OF PROJECT MANAGEMENT (2004). *National Competency Standards for Project Management*. Canberra: Innovation and Business Skills.

BETTS, M., and LANSLEY, P. (1995). "International journal of project management: a review of the first ten years," *International Journal of Project Management*, 13: 207–17.

BREDILLET, C. N. (2006). "The future of project management: mapping the dynamics of project management field in action," in D. I. Cleland and R. Gareis (eds.), *Global Project Management Handbook: Planning, Organizing, and Controlling International Projects*, 2nd edn. New York: McGraw-Hill.

——(2009). "Mapping the dynamics of the project management field: project management in action (part 3)," *Project Management Journal*, 40/3: 2–5.

CRAWFORD, L., POLLACK, J., and ENGLAND, D. (2006). "Uncovering the trends in project management journal emphasis over the last 10 years," *International Journal of Project Management*, 24: 175–84.

EKSTEDT, E., LUNDIN, R. A., SÖDERHOLM, A., and WIRDENIUS, H. (1999). *Neo-industrial Organising*. London: Routledge.

INTERNATIONAL PROJECT MANAGEMENT ASSOCIATION (2006). *ICB: IPMA Competence Baseline: The Eye of Competence*, 3rd edn. (1st edn. 1999). Zurich: International Project Management Association.

KERZNER, H. (2009). *Project Management: A Systems Approach to Planning, Scheduling and Controlling*, 10th edn. Hoboken, NJ: Wiley.

KLOPPENBORG, T., and OPFER, W. A. (2002). "The current state of project management research: trends, interpretations and predictions," *Project Management Journal*, 33/2: 5–19.

KWAK, Y. H., and ANBARI, F. T. (2009). "Analyzing project management research: perspectives from top management journals," *International Journal of Project Management*, 27: 435–46.

MIDLER, C. (1995). "Projectification of the firm: the Renault case," *Scandinavian Journal of Management*, 11/4: 363–76.

MORRIS, P. W. G. (2001). "Research trends in the 1990s and the need to focus on the business benefit of project management in project management research," in D. P. Slevin, D. I. Cleland, and J. K. Pinto (eds.), *Project Management Research at the Turn of the Millennium: Proceedings of PMI Research Conference 2000*. Newton Square, PA: Project Management Institute.

PROJECT MANAGEMENT INSTITUTE (1987). *The Project Management Body of Knowledge*. Newtown Square, PA: Project Management Institute.

——(2008). *A Guide to the Project Management Body of Knowledge*, 4th edn. (1st edn. 1996). Newtown Square, PA: Project Management Institute.

SÖDERLUND, J. (2004a). "Building theories of project management: past research, questions for the future," *International Journal of Project Management*, 22: 183–91.

——(2004b). "On the broadening scope of the research on projects: a review and a model for analysis," *International Journal of Project Management*, 22: 655–67.

THEMISTOCLEOUS, G., and WEARNE, S. H. (2000). "Project management topic coverage in journals," *International Journal of Project Management*, 18: 7–12.

TURNER, J. R., HUEMANN, M., ANBARI, F. N., and BREDILLET, C. B. (2010). *Perspectives on Projects*. London: Routledge (to appear).

CHAPTER 4

PROSPECTS FOR PROFESSIONALISM IN PROJECT MANAGEMENT

DAMIAN HODGSON

DANIEL MUZIO

INTRODUCTION

There has been in recent years a marked upsurge in interest in professionalism in project management. The professionalization of project management is apparently demanded by employers, clients, and sponsors alike, seeking guarantees of competence in the delivery of projects. Equally, there appears to be significant demand on the part of project management (PM) practitioners seeking more secure and transferable credentials to act as guarantees of competence and to build a more reliable, informed, and effective knowledge base in what is often an "accidental" or secondary profession. Nonetheless, skepticism persists regarding the depth and breadth of project management's institutionalized knowledge base, and the potential for the field to attain the levels of internal organization, legitimacy, and influence achieved by other, more established professions.

Key to this debate are the activities of the various professional associations which represent project management. In an era where traditional tactics of monopolistic closure, restrictive practices, and self-regulation are often regarded as neither desirable nor achievable, these professional associations appear to be attempting to professionalize by employing, to varying degrees, distinctive entrepreneurial tactics based around marketable services and an active engagement with corporate interests. These tactics, which will be reviewed in the course of this analysis, include an increasingly international orientation, an intense focus on the body of knowledge, the development of diversified and stratified accreditation, an emphasis on corporate membership and client value, and the forging of distinctive relationships with broader stakeholders.

Through an analysis of the tactics of professionalization employed within the field of project management, we trace out the implications of an emergent form of organizational/corporate professionalism, predicated by "the market" rather than the state, and structured by the international activities of major employers and clients as "institutional entrepreneurs." An understanding of what professionalism means for the field of project management requires some context regarding the contested nature of professionalism, the different forms which professionalism has taken, historically and in contemporary society, and questions regarding the relevance of professions in the twenty-first century. We will address this context in the following section, establishing a lens through which the specific nature of professionalism in project management may be established, identifying the dimensions along which it differs both from traditional forms of professionalism and from the approaches taken by other "new" professions. The chapter then concludes with an examination of the implications of the route taken by agencies within the field of project management, and in light of this, of the prospects for a project management profession.

PROFESSIONALISM AS AN "OCCUPATIONAL PROJECT"

The terms profession, professional, and professionalism are contested and invested with multiple meanings (Kritzer 1999), owing perhaps to the status benefits they confer. At a most basic folk level, they represent a shorthand for any form of intellectual or even high-status occupation. Such definitions are often loaded with a series of positive traits including: a developed and systematic knowledge base, high levels of training and commitment, autonomy and independence of judgment, and a public-spirited orientation (Macdonald 1995). The implicit assumption here is that these traits are functional to the proper delivery of what are crucial individual and public services. Rather differently, in current management talk, the term professional is often used to invoke commitment, effort, and dedication, in a disciplinary or normative fashion (Anderson-Gough et al. 2000; Grey 1997, 1998; Fournier 1999). In this chapter, we use these terms in their more sociological meaning, as referring to a specific way of organizing work (Johnson 1972), one in which an occupation, through its professional association, exercises a significant degree of control over its own work, including its definition, regulation, execution, and evaluation, with the joint aim of enhancing the quality and perceived value of such work, and thus improving the status of the occupation. This contrasts with alternative occupational solutions such as entrepreneurship and managerialism where activities are regulated through contractual exchanges in a relatively open market, or else through directed coordination in organizational hierarchies (Freidson 1994). Of course, reality does not neatly conform to such essential categories; however, as ideal types, these opposing principles for organizing occupations draw our attention to some of the salient features of specific occupations. Furthermore, it is also important to remain alert to the international differences between definitions of professions and professionalism (Sciulli 2005; Evetts 2003); as Ackroyd argues, "much of what has passed for the sociology of the professions published in English actually describes something culturally specific, primarily relating to Anglo-American experience" (1996: 600).

Professionalism has historically been legitimized in terms of public interest and the guarantees of quality, competence, and integrity it offers with regards to crucial individual and social services (Parsons 1954; Greenwood 1957). Aside from its value to the public, it is clear that professionalism offers some advantages to the producers of such services as it offers avenues to restrict supply in their markets and therefore increase the economic value of their work as well as the status and social standing connected with their occupational role (Larson 1977). In this context and in light of the interests at stake, it is useful to think of professionalism and its outcomes not as a historical accident nor as a functional requirement for specific types of work but as the result of a concerted and sustained political endeavor, described by Larson (1977) as a "professional project."

The essence of a "professional project" is normally best understood as the attempt "to translate a scarce set of cultural and technical resources into a secure and institutionalized system of social and financial rewards" (Larson 1977: xvii). This historically is centered around notions and processes of occupational closure (Parkin 1979; Murphy 1988; Macdonald 1995; Muzio, Ackroyd, and Chanlat 2007) as professions seek to control entry to and competition within labor markets, while at the same time ensuring some degree of "institutional autonomy" (Evetts 2003) to regulate their own affairs. Crucial to many such professional projects is the ability to monopolize specific jurisdictions of work, creating and defining core knowledge (usually in conjunction with universities) while also maintaining skill scarcity by managing and often restricting access to training, accreditation, and thus labor market opportunities (Larson 1977). Also important are wider legitimacy claims of professions and the extent to which they have been able to forge a "coherent ideology" to justify their special privileges both on the grounds of technical competency and the trusteeship of socially valuable forms of knowledge (Brint 1994; Collins 1990). Thus, ultimately the objective is to achieve degrees of regulation over a field of practice, in terms of controlling both the supply of expert labor *and* the conduct of these experts (Abel 1988). This is most accomplished in the case of showcase professions such as law and medicine in Anglo-Saxon societies (Evetts 2003); yet a wide range of occupations have over the years staged elements of professionalization with differing degrees of success.

Such processes have been steeped in the negotiations between professions and other key actors in their field (Burrage and Torstendahl 1990; Krause 1996) over time. These interactions constitute an inevitably political process as different agents attempt to negotiate favorable settlements with the profession. In studies of professionalization, attention is given in particular to the role played by universities (Burrage and Torstendahl 1990); by clients and consumers of professional services; by other competing professions equipped with alternative knowledge claims and forms of cultural capital (Abbott 1988); and, most important of all, by the state (Burrage and Torstendahl 1990; Torstendahl and Burrage 1990; Macdonald 1995). Successful professionalization, it is argued, requires the effective negotiation of a "regulative bargain" "whereby the state protects professionals from unfettered competition but trusts them to put public interest before their own" (Freidson 1994: 202). Crucial to this has been the ability of a profession to present itself as trustee of valuable and socially relevant forms of expertise (Brint 1994) whose regulation is actually in the public interest. This acts as a powerful ideological legitimization for monopoly and other restrictive arrangements which would not normally be tolerated. As shall be discussed below, for various socio-political reasons, prospects for such "regulative bargains" seem particularly dim in the current era.

This contextualization of project management as a profession may be further refined by drawing on the influential taxonomy of expert occupations developed by Reed (1996) where he differentiates between three kinds of knowledge-based occupations in late modernity; *liberal professions, organizational professions*, and *entrepreneurial professions* (Reed, 1996) (see Figure 4.1).

The *liberal* or *collegiate professions* refer to what are generally recognized as the established professions such as law and architecture, and (historically) medicine. For such groups, professional identity is strong, members tend to work in partnerships rather than as employees of an organization, and their power is drawn from their ability to monopolize and to police a field of abstract knowledge and a set of applied skills, which are valued by clients. By contrast, *organizational professions*, such as human resource managers, engineers, teachers, social workers, and nowadays doctors, are employed by public or private sector organizations and work within the bureaucracy of these organizations. Such professionals enjoy the support of strong professional bodies, and have a degree of professional autonomy in the application of discretion and judgment in their work. However, overall, they are subject to what Ackroyd (1996) terms "double closure," in that their activities are structured by the professional associations to which they belong but also by the requirements of their employer, on whom they rely for rewards and promotion.

Expert groups	Knowledge base	Power strategy	Organizational form	Occupational types
Independent/Liberal Professions	Abstract; Codified; Cosmopolitan; Rational	Monopolization	Collegiate	Doctors, Architects, Lawyers
Organizational Professions	Technical; Tacit; Local; Political	Credentialism	Bureaucracy	Managers, Administrators, Lawyers
Entrepreneurial Professions	Esoteric; Non-Substitutable; Global; Analytical	Marketization	Network	Financial, Business Consultants, Project/R&D Engineers, Computer/IT Analysts

Fig. 4.1 Expert groups and their power strategies

Source: Reed (1996: 586).

Nonetheless, they often gain status and influence in their employing organizations through the possession of credentials, awarded by their respective professional bodies, which mark the mastery of a diverse set of techniques and managerial practices which must, however, be adapted for application in their local contexts. Finally, *entrepreneurial professionals*, such as management and financial consultants or IT specialists, are typically employed either in large bureaucracies or small firms, and belong to weak professional associations (or indeed, no professional association at all). This group draws upon specialized technical or cognitive skills valued in the labor market, rather than any formal credentials. Nonetheless, for these professionals, in the absence of strong professional bodies, their activities are largely bounded by the demands of clients and their employers.

Recent debates on the professions have stressed the impact of broader changes in the political economy on both established professions and professionalizing occupations (Hanlon 1999; Muzio and Ackroyd 2005). As neo-liberal and increasingly budget-conscious governments redirected their priorities from the Keynesian preoccupation with welfare to the post-Keynesian preoccupation with efficiency, financial rigor, and international competitiveness (Jessop 1994), the professions have found themselves on the receiving end of an increasing number of deregulatory interventions and cost-cutting exercises (Abel 2003; Muzio and Ackroyd 2005). In private sector professions such as law we have witnessed in the UK the progressive challenge to monopolies (such as the partial liberalization of the key conveyancing market) and restrictive arrangements (the lifting of advertising bans, set fees, and most recently, with the Legal Services Act, restriction on ownership and governance structures), as well as drastic cuts to public funding for these services (see cuts to Legal Aid eligibility). In the public sector, reforms followed a comparable and equally significant route, as governments attempted to inject market discipline by reorganizing public services around "quasi-markets" (Lucio and Kirkpatrick 1995) in which providers compete over resources and end-users. In parallel, private sector practices and techniques have been introduced under the guise of New Public Management (Clarke and Newman 1997). In all of these cases, the assumption is that traditional professionalism as a way of organizing work is inefficient and less virtuous when compared with alternatives such as managerialism and entrepreneurship. Whilst there is ongoing debate on the extent of these challenges and on the effectiveness of defense mechanisms (Muzio, Ackroyd, and Chanlat 2007), governmental action has certainly shaken if not dismantled the normative, regulatory, and institutional scaffolding that supported the system of the professions. As the golden age (Aronowitz and Di Fazio 1994; Burris 1993; Derber, Schwartz, and Magrass 1990; Reed 2006) of professionalism seems to be over, the prospects for the institutionalization and development of new professional occupations, such as project management, are widely assumed to be rather limited.

Project management represents a challenging case insofar as its developmental trajectory, and its explicit pursuit of professional status, differs from the path followed by many other new expert occupations (Hodgson 2007). This raises the possibility that project management points to the emergence of a new corporate form of professionalization which may be better suited for the contemporary realities of its work and context.

THE RISE OF PROJECT MANAGEMENT

While the prehistory of project management extends back to the nineteenth century and arguably earlier (see Morris 1997), project management as a recognized and named field of activity can be reliably traced back only as far as the mid twentieth century (Engwall 1995; Morris 1997; Chapter 1), being born out of the technological advances of the 1940s/1950s onwards in engineering, and in particular in the

US military and defense sectors. The profile of the field and its associated techniques benefited greatly from its contribution to the delivery of a number of high-profile "mega-projects" in the USA through this period and into the 1960s and 1970s, particularly the various Apollo space missions and other activities of NASA and the US military–industrial complex (Hughes 1998). It is only, however, in recent years that realistic aspirations to a stand-alone professional status for project management have emerged, with professional associations achieving some kind of prominence by the start of the 1990s (Blomquist and Söderholm 2002). The emergence of these associations as important institutional actors coincides with an era in which the tools, techniques, and principles of project management have been widely promoted as a vital organizational capability, not just in engineering and heavy industry but across the gamut of knowledge-intensive business environments. Project teams have been identified as one of the major elements of restructuring through the 1990s across European, US, and Japanese corporations in a variety of industries and sectors (Whittington et al. 1999). In the same period, the expansion of project working and project management has made particular gains within IS/IT and in New Media, as well as benefiting from New Public Management (NPM) and the increased public sector reliance upon fixed-term public–private partnerships and targeted funding.[1] These diverse shifts have led to a promising climate for the development of project management as a discipline and for the staging of its own "professionalisation project" (Zwerman et al. 2004). Broadly speaking, it is possible to speak of the field of project management being engaged in what Larson (1977) would describe as a process of "occupational mobility," encompassing specific attempts to promote a particular conception of project management, and to persuade various stakeholders of the value of project management (see Blomquist and Söderholm 2002; also Thomas and Mullaly 2008). The various professional associations, inevitably, take on a key role in this project. Specifically, one can identify a set of strategies, policies, and tactics employed by professional associations to validate the field and to enhance its status and influence across various domains of activity.

Globally, project management as a discipline tends to be represented by national associations, which vary widely in size, influence, and respectability, with the US-based Project Management Institute (PMI) and the British Association for Project Management (APM) representing the largest and most influential. PMI was founded in 1969 and saw steady but unspectacular growth until the late 1980s; in 1988 the adoption of a formal policy on professionalization, encompassing standards, certification, education, and research, marked the beginning of a period of increasingly rapid expansion and growing influence for the PMI. By 2009, from around 8,000 members in 1992, PMI had 290,000 members and 320,000 certified professionals on their books.[2] Across a similar time-span, APM grew from a collection of practitioners interested in network analysis in the early 1970s, gradually but slowly expanding its membership through the 1980s but acting primarily as a club for members with similar interests rather than a professional association. In recent years, the APM has undergone rebranding and modernization, has moved to a new national headquarters, and has rapidly expanded the number of corporate members, including several arms of local and national government. This corporate and state patronage has encouraged the Association to pursue a Royal Charter, a process initiated in April 2008. The growth in both associations since the early 1990s has been dramatic, particularly in the case of PMI; APM's 17,500 is a significant increase on the 5,000 members it had in 1992 (see Figures 4.2 and 4.3).

Both associations, but again PMI in particular, have benefited from sectoral shifts, notably the growth in IS/IT and therefore in the management of IS/IT-related projects, in the last fifteen years. However, for both associations, a significant pro-portion of their membership is located in consultancy/business services. For both associations, their rapid growth begins around the time that they begin to accredit members, supported by the creation and publication of their first substantive "body of knowledge"; for PMI, the first Project Management Body of Knowledge (or "PMBoK") was published in August 1987, shortly followed by the APM in 1992. Although PMI did accredit individuals from the early 1980s, the vigorous pursuit of credentialism for both associations stems back to the period between 1988 and 1992, opening up the possibility of accreditation of individuals and thus control of the "production of producers" (Abel 2003). Serving as touchstone, syllabus, guide-book, and lexicon, the "bodies of knowledge" of the APM and PMI (and those of the other major associations globally) represent a vital element in any explanation of the growth and institutional legitimacy of the field of project management—

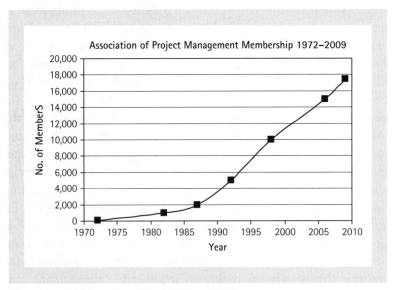

Fig. 4.2 APM membership (1972–2009)

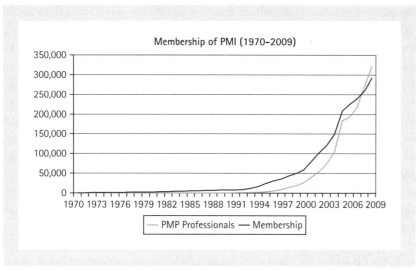

Fig. 4.3 PMI membership (1970–2009)

more so than in many other professional fields, where often there is no single comprehensive document or guide document to the knowledge base of the discipline.
For this reason, their importance will be analyzed in more detail below, alongside
other distinctive characteristics and tactics of professionalization in project
management.

ANALYZING PROJECT MANAGEMENT
PROFESSIONALISM

Project management can be broadly defined as one of a number of contemporary
"expert occupations" (Reed 1996) or forms of "knowledge work" (Blackler 1995),
with a significant managerial component alongside the more technical dimensions
of its role. However, unlike many comparable occupations, project management
globally has pursued and promoted professional status. This ongoing process of
professionalization in project management runs directly against the general consensus in the literature on the sociology of the professions (Blackler, Reed, and
Whitaker 1993; Broadbent, Dietrich, and Roberts 1997; Reed 1996, 2006) which
views professionalism as an increasingly unlikely strategy in today's political economy, with its emphasis on entrepreneurship, de-regulation, and managerialism.
This is thought to be particularly so with regards to new forms of expert occupations,

such as project management, which differ in significant ways from the established professions.

Liberal professions such as law and medicine flourished in situations where knowledgeable, organized, and relatively homogeneous producers were confronted by fragmented, heterogeneous, and uninformed consumers who were not in a position to define their needs and how these should be met nor indeed to evaluate service quality. The situation in which project management operates is radically different. Project managers are largely employed within large organizations, where they help to support and realize the commercial objectives of their employers, with only a minority serving such organizations from independent and relatively small consultancies (Zwerman et al. 2004). In both cases, project managers lack a distinctively deep and esoteric knowledge base, as other groups such as architects, engineers, management consultants, quantity surveyors, and IT specialists can and do claim project management expertise. Indeed the extent to which they can claim an independent expertise can be considered dubious with much of their knowledge being contextual, situated and embedded in organizationally specific processes, procedures, and frameworks. Furthermore, in this context power politics clearly favors the consumer—who often happens also to be the employer. In most cases, the employer and/or client is a powerful organization with considerable resources and multiple alternatives on how to meet its project management requirements, including direct influence over the professional associations themselves.

Thus, as examples of Reed's "organizational professions" (1996), project managers are subjected to corporate priorities, strategies, and structures which in turn they help to reproduce and legitimize. This is not a particularly fertile ground for traditional professional projects based on occupational closure and self-regulation; rather these occupations are expected to prosper through their ability to close off and monopolize "relatively powerful and privileged positions within [the] technical and status hierarchies" they inhabit (Reed 1996: 585). Their success is ultimately based not on their role as independent advisers but on their ability to "show value" by solving technical and to some extent managerial problems for their employers, who define the parameters, objectives, and evaluation criteria for their work (project) as well as their broader conditions of employment. In this context, operating within the parameters provided by their employers, project managers have little scope to control the moral or even the technical content of their own work. This is far removed from ideal-typical conceptions of professionalism which stress the abilities of an occupation to retain control over the definition, execution, and evaluation of its own work.

Given these considerations, the professionalization of project management raises some interesting questions. How is this occupation accomplishing professionalism? How does this professional project differ from the traditional professions of the past? What new tactics are being deployed, with what measure of success? Does the experience of project management point to a new pattern of professionalization and what are its distinctive characteristics? And what are the likely implications of these developments for the practice of project management? In the next section we attempt to address these questions by reviewing the distinctive characteristics of this professional project.

TACTICS OF PROFESSIONALIZATION
IN PROJECT MANAGEMENT

In this section, then, we will describe the distinguishing features of project management's professionalization, covering (1) the international character of professionalization, (2) the centrality of bodies of knowledge in this process, (3) the development of diversified and stratified accreditation, (4) the emphasis on corporate membership and client value, and (5) the distinctive relationship forged with broader stakeholders including the state and higher education.

The first relevant characteristic is the international scope of this project which breaks away from the traditional link between professionalization and national jurisdictions.

The international scope of project management professionalism

Most national associations for project management, including the APM, are themselves members of an international umbrella body, the International Project Management Association (IPMA). The IPMA provides a forum for dialogue, knowledge-sharing, and coordination of the activities of its member associations, as well as providing an international framework for project management formation and accreditation. At the same time, acting for all members, the IPMA implicitly discourages international expansionism on the part of any member association, working on the principle that there should be one association to represent each nation. The sustainability of this position in an era of globalization is open to question, as project managers move internationally within and between multinational firms, and routinely coordinate cross-border activity. One significant challenge to multinational visions of project management professionalism is PMI; PMI is not a member of IPMA and has a more aggressive globalization strategy, having established substantial chapters in over sixty-five countries to date (PMI 2009). While the potential for PMI to become the primary association for project managers in many European countries, such as the UK, Germany, and France, is constrained by the established presence of national associations, PMI has managed to build a more dominant position elsewhere in Europe such as Greece and several central and Eastern European states. Outside of Europe, PMI has in recent years established a significant presence in Japan, China, and India, and has seen rapid growth in other areas such as Malaysia, Pakistan, Peru, and Kuwait. Despite this global reach, it remains the case that around 70 percent of PMI members and PMI certified professionals are located in the USA and Canada, and the vast majority of these are based in the USA (PMI 2007).

The varying responses to globalization from the various associations (coordination through an umbrella organization such as the IPMA or direct expansion as in the case of the PMI) lends some support to Evetts's prediction of an evolving remit for professional bodies, "to continue the guardianship of the professions' expertise and interest, to develop international arrangements for the acquisition of qualifications, to engage in the competitions over jurisdictions and to maintain systems of professional regulation, this time within transnational markets and international divisions of labour" (Evetts 1995: 772). A consequence of this is the shifting network of cooperation and competition between professional associations where boundaries overlap, as reflected in the variegated pattern of expansion of PMI in recent years. In other words, as clients and economic activity globalize, the professional project follows suit acquiring an international dimension.

The development of diversified and stratified accreditation

Another key role of the various bodies of knowledge is to support and to structure the certification procedures of the professional associations within the field; the success of credentialism in the context of project management emerges clearly from the rapid growth in membership resulting from the introduction of accreditation by the PMI and APM. Both organizations launched their accreditation in the early 1990s with a single entry point qualification, in line with the practice of traditional professions; for PMI, the PMP (Project Management Professional), and for APM, the CPM (Certificated Project Manager). Both were based primarily on testing formal knowledge (as enshrined in the respective bodies of knowledge). However, the accreditation policies of the PMI, APM, and IPMA have diversified since in two main regards. First, new qualifications have been added to the initial single point, both horizontally (through the creation of specialized qualifications, such as the PMI's PMI-SP (Scheduling Professional) qualification) and vertically, through the creation of a hierarchy of qualifications (see Figure 4.4).

This may be interpreted both as a recognition of the diversity of the field, and also as a stratification of the profession, reflecting but also institutionalizing a hierarchy within this area of practice. Secondly, the new qualifications, and increasingly the "higher-level" credentials, rely upon a testing of competency, rather than formal knowledge, and demand evidence of ability in the form of CVs, portfolios, and other testimonies of job-related performance. Hence, as one progresses through the hierarchy of qualifications there is a shift from input- to output-based measures, and also a recognition of the diversity of contexts in which project management is practiced. This move towards tiered membership

Level	APM	IPMA	PMI[a]	PMAJ[a]
A		Certified Projects Director (CPD)		
B	Certificated Project Manager (CPM)	Certified Senior Project Manager (CSPM)	Program Management Professional (PgMP)	Program Management Architect (PMA)
C	Practitioner Qualification (PQ)	Certified Project Manager (CPM)	Project Management Professional (PMP)	Project Management Registered (PMR)
D	APMP	Certified Project Management Associate (CPMA)	Certified Associate in Project Management (CAPM)	PM Specialist (PMS)
	Introductory Certificate (IC)			
Other	Risk Management (PRMC)		PMI-SP (Scheduling Professional) PMI-RMP (Risk Mgt Professional)	

Fig. 4.4 Qualification frameworks comparison

[a]The structures for PMI and PMAJ do not conform directly to the four-level framework established by the IPMA, as they are not IPMA member associations.

propositions and competence-based closure echoes similar developments in other forms of expert labor such as consultancy and indicates an attempt to develop more suited qualification paths in occupations characterized by a more elusive and situated knowledge base.

That said, it is important to remain aware of the commercial imperative underpinning the drive towards certification. Clearly, as Morris et al. note (2006: 713), for the professional associations, certification "is a highly effective means of attracting membership and increasing influence," and indeed, for PMI, the exponential increase in membership appears in itself to be vindication of the effectiveness of these tactics. Membership brings not only status and influence but also revenue.

The centrality of the bodies of knowledge

A more traditional feature of this professionalization project has been the relative success of project management compared to other expert occupations such as consultancy[3] in developing and establishing a coherent and formalized body of codified knowledge. As noted, the creation, delimitation, and definition of a sphere of knowledge, which can be embodied in official credentials, is a key element in the evolution of established professions. As Morris, Patel, and Wearne (2000: 156) note, "The Body of Knowledge...reflects the ontology of the profession; the set of words, relationships and meanings that describe the philosophy of project management." Numerous other semi-professions, such as nursing and teaching, perceive the lack of a proprietary, codified, and bounded knowledge base to be a major impediment to their aspirations to professionalize (Zwerman et al. 2004); with project management the body of knowledge is seen as an important and necessary but not sufficient condition for professionalization (Morris et al. 2006). Three significant bodies of knowledge are identified by Morris, Jamieson, and Shepherd (2006); those of the PMI (the PMBoK "Guide"), APM (APM BoK), and PMAJ (P2M). A fourth, the IPMA Competence Baseline (ICB), is a composite of the documents of various European associations, and is intended to act as a framework within which national associations can build their own body of knowledge documents (Crawford 2004).[4] Of these documents, the PMBoK is most restrictive in its definition of the scope of project management (Crawford 2004; Morris, Jamieson, and Shepherd 2006); it is also arguably the most influential document, PMI claiming that there are over two million copies of their PMBoK in circulation. While all of the major bodies of knowledge have been intermittently updated since the early 1990s, this typically involves expanding their scope through the inclusion of additional elements, such as program or portfolio management. However, these revisions regularly fall short of the more fundamental, disruptive, and costly restructuring of the knowledge domain which two decades of "empirically derived information and theoretically informed critique" might necessitate (Morris et al. 2006: 715). The institutionalization of the bodies of knowledge—in textbooks, training programmes, appraisal criteria—therefore represents a temporal freezing of debates on the underpinning knowledge and practices in this domain (Hodgson and Cicmil 2006).

The formation of a body of knowledge is traditionally seen as an obligatory step in the move towards professional status, both for the legitimization of a profession's knowledge base and for the support of closure regimes, restricting access to job markets to a limited circle who have mastered the relevant knowledge base (Parkin 1979). While this legitimacy relies upon the codification of knowledge, however, codified and codifiable knowledge remains only a subset of knowledge (Lave and Wenger 1991; Nonaka and Takeuchi 1995), and a minor subset of what might be termed "professional expertise," which relies upon the expertise of the professional to interpret and relate to the complexities of reality (Boreham 1983; Schön 1995; Cook and Seely Brown 1999). Ongoing debates over the structure, form, and content of the various bodies of knowledge reflect this tension between indeterminacy (maintaining the mystique of professional expertise) and technicality (codifying professional knowledge as generalizable principles and methodologies) (Jamous and Pelloile 1970). While an explicit body of knowledge helps to legitimize project management as an expert occupation with ownership of a recognized technical base, aspirations of enhanced professional status and professional autonomy are not helped by the commodification of project management expertise through more detailed and prescriptive bodies of knowledge.

This tension is further complicated in the field by the distinctive ontologies represented by the various bodies of knowledge. While for some in the field, the existence of divergent views on core aspects of project management reflects the comparative immaturity of the field, conversely, it may be argued that "a mature discipline is one which allows space for differences of opinion and views about even quite fundamental matters.... The search for an authoritative, unitary position on all matters relating to projects may thus be a symptom of immaturity" (Morris et al. 2006: 718). It would, however, be naive to ignore the competitive dynamics underpinning the variation in bodies of knowledge; that the professional associations are engaged in a form of competition for legitimacy, influence, membership, and patronage and, in this regard, the bodies of knowledge represent one of their respective "unique selling points" for providers of education and training.

Focus on corporate membership and client value

The relationship of professional associations to major employers/clients is a complex one, marking a shift away from traditional professionalization based around a compact with the state towards new corporate forms of professionalism predicated on market value as indexed by the "buy-in" of major corporations in the field (Kirkpatrick and Ackroyd 2003). In this way, project management exemplifies a broader tendency described by Brint (1994) as the shift from a "social trusteeship" to an "expert" conception of professionalism, whereby technical knowledge and service to the client rather than value to society and public service mark out professionalism. Developing this argument, project management bears a strong resemblance to Hanlon's description of the "commercialized professionalism" (Hanlon 1998), in that its claims to expertise rely upon three specific elements; "technical ability, managerial competency and *in particular the delivery of economic benefits by the project manager for his or her client*" (Morris et al. 2006: 711, emphasis added). In this regard, it is interesting to note that the PMI tagline "Building Professionalism in Project Management" was changed in July 2004 to "Making Project Management Indispensable for Business Results," underlining and making explicit the "commercialized profession" orientation of PMI. The most substantial research project funded to date by PMI into the "Value of Project Management" (Thomas and Mullaly 2008) serves as further evidence of the vital importance of making a firm connection between project management and corporate success.

Since 2000, APM has worked to increase the number of corporate members, in a concerted drive to directly involve major companies for whom projects form a key element of their activities. As a result, APM corporate membership has increased from 150 member firms in 2001 to nearly 500 in 2009. Interestingly, PMI does not have a comparable category of corporate members; currently, all PMI members are individuals. However, in recent years PMI has established a Corporate Council, which in 2009 was composed of nearly thirty members, most of whom were US-based multinationals drawn from a range of industries, from consulting and finance to IT and aerospace. This reorientation towards employer and client organizations, mirrored by other contemporary professionalizing occupations such as management consulting, reflects a shift in power in professional associations, where the state plays a part, but only as one of many corporate sponsors (see next section), and where individual members are but one constituency. Evetts, for example, distinguishes between professionalization "from within," the traditional mode whereby practitioners organize to insulate themselves from the market, and professionalization "from above," where the process is instigated and controlled by employers of professionals, often with the agreement of members who see their interests at least partly served by the employing organizations (Evetts 2003).

Shifting relations with academia, government, and NGOs

The distinctiveness of the project management professionalization process can be illustrated also by a consideration of the relations between project management professional associations and other important stakeholders, particularly those institutions such as universities, and the various arms of government, which hold, or have held, pivotal roles in the recognition of traditional professions.

Both PMI and APM have in recent years developed relations with universities and higher education institutions, in various forms; however, in comparison to traditional professions, these academic links appear very late in the professionalization process, and there is little sign to date of the associations relying heavily upon academic research for legitimacy. The reverse is rather the case as universities appear to draw on the professional associations for their own market legitimacy. Indeed professional associations accredit particular academic training programmes through, for example, the PMI Global Accreditation Center, which recognizes programmes in some twenty-five institutions worldwide. By accepting and incorporating the professional associations' conceptions of project management, universities can increase the appeal and market value of their degree programmes, and at the same time implicitly legitimize the professional associations' view of the discipline.

In recent years relations between the associations and higher education establishments have extended to include the provision of more substantial support for research activities. The resources available to the professional associations, both financial and symbolic, certainly offer the potential for leadership and direction of the emergent research agenda in this field. PMI in particular has invested significantly in research funding, the most notable example being the $2.5 million awarded for the Value of Project Management project. At the same time, organizing and supporting research conferences (e.g. the PMI research conference) affords another means to guide research in the discipline (Blomquist and Söderholm 2002). Yet, ultimately, it remains the case that "research has thus so far played a modest role in the development and formalisation of the discipline as represented by the Bodies of Knowledge" (Morris et al. 2006: 715), although this in itself is far from unusual where academia and professional practice intersect (Barley, Meyer, and Gash 1988).

Conspicuous by its absence, however, is evidence of a "regulative bargain" between any professional association and specific nation states. In several cases, specific departments or quasi-governmental organizations have formal relations with a professional association—hence APM counts among its corporate members numerous agencies such as HM Treasury, the Ministry of Defence, the Department of Health, the UK Government Communications Headquarters (GCHQ), and various local government bodies, and the PMI's corporate council includes the US Department of Energy's Office of Engineering and Construction Management. These good relations, however, do not amount to an affordance of monopolistic privileges, as might have been achieved by the liberal professions. The recent decision by APM to pursue chartered status (announced December 2007), however, invites a more robust level of support from the British state for the association, and if successful, opens the way to the introduction of something approaching a "license to practice," guaranteed by the APM.

As a final comment on the settlements negotiated between the professional associations and powerful external agencies, one might observe tentative attempts to establish agreements with supra-national and non-governmental organizations, including important standard-setters (Hodgson and Cicmil 2006) such as the International Standards Organization (ISO), British Standards Institute (BSI), the American National Standards Institute (ANSI), and over a dozen others (see Crawford 2004 for a detailed comparison). At present, the PMI PMBoK has been recognized as an ANSI standard, while the BSI has also developed a British standard for project management, BS 6079–1. The creation of an international standard for project management, under the auspices of the ISO, is currently under way, and involves negotiations between the different professional associations, national standards associations, and representatives of a vast range of industries regarding the form and scope of the standard. Arguably, returning to the initial issue of globalization, this negotiation forms a vital new terrain of competition between not only project management professional associations, but also regions, industries, and corporations.

DISCUSSION

Project management at the end of the first decade of the twenty-first century occupies an intriguing position as an aspirant profession, caught between the paradigmatic models of professionalism provided by the liberal professions and a fundamentally different institutional and competitive location in the contemporary work environment. Professional status and the acquisition of accredited knowledge and competences in managing projects is seen by many practitioners as invaluable, not only as guidance to everyday practice in a challenging occupation but also as providing a route to status, influence, material rewards, and legitimization. The outcomes of professionalization are even more important for the many who have moved into project management "accidentally," often later in their careers, and lack formal training in their new role.

The ongoing transformation of project management into a discipline broadly recognized as a modern profession departs in significant ways from traditional models of professionalization. Given that professionalism has constantly evolved as "the product of a dialectical relationship with its environment" (Hanlon 1999: 3), it is no surprise that the key institutional actors in the project management field, the professional associations, have adopted innovative tactics to enhance the status and influence of project managers and to acquire recognition as a profession. Distinctive tactics include (1) an exceptionally international dimension to the professionalization project, (2) a focus on knowledge legitimization through the promotion of written bodies of knowledge (at the implicit expense of uncodified/uncodifiable knowledge or interpretive practice), (3) a move towards diversified and stratified modes of accreditation, (4) a marked emphasis on corporate membership and client engagement, and (5) an attenuated relationship to those traditional bedrocks of professionalism, the state and higher education institutions. These tactics may be seen to be specifically designed to counter the functional difficulties presented by project management as a discipline and occupation, its interdisciplinary and porous scope of operation, the location of project managers as employees within large public and private organizations, as well as the broader challenges of a more hostile historical context toward professional claims of all kinds. That project management has increased its profile, influence, and status through these tactics in the current social and political climate is itself a remarkable achievement which merits closer analytical attention. There are at the same time critical concerns implied by the specific form professionalization has taken for project management, and the power dynamics which shape the actions of the various players in the field. We will therefore highlight four particularly salient issues implied by our reading.

First, as the analysis above leads us to characterize contemporary project management as an amalgam of organizational and corporate professionalism in Reed's terms, one may infer a relatively weak position for the individual project management practitioner compared to many traditional professionals. Reliant upon market-recognized "expertise" rather than strong claims of "social trusteeship," the project manager is simultaneously structured by his/her location within organizational bureaucracies and career structures, and is also indirectly subject to their employers' influence over the professional associations themselves, leading to a double (or indeed triple) closure. This multiple dependency of the project management professional is simultaneously the source of her/his strength and weakness; that is, the achievement of a broadly recognized professional status for the field depends upon, and may at the same time be undermined by, embracing the agenda and priorities of employers and clients.

Secondly, and relatedly, the reliance upon the market for legitimacy lends a particular power to major employers and consumers of project management services in shaping the future of the nascent profession. Due to the growing membership, both individual and corporate, of these associations, their aspirations to control both the "production of producers" and "production by producers" in this field (Abel 1988) appears increasingly feasible. As described above, the reference point for the major professional associations, particularly PMI, is not the state (except in its increasingly relevant capacity as a large consumer of expert services) but the market, with the building of market consensus rather than the achievement of statutory recognition as the key objective. In other words, the associations set out to build a critical mass of consensus around the professionalization project by persuading a sufficiently large number of employers and clients of project management of the merits of professional membership, accreditation, and regulation. Once a sufficiently large share of the market has been won over, professional affiliation would be routinely expected and indeed requested by both clients and employers in their procurement and recruitment process; thus, de facto, delivering a market form of occupational closure, produced not by the state but by major corporations in this field.

Furthermore, the strength of such links with major employers and clients of project managers mean that professionalism in this field increasingly resembles "professionalism from above" rather than the collegial "professionalization from within" (Evetts 2003). The prospect of a countervailing force from project management practitioners is undermined by the creation of a hierarchy of professionals, formally structured through a ladder of qualifications. This stratification of the field marks another break with the classical collegiate model of professionalism as a cadre with one entry point and allegedly equal levels of competence, and lays open the possibility for a polarized and fragmented occupation, a development mirrored in other professions and expert occupations such as human resource management.

Finally, in light of these developments, the question of the effectiveness of professional project management—whether or not professionalization within the field has delivered projects more effectively or more reliably—remains moot, and may be arguably seen as a second-order concern for some actors in the field, as the absence of this "silver bullet" does not appear to have significantly impeded the recent expansion of the field. Whether current research endeavors (such as PMI's Value of Project Management programme) can provide this silver bullet, or whether project management can build upon its current status without convincing evidence of this link, is a pressing concern.

While this chapter provides a broad "snapshot" of the current mode of organization of project management, more longitudinal analysis of the dynamics within the field in future research is necessary to measure the projected transformation of project management towards full organizational professionalism whilst at the same time more research effort could be placed on establishing the benefits of professionalization to practitioners, employers, and end-users. A deeper ethnographic examination of practitioner motivations regarding professional status is also a research priority, looking in detail at values, orientations, and conduct of both members and non-members of professional associations across a range of sectors. Finally, research would benefit from a more international perspective in order to broaden our understanding of professionalization outside of Anglo-Saxon economies. Such research is vital for an accurate understanding of the power relations in the field, with implications for the evolution of project management knowledge, the relation between practice and theoretical and empirical research, as well as the evolving career structure of project managers in a global economy.

NOTES

1. The largest source of corporate members of the Association for Project Management after construction, consulting, and training are government and IS/IT.
2. To establish the comparative size of the PM professional associations, the Institute of Electrical and Electronics Engineers (IEEE) in 2009 had around 365,000 members; the Association of Chartered Certified Accountants (ACCA) had 131,500 members, the UK-based Chartered Institute of Personnel and Development (CIPD) had 133,000 members, while the US-based Society for Human Resource Management (SHRM) had 250,000.
3. For a more detailed examination of the relationship between the occupations of project management and consulting, see Muzio et al. (2011).
4. As Morris et al. (2006) note, the ICB is formed by combining the British, German, and French bodies of knowledge; "the French and German BOKs are modelled closely on the APM BOK as, in consequence, is the IPMA structure" (2006: 712).

REFERENCES

ABBOTT, A. D. (1988). *The System of Professions: An Essay on the Division of Expert Labor.* Chicago: University of Chicago Press.
ABEL, R. L. (1988). *The Legal Profession in England and Wales.* New York: Blackwell.

—— (2003). *The Politics of Professionalism: Lawyers between Markets and State, from the Green Papers to the Access of Justice Act.* Oxford: Oxford University Press.

ACKROYD, S. (1996). "Organization contra organizations: professions and organizational change in the United Kingdom," *Organization Studies*, 17/4: 599–621.

—— (2009) "Redirection in the study of expert labour," paper delivered at ESRC Workshop "Professions and Professionalism in the 21st Century: Meanings, Challenges and Prospects," Lancaster University, January 2009.

ADLER, P. S. (2001). "Market, hierarchy, and trust: the knowledge economy and the future of capitalism," *Organization Science*, 12/2: 215–34.

ANDERSON-GOUGH, F., et al. (2000). "In the name of the client: the service ethic in two professional services firms," *Human Relations*, 53/9: 1151–74.

ARONOWITZ, S., and DI FAZIO, W. (1994). *The Jobless Future: Sci-tech and the Dogma of Work.* Minneapolis: University of Minnesota Press.

BAER, W. C. (1986). "Expertise and professional standards," *Work and Occupations*, 13/4: 532–52.

BARLEY, S. R., MEYER, G., and GASH, D. (1988). "Cultures of culture: academics, practitioners and the pragmatics of normative control," *Administrative Science Quarterly*, 33/1: 24–60.

BLACKLER, F. (1995). "Knowledge, knowledge work and organizations: an overview and interpretation," *Organization Studies*, 16/6: 1021–46.

—— REED, M. I., and WHITAKER, A. (1993). "Editorial introduction: knowledge workers and contemporary organizations," *Journal of Management Studies*, 30/6: 851–62.

BLOMQUIST, T., and SÖDERHOLM, A. (2002). "How project management got carried away," in K. Sahlin-Andersson and A. Söderholm (eds.), *Beyond Project Management: New Perspectives on the Temporary–Permanent Dilemma.* Copenhagen: Copenhagen Business School Press.

BOREHAM, P. (1983). "Indetermination: professional knowledge, organization and control," *Sociological Review*, 31/4: 693–718.

BRINT, S. G. (1994). *In an Age of Experts: The Changing Role of Professionals in Politics and Public Life.* Princeton: Princeton University Press.

BROADBENT, J., DIETRICH, M., and ROBERTS, J. (eds.) (1997). *The End of the Professions? The Restructuring of Professional Work.* London: Routledge.

BURRAGE, M., and TORSTENDAHL, R. (eds.) (1990). *Professions in Theory and History: Rethinking the Study of the Professions.* London: Sage.

BURRIS, B. (1993). *Technocracy at Work.* Albany, NY: State University of New York Press.

CLARKE, J., and NEWMAN, J. (1997). *The Managerial State.* London: Sage.

COLLINS, H. M. (1990). *Artificial Experts: Social Knowledge and Intelligent Machines.* Cambridge, MA: MIT Press.

COOK, S. D. N., and SEELY BROWN, J. (1999). "Bridging epistemologies: the generative dance between organizational knowledge and organizational knowing," *Organization Science*, 10/4: 381–400.

CRAWFORD, L. (2004). "Project management standards and guides," in P. W. G. Morris and J. K. Pinto (eds.), *The Wiley Guide to Managing Projects.* Hoboken, NJ: John Wiley and Sons, 1150–96.

DERBER, C., SCHWARTZ, W. A., and MAGRASS, Y. R. (1990). *Power in the Highest Degree: Professionals and the Rise of a New Mandarin Order.* New York: Oxford University Press.

ENGWALL, M. (1995). *Jakten på det Effektiva Projektet.* Stockholm: Nerenius and Santérus.

EVETTS, J. (1995). "International professional associations: the new context for professional projects," *Work Employment and Society*, 9/4: 763–72.

—— (2003). "The sociological analysis of professionalism: occupational change in the modern world," *International Sociology*, 18/2: 395–415.

FINCHAM, R. (2006). "Knowledge work as occupational strategy: comparing IT and management consulting," *New Technology, Work and Employment*, 21/1: 16–28.

FOURNIER, V. (1999). "The appeal to 'professionalism' as a disciplinary mechanism," *Sociological Review*, 47/2: 280–307.

FREIDSON, E. (1994). *Professionalism Reborn: Theory, Prophecy and Policy*. Cambridge: Polity Press.

FURUSTEN, S., and GARSTEN, C. (2005). "New professionalism," in S. Furusten and A. Werr (eds.), *Dealing with Confidence*. Copenhagen: CBS Press.

GREENWOOD, E. (1957). "The attributes of a profession," *Social Work*, 2: 45–55.

GREY, C. (1997). "Management as a technical practice: professionalization or responsibilization?," *Systems Practice*, 10/6: 703–25.

—— (1998). "On being a professional in a 'big six' firm," *Accounting Organizations and Society*, 23/5–6: 569–87.

HANLON, G. (1998). "Professionalism as enterprise: service class politics and the redefinition of professionalism," *Sociology*, 32/1: 43–63.

—— (1999). *Lawyers, the State and the Market: Professionalism Revisited*. Basingstoke: Macmillan Business.

HODGSON, D. E. (2002). "Disciplining the professional: the case of project management," *Journal of Management Studies*, 39/6: 803–21.

—— (2007). "The new professionals: professionalisation and the struggle for occupational control in the field of project management," in D. Muzio, S. Ackroyd, and J. F. Chanlat (eds.), *Redirections in the Study of Expert Labour: Medicine, Law and Management Consultancy*. Basingstoke: Palgrave.

—— and CICMIL, S. (2006). *Making Projects Critical*. Basingstoke: Palgrave.

—— —— (2007). "The politics of standards in modern management: making 'the project' a reality," *Journal of Management Studies*, 44/3: 431–50.

HUGHES, T. P. (1998). *Rescuing Prometheus: Four Monumental Projects That Changed the Modern World*. New York: Pantheon Books.

JAMOUS, H., and PELLOILE, B. (1970). "Changes in the French university-hospital system," in J. Jackson (ed.), *Professions and Professionalization*. Cambridge: Cambridge University Press.

JESSOP, B. (1994). "The transition to post-Fordism and the Schumpeterian welfare state," in R. Burrows and B. Loader (eds.), *Towards a Post-Fordist Welfare State?* London: Routledge.

JOHNSON, T. J. (1972). *Professions and Power*. London: Macmillan.

KIRKPATRICK, I., and ACKROYD, S. (2003). "Archetype theory and the changing professional organization: a critique and alternative," *Organization*, 10/4: 731–50.

KRAUSE, E. A. (1996). *Death of the Guilds: Professions, States, and the Advance of Capitalism, 1930 to the Present*. New Haven: Yale University Press.

KRITZER, H. M. (1999). "The professions are dead, long live the professions: legal practice in a postprofessional world," *Law and Society Review*, 33/3: 713–59.

LARSON, M. S. (1977). *The Rise of Professionalism: A Sociological Analysis*. Berkeley and Los Angeles: University of California Press.

LAVE, J., and WENGER, E. (1991). *Situated Learning: Legitimate Peripheral Participation.* Cambridge: Cambridge University Press.

LUCIO, M. M., and KIRKPATRICK, I. (1995). *The Politics of Quality and the Management of Change in the Public Sector.* London: Routledge.

MACDONALD, K. M. (1995). *The Sociology of the Professions.* London: Sage.

MORRIS, P. W. G. (1997). *The Management of Projects.* London: T. Telford.

——JAMIESON, H. A., and SHEPHERD, M. M. (2006). "Research updating the APM Body of Knowledge 4th edition," *International Journal of Project Management,* 24/6: 461–73.

——PATEL, M. B., and WEARNE, S. H. (2000). "Research into revising the APM Project Management Body of Knowledge," *International Journal of Project Management,* 18/3: 155–64.

——CRAWFORD, L., HODGSON, D., SHEPHERD, M. M., and THOMAS, J. (2006). "Exploring the role of formal bodies of knowledge in defining a profession: the case of project management," *International Journal of Project Management,* 24/8: 710–21.

MURPHY, R. (1988). *Social Closure: The Theory of Monopolization and Exclusion.* Oxford: Clarendon Press.

MUZIO, D., and ACKROYD, S. (2005). "On the consequences of defensive professionalism: recent changes in the legal labour process," *Journal of Law and Society,* 32/4: 615–42.

————and CHANLAT, J. F. (eds.) (2007). *Redirections in the Study of Expert Labour: Established Professions and New Expert Occupations.* Basingstoke: Palgrave.

——BEAVERSTOCK, J., FAULCONBRIDGE, J., HALL, S., and HODGSON, D. E. (2011). "Towards corporate professionalization: the case of project management, management consultancy and executive search," *Current Sociology* (forthcoming).

NONAKA, I., and TAKEUCHI, H. (1995). *The Knowledge Creating Company.* Oxford: Oxford University Press.

NOORDEGRAAF, M. (2007). "From 'pure' to 'hybrid' professionalism: present-day professionalism in ambiguous public domains", *Administration and Society,* 39/6: 761–85.

PARKIN, F. (1979). *Marxism and Class Theory: A Bourgeois Critique.* London: Tavistock Publications.

PARSONS, T. (1954). *The Professions and Social Structure: Essays in Sociological Theory.* New York: Free Press.

PMI (2004). *A Guide to the Project Management Body of Knowledge,* 3rd edn. Newtown Square, PA: Project Management Institute Inc.

——(2007). "PMI fact sheet March 2007," http://www.wipmsig.org/documents/ PMI Fact Sheet.pdf. Accessed 27 July 2009.

——(2009) "PMI chapters," http://www.pmi.org/GetInvolved/Pages/PMI-Chapters.aspx. Accessed 27 July 2009.

REED, M. I. (1996). "Expert power and control in late modernity: an empirical review and theoretical synthesis," *Organization Studies,* 17/4: 573–97.

——(2006). "Engineers of human souls, faceless technocrats or merchants of morality? Changing professional forms and identities in the face of the neoliberal challenge," in A. H. Pinnington, R. Macklin, and T. Campbell (eds.), *Human Resource Management: Ethics and Employment.* Oxford: Oxford University Press.

SCHÖN, D. A. (1995). *Reflective Practitioner: How Professionals Think in Action.* Aldershot: Arena.

SCIULLI, D. (2005). "Continental sociology of professions today: conceptual contributions," *Current Sociology,* 53/6: 915–42.

SUGARMAN, D. (1996). "Bourgeois collectivism, professional power and the boundaries of the state: the private and public life of the Law Society, 1825 to 1914," *International Journal of the Legal Profession*, March 3/1–2: 81–135.

THOMAS, J., and MULLALY, M. (2008). *Researching the Value of Project Management*. Newtown Square, PA: PMI.

TORSTENDAHL, R., and BURRAGE, M. (1990). *Professions in Theory and History: Rethinking the Study of the Professions*. London: Sage Publications.

WHITTINGTON, R., PETTIGREW, A., PECK, S., FENTON, E., and CONYON, M. (1999). "Change and complementarities in the new competitive landscape: a European panel study, 1992–1996," *Organization Science*, 10/5: 583–600.

ZWERMAN, B. L., THOMAS, J. L., HAYDT, S., and WILLIAMS, T. A. (2004). *Professionalization of Project Management: Exploring the Past to Map the Future*. Newtown Square, PA: PMI.

PART II

INDUSTRY AND CONTEXT

CHAPTER 5

THE PROJECT BUSINESS

ANALYTICAL FRAMEWORK AND RESEARCH OPPORTUNITIES

KARLOS ARTTO

ANDREW DAVIES

JAAKKO KUJALA

ANDREA PRENCIPE

INTRODUCTION

Project business is an emerging research field, which adopts a business-centric view to the management of projects, firms, and networks of projects and firms. Project business has been defined as "the part of business that relates directly or indirectly to projects, with the purpose of achieving objectives of a firm or several firms" (Artto and Wikström 2005). Relying on existing research, this chapter identifies (a) the managerial challenges for successful management of projects and project-based firms and (b) the research themes and opportunities that may enhance our understanding of project business. We use the term "project-based firm" to refer *both* to firms that conduct part of their operations using projects *and* to firms that organize most of their internal and external activities in projects. Project-based firms and organizations are found in a wide range of industries, such as consulting and professional services, cultural industries, high technology, and complex products and systems. A project represents a delivery system of a firm's internal development or external business activities. In addition, a project may cross the boundaries of two firms (e.g. designing of products and services jointly by the project contractor firm and its client) or several firms working in alliances or coalitions, or as multi-organization enterprises, project networks, or project ecologies.

THE PROJECT BUSINESS FRAMEWORK: FOUR DISTINCTIVE MANAGEMENT AREAS

Project business includes activities positioned within the boundaries of projects and firms as well as aspects of collaboration within whole networks of multiple firms. Söderlund (2004) introduced a framework with the dimensions of single vs. multiple projects, and single vs. multiple firms to analyze project management research. We extend his framework arguing that any project may cross one or several firms' boundaries and business activities, and vice versa, any firm may cross one or several projects' boundaries and business activities. The four areas of project business (Figure 5.1) vary depending upon whether management is concerned with a project, a project-based firm, a project network, or a business network (Artto and Kujala 2008):

- *Management of a project*—addresses a single project.
- *Management of a project-based firm*—addresses activities of a firm involved in governing/managing multiple simultaneous or sequential projects for the firm's business purposes.
- *Management of a project network* area—addresses the management of the temporary project organization across multiple participating firms and other actors each of which have their own objectives, interests, and expectations from the project.
- *Management of a business network* area—includes activities in the business marketplace including several firms and their business interests, often involving multiple projects that serve as temporary business vehicles to achieve each firm's permanent businesses.

The project business framework in Figure 5.1 represents a business-centric view to project research and its empirical applications. The framework highlights that projects and firms are both independent entities and interdependent networked organizations. It recognizes the variety of firms that organize their activities in projects. Some firms also run their businesses through other strategic business activities that are only indirectly project related. For example, Nokia Siemens Networks (NSN) offers major telecom network implementation projects for its customers, but also a wide range of services (that may be more related to customers' businesses rather than projects), such as business consulting and outsourcing.

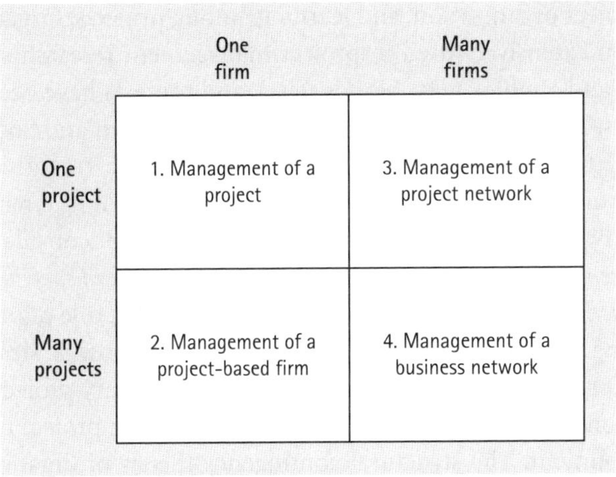

	One firm	Many firms
One project	1. Management of a project	3. Management of a project network
Many projects	2. Management of a project-based firm	4. Management of a business network

Fig. 5.1 Framework of project business: four distinctive management areas

In Figure 5.1, we refer to "many firms" as when there are multiple private organizations involved in projects such as project contractors, subcontractors, designers, architects, and financiers. In addition to many firms, project networks and business networks may also include public sector organizations such as government ministries, universities, and NGOs. All these firms and other organizations are relevant *stakeholders* interacting with projects and project-based firms in the marketplace.

MANAGEMENT OF A PROJECT

The *management of a project* is a well-researched area and can be briefly summarized. Project management knowledge has been developed since the emergence of the modern project and program management in the 1950s and 1960s. The contemporary standard documents of project management represent an excellent overview of what the application of management of a single project includes (ISO 1997; PMI 2008; IPMA 2006; APM 2006). Such standard documents cover knowledge areas (or processes) useful for project management practitioners and for company users (Morris et al. 2006). Much of the existing project management literature adopts a practice-oriented view where the project is seen as a development process guided by plans and working within pre-established constraints of time, cost, and specification. More recently, the emphasis has shifted from the technical-tactical management of specific projects' tasks (with e.g. CPM and PERT as described by Moder and Phillips 1964), first organizationally to the management of the project team and people and project organization, and learning among projects. Organizational theories have been extensively used in project management research since the 1960s (Stinchcombe and Heimer 1985; Morris 1994), and projects have been increasingly defined and researched as temporary organizations (Lundin and Söderholm 1995). Organizational theories such as contingency theory have recently been used to emphasize a project's role as an independent organization in its environment.

More recently, project management has been criticized for considering *projects as working to "given" pre-determined constraints of time, cost, and specified scope guided by predetermined plans* (Morris et al. 2006). Increasingly the role of project management in shaping the front-end and in linking with the sponsors' strategies is being recognized (Morris 1994, 2009). But in general, contemporary project management rarely focuses on ensuring beneficial *business outcomes* of a project in an uncertain external environment. The structural contingency theory of organizations asserts that the effectiveness of an organization is contingent upon the fit between structural and environmental variables (Lawrence and Lorsch 1967; Donaldson 2001). Shenhar (2001) compared the effectiveness of different project management approaches in different environments, but the *contingency* aspect tends to be more focused on the project's internal characteristics rather than contingencies in the business environment. However, as Engwall (2003) argues, the environment is not exclusively on the outside of the organization but organizational actions take place within a *complex societal web* of structures, resources, values, and players.

Based on the above analysis, we call for a greater outcome orientation in the management of projects. This requires an *open systems view* where the project is an organic and purposeful business vehicle, interrelated with one (e.g. the parent organization) or many other organizational entities (Von Bertalanffy 1950; Emery and Trist 1965; Katz and Kahn 1966). Future research, should focus inter alia on *contingencies represented by factors and variables exogenous to the project* (Miller and Lessard 2001a). Not only is the fit of the project's management to the environment important, the project's aspirations concerning the outcome in terms of its short- and long-term business implications set requirements for the appropriate project management approach.

This brings us to the literature on *project strategy,* which typically assumes that the project is subordinated to a single parent firm and there is a link between the strategies of the parent and the project (Morris and Jamieson 2004; Shenhar et al. 2005). However, in a complex *stakeholder* environment, a project strategy of an autonomous project may to some extent be self-established by the project itself, as affected by how the project defines its success criteria, and how the project perceives its context (Artto et al. 2008a). Therefore, as far as a project's strategy is concerned, we suggest that a project is comparable to a firm (which has a strategy of its own: its strategy helps shape its environment and the emergent strategies of its stakeholders), and in this respect a project also faces its own business environment with both collaborative and competitive forces. In conclusion, the "management of a project" research area addresses questions such as "how does the project dynamically define its desired business outcome and how is the outcome achieved in the changing business environment with multiple internal and external business players?," or "what is a single project's strategy in relation to its multiple stakeholder organizations' strategies and how does each stakeholder [including the project's parent] affect the project's strategy formulation?," or "what are the contingencies in a project's internal or external environment that affect the project's strategy and the process of its formulation?" These questions relate to our argument that projects must be considered as business entities themselves, and that focusing on the business outcome of the project in its management activities is critical. Future project management should move towards managing the delivery of the ultimate [business] outcome of the project within its dynamic business environment. A relevant further approach to such an aspect is introduced by the integrated solutions and modularity discussions conducted later in this chapter.

MANAGEMENT OF A PROJECT-BASED FIRM

The *management of a project-based firm* is an area addressing the managerial issues of a firm that uses projects to conduct either a majority or just a specific part of its activities. Project-based firms include technology-based and service-providing firms which organize their operational activities in customer delivery type projects and firms which organize their internal development activities as projects. Research on project-based firms focuses on the project-based firm's ability to sell and deliver projects to its customers (Hobday 2000; Cova, Ghauri, and Salle 2002; Whitley 2006), on the management of innovation (Gann and Salter 2000; Keegan and Turner 2002; Lindkvist 2004), on learning (Prencipe and Tell 2001), and on project portfolio management (Cooper, Edgett, and Kleinschmidt 1997a, 1997b).

Whitley (2006) introduces a typology of project-based firms by categorizing them conceptually through two dimensions: stability of work roles, and singularity of outputs. We argue that Whitley's typology introduces interesting aspects of what could be called "*frequency* of repeating" (works and/or outputs). The concept of frequency can be considered as a central feature in a project-based firm's business. The strategic objective of the project-based contractors, for example, is to create, maintain, and manage multiple relationships with customer and other parties that enable or support the construction of future demand for projects (Cova and Hoskins 1997; Tikkanen, Kujala, and Artto 2007). In a similar manner, the project contractor creates and maintains multiple non-project-specific relationships with potential subcontractors in order to guarantee the effective sales and delivery of projects (Skaates and Tikkanen 2003). Through good relationships with certain subcontractors a project contractor *signals to the customer that capable resources are available* (Artto, Eloranta, and Kujala 2008). Procurement as well as subcontractor and supplier network management is important due to the trend of increased subcontracting and the focus being placed on a firm's core capabilities, so that *firms and projects are progressively more dependent on their suppliers* (Walker and Rowlinson 2008). Turner and Keegan (2001) analyze the organization of a project-based firm through aspects of internal governance and especially how the organization manages the interfaces with external customers through "brokers" (as customer account managers) and the customers' interfaces further down internally to projects through "stewards" (as coordinators of multiple projects belonging to what can be considered as the strategic center of Davies, Brady, and Hobday 2006).

In a project-based contractor firm, *products and their modularity not only cover the physical products*, but also the project *processes and project organization*, which represent the ultimate *capacity and capability* to create the desired solution as the outcome of the project. Gaddis (1959) suggested that the job of the project manager is to create the product. The interaction often creates great interdependency, not only from an engineering design perspective, but also in an *organizational sense* (see e.g. Bonaccorsi, Pammolli, and Tani 1996; Sosa, Eppinger, and Rowles 2004). The nature of the product plays an important role in shaping industrial organization (Hobday 1998). The choice of *product structure and organizational architecture interact* (Sanchez and Mahoney 1996). This means that product interdependencies translate with fairly good accuracy into design team interaction, thus providing a structured basis for managing project processes (Brusoni 2005).

In conclusion, recent research has addressed the distinctive characteristics of the management of a project-based firm. Such characteristics include the firm's organizational fragmentation into several independent projects, small number bargaining or low frequency of repeating works and outputs, relational context of projects with an emphasis on customer and supplier relationships, the complicated interrelatedness of product structure and organizational structure, and the systemic nature of business with activities and capabilities crossing organizational boundaries of firms and projects. We suggest that the research on project-based firms could also be applied to understanding the management of those public sector organizations that organize their activities in the project form.

MANAGEMENT OF A PROJECT NETWORK

The *management of a project network* area covers a network of several firms and other organizations from different businesses and institutional environments that participate in a project. The increasing externalization of activities to suppliers' networks (Cox and Ireland 2006) characterizes both firms and projects. The *systems integration capability* is relevant for constructing a supply organization for a multi-firm project with multiple subcontractors, suppliers, and other business and non-business players. The network of organizations participating in a single project has been defined as a *project network* (Hellgren and Stjernberg 1995), project-based enterprise (DeFillippi and Arthur 1998), *multi-organization enterprise* (Grün 2004), or a project coalition (Winch 2006). Such a project setting creates a challenge for achieving an alignment of often conflicting objectives and interests among the multiple stakeholders involved in a project network. Research on large projects and global projects captures the idea of the network of organizations from different businesses and from *different institutional environments* participating in the project (Morris and Hough 1987; Miller and Lessard 2001a, 2001b). The *dynamic nature of a project network* is emphasized by the fact that the project network is a temporary endeavor which includes several distinctive phases (Morris 1983) each of which has a continuously changing constellation of actors in ever-changing roles (Dubois and Gadde 2000).

Further research is required to develop a novel *theory of governance in project networks* (or in large multi-firm projects) by adopting a project network which goes beyond organizational forms that cut across the traditional firm–market dichotomy (see e.g. Jones, Hesterly, and Borgatti 1997). Indeed, we suggest that in the governance of multi-firm project networks, any of the prevalent governance approaches that rely on market, hierarchy, or hybrid forms is not sufficient, because they fail to grasp how a *project is managed as a temporary enterprise* involving multiple participating firms (DeFillippi and Arthur 1998), while simultaneously managing its *external network of stakeholders*.

A network view on a project emphasizes the existence of *relationships* or *ties* (Uzzi 1997) in different kinds of *network structures,* where no actor alone has total control over the network (Powell 1990). The network view on a project represents a new *organizational design* that puts emphasis on the *relationships* between the organizations in the project's network. The need to achieve goal alignment between the owner and the contractor, and to reduce the chance and benefit for *opportunism* by the owner or contractor, have been considered as the most significant issues when choosing the type and content of the contract between the parties (Turner and Simister 2001). For a dyadic contractual relationship the selection of appropriate management approaches for a project should be based on *incentivization* through contracts (Levitt and March 1995). The purpose of a contract is to create a project organization, and it should be based on a system of *cooperation instead of conflict,* and therefore the need for goal alignment is more significant (Levitt and March 1995; Turner and Simister 2001).

The more complex the product (and the project) under creation, the more important *systems integration* becomes as a means of coordination. Sosa, Eppinger, and Rowles (2004) show a practical dimension of systems integration when they distinguish between "modular and integrative systems" in a product. This has important practical implications for *managing technical team interaction*, or what McCord and Eppinger (1993) term "the integration problem of concurrent engineering." *Modular product and process structures* further enable system integrators to rely on more unstable *organizational structures* in the form of a network of suppliers. Brusoni, Prencipe, and Pavitt (2001) emphasize the importance of *systems integration capability* for tightening the links within such a loosely coupled network of firms.

In conclusion, the network view on projects draws attention to relationships both within and across organizations. In this respect, systems integration capability for integrating a network of multiple subcontractor and supplier firms is most relevant. The ultimate integrated capability within a single project therefore consists of capabilities that reside in multiple specialist firms within a project. We argue that within this line of research it would be appropriate to pursue a temporary supply chain view of project networks as it helps understand projects as delivery networks comprising multiple firms and their [sub]projects.

MANAGEMENT OF A BUSINESS NETWORK

The *management of a business network* area includes research themes that relate to several firms' activities, where the firms engage from time to time in mutual projects. A business network is a "permanent" *constellation of actors that are or could be involved in each other's current or future project activities*, such as competitors, financiers, customers and their clients, contractors and their subcontractors, suppliers, designers, architects, manufacturers, service providers, integrators, and consultants. In a business network, the aim of each firm is to maintain its efficiency and innovativeness in the network, and to *position the firm strategically in the value network of all business players. In addition,* facilitating *government or institutional agencies* may serve in the central role of business incubators that affect the project constellations (Doz and Hamel 1998; Porter 1998). The actors in the business network, as well as in the project network, can have aims that are synergistic, and accordingly, there is room for *partnership and collaboration* (Davis and Walker 2008) as well as contradictory and conflicting behavior. Grabher (2002, 2004) acknowledges the importance of *project ecologies* or regional agglomerations of project-based organizational and institutional participants; the "project ecologies" arena is where economic geographers are contributing to understanding project business as an inter-organizational phenomena.

Networked firms in the permanent business network and their (long-term) business relationships affect the selection of participating firms in a project (temporary, or short-term) and vice versa (Hellgren and Stjernberg 1995; Sydow and Staber 2002; Ahola et al. 2006). Bengtson, Havila, and Åberg (2001) argue that some *inter-organizational relationships do survive after the end of the project* and the project may even create dependencies among project actors. For example, Eccles (1981) discovered that the construction industry tends to form *quasifirms*. Indeed, experiences in the business network obtained during past projects can affect the selection of actors for a future project network, which phenomenon can be called a *shadow of the past* (Poppo, Zhou, and Ryu 2008). On the other hand, expectations of future collaboration in business affect the behavior of firms participating in a project network and for this phenomenon we can use the term *shadow of the future*, according to Heider and Miner (1992). Framework agreements are concrete vehicles for constructing positive expectations for long-term future collaboration and thereby effectiveness among the network parties over single projects (Walker, Bourne, and Rowlinson 2008). Long-term collaboration with a relatively stable set of suppliers *lowers the transaction costs and affords interactive learning processes* that benefit the partners (Grabher 2004). On the other hand, lack of long-term inter-organizational relationships between participating firms in a project network can even lead to a project failure.

From a project supplier perspective, also the *sleeping phase of the relationship between projects has to be managed actively in order to maintain a good relational position for future project deliveries* (Cova, Ghauri, and Salle 2002). In order to overcome the challenges caused by *discontinuity* of relationships in project deliveries, *many project contractor firms have included a wide set of services in their offering*. One purpose of such wide service offering is to make the firm's activities and *business relationships* with other parties—and especially with their customers—*more continuous* within the permanent but dynamic business network. Furthermore, the customer relationships are made more continuous by providing maintenance, support, or operation services for the effective operation of a customer's installed base. Artto et al. (2008b) distinguish six different impact types for *the provided service's impact on the contractor firm's business model*; for example, the "customer entry" impact type indicates that a service is delivered in order to acquire customer entry in future project deliveries, or for maintaining the customer relationship.

In conclusion, the business network and a project network of a single project are interrelated. There are two-way impacts between the permanent (or long-term) business network and the temporary (or short-term) project network. A firm's relationship position in the overall business network affects the risks and opportunities arising at the level of single projects. Furthermore, the opposite can occur when the relationships at the level of single projects affect the risks and opportunities arising at a higher business level, i.e. when single projects have implications for long-term business performance. Sustainable competitive advantage of a whole business network occurs through selection and development of both collaborative partnerships and arm's-length contractual relationships, while balancing the short-term and long-term views in the overall business, and from several firms' perspectives.

DISCUSSION OF MANAGERIAL CHALLENGES AND RESEARCH THEMES

Each of the management areas of the project business framework has its unique context and challenges which need to be taken into account for creating better managerial approaches in the project business. The main managerial challenges and issues characterizing complex organizational context for each management area are presented in Table 5.1.

Research on the project business should address the managerial challenges presented in Table 5.1, taking into account the specific complex organizational context of each management area. Based on our analysis, we suggest that, at a minimum, future research should address the following four research themes, which cut across the management areas of the project business framework:

- Theme 1: Managing in challenging institutional environments,
- Theme 2: Risks and their management in complex organizations and networks,
- Theme 3: Learning and capabilities in project-based organizations, and
- Theme 4: Business logic in project-based organizations.

The intersections of these themes and the management areas include more specific research opportunities within each of the four themes

THEME 1: MANAGING IN CHALLENGING INSTITUTIONAL ENVIRONMENTS

While many project-based firms are global, project work usually has strong local orientation and firms in project business must have the capability to adapt to *local business environments*. Mechanisms for adaptation include, among others, local presence or use of local partners. Ultimately, a single project and the project specificity of its business model represent an ultimately local micro-market with one single customer. A local market for a project contractor consists of multiple firms and projects with a web of simultaneous, controversial, and *dynamic collaborative and competitive relationships*. The management of participating actors from different institutional environments is a challenge for any project and firm. The important

Table 5.1 The main managerial challenges in the four areas of the project business

	Unit of analysis	The managerial challenge is...	Issues from the analysis that characterize the complex organizational context
Management of a project	A project as a business entity	...to manage a single project effectively in its environment by taking into account that the project is a purposeful business entity and the management of its inherent business content can be compared to the management of a firm's business.	Project as an organization with its distinctive goals and objectives, multiple stakeholders, and contingencies in external environment, project's internal contingencies (e.g. uniqueness, complexity)
Management of a project-based firm	A firm or a portfolio of projects	...to manage a firm and its multiple projects as a whole, by ensuring that projects support the strategy and business objectives of the firm, by simultaneously allocating the firm's scarce resources to projects.	Decentralization of the firm's business into projects, interdependencies between projects, frequency of repeating works and/or outputs, discontinuity of relationships with customers and suppliers
Management of a project network	A project as a multi-firm network	...to manage a project as a multi-firm enterprise through managing multiple firms participating in the project, by creating a contractual or an organizational arrangement that enhances goal alignment and coordination across multiple firms.	Asymmetry of participating firms' objectives, diverse interests and identities, dynamism in the network, coordination of actors from different cultural and institutional environments
Management of a business network	A network of firms and their relationships	...to manage a network of actors and their relationships in an open and competitive business marketplace where the firms may or may not engage in joint projects with other firms. From a single firm's or project's viewpoint, maintaining efficiency and innovativeness in the network is central, and is affected by how the firms and projects decide to position themselves in the value network of all business players and non-business actors.	Simultaneous collaboration and competition, projects as intermediaries building bridges between organizations, conflicting short- and long-term interests, interplay between short-term project network and long-term business network, various network positions depending on other actors' positions and strategies, servitization and continuous change of firms' business models

role of different stakeholders and respective differences in their institutional settings becomes especially important in large and global projects and international project-based firms. *Complex social networks of relationship*s as described by Granovetter (1985), and different competitive strategies that business organizations may adopt (as described by Miles and Snow 1986) in a *dynamic network of organizations*, become relevant for understanding how projects should be managed effectively in their environments.

Many projects face the challenge of managing an internal network of multiple organizations while still being always interconnected to the outside world's *stakeholders, institutions*, and *events*. The research on *large projects* and *global projects* identifies the importance of managing a *wider socio-political environment*. Floricel and Miller (2001) discuss *risks* that are embedded in the global network of actors, by referring to what they call *social and institutional risks*, while Orr and Scott (2008) analyze *institutional exceptions* in global projects that result from the *institutional differences* of organizations participating in a project.

Research on *stakeholders* and *stakeholder networks* is a fruitful basis for interpreting the challenging institutional environments of networked projects (Aaltonen, Kujala, and Oijala 2008). As project stakeholders (including the firm's local units) in different institutional settings interpret the projects' goals and business objectives differently, the communication in such organizational structures is challenging. An information-processing perspective (Daft and Lengel 1986) would also provide appropriate avenues for further studies on global project-based firms, networks, and projects.

THEME 2: RISKS AND THEIR MANAGEMENT IN COMPLEX ORGANIZATIONS AND NETWORKS

Project networks are complex and dynamic structures that introduce risk and uncertainty to projects. Uncertainties in project networks are due to: network effects such as dependence on other actors; *interest asymmetries*; different identities; nonexistence of information; *information asymmetry in the network*; *social and institutional risks, network risks*; trying to behave rationally; and risk management procedures that do not fit into the networked context. Research on networked projects and network-related risks introduce different requirements into a project's risk management than what the traditional and rather decision-analysis-oriented project risk management area represents. Such *new risk management schemes* would require putting appropriate *governance structures* and learning schemes in place among several actors within the network.

In order to widen the existing narrow decision analysis orientation in project risk management, we refer to two notions introduced by Floricel and Miller (2001) called respectively robustness and governability. *Robustness* refers to the properties of a strategic system that enable the project to deal with anticipated risks. *Governability* refers to a group of properties that enables the project to react to unexpected events. Governability develops and complements Bettis and Hitt's (1995) notion of flexibility. Furthermore, project risk management should adopt a wider (than the rational decision analysis-oriented) view by adopting managerial approaches from general management.

The *nature of the project business and the dynamism due to varying roles of firms from one project to the next* may cause additional challenges of *how to manage risk in the short and long terms*: for example, a short-term partner in one project may become a competitor in future projects, and vice versa. From a project contractor firm's *business model* point of view, one could ask the following questions related to risk-taking related to the *servitization*: How far into operational services (or even asset-sharing) can a project contractor go for taking responsibilities for customers' businesses activities; and how much responsibility can a project contractor take on operating competitors' equipment for the customer (with competitors' proprietary IPRs, spare parts, etc.)? Concerning purchasing from subcontractors, there is an abundance of papers discussing the vertical dyadic inter-organizational buyer–sub-contractor relationships. But the focus on existing subcontracting models is too often limited to an analysis of the individual subcontractor's ability to deliver in a single project in a dyadic, project-centric buyer–seller setting. Instead, the business relationships should be considered in a more complex setting of a network of sub-contractors, where subcontractors' mutual relationships with each other, or a sub-contractor's direct relationships to the contractor's customer or competitor, might introduce a major risk or opportunity to the project or to the contractor firm's long-term business.

THEME 3: LEARNING AND CAPABILITIES IN PROJECT-BASED ORGANIZATIONS

Research needs to continue to address the learning involved within and between temporary and permanent organizations. *Knowledge-sharing* has a central role in learning (Davies and Brady 2000; Sydow, Lindkvist, and DeFillippi 2004). In the case of complex project networks, the *inside-project learning* during the project is a relevant theme to be researched. Inside-project learning contributes to the building of the required capability within the network and to achieving a successful *collective performance*. Learning within the project network is emphasized as an internal capability-building device for project enterprises that helps the network's actors to accomplish the project's goals jointly. Learning is a precondition for the team comprised of representatives of multiple firms needing to understand the ultimate outcome of the project and its composition as based on the composition of each party's objectives. However, in addition to understanding the outcome, the various players in the network must also make sense together about the method of project execution and each party's role in it. Miscommunication, or lack of communication among the firms in a project, may impede the collective learning process and mutual understanding among the firms of the project's goal and goal achievement approaches, thus disrupting the effective project implementation.

Ruuska (2005) found that successful projects are those that are able to achieve *collective competence*. Collective competence is described as a group's ability to *work together* towards a common goal and results in the creation of a collective outcome. For the management of innovation projects which create new business with uncertain outcomes, McGrath and MacMillan (2000) introduce a *discovery-oriented project management* scheme for intra-project learning. Furthermore, Brady and Davies (2004) introduce a *project capability-building model* which is based on the learning scheme within the firm. Project-led learning occurs in the early phases of the project: this learning is led by an exploratory "vanguard project" phase that contributes to later project phases that are responsible for increasing the firm's project capabilities (Brady and Davies 2004).

THEME 4: BUSINESS LOGIC IN PROJECT-BASED ORGANIZATIONS

There is a need for research on projects using a cross-disciplinary foundation of theories from business strategy and other related areas. For example, the concept of a business model can be used to explain not only the business logic of a project-based firm, but the inherent business logic of a project as well. Project-specific business models might introduce a whole new business-centric paradigm to the management of a single project. However, it is not clear how project-level and firm-level business models work together in project-based firms. Further research is also needed on the choice of a specific business model and the relationship between the contingency variables and the business model's performance: Which factors affect the effectiveness of a specific business model?

Finally, more research is needed on how business models evolve. Trends such as *servitization* (Vandermerwe and Rada 1988; Wikström et al. 2009) explain the emergence of new business models through increased offering of integrated bundles of products and services in the form of solutions and operational services in the *value stream* (Davies 2004). For example, a power plant contractor firm that previously has delivered power plants to its customers might face a situation where it now delivers through a servitized delivery scheme the mere energy capacity (MWh), the production of which previously used to be the customer's business. In this way, by occupying a *larger share and responsibility of the customers' businesses* with their service offering, project contractors are also given the possibility of capturing a larger portion of the overall *value stream* and to gain more profits. The evolution of business logic in project-based firms has been analyzed from several different perspectives, opening up promising avenues for further research. Drawing on *contingency theory*, Ceci and Prencipe (2008) examine the organizational and environmental/market factors in firms delivering integrated solutions, showing that the co-evolution of firms' strategy and distinct strategic decisions lead to differences in capabilities configurations. Lindkvist (2008) looks at the *evolution of project-based firms' business logic* through analyzing how project-level processes in project-based firms display features of an evolutionary learning process, with pre-selection, variation, and retention. The conclusion is that projects can be seen as experiments within trial-and-error-based strategic *learning*. Concerning the evolution of business in firms, Bonaccorsi, Pammolli, and Tani (1996) analyze the change of boundaries and respectively the business logic in system companies by conceptualizing the companies' interactions between market conditions and long-term technology problems. Prencipe (1997) elaborates a similar problem through considering how a system company would master the product's evolutionary dynamics through guaranteeing in-house or external technological competencies for managing the boundaries of product systems that may threaten the viability of control.

Conclusion

Project business is an emerging research field, which adopts a business-centric view of the management of projects, firms, and networks of projects and firms. The main focus is on how firms survive and ensure their competitive advantage in a complex networked business environment. Projects may cross several firms' organizational boundaries. Depending on the independence of a project, a project can serve as a resource for one or several firms, or vice versa, a project may be the major business player which uses one or several firms as resources for accomplishing its business purposes. A project is a different organizational entity than its stakeholder firms (including its parent firm as one of the stakeholders). Therefore, a project's goals are different from those of its stakeholder firms and the project's goals may be in conflict with a stakeholder firm's goals. Goal alignment between firms and projects is the aim if alliances are desirable. However, conflict, competition, and rivalry exist among projects and firms and must be carefully managed to guarantee the success of a project, firm, or network of firms.

The business-centric view complements traditional approaches and is focused on how to organize projects and operations of a project-based firm. Managerial challenges are different in the four distinctive management areas of our project business framework: (1) management of a project; (2) management of a project-based firm; (3) management of a project network; and (4) management of a business network. Our analysis suggests four research themes that are relevant for addressing the managerial challenges in each of the four areas. The four themes emerged from our review of the literature which help to resolve these challenges:

- managing in challenging institutional environments
- risks and their management in complex organizations
- learning and capabilities in project-based organizations
- business logic in project-based organizations.

These themes represent fruitful areas for future research on the project business.

REFERENCES

AALTONEN, K., KUJALA, J., and OIJALA, T. (2008). "Stakeholder salience in global projects," *International Journal of Project Management*, 26/5: 509–16.

AHOLA, T., KUJALA, J., LAAKSONEN, T., and ELORANTA, K. (2006). "The long-term inter-organizational relationships in project business," *Proceedings of the Seventh International Conference of the International Research Network on Organising by Projects IRNOP VII*, October 11–13, 2006, Xi'an, China, 52–69.

APM (2006). *Association for Project Management: APM Body of Knowledge*, 5th edn. High Wycombe: Association for Project Management.

ARTTO, K., ELORANTA, K., and KUJALA, J. (2008b). "Subcontractors' business relationships as risk sources in project networks," *International Journal of Managing Projects in Business*, 1/1: 88–105.

——and KUJALA, J. (2008). "Project business as a research field," *International Journal of Managing Projects in Business*, 1/4: 469–97.

——and WIKSTRÖM K. (2005). "What is project business?" *International Journal of Project Management*, 23/5: 343–53.

——Kujala, J., Dietrich, P., and Martinsuo, M. (2008a). "What is project strategy?" *International Journal of Project Management*, 26/1: 4–12.

——Wikström, K., Hellström, M., and Kujala, J. (2008b). "Impact of services on project business," *International Journal of Project Management*, 26/5: 497–508.

Bengtson, A., Havila, V., and Åberg, S. (2001). "Network dependencies and project termination: why some relationships survive the end of the project," 17th annual IMP Conference, Oslo.

Bettis, R. A., and Hitt, M. A. (1995). "The new competitive landscape," *Strategic Management Journal*, 16: 7–19.

Bonaccorsi, A., Pammolli, F., and Tani, S. (1996). "The changing boundaries of system companies," *International Business Review*, 5: 539–60.

Brady, T., and Davies, A. (2004). "Building project capabilities: from exploratory to exploitative learning," *Organization Studies*, 25/9: 1601–21.

Brusoni, S. (2005). "The limits to specialization: problem solving and coordination in 'modular networks'," *Organization Studies*, 26/12: 1885–907.

——Prencipe, A., and Pavitt, K. (2001). "Knowledge specialization, organizational coupling, and the boundaries of the firm: why do firms know more than they make?" *Administrative Science Quarterly*, 46: 597–621.

Ceci, F., and Prencipe, A. (2008). "Configuring capabilities for integrated solutions: evidence from the IT sector," *Industry and Innovation*, 15/3: 277–96.

Cooper, R. G., Edgett, S. J., and Kleinschmidt, E. J. (1997a). "Portfolio management in new product development: lessons from the leaders—I," *Research Technology Management*, September–October: 16–28.

——————(1997b). "Portfolio management in new product development: lessons from the leaders—II," *Research Technology Management*, November–December: 43–52.

Cova, B., Ghauri, P., and Salle, R. (2002). *Project Marketing: Beyond Competitive Bidding*. London: John Wiley & Sons Ltd.

——and Hoskins, S. (1997). "A twin-track networking approach to project marketing," *European Management Journal*, 15/5: 546–56.

Cox, A., and Ireland, P. (2006). "Strategic purchasing and supply chain management in the project environment—theory and practice," in D. Lowe and R. Leiringer (eds.), *Commercial Management of Projects: Defining the Discipline*. Oxford: Blackwell Publishing, 390–416.

Daft, R. L., and Lengel, R. H. (1986). "Organizational information requirements, media richness and structural design," *Management Science*, 32/5: 554–71.

Davies A. (2004). "Moving base into high-value integrated solutions: a value stream approach," *Industrial and Corporate Change*, 13: 727–56.

——and Brady, T. (2000). "Organisational capabilities and learning in complex products and systems: towards repeatable solutions," *Research Policy*, 29/7–8: 931–53.

——and Hobday, M. (2006). "Charting a path toward integrated solutions," *MIT Sloan Management Review*, Spring: 39–48.

Davis, P. R., and Walker, D. H. T. (2008). "Case study: trust, commitment and mutual goals in alliances," in D. H. T. Walker and S. Rowlinson (eds.), *Procurement Systems: A Cross Industry Project Management Perspective*. Abingdon: Taylor and Francis, 378–99.

DeFillippi, R. J., and Arthur, M. B. (1998). "Paradox in project-based enterprise: the case of film making," *California Management Review*, 40/2: 125–39.

Donaldson, L. (2001). *The Contingency Theory of Organizations*. Thousand Oaks, CA: Sage Publications.

Doz, Y. L., and Hamel, G. (1998). *Alliance Advantage: The Art of Creating Value through Partnering*. Boston: Harvard Business School Press.

Dubois, A., and Gadde, L.-E. (2000). "Supply strategy and network effects: purchasing behaviour in the construction industry," *European Journal of Purchasing and Supply Management*, 6: 207–15.

Eccles, R. (1981). "The quasifirm in the construction industry," *Journal of Economic Behavior and Organization*, 2: 335–57.

Emery, F. E., and Trist, E. L. (1965). "The causal texture of organisational environments," *Human Relations*, 18/1965: 21–32.

Engwall, M. (2003). "No project is an island: linking projects to history and context," *Research Policy*, 32/5: 789–808.

Floricel, S., and Miller, R. (2001). "Strategizing for anticipated risks and turbulence in large-scale engineering projects," *International Journal of Project Management*, 19: 445–55.

Gaddis, P. O. (1959). "The project manager," *Harvard Business Review*, 9: 89–97.

Gann, D., and Salter, A. (2000). "Innovation in project-based, service-enhanced firms: the construction of complex products and systems," *Research Policy*, 29/7–8: 955–72.

Grabher, G. (2002). "The project ecology of advertising: tasks, talents, and teams," *Regional Studies*, 36/3: 245–62.

——(2004). "Architectures of project-based learning: creating and sedimenting knowledge in project ecologies," *Organization Studies*, 25/9: 1491–514.

Granovetter, M. (1985). "Economic action and social structure: the problem of embeddedness," *American Journal of Sociology*, 91/3: 481–510.

Grün, O. (2004). *Taming Giant Projects: Management of Multi-organization Enterprises*. Berlin: Springer.

Heide, J., and Miner, A. (1992). "The shadow of the future: effects of anticipated interaction and frequency of contact on buyer–seller cooperation," *Academy of Management Journal*, 35/2: 265–91.

Hellgren, B., and Stjernberg, T. (1995). "Design and implementation in major investments: a project network approach," *Scandinavian Journal of Management*, 11/4: 377–94.

Hobday, M. (1998). "Product complexity, innovation and industrial organisation," *Research Policy*, 26: 689–710.

——(2000). "The project-based organisation: an ideal form for managing complex products and systems?" *Research Policy*, 29: 871–93.

IPMA (2006). *International Project Management Association, ICB—IPMA Competence Baseline*, ed. G. Caupin, H. Knöpfel, G. Koch, F. Pérez-Polo, and C. Seabury, 2006–Version 3.0. Monmouth: International Project Management Association (IPMA).

ISO (1997). *ISO 10006: Quality Management—Guidelines to Quality in Project Management*, ISO 10006:1997(E). Geneva: International Organization for Standardization (ISO).

Jones, C., Hesterly, W. S., and Borgatti, S. P. (1997). "A general theory of network governance: exchange conditions and social mechanisms," *Academy of Management Review*, 22/4: 911–45.

Katz, D., and Kahn, R. L. (1966). *The Social Psychology of Organizations*. New York: Wiley.

Keegan, A., and Turner, J. R. (2002). "The management of innovation in project-based firms," *Long Range Planning*, 35: 367–88.

Lawrence, P. R., and Lorsch, J. W. (1967). *Organization and Environment: Managing Differentiation and Integration*. Boston: Harvard Business School Press.

LEVITT, B., and MARCH, J. G. (1995). "Chester I. Barnard and the intelligence of learning," in O. E. WILLIAMSON (ed.), *Organization Theory: From Chester Barnard to the Present and Beyond*. New York: Oxford University Press, 11–37.

LINDKVIST L. (2004). "Governing project-based firms: promoting market-like processes within hierarchies," *Journal of Management and Governance*, 8: 3–25.

——(2008). "Project organization: exploring its adaptation properties," *International Journal of Project Management*, 26: 13–20.

LUNDIN, R. A., and SÖDERHOLM, A. (1995). "A theory of temporary organization," *Scandinavian Journal of Management*, 11/4: 437–55.

McCORD, K., and EPPINGER, S. (1993). "Managing the integration problem in concurrent engineering," working paper, Cambridge, MA.

McGRATH, R. G., and MacMILLAN, I. (2000). *The Entrepreneurial Mindset: Strategies for Continuously Creating Opportunity in an Age of Uncertainty*. Boston: Harvard Business School Press.

MILES, R., and SNOW, C. (1986). "Organizations: new concepts for new forms," *California Management Review*, 28/2: 68–73.

MILLER, R., and LESSARD, D. (2001a). *The Strategic Management of Large Engineering Projects: Shaping Risks, Institutions and Governance*. Cambridge, MA: MIT Press.

——(2001b). "Understanding and managing risks in large engineering projects," *International Journal of Project Management*, 19: 437–43.

MODER, J. J., and PHILLIPS, C. R. (1964). *Project Management with CPM and PERT*. New York: Van Nostrand Reinhold.

MORRIS, P. W. G. (1983). "Managing project interfaces: key points for project success," in D. I. Cleland and W. R. King (eds.), *Project Management Handbook*. New York: Van Nostrand, 3–36.

——(1994). *The Management of Projects*. London: Thomas Telford.

——(2009). "Implementing business strategy via project management," in T. M. Williams, K. Samset, and K. J. Sunnevåg (eds.), *Making Essential Choices with Scant Information: Front-End Decision-Making in Major Projects*. Basingstoke: Palgrave Macmillan.

——and HOUGH, G. H. (1987). *The Anatomy of Major Projects: A Study of the Reality of Project Management*. Chichester: John Wiley & Sons.

——and JAMIESON, A. (2004). *Translating Corporate Strategy into Project Strategy: Realizing Corporate Strategy through Project Management*. Newtown Square, PA: Project Management Institute.

——CRAWFORD, L., HODGSON, D., SHEPHERD, M. M., and THOMAS, J. (2006). "Exploring the role of formal bodies of knowledge in defining a profession: the case of project management," *International Journal of Project Management*, 24: 710–21.

ORR, R. J., and SCOTT, W. R. (2008). "Institutional exceptions on global projects: a process model," *Journal of International Business Studies*, 39: 562–88.

PMI (2008). *A Guide to the Project Management Body of Knowledge (PMBOK)*, 4th edn. Project Management Institute (PMI).

POPPO, L., ZHOU, K., and RYU, S. (2008). "Alternative origins to interorganizational trust: an interdependence perspective on the shadow of the past and the shadow of the future," *Organization Science*, 19/1: 39–55.

PORTER, M. E. (1998). "Clusters and the new economics of competition," *Harvard Business Review*, 76/6: 77–90.

POWELL, W. W. (1990). "Neither market nor hierarchy: network forms of organization," *Research in Organizational Behavior*, 12: 295–336.

PRENCIPE, A. (1997). "Technological competencies and product's evolutionary dynamics: a case study from the aero-engine industry," *Research Policy*, 25: 1261–76.

——and TELL, F. (2001). "Inter-project learning: processes and outcomes of knowledge codification in project-based firms," *Research Policy*, 30/9: 1373–94.

RUUSKA, I. (2005). "Social structures as communities for knowledge sharing in project-based environments," Helsinki University of Technology, Work Psychology and Leadership, Doctoral Dissertation Series 2005/3, Espoo.

SANCHEZ, R., and MAHONEY, J. T. (1996). "Modularity, flexibility, and knowledge management in product and organization design," *Strategic Management Journal*, Special issue on knowledge and the firm, 17/Winter: 63–76.

SHENHAR, A. J. (2001). "One size does not fit all projects: exploring classical contingency domains," *Management Science*, 47/3: 394–414.

——DVIR, D., GUTH, W., LECHLER, T., MILOSEVIC, D., PATANAKUL, P., POLI, M., and STEFANOVIC, J. (2005). "Project strategy: the missing link," paper presented at the annual Academy of Management meeting, August, 5–10 Honolulu, HI.

SKAATES, M. A., and TIKKANEN, H. (2003). "International project marketing as an area of study: a literature review with suggestions for research and practice," *International Journal of Project Management*, 21/1: 503–10.

SÖDERLUND, J. (2004). "On the broadening scope of the research on projects: a review and a model for analysis," *International Journal of Project Management*, 22/8: 655–67.

SOSA, M. E., EPPINGER, S. D., and ROWLES, C. M. (2004). "The misalignment of product architecture and organizational structure in complex product development," *Management Science*, 50/12: 1674–89.

STINCHCOMBE, A. L., and HEIMER, C. A. (1985). *Organization Theory and Project Management: Administering Uncertainty in Norwegian Offshore Oil*. Oslo: Norwegian University Press.

SYDOW, J., LINDKVIST, L., and DEFILIPPI, R. (2004). "Project-based organizations, embeddedness and repositories of knowledge," *Organization Studies*, 25/9: 1475–90.

——and STABER, U. (2002). "The institutional embeddedness of project networks: the case of content production in German television," *Regional Studies*, 36/3: 215–27.

TIKKANEN, H., KUJALA, J., and ARTTO, K. (2007). "The marketing strategy of a project-based firm: the four portfolios framework," *Industrial Marketing Management*, 36: 194–205.

TURNER, J. R., and KEEGAN, A. (2001). "Mechanisms of governance in the project-based organization: roles of the broker and steward," *European Management Journal*, 19/3: 254–67.

——and SIMISTER, S. J. (2001). "Project contract management and theory of organization," *International Journal of Project Management*, 19: 457–64.

UZZI, B. (1997). "Social structure and competition in interfirm networks: the paradox of embeddedness," *Administrative Science Quarterly*, 42/1: 35–67.

VANDERMERWE, S., and RADA, J. (1988). "Servitization of business: adding value by adding services," *European Management Journal*, 6: 314–24.

VON BERTALANFFY, L. (1950). "The theory of open systems in physics and biology," *Science*, NS 111/2872: 23–9.

WALKER, D. H. T., BOURNE, L., and ROWLINSON, S. (2008). "Stakeholders and the supply chain," in D. H. T. Walker and S. Rowlinson (eds.), *Procurement Systems: A Cross Industry Project Management Perspective*. Abingdon: Taylor & Francis.

——and ROWLINSON, S. (eds.) (2008). *Procurement Systems: A Cross Industry Project Management Perspective*. Abingdon: Taylor & Francis.

WHITLEY, R. (2006). "Project-based firms: new organizational form or variations on a theme?" *Industrial and Corporate Change*, 15/1: 77–99.

WIKSTRÖM, K., HELLSTRÖM, M., ARTTO, K., KUJALA, J., and KUJALA, S. (2009). "Services in project-based firms: four types of business logics," *International Journal of Project Management*, 27/2: 113–22.

WINCH, G. M. (2006). "The governance of project coalitions: towards a research agenda," in D. Lowe and R. Leiringer (eds.), *Commercial Management of Projects: Defining the Discipline*. Oxford: Blackwell Publishing, 324–43.

CHAPTER 6

....

PROJECTS AND PARTNERSHIPS

INSTITUTIONAL PROCESSES AND EMERGENT PRACTICES

....

MIKE BRESNEN

NICK MARSHALL

INTRODUCTION

....

Projects have always required effective collaboration between the individuals and organizations that are brought together under various forms of project-based organization to achieve specific project objectives (Morris 1994). Whether we are talking about engineering projects (including construction and aerospace), R&D activity, new product development, film-making and the performing arts, or advertising campaigns, there has always been the need to combine expertise and other resources that are not only professionally/technically specialized, but also often organizationally distributed (Bresnen 1990; Hobday 2000; Jones and Lichtenstein 2008).

However, the complexities of project tasks and the challenges created by the project-based forms of organization they give rise to (Whitley 2006) combine to make achieving such collaboration a perennial problem (e.g. Grabher 2002: 207–8). Projects not only require effective inter-professional and/or inter-organizational collaboration, they are also faced with the need for this to happen with clearly focused (but often ambiguous and negotiated) task objectives in mind, over comparatively short timescales, and according to complex divisions of labor between those involved in conceptualizing, commissioning, designing, producing, and delivering the work. Project tasks can be highly uncertain and there may be an expectation of little, if any, follow-on work or longevity in the relationship between project participants and few opportunities for knowledge and learning to pass from one project to the next (Sydow, Lindkvist, and DeFillippi 2004).

Given these task and organizational conditions (which vary significantly, of course, across types of project), an additional layer of complexity is added by virtue of the correspondingly complex institutional contexts within which projects are often embedded (Ekstedt et al. 1999; Grabher 2002). It has long been recognized that projects are not stand-alone entities and are strongly influenced by the historical and organizational context in which they operate (Engwall 2003). However, projects also frequently occur in multi-organizational settings and are also constrained by their transient characteristics (Bresnen 1990; Jones and Lichtenstein 2008). This requires attention to be drawn not only to the different organizational interests represented, but also to the influence of the diverse and relatively more permanent institutional structures that influence project interactions. Project management in the biomedical domain, for example, involves complex patterns of interaction between scientists, clinicians, corporations, small-scale entrepreneurs, social scientists, ethicists, and regulators—each of which will be guided by their own interests (scientific, clinical, commercial) and distinct and established epistemic practices (Newell et al. 2008). Similarly, in construction, project management can be viewed as a contested terrain, in which the different professional norms and values articulated by architects, engineers, surveyors, and builders have historically competed for influence (Bresnen 1996).

Grabher (2002) has introduced the concept of "project ecology" to refer to the conditions in which projects are embedded. Importantly, conditions in such project contexts are institutionally highly complex and this, in turn, has an important bearing upon the development of project management knowledge, upon professional orientations to the project management process, and upon the development and diffusion of managerial practices concerned with improving project performance (including mechanisms designed to promote collaboration). Project management techniques may constitute an emerging body of knowledge that has become increasingly sophisticated in recent years in line with growing professionalization (Hodgson and Cicmil 2007). However, its origins lie in a very specific type of project environment (large-scale engineering work), and the professional bodies that articulate and promote this body of knowledge are also much less established and influential than those in other management disciplines (e.g. accountancy) in guiding practice across the range of conditions in which projects occur (Morris 1994). In the absence of a more unifying knowledge base and set of agreed upon practices for organizing and managing projects, it consequently becomes important to explore the effects on action and knowledge formation of the complex and fragmented institutional conditions within which such projects are embedded (Ekstedt et al. 1999). In construction and engineering, for example, Winch (1998) has argued that institutional-level effects (diverse professions and institutions) combine with operational circumstances (project-basing, complex products) to militate against the spread of innovative practices.

The aim of this chapter, then, is to explore the contribution that an understanding of institutional context and institutional processes can make to understanding the development and change of project management processes and practices—specifically those concerned with improving collaboration on projects. To date, there have been relatively few attempts made to apply institutional theory (DiMaggio and Powell 1983) to try to understand the development of collaboration in the peculiar (multi-)organizational context of complex projects. Given tendencies towards institutional fragmentation, there can be immense value in trying to understand the ways in which new management practices that promote collaboration are diffused and legitimized within project environments and how their sedimentation in project management practices is affected by inter-organizational and inter-professional relationships. Recently, work has started to explore the institutional conditions affecting integration across cross-national projects (Orr and Scott 2008) and, in fields such as biotechnology, an interest in examining network forms of organization as a mode of governance from an institutional perspective is already well established (Powell et al. 2005). However, rarely has there been any attempt to try to understand the recursive relationship between institutional processes and emergent changes in management practice in the context of project "ecologies" that are institutionally complex (for exceptions see Sydow and Staber 2002; Newell et al. 2008). How, for example, do more collaborative forms of interaction emerge, diffuse, and become institutionalized in an existing institutional field that is highly fragmented and in which interaction is often focused on specific project tasks that are transient in nature and which require the input of a range of participants operating according to highly diverse (and very often conflicting) norms and values? Even if participating organizations are themselves more permanent and institutional arrangements well established—as is the case in project settings that could be characterized as "organizational" (Whitley 2006)—how do new forms of contractual interaction emerge given the isomorphic pressures that institutional theory would lead us to suspect might inhibit the transition from one mode of contracting to another (cf. DiMaggio and Powell 1983)? Or does the lack of institutional constraints found in some complex project ecologies allow greater flexibility and so generate opportunities for introducing change (cf. Ekstedt et al. 1999)? Does this, in turn, mean that they constitute relatively fragile conditions for the deep embedding of such initiatives in management practices? And what implications do these varying conditions have for the development of project management knowledge more widely?

In order to shed some light on these questions, this chapter focuses on the particular example of the emergence of partnering in the UK construction industry. The construction industry is an important exemplar of the problems of inter-organizational collaboration in complex institutional settings—not only because of the scale of project-based working in the sector, but also because of continuing problems of achieving collaboration across the "temporary multi-organization" that links clients, designers, contractors, and suppliers in the management of projects (Cherns and Bryant 1984). It is also a very topical case, due to the efforts made in recent years to shift the basis of interaction away from adversarial contracting towards relational contracting based on partnering principles (e.g. Bennett and Jayes 1995). Indeed, it could be classified as a type of project context within which the repeated relations that occur—albeit of varying length and intensity (Jones and Lichtenstein 2008)—create tensions around the use of collaborative and competitive mechanisms (Bresnen 2007). Although construction contracting arguably represents only one type of project-based activity (which is itself quite varied), it nevertheless allows us to say something more general about institutionalization processes that relate to projects undertaken under similar conditions of high separation/stability of roles and yet high singularity of goals/outputs (Whitley 2006).

The analysis of the early stage transition from traditional, more adversarial approaches to greater cooperation between clients and contractors is informed by a historical overview and retrospective analysis of secondary material combined with primary research data collected on a number of prominent case-study projects that were investigated by the authors (see Bresnen and Marshall 2000 for further details). Importantly, the research was conducted at a time (the late 1990s) when partnering was increasingly being adopted in the UK by clients keen to improve their working relationships with their contractors, as well as directly benefit from what the approach had to offer. Most of the case-study projects we looked at were presented as exemplars of novel, more collaborative ways of organizing projects. At the same time, heated debates (now considerably abated) raged within the industry about the value and benefits of partnering. Consequently, this was a period of relatively low levels of institutionalization of partnering within the UK and relatively high levels of disagreement about its merits (cf. Colyvas and Powell 2006). As such, it offers an ideal opportunity to explore, in a historical context but using real-time data, the early to mid-stage processes of institutionalization associated with the emergence of a new, alternative institutional logic to that based on arm's-length, adversarial contracting.

The framing of the analysis draws upon recent developments within a particular strand of institutional theory that has tended to focus attention more on processes of institutional change than on conditions of isomorphism and stability within institutional fields (e.g. Colyvas and Powell 2006; Lounsbury 2007; Reay and Hinings 2005). Using this approach allows us to draw attention to the competing institutional "logics" associated with adversarialism and collaboration in construction (cf. Friedland and Alford 1991) and how the dialectical tensions that were created were mobilized to effect change at both institutional and (project) organizational levels (Seo and Creed 2002). It also allows us to explore the recursive relationship between institutional developments at the level of the sector as a whole and how these were reflected (or not) in emerging project management practices associated with the introduction of partnering on particular projects—thus allowing an exploration of the translation of the concept of partnering into practice (and, in turn, the influence of emergent practice on industry conceptions of partnering).

The analysis also draws attention to the prospect that project organization in construction (and similar project contexts) constitutes precisely the sort of conditions which encourage the "co-mingling" of institutional logics (Smith-Doerr 2005) that allows, for example, the coexistence of cooperation and competition. Moreover, such institutional ambiguities and complexities not only influence the nature, extent, and speed of transition from one mode of contracting to another (depending upon the interests, power, and actions of the diverse groups involved), they also have a profound influence upon the extent to which new modes of collaboration take different forms, how new project management practices are legitimized and taken for granted, and how old management practices are superseded, incorporated, or suppressed (Colyvas and Powell 2006; Reay and Hinings 2005).

AN INSTITUTIONAL THEORY PERSPECTIVE

An institutional theory perspective can therefore potentially throw important light upon the dynamics of change associated with the attempted transition to collaborative contracting in project environments. As already noted, recent developments in (neo-)institutional theory have shifted attention towards understanding processes of change within *existing* institutional fields and how they are associated with a transition from one institutional "logic" to another (Friedland and Alford 1991; Colyvas and Powell 2006; Lounsbury 2007; Maguire, Hardy, and Lawrence 2004; Reay and Hinings 2005). Institutional "field" can be defined as "...key suppliers, resource and product consumers, regulatory agencies and other organizations that produce similar services or products" (DiMaggio and Powell 1983: 148–9). Institutional "logics" (Friedland and Alford 1991) refer to "broader cultural beliefs and rules that structure cognition and guide decision-making in a field" (Lounsbury 2007: 289). They represent a deeper way of looking at institutional processes than is suggested by a focus purely on structural arrangements and draw attention to the belief systems and associated practices that make certain actions or solutions legitimate. Consequently, it is difficult to understand change in an established field without consideration of both structural change and change in institutional logics (Reay and Hinings 2005: 352).

Early work within neo-institutional theory tended to assume that any shift from one prevailing logic to another would be triggered by exogenous factors (e.g. changed market conditions), proceed through a number of broad stages or phases, involve the (gradual or rapid) displacement of an older institutional logic with another, and also be essentially non-conflictual (e.g. Scott et al. 2000). However, recent work that has looked at change in such diverse fields as health-care (Reay and Hinings 2005) and banking (Lounsbury 2007) has challenged these assumptions and suggested instead that pressures for change can be endogenous (Colyvas and Powell 2006), that institutional fields can be highly fragmented and exhibit wide variations in practice (Lounsbury 2007), that it is quite possible (and indeed likely) that competing logics can arise and coexist within the same institutional field (Friedland and Alford 1991), and that the process of change is often associated with the exercise of power and high levels of resistance and conflict. Colyvas and Powell (2006), for example, in a study of technology transfer activity at Stanford University, examine how the elaboration of new detailed standards, languages, and norms (signaling greater legitimacy) emerged hand in hand with the development of tacit understandings associated with the embedding of new norms and values in ongoing practices and routines (signaling greater "taken-for-grantedness"). Although they argue that these proc-esses are complementary, they importantly stress that institutionalization is not necessarily a smooth, linear, and uncontested process, and that it involves active engagement by those affected.

Work in this area also often highlights the conditions under which competing logics can be expected to arise (and thrive). Smith-Doerr (2005), for example, observes that certain forms of structural arrangement—notably, network forms of organization, of the type found in biosciences (cf. Powell et al. 2005; Pisano 2006)—provide the type of context in which institutional logics are able to "co-mingle," in ways that allow apparently contradictory, taken-for-granted practices to coexist. So, for example, she highlights how scientists are able to reconcile different, and contra-dictory, ways of working into frames that are "logically disjointed, but narratively seamless" (2005: 285)—for example, by legitimizing more applied research through the access it gives to resources to conduct basic research. At the same time, this link between changing institutional logics and professional/managerial identity pro-vides some of the driving force for conflict between alternative institutional logics operating in the same field. Indeed, many highlight the importance of jurisdictional struggles in ways that resonate with the metaphor of a "battlefield" in the depiction of competing institutional logics and the power relationships and conflict involved in change (e.g. Reay and Hinings 2005).

Importantly, however, while established institutional logics are often challenged and subordinated, they are not always or necessarily displaced. Instead, they can coexist—especially in certain types of structural or cultural context (Smith-Doerr 2005). In such circumstances, change may be continually contested, partial, or only skin-deep. Reay and Hinings (2005), for example, characterize change as a process that develops in stages—from relative stability, to attempts to promulgate change, to responses involving resistance, acquiescence, or acceptance, and thence to some degree of stability (which they categorize as uneasy truce and subjugation).

Consequently, it is important to understand not only the conditions enabling institutional logics to coexist and compete, but also the dynamics promoting conservatism or change. Seo and Creed (2002) suggest that change occurs as a result of the dialectical tensions created through institutionalization, which surface when alternative logics collide. They argue that the processes of structuration associated with institutionalization give rise to internal contradictions due to resultant inefficiencies in operation, lack of adaptability, over-elaboration of structures/processes, and isomorphic pressures towards conformity. However, for change to occur, actors have to be aware of the need for change, able to mobilize alternative logics, and able to take (collective) action (2002: 237). This "active and artful exploitation of institutional contradictions" is therefore the direct result of the divergent interests that institutionalization inevitably gives rise to and which it tries to suppress. Actors operate as "carriers" of institutions, having the power to infuse change with meaning and to use institutional meaning as a political resource in introducing change (e.g. Maguire, Hardy, and Lawrence 2004).

Exploring the institutionalization of partnering in the UK

Arguably, the degree of inter-organizational and inter-professional interaction long associated with the management of projects—particularly those found in the construction context (Bresnen 1990)—provides precisely the sorts of conditions in which one would expect to encounter (dialectical) tensions between conflict and collaboration that generate action from time to time, as leading actors within the sector are driven to champion change. Indeed, policy- and practice-driven interventions in the organization and management of the construction process have been frequent since early work at the Tavistock Institute and elsewhere (e.g. Higgin and Jessop 1965) bemoaned the lack of communication and cooperation found in the sector and called for a more integrated approach to managing projects.

Despite the profusion over the years of policy and practical initiatives within the sector designed to enhance cooperation (e.g. design-build contracting), it is not, however, until the emergence of partnering that we see such structural changes being accompanied by anything like the sort of profound change in logic that would be needed to meet the aspirations of early advocates of greater project integration. However, although partnering has undoubtedly now become a much more widespread feature of global construction management practice (e.g. Chan, Chan, and

Ho 2003; Wood and Ellis 2005), its diffusion has not been as extensive as might be expected and research continues to pose questions about the spread of partnering across different national and cultural contexts (Phua 2006) as well as raise doubts about the extent of internalization and institutionalization of partnering practices by construction companies (Ng et al. 2002; Kadefors, Bjorlingson, and Karsson 2007). Consequently, despite its presumed benefits, partnering is by no means as pervasive or taken for granted as its early advocates would have liked. Looking back at the emergence and development of partnering can help explain why this might be the case.

A new institutional logic emerges?

Partnering in the construction industry—broadly defined as involving a commitment by organizations to cooperate to achieve common business objectives (CII 1989: 2)—arose out of a series of early industry- and government-sponsored reports in the USA, the UK, and elsewhere which emphasized the problems caused by fragmentation and conflict within the industry and which saw partnering as a way of overcoming the adversarialism commonly associated with construction contracting. So, for example, influential reports from the Construction Industry Institute (CII 1989) in the USA and the National Economic Development Office (NEDO 1991) in the UK both attributed poor performance to fragmentation and a lack of trust and cooperation between contractual partners. The CII, for instance, called for: "changing traditional relationships to a shared culture without regard to organizational boundaries [where the] relationship is based on trust, dedication to common goals and an understanding of each other's individual expectations and values" (CII 1989: 2). Echoing these conclusions were the recommendations of the later Latham (1994) and Egan (1998) reports in the UK, both of which called for improved working relationships and greater supply chain integration.

   These attempts at legitimizing partnering and the "meaning-making" associated with developing partnering in practice brought together a number of leading industry, academic, and governmental actors who not only occupied influential positions within the industry, but who were also closely interconnected through wider industry networks. So, for example, in the foreword to an influential report from the Centre for Strategic Studies in Construction (CSSC), Sir Michael Latham commented that: "[t]heir work offers hard evidence to support my recommendation that the industry should make greater use of partnering" (Bennett and Jayes 1995: ii). The CSSC was, in turn, commissioned to provide a report on partnering to one of the twelve groups established by the Construction Industry Board (CIB) set up to implement the main recommendations of the Latham Report (Bennett, Ingram, and Jayes 1996).

Although such leading practitioners clearly had a significant personal impact as opinion leaders, it was the enrollment of well-established institutional bodies within the sector (such as the Construction Industry Council, the Building Research Establishment, and professional associations such as the Institution of Civil Engineers and the Chartered Institute of Building) that led to the message of partnering being carried forward. Linking these institutional bodies were large numbers of working parties and committees, often with overlapping membership, which were set up to develop the concept and practice of partnering and transmit the message throughout industry (e.g. CRINE 1994; ACTIVE 1996). Workshops and seminars bringing together industry, academic, and government policy groups also became commonplace in the 1990s, including newly created networks such as the Construction Productivity Network.

At the level of individual firms, it was clear too that partnering was becoming increasingly important. In the projects we investigated, the principle of collaboration was accepted by senior client and contractor managers as a primary goal. Clients were the prime movers in the decision to establish some form of collaborative arrangement, and knowledge about partnering often circulated through informal social networks. A sense of dissatisfaction with the status quo was a general feeling among the managers we interviewed. Senior managers often spoke of a persistent failure to achieve performance targets. There was thus a general receptivity towards change among key decision-makers, even if the precise course that it should take was not that clear.

Fragmented fields, divergent interests

The significance of these networks of meaning construction and dissemination is that they depended upon and, in turn, selectively reinforced existing relations of power and influence. Cox and Townsend (1998: 146, 157), for example, argue that the process of consultation which informed the Latham Report involved only "those with vested interests in retaining the status quo ... [and so] ... would never provide the radical solutions required to fully address the industry's problems." That is not to say that each interest group was equally successful in encouraging its views to be reflected in the final report. Those that stood to gain the most from seeing partnering and the other Latham recommendations implemented were large clients with extensive and regular capital outlays for construction and major contractors hoping to secure ongoing streams of work by entering into long-term relationships with them (Barlow et al. 1997). Not surprisingly, it was precisely such groups which exerted the greatest influence over the way the partnering concept was framed.

The growing popularity among clients of partnering and alliancing in the first half of the 1990s also coincided with a period of recession in demand for construction services which meant that clients could use their market power to encourage contractors to comply with their preferred practices. Green (1999: 7) has even suggested that behind the "rhetoric of seduction" was the "iron fist" of client market power. He quotes from the Construction Clients' Forum, whose members contribute 80 percent of the UK market for construction services: "*The message from the CCF is clear. If this Pact is concluded, clients represented on the CCF will seek to place their £40bn of business with companies that are seen to follow the approach described in this document*" (Green 1999: 7, emphasis in original). Other groups, in contrast, were less successful in communicating their views. For small subcontractors and specialist trades, where collective action is undermined by extreme fragmentation, this is perhaps not so surprising and is reflected in their continuing ambivalence towards partnering (Ng et al. 2002). However, architects have also been less active in shaping such developments in their favor and it could be argued that close partnering relationships between clients and contractors further marginalize them from the project management process (Bresnen 1996).

The net effect was that, whether or not senior managers within contracting companies were enthusiastic about partnering, there was little they could do to resist clients' desires to foster collaboration. One of our projects, for example, was part of a five-year framework agreement to provide airfield civil engineering services. Given the significance of the client, and the possibility of missing out on this lucrative market, the contractor was not slow to realize the implications of failing to agree with the client's preferred vision of collaboration. The self-discipline required to respond to the demands of clients could also be actively used by contractors in their bidding. Realizing the growing importance of collaboration, some contractors were using their enthusiasm for, and experiences of, partnering as marketing tools designed to win work. This was part of an explicit strategy by one main contractor who aimed to increase the proportion of turnover contributed by collaborative projects from its current level of 65 percent to 75 percent over the following two years. In some of our projects, contractors were even willing to absorb increased costs or allow late design changes (without registering these as formal variations), in order to stay within the "spirit" of the agreement.

Internal tensions in the logic of partnering

Debate is still rife within the industry about what partnering actually involves, with many different approaches relying upon various combinations of contracts and incentives, performance improvement tools, and techniques and mechanisms for integrating project teams (Nystrom 2005). However, early practical prescriptions for partnering very rapidly converged on the use of tools and techniques, such as formal workshops, teambuilding, and incentive systems, designed to promote pre-ferred forms of behavior (e.g. CII 1989). Some even suggested that, given the correct "tools", collaboration could be achieved in the more limited timescale of a single project (e.g. Bennett and Jayes 1995). Arguably, this reflects a highly "instrumental" rationality or logic that emphasizes practical problem-solving and an underpinning systems view of the world (cf. Townley 2002).

However, this belief in being able to "engineer" culture represents something of a contradiction between different logics of action, as many proponents of partnering also recognized that there was a strong "cultural" component to the problems faced by the construction industry, characterized as entrenched attitudes leading to short-termism and uncooperative behavior (e.g. Bennett, Ingram, and Jayes 1996: 8). Consequently, a reliance upon tools and techniques to generate the required levels of collaboration (inducing *behavioral* change) contrasted with the emphasis placed on changing deeper values and belief systems (Barlow et al. 1997: 3).

From our own cases, it was clear that practitioners were well aware of this uneasy coexistence between the instrumental logic driving attempts to implement partner-ing and the required "cultural change" at the heart of the approach. One design man-ager, for example, recognized that "attitudes can be pretty set" and observed that they were still "experiencing many of the same problems as before"—suggesting that there were continuing limitations posed by entrenched norms and values. Indeed, as Green, Fernie, and Weller (2005) have noted, existing institutional norms within construction are strong and, in contrasting orientations towards supply chain man-agement in construction and aerospace sectors, they identify a number of significant differences. Specifically, in construction, they see more of an emphasis on improving bottom-line project performance (i.e. reducing costs and increasing margins), mean-ing that supply chain integration is seen more in operational than strategic terms. They also highlight how more emphasis tends to be placed on the difficulties in improving relationships given the scale of "cultural" change required.

Moreover, the adoption of collaborative strategies by clients was often framed in overtly rationalistic terms. The anticipated benefits of improved cooperation were included in the business plan for one of our cases and played a key role in persuad-ing the client board to sanction the project (the likelihood of reducing capital expenditure and shortening the lead-time before bringing production on line, were offered as key inducements to proceed with developing an extremely marginal off-shore gas reserve). However, in several cases, the appeal to "objective" arguments was based on a speculative and frequently undemonstrated relationship between enhanced cooperation and performance. One manager described the decision to implement partnering as a "leap of faith" which cast his organization into a pro-longed period of experimentation and learning. In other instances, the adoption of collaborative arrangements was influenced by wider change programmes being implemented in the client's core business (for example, positive experiences on off-shore projects led one client to establish an alliance for an onshore oil refinery).

While most client managers accepted the principle of collaboration, there was, however, considerable variation in the practices and techniques used to achieve it. One noticeable difference was between those who thought cooperation could be encouraged over relatively short timescales and those who considered it to be the result of much longer and continuous interaction. Managers who believed that collaboration could be developed in the short term were also ambivalent about the continued benefits of cooperation. Fears were expressed that "cosy relationships" could develop and it was felt important to "go back to the market" to ensure that project procurement remained competitive. More generally, there was recognition of a trade-off between the benefits of collaboration and of competition. While those in favor of project-specific relationships tended to regard these as mutually incompatible over the long term, those pursuing longer-term partnerships felt that this tension could be overcome, by introducing quasi-competitive techniques, such as internal and external benchmarking, stretch targets, and continuous improvement procedures.

Coexisting and co-mingling institutional logics

Project management practices in construction have traditionally involved a combination of arm's-length and direct techniques of control—the former through formal contractual means, the latter through direct and continuous surveillance of activity (using clerks of works, quantity surveyors, etc.). However, such a combination involves a considerable outlay of resources by clients in what one manager described as "man-to-man marking" of contractors' activities. Collaborative approaches are a more informal and less direct way of controlling the construction process, which seemingly give contractors greater scope for autonomous, self-governing activity. At the same time, they also appeal to clients faced with having to reduce staffing levels in project departments. Heavy personnel reductions were common in our cases, but concerns were also raised about the loss of expertise and specialist knowledge that could affect clients' ability to regulate their suppliers, and this sometimes resulted in design capabilities being retained in-house.

The building of high levels of mutual trust was therefore often viewed by clients as an important accompaniment to collaborative arrangements. However, there were also strict limits to the level and quality of trust and, despite the increased use of more informal and quasi-contractual agreements to regulate inter-firm relations (memoranda of understanding, charters, etc.), formal standard contracts would come into force in the event of the agreement failing. It is also doubtful whether one could describe such agreements as being founded primarily on principles of trust, as it was evident from the commercial terms and conditions that they included mechanisms to minimize the likelihood of opportunism—usually involving some type of risk/reward formula. Consequently, rather than unqualified trust being the primary basis for regulating relations, an emphasis was placed on carefully designed commercial mechanisms to promote concerted efforts to improve project performance.

Moreover, there were clear limits to the nature and extent of autonomy and self-governance. Even if collaborative approaches did appear to involve much lower levels of direct supervision, this did not mean that techniques of surveillance had been removed. Emphasis instead shifted towards the use of auditing. Audit is a subtle practice of control, a "technology of mistrust" (Power 1994), in which those audited have to demonstrate their accountability by making their practices transparent and auditable. In a number of projects, we found a strong emphasis on "open-book" relationships, which encouraged clients to engage in periodic audits of their contractual partners. In one case, a decision had been taken to reduce task duplication in the site office by assigning the role of commercial management to the contractor. At a periodic audit a number of discrepancies were detected and this led to the reintegration of commercial functions back into the client body. Auditing clearly represents an important limitation on trust-based relations, which may break down entirely if practices are discovered that do not comply with the auditor's requirements.

There was also considerable evidence of the persistence of practices more commonly associated with conventional approaches to contracting. Although many managers recognized the importance of transmitting messages of change to site level, there were also those who stressed that there should be limits to decentralization, where senior managers' expectations were not shared by others across the organization. Site staff also often felt that their day-to-day activities were little affected by company initiatives on collaboration and, where individuals engaged in what managers considered "inappropriate" forms of behavior, they were reassigned to more conventional projects. It was also apparent that ingrained patterns of behavior could be extremely difficult to overturn and this could lead to significant conflict where, for example, site managers found it difficult to accept that other contractors were on an equal footing within the alliance.

Taken-for-grantedness, acquiescence, or uneasy truce?

The above discussion suggests that traditional practices, approaches, and attitudes could coexist with the logic of collaboration, often at different locations within the extended project organization and often in ways that combined the rhetoric of cooperation with the reality of more subtle means of control.

Even where a high level of consensus and integration appears to have developed, this did not mean that conflicts and resistance were eliminated. In one project, for example, conflicts occurred not so much within the project team, but between the team and other client groups. The project team in this case felt that it was habitually sidelined by other client departments, at least until the appointment of a senior manager with sufficient influence to act as a project champion. Similar internal political difficulties facing relatively cohesive and united project teams were reported on other projects.

Conflict was also not necessarily viewed in negative terms. Some client managers tried to harness conflict creatively to improve project performance. The use of target cost incentives, for example, was often seen as a way of channeling conflict constructively since, through the early negotiation of an "acceptable" target cost, disagreements could be brought out into the open rather than being suppressed or allowed to lie dormant until later stages of the project (when they could do more damage). Such early conflict could also help the parties "buy in" to mutually agreed objectives and performance targets.

Furthermore, it was clear that an espoused commitment to partnering did not necessarily mean any lack of continuing, real tensions. The relocation of "unsuitable" individuals referred to above clearly indicates that, regardless of whether or not individuals privately believed in partnering, it was clearly advantageous to profess public adherence to the idea. After all, who would wish to be associated with the adversarialism and confrontation that were being demonized in partnering discourse? Consequently, the partnering concept contained carefully constructed rhetorical devices designed to promote its acceptance. A similar observation can be made at an organizational level, where divergent interests could be temporarily suppressed (and disbelief suspended?) in the interests of short-term collaboration for longer-term commercial gain. Yet continuing tensions were apparent, as in one case, where the client, having used alliance arrangements for several years, was planning to return to more conventional competitively tendered, lump sum arrangements—partly due to the failure of a major alliance project to meet performance expectations.

CONCLUDING DISCUSSION

This analysis of the early stage development of partnering in the UK construction industry has attempted to chart the processes of institutionalization associated with attempts to invest partnering with legitimacy and to harness the dialectical contradictions that had long been associated with the adversarialism said to prevail within the sector. Clearly, the development of partnering emerged out of a complex process of interaction involving industry, government, academic, and other groups, each of which has attempted to promote its own views as *the* legitimate expression of partnering, with the weight of existing institutions being used to lend authority to their claims and coalitions of interest being built through various cross-sectoral initiatives. Understanding the dynamics of attempts at change within the sector towards the institutional logic of partnering thus highlights a number of important features.

First, that the mobilization of interest in pursuit of partnering involved the artful exploitation by leading actors and organizations of a combination of circumstances within the sector at the time (cf. Seo and Creed 2002). These conditions included a lack of satisfaction with the status quo within the industry, the availability of an alternative collaborative discourse (influenced by developments within the automotive sector), the combination of market conditions which enabled clients to take the initiative, and the active mobilization of bias within established and newly emerging industry networks.

Second, that partnering in practice took on (and takes on) different forms that reflect variation in localized interpretation and enactment of the approach. Early debates about the nature of partnering—about whether it could be long or short term and "engineered" or more emergent—also created alternative conceptions of how partnering works in practice that not only suggest competing logics of action that can be used as a practical point of reference, but which also have a resonance today in continuing debates about the nature, meaning, and extent of partnering. Indeed, much current research is still driven by the search for an all-embracing definition and a generalizable set of performance metrics (e.g. Anvuur and Kumuraswamy 2007).

Third, that the development of partnering shows not only how variations in practice could proliferate (Nystrom 2005), but also how the new partnering logic could coexist and co-mingle with a prevailing logic associated with existing institutional norms and values—the rhetoric of autonomy and self-governance for example often masking the reality of more subtle forms of control based on self-discipline and audit (cf. Marshall 2006). Consequently, rather than representing the transition to an entirely new mode of working, partnering has developed with the flexibility that enables it to incorporate established modes of action—including those strongly associated with adversarial contracting.

In attempting to explain the tension between acceptance and skepticism which has characterized the spread of partnering, we would therefore suggest that there was (and, to a certain extent, still is) a shifting dialogue between different institutional logics of competition and collaboration due to the underlying tensions between them (Lounsbury 2007). On the one hand, interest in partnering has been sustained through processes of institutional legitimization, through its rhetorical management of meaning, and because it supplies individuals and organizations with the basis for a positive presentation of their actions. On the other hand, its validity claims are constantly being challenged through practitioners' experiences of attempting to implement the idea. In some cases, the means–ends logic of instrumental reason triumphs: the "leap of faith" which is often claimed by proponents as necessary to embark on the "partnering journey" comes up against the measurement of effectiveness in terms of cost, schedule, and quality. In other cases, success in pursuing collaboration lends strength to making the approach increasingly taken for granted.

These tensions and dynamics are reflected in the continuing lack of clear-cut evidence of the performance benefits of partnering. Early research stressed quite strongly the benefits and value of collaboration through partnering (e.g. Bennett, Ingram, and Jayes 1996) and this proselytizing is still found in some recent accounts (e.g. Li et al. 2001). However, others have highlighted instead the difficulties in implementing partnering in practice (e.g. Ng et al. 2002; Bresnen 2007), as well as problems in measuring performance effects and in attributing improvements in project performance unambiguously to a partnering arrangement (e.g. Nystrom 2008).

More generally, there is a clear sense in which the underlying tensions and contradictions that belie partnering (Bresnen 2007) provide a set of latent influences that, depending on changing commercial and other conditions, may at any time provide the dialectical impulse that motivates key actors and institutions to promote alternative (and possibly retrogressive?) ways of working. In other words, even if partnering were to be now seemingly "taken for granted" in particular institutional settings, it does not mean that it will necessarily continue to be so—insofar as it encapsulates real contradictions between, say, the benefits of collaboration and competition. So, for example, although partnering may now be more established and "taken for granted" this does not mean that it is any less important to understand the residual dialectical tensions and contradictions that may have been suppressed by this new institutional logic (e.g. Green 1999; Bresnen 2007). This may be even more the case in places, such as the UK, where the greater exposure to partnering over time has inevitably laid bare its actual costs, as much as its espoused benefits (e.g. the loss of benefits of competitive tender). Moreover, the fact that collaboration is not purely a consequence of partnering and can be found on more traditional, supposedly adversarial, contracts provides a further rationale for those motivated to question the new institutional logic of collaboration.

Further, there are a number of implications that derive from the above discussion for an understanding of project management and organization more generally. First, by combining an analysis of changing discourse at an industry level with changing practice at the project level, the analysis has attempted to demonstrate how susceptible the realm of project management is to the coexistence and co-mingling of institutional logics—particularly through the fragmented institutional structures within which complex projects are often undertaken. A comparable situation can be found in other institutionally complex project-based environments, such as biotechnology, where scientific and commercial logics often coexist and combine in the production of new drugs and process innovations (Powell et al. 2005). Existing work suggests that network forms of organization may be conducive to the co-mingling of institutional logics through allowing space for different norms and values to thrive and combine (Smith-Doerr 2005). However, it may be in transient project-based forms of organization—where the basis for action is the one-off project task (Ekstedt et al. 1999)—that the circumstances exist to make such processes and tensions more prominent and salient. This may be particularly the case in project forms of organization that could be classified as "radical" (Lindkvist 2004) or "precarious" (Whitley 2006) and hence more susceptible to divergent influences and pressures towards change. Clearly, more work is needed not only to explore changing institutional logics within project-based settings, but also to explore the propositions suggested here—that project-based organization is particularly prone to the coexistence and co-mingling of institutional logics associated with changing management practices and that the more fragmented the institutional context, the more likely this is to be the case.

Second, recent work in institutional theory has also started to address the relationship between changing institutional logics and professional identity. Lounsbury (2007: 302), for example, concludes by calling for more research on how broader symbolic meaning systems associated with particular institutional logics relate recursively to localized practices and the construction of managerial and professional identity. As this chapter has been concerned with understanding interrelationships between industry discourse and practical case examples of partnering, it has not been possible to explore the dynamics of identity construction in any great depth and more research is clearly needed in this area. However, the analysis has several times touched upon the impact that the transition to partnering had upon individuals' and organizations' sense of their own identities and appropriate professional/managerial behavior, suggesting that there are important limits to the legitimacy and taken-for-grantedness of existing institutionalized roles and managerial practices that are placed in sharp relief in project organizations faced with processes of institutional change. Returning to the proposal above—that project-based organizations in fragmented institutional contexts may be prime sites for examining the co-mingling of institutional projects—there is also a great deal to be learned here about what the conditions found in project environments mean for the development and change of professional/managerial identity. For example, given the variation in patterns of expertise associated with different forms of project organization (Whitley 2006: 90), may the implications for managerial identity implied here be even more pronounced and radical in more fluid types of project setting?

Third, the analysis embarked on here demonstrates the value of combining an exploration of change at the institutional level with changing practice at the level of individual projects. Research into project-based forms of organization often tends to explore them purely at the institutional level (e.g. Powell et al. 2005; Whitley

2006) or, alternatively, at the organizational level—examining connections between project and organizational management practices, for example (e.g. Dubois and Gadde 2002; Sapsed and Salter 2004). This chapter has instead drawn upon a strand of institutional analysis that allows a "drilling down" through levels of analysis to assess more deeply and practically the effects of institutional-level change on practice (and vice versa). Consequently, there may be added value in taking a more multi-level analytical approach to understand the recursive relationship between institutional processes and emergent management practices (cf. Sydow, Lindkvist, and DeFillippi 2004). So, for example, it becomes possible to examine to what extent developments in project management knowledge are invested with the legitimacy they need in order to translate into practice and become taken for granted across the range of competing institutional influences that govern the field. Although such an approach is a very challenging one, it does offer the prospect of a much deeper understanding of the dynamics of collaboration under project-based forms of organization than is currently available.

Last but not least, it also offers the prospect of understanding more fully the problems of, and prospects for, developing and institutionalizing a body of knowledge which constitutes a clear and unitary frame of reference for guiding behavior in complex project settings. As already noted, the development of a project management body of knowledge (which will include consideration of different approaches to collaboration) has proved a difficult venture and it could be argued that this is perhaps inevitable given the very different institutional logics that prevail within complex project ecologies. However, the above analysis also suggests that this is not necessarily the case and that, if institutional conditions are right, then the tensions generated by internal institutional contradictions can promote new modes of working that, in turn, challenge and add to existing knowledge bases. The problem is perhaps in assuming a more static view, where the aim is to develop a more definitive, but still abstract, body of knowledge that tries to cut across institutional differences and which is then superimposed upon practice. The above analysis has suggested instead that, in the conditions of institutional fragmentation found in many types of project settings, it is the process of institutional change, rather than the process of institutional isomorphism, that is the relevant dynamic to explore and understand if one is interested in the development of project management knowledge and its embedding in project management practice.

Acknowledgements

The research reported in this chapter was supported by EPSRC grant reference GR/L01206.

REFERENCES

ACTIVE (1996). *ACTIVE Engineering Construction Initiative: The Action Plan*. London: ACTIVE.

ANVUUR, A. M., and KUMURASWAMY, M. M. (2007). "Conceptual model of partnering and alliancing," *Journal of Construction Engineering and Management*, 133/3: 225–34.

BARLOW, J., COHEN, M., JASHAPARA, A., and SIMPSON, Y. (1997). *Towards Positive Partnering*. Bristol: Policy Press.

BENNETT, J., and JAYES, S. (1995). *Trusting the Team: The Best Practice Guide to Partnering in Construction*. Reading: Centre for Strategic Studies in Construction/Reading Construction Forum.

——INGRAM, I., and JAYES, S. (1996). *Partnering for Construction*. Reading: Centre for Strategic Studies in Construction, Reading University.

BRESNEN, M. (1990). *Organising Construction*. London: Routledge.

——(1996). "Traditional and emergent professionals in the construction industry: competition and control over the building process," in I. Glover and M. Hughes (eds.), *The Professional-Managerial Class: Contemporary British Management in the Pursuer Mode*. Aldershot: Avebury, 245–68.

——(2007). "Deconstructing partnering in project-based organisation: seven pillars, seven paradoxes and seven deadly sins," *International Journal of Project Management*, 25/4: 365–74.

——and MARSHALL, N. (2000). "Building partnerships: case studies of client–contractor collaboration in the UK construction industry," *Construction Management and Economics*, 18/7: 819–32.

CHAN, A. P. C., CHAN, D. W. M., and HO, K. S. K. (2003). "An empirical study of the benefits of construction partnering in Hong Kong," *Construction Management and Economics*, 21/5: 523–33.

CHERNS, A., and BRYANT, D. (1984). "Studying the client's role in construction management," *Construction Management and Economics*, 2: 177–84.

COLYVAS, J. A., and POWELL, W. W. (2006). "Roads to institutionalisation: the re-making of boundaries between public and private science," *Research in Organisational Behaviour*, 27: 305–53.

CONSTRUCTION INDUSTRY INSTITUTE (1989). *Partnering: Meeting the Challenges of the Future*. Austin, TX: Construction Industry Institute.

COX, A., and TOWNSEND, M. (1998). *Strategic Procurement in Construction: Towards Better Practice in the Management of Construction Supply Chains*. London: Thomas Telford.

CRINE (1994). *CRINE Report*. London: Institute of Petroleum.

DIMAGGIO, P., and POWELL, W. (1983). "The iron cage revisited: institutional isomorphism and collective rationality in organizational fields," *American Sociological Review*, 48: 147–60.

DUBOIS, A., and GADDE, L.-E. (2002). "The construction industry as a loosely coupled system: implications for productivity and innovation," *Construction Management and Economics*, 20/7: 621–31.

EGAN, J. (1998). *Rethinking Construction*. London: DETR.

EKSTEDT, E., LUNDIN, R., SÖDERHOLM, A., and WIRDENIUS, H. (1999). *Neo-industrial Organizing: Renewal by Action and Knowledge Formation in a Project-Intensive Economy*. London: Routledge.

ENGWALL, M. (2003). "No project is an island: linking projects to history and context," *Research Policy*, 32/5: 789–808.

FRIEDLAND, R., and ALFORD, R. R. (1991). "Bringing society back in: symbols, practices, and institutional contradictions," in W. W. Powell and P. J. DiMaggio(eds.), *The New Institutionalism in Organizational Analysis*. Chicago: University of Chicago Press.

GRABHER, G. (2002). "The project ecology of advertising: tasks, talents and teams," *Regional Studies*, 36/3: 245–62.

GREEN, S. D. (1999). "Partnering: the propaganda of corporatism?" in S. O. Ogunlana (ed.), *Profitable Partnering in Construction Procurement*. London: E. & F. N. Spon, 3–13.

——FERNIE, S., and WELLER, S. (2005). "Making sense of supply chain management: a comparative study of aerospace and construction," *Construction Management and Economics*, 23: 579–93.

HIGGIN, J., and JESSOP, N. (1965). *Communications in the Building Industry*. London: Tavistock Publications.

HOBDAY, M. (2000). "The project-based organization: an ideal form for managing complex products and systems?" *Research Policy*, 29: 871–93.

HODGSON, D., and CICMIL, S. (2007). "The politics of standards in modern management: making 'the project' a reality." *Journal of Management Studies*, 44/3: 431–50.

JONES, C., and LICHTENSTEIN, B. (2008). "Temporary inter-organizational projects: how temporal and social embeddedness enhance coordination and manage uncertainty," in S. Cropper, M. Ebers, C. Huxham, and P. S. Ring (eds.), *Oxford Handbook of Inter-organizational Relations*. Oxford: Oxford University Press.

KADEFORS, A., BJORLINGSON, E., and KARSSON, A. (2007). "Procuring service innovations: contractor selection for partnering projects," *International Journal of Project Management*, 25: 375–85.

LATHAM, M. (1994). *Constructing the Team*. London: HMSO.

LI, H., CHENG, E., LOVE, P., and IRANI, Z. (2001). "Co-operative benchmarking: a tool for partnering excellence in construction," *International Journal of Project Management*, 19/3: 171–9.

LINDKVIST, L. (2004). "Governing project-based firms: promoting market-like processes within hierarchies," *Journal of Management and Governance*, 8: 3–25.

LOUNSBURY, M. (2007). "A tale of two cities: competing logics and practice variation in the professionalizing of mutual funds," *Academy of Management Journal*, 50/2: 280–307.

MAGUIRE, S., HARDY, C., and LAWRENCE, T. B. (2004). "Institutional entrepreneurship in emerging fields: HIV/AIDS treatment advocacy in Canada," *Academy of Management Journal*, 47: 657–79.

MARSHALL, N. (2006). "Understanding power in project settings," in D. Hodgson and S. Cicmil (eds.), *Making Projects Critical*. Basingstoke: Palgrave Macmillan, 207–31.

MORRIS, P. W. G. (1994). *The Management of Projects*. London: Thomas Telford.

NEDO (1991). *Partnering: Contracting without Conflict*. London: HMSO.

NEWELL, S., GOUSSEVSKAIA, A., SWAN, J., BRESNEN, M., and OBEMBE, A. (2008). "Managing interdependencies in complex project ecologies: the case of biomedical innovation," *Long Range Planning*, 41/1: 33–54.

NG, T., ROSE, T., MAK, M., and CHEN, S. E. (2002). "Problematic issues associated with project partnering: the contractor perspective," *International Journal of Project Management*, 20/6: 437–49.

NYSTROM, J. (2005). "The definition of partnering as a Wittgenstein family-resemblance concept," *Construction Management and Economics*, 23/5: 473–81.

NYSTROM, J. (2008). "A quasi-experimental evaluation of partnering," *Construction Management and Economics*, 26: 531–41.

ORR, R. J., and SCOTT, W. R. (2008). "Institutional exceptions on global projects: a process model," *Journal of International Business Studies*, 39: 562–88.

PHUA, F. T. T. (2006). "When is construction partnering likely to happen? An empirical examination of the role of institutional norms," *Construction Management and Economics*, 24/6: 615–24.

PISANO, G. (2006). "Can science be a business? Lessons from biotech," *Harvard Business Review*, 1 October: 114–25.

POWELL, W. W., WHITE, D. R., KOPUT, K. W., and OWEN-SMITH, J. (2005). "Network dynamics and field evolution: the growth of interorganizational collaboration in the life sciences," *American Journal of Sociology*, 110: 1132–205.

POWER, M. (1994). "The audit society," in A. G. Hopwood and P. Miller (eds.), *Accounting as Social and Institutional Practice*. Cambridge: Cambridge University Press, 299–316.

REAY, T., and HININGS, C. R. (2005). "The recomposition of an organizational field: health care in Alberta," *Organization Studies*, 26/3: 351–84.

SAPSED, J., and SALTER, A. (2004). "Postcards from the edge: local communities, global programmes and boundary objects," *Organisation Studies*, 25/9: 1515–34.

SCOTT, W., RUEF, M., MENDEL, P., and CARONNA, C. (2000). *Institutional Change and Healthcare Organizations: From Professional Dominance to Managed Care*. Chicago: University of Chicago Press.

SEO, M. G., and CREED, W. E. D. (2002). "Institutional contradictions, praxis and institutional change: a dialectical perspective," *Academy of Management Review*, 27: 222–47.

SMITH-DOERR, L. (2005). "Institutionalising the network form: how life scientists legitimate work in the biotechnology industry," *Sociological Forum*, 20/2: 271–99.

SYDOW, J., and STABER, U. (2002). "The institutional embeddedness of project networks: the case of content production in German television," *Regional Studies*, 36/3: 215–28.

——LINDKVIST, L., and DEFILLIPPI, R. (2004). "Project-based organisations, embeddedness and repositories of knowledge," *Organization Studies*, 25/9: 1475–89.

TOWNLEY, B. (2002). "The role of competing rationalities in institutional change," *Academy of Management Journal*, 45: 163–79.

WHITLEY, R. (2006). "Project-based firms: new organizational forms or variations on a theme?" *Industrial and Corporate Change*, 15/1: 77–99.

WINCH, G. M. (1998). "Zephyrs of creative destruction: understanding the management of innovation in construction," *Building Research and Information*, 26/5: 268–79.

WOOD, G. D., and ELLIS, R. C. T. (2005). "Main contractor experiences of partnering relationships on UK construction projects," *Construction Management and Economics*, 23/3: 317–25.

CHAPTER 7

PROJECT ECOLOGIES

A CONTEXTUAL VIEW ON TEMPORARY ORGANIZATIONS

GERNOT GRABHER

OLIVER IBERT

INTRODUCTION

Projects, it seems, are able to enact their own small worlds. As "temporary organizations" (Lundin and Söderholm 1995) and one-off ventures they appear as unique phenomena without predecessors or future perspectives. As goal-oriented organizations (Turner and Müller 2003) they evoke separate systems of relevance. Projects are strongly focused in scope and the involved actors are selected according to their contribution to the project's aims. Moreover, projects are from the outset well defined in terms of budget and other resources. These reiterated emphases on strict organizational boundaries and clear-cut distinctions between inside and outside have been suggestive to a perspective on temporary organizations which preferably concentrated on internal processes of project management.

More recently, though, a contextual view on projects (see Blomquist and Packendorff 1998; Ekstedt et al. 1999; Gann and Salter 2000; Grabher 2002a; Sydow and Staber 2002; Asheim 2002; Engwall 2003; Brady and Davies 2004; Söderlund 2004; Davies and Hobday 2005) has gained momentum, which problematizes the shortcomings of this conventional perspective. Instead of treating projects as

a isolated from their history, stripped off their contemporary social and
ɪtext, and independent of the future, this literature highlights that tempor-
ɪizations continually interact with their wider context. For instance, aims
ɪe of a project have to be interpreted against the background of its stakehold-
ᴄ. ɪory and future perspectives (Engwall 2003). Personal expertise needed in the
course of a project is flexibly obtained from local labor markets (Jones 1996; DeFillippi
and Arthur 1998). Project-based firms usually manage a whole portfolio of interrelated projects (Anell 2000), some of which compete for resources while others
might cross-subsidize each other. Mutual trust, which is always at risk in a temporary
organization, might be derived from common personal experiences gained in former
collaboration but also on short notice from existing institutional settings and established professional standards ("swift trust"; Meyerson, Weick, and Kramer 1996).

The notion "project ecology" (Grabher 2002a, 2002b, 2002c, 2004a, 2004b;
Grabher and Ibert 2006; Ibert 2004) provides a conceptual framework for analyzing
projects from a contextual view. In short, project ecologies denote a relational space
which affords the personal, organizational, and institutional resources for performing projects. This relational space encompasses social layers on multiple scales, from
the micro level of interpersonal networks to the meso level of intra- and inter-organizational collaboration to the macro level of wider institutional settings.
Moreover, it unfolds a complex geography, which explicitly is not reduced to local
clusters but also extends to more distanced individuals and organizations or a-spa-
tial institutions (DeFillippi and Arthur 1998; Grabher 2002b; Asheim 2002; Sapsed
and Salter 2004; Grabher and Ibert 2006).

One of the main fields in which the contextual view generated new insights is the
topic of project-based learning (Schwab and Miner 2008). Through their trans-
disciplinarity and transience, projects appear as a most pertinent form for creating
knowledge in the context of application (Amin and Cohendet 2004). The temporal
limitation of projects, however, also causes a cardinal limitation of any transient
organizational form in sedimenting knowledge. Knowledge accumulated in the
course of a project is at risk of being dispersed as soon as the project team is dissolved and members are assigned to a different task, another team, a new deadline
(DeFillippi and Arthur 1998; Prencipe and Tell 2001). The overarching focus on
deadlines hardly leaves time to reflect on previous assignments (Hobday 2000;
Brady and Davies 2004).

Projects, viewed as singular ventures, combine diverse knowledges effectively;
apparently, however, they also tend to forget quickly. This notorious syndrome of
"organizational amnesia" has increasingly drawn the attention from the singular
venture to the wider social context in which projects are embedded (Hobday 2000;
Prencipe and Tell 2001; Brady and Davies 2004; Sydow, Lindkvist, and DeFillippi
2004; Cacciatori 2008). Essential processes of creating and sedimenting knowledge
are seen to arise at the interface between projects and the organizations, networks,
and institutions in and through which projects operate (Scarbrough et al. 2003;

Schwab and Miner 2008). This chapter reveals the multilayered architecture of project ecologies by consecutively disentangling the social layers which are constitutive for project-based learning; the core team, the firm, the epistemic community, and the personal networks.

After differentiating cumulative and disruptive learning regimes we explore in the second part of the chapter the basic organizational unit and the elementary learning arena of projects, the core team. It embodies temporal continuity and bears chief responsibility during the course of the entire project (DeFillippi and Arthur 1998). By moving from the core team to the firm, the analysis shifts (in the third part) from the level of the individual project to learning processes that accrue from the management of portfolios of projects. By handling subsequent and related projects, firms in project ecologies thus acquire particular "project capabilities" (Davies and Brady 2000).

The actual locus of project-based learning extends beyond the boundaries of the individual firm. The perforation of firm boundaries in fact is an emblematic feature of project ecologies. Project-specific knowledge creation ensues in the epistemic community (fourth part). The epistemic community involves all project participants who contribute to the production of knowledge to accomplish the specific task, even if only temporarily and partially (see also Knorr Cetina 1981, 1999; Amin and Cohendet 2004: 75). Most importantly, they comprise clients and suppliers but increasingly also major corporate groups to which project ecologies become affiliated.

Core team, firm, and epistemic community represent the organizational layers that are temporarily tied together for the completion of a specific project. Beyond this manifest pattern of organizational networks, project ecologies also unfold a wider fabric of personal networks that endure and stretch out beyond the actual project (fifth part). Although these more latent networks can be activated to solve project-specific problems, they typically remain in the project background and sustain ongoing learning processes of the individual project members (see also Starkey, Barnatt, and Tempest 2000; Wittel 2001). The chapter concludes by sketching some avenues for future research.

The basic idea of project ecology has been developed in close dialogue between theory and empirical fieldwork. Two successive research projects contributed to its stepwise exploration. The first research project was a longitudinal empirical study of project-based organizing in the London advertising industry that comprised 78 semi-structured interviews (with an average duration of 120 minutes) in advertising agencies (with account managers, account planners, and art directors) and in collaborating film and post-production companies. By using inductive qualitative techniques to analyze the data (Eisenhardt 1989), the findings were aggregated and synthesized in a first conceptualization of the notion of the project ecology (Grabher 2002a, 2002b, 2003). On this basis, a second research endeavor aimed at a systematic comparison between two distinct yet comparable ecologies, the software ecology in

Munich and the advertising ecology in Hamburg. The empirical material on the Munich software ecology comprises thirty-eight semi-structured interviews (with project managers, software engineers, and key management personnel), the data on the Hamburg advertising ecology embraces twenty-nine interviews (with creative staff, account managers, and planners). These two bodies of research material provided the empirical basis of the comparative conceptualization of project ecologies (Grabher 2004a, 2004b; Grabher and Ibert 2006).

Contrasting project ecologies: cumulative vs. disruptive learning

We elucidate the conceptual framework by comparing two kinds of project ecologies that are driven by opposing logics and organizational practices of creating and sedimenting knowledge.

The key imperative in the software ecology is modularization (de Waard and Kramer 2008). Knowledge practices in this mode are rooted in the fundamental association between learning and repetition: repeated cycles of interaction within the organization and between the organization and the environment form the basis of learning. Project organizing is geared towards moving from the singular one-off venture to repeatable solutions (see also Davies and Brady 2000; Brady and Davies 2004; Davies and Hobday 2005; Frederiksen and Davies 2008; Schwab and Miner 2008). Software production in Munich exemplifies this cumulative learning regime.

The logic of modularization will be juxtaposed with a learning mode that is organized around the imperative of originality. Although learning by repetition also plays an important role, learning by switching ties both within and across organizations signifies the characteristic knowledge practice in this type of ecology. The advertising ecologies of London and Hamburg epitomize such a disruptive learning regime in which the overarching demand for originality minimizes the scope for repeatable solutions and convention defying is encouraged as a convention (Nov and Jones 2003: 9).

The chief aim of the following sections is neither to provide in-depth idiographic accounts of the local clusters in Munich, Hamburg, or London nor aimed at an exhaustive sectoral analysis of the software and advertising businesses. At issue is an empirically grounded conceptualization (see Glaser and Strauss 1967) of two types of project ecologies, a cumulative project ecology (derived from research on software in Munich) and a disruptive project ecology (based on the study of advertising in Hamburg and London). The argument occasionally risks brushing over idiosyncrasies of the empirical cases for the sake of the consistency and usefulness of a conceptual template for studying the multilayered architecture of different types of project ecologies (see also Whitley 2006: 84).

THE CORE TEAM: REDUCING VS. PRESERVING COGNITIVE DISTANCE

The core team epitomizes temporal continuity and accountability (DeFillippi and Arthur 1998) and typifies the elementary learning arena (Söderlund, Vaagaasar, and Andersen 2008). Although the concrete personal constellations will hardly recur in successive projects, temporary organizations still are "organized around enduring structured role systems whose nuances are negotiated in situ" (Bechky 2006: 4). Abstracting from the idiosyncrasies of the production process, the respective core teams in the disruptive and the cumulative ecologies comprise a set of professional profiles and skills that share some generic features. The service logic of solving a specific problem of the client is, or at least ought to be, the prime logic of a project. The client-specific tasks, demands, and expectations have to be balanced against the management logic of the project which aims at keeping the project within key parameters such as time and budget. The fragile balance between the service logic (of solving the client's business problem) and the management logic (of keeping the project on track) provides the organizational coordinates within which the professional logic of the expert knowledge can unfold.

These generic imperatives of project organizing are embodied in and balanced by different trade-specific professional profiles and occupations (on software, see Ibert 2004; on advertising, see Pratt 2006: 6–12). Each professional profile signifies a specific work ethos and perspective which implies a certain "cognitive distance" between these professions (see Nooteboom 2000). Meaningful interaction and fruitful collaboration across cognitive distance, of course, is possible as long as the participants can make sense of each other's perspectives. In both kinds of project ecologies, however, cognitive distance is enacted in fundamentally different ways. Whereas the interactions and practices of the core team in the cumulative ecology are geared towards reducing cognitive distance, project organizing in the disruptive ecologies rather is aimed at preserving cognitive distance.

The organizational repertoire to reduce cognitive distance in the cumulative ecology includes a range of organizational practices and conventions. First, professionals in the course of their careers, sometimes even in the course of a project, switch roles. "There are no clear-cut categories of software workers, such as designers, coders, and testers. Designations do not provide job descriptions in the organizational structure—job description is ambiguous" (Ilvarasan and Sharma 2003: 3).

The practice of switching roles is also facilitated by non-discriminating training: candidates with graduate degrees in engineering and technology (in a broad range of disciplines) typically are selected by firms for a broad array of jobs and roles. Secondly, the composition of core teams characteristically remains stable over several project cycles. Collaboration within the team thus evolves from an interaction between strict professional roles into relationships between acquainted colleagues. Collaboration in the project, generally, seems more strongly molded by the service logic of joint problem-solving than by the particular professional ethos. The predominant collaborative ethos thus harshly clashes with the cliché of the red-eyed, antisocial coder hidden in a silent cubicle.

In the disruptive ecologies, in contrast, professional identities crystallize into "creeds" whose distinctiveness is reiterated through organizational practices, professional styles, and distinct dress and language codes (Grabher 2002b: 248; see also Bilton and Leary 2002: 56–7). Professionals hardly change roles within the core team. Although professionals are recruited from a broad range of educational and biographical backgrounds, further training appears more discriminating between different occupations since it is provided by professional associations (like the Account Planning Group) rather than by individual agencies. Moreover, the personal composition of teams is deliberately altered from time to time to trigger novel and unexpected confrontations of different perspectives. Interactions within the team are, comparatively speaking, more strongly shaped by antagonistic professional identities than by the joint project task. For creative individuals, for example, market researchers and strategic planners in the core team notoriously represent a permanent restriction of their imagination, and inspiration by those "who lack passion for advertising" (Shelbourne and Baskin 1998: 78). Creative sparks ignite, as the business mantra goes, in this rivalry between strong professional identities.

THE FIRM: ECONOMIES OF REPETITION VS. ECONOMIES OF RECOMBINATION

Economies of repetition: tools, cultures, stories

Despite the extensive projectification of production, the cumulative as well as the disruptive ecologies are quite obviously populated by firms. Firms sustain ongoing and repetitive business processes that are instrumental in managing project portfolios (Gann and Salter 2000; Geraldi 2008; Blichfeldt and Eskerod 2008; Ariuta, Smith, and Bower 2009). By handling a range of consecutive and related projects, firms in both kinds of ecologies in fact aim at enhancing and accumulating particular "project capabilities" (Davies and Brady 2000; Brady and Davies 2004).

In disruptive as well as cumulative ecologies firm-specific best practice is codified in tools which align collective effort by providing menus and checklists for risk assessment, costing, project design, scheduling, and contractual agreements. Moreover, firms aim at reinforcing and extending the reach of codified tools with (less codified) culture. Corporate culture in both trades is colored by idiosyncratic personal constellations, less visible in the cumulative ecology but much more palpable in the disruptive ecologies around the "stars" and agency founders (after whom, symptomatically, agencies are named). Most recent contributions to the project literature indicate that codified knowledge also materializes in knowledge artifacts which in turn perpetuate corporate cultures. For instance, routines that are stored in manuals, checklists, or excel charts (Cacciatori 2008) are frequently re-enacted in consecutive projects. New managerial practices are not only illustrated but also invoked and mediated by alternative ways of representing organizational charts (Taxén and Lilliesköld 2008).

Economies of recombination: modules, products

While in our ecologies project-to-project and project-to-business learning allows firms to reap "economies of repetition" (Davies and Brady 2000), only the cumulative ecology benefits from economies of recombination to a substantial degree. These economies emanate from the ability to balance the contradictory demands of offering a problem-specific solution to the client and yet, at the same time, to reuse and sediment project knowledge into "modules" that can be recombined in subsequent or related projects. Modules epitomize the proverbial "black box," a component that produces a particular output from a certain input while the internal functioning remains largely irrelevant (Brusoni and Prencipe 2001; de Waard and Kramer 2008).

Economies of recombination accrue from not offering one-off solutions in the strict sense of the word. On an ad hoc project-to-project level, they flow from the creation of novel combinations of familiar elements and by-products from previous projects (Hansen, Nohria, and Tierney 1999). On a more strategic level, firms realize economies of recombination by engaging in a process of moving from first-of-its-kind projects to the execution of portfolios of related projects (Davies and Brady 2000: 952; Frederiksen and Davies 2008). This move widens the scope for reuse in the sense of increasing the "utility" (by enhancing ease of modification) and/or "variability" of code (by boosting adaptability to different contexts). Learning by recombination, however, is rather ambiguous. Extra effort has to be spent on standardization, codification, administration, and coordination. The related costs come at the expense of the respective project budgets (Ibert 2004; de Waard and Kramer 2008).

Furthermore, at the time knowledge is preserved it is difficult if not impossible to anticipate the concrete situation in which this knowledge will be retrieved. The future value of knowledge stored in modules is highly uncertain.

In the Munich ecology, for instance, organizational routines to systematically reuse components seem largely confined to the library model (in which centralized repositories of components are set up) and, in a few exceptions, simple versions of a curator model (where the specialists managing repositories of components are also assigned a quality certification role; see also Fichman and Kemerer 2001). Primarily large corporations offer their repository in a, so to speak, crystallized version of a product, that is, a standardized software program. However, even for firms who specialize in products, projects remain of vital importance. Projects provide crucial learning opportunities to refine products or to broaden the domain of their applicability (Fichman and Kemerer 2001). Projects, in other words, are client-sponsored external R&D laboratories of firms who specialize in products.

The logic of reusing knowledge on the level of the product seems diametrically opposed to the overarching imperative of freshness in the disruptive ecologies. In advertising, for instance, individual campaigns have to be in tune with the registers of a brand identity comprising aesthetic details such as color schemes, graphic elements, tonality of images and sounds, as well as the conceived character of the brand as conveying an air of youthfulness, trustworthiness, or inexpensiveness, for example. Within these parameters the professional ethos of creativity as well as the explicit demands of the clients for fresh ideas limits the scope for reuse to an absolute minimum. Moreover, the individual aesthetic and semantic registers of one brand (like a color scheme) cannot simply be recombined like chunks of software code to design a second brand identity. Economies of recombination are not a viable learning strategy in disruptive ecologies.

Epistemic community: clients, suppliers, corporate groups

The actual locus of knowledge production, of course, extends beyond the boundaries of the firm and involves communities "[w]ho are in contact with the environment and involved in interpretive sense making, congruence finding and adapting. It is from any site of such interactions that new insights can be coproduced" (Brown and Duguid 1991: 53). Deliberate knowledge creation more specifically ensues in "epistemic communities" (Knorr Cetina 1981, 1999). Epistemic communities are organized around the specific project task and a mutually

recognized subset of knowledge issues. They are governed by a procedural authority endowed internally or externally to fulfill the project goal (see Cowan, David,
and Foray 2000). Individuals accumulate knowledge according to their own experience and validation is made according to the procedural authority: what is evaluated is the contribution of the member to the cognitive goal with regard to the
criteria set by the procedural authority (Amin and Cohendet 2004: 75). Epistemic
communities in disruptive and in cumulative ecologies extend beyond the firm to
involve the same set of actors, that is, clients, suppliers, and corporate groups.

The very notion of the "community" evokes a sense of persistence, coherence,
and harmony that not only seems absent but even not desired in the originality-
fixated advertising ecology. The rivalry in the antagonistic learning practices and
transience of ties in the disruptive learning regime might collectively be called epistemic (Lindkvist 2005). Since our focus here however is on the basic architecture of
project ecologies we will retrain from elucidating this differentiation in this chapter.
(For further details, see Grabher 2004: 1498).

Clients: technical vs. personal lock-in

Clients play a central role in knowledge production that is not confined to initiating
and sponsoring the entire venture. Both kinds of ecologies are driven by the strategic goal to transform a single project into a lasting relationship. In both contexts,
projects thus are strongly conceived as strategic pivots from which to leverage a
continuous stream of business. Apart from sharing an interest in transforming
projects into relationships, disruptive as well as cumulative ecologies rely on different practices to "lock-in" clients.

In the cumulative software ecology, user participation appears particularly deep
(see Lehrer 2000: 592; Petter 2008). Software projects frequently are carried out on
site in ongoing conversation with the IT units as well as the end-users in the client's
organization. The client's expectations, although specified in the brief, typically do
not consolidate before the project process has yielded some interim variants. And as
the software becomes more complex in the course of the project, so do the implications of even seemingly simple changes that ramify throughout the entire client
organization and its "legacy system" operating on older software platforms.

Even within shorter project cycles project specifications as a consequence are "rack-
eting up" (Girard and Stark 2002: 1940). Such "scope creep" (Jurison 1999: 33) notoriously puts pre-calculated plans of resource allocation at risk. Viewed from a more
strategic point of view, however, scope creep might not only benefit the usefulness of
the software. It also opens up prospects for turning the single project into a lasting tie
(Casper and Whitley 2002: 24). The repertoire for this sort of strategic scope creep
(that is, to deliberately lock-in clients by increasing interdependencies) in the cumulative ecology ranges from training the client's staff, stand-by advice through a hot-line,
to technical maintenance, including regular updates and debugging.

The less intense client involvement in the disruptive advertising ecologies is inter-related with lower degrees of technical interdependencies of the project output with the existing business of the client. Of course, individual campaigns have to correspond to brand identities. Such interdependencies, however, are more an issue of interpretive plausibility than of technical compatibility. Consequently, the leeway for strategic scope creep in the disruptive ecology is limited and confined to establishing personal trustful relationships. In a context in which interaction resembles less the "facts-and-figures" exchange of business parlance but is strongly colored by individual taste and esthetic preferences, trust in the expert's judgment is of considerable value.

Trust does not equal involvement though. On the contrary, high levels of trust afford lower degrees of controlling the creative process. Trust, among others, is nur-tured through a practice that in the London advertising ecology has been referred to as "educating clients" (Grabher 2002b: 250). This practice encompasses, besides agreeing on basic esthetic parameters, clarifying the division of labor that is rooted in mutual respect for professional competencies. Whereas client involvement in the cumulative ecology is strongly driven by the necessities and (leveraged opportuni-ties) to integrate the project output into "legacy systems," client participation in the disruptive ecologies is limited by the creative ethos that demands at least temporary independence from the interference of clients who characteristically are seen to associate creativity with risk (Shelbourne and Baskin 1998).

Suppliers: orchestration vs. improvisation

The different degrees of client involvement correspond with inverted roles of sup-pliers. In the cumulative ecology the higher degree of client involvement corre-sponds with a relatively lower intensity of ties with external collaborators. While larger product-oriented corporations rely on supplier networks for recurring cycles of client-specific implementation, smaller, projects-only specialists seem to prefer in-house solutions vis-à-vis extended supplier networks. In fact, freelancing is fre-quently derogated as "body-leasing" by smaller service providers.

The modularization of projects as well as the analytical professional ethos favors a partition of jobs among project collaborators that resembles orchestration. In organizational terms, orchestration involves a clearly defined role of a single leader, a clear assignment of task and responsibilities, and exact timing. Due to the size and technical complexities of projects (see also Fichman and Kemerer 2001: 58), a high premium is again placed on continuity. Long-term collaboration with a relatively stable set of suppliers additionally not only lowers transaction costs but also affords interactive learning processes that benefit the subsequent maintenance and upgrad-ing of software.

In the disruptive ecologies the participation of technical specialists follows similar principles of hierarchical synchronization and modularization of tasks. The collabora-tion with creative professionals, though, involves turbulence, ambiguity, and ongoing "redistribution of improvisation rights" (Weick 1998: 549). Collaboration with creative suppliers mimics organizational features of (jazz) improvisation, a "prototype organization" designed to maximize innovation (Hatch 1999). Improvisation implies a rotation of leadership during performance and a deliberate interruption of habit patterns. In the same way as jazz bands vary their composition of players, ties of agencies with suppliers are reconfigured from time to time around a relatively stable set of core relationships. This variance in composition reflects, on the one hand, the demand for a project-specific set of skills; on the other hand, collaborative ties with suppliers are also deliberately interrupted or terminated for the sake of freshness. New team members hold the promise of new ideas (Grabher 2001: 367–9; see also Perretti and Negro 2007).

Corporate groups: product vs. client-centered affiliation

The knowledge practices, more and more, are molded by corporate groups into which the ecologies increasingly become tied. In the cumulative ecology the importance of corporate groups is immediately obvious through the presence of truly global software brand names like SAP, Oracle, or Microsoft. Beyond direct ownership, smaller firms are often tied to corporate groups through license agreements which primarily refer to the client-specific adaptations of the product portfolio of the large corporations in the context of recurrent projects. License agreements typically aim at generating feedback from the front line of application projects to the refinement of corporate tools and the further evolution of the product portfolio. This continuous inflow of corporate methods, standards, and tools yields positive reputation effects through which for instance the label "Oracle approved" facilitates access to additional clients.

The significance of the large corporate domain in the disruptive ecologies is far less perceptible, and deliberately so. Since affiliation of London advertising agencies with the three leading global communication groups, Interpublic, Omnicom, and WPP, often is limited to financial control, these ownership links provide only comparatively narrow channels through which corporate tools and cultures diffuse into the ecology and project experience is fed back into the corporate group. Although corporate groups, like WPP for example, set up "knowledge communities" which share non-confidential insights and case-study evidence (WPP Group Navigator 2008), the scope for post- and cross-project learning within the corporate network is considerably smaller, not least due to the pronounced variety of agency cultures within these federated groups.

Whereas the corporate groups in the cumulative ecology crystallize primarily around products, they evolve around clients in the advertising ecologies. In advertising, for instance, the key rationale is to provide clients with a "one-stop" service on a global scale and in a cross-disciplinary fashion including the entire spectrum of communication services, ranging from classical advertising to direct marketing, sponsorship, PR, to design service. For software firms the involvement with a group encompasses both the range of modules and the portfolio of skills; for advertising agencies group affiliation only broadens the spectrum of skills from which to compose core teams whereas the transfer of modules within the corporate group is restricted by the imperative of originality.

Although the backing of a corporate group facilitates the acquisition of global clients, the association with a "Wall Street behemoth" degrades creative reputation in the disruptive ecologies conspicuously. For the creatives, the "hearts," the efficiency-driven manuals and standardized corporate toolkits inevitably thwart the creative process which demands distance not only from client interference but also from the uniform corporate principles of the "suits" (see also Pratt 2006).

PERSONAL NETWORKS: COMMUNALITY AND CONNECTIVITY VS. SOCIALITY

Epistemic communities are built around actual organizational networks that represent the "plumbing" of the project ecologies (see also Podolny 2001; Owen-Smith and Powell 2004). Each project prompts a reconfiguration of the "pipes" through which resources are conveyed to achieve the specific project aim. Project ecologies however also comprise personal networks that endure and stretch out beyond the manifest pattern of the actual production networks. Although these more latent personal ties can be activated to solve specific problems in the actual project (Starkey, Barnatt, and Tempest 2000; Söderlund, Vaagaasar, and Andersen 2008) they more typically remain in the project background and provide lasting support for the individual members in multiple ways.

In the disruptive and cumulative ecologies members seem to rely on personal networks that systematically differ with respect to their governance principle and their architectures. The proposed differentiation of network types reflects different degrees of social embeddedness (Granovetter 1985) as indicated by the multiplexity of ties (Uzzi 1997; Uzzi and Gillespie 2002). While network communality intricately interweaves private with professional dimensions of social exchange (high multiplexity) and network sociality is dominated by professional agendas that are merely underpinned by private aspects, network connectivity is almost exclusively professionally oriented (low multiplexity). The three network types, phrased differently, range from the socially thick, friendship-like relations of communality to the socially thin, workmate-like relations of connectivity with sociality occupying an intermediate position. The proposed differentiation of network ties is an inductive typology employed to systematize empirical observations and direct further theoretical imaginations on latent personal networks in cumulative and disruptive ecologies (Table 7.1).

Table 7.1 The nature and functions of personal networks in cumulative and disruptive project ecologies

	Communality	Sociality	Connectivity
	Cumulative	Disruptive	Cumulative
Nature of ties	Lasting, intense	Ephemeral, intense	Ephemeral, weak
Social realm	Private cum professional	Professional cum private	Professional
Governance	Trust	Networked reputation	Professional ethos
Contents	Experience	Know-whom	Know-how

Communality: exchanging experience

The notion of communality denotes robust and thick ties that are firmly rooted in personal familiarity and social coherence. Communality appears of higher relevance in the cumulative ecology. The cumulative learning regime translates into comparatively long affiliations with firms which in turn reduce the likelihood that network ties with former colleagues from school and university or with long-term workmates are disrupted by inter-firm and inter-regional mobility. Long-term organizational affiliations and a comparatively strong attachment to the locality engender the evolution of personalized experience-based trust as the chief governance principle. The robust architecture based on common personal experience limits the number of relationships (see also Granovetter 1985; Uzzi 1997), characteristically to between three and six ties in the Munich ecology. The strength of personal ties, however, does not necessarily imply high frequency of interaction. On the contrary, these networks typically can remain dormant over long periods of time and can be reactivated without much social effort.

Since communality is rooted in social coherence rather than in professional identity, the scope for project-specific support is naturally rather limited. Network communality typically provides backing in dealing with personal issues when these ties, for example, are used as a sounding board for contemplating career decisions or discussing conflicts within the core team.

Sociality: acquiring know-whom

In contrast to the strong and lasting relations in communality, the notion of sociality emphasizes ephemeral, yet intense, networking that is primarily driven by professional motivations (Wittel 2001). Sociality represents the archetypical form of networking in the disruptive ecologies. Whereas communality evolves through stability and long-term commitments, sociality is driven by the canonical compulsion of mobility and flexibility. Short project cycles hardly leave time to develop personalized trust based on shared experience, familiarity, or social coherence. Instead, sociality essentially relies on "networked reputation" (Glückler and Armbrüster 2003) as a chief governing principle. In the absence of personal experience with a particular person or firm, project members rely on word-of-mouth judgments of friends or trusted collaborators.

The more complex architecture of network sociality is primarily constructed around professional complementarity. Sociality comprises relationships with practitioners who, potentially, could complement a core team or a supplier network in a future project. Since the private dimension of these ties (such as personal sympathy, affinity to certain hobbies, or joint acquaintances) is primarily seen as instrumental for easing professional agendas it typically remains superficial. Hence, sociality is less limited than communality and involves several dozen to a few hundred ties.

In the disruptive ecologies sociality fulfills indispensable functions. Most importantly, sociality provides critical information of job opportunities for the nomadic project worker as well as on pending accounts, forthcoming pitches, and available cooperation partners (see also DeFillippi and Arthur 1998; Tempest and Starkey 2004; Pratt 2006). The circulating know-whom is not confined to information on mere availability but also refers to generic project skills like reliability and stress tolerance.

Connectivity: upgrading know-how

The concept of connectivity denotes the socially thinnest and culturally most neutral, in a sense, the most weakly embedded mode of networking. Connectivity is relatively distant from the personal realm; relations are almost purely informational. As much the cause as the result of the low level of social embeddedness, connectivity primarily unfolds in virtual forms of interaction while communality and sociality represent predominantly face-to-face modes of networking. These virtual and ephemeral forms of exchange hardly seem to engender personalized trust nor do they unfold the dynamics of networked reputation. Nevertheless, online networks depend on a sort of generalized reciprocity to preserve the collectively accumulated knowledge from excessive free-riding. Under conditions of (close to) anonymous exchange connectivity seems to be governed by professional norms and ethos (see also Grabher and Maintz 2006). Despite the vast extension of the ties, the architecture follows a straightforward construction principle: participation is bound to a certain level of expertise which allows meaningful interaction with other participants. The far-reaching connectivity complements the restricted communality in the cumulative ecology.

While communality provides a sounding board for conveying personal experience beyond the specific project, connectivity yields essential continuing learning processes related to the substance matter of software projects, which is coding. First, particularly in the context of open-source code like Linux, connectivity provides a virtual construction site where code is updated, modified, and repaired, that is, a place where software developers do the actual programming work. Second connectivity is a most effective vehicle for upgrading and reformatting software skills on a day-to-day basis. By stretching out far beyond the knowledge range of the core team and firm, connectivity thus opens up a wide horizon for a continuous further (self-) education and the upgrading of the individual know-how basis (see also Amin and Roberts 2008).

SUMMARY AND DISCUSSION

Inspired by a contextual perspective on projects (Blomquist and Packendorff 1998; Ekstedt et al. 1999; Gann and Salter 2000; Grabher 2002a; Sydow and Staber 2002; Engwall 2003; Brady and Davies 2004; Scarbrough et al. 2003; Söderlund 2004; Davies and Hobday 2005; Frederiksen and Davies 2008; Schwab and Miner 2008), this chapter set out to unfold a conceptual framework for analyzing processes of project-based learning. This framework has been built around the notion of project ecology (Grabher 2002a, 2002b, 2002c, 2004a, 2004b; Grabher and Ibert 2006; Ibert 2004). By consecutively probing into the constitutive layers of project ecologies—the core team, the firm, the epistemic community, and personal networks—the multilayered organizational architecture of project ecologies was revealed. This architecture provides the theoretical template for a comparative exploration of the cumulative and the disruptive ecologies (see Table 7.2).

Starting with the basic organizational layer of the project ecology, the core team represents the elementary learning arena. While the software ecology seeks to facilitate cumulative learning through reducing cognitive distance within the core team, the advertising ecologies cultivate rivalries and maintain cognitive distance between team members to trigger creativity.

By subsequently moving from the core team to the firm, the analysis shifted from learning in the individual project to learning that accrues from the management of project portfolios. In both kinds of ecologies firms reap "economies of repetition" (Davies and Brady 2000) by transferring lessons from individual projects into a firm-specific set of organizational tools, a distinctive culture, and a repertoire of stories. The cumulative ecology, though, in addition benefits from "economies of recombination" that arise from accumulating knowledge into modules that can efficiently be recombined in subsequent projects.

The actual locus of project-specific knowledge production in both kinds of ecology is the epistemic community that extends beyond the firm and involves clients, suppliers, and global corporate groups. Reflecting the different degrees of client involvement, projects in the cumulative ecology might more aptly be described as being performed *with* the client, whereas advertising projects are closer to being realized *for* the client (Girard and Stark 2002). On the level of supplier relations, the contrasting learning logics play out as the opposition between the commonsense "never change a winning team" in the cumulative ecology and the challenge to "always change a winning team" (Mayer 2008: 137) for the sake of freshness in the disruptive ecologies. The increasing affiliation with global corporate groups implies for the cumulative ecology a widening of the portfolio of modules and skills, whereas group affiliation in the disruptive ecologies basically broadens the spectrum of skills from which to compose core teams.

Core team, firm, and epistemic community represent organizational layers that are temporarily tied together for the completion of a specific project. Beyond these temporarily manifest organizational networks, ecologies also unfold a wide and latent though more enduring fabric of personal networks. The cumulative learning mode of the software ecology translates on the one hand into dense, though constrained webs of lasting and intense ties (communality) for the exchange of personal experience; on the other hand into socially thin and vast virtual networks (connectivity) that afford a continuous upgrading of skills and the occasional exchange of specific know-how. The disruptive learning regime that predominates in the advertising ecologies of Hamburg and London, in contrast, favors ephemeral, yet intense variants of networks (sociality). Sociality, suggestive of a commodification of networks, is instrumental for building up know-whom.

The constitutive organizational layers, however, do not only support distinctive dynamics of creating and sedimenting knowledge (as revealed by reading Table 7.2, line by line). Moreover, the two kinds of ecologies differ qualitatively with regard to the relative weight and specific role of the individual layers in the overall architecture of each (as a column-by-column reading of Table 7.2 suggests). Although practices to curb the notorious amnesia of project-based organizing are ingrained in all layers, the firm appears to play a more significant role for knowledge sedimentation in the cumulative ecology. The firm is not only a prime locus of accumulating generic project capabilities, it also affords a chief repository of specific project know-how that is sedimented in modules and products. The firm thus embodies key memory functions in the cumulative ecology (Ibert 2004). In the disruptive ecologies, in contrast, the firm primarily functions as repository of project capabilities whereas the prevailing imperative of originality limits the scope for modularization of project knowledge. In addition, network sociality provides a distributed repository for know-whom that is indispensable for the relentless

Table 7.2 The multilayered architecture of cumulative and disruptive project ecologies

Cumulative ecology	Disruptive ecology
Core team	**Core team**
Reducing cognitive distance	Preserving cognitive distance
Switching roles	Stable roles
Stable teams	Switching teams
Firm	**Firm**
Economies of repetition	Economies of repetition
Tools, culture	Culture, tools
Economies of recombination	Economies of recombination
Modules, products	—
Epistemic community	**Epistemic collective**
Clients	*Clients*
Projects with clients	Projects for clients
Technical lock-in	Personal lock-in
Suppliers	*Suppliers*
Orchestration	Improvisation
Never change a winning team	Always change a winning team
Corporate groups	*Corporate groups*
Product-centered	Client-centered
Portfolio of skills and modules	Portfolio of skills
Personal networks	**Personal networks**
Communality	Sociality
Experience	Know-whom
Connectivity	
Know-how	

rewiring of ties and recombination of teams. In this sense, the repositories of knowledge in the disruptive ecology are located in both the firm and the personal networks.

Regardless of industry-specific differences, the notion of the project ecology seems a useful conceptual template for at least three reasons. First, context and projects are regarded as co-constitutive. The notion thus overcomes the weaknesses of both, traditional approaches of project management and institutional views on organizing. Whereas the former tend to neglect the manifold interactions between project and context at all, the latter tend to privilege, implicitly at least, a one-directional influence of an (a priori given) institutional context onto organizations. The notion of project ecology, similarly to structurationist perspectives (see, for example, Sydow and Staber 2002), puts the accent on the recursive co-production and mutual configuration of project and ecology. Collaboration in projects, for example, might engender a personal network that subsequently provides the basis for a core team in which a follow-up project is anchored. Personal networks, in a sense, are both context and project. The intricate concoction of core team, firm, epistemic community, and personal networks thus repudiates any straightforward categorization into the static dualism of project and context.

Second, the notion of the ecology accentuates diversity. A project ecology not only comprises a diverse ensemble of organizations, communities, and personal networks, indeed, it also signifies a diverse ecology of professional ethos, social logics, organizational principles, and cultures. By deliberately embracing such diversity, the analysis becomes more sensitive to internal tensions and conflicts. Instead of constructing the layers of the ecologies exclusively in terms of neat complementarities, the analytical framework offered here accommodates incoherence. Symptomatically, for example, individual project participants are faced with the challenge of aligning their conflicting loyalties to the project, the firm, and their personal professional aspirations (Grabher and Ibert 2006). The notion of project ecology avoids the functionalism of "best practice" approaches and instead brings to light the hidden costs and paradoxes of the project business (see also Hodgson and Cicmil 2006).

Finally, the notion of project ecologies appreciates the diffuse sphere of networks that outlast the particular project. By appreciating a range of latent ties networks are not only perceived as "pipes" through which resources are conveyed but also as "prisms" through which other members of the ecology are observed and assessed (Podolny 2001). These latent networks moreover epitomize potentiality (Wittel 2001: 71); they sustain contacts to potential future collaborators and keep open information channels that potentially provide access to upcoming project opportunities. The notion of project ecology, taken together, thus could afford a conceptual template that allows us to advance a less functionalist, more differentiated, and dynamic understanding of project embeddedness.

Future directions

Our juxtaposition of cumulative and disruptive ecologies is based on and illustrated with the software ecology in Munich and the advertising ecologies in London and Hamburg. However, we contend that the notion of project ecologies can be usefully applied to explore the multilayered organizational architecture of project-based organizing in different industrial settings (see also Ekstedt et al. 1999: 192; Asheim 2002; Whitley 2006). In our view, research in two fields might be particularly rewarding.

First, the project literature to a considerable degree focused on ecologies that are anchored in firms. The quintessential example is the construction industry that for a long period of time represented the privileged field to study and to conceptualize project organization. The quintessential role of project organization in the construction industry is reflected in the fact that 46 percent of all papers in the *International Journal of Project Management* between 1984 and 1998 were devoted to this industry (Themistocleous and Wearne 2000: 11). Against the background of the enormous upsurge of interest in the creative and cultural industries more broadly, the literature on project organizing has also theoretically engaged with the organizational anatomy of ecologies that are embedded in firms and networks, like feature-film production (for example, Jones 1996; Bechky 2006; Schwab and Miner 2008). Ecologies that basically evolve around networks and in which firms play only a minor role have attracted less attention so far. Possible cases are certain segments of the video-game industry or open-source projects in which latent and more informal layers of a project ecology seem to play an overarching role not just as a passive background but as essential source of personnel, organizational, motivational, and knowledge resources.

Second, project research has accumulated a considerable body of knowledge on the management of single major events (like world exhibitions or world championships) or (infrastructural) mega-projects. This literature often took issue with the managerial practices of coping with the organizational (ir)rationalities of managing complex projects with large numbers of contributors, long time-spans, and/or considerable degrees of technical complexity and interdependence under tight budgetary and time constraints (see, for example, Flyvbjerg, Bruzelius, and Rothengatter 2003; Pitsis et al. 2003; Marrewijk et al. 2008). Contextual views have been rarely employed for this type of projects. In particular, the question of learning from major single or rare events (as diverse as natural disasters, major infrastructural breakdowns, or economic crises) has so far hardly been dealt with in a systematic fashion (for an important exception, see Lampel, Shamsie, and Shapira 2009). The notion of project ecology, we maintain, might be a useful template to explore how actors in such events mobilize resources from personal networks, rely on proven sets of organizations to mobilize knowledge resources and to sediment experience (Cacciatori, Grabher, and Prencipe 2007). The specific challenge in these cases seems not only the mobilization and enactment of a familiar context but to select appropriate contexts that enhance learning beyond the routinized cognitive repertoire and familiar post hoc rationalizations (Lampel, Shamsie, and Shapira 2009).

ACKNOWLEDGEMENTS

This chapter draws on the conceptualization of project ecologies as first published in Grabher 2004b. The authors gratefully acknowledge financial support of the Deutsche Forschungsgemeinschaft (DFG: GR 1913/3).

REFERENCES

AMIN, A., and COHENDET, P. (2004). *Architectures of Knowledge: Firms, Capabilities, and Communities.* Oxford: Oxford University Press.

——and ROBERTS, J. (2008). "Knowing in action: beyond communities of practice," *Research Policy,* 37/2: 353–69.

ANELL, B. (2000). "Managing project portfolios," in R. A. Lundin and F. Hartman (eds.), *Project as Business Constituents and Guiding Motives.* Boston: Kluwer Academic Publishers, 77–88.

ARIUTA, B., SMITH, N., and BOWER, D. (2009). "Construction client multi-projects: a complex adaptive system," *International Journal of Project Management,* 27/1: 72–9.

ASHEIM, B. (2002). "Temporary organizations and spatial embeddedness of learning and knowledge creation," *Geografiska Annaler,* 84(B)/2: 111–24.

BECHKY, B. A. (2006). "Gaffers, gofers, and grips: role-based coordination in temporary organizations," *Organization Science,* 17/1: 3–21.

BILTON, C., and LEARY, R. (2002). "What can managers do for creativity? Brokering creativity in the creative industries," *International Journal of Cultural Policy,* 8/1: 49–64.

BLICHFELDT, B. S., and ESKEROD, P. (2008). "Project portfolio management: there's more to it than what management enacts," *International Journal of Project Management,* 26/4: 357–65.

BLOMQUIST, T., and PACKENDORFF, J. (1998). "Learning from renewal projects: content, context and embeddedness," in R. A. Lundin and C. Midler (eds.), *Projects as Arenas for Renewal and Learning Processes.* Boston: Kluwer Academic Publishers.

BRADY, T., and DAVIES, A. (2004). "Building project capabilities: from exploratory to exploitative learning," *Organization Studies,* 25/9, Special Issue on "Project-Based Organizations, Embeddedness and Repositories of Knowledge": 1601–22.

BROWN, J. S., and DUGUID, P. (1991). "Organizational learning and communities of practice: towards a unified view of working, learning, and innovation," *Organization Science,* 2/1: 40–57.

BRUSONI, S., and PRENCIPE, A. (2001). "Unpacking the black box of modularity: technology, product, and organisation," *Industrial and Corporate Change*, 10/1: 179–205.

CACCIATORI, E. (2008). "Memory objects in project environments: storing, retrieving and adapting learning in project-based firms," *Research Policy*, 37: 1591–601.

——GRABHER, G., and PRENCIPE, A. (2007). "Continuity in project-based organizing: antecedents, artifacts, and adaptiveness," paper presented at the VII. IRNOP Conference, September 19–21, Brighton.

CASPER, S., and WHITLEY, R. (2002). "Managing competences in entrepreneurial technology firms: a comparative institutional analysis of Germany, Sweden and the UK," Working Paper No. 230. ESRC Centre for Business Research, University of Cambridge.

COWAN, R., DAVID, P. A., and FORAY, D. (2000). "The explicit economics of knowledge codification and tacitness," *Industrial and Corporate Change*, 9/2: 212–53.

DAVIES, A., and BRADY, T. (2000). "Organizational capabilities and learning in complex product systems: towards repeatable solutions," *Research Policy*, 29/7–8: 931–53.

——and HOBDAY, M. (2005). *The Business of Projects: Managing Innovation in Complex Businesses and Products*. Cambridge: Cambridge University Press.

DEFILLIPPI, R. J., and ARTHUR, M. B. (1998). "Paradox in project-based enterprise: the case of film making," *California Management Review*, 40/2: 125–38.

DE WAARD, E. J., and KRAMER, E.-H. (2008). "Tailored task forces: temporary organizations and modularity," *International Journal of Project Management*, 26/5: 537–46.

EISENHARDT, K. M. (1989). "Building theories from case study research," *Academy of Management Review*, 14/4: 532–50.

EKSTEDT, E., LUNDIN, R. A., SÖDERHOLM, A., and WIRDENIUS, H. (1999). *Neo-Industrial Organizing: Renewal by Action and Knowledge in a Project-Intensive Economy*. London: Routledge.

ENGWALL, M. (2003). "No project is an island: linking projects to history and context," *Research Policy*, 32/5: 789–808.

FICHMAN, R. G., and KEMERER, C. F. (2001). "Incentive compatibility and systematic software reuse," *Journal of Systems and Software*, 57/1: 45–60.

FLYVBJERG, B., BRUZELIUS, N., and ROTHENGATTER, W. (2003). *Megaprojects and Risk: An Anatomy of Ambition*. Cambridge: Cambridge University Press.

FREDERIKSEN, L., and DAVIES, A. (2008). "Vanguards and ventures: projects as vehicles for corporate entrepreneurship," *International Journal of Project Management*, 26/5: 487–96.

GANN, D. M., and SALTER, A. J. (2000). "Innovation in project-based, service-enhanced firms: the construction of complex products and systems," *Research Policy*, 29/7–8: 955–72.

GERALDI, J. G. (2008). "The balance between order and chaos in multi-project firms: a conceptual model," *International Journal of Project Management*, 26/4: 348–56.

GIRARD, M., and STARK, D. (2002). "Distributed intelligence and organizing diversity in new media projects," in G. Grabher (ed.), "Fragile sector, robust practice: project ecologies in new media," *Environment and Planning: A Theme Issue*, 34/11: 1927–49.

GLASER, B. G., and STRAUSS, A. L. (1967). *The Discovery of Grounded Theory: Strategies for Qualitative Research*. New York: Aldine Publishing.

GLÜCKLER, J., and ARMBRÜSTER, T. (2003). "Bridging uncertainty in management consulting: the mechanisms of trust and networked reputation," *Organization Studies*, 24/2: 269–97.

GRABHER, G. (2001). "Ecologies of creativity: the village, the group, and the heterarchic organisation of the British advertising industry," *Environment and Planning A*, 33/2: 351–74.

GRABHER, G. (2002a). "Cool projects, boring institutions: temporary collaboration in social context," in G. Grabher (ed.), "Production in projects: economic geographies of temporary collaboration," *Regional Studies*, Special Issue, 36/3: 205–15.

—— (2002b). "The project ecology of advertising: tasks, talents and teams," in G. Grabher (ed.), "Production in projects: economic geographies of temporary collaboration," *Regional Studies,* Special Issue, 36/3: 245–63.

—— (2002c). "Fragile sector, robust practice: project ecologies in new media," in G. Grabher (ed.), *Environment and Planning: A Theme Issue,* 34/11: 1903–2092.

—— (2003). "Switching ties, recombining teams: avoiding lock-in through project organization?" in G. Fuchs and P. Shapira (eds.), *Rethinking Regional Innovation and Change: Path Dependency or Regional Breakthrough?* Boston: Kluwer Academic Publishers.

—— (2004a). "Learning in projects, remembering in networks?" *European Urban and Regional Studies,* 11/2: 103–23.

—— (2004b). "Temporary architectures of learning: knowledge governance in project ecologies," *Organization Studies,* 25/9: 1491–514.

—— and IBERT, O. (2006). "Bad company? The ambiguity of personal knowledge networks," *Journal of Economic Geography,* 6/3: 251–71.

—— and MAINTZ, J. (2006). "Learning in personal networks: collaborative knowledge production in virtual forums," Working Paper Series. Columbia University, New York: Center on Organizational nnovation. Available online at: http://www.coi.columbia.edu/workingpapers.html.

GRANOVETTER, M. (1985). "Economic action and economic structure: the problem of embeddedness," *American Journal of Sociology,* 91/3: 481–510.

HANSEN, M. T., NOHRIA, N., and TIERNEY, T. (1999). "What's your strategy for managing knowledge?" *Harvard Business Review,* 77/2: 106–16.

HATCH, M. J. (1999). "Exploring the empty spaces of organizing: how improvisational jazz helps redescribe organizational structure," *Organization Studies,* 20/1: 75–100.

HOBDAY, M. (2000). "The project-based organisation: an ideal form for management of complex products and systems?" *Research Policy,* 29/7–8: 871–93.

HODGSON, D., and CICMIL, S. (2006). *Making Projects Critical.* Basingstoke: Palgrave Macmillan.

IBERT, O. (2004). "Projects and firms as discordant complements: organisational learning in the Munich software ecology," *Research Policy,* 33/10: 1529–46.

ILVARASAN, P. V., and SHARMA, A. K. (2003). "Is software work routinized? Some empirical observations from the Indian software industry," *Journal of Systems and Software,* 66/1: 1–6.

JONES, C. (1996). "Careers in project networks: the case of the film industry," in M. B. Arthur and D. M. Rousseau (eds.), *The Boundaryless Career.* Oxford: Oxford University Press, 58–75.

JURISON, J. (1999). "Software project management: the manager's view," *Communications of the Association for Information Systems,* 2/17.

KNORR CETINA, K. (1981). *The Manufacture of Knowledge.* Oxford: Pergamon Press.

—— (1999). *Epistemic Cultures: How the Sciences Make Knowledge.* Cambridge: Cambridge University Press.

LAMPEL, J., SHAMSIE, J., and SHAPIRA, Z. (2009). "Experiencing the improbable: rare events and organizational learning," *Organization Science,* 20/5: 835–45.

LEHRER, M. (2000). "From factor of production to autonomous industry: the transformation of Germany's software sector," *Vierteljahreshefte für Wirtschaftsforschung,* 69/4: 587–600.

LINDKVIST, L. (2005). "Knowledge communities and knowledge collectivities: a typology of knowledge work in groups," *Journal of Management Studies*, 42/6: 1189–210.

LUNDIN, R. A., and SÖDERHOLM, A. (1995). "A theory of the temporary organization," *Scandinavian Journal of Management*, 11/4: 437–55.

MARREWIJK, A. VAN, CLEGG, S. R., PITSIS, T. S., and VEENSWIJK, M. (2008). "Managing public–private megaprojects: paradoxes, complexity, and project design," *International Journal of Project Management*, 26/6: 591–600.

MAYER, H.-N. (2008). "Mit Projekten Planen," in A. Hamedinger, O. Frey, J. Dangschat, and A. Breitfuss (eds.), *Strategieorientierte Planung im Kooperativen Staat*. Wiesbaden: VS Verlag für Sozialwissenschaften, 128–50.

MEYERSON, D., WEICK, K. E., and KRAMER, R. M. (1996). "Swift trust and temporary groups," in R. M. Kramer and T. R. Tyler (eds.), *Trust in Organizations: Frontiers of Theory and Research*. Thousand Oaks, CA: Sage, 166–95.

NOOTEBOOM, B. (2000). "Learning by interaction: absorptive capacity, cognitive distance and governance," *Journal of Management and Governance*, 4/1–2: 69–92.

NOV, O., and JONES, M. (2003). "Ordering creativity? Knowledge, creativity, and social interaction in the advertising industry," Working Paper, Judge Institute of Management, Cambridge University.

OWEN-SMITH, J., and POWELL, W. W. (2004). "Knowledge networks as channels and conduits: the effects of spillovers in the Boston biotechnology community," *Organization Science*, 15/1: 2–21.

PERRETTI, F., and NEGRO, G. (2007). "Mixing genres and matching people: a study in innovation and team composition in Hollywood," *Journal of Organizational Behavior*, 28/5: 563–86.

PETTER, S. (2008). "Managing user expectations on software projects: lessons from the trenches," *International Journal of Project Management*, 26/7: 700–12.

PITSIS, T., CLEGG, S., MAROSSZEKY, M., and RURA-POLLEY, T. (2003). "Constructing the Olympic dream: a future perfect strategy of project management," *Organization Science*, 14/5: 574–90.

PODOLNY, J. M. (2001). "Networks as pipes and prisms of the market," *American Journal of Sociology*, 107/1: 33–60.

PRATT, A. C. (2006). "Advertising and creativity, a governance approach: a case study of creative agencies in London," *Environment and Planning A*, 38/10: 1883–99.

PRENCIPE, A., and TELL, F. (2001). "Inter-project learning: processes and outcomes of knowledge codification in project-based firms," *Research Policy*, 30/9: 1373–94.

SAPSED, J., and SALTER, A. (2004). "Postcards from the edge: local communities, global programs and boundary objects," *Organization Studies*, 25/9: 1475–89.

SCARBROUGH, H., LAURENT, S., BRESNEN, M., EDELMAN, L., NEWELL, S., and SWAN, J. (2003). "Developing the contextual view of project-based learning: analysis of case-studies," paper presented at the 19th EGOS Colloquium, Copenhagen Business School, July 3–5.

SCHWAB, A., and MINER, A. S. (2008). "Learning in hybrid project systems: the effects of project performance on repeated collaboration," *Academy of Management Journal*, 51/6: 1117–49.

SHELBOURNE, J., and BASKIN, M. (1998). "The requirements for creativity: a director's perspective," in A. Cooper (ed.), *How to Plan Advertising*. London: Cassell/The Account Planning Group, 64–80.

SÖDERLUND, J. (2004). "Building theories of project management: past research, questions for the future," *International Journal of Project Management*, 22/3: 183–91.

——VAAGAASAR, A. L., and ANDERSEN, E. S. (2008). "Relating reflecting and routinizing: developing project competence in cooperation with others," *International Journal of Project Management*, 26/5: 517–26.

STARKEY, K., BARNATT, C., and TEMPEST, S. (2000) "Beyond networks and hierarchies: latent organizations in the U.K. television industry," *Organization Science*, 11/3: 299–305.

SYDOW, J., and STABER, U. (2002). "The institutional embeddedness of project networks: the case of content production in German television," in G. Grabher (ed.), "Production in projects: economic geographies of temporary collaboration," *Regional Studies*, Special Issue 36/3: 215–27.

——LINDKVIST, L., and DEFILLIPPI, R. (2004). "Project-based organizations, embeddedness and repositories of knowledge: editorial," *Organization Studies*, 25/9: 1475–89.

TAXÉN, L., and LILLIESKÖLD, J. (2008). "Images as action instruments in complex projects," *International Journal of Project Management*, 26/5: 527–36.

TEMPEST, S., and STARKEY, K. (2004). "The effects of liminality on individual and organizational learning," *Organization Studies*, 25/4: 507–27.

THEMISTOCLEOUS, G., and WEARNE, S. H. (2000). "Project management topic coverage in journals," *International Journal of Project Management*, 23/1: 1–45.

TURNER, R. J., and MÜLLER, R. (2003). "On the nature of projects as temporary organizations," *International Journal of Project Management*, 21/1: 1–8.

UZZI, B. (1997). "Social structure and competition in interfirm networks: the paradox of embeddedness," *Administrative Science Quarterly*, 42: 35–67.

——and GILLESPIE, J. J. (2002). "Knowledge spillovers in corporate financing networks: embeddedness and the firm's debt performance," *Strategic Management Journal*, 23/7: 595–618.

WEICK, K. E. (1998). "Improvisation as a mindset for organizational analysis," *Organization Science*, 9/5: 543–55.

WHITLEY, R. (2006). "Project-based firms: new organizational form or variations on a theme?" *Industrial and Corporate Change*, 15/1: 77–99.

WITTEL, A. (2001). "Toward a network sociality," *Theory, Culture & Society*, 18/6: 51–76.

WPP GROUP (2008). WPP Group Navigator. http://www.wpp.com/wpp/.

PART III

STRATEGY AND DECISION-MAKING

CHAPTER 8

THE P-FORM CORPORATION

CONTINGENCIES, CHARACTERISTICS, AND CHALLENGES

JONAS SÖDERLUND

FREDRIK TELL

INTRODUCTION

To a great extent the attractiveness of projects lies in their capacity to integrate diverse knowledge bases and expertise. This capacity has become increasingly important as industries and firms turn to business models involving "complex product systems" and "integrated solutions," which require R&D initiatives and implementation efforts to span across knowledge domains and organizational boundaries. Such developments have led firms to explore the use and value of projects as a key feature of their organizational design and growth trajectories. In that respect, projects are not only measures for integrating knowledge from diverse sources, but they also allow for low-cost and flexible resource commitments (Sydow, Lindkvist, and DeFillippi 2004).

The advent of projects as a key feature in organizational practice has attracted researchers to investigate a broad range of issues. Previous literature exploring the nature of project-based organizations/firms can be grouped into three themes (see also Davies and Frederiksen 2010): (1) "single project firms," typically mega-projects carried out by multi-firm consortia, inter-organizational collaboration where the primary focus is on the single project that is formed and dissolved for its own sake, (2) "project-led organizations," organizations that operate internally to supply the firm with new knowledge, services, and products, typically found in the R&D part of the corporation (Hobday 2000), and (3) project-based firms, i.e. firms that earn their income from selling and delivering projects and complex systems to external clients, and that are often found in industries like construction, power systems, telecommunication, consulting, and media.

Our contention in this chapter is to discuss these latter project-based firms, i.e. firms that operate as permanent organizations and carry out their main activities in projects and where projects are the primary so-called "unit of production." We want to demarcate such firms both from "single project firms" that—in their entirety—are composed for the execution of a specific task and then dissolve, as well as from those firms where projects are of significant importance but not the primary unit of production. We thus align with Hobday (2000) and Whitley (2006) and their general analyses of project-based firms as having unique and specific properties. Accordingly, this chapter is concerned with Mintzberg's (1979) "operating adhocracy" and so-called "Type 1 firms" that "carry out projects directly on behalf of clients, delivering to the external market..." (Keegan and Turner 2002: 370). Such firms are common in the EPC (Engineering, Procurement, and Construction) industries and in complex product systems industries (Hobday 1998), but we also find them in, *inter alia*, the advertising, software engineering, consulting, and media sectors. The common denominator is that they are all involved in complex problem-solving, integrating knowledge from different areas of expertise with high degrees of output singularity (Whitley 2006). This forces the firms to continuously reconfigure their units of production to fit the specific needs at hand. In several ways, due to technology development, many project-based firms have undergone changes to harness an increasing amount of complexity, drawing upon a multitude of knowledge bases and sub-systems to produce their outputs. This development has made systems, organizational, and knowledge integration increasingly important and difficult matters.

One of the main arguments in this chapter is that this kind of firm has received scant attention in previous research. This is especially true considering the much-researched M-form (multi-divisional form) corporation, investigated by Chandler (1962). The M-form is a popular topic in the strategy literature and frequently used to understand the growth of large industrial enterprises, internationalization trajectories, and corporate diversification (see for instance Bartlett and Ghoshal 1993; Collis, Young, and Gould 2007; Galan and Sanchez-Bueno 2009). However, despite the many reports that projects constitute significant organizational pillars and that "projects" to some extent play a similar role as the one played by "divisions" in the

M-form, the "project-form" (P-form) characteristics have not been explicitly addressed and examined in previous research. (In this chapter, we are particularly concerned with formal organizational structures, hence we use the "-form" annotation. Such a choice naturally excludes analysis of important facets of project-based organizing, but hopefully the chosen focus facilitates clarity in exposition.) For this reason, this chapter builds further on the research on project-based firms including Hobday (2000), Gann and Salter (1998), Lindkvist (2004), and Whitley (2006), to conduct a comparison between the M-form and the P-form. Thus, we engage in the three primary questions to explore the nature of P-form corporations: (a) where do we find them (i.e. under what contingencies do they operate), (b) how do they look (i.e. what are their significant characteristics), and (c) what are their problems (i.e. what challenges are associated with their implementation and operation)?

To answer these questions, the chapter is structured in the following way. In the next section we compare the P-form corporation with the M-form corporation. The focus will be on a selected number of contingencies and structural characteristics that are particularly important if we are to address the specific challenges of P-form corporations. A central tenet in our argument is that the P-form corporation enhances idiosyncratic learning and accumulation of capabilities through mechanisms of simplification and the facilitation of temporally and locally constrained, but interdisciplinary, learning (Levinthal and March 1993). The main argument is that the P-form corporation allows for "temporary decentralization" in the problem-solving activities of the firm (Siggelkow and Levinthal 2003). Therefore, in the final part of the chapter, we focus specifically on temporary decentralization and some of its challenges as applied in the P-form corporation. The chapter ends with suggestions for future research.

THE P-FORM CORPORATION
AND THE M-FORM CORPORATION

In historical analyses formal organizations have been discussed in terms of managerial hierarchies (Chandler and Daems 1980). In Chandler's (1962, 1990) analysis, the M-form had a profound role in the explanation of growth and capability-building in large corporations from the 1920s until the 1970s. Previously, investments in the hierarchies of the unitary form (U-form) enabled American companies in the late nineteenth century to exploit advantages of general technologies, standardization of operations, and the emergence of mass markets. Essentially, the U-form centered on grouping units according to functions (Walker and Lorsch 1968) to exploit the economies of specialization and scale associated with such organizational forms. With the increasing proliferation of markets, the M-form came to supplant the

U-form. The prime reason was that the division into (semi-) autonomous units, governed by central headquarters, allowed for the utilization of related diversification strategies complementing economies of scale with economies of scope. Thus an important rationale underpinning the M-form was still so-called "economies of throughput" requiring substantial investments in fixed capital equipment for the manufacturing of high volumes and subsequent low unit cost (Nightingale et al. 2003). Chandler (1962) documented the emergence of organizational structures with divisions operating on distinct product markets as a common response to growth requirements and market and technology segmentations. Hence, divisions, which not only catered for local responsiveness but also alleviated administrative burdens at corporate headquarters, were the fundamental cornerstones of M-form corporations. The M-form idea was presented as an ideal type as it incorporated the divisionalization and decomposition of companies to promote the evolution of managerial and leadership capabilities. It generally paved the way for an elaborate understanding of large businesses, their growth, and core capabilities.

To respond to the empirical realities and challenges of large enterprises, writers have argued for the need to move beyond conventional images of the M-form corporation. An important argument in this line of research is that the M-form corporation is less effective in making use of its knowledge and core capabilities (Chandler 1990; Prahalad and Hamel 1990). For instance, Hedlund (1994) suggests that some of the drawbacks of the M-form are associated with its strong focus on division, permanent structures, top management, vertical communication, and hierarchy. Hedlund's critique also applies to firms that largely depend on projects for their ongoing operations, something which calls, among other things, for cross-functional integration, horizontal communication, and temporary structures.

It is important to complement the conventional idea of large corporations and consider the role that projects have played for growth potentials and the enhancement of organizational capabilities. There are two reasons for this standpoint. First, many large corporations have relied heavily on utilizing the P-form to manage their operations. For instance, in a study of Asea Brown Boveri (ABB), one of the global leaders in power transmission systems, Söderlund and Tell (2009) highlight the fact that project managers and project directors played a fundamental role in the growth of the company since the 1950s. Of importance to ABB's international expansion were hundreds of "global project managers" who had the responsibility to supply leadership capabilities and handle integration efforts across divisions. Nevertheless, many analyses of companies similar to ABB—a company highly dependent upon large-scale engineering projects—frequently downplay the role of projects as organizational forms and of project managers as important "agents" in the capability-building process. Second, many growth industries are project based (Sydow, Lindkvist, and DeFillippi 2004; Davies and Hobday 2005). In these industries, corporate divisions play a less significant role. Instead, projects in different shapes and sizes often fill the need for "division" in fast-paced environments (Eisenhardt and

Brown 1997). In project-based firms, corporate strategy tends to assume temporary features, which favor the use of "temporary systems" as significant organizational cornerstones. In this respect, exploring the contingencies, characteristics, and challenges of the P-form corporation may improve the analysis of the differences between two fundamental organizational ideal types (M-form and P-form) and address some of the challenges in both mature and non-mature project-based industries.

CONTINGENCIES OF THE P-FORM CORPORATION

What then are the differences between the P-form and the M-form corporation with regards to their contingencies and situational factors? In outlining the analysis, we begin in Table 8.1 by depicting some contingencies that are conspicuous candidates for being the causes for the emergence and sustainability of the P-form corporation in comparison with the M-form. Generally, these contingencies focus on the situations where we find P-form corporations, particularly in terms of market environment, technological interdependence, mode of production, and

Table 8.1 Contingencies of P-form and M-form corporations

Contingencies	P-form corporation	M-form corporation
Market conditions	Differentiated and dynamic	Differentiated and stable
Output type	Customized products, systems and services	Standardized products sold in diverse markets
User involvement	High degree of user involvement in the innovation process	Low degree of user involvement in the innovation process
Time-orientation	Deadline-focused	Continuous
System of production	Unit production and small batch	Large batch and mass production
Economic rationale	Economies of system	Economies of scale and scope
Technology type	Engineering (and non-routine)	Routine
Primary type of interdependencies	Reciprocal interdependence	Pooled and sequential interdependencies
Nature of tasks	Heterogeneous, infrequent, causally ambiguous	Homogeneous, frequent, causally non-ambiguous
Dimensions of knowledge specialization	Breadth and depth	(Breadth and) depth
Problem character	Nearly and non-decomposable	Decomposable

economic rationale. Below, we review each of these contingencies and compare them across the P-form and M-form corporation, respectively. The analysis is inspired by Hedlund (1994) and Söderlund and Tell (2009) and provides an extension of their ideas.

We first recognize the organizational environment and especially the importance of market conditions for organizational adaptation. Mintzberg's (1979) synthesis of structural contingency theory recognizes two dimensions of market conditions as influencing organizational design. The first dimension deals with market dynamics (dynamic/stable) and the second dimension concerns market differentiation (high/low). While the M-form primarily emerged as a response to increased differentiation and proliferation of markets (utilizing economies of scope by utilizing complementary assets, see Teece 1980), each self-contained division was also designed to reap economies of scale and efficiencies in clearly defined market segments where the rate of change could be more or less planned for. In contrast, when markets are both differentiated and dynamic, there is a need for innovation and recombination of knowledge and competencies in order to meet new consumer preferences, as well as to proactively induce new demand. When products are highly customized or made-to-order (rather than made-to-stock and with pre-defined specifications) this calls for swift combination and integration, for instance, of components and services to deliver tailor-made solutions. This is typically the case in the production of "client projects" or "business projects" where specific offerings of product–service combinations are made to customers. Such customization and intense customer involvement in the innovation and delivery process are common in project production, including complex products and systems and IT systems implementation (Hobday 1998). Unlike the contingencies of standardization and arm's-length transactions with customers typical for M-form corporations, increased user–producer interactions and complex offerings, paired with a wide range of customer "options," generally point to the possible benefits of accruing organizational forms that support the rapid integration of multiple specialized knowledge bases. In these respects, the M-form and P-form differ sharply.

Time orientation is another important contingency factor where differences are observed. The P-form seems appropriate in situations characterized by tight deadlines and clear objectives (Lindkvist, Söderlund, and Tell 1998). The logic is one of a "paced" environment which requires an organization that is able to partition time into discrete events and respond accordingly. This can be contrasted to the continuous "learning-curve logic" of M-form corporations that economize on high continuous throughput and scale and scope effects (Chandler 1990). As elaborated by Nightingale et al. (2003), contexts where such economic rationales for the M-form prevail can also be juxtaposed with cases characterized by instances of so-called "economies of system" where performance is improved "by increasing the utilization of a fixed amount of installed capacity, over a given period of time, even when the scale, scope and speed of production are constant" (Nightingale et al. 2003: 479).

Economies of system can be utilized when firms are able to learn more about the interacting properties of systems and can, for example, develop technical control systems that better utilize an infrastructure as a whole. Such learning necessitates the multi-disciplinary organizational interaction which is one of the trademarks of project organizing.

Woodward (1965) investigated the relationship between technology (understood as systems of production) and organizational form. To classify technology, she used the terminology of "small batch and unit production," "large batch and mass production," and "process production." She contended that these three groups of technologies were associated with amplified rates of technical complexity (Woodward 1965: 40–4), and found that organic organizational forms (Burns and Stalker 1961: 121–2) such as those found in adhocracies and project-based organizations are more aligned with small batch and unit production, while on the other hand mechanistic organizational forms were more fit in large batch and mass production (Woodward 1965: 64). Extending this analysis, Perrow (1970) developed a typology based on task variability (high/low) and task analyzability (high/low). Task variability refers to the number of exceptions encountered when conducting a specific task, while task analyzability denotes the extent to which search activities are required in solving problems associated with performing the task. Based on this distinction, we suggest that P-form corporations are appropriate in situations where task variability is high, although task analyzability may differ across P-form corporations (cf. Lindkvist, Söderlund, and Tell 1998). In addition, technology considerations arise because of the interdependencies involved in the production process. Using the terminology developed by Thompson (1967), we can distinguish contingencies characterized by "reciprocal interdependencies" where all the elements in the production process are dependent on each other. Such a situation calls for mutual adjustment of the organizational members involved, something which is often facilitated through interdisciplinary project teams with experts from different areas of expertise found in P-form corporations. Correspondingly, the M-form corporation draws upon its ability to cater for the "pooled interdependence" among divisions with regard to the organizational headquarters and to those staff functions used in common, but at the same time exploits sequential interdependencies in the production process of the divisions.

In furthering the analysis of the P-form corporation and its particular technological and knowledge-related difficulties, Zollo and Winter (2002) single out three distinct task features. According to these authors, these features influence the extent to which knowledge is articulated and codified in the organization. They suggest that due to the cognitive investments required, knowledge articulation and codification will be found in contexts characterized by task heterogeneity, task infrequency, and task causal ambiguity. These are task features typically associated with P-form corporations with their unique output, low procurement frequency, and difficulties to standardize processes. Moreover, Brusoni, Criscuolo, and Geuna (2005) suggest that firms producing complex products and systems require both breadth and depth of knowledge. While we agree with this proposition in general, we also argue that these requirements operate in both the M-form and the P-form corporation. A more fine-grained analysis can, however, be obtained by considering the so-called "system-relevant problem character" and the specific problem-solving strategy at hand. Using the terminology developed by Simon (1962), we distinguish between three kinds of problems: decomposable, nearly decomposable, and non-decomposable. The problem-solving strategy in the M-form corporation is one of decomposing "problems" into separate units that are denoted divisions, where one can rely on depth (specialization), in particular with regard to the distinctive environmental conditions prevailing in that specific unit. However, as argued by Simon (1996: 198): "(1) In a nearly decomposable system the short-run behaviour of each component sub-system is approximately independent of the short run behaviour of the other components; (2) in the long run the behaviour of components depends in only an aggregate way on the behaviour of the other components." In situations where system properties are nearly decomposable, there is a need to develop organizational designs that can account both for specialization and depth, as well as for sufficient breadth to be able to take into consideration effects on the overall system (Yakob and Tell 2009). Based on this analysis, we suggest that the P-form corporation exhibits certain characteristics that make it a potent candidate for solving so-called "nearly decomposable problems" and "non-decomposable problems" (Siggelkow and Levinthal 2003; Nickerson and Zenger 2004).

As evidenced in the above comparative analysis, the P-form and M-form corporations differ on important grounds. They typically operate in quite different environmental and organizational conditions. These conditions, we argue, have fundamental effects on the way the corporation ensures the supply and maintenance of organizational capabilities—what capabilities are critical and what difficulties are associated with capability-building in the two organizational ideal types discussed here. To address these challenges, we will first explore further the characteristics of each ideal type.

CHARACTERISTICS OF THE P-FORM CORPORATION

In this section, we focus on the structural characteristics that are needed to cope with the contingency factors discussed above. In particular, we center on the unit of production, the grouping principle, the type of communication and capabilities, and the decision structure.

A fundamental issue in organization theory relates to the question whether organizational units should be grouped by product/market or function (Walker and Lorsch 1968). The classic functional organization focuses on function as the main design feature and thereby the advantages of economies of scale. One of the novelties introduced in the M-form corporation was the idea of dividing by product/market, facilitating intra-unit coordination at the expense of scale, while at the same time utilizing economies of scale and scope through centralized functions. Similar to the matrix structure, the P-form corporation relies on a concurrent grouping by product/market and function, as projects are often defined in terms of product or market outcomes, but draw upon organizational members located in, or at least affiliated with, functional departments. This cross-disciplinarity conjoint with a product/market focus allows for the exploitation of economies of scale and specialization, while at the same time providing a mechanism for organizational coordination and integration.

In the P-form corporation, communication is characterized by horizontal/lateral linkages between organizational members, resembling the network structures found by Burns and Stalker (1961) in their analysis of organic structures. In contrast, the M-form corporation is characterized by vertical information and communication flows between headquarters and divisions as well within the divisions (Hedlund 1994). In Table 8.2 below, we outline some of the structural characteristics of the P-form corporation in contrast to those of the M-form corporation.

As touched upon earlier, the M-form corporation draws upon a particular type of knowledge specialization, namely the one related to certain products and markets. Within each division, knowledge is integrated to produce specific goods that serve designated markets, but there is no support for knowledge integration across divisions (Prahalad and Hamel 1990). In contrast, the P-form corporation, with its strong emphasis on cross-functional work and the organization of expertise in designated projects, can generally be conceived as a solution for combining and integrating differentiated and complex knowledge (Grandori 2001). Thus, the P-form corporation generally supports the evolution of "combinative capabilities" (Kogut

Table 8.2 Characteristics of P-form and M-form corporations

Characteristics	P-form corporation	M-form corporation
Production unit	Project	Division/business unit
Grouping principle	Market and function	Market
Communication	Horizontal	Vertical
Capabilities	Knowledge specialization and integration	Knowledge specialization
Decision structure	Temporarily decentralized	Partially decentralized

and Zander 1992) and arenas for "knowledge integration" (Grant 1996), in which both the specialization and integration of knowledge are considered to be critical (Lindkvist 2005).

Another conspicuous characteristic of the M-form corporation is its ability to draw upon the partial decentralization of strategic decisions from corporate head-quarters to division managers, while still relying on centralized functions, such as R&D and marketing. This follows from the assumption that product markets can be clearly distinguished and managed autonomously. There are two important ramifications of decentralization for the subsequent analysis. First, decentraliza-tion suggests that decision-making is disaggregated to sub-units. Second, when choices regarding activities can be grouped together in separate units, so that inter-dependencies with other sub-units are mitigated, the overall design problem for a firm can be denoted as "decomposable" (Simon 1962).

The structural characteristics of P-form corporations focus on the two variables of decentralization of decision-making (distribution of decision rights) and the decom-posability of problems (decision problems). In light of the notion of temporary decentralization, projects represent new "activity configurations" to decompose deci-sion-making and search problems. In Siggelkow and Levinthal's framework, an organi-zational structure is decentralized when "decision making has been disaggregated into a number of subunits, or divisions, each making its own decisions" (2003: 651). In con-trast, a centralized organizational structure is characterized by decision-making being placed only at the firm level as a whole. Following this framework, firms are conceptu-alized as systems of interdependent activities, and accordingly, projects are conceptual-ized as temporary systems of interdependent activities. This implies that the degree and pattern of interactions among the activities is critical for the analysis of why firms turn to projects as a solution to an organizational problem. If the problem that the firm is facing can be grouped in a way that allows for all interactions to be captured within separate units or divisions, and no interdependencies exist across divisions, the overall decision problem that the firm is facing is "decomposable." However, as is well known from empirical research, many organizational and managerial problems are far from decomposable. For instance, in the case of P-form corporations, there are a number of examples of the challenges to decomposition and decision rights to individual projects. These include the sharing of resources, long-term maintenance responsibilities, cross-project communication, and marketing activities that need to be coordinated across projects. As a result, "if interactions among a firm's activities are non-decomposable, neither a decentralized nor a permanently decentralized organizational structure leads to high performance" (Siggelkow and Levinthal 2003: 652). In such situations, an organ-izing principle with temporary decentralization and subsequent reintegration yields the highest long-term performance, a principle which summarizes some of the funda-mentals of the P-form corporation.

In Siggelkow and Levinthal's (2003) analysis of temporary decentralization, organizational structure is essentially a matter of the distribution of decision rights.

Decision rights could be seen as being either centralized or decentralized. As in the case of the creation of (permanent) divisions in the M-form corporation, (temporary) projects in general can be conceived of as a decentralization effort into new departmental forms. This is the classic case of the so-called "tiger team" and "autonomous team" structure discussed in innovation and product development literatures (Clark and Fujimoto 1991). As organizational solutions, they allow for low-cost experimentation that does not necessarily pose the same threat to vested interests that is often associated with the creation of permanent organizations, such as divisions, functional departments, or business units (Sydow, Lindkvist, and DeFillippi 2004: 1475). As argued by Lindkvist, Söderlund, and Tell (1998), organizing activities in projects may then generally be seen as a way to decouple activities and organizational processes from the rest of the organization. In that respect projects as an organizational form are similar to other kinds of decentralization and departmentalization efforts, although we are here dealing with a particular kind of decentralization endeavor, since there are essential temporalities involved.

Like other kinds of departmentalization arrangements, projects have the potential to produce a simplification by more or less severing relationships and interactions; a cut-off that makes it possible to handle existing problems within the limited cognitive abilities given to man (Levinthal and March 1993). Such simplification seems critical, given the mounting complexity apparent in many contemporary projects with a number of specialists, technologies, and sub-systems involved. Thus, projects may reduce (and in some situations even allow for) the escape of complexity, which would trigger action and improve the possibilities to learn from experience and integrate across knowledge bases. This learning is made possible thanks to a narrowness of focus on the specific project targets at hand. To focus on a particular client, deadline, budget, quality, and similar targets typically associated with project management, is something which simplifies things, and, as is well known from theories of learning, simplicity and focus are fundamental principles to be able to learn from experience. However, what *ceteris paribus* will result is "local learning" that has a number of advantages, but, which also comes at certain costs and risks. The obvious advantage is the focus and the possibility to reap the benefits of economies of system. In this respect, cross-functional and team-based units such as projects also provide opportunities of "exploratory jumps" because of the inherent possibilities to recombine complementary knowledge of specialists (Levinthal and Warglien 1999). In line with Allen (1995), the costs depend on the rate of change of disciplinary knowledge development—high disciplinary knowledge development would mean that people involved in a project run the risk of losing specific expertise since they are not "connected" to their home base and may miss out on the latest technologies, innovations, and ideas within their respective disciplinary domain. The other risk relates to the decentralization effort as such, as it may lead to a general disconnection between overall organizational goals and decisions made within the decentralized unit. In the area of project management this has been referred to as a problem of drifting and that projects tend to "go away" (e.g. Clark and Fujimoto 1991). In the P-form corporation markets and external clients play an important part. However, clients can work in two very different directions with regard to the project: to trigger the drift (require adjustments, change specifications, or push for decisions that give priority to short-term matters) or to control the drift (delimit decision opportunities for project managers, control progress according to preset plans, etc.).

Decision problems in the P-form corporation generally concern system complexity and interdependencies. Accordingly, decision problems are fundamental for the understanding of projects and project organizing. As stated earlier, the guiding parameter is whether this organizational problem can be treated as decomposable, nearly decomposable, or non-decomposable, corresponding to an increasing degree of complexity (Nickerson and Zenger 2004). Previous works within the knowledge-based theory of the firm highlight the creation of interdependencies to generate new knowledge (Grant 1996). Where knowledge complexity and differentiated knowledge bases abound, team-based knowledge integration in cross-functional projects is generally seen as a viable organizing mechanism (Grandori 2001). Hence, projects are not only ways to solve decision problems in a Simonian way, but also about making interdependencies come about. In the latter case, the development of knowledge integration capabilities is a central feature, which is one explanation for why so many P-form corporations distinguish activities such as systems integration, project management, and complex problem-solving as their core competence (Davies and Hobday 2005; Söderlund 2005).

The complexity of broad-scale integration common in projects also creates more profound causal ambiguities and higher barriers against imitation. A key management task in the P-form corporation, besides the facilitation and stimulation of mechanisms for the integration of specialist knowledge, is therefore the ongoing improvement of the architecture of organizational capabilities (Grant 1996). If firms are conceived as adaptive systems, then organizational design becomes a task of structuring the interdependencies involved. A fundamental problem here is how to exploit past experience and at the same time explore new opportunities (March 1991; Levinthal and Warglien 1999). This problem is summarized by Siggelkow and Levinthal:

Perspectives differ, however, on the suggested organizational structure to manage this process. On one hand, firms need to search broadly for new activity configurations. On the other hand, firms need to coordinate across their interdependent activities to avoid misfits and instability. While the call to balance search and coordination has been well understood, there is still little known about how different organizations structures moderate this balance. (Siggelkow and Levinthal 2003: 651)

P-form corporations could then be viewed as operating on two distinct organizational levels, one being the project level (the temporary system/team/organization) and the other the firm level (the permanent system/firm/corporation). These organizational levels work jointly in the development and evolution of the firm.

New ideas and new challenges are dealt with in temporary systems and learning from experience is transferred to the permanent system. Adaptation is thus not primarily a matter for the individual project, but rather a property of populations of temporary systems/projects, i.e. at the firm level. Therefore, the firm adapts through a selection among "non-adaptive, efficient and legitimate" temporary systems (March 1995: 434). The P-form corporation tries to sort out the problem of exploitation by launching yet another new organization to respond to the new challenges, meaning that one project is replaced by another project. As March (1995: 434) argues, in such contexts "organizations lose important elements of permanence."

Hitherto most studies on project-based organizations have argued that the choice of using projects as an organizational form is contingent upon increasing environmental complexity or because problem-solving/tasks have become more complex and require the integration of a diverse set of specialist skills, knowledge bases, and sub-systems (see for instance Hobday 2000). In other words, projects are used to match the external environmental contingencies; to guarantee flexibility and responsiveness. However, in our version, which draws on the idea of adaptation in changing environments, projects are not only a mechanism simply to match external complexity, but also an organizational design mechanism to structure and manipulate interdependencies (Levinthal and Warglien 1999). This idea is also evident in the research on time-pacing by Eisenhardt and Brown (1997), which indicates the importance of time-based control and so-called "semi-structures" in highly complex situations. A typical case here is the setting of fixed deadlines and time-critical contracts with serious consequences involved—measures that have significant effects on the pacing of organizational activities.

Despite its temporary nature, a key rationale of the P-form corporation resides, somewhat paradoxically, in its capacity to benefit from permanent activities, be it search activities, the generation and identification of new opportunities/projects, decentralization efforts, or the reintegration of results and local learning. If not, then, in line with Whitley (2006), the P-form corporation would have few possibilities of creating a sustainable competitive advantage. Thus in such cases, the P-form corporation would only function as "little more than an administrative convenience" (DeFillippi and Arthur 1998: 137) without capabilities to deal with industry volatility. The effect would eventually become "enterprise failure" (ibid.) or at best a "precarious project-based firm" (Whitley 2006).

The P-form corporation is based on a capacity to achieve efficiency at the project level and to manage adequate explorations among its total set of projects. What is important here is the continuous stream of "mutant organizations," i.e. the creation of related variation in the portfolio of projects carried out by the firm. In other words, a P-form corporation would strive towards "having families of sequentially related projects" (DeFillippi and Arthur 1998: 126). In this regard, P-form corporations may function as sustainable, adaptive systems only if there is a reliable process for generating new projects that differ from existing ones but which equally take advantage of the possible combinations of previous learning in executed projects. This creates opportunities for differentiated search as well as the reintegration and recombination of knowledge. In other words, P-form corporations are particularly appropriate in contexts where problems are non-decomposable and nearly decomposable, although establishing and managing of organizational forms under such circumstances poses a set of significant challenges.

CHALLENGES FOR THE P-FORM CORPORATION

In the previous sections, we examined the contingencies and characteristics of the P-form corporation. The analysis of characteristics centered on the project as the basic production unit, organizational grouping according to market and function, and the centrality of horizontal communication and knowledge integration. We also emphasized the distinctive characteristic of the P-form corporation as pertaining to temporary decentralization—a theoretical lens we argue is important for analyzing the advantages and disadvantages of P-form corporations, something which also might enhance the understanding of when and where to organize activities by projects (see Söderlund 2004).

Advantages of the aforementioned P-form characteristics include flexible resource commitment and the general ability to solve complex problems adapted to distinctive circumstances. Inherent in the combination of these characteristics are also, of course, a set of challenges. As earlier mentioned, Zollo and Winter (2002) classify task features into causal ambiguity (complexity), heterogeneity, infrequency. Firms operating through projects score high on all these features and many of the challenges arise out of the way they are designed to deal with complexity in problem-solving situations, the autonomy and heterogeneity of projects and inter-temporal considerations associated with the frequency of projects. We suggest that these three challenges all are related to a fourth challenge of reintegration and recombination. In the following, we emphasize these four challenges: (1) decomposition, (2) temporary decentralization, (3) time orientation, and (4) reintegration.

Challenge 1: decomposition

The first challenge addressed arises as a consequence of the P-form corporation relying on decomposition in complex problem-solving situations. Just like any other organizational effort aimed at simplification (cf. Levinthal and March 1993), project organization "decouples" activities from their environment and puts autonomous groups in charge of pre-specified tasks. The P-form corporation at the operational level then ignores interdependencies for a while which might be beneficial for long-term performance (Siggelkow and Levinthal 2003: 664). Such decomposition into projects with explicit goals, task structures, and deadlines creates opportunities for in-depth learning and problem-solving within projects. Moreover, projects may also be regarded as "knowledge collectivities" (Lindkvist 2005) that mirror overarching organizational interdependencies. In that respect, projects constitute an important solution in a world of nearly decomposable systems, particularly as they make it possible to break away from current routines and practices. Due to their interdisciplinary and temporary character, projects may alleviate the local myopia generally associated with organizational simplification, specialization, and communities of practice. Instead of only promoting knowledge-based similarity, which is an important feature of functional specialization and communal knowledge development, organizing by projects implies less longevity in relationships among homogeneous organizational members. However, decomposition comes at a cost. Just like any other organizational practice, projects may lead a life of their own. As discussed in Sapsed and Salter (2004), these organizations run the risk of creating "balkanized project practices" as projects are distributed in the organization. Consequently, among the main challenges for project-based organizations, suggested by for instance Prencipe and Tell (2001), are learning across projects and between projects and the organization.

Challenge 2: temporary decentralization

The second challenge for P-form corporations is derived from the temporary decentralized distribution of decision rights. Not only is the P-form corporation a decomposition response to the cognitive challenge of problem-solving, but it also introduces market-based governance structures in the sense that as project objectives are fairly clearly established, there are opportunities for creating incentive structures associated with the attainment of project goals. Given that projects and project managers are granted substantial autonomy in making decisions about how to attain project goals, management can assess this behavior on the basis of project outcomes. As discussed by Nonaka and Takeuchi (1995) such project autonomy facilitates knowledge creation, as decentralization and performance-based control induce opportunities for variation in organizational behavior. Challenges for management may however arise out of the use of temporary decentralization and, correspondingly, temporary centralization. Two of the ramifications of temporary decentralization pertain to what to decentralize/centralize and when to decentralize/centralize. The former issue relates to the content and jurisdiction of autonomy distributed to projects and project managers. The latter issue points to the difficulty in finding the right time to diffuse authority to projects and when to withhold decision rights and adhere to more centralized rules and directives (as, for instance, in the promulgation of standardized project management models).

Challenge 3: time orientation

The third challenge draws upon the previous, and centers on time orientation and deadlines. First, and in line with the underlying rationale of decomposition and decentralization, the P-form corporation is largely driven by the underlying control of time and deadlines. As discussed in the literature on project management, the distinctive feature of projects compared to other organizational forms is the dead-line—and the fact that projects are "intentionally temporary." This is also apparent in the idea of temporary decentralization. This has some important effects. As suggested by Gersick (1995), a deadline tends to produce a kind of rationalistic break that breaks the spell—that tells the individuals to think for themselves. Such breaks can produce strategic rethinking and reflective means–ends analyses. In such situations, time-based control mechanisms, and thereby project organizing, tend to replace bureaucratic principles and the "logic of appropriateness" with the more project-oriented "logic of consequentiality" (March and Olsen 1989). However, taking into account the inter-temporal features of project-based learning processes, it may be suggested that the infrequency of projects constitutes a problem for the P-form corporation (Prencipe and Tell 2001), especially from the perspective of routine development and experience accumulation. If each project in a P-form corporation represents an infrequent (and rare) event in which project members were able to think in novel ways, the challenge for the firm thus lies in maintaining the memory of that rare event. However, there is also a challenge pertaining to the temporality of P-form corporations. Not only may the firm forget rare events, but just as there are difficulties regarding the commonality across separated and decentralized projects, there is a "timing" issue with respect to the "global time" of the firm and to how individual projects relate to this global time (Söderlund 2002). Just as pacing needs to be matched in particular projects, time needs to be harmonized in the firm as a whole.

These three challenges demonstrate the consequences of decomposition, temporary decentralization, and time orientation associated with the P-form corporation. Taken together, these challenges illustrate a common theme, namely that of balancing exploration and exploitation (March 1991). In short, while the P-form may be conducive to the former, there may be a lack of consideration for the latter. In line with this reasoning, Brady and Davies (2004) suggest that project-based firms such as Ericsson and AT&T build capabilities by organizing for a sequence of moving from initial exploration activities to subsequent exploitation activities. However, the so-called "economies of repetition" and "repeatable solutions" are ongoing difficulties in the P-form corporation (Davies and Brady 2000).

Challenge 4: reintegration

The fourth challenge for P-form corporations complements Brady and Davies's (2004) somewhat linear way of framing the problem. Instead, we propose that the challenge is more generally in knowledge recombination and reintegration, and more specifically in temporality. As such, the challenge of reintegration is a consequence of the three challenges discussed above, as it highlights company-wide integration across projects separated in terms of problem focus, authority, and time. While organizing by projects may create impediments to organizational learning in the sense of exploiting repetitive experience among organizational members, it has been argued that the more market-like processes of participation in projects by organizational members, guided by a strong project goal and specific time limits, foster the utilization of new knowledge combinations. The establishment of a "developed mind" in project teams in the sense of "knowing who knows what" rather than "knowing what everyone else knows" (cf. Lindkvist 2005) is a critical issue here. Thus, utilizing such strong complementarities between knowledge bases is an important trait of knowledge integration (Enberg, Lindkvist, and Tell 2006). But how can such "project features" be mirrored at the organizational level where projects are distributed in terms of knowledge, decision rights, and temporality in the organization?

This challenge goes back to Siggelkow and Levinthal's (2003) original notion of temporary decentralization. We argue that this notion is instructive—although possibly somewhat misleading—in the context of P-form corporations. We argue that one of the main potentials of the concept lies in the way it highlights not decentralization, but *temporary* decentralization. While the challenge of decentralization is well known and also illustrated in our discussion above, the main challenge for P-form corporations lies precisely in the management of the temporality of decentralization. The timing of decentralization vs. centralization suggests that P-form corporations need mechanisms for "pacing" the organization vis-à-vis the projects (cf. Eisenhardt and Brown 1997).

In sum, P-form corporations in their ideal form may have unique opportunities to balance the dilemma of exploration and exploitation. Projects are decoupled from organizational rules and routines to focus on a particular problem, be it tailor-made designs or client interactions. Such decentralization effort and decomposition of tasks normally come with managerial authority to respond to opportunities that are associated with complexity reduction. This tends to lead to local problem-solving, local search, and situated learning processes. As discussed earlier, one consequence is the difficulty of transferring local knowledge for use in other contexts. What is significant in this case is the role of strategy and management to create synergies across the family of projects and the development and sustainability of core competences needed to reap the benefits of previous learning. Thus, P-form corporations must develop core competencies that make them more than merely an "administrative convenience" and a "financial portfolio" of separate projects. This would stress the importance of good general management if efficiencies at the system-wide and top level of the firm are to be reaped. Of course, management at the project-level is a critical issue; however to deal with market dynamics and industry volatility, managing the P-form corporation is much more than the management of individual projects.

CONCLUDING REMARKS

One might ask whether the P-form is replacing or complementing the M-form, whether they can exist together or whether they are conflicting. In large organizations, it is most likely that the M-form will coexist with the P-form as there is a need to create separate business areas and divisions, and where the P-form corporation exists within the M-form. This was evident in ABB, where both M-form and P-form characteristics played an important role in the evolution of the company (Söderlund and Tell 2009). Still, the permanent division would then need to be "strong enough" for cross-divisional work not to be necessary and so that the permanent guideline can be established without too many and frequent changes needed. There is a fundamental difference between the two forms—the strength and permanence of decentralization—if it is not possible to create such permanence, then organizations may opt for the P-form despite having contingencies that would speak in favor of the M-form logic.

In this chapter, we focused on the challenges related to local search and learning, temporary decentralization, time orientation, and system-wide transfer of knowledge. In the analysis put forward, the project process was depicted as a process of temporary decentralization and ensuing reintegration. The "temporary system" as such is controlled by a set of organizing mechanisms, including time limits and project goals which delineate the boundaries of the temporary system—within these boundaries, a decentralized knowledge process can evolve adapted to local needs and priorities. A general concern would then be the boundaries surrounding this temporary system. In the suggested analysis, boundaries at the project level are fundamental for handling adaptation at the firm level; boundaries that cut off interdependencies with the rest of the environment and the parallel projects. In other words, decentralization would lead to an ignorance of interdependencies, yet simultaneously allow for the bundling of interdependencies at the project level.

The aim of this chapter has been to pinpoint the contingencies, characteristics, and challenges of the P-form corporation. The ensuing analysis very much echoed problems and features tied to temporary decentralization. We believe temporary decentralization is an important idea that carries with it both managerial and theoretical implications. This kind of analysis also seems fitting in times when it has become difficult to predict the future, to set out plans that will hold and formulate valid scenarios and permanent decentralization measures that will exist for more than a few months. Given the significance of temporary decentralization based on deadlines as control mechanisms, we would assume that deadlines have a significant role in P-form corporations, not only for purposes of control but also for "strategic reflection," cooperation modes, and system-wide efficiencies. Besides this "deadline mentality," temporary decentralization and project organization typically also involve some kind of logic of "temporary organizing" (Goodman and Goodman 1976; Lundin and Söderholm 1995) where new people are brought in and current project members leave to be able to solve unique problems and achieve system-wide efficiencies. In other words, P-form corporations curb problems of "group longevity" (Katz 1982), which can have positive effects on individuals' external awareness and creativity (Skilton and Dooley 2010). In that respect, the P-form corporation is able to escape some of the problems associated with the stylized version of the M-form corporation. However, it would need to make sure that people have some kind of "common knowledge" to be able to establish cooperation and coordination procedures, build swift trust, and communicate efficiently (cf. Meyerson, Weick, and Kramer 1996).

To conclude this chapter, we argue that there are several important research openings lying ahead in the analysis of the nature and dynamics of P-form corporations:

- *The nature of P-form corporations.* This calls for a closer examination of different types of P-form corporations and the variations across industries and institutional contexts. Drawing on Whitley (2006), a starting point would be to make a distinction in terms of their singularity and the stability and separation of work roles. This speaks in favor of a closer examination of the institutional setting in which P-form corporations operate: how can P-form corporations be developed and sustained despite institutional drivers and factors that seem to hinder their development?
- *The formation of P-form corporations.* This involves questions associated with the history and early evolution of P-form corporations and relates to the drivers of external contingencies and how firms respond to such requirements, for instance with increasingly differentiated and dynamic markets. In that respect, we can think of firms with two very different trajectories: one that is founded in line with the P-form characteristics, and one that is primarily molded in a different form, be that U-form or M-form logics, which gradually adopts characteristics resembling the P-form corporation. The question would then be tied to the path dependencies of firms and the possibilities to bring about P-form corporations, despite routines and capabilities that would drive the organization in a different direction.
- *The growth of P-form corporations.* This builds on work within the capability literature that has specifically addressed the importance of "project capabilities" and "project competence" (Söderlund 2008). How are core competences developed in the P-form corporation, what core competences are critical, and how does their

criticality vary over time? How do project-level capabilities match firm-level capabilities? How do P-form corporations build leadership capabilities at different levels and how do these different levels work together to build sustainable P-form corporations that are able to deal with technological discontinuities and radical innovation? What specific growth problems are related to rigidities in the P-form corporations? Are there limits to the scalability of the size of P-form corporations?

REFERENCES

ALLEN, T. J. (1995). "Organization and architecture for product development," Working Paper, MIT Sloan School of Management.

BARTLETT, C., and GHOSHAL, S. (1993). "Beyond the M-form: toward a managerial theory of the firm," *Strategic Management Journal*, 14: 23–46.

BRADY, T., and DAVIES, A. (2004). "Building project capabilities: from exploratory to exploitative learning," *Organization Studies*, 25/9: 1601–21.

BRUSONI, S., CRISCUOLO, P., and GEUNA, A. (2005). "The knowledge bases of the world's largest pharmaceutical groups: what do patent citations to non-patent literature reveal?" *Economics of Innovation and New Technology*, 14/5: 395–415.

BURNS, T., and STALKER, G. M. (1961). *The Management of Innovation*. London: Tavistock.

CHANDLER, A. D. (1962). *Strategy and Structure: Chapters in the History of Industrial Enterprise*. Cambridge, MA: MIT Press.

——(1990). *Scale and Scope: The Dynamics of Industrial Capitalism*. Cambridge, MA: The Belknap Press of Harvard University.

——and DAEMS, H. (eds.) (1980). *Managerial Hierarchies: Comparative Perspectives on the Rise of the Modern Industrial Enterprise*. Cambridge, MA: Harvard University Press.

CLARK, K. B., and FUJIMOTO, T. (1991). *Product Development Performance: Strategy, Organization and Management in the World Auto Industry*. Boston: Harvard Business School Press.

COLLIS, D., YOUNG, D., and GOULD, M. (2007). "The size, structure and performance of corporate headquarters," *Strategic Management Journal*, 28: 383–405.

DAVIES, A., and BRADY, T. (2000). "Organisational capabilities and learning in complex product systems: towards repeatable solutions," *Research Policy*, 29: 931–53.

——and FREDERIKSEN, L. (2010). "Project-based innovation: the world after Woodward," in *Technology and Organization: Essays in Honour of Joan Woodward*. Research in the Sociology of Organizations Series.

——and HOBDAY, M. (2005). *The Business of Projects: Managing Innovation in Complex Products and Systems*. Cambridge: Cambridge University Press.

DEFILLIPPI, R. J., and ARTHUR, M. B. (1998). "Paradox in project-based enterprise: the case of film making," *California Management Review*, 40/2: 125–39.

EISENHARDT, K. M., and BROWN, S. L. (1997). "The art of continuous change: linking complexity theory and time-paced evolution in relentlessly shifting organizations," *Administrative Science Quarterly*, 42/2: 1–34.

ENBERG, C., LINDKVIST, L., and TELL, F. (2006). "Exploring the dynamics of knowledge integration: acting and interacting in project teams," *Management Learning*, 37/2: 143–65.

GALAN, J. I., and SANCHEZ-BUENO, M. J. (2009). "The continuing validity of the strategy-structure nexus: new findings 1993–2003," *Strategic Management Journal*, 30: 1234–43.

GANN, D., and SALTER, A. (1998). "Learning and innovation management in project-based, service-enhanced firms," *International Journal of Innovation Management*, 2/4: 431–54.

GERSICK, C. (1995). "Everything new under the gun: creativity and deadlines," in C. M. Ford and D. A. Gioia (eds.), *Creative Action in Organizations*. Thousand Oaks, CA: Sage.

GOODMAN, R. A., and GOODMAN, L. P. (1976). "Some management issues in temporary systems: a study of professional development and manpower—the theater case," *Administrative Science Quarterly*, 21/3: 494–501.

GRANDORI, A. (2001). "Neither market nor identity: knowledge-governance mechanisms and the theory of the firm," *Journal of Management and Governance*, 5: 381–99.

GRANT, R. M. (1996). "Toward a knowledge-based theory of the firm," *Strategic Management Journal*, 17, Special Issue: 109–22.

HEDLUND, G. (1994). "A model of knowledge management and the N-form corporation," *Strategic Management Journal*, 14: 73–90.

HOBDAY, M. (1998). "Product complexity, innovation and industrial organisation," *Research Policy*, 26: 689–710.

——(2000). "The project-based organization: an ideal form for management of complex products and systems?" *Research Policy*, 29: 871–93.

KATZ, R. (1982). "The effects of group longevity on project communication and performance," *Administrative Science Quarterly*, 27/1: 81–104.

KEEGAN, A., and TURNER, J. R. (2002). "The management of innovation in project-based firms," *Long Range Planning*, 35: 367–88.

KOGUT, B., and ZANDER, U. (1992). "Knowledge of the firm, combinative capabilities and the replication of technology," *Organization Science*, 3/3: 383–97.

LEVINTHAL, D., and MARCH, J. G. (1993). "The myopia of learning," *Strategic Management Journal*, 14, Special Issue: 95–112.

——and WARGLIEN, M. (1999). "Landscape design: designing for local action in complex worlds," *Organization Science*, 10/3, Special Issue: Application of Complexity Theory to Organization Science: 342–57.

LINDKVIST, L. (2004). "Governing project-based firms: promoting market-like processes within hierarchies," *Journal of Management and Governance*, 8/1: 3–25.

——(2005). "Knowledge communities and knowledge collectivities: a typology of knowledge work in groups," *Journal of Management Studies*, 42/6: 1189–210.

——SÖDERLUND, J., and TELL, F. (1998). "Managing product development projects: on the significance of fountains and deadlines," *Organization Studies*, 19/6: 931–51.

LUNDIN, R., and SÖDERHOLM, A. (1995). "A theory of the temporary organization," *Scandinavian Journal of Management*, 11/4: 437–55.

MARCH, J. G. (1991). "Exploration and exploitation in organizational learning," *Organization Science*, 2/1: 71–87.

——(1995). "The future, disposable organizations and the rigidities of imagination," *Organization*, 2/3–4: 427–40.

——and OLSEN, J. P. (1989). *Rediscovering Institutions: The Organizational Basis of Politics*. New York: Free Press.

MEYERSON, D., WEICK, K. E., and KRAMER, R. M. (1996). "Swift trust and temporary groups," in R. H. Kramer and T. R. Tyler (eds.), *Trust in Organizations*. Thousand Oaks, CA: Sage.

MINTZBERG, H. (1979). *The Structuring of Organizations*. New York: Prentice Hall.

NICKERSON, J., and ZENGER, T. (2004). "A knowledge-based theory of the firm: the problem-solving perspective," *Organization Science*, 15: 617–32.

NIGHTINGALE, P., BRADY, T., DAVIES, A., and HALL, J. (2003). "Capacity utilization revisited: software, control and the growth of large technical systems," *Industrial and Corporate Change*, 12/3: 477–51.

NONAKA, I., and TAKEUCHI, H. (1995). *The Knowledge Creating Company*. New York: Oxford University Press.

PERROW, C. (1970). *Organizational Analysis: A Sociological Review*. Belmont, CA: Wadsworth.

PRAHALAD, C., and HAMEL, G. (1990). "The core competence of the corporation," *Harvard Business Review*, May–June: 79–91.

PRENCIPE, A., and TELL, F. (2001). "Inter-project learning: processes and outcomes of knowledge codification in project-based firms," *Research Policy*, 30: 1373–94.

SAPSED, J., and SALTER, A. (2004). "Postcards from the edges: local communities, global programs and boundary objects," *Organization Studies*, 25/9: 1515–34.

SIGGELKOW, S., and LEVINTHAL, D. A. (2003). "Temporarily divide to conquer: centralized, decentralized, and reintegrated organizational approaches to exploration and adaptation," *Organization Science*, 14/6: 650–69.

SIMON, H. (1962). "The architecture of complexity," *Proceedings of the American Philosophical Society*, 106/6: 467–82.

——(1996). *The Sciences of the Artificial*, 3rd edn. Boston: MIT Press.

SKILTON, P., and DOOLEY, K. (2010). "The effects of repeat collaboration on creative abrasion," *Academy of Management Review*, 35/1: 118–34.

SÖDERLUND, J. (2002). "Managing complex development projects: arenas, knowledge processes and time," *R&D Management*, 32/5: 419–30.

——(2004). "Building theories of project management: past research, questions for the future," *International Journal of Project Management*, 22/3: 183–91.

——(2005). "Developing project competence: empirical regularities in competitive project operations," *International Journal of Innovation Management*, 9/4: 451–80.

——(2008). "Competence dynamics and learning processes in project-based firms: shifting, adapting and leveraging," *International Journal of Innovation Management*, 12/1: 41–67.

——and TELL, F. (2009). "The P-form organization and the dynamics of project competence: project epochs in Asea/ABB, 1950–2000," *International Journal of Project Management*, 27: 101–12.

SYDOW, J., LINDKVIST, L., and DEFILLIPPI, R. (2004). "Project-based organizations, embeddedness and repositories of knowledge: editorial, special issue," *Organization Studies*, 25/9: 1475–89.

TEECE, D. (1980). "Economics of scope and the scope of an enterprise," *Journal of Economic Behavior and Organization*, 1: 223–47.

THOMPSON, J. D. (1967). *Organisations in Action*. New York: McGraw-Hill Book Company.

WALKER, A. H., and LORSCH, J. W. (1968). "Organizational choice, product versus function," *Harvard Business Review*, November/December: 129–38.

WHITLEY, R. (2006). "Project-based firms: new organizational form or variations on a theme," *Industrial and Corporate Change*, 15/1: 77–99.

WOODWARD, J. (1965). *Industrial Organization: Theory and Practice*. London: Oxford University Press.

YAKOB, R., and TELL, F. (2009). "Detecting errors early: management of problem-solving in product platform projects," in A. Gawer (ed.), *Platforms, Markets and Innovation*. Cheltenham: Edward Elgar.

ZOLLO, M., and WINTER, S. G. (2002). "Deliberate learning and the evolution of dynamic capabilities," *Organization Science*, 13/3: 339–51.

CHAPTER 9

IMPLEMENTING STRATEGY THROUGH PROJECTS

CHRISTOPH LOCH
STYLIANOS KAVADIAS

PROJECT MANAGEMENT: STRATEGY SHAPING OR EXECUTION?

The linguistic root of the word *project* is the Latin word *projectum*, which means "something that is thrown forward." This word suggests a forward-looking emphasis more than a tactical execution emphasis. Although many of the tools of project management were developed in the early US missile programs like Polaris, closer examination suggests that the Polaris program revolved much more around strategic choices than around project management techniques. In 1955, the Navy's Fleet Ballistic Missile (FBM) program aimed to "get a share of the ballistic missile 'pie'" (Spinardi 1994: 25): Admiral Burke believed that "the first service that demonstrates a capability for this is very likely to continue the project and others may very well drop out" (1994: 26). The result was a clear prioritization of schedule over cost and specifications. (Indeed, the first two deployed versions of the Polaris missile had less than the desired range and explosive capacity.) The specifications were carefully differentiated from the competing Air Force systems, emphasizing the destruction of urban centers with limited required accuracy—as opposed to the Air Force's goals of destroying hardened targets, which required less power but more accuracy (1994: 34).

Even the PERT (Program Evaluation and Review Technique, a formal planning method developed by Polaris) served less for improving project control than for "offering technological pizzazz that was valuable in selling the program....The image of managerial efficiency helped the project. It mattered not whether parts of the system functioned or even existed; it mattered only that certain people for a certain period of time believed that they did" (Spinardi 1994: 36). In summary, the operational definitions, priorities, actions, and even "efficiency" itself were repeatedly changed and subordinated to the Navy's strategic organizational goal: securing resources in competition with the Air Force.

This strategic dimension, however, has diminished within the project management (PM) discipline. Project management has shifted towards a focus on the execution of projects, assuming (usually) a "written in stone" mission and externally set goals (see Chapter 1 in this book). For example, the Project Management Institute's *PMBoK Guide* (PMI 2004) defined PM as the application of knowledge, skills, tools, and techniques to project activities in order to meet or exceed stakeholder needs and expectations from a project. This involves balancing competing demands among scope, time, cost, and quality, and among stakeholders with differing needs and expectations, including identified requirements (needs) and unidentified requirements (expectations) (PMI 2004). Similarly, the definitions of two representative textbooks (Kerzner 2003: 3; Meredith and Mantle 2003: 9) exclude decisions about a project's scope from the definition of project management.

Thus, the historical evolution of project management contains a hint of irony: although the Polaris program is widely cited as having made an important contribution to the birth of project management, the discipline has divorced itself from the strategic types of action that drove the success of the Polaris development.

Recently, this "narrowing down" has begun to reverse. Several scholars have called for improving the link between project management and strategy. Morris (2006) characterized project definition and an appropriate embedding of the project in its environment as the "most important drivers of success." Artto and Dietrich (2004) summarized project portfolio tools as a way of strategic management of projects. New textbooks devote space to the discussion of how projects are (or should be) embedded in strategy (cf. Pinto 2006); even the "conservative" PMI *PMBoK Guide* (PMI 2004) has begun to acknowledge that "projects are often utilized as a means of achieving an organization's strategic plan," and that projects are "authorized as a result of...strategic considerations" (2004: 7).

Thus, the realization is growing that projects fail not only because of incompetent execution, but also, and frequently, because of a muddled strategic context, inadequate scope, or unarticulated—and thus unresolved—tensions and/or trade-offs among the project stakeholders (see Morris 2006 and Chapter 1 in this book). This realization has a straightforward message: project managers could benefit a great deal from expanding their activity to account for strategy alignment and organizational enablers.

In this chapter, we propose that this view, although a step forward, still decouples project management from strategy-making. It implies that the business people set the outcomes and charter, and project management executes. Yet, this view misses the fact that strategy is not made only "at the top" and then cascaded down. In a world of increasing uncertainty, volatility, and interdependence across forms, industries, and countries, strategy is emergent; it has to adjust to events as they occur (Mintzberg 1978). Strategy is therefore top down as well as bottom up. The discipline of project management cannot retreat and say, "We accept that we need to be informed about strategy so we can implement it better, but we leave the big decisions to the big people!" Project management should raise its sights to a higher-impact role by participating in strategy formulation itself.

Top-down and bottom-up contribution
of projects: search theory

Challenging organizational problems require complex projects to achieve a solution. The literature has abstracted them as optimizations of complex functions—(bold symbols stand for vectors) (Loch and Terwiesch 2007; Mihm, Loch, and Huchzermeier 2003; Rivkin and Siggelkow 2003):

$$\text{Max}_x P(x,a)$$

In this abstract formula, the vector x represents a set of decision variables. For example, building a new iron-ore-reduction facility demands designing thousands of components grouped in hundreds of sub-systems, for which design parameters must be set. Thus, the vector $x = (x_1, \ldots, x_n)$ might consist of tens of thousands of variables. The function P represents the performance metric considered for the particular project (e.g. financial, technical, reputation). It represents the causal effects of the variables—for example, whether a variable increases or diminishes performance, and the interactions among the x_i's. The shape of P could be influenced by a multitude of exogenous parameters, denoted by the vector a, that are not under the control of the project management team. These parameters may change over time in possibly unforeseeable ways (for example, a change in customer needs because of an economic change in a downstream industry, material characteristics, or a regulatory change). In principle, P maps every element of the set of problem solutions $\{x\}$ to a real number (usually a dollar value) that can be used to perform comparisons. The choice of the "right" metric reflects the major dimensions of industry competition. Figure 9.1 summarizes this abstract representation of a project.

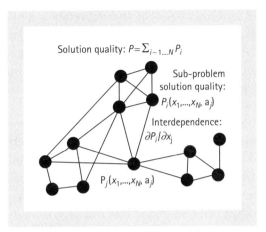

Fig. 9.1 A complex problem with interdependent sub-problems

The variables that determine the project performance may "interact in non-sim-
ple ways [such that] given the properties of the parts and the laws of their interactions, it is not a trivial matter to infer the properties of the whole" (Simon 1969: 195).
Then the performance landscape that results from the mapping P is *rugged*; that is,
it exhibits *many local maxima*. (A *local maximum* is a solution x from which no
small deviation along any decision x_i offers an improvement.) When the performance function P is rugged, local search through small modifications cannot find the
global optimum, the overall best solution. In addition, the different decision variables, x_i, may require various domains of expertise to assess them and meaningfully
choose new values. Typically, no "mastermind" holds all these competences and
understands the overall performance function P well enough to be able to "optimize" on all dimensions (Kavadias and Sommer 2009).

As a response to such problem-solving challenges, organizations typically resort
to two main search strategies: (i) the distribution of the necessary tasks across multiple actors (delegation and distributed problem-solving) and (ii) the establishment
of iterative processes that enhance the ability to quickly find a better (according to
the given metric) solution.

Search is usually distributed across many actors, because the deep knowledge
about sub-problems and components is held by specialists (Simon 1969; Loch and
Terwiesch 2007). In our formal abstraction, the overall performance P results from
"smaller" pieces: $P=\sum_i P_i(x_1, \ldots ,x_N, a_i; d)$. Each sub-problem P_i is delegated to an
actor i, such as a sub-team or a specialized subcontractor. The parameter vector d
represents repeatedly executed analyses, tests, component designs, management
coordination activities, etc., which are institutionalized in formally established
"rules" (also known as processes) that ensure effectiveness at the organizational
level (Nelson and Winter 1982). For example, subcontractors are often subject to

detailed contractual agreements about the deliverables and specifications that ensure their proper contribution towards the overall performance. Well-known processes, such as the project life cycle (or the corresponding stage gate process in product development projects), are precisely this: institutionalized sets of rules that dictate how to proceed towards a solution, that is, the steps from a current solution x to a new one y.

Processes are also needed to ensure coordination and/or communication given that sub-problems usually depend on one another (represented by the interdependence lines with cross-partial derivatives in Figure 9.1), and thus organizations consist of more or less tightly coupled groups (Cyert and March 1963).

In summary, search theory characterizes project work as a sequence of successive iterations of sub-problem trial solutions that converge towards a system solution. For such complex projects, search theory has produced relevant insights:

- Senior management does not perform detailed problem-solving. Sub-problem (component, module) decisions should be delegated down to the lowest possible level, along with the right front-line problem-solving structure (Rivkin and Siggelkow 2003; Mihm et al. 2010).
- Senior management channels and checks the solutions produced at the front line for their contribution to overall performance: it sets in place the necessary structures (sub-team communication and coordination mechanisms, alignment checks between lower-level solutions and top-level priorities, and deadlock-resolution rules). Top management needs to empower; over-control from the top reduces the quality of the solutions produced (Rivkin and Siggelkow 2003).

Thus, search theory suggests an effective allocation of decision rights when it comes to project management tasks: since senior management *does not know* what the right execution decisions are, these decisions need to be taken at the front line, with full knowledge of the operational context. However, senior managers do have the oversight to determine what the right performance metrics are, and to identify effective institutionalized processes and rules—these, of course, are also subject to modifications and emerging changes as the environment shifts and the organization learns. In other words, there exists a second search process that happens in parallel at the senior management level. This top management search process constrains the operational (project-level) search process, but is itself changed by the operational-level results as they produce learning about effectiveness in an evolving environment. Through these two interlocking search processes, top-down and bottom-up management are intertwined, and they need to be considered simultaneously.

A body of theory is available to characterize and understand the two search processes, namely *hierarchically nested evolutionary cycles*, as in evolutionary biology and anthropology (Sober and Wilson 1999; Boyd and Richerson 2005). We summarize this view with our terminology in Figure 9.2 (adapted from Loch and Kavadias 2007).

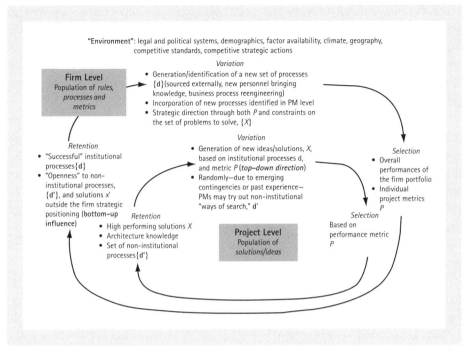

Fig. 9.2 Two-level evolutionary view of projects in the organization

Figure 9.2 shows two levels of search processes, or evolutionary cycles, each consisting of the three stages of evolution: variation, selection, and retention to the next generation. The lower-level operational cycle operates *at the project manager level*. This is where "content" problem-solving occurs: novel solutions are created for problems facing the organization, through "creative" (partially random) idea combinations from differing areas of expertise and knowledge, shaped and constrained by the institutional process above it. The transformation of ideas into outcomes (products or production processes), is well known to exhibit the evolutionary steps of creative search, namely idea generation, selection (based on pre-determined metrics that reflect the strategic objectives), and retention in artifacts or prototypes, or even through an explicit technology database (e.g. Hargadon and Sutton 1997; Thomke 2003; Fleming and Mingo 2007).

At the higher level in Figure 9.2, we find the institutionalized processes and routines that govern project work and reflect "the way the organization does things." Such processes may arise within the organization in ways that are not always fully conscious (Nelson and Winter 1982). They may emerge from trials within existing projects (a bottom-up effect) or arise from the imitation of outside benchmarking examples or professional practices. Processes are selected by their performance, which is often difficult to measure (success is stochastic and causally ambiguous and can be assessed only in the long term), so selection is noisy. It does happen in organizations that processes are chosen or eliminated based on spurious outcomes, after assigning erroneous causal links. Processes that are "selected out" may be officially discontinued or fall into disuse, but processes also have strong inheritance persisting over time.

The two levels of evolution interact: the lower level "makes up" the higher level (e.g. the process landscape of the firm is made up by the practices within the projects), and in turn, the structure of the higher level influences the creation, selection criteria, and inheritance of the lower level. The levels may contradict one another: what is adaptive at the lower level may not be adaptive for the higher level (Sober and Wilson 1999: 27). At the same time, the bottom-up interactions between the two processes depend heavily on the "openness" of senior management to allow successful practices to "bubble up" from the lower ranks of the organization, integrate them, and eventually shape its subsequent direction and performance.

Figure 9.2 highlights two key implications: progress accumulates iteratively, not by executing toward a fixed and well-known goal, and strategy-making and project execution are one system and must be managed in an integrated way. These implications echo previous observations about the differences between *induced* and *emergent* strategy (Mintzberg 1978; Burgelman 1991). Therefore, projects are more than mere "aligned mechanisms to execute strategy"; they need to play an integral part in "strategy-finding."

In the remaining two sections, we first present widely used tools for strategy-cascading and project alignment, and then we provide an overview of (necessary but less widely used) tools that help to use projects as strategy-making devices.

LINKING BUSINESS STRATEGY AND PROJECT EXECUTION: TOP-DOWN CASCADING TOOLS

Several tools and methods allow project managers to create and maintain the link between strategy and project execution. Here, we briefly present three distinct categories of tools that have proven useful in practice: (1) strategy-cascading tools, which facilitate translation of the business strategy into specific project objectives; (2) project portfolio diagrams, which facilitate the explicit identification of trade-offs during the allocation of resources across projects and also enable more accurate valuation of individual projects; and (3) formal tools for influencing stakeholders and negotiating, which facilitate the identification and negotiation of friction points during project execution. No specific tool gives "an answer" (in the sense of an optimization algorithm). Tools help to establish a common language within an organization, a language that consistently articulates the relationship between operational goals and strategic objectives. This allows actors to exchange information efficiently and to act in a coordinated fashion.

Strategy-cascading

We present three strategy-cascading tools: the ratio tree, the balanced scorecard, and Markides' five-questions strategy framework.

The first tool is the *financial ratio tree* developed in 1985 by Richard Foster and colleagues. It draws on the famous DuPont financial ratio tree developed by F. D. Brown, a DuPont engineer, as early as 1914. The elegant idea is that the firm's key financial return on investment (from R&D) can be broken into a "technical performance" part and a "commercialization" part. Technical progress is measured by improvements in operating performance (e.g. product features, or process efficiency or quality) and commercialization success by returns (e.g. market share and price earned) from a given offering (see Figure 9.3).

The R&D return tree is an elegant conceptual tool that contributes to a clear understanding of cause and effect, especially in conceptually separating the entangled effects of R&D versus commercial activities. Although it is well known and

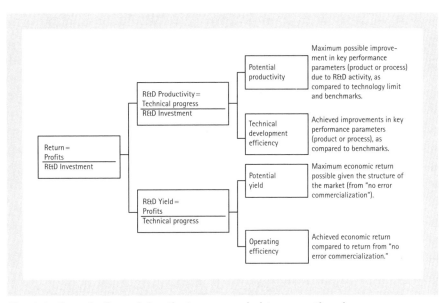

Fig. 9.3 Generic financial ratio tree cascaded to operational measures

Source: Adapted from Foster et al. (1985).

often cited, it is only rarely used because (a) the measures are very difficult to obtain (and easily the subject of endless interpretation battles), and (b) its complexity mounts as one expands the tree to more and more operational measures.

The second tool is the widely used *balanced scorecard* (see Figure 9.4) introduced by Kaplan and Norton (1996, 2000). It evaluates a (sub)organization's activities according to financial, customer, business process, and "learning" or competence-building goals. The scorecard offers a comprehensive summary of four types of organizational goals, and it allows for the possibility of breaking them down to lower levels of the organization.

The balanced scorecard tool has two key limitations. First, due to the "generic" nature of the sets of criteria (financial, customer, processes, and learning), the tool very easily reverts into a standardized measure mechanism. In principle these criteria should be adjustable, but in practice they often become standardized (as in "best practices" of customer and process metrics, which end up being just the ones most commonly used) and thus fail to capture the individual organization's true strategy. Second, the scorecard is typically implemented with a strong top-down flavor, neglecting the bottom-up feedback cycle emphasized in this chapter. In principle, responses to both objections can be incorporated into the tool, but only at a significant cost in increased complexity. This is why there are fewer implementations of

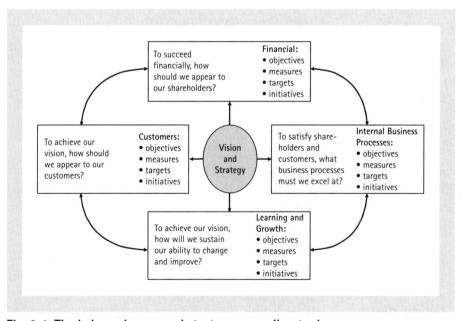

Fig. 9.4 The balanced scorecard strategy–cascading tool

Source: Adapted from Kaplan and Norton (1996).

the balanced scorecard in project management than in sales or manufacturing, where performance is easier to measure.

A third tool, related to the balanced scorecard but less widely applied, adapts the five questions of a generic framework introduced by Markides (1999) to a project management context (see Figure 9.5). In contrast to the balanced scorecard, this tool adopts an explicitly strategic view and begins by articulating the business unit's strategy via five straightforward questions:

1. *What* products are we offering? Answering such a question is far from trivial; it requires answering tough related questions such as: Do we offer support services? Why or why not? Do we offer a solution or a product/component? And so on.
2. *Who* are the customers that pay? Answers to this question may reveal a distinction between customers (parties that pay for the product) and end-users (parties that actually use the product and may influence the purchasers) as well as a better understanding of which project specification addresses which party's requirements.
3. *How* is our organization able to deliver the product/service? This question aims to elucidate the organization's core processes (i.e. activities based on core competences and knowledge). Projects may represent one of the core activities—for delivering solutions in some organizations, for executing change in others.

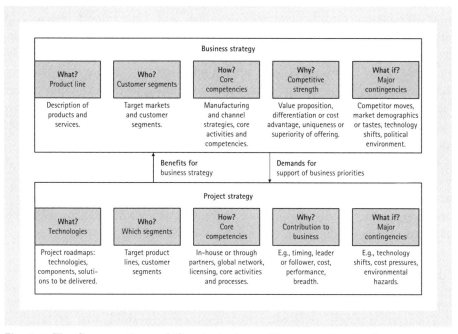

Fig. 9.5 The five questions of the strategic position cascading tool

Source: Adapted from Markides (1999).

4. *Why* do customers buy from us rather than from the competition or not at all? This question seeks a clear articulation of the value proposition of the product/service offering.
5. *What if* the environment changes? Will the competitive logic change the required market offering and/or the processes used in the organization?

The project strategy then articulates what the project contributes in business terms: what scope to offer, what "customers" to satisfy, what PM methods and processes to employ, what specific value does the project contribute to any of the firm's priorities? Finally, what changes may force the project team to modify its scope or approach later?

The business strategy places demands and financial constraints on the project scope. In turn, the project strategy places feasibility constraints on—while also offering new opportunities or modifications to—the business strategy. The Markides framework is able to capture a productive top-down and bottom-up dialogue. This tool is somewhat more complicated than the balanced scorecard, but it lends itself more easily to capturing the precise business strategy an organization is following. At the same time, it facilitates the articulation of the rules and processes *d* in our introductory evolutionary framework. Loch and Tapper (2002) described a detailed application example in the advanced development department of a small diamond company.

In summary, all three strategy-cascading tools emphasize the importance of alignment. Misalignment is responsible for the pursuit of technical feats (by engineers who infamously dither with over-designed, "gold-plated" solutions), for running after the competition's innovations without ever catching up, and for faking the business numbers ("chasing the hockey stick": the breakthrough revenue explosion is always two years away). Project team members who are not knowledgeable about strategy are thus unable to articulate the consequences and value of their decisions; as a result, they may lose motivation and no longer contribute all their knowledge, or they may start pursuing their own personal goals rather than supporting the organization.

The key benefits of explicitly articulating a project strategy extend far beyond its use as a "control tool." Indeed, which tool is used matters less than whether management strives to use it to foster dialogue and motivation. The benefits of strategy cascading can be broadly summarized as clarity, guidance in assessing trade-offs, and motivation and empowerment of project workers (Loch 2008).

Portfolio views

A key element of turning any strategic vision from hopeful statement into concrete plan of action is the effective allocation of resources across initiatives and tasks that aim to fulfill the strategic objectives. Portfolio views offer a holistic perspective on the organization's efforts to promote evolution of the business strategy. Portfolios are acknowledged in some project management textbooks (e.g. Meredith and Mantel 2003; Pinto 2006), but only qualitatively or with financial ratios (such as returns or cash flows). An important perspective missing from these accounts is that a project's value in terms of contribution to the firm often depends on the entire portfolio and is not merely a project-level feature (Girotra, Terwiesch, and Ulrich 2007).

Project managers can better communicate their projects' performance when they are armed with a deep understanding of the entire collection of projects. Recognizing project interactions enables better knowledge of an individual project's contribution to strategy as well as more focused and reliable execution. The portfolio embodies how the organization is pursuing its strategic objectives. The project team should clearly understand what strategic domain its project covers, what its role is, whether there is a duplicate or backup, and what interdependencies exist with other projects.

There are many portfolio representation tools and frameworks; here we offer two widely used visual tools (Figure 9.6) as examples. We argue that the portfolio should be customized to the organization and should not be restricted to standard views (Hutchison-Krupat and Kavadias 2009). The left diagram of Figure 9.6 emphasizes project novelty (and hence risk) in terms of technology used and markets addressed. The right diagram classifies projects by market segment and the firm's competitive position within those segments.

In the left diagram of Figure 9.6, projects with low novelty on both dimensions (technology and market) represent "continuous improvement" efforts (e.g. support or upgrade projects for the customer) or Six Sigma improvement projects inside certain organizational processes. Continuous improvement projects are often important for the organization: software upgrades can generate a lot of money; customer support projects earn substantial revenues in engineering services and

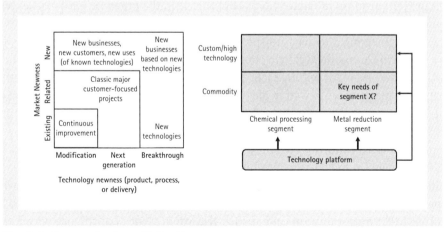

Fig. 9.6 Two project portfolio diagrams

build brand equity; and internal continuous improvement projects drive productivity growth, the lifeblood of margin protection. Such projects also exhibit very low
risk. Yet they suffer from a low "glamour factor" and thus attract minimal attention
from top management, which results in a control-focused "autopilot" approach.
Moreover, formalized professional project management methods may be too heavy-
handed for such projects: for example, a Six Sigma project may involve four person-
weeks of effort spread over a team of five people. In this situation, at issue is not
formal coordination and tracking of milestones, which are quite simple. Instead the
challenge is motivating operations people to be engaged and to offer their ideas and
tacit knowledge. An exaggerated emphasis on control may squeeze such initiatives
to death.

Projects in the middle zone of the left diagram are the challenging projects one
typically encounters in project management stories and examples: they address new
customers and/or locations (although within similar segments), which increases
the risk of misunderstandings and resultant tensions with customers, and they
embody some novel technologies, which increases the risks associated with timely
delivery and system integration. These projects pose substantial risks, and it is in
this area where professional and disciplined methods for planning, requirements
negotiation and "freezing," monitoring, and risk management offer value.

Finally, some projects break into fundamentally new territory for the organization. New territory can mean addressing a new category of customers (e.g. a fluid-
bed reactor engineering contractor who has worked with metal reduction and who
now addresses chemical companies about designing chemical reactor vessels). It can
also mean incorporating radically novel platform technologies into a project (e.g.
integrating a continuous variable transmission [CVT] powertrain into an SUV and
altering an entire product category). Such projects offer the potential of high returns
but are also quite risky. Moreover, the effectiveness of established formal project
management methods comes into question.

The right diagram in Figure 9.6 places projects in the organization's market segments and the strategic role of those segments. With reference to our fluid-bed
reactor engineering, the diagram shows two segments, metal and chemical, as well
as a standard commodity (existing business) versus a high-end customization (new
business) sub-segment within each. Looking at the organization's projects in this
matrix illuminates two key strategic decisions. First is the de facto prioritization of
the business segments: which one should receive more resources to fund more initiatives? Which segment has unfulfilled market demand or unpursued growth
opportunities? Second, does the project "defend" the ongoing business objectives or
does it rather aim to generate new business? The answers to these questions determine the risk profile, since adapting previous approaches is less risky than entering
a new market. In that context, our previous CVT SUV example could be viewed as
a project that meant to position a firm at the forefront of performance within the
SUV segment. Once more, the objective is to assess not the attractiveness of

individual projects but instead whether the initiatives combine to address the organization's markets and support its business strategy.

Such portfolio views prompt senior management to ask questions of *balance*: are we undertaking too few (or too many) innovative, high-risk projects? The benchmark is fewer than 10 percent in most organizations, since undertaking more would pose excessive risks overall. Are we investing enough of our project management resources in continuous improvement projects? If we do too little, our organizational methods and processes may not be improving aggressively enough to achieve productivity goals and cost competitiveness. If we focus on this category too much, we may become too incremental and too oriented towards the short term. In other words, portfolio tools should ask *questions* about the prioritization of resource investments in project initiatives, with responses articulating how the projects contribute to the business. The left-hand portfolio in Figure 9.6 asks: How much do we want to invest in improvement of current products and processes, next-generation projects, and breakthrough projects, and how much risk are we willing to take? The right-hand portfolio asks: On which market segments are we focusing our efforts, and what balance are we striking between current business growth and new business development?

In addition, the holistic perspective of portfolio tools allows the evaluation of individual projects not only in absolute terms but also relative to one other. Project rankings based on standard financial metrics may favor some initiatives, but this in itself does not imply that those initiatives should be in the portfolio, because the organization may have decided to break ground in another market. The major limitation of a bottom-up approach to portfolio management is that it risks including "attractive" projects that do not support the organization's strategic interest. Put differently, the whole portfolio should be more valuable than the sum of the parts [projects] as seen individually. It is senior management's responsibility to set the desired balance of improvement, next-generation, and high-risk innovative projects. No method can actually "derive" the right portfolio because senior management sets the business priorities. However, project managers must actively participate because it is their detailed knowledge that's needed when appraising the potential of proposed projects.

Unfortunately, most organizations—even the sophisticated ones that employ project portfolio tools—use "generic" portfolios that have been offered in the literature (e.g. Wheelwright and Clark 1992; Artto and Dietrich 2004; Kavadias and Chao 2007); examples include risk versus return and market growth versus market size (the classic Boston Consulting Group's strategy portfolio). It would be appropriate for two different organizations to use the same generic portfolio only if the organizations had the same strategy. For example, an engineering contractor that competes by offering fast, low-cost implementation of standardized facilities should not have the same project portfolio as one that deals with customized high-tech facilities.

Negotiation and stakeholders

Stakeholders are the various parties who may not necessarily have an official role but nevertheless have an interest in the direction of a project. As we argued at the start of this section, both the overall business strategy and the individual project strategies tend to be compromises among relevant trade-offs; it often happens that stakeholders (inside or outside the boundaries of the organization) may have different interests or perceive these compromises in different ways, because of interest conflicts, but also because they are driven by different "thought worlds" (Dougherty 1992). For example, the government may aim to subsidize the development of a new "green" technology or a major infrastructure project in order to increase social welfare, whereas the project subcontractors undertake the effort with the objective of making a profit.

Two widely used tools that enable the formal representation of stakeholder interactions are *stakeholder maps* and *power/interest matrices* (Freeman 1984; Elias, Cavana, and Jackson 2002; Winch and Bonke 2002). A *stakeholder map*, or a list of all stakeholders with their interests, indicates for whom the project causes problems (opponents) or offers something attractive (proponents). The *power/interest matrix* offers a categorization of the stakeholders that suggests in which order they should be approached (Figure 9.7).

The power/interest matrix acknowledges the relationship networks that exist in organizations (Rowley 1997). No one decides in isolation; we all ask people whom we know and trust for advice. Thus, a stakeholder strategy must account for the influential

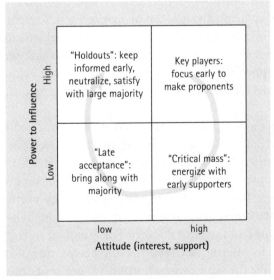

Fig. 9.7 Stakeholder power/interest matrix

"brokers" in the stakeholder network. If you can get influential stakeholders on your side their network will "work for you"; this dynamic represents a non-linear feedback process that can result in an "epidemic of support" (or of resistance).

According to this social network logic, the power/interest matrix suggests the order of approach: network-central, and thus influential, stakeholders who happen to like the project are natural early allies. Once they are willing to speak up for the project, the "critical mass" of less influential but positive stakeholders can be mobilized, and they then pull along the slightly negative players in a "social contagion" (Rowley 1997; Krackhard and Hanson 1993). Each of these stakeholder categories requires its own attention and approach.

Whereas the stakeholder map and the power/influence matrix offer a comprehensive representation of the stakeholder network and its members' intentions, they consider only one underlying source of those intentions, namely the rationally driven "conflicting interests"; however, two additional sources of stakeholder intentions are relevant here: the less conscious and more subtle issues of culture and/or emotional aspects of social transactions (the lower-level gray layers in Figure 9.8).

The layer below the network influence layer is the cultural layer of "what is appropriate." Culture refers to the socially learned routines and assumptions of

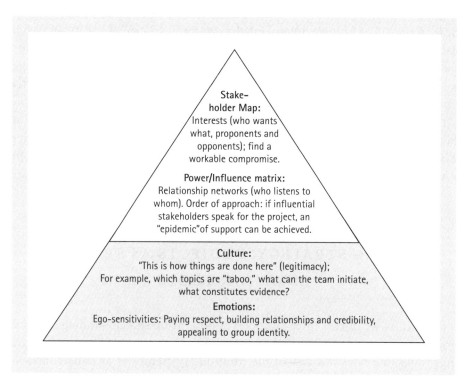

Fig. 9.8 Levels of influencing stakeholders

social integration and problem-solving that successive generations of a group's members inherit (Schein 2004; Boyd and Richerson 2005). In our previous terminology, this means that the rules/processes d are not always consciously derived by some kind of optimization, but arise as cultural habits and unspoken assumptions. Thus, changes may also arise in unconscious cultural shifts, and rules may be enforced not only by official incentives and sanctions but also by social norms and peer pressure. Examples abound across different types of projects: does your project usurp an activity that, within a particular country, the government or a local power broker "owns"? Does it sufficiently consult local people so they feel respected? Project specifications must sometimes be adjusted in order to locate the project within the range of socially acceptable configurations and outcomes.

Even deeper lies the layer of emotions. Specifically, when status feelings, and an associated desire to "win," creep into interactions, stakeholders may harden their positions and demands; if, however, a relationship can be built, or a feeling of "we" based on some kind of common identity can be emphasized, people become more cooperative. Such behavioral influences are robust and often economically large (Loch and Wu 2008). In stakeholder management, this implies that individuals may find the project fundamentally beneficial yet still resist or impede its progress simply because the project manager did not ask for advice at a critical juncture, did not invite them to the milestone ceremony, or did not refer to them in an interview with the local press. The attitude of local inhabitants toward a project may be swayed by making the effort to engage local experts on the steering committee or on the project itself (thus giving respect and building a relationship). Once people see the project as "theirs," they may naturally swing toward support, regardless of the objective project specifications.

The two lower layers in Figure 9.8 cover the underlying bases of understanding stakeholder interests and the political influence landscape; understanding sources of strong emotions may help the project manager mobilize support in some situations.

SHAPING STRATEGY: PROJECTS AS STRATEGY CREATION TOOLS

In this section we discuss three examples of bottom-up strategy-finding roles that projects can play, as we discussed in Figure 9.2. They can be categorized on two dimensions: the type of search at the front line (incremental or radical) and the extent of bottom-up initiatives allowed. The type of search processes/actions that drive highly novel solutions has been classified in two main categories: parallel searches (ecologies of experiments) and trial-and-error iterations (Loch, Pich, and De Meyer 2006). Based on this categorization:

- We discuss how an ecology of small parallel emerging projects can cumulatively result in a business strategy shift.
- We show how large projects that develop significantly novel solutions and through which significant strategy changes emerge should be managed.
- We give an example of a radical project that in itself represented a major emergent shift in the strategy of the organization.

Managing change through small projects

We saw earlier that high-performance organizational search projects should contribute to strategy, shaping it rather than merely executing given targets. This can be done even in manufacturing organizations (often characterized by little tolerance for bottom-up initiatives) if the individual projects are small and relatively simple. Sting and Loch (2009) studied strategy deployment in six manufacturing organizations and found that strategy was shaped by the collection of improvement projects.

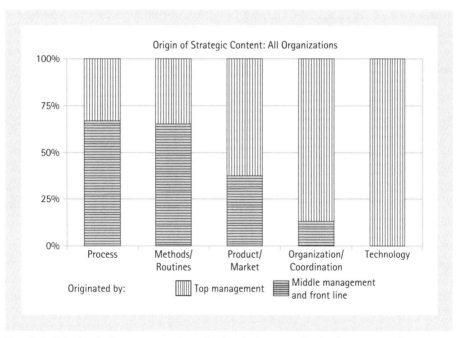

Fig. 9.9 Strategic improvement projects at six manufacturing companies

For example, each organization had about ten to twenty "strategic" improvement projects that were driven and followed up by senior management (in addition to many smaller projects driven at the line or department levels). Figure 9.9 categorizes these projects by problem domain and shows that many of them originated at the bottom of the organization, not the top. Significant (manufacturing process) technology investments were so expensive that they were initiated at the top (right bar in the figure), but product/market and organizational projects came from the bottom to some degree.

In addition, four of the six organizations were flexible in their strategic targets, willing to adjust them depending on the results. For example, one organization changed its technology trajectory because of inputs from a workshop that brought together product and process engineers and experienced manufacturing craftspeople. Another organization put in place an experimental production line staffed by older workers, initiated by a department manager triggered by the observation in a senior management meeting that the workforce was getting older, which threatened productivity goals. The production line personnel developed, entirely bottom up, an integrated system of ergonomic, work schedule, and health management support actions that brought productivity up to the level of a young workforce; this system was adopted by the company as a whole and thus changed the company's HR strategy (Loch et al. 2010).

The key to these organizations' ability to shape strategy through projects from the bottom lies in their willingness to articulate problems at the top, but to allow initiatives to "bubble up," monitoring only for coordination across departments and for the existence of results. These results are allowed to be useful in unexpected directions. The individual projects are relatively small (usually less than one person-year), but collectively they add up to emerging strategic effects.

Iteration and parallel trials in emerging uncertain projects

Larger, complex projects with the ambition to contribute to strategy must accept a higher level of risk internally to the project (for example, a new technology or a new market). Worse, such projects must accept that risks may arise that are unforeseeable at the outset. The following quote from Drucker (1985: 189) illustrates this idea well:

When a new venture does succeed, more often than not it is in a market other than the one it was originally intended to serve, with products and services not quite those with which it had set out, bought in large part by customers it did not even think of when it started, and used for a host of purposes besides the ones for which the products were first designed.

Economists have called this "unawareness" or "unforeseen contingencies" (Modica and Rustichini 1994); scholars in public policy term it "wicked problems" (Rittel and

Webber 1973); project management professionals have used the term "unknown unknowns," or "unk unks" (Wideman 1992). When a project develops a new technology or tackles a new market, unknown unknowns are rampant (Loch, Pich, and De Meyer 2006).

When unk unks are so fundamental that the project goal and path are themselves fundamentally unknown, risk management and local flexibility are insufficient. Any plan will run into major surprises, and the project team will be required to abandon assumptions and look for solutions in non-anticipated places (Miller and Lessard 2000; Loch, Pich, and De Meyer 2006).

Of course, the project team should attempt to convert unknown unknowns into risk by performing careful upfront feasibility and risk analyses—competent risk management and project planning are still required and should be used as much as possible. However, in novel or breakthrough projects, this is simply not sufficient, no matter how hard one tries. The necessity for adopting a flexible mindset can indeed be identified at the outset of the project: while the unk unks themselves cannot be foreseen, the *situation that bears their presence may well be diagnosable*. For example, discovery-driven planning (McGrath and MacMillan 1995, 2000) proposes to explicitly acknowledge that unknown unknowns exist and to uncover them with analyses such as assumptions checklists. Similarly, Loch et al. (2008) illustrated with the example of a start-up venture project how the presence of unknown unknowns can be diagnosed by systematically probing what one knows about the project, and where one has the intuition of being on unsafe ground.

Two fundamental approaches exist for this level of unforeseeable uncertainty: trial-and-error learning and selectionism (Pich et al. 2002; Leonard-Barton 1995).

Under **trial-and-error learning**, the team starts moving towards one outcome (the best it can identify), but is prepared to repeatedly and fundamentally change both the outcome and the course of action as new information becomes available. Exploratory experiments, aimed at gaining information without necessarily contributing "progress," are an important part of this approach; failure of such experiments is a source of learning rather than a mistake. It is therefore important to track the learning and reduction in knowledge gaps rather than tracking only the progress towards a target. The approach has been described under various names by numerous authors in technology transfer, new product development, engineering projects, and new ventures (for an overview, see Sommer and Loch 2009).

Alternatively, the team might choose to "hedge" and opt for **selectionism**, or pursuing multiple approaches in parallel, observing what works and what doesn't (without necessarily having a full explanation why) and choosing the best approach ex post facto. Examples of this approach abound, including Microsoft's pursuit of several operating systems during the 1980s (Beinhocker 1999), Toyota's "set-based engineering" (Sobek, Ward, and Liker 1999), and "product churning" by the Japanese consumer electronics companies in the early 1990s (Stalk and Webber 1993).

		Complexity	
		Low	High
	High	**Learning** Flexibility to fundamentally re-define business plan and venture model	**Selectionism** Selectionism is most effective *if* choice of best trial can be deferred until unk unks have emerged (true market response is known)
	Low	**Planning** • Execute plan toward target • Risk identification and risk management • Learning and updating	**Selectionism** • Plan as much as possible • Try out several alternative solutions and choose the best as soon as possible

(Left axis: Unforeseeable Uncertainty)

Fig. 9.10 When to choose trial–and–error learning versus selectionism

In a large-scale empirical study of sixty-five new venture projects, Sommer and Loch (2009) showed that the best combination of learning and selectionism, as measured by their effect on project success, depends on the level of unforeseeable uncertainty in the project and the complexity of the project (Figure 9.10). When both uncertainty and complexity are low (lower left quadrant), planning and standard risk management are up to the task and the most efficient. When unforeseeable uncertainty looms large, be flexible and apply trial and error. When complexity is high, use parallel trials and narrow the field down to the best as soon as possible. The hardest situation is in the upper right quadrant, where unforeseeable uncertainty and project complexity combine. It turned out that the highest success level was associated with parallel trials if they could be kept alive until uncertainty had been reduced to the point that all important risks were known. Otherwise, trial and error performed better. Of course, in any large project, trial and error and selectionism can be combined and applied differently to different sub-projects.

Shaping and evolving the project's strategic mission: an example

Finally, we discuss an extreme example of a project, in which the events in the project led to a change in the organization's strategy. This example illustrates that a project's mission is rarely objective, and that the strategy the project is supposed to support does not exist or is in flux because the environment is changing. Although the specifications are articulated in technical terms, one begins always with a social construction that reflects a "wish" that is in some way shared by stakeholders (and that can be explained to support the organization's strategy). This strategy is often emergent and evolving over time, and it sometimes depends on fickle and fleeting alliances among multiple players. Projects in the public domain are especially prone to such ambiguity, but projects in large organizations can also reflect this level of emergent goals (Rittel and Webber 1973). For such emergent strategic projects, where stakeholder priorities are fluid and may shift before the project is completed, the organization is often faced with a delicate question: Does the organization attempt to enforce the preset compromise between stakeholders or is renegotiation inevitable, putting the project's benefits at risk?

The answer is that stakeholder shifts may be unavoidable: the project goals may drift to reflect changing social consensus and alliances. The organization can rarely force stakeholders to stand by prior compromises; it must allow the goals to drift but should try to steer or nudge this drift toward a configuration that continues to support (albeit in a possibly modified way) the organization's strategy. This task is difficult and requires as much diplomacy and political skills as traditional project management, and it certainly requires the full support and detailed involvement of the organization's senior management. Thus, for emergent projects a key ability of the organization is maintaining a disciplined *focus on the strategic role of the project* for the organization.

Consider the recent example (Loch and Mihm 2008) of Eurocontrol, the European agency for air traffic control. The agency reports to the Council of European Transport Ministers and, with its 2,500 employees, coordinates traffic control across the European Union (EU). The agency's task is complex because each of the thirty-five member countries owns part of the European airspace; moreover, air traffic control in each country is performed with local systems that are mutually incompatible. Personnel certifications and policies also differ from country to country. This complexity makes air traffic control in Europe more expensive than in the United States and also vulnerable to flight delays due to coordination failures.

Since the mid 1990s, various parties have informally discussed frameworks for system configurations of a Europe-wide compatible ATC system. In 2001, RDC (Eurocontrol's R&D and system simulation organization) started a project to develop an "operational concept" of European ATC for 2020 and beyond. An operational concept is a high-level description of the flows and processes used to guide planes but without any technical description of how the functionality would actually be achieved. The project had two rationales: (1) such a concept was a genuine part of RDC's mission to move ATC forward, and (2) the RDC wanted to place itself more centrally in the network of relevant stakeholders (governments, national ATC providers that were half public and half private, airlines, airports, and ATC equipment manufacturers). The RDC formed a research consortium together with some equipment manufacturers and national ATC providers, and they obtained research funding from the European Commission as part of its five-yearly

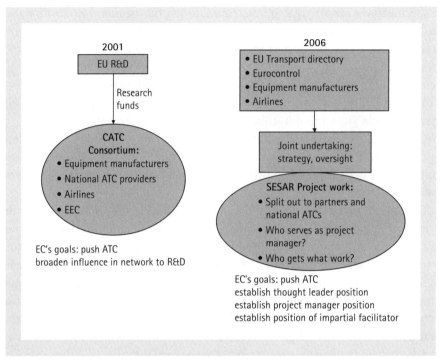

Fig. 9.11 Evolution of the RDC's ATC project

Source: Adapted from Loch and Mihm (2008).

framework R&D fund. In 2004, the consortium delivered a first-stage high-level concept. This project, called CATC (Collaborative ATC), is shown on the left-hand side of Figure 9.11.

However, stakeholder coalitions evolved over the course of these three years. The national ATC providers and airlines decided that CATC was too important to be left to R&D people—particularly under the auspices of Eurocontrol and RDC, a central body representing the EC rather than national constituencies. A broader consortium was founded, one driven by business people rather than R&D people; the RDC managed to become a member of this consortium so as not to be left out. The new consortium quickly rejected the CATC operational concept as too inflexible. They dubbed their effort SESAR (Single European Sky Advanced Research), which by 2008 became the unifying term for the attempt to restructure European air traffic control. SESAR set out to produce an improved operational concept by 2006. Yet no advancement occurred until mid-2007, and the effort largely reproduced CATC—evidence that technical criteria were not the only ones in play.

The SESAR project is shown on the right-hand side of Figure 9.11. It would receive two billion in funding over twelve years from the EC and Eurocontrol, and it would be run by a new entity (a project steering committee) known as the Joint Undertaking. Although the technical goals of the SESAR project were not much different from those of the original CATC, the project had assumed a different mission and was run differently. The RDC would be working for the Joint Undertaking in a role that was still to be defined: possibly as an operational project manager that would coordinate various players and work packages, as a subcontractor for certain R&D and simulation work, or some combination of both.

How should the RDC respond to this changed project context? Its original strategic vision was no longer valid. However, the RDC could still contribute to the greater whole, while extracting value for its own organization, by advantageously placing itself in the stakeholder network. The value proposition to the RDC's constituencies—as well as the strategic role of the project for the RDC itself—would have to change. Despite the radical changes, there was still a strategic role to be played in this project by the RDC: to establish the RDC as a "thought leader" on the concept for 2020; as a project manager with the capacity to coordinate partners as different as national ATC providers, airlines, and equipment manufacturers; and as an impartial arbiter that could help stakeholders identify win-win compromises. If played right, the new project (because it was broader) might help the RDC even more than the original project. However, this would require RDC's senior management to become explicitly involved in order to steer SESAR activities in this direction. This was not a project with deliverables but rather a strategic initiative that might change the organization's size, structure, and external position.

In summary, this example shows that the classic approach to project management—where "specifications" are taken as given and changing them is viewed as a catastrophic disruption—may paralyze an organization involved in large, novel strategic projects. In such projects, the goals may be a social construction born out of consensus rather than a "technical solution to a defined problem." As a result, top management must be involved in guiding the emergent process of "morphing" the consensus mission over time. If this is done well (even at the cost of operational project management inefficiencies due to changes), the project may become a great strategic asset, as we see in the example of SESAR. If the organization does not see this opportunity, the project may become a lost opportunity, or worse, a failure that hurts the organization's credibility and standing. The Eurocontrol project is a vivid showcase of the importance of senior management's "openness" to emergent (unforeseeable) influences in major projects, and of the importance of monitoring not simply progress but also governance, priorities, and the project's position in a changing environment. Monitoring must include key stakeholders— only if they agree on how to view the changes can the project evolve in ways that further the organization's strategy rather than cause strife and conflict.

This last point is linked to the strategy framework in Figure 9.2. The "what if" contingency dimension of strategy is not only a high-level search for new macroeconomic trends but is also informed by events within the projects themselves.

That is, an organization's projects can and should be used as sources of warning signals about emerging changes in the behavior of customers, stakeholders, competitors, and markets.

CONCLUSION

Traditionally, a project's scope, objectives, and specifications have been viewed as a mandate with which project managers must operate and succeed. Newer work in project management has rediscovered the systematic use of projects as implementation "vehicles" for an organization's strategy. Three strategy alignment tools are widely used and being integrated into project management; we have provided an overview of these tools:

1. A systematic translation of the business strategy into project targets with cascading tools.
2. A portfolio-level assessment of the organization's projects. Projects interact in their effects on the business, and the portfolio view clarifies existing priorities.
3. A thorough understanding of the "map" of stakeholders and their respective objectives. This is an integral part of strategic alignment.

However, projects also create and shape strategy from the bottom up. As organizations do not optimize strategy but search for acceptable solutions, projects play an integral part in this search. Examples of bottom-up strategy shaping include:

1. A portfolio of small improvement projects that can change and enhance strategy if senior management is willing to accept useful but unexpected results.
2. Larger projects that have the ambition to contribute to emerging strategy but which must accept unforeseeable uncertainty as part of their mission. This requires trial-and-error and selectionism (parallel trials) project management.

Project management has a larger role to play in organizations as the vehicle for strategic trials and change. To fulfill this role, the bottom-up tools sketched in this chapter need to be formalized and consistently applied.

REFERENCES

ARTTO, K. A., and DIETRICH P. H. (2004). "Strategic business management through multiple projects," in P. W. G. Morris and J. K. Pinto (eds.), *The Wiley Guide to Managing Projects*. London: John Wiley & Sons Inc., 144–76.

BEINHOCKER, E. D. (1999). "Robust adaptive strategies," *Sloan Management Review*, 40/3: 95–106.

BOYD, R., and RICHERSON, P. J. (2005). *The Origin and Evolution of Cultures.* Oxford: Oxford University Press.

BURGELMAN, R. A. (1991). "Intraorganizational ecology of strategy making and organizational adaptation: theory and field research," *Organization Science*, 2/3: 239–62.

CYERT, R. M., and MARCH, J. (1963). *A Behavioral Theory of the Firm.* Englewood Cliffs, NJ: Wiley Blackwell.

DOUGHERTY, D. (1992). "Interpretive barriers to successful product innovation in large firms," *Organization Science*, 3/2: 179–203.

DRUCKER, P. F. (1985). *Innovation and Entrepreneurship.* New York: Harper Collins.

ELIAS, A. A., CAVANA, R. Y., and JACKSON, L. S. (2002). "Stakeholder analysis for R&D project management," *R&D Management*, 32: 301–10.

FLEMING, L., and MINGO, S. (2007). "Creativity in new product development: an evolutionary integration," in C. H. Loch and S. Kavadias (eds.), *Handbook of New Product Development Management.* Oxford: Butterworth/Heinemann, 113–34.

FOSTER, R. N., LINDEN, L. H., WHITELEY, R. L., and KANTROW, A. M. (1985). "Improving the return on R&D I," *Research Technology Management*, January–February: 12–17.

FREEMAN, R. E. (1984). *Strategic Management: A Stakeholder Approach.* Boston: Pitman.

GIROTRA, K., TERWIESCH, C. K., and ULRICH, T. (2007). "Valuing R&D projects in a portfolio: evidence from the pharmaceutical industry," *Management Science*, 53/9: 1452–66.

HARGADON, A., and SUTTON, R. I. (1997). "Technology brokering and innovation in a product development firm," *Administrative Science Quarterly*, 42: 716–49.

HUTCHISON-KRUPAT, J., and KAVADIAS, S. (2009). "Organizational enablers for NPD portfolio selection," Georgia Tech Working Paper.

KAPLAN, R. S., and NORTON, D. P. (1996). *The Balanced Scorecard.* Boston: Harvard Business School Press.

————(2000). "Having trouble with your strategy? Then map it," *Harvard Business Review*, September–October: 167–76.

KAVADIAS, S., and CHAO, R. (2007). "Resource allocation and new product development portfolio management," in C. H. Loch and S. Kavadias (eds.), *Handbook of New Product Development Management.* Oxford: Butterworth Heinemann Elsevier.

——and SOMMER, S. (2009). "The effects of problem structure and team expertise on brainstorming effectiveness," *Management Science* (forthcoming).

KERZNER, H. (2003). *Project Management: A Systems Approach to Planning, Scheduling and Controlling*, 8th edn. Hoboken, NJ: Wiley.

KRACKHARD, D., and HANSON, J. R. (1993). "Informal networks: the company behind the chart," *Harvard Business Review*, July–August.

LEONARD-BARTON, D. (1995). *Wellsprings of Knowledge.* Cambridge, MA: Harvard Business School Press.

LOCH, C. H. (2008). "Mobilizing an R&D organization through strategy cascading," *Research Technology Management*, September–October: 1–9.

——and KAVADIAS, S. (2007). "Managing new product development: a framework," in C. H. Loch and S. Kavadias (eds.), *Handbook of New Product Development Management.* Oxford: Butterworth Heinemann/Elsevier, chapter 1.

——and MIHM, J. (2008). "Eurocontrol's experimental center," INSEAD Case Study.

——and TAPPER, U. A. S. (2002). "Implementing a strategy-driven performance measurement system for an applied research group," *Journal of Product Innovation Management,* 19: 185–98.

——and TERWIESCH, C. (2007). "Coordination and information exchange," in C. H. Loch and S. Kavadias (eds.), *Handbook of New Product Development Management.* Oxford: Butterworth Heinemann/Elsevier, chapter 12.

——and WU, Y. (2008). "Social preferences and supply chain performance: an experimental study," *Management Science,* 54/11: 1835–49.

——PICH, M. T., and DE MEYER, A. (2006). *Managing the Unknown: A New Approach to Managing Projects under High Uncertainty.* Hoboken, NJ: Wiley.

——SOLT, M. E., and BAILEY, E. (2008). "Diagnosing unforeseeable uncertainty in a new venture," *Journal of Product Innovation Management,* 25/1: 28–46.

——STING, F., BAUER, N., and MAUERMANN, H. (2010). "Mobilized productivity knows no age," *Harvard Business Review,* March: 99–104.

MCGRATH, R. G., and MACMILLAN, I. (1995). "Discovery driven planning," *Harvard Business Review,* July–August: 44–54.

——(2000). *The Entrepreneurial Mindset: Strategies for Continuously Creating Opportunity in the Age of Uncertainty.* Cambridge, MA: Harvard Business Press.

MARKIDES, C. C. (1999). "A dynamic view of strategy," *Sloan Management Review,* Spring: 55–63.

MEREDITH, J. R., and MANTEL, S. J. (2003). *Project Management: A Managerial Approach.* Hoboken, NJ: Wiley.

MIHM J., LOCH, C. H., and HUCHZERMEIER, A. (2003). "Problem-solving oscillations in complex engineering projects," *Management Science,* 49/6: 733–50.

————WILKINSON, D., and HUBERMAN, A. (2010). "Hierarchical structure and search in complex organizations," *Management Science* (forthcoming).

MILLER, R., and LESSARD, D. R. (2000). *The Strategic Management of Large Engineering Projects: Shaping Institutions, Risk and Governance.* Cambridge, MA: MIT Press.

MINTZBERG, H. (1978). "Patterns in strategy formation," *Management Science,* 24/9: 934–48.

MODICA, S., and RUSTICHINI, A. (1994). "Awareness and partitional information structure," *Theory and Decision,* 37: 107–24.

MORRIS, P. W. G. (2006). "Initiation strategies for managing major projects," in P. C. Dinsmore and J. Cabanis-Brewin (eds.), *The AMA Handbook of Project Management.* New York: AMACOM, chapter 4.

NELSON, R. S., and WINTER, S. G. (1982). *An Evolutionary Theory of Economic Change.* Cambridge, MA: Harvard University Press.

PICH, M. T., LOCH, C. H., and DE MEYER, A. (2002). "On uncertainty, ambiguity and complexity in project management," *Management Science,* 48/8: 1008–23.

PINTO, J. K. (2006). *Project Management: Achieving Competitive Advantage.* Englewood Cliffs, NJ: Prentice Hall, Pearson Education.

PMI (2004). *A Guide to the Project Management Body of Knowledge (PMBOK Guide),* 3rd edn. Newton Square, PA: Project Management Institute.

RITTEL, H. W., and WEBBER, M. M. (1973). "Dilemmas in a general theory of planning," *Policy Sciences,* 4: 155–69.

RIVKIN, J. W., and SIGGELKOW, N. (2003). "Balancing search and stability: interdependencies among elements of organizational design," *Management Science,* 49/2: 290–311.

Rowley, T. J. (1997). "Moving beyond dyadic ties: a network theory of stakeholder influences," *Academy of Management Journal*, 22/4: 887–910.

Schein, E. H. (2004). *Organizational Culture and Leadership*. San Francisco: Jossey-Bass.

Simon, H. A. (1969). *The Sciences of the Artificial*, 2nd edn. Cambridge, MA: MIT Press.

Sobek, D. K., II, Ward, A. C., and Liker, J. K. (1999). "Toyota's principles of set-based concurrent engineering," *Sloan Management Review*, 40/2: 67–83.

Sober, E., and Wilson, D. S. (1999). *Unto Others: The Evolution and Psychology of Unselfish Behavior*. Boston: Harvard University Press.

Sommer, S. C., and Loch, C. H. (2009). "Project management under high uncertainty," in V. K. Narayanan and G. O'Connor (eds.), *Technology and Innovation Management Encyclopedia*. Oxford: Blackwell.

——— and Dong, J. (2009). "Managing complexity and unforeseeable uncertainty in startup companies: an empirical study," *Organization Science*, 20/1: 118–33.

Spinardi, G. (1994). *From Polaris to Trident: The Development of US Fleet Ballistic Missile Technology*. Cambridge: Cambridge University Press.

Stalk, G., and Webber, A. M. (1993). "Japan's dark side of time," *Harvard Business Review*, July–August: 93–102.

Sting, F., and Loch, C. H. (2009). "Where top-down and bottom-up meet: a study of strategy deployment at five manufacturing organizations," INSEAD Working Paper, August.

Thomke, S. H. (2003). *Experimentation Matters*. Cambridge, MA: Harvard Business School Press.

Wheelwright, S. C., and Clark, K. B. (1992). *Revolutionizing Product Development*. Boston: Harvard Business School Press.

Wideman, R. W. (1992). *Project and Program Risk Management: A Guide to Managing Project Risks and Opportunities*. Newtown Square, PA: Project Management Institute.

Winch, G. M., and Bonke, S. (2002). "Project stakeholder mapping: analyzing the interests of project stakeholders," in D. P. Slevin, D. I. Cleland, and J. K. Pinto (eds.), *The Frontiers of Project Management Research*. Newton Square, PA: Project Management Institute, 385–403.

CHAPTER 10

PROGRAM MANAGEMENT

AN EMERGING OPPORTUNITY FOR RESEARCH AND SCHOLARSHIP

SERGIO PELLEGRINELLI

DAVID PARTINGTON

JOANA G. GERALDI

INTRODUCTION

The rise of the professional discipline of project management has been accompanied by a growth in the number of project management academics who seek to publish their work in highly rated management journals, especially those that require research to be positioned within an established theoretical field. A growing number of scholars have used project management as the context within which to conduct such theory-based inquiry from other perspectives. Important theory-based contributions to management practice have been achieved.

In this chapter we argue that programs and program management provide further opportunities for researchers to apply and extend theory, thereby informing management practice in a number of ways and adding to an important body of knowledge. Program management has developed, and continues to evolve, as a managerial approach for coordinating primarily project-based activities and marshalling resources, and for the realization of complex, emergent endeavors. The term program is applied to a wide range of working arrangements, organizing frameworks, processes of change, and mechanisms for creating capabilities. We review attempts to define program management, and the debates on whether it is an extension of project management or a distinct discipline. We argue that programs and program management, though still emerging as a field of study and practice, are distinctive, and we offer our synthesis of the principal characteristics of programs (or programmes) and program management.

Based on our personal experiences and research interests, we then identify five areas—organization theory, organizational change, strategic management, leadership, and competence—that offer a rich domain for scholarly management research.

Scholarship and publishing project management research

We are surrounded by projects and project work, from the construction of iconic buildings to the writing of researched essays by schoolchildren. Projects have become such an ingrained way of working for many organizations that commentators have coined the term projectification to describe this phenomenon (Midler 1995). Project management, as a formal management discipline, has its origins in aerospace and defense (Morris 1994). Its scope has expanded beyond the fields of operations management and engineering and the traditional tools and techniques still closely associated with project management, such as work breakdown structures, networks, critical path method, and cost and schedule tracking. It now embraces topics such as procurement, team development, stakeholder management, and project leadership. While there is still debate about the scope of project management, it can be and is seen as a broad management approach rather than an execution-only discipline (Morris 1994, 2009).

In the academic world, a parallel development has taken place. Project management has become a core component of most business and management degrees, as well as a specialist degree subject at both undergraduate and postgraduate levels. The academic spread of project management has been accompanied by a steady growth in the number of academics who teach the subject and conduct research that aims to contribute to the development of its knowledge base. The research has broadly followed the developing interests in the field and the application of project management in diverse contexts and industries. While still focused on praxis and helping practitioners, the development of the discipline has become more theoretically informed and grounded, and research into project management has become more rigorous and systematic. A greater plurality of ontological and epistemological assumptions and theoretical lenses has informed the academic work in the field in the last decade or so. Some of this work has been published in highly ranked journals from other established academic fields and provides a richer, deeper, and more theoretically informed understanding of projects and project management (e.g. Brown and Eisenhardt 1997; Hodgson 2002, 2004; Hodgson and Cicmil 2007; Pich, Loch, and De Meyer 2002; Söderlund and Bredin 2006). It has advanced the knowledge base and raised academic and practitioner awareness in what had previously been a rather atheoretical, insular, and self-referential community. It has taken the study of project management beyond the largely prescriptive, instrumental, and unreflective nature of early work, codified in professional bodies of knowledge, which was overly reliant on an unquestioned rationalist paradigm (Williams 2005).

Programs and program management offer another opportunity for similarly rigorous and systematic research that generates or extends theory and improves program management practice. Such scholarship can build upon and contribute to knowledge and debates in more established fields, be published in highly ranked journals, and enrich our understanding of an increasingly important management approach.

CONCEPTUALIZATIONS OF PROGRAM MANAGEMENT

The growth of projects as an important or principal method for undertaking work in or by organizations was accompanied by a perceived need for coordination and effective resource deployment, and mechanisms for balancing diverse interests and priorities between projects. Program management was seen as, and still has a role to play as, a way of coordinating and directing projects (Ferns 1991; Gray 1997). More recently, Maylor et al. suggest that "programs and portfolios of programs are being used as a unit of activity in order to provide managerial sense-making and control when running complex organizations" (2006: 671), and have coined the term programmification. Probably not all complex organizations would benefit from management by programs, but programs and program management are widely used to realize complex undertakings. Others, in a more normative vein, have promoted the concept of enterprise program management—structures and processes conceived to create tight linkages between an organization's strategy and the totality of its projects and related change activity (Williams and Parr 2004; Gaddie 2003). The purported merits of this all-embracing approach are that it provides greater clarity and control over spending, and better deployment of resources, and so gives organizations greater chances of realizing their strategies and achieving the desired benefits from their programs and projects.

Professional bodies, such as the Project Management Institute (PMI) and the UK Association for Project Management (APM), echoed the conceptualization of programs as the means of coordinating projects (and non-projects) activities. The APM Body of Knowledge defines programs as the "coordinated management of related projects, which may include related business as usual activities that together achieve a beneficial change of a strategic nature for an organization"(APM 2006: 6). The PMI Body of Knowledge sees programs as "a group of related projects managed in a coordinated way to obtain benefits and control not available from managing them individually" (PMI 2006: 16). Within these professional bodies, there has been, and still remains to some degree, an implicit assumption that program management is part of, or an extension of, project management. The underpinning assumptions of rationality, control, efficient resource utilization, and effective delivery that have informed project management bodies of knowledge have often been imputed to program management. Programs have sometimes been conceived as scaled-up versions of projects—mega-projects. Sometimes the words project and program are used interchangeably.

Programs have also taken on a meaning beyond coordinating frameworks, assuming a broader notion and encompassing the initiation and shaping of the projects falling within the program (Pellegrinelli 1997) and a process for the realization of broader strategic or tactical benefits (Murray-Webster and Thiry 2000). Programs and program management are being cast as the management approach for bringing about societal change and organizational transformations (OGC 2003, 2007). The work associated with acquiring, developing, maintaining, and enhancing a capability has long been called a program(me) within the Aerospace and Defense sectors (Meier 2008; Sapolsky 1972), and driven largely by the US Department of Defense, this conception of "program" management has dominated the US literature. The latest version of Japan's foremost guide to project and program management, P2M, suggests program and program management as a "practical capability" to respond to external changes, allow flexibility, and cope with ambiguity, complexity, uncertainty, and expandability. The P2M guide covers a wide range of program types where previous editions had concentrated on externally focused programs, including mega-projects and major infrastructure developments (P2M 2008).

Typologies and classifications have been put forward to make sense of the variety of forms programs take. Ferns (1991) connected programs with organizational change and classified these as: strategic programs, involving changes in mission of the organization such as mergers and privatization; business cycle related with continuous changes in the business processes, and single-objective programs which are actually not more than large projects. Wheelwright and Clark (1992) offered a framework for classifying product development projects based on two dimensions of product change and process change: derivative, platform, breakthrough, and (outside their main grid) R&D. They argued that a balanced development portfolio or "aggregate project plan" yields better results given limited resources and competing priorities. Pellegrinelli (1997) proposed three program configurations: portfolio, goal oriented, and heartbeat, based on empirically observed organizational arrangements at a large telecommunications company. While criticized for not being a robust or comprehensive typology (Vereecke et al. 2003), the configurations highlight the range of purposes that programs might and do serve. The configurations describe the relationship between the program and its constituent projects: the synergistic coordination of relatively independent projects (portfolio); the active initiation, shaping, and management of component projects (goal oriented); the assembly of discrete work packages into a project and its efficient execution (heartbeat). The typology offered by Vereecke et al. (2003) classified programs according to two dimensions: extent to which the projects exist at launch, and degree of change in the expected outcome of the program. Evaristo and van Fenema (1999) classify programs according to the number of projects and their locations: co-located projects, distributed projects, and traditional projects (single project in single location). In a similar line, Maylor et al. (2006) proposed a classification based on the interrelationships between projects within a program in chain (sequential), portfolio (concurrent), and network (interdependent).

The goal-oriented configuration or program rationale (Pellegrinelli 1997) has been the focus of attention of most commentators and authors, with the other two configurations regarded as a form of multi-project management and an extension of operations management. In keeping with the principal understanding and rationale of a program, our main focus in the remainder of the chapter is the goal-oriented program.

PROGRAM MANAGEMENT: A SYNTHESIS

At present, and despite their ever-increasing use, there is a lack of consensus on the nature and purpose of programs and program management. The development of ideas and practice is fragmented and commentators on program management have not built well on previous knowledge.

Advocates of a distinct program management discipline have sought to distance it from the embrace of the execution-oriented project management approach and mindset (Thiry 2002, 2004; Pellegrinelli and Partington 2006; Pellegrinelli 1997, 2002, 2008), staking out program "ground" and urging program practitioners to approach their work differently. Lycett, Rassau, and Danson (2004) have suggested that the shortcomings in standard program management approaches can be traced to two flawed assumptions. The first is that program management is a scaled-up version of project management, still implied by project management professional bodies of knowledge. The second is that a "one size fits all" approach to program management is appropriate.

Sceptics question the uniqueness of features attributed to program management in many texts, and its claimed primacy or mediating role in relation to the translation and implementation of strategy. Good project managers are aware of how their work affects the organization and what needs to happen for benefits to be realized. They understand strategy and seek to connect their work to strategic goals, have dealt with stakeholders and suppliers, have communicated and consulted, and have established governance arrangements. These activities are not new, nor exclusive to program management, particularly from the perspective of project management as a holistic management approach. Project management is not merely an execution-only function, subordinate to program management (Morris 2009). The challenges of managing a mega-project have much in common with those of managing a program.

Our position is that projects can and often do stand alone, outside a program framework, and that managers of such independent projects strive to achieve their objectives within their business and societal contexts. Not all projects are, nor need be, components of a program, bereft of their own strategy and direct contribution to important organizational or societal goals. But there are, as yet, no truly shared answers to some fundamental questions. How is a project similar to and different from a program? For instance, if you substitute work package for component project and work package manager for project manager, what is substantially different in terms of approach and management coordination? Don't programs exist simply because people have been seduced by program management's implied proximity to strategy and therefore greater importance, status, and prestige?

We contend that projects and programs, and their associated management approaches, are part of a wider field of purposeful (i.e. desired and mandated to some degree) and structured (i.e. planned and controlled to some degree) change. The change may relate to an organization's assets, structures, infrastructure, systems, and/or processes, to the development of some form of operating capability (e.g. defense), to the creation of new social institutions (e.g. replacing failing secondary schools with new, reinvigorated schooling (facilities, staff, and curriculum) linked to or sponsored by private companies), or to the transformation of a nation's infrastructure (e.g. road and rail networks). The diversity of instances of such changes points to myriad practices one might expect, and can actually find, employed to deal with specific circumstances.

While acknowledging the overlap and without diminishing the value and importance of project management, our contention is that there are subtle but important qualitative differences between what we would term projects and programs. Program management as a set of management practices emerged initially from project management but now encompasses and continues to draw insights, theories, and techniques from other fields and disciplines. It has evolved to cope with instances of purposeful and structured change beyond even an inclusive, holistic conception of project management. The features of the change and its context that program management seeks to deal with include, but are not limited to, environmental uncertainty and/or ambiguity, complexity, embeddedness, and sheer scale.

Program management's leading exponents have qualitatively different conceptions of and approaches to their work compared to their project counterparts. Along some attributes or dimensions, their conceptions and practices build on core project management concepts and along others there are marked discontinuities (Partington, Pellegrinelli, and Young 2005). We contend that exemplary program management is underpinned by some different, as yet not fully explored, assumptions and considerations from those of project management. From a practice perspective, subsuming program management as a subset or a linear extension of project management risks triggering in managers a set of expectations, routines, and processes which may hinder the realization of the fundamental aim of the endeavor (Pellegrinelli and Partington 2006). From a research perspective, it risks impeding the accumulation of knowledge and development of theory by conflating different phenomena.

Research over the last few years has already shed light on programs and program management. For instance, Pellegrinelli et al. (2007) studied the extent to which the practices of program management follow the OGC MSP (Management Successful Programs) framework, one of the most recognized guides and used on UK public sector programs. The research showed that program management practices are embedded in and shaped by its context and do not comply to the guide/framework, even when this is mandated. Martinsuo and Lehtonen (2007) explore program initiation from a sense-making perspective (Weick 1995). Lehtonen and Martinsuo (2008, 2009) draw upon organization theory to analyze the creation and maintenance of program boundaries and the integration of a program within its parent organization. Partington, Pellegrinelli, and Young (2005) describe the conceptions of program managers using the phenomenographic method. This work provides rich insights and augments the various texts and guidance on programs and program management. This research-based work highlights the discrepancy between actual practice and the largely normative guidance to practitioners, and starts to build a theoretically informed and empirically grounded body of knowledge.

Without wishing to engage in a debate on definitions, which is likely to prove sterile and to grate with practitioners' lived experiences of projects and programs, or unnecessarily reify a subtle, context-dependent, and multi-faceted phenomenon, we set out our synthesis of the distinctive characteristics of programs and program management. We offer this synthesis, distilled from the literature, our research, and personal experiences of working alongside practitioners, as a step in understanding the essence of programs and mapping the emergent discipline of program management.

Programs are frameworks (of various configurations) to coordinate, communicate, align, manage, and control (primarily "project") activities to achieve a desired synergy, benefits, outcome, or vision. A (goal-oriented) program's vision and hence its success criteria are usually more strategic, such as the creation of competitive advantage, national security, or enhanced social welfare, and so program outcomes are less tangible then might be found in or desired of projects. Compared to projects, programs are emergent in terms of their content, scope, and final outcome, have a far less definite time horizon (and so less temporary in nature), and are far more embedded (so less insular and generic/standardized) within the political, cultural, and governance norms of the organization or community they seek to serve. They have porous, malleable boundaries, and are often embedded within ongoing routines, operations, and decision-making processes. They draw upon the contribution and participation of diverse stakeholders. Programs and their managers cope with business and societal environments that are inherently complex, ambiguous, fluid, and unstable. Consequently, managers of programs strive to accommodate shifting agendas, flex to changing circumstances, reconcile divergent interests and aspirations, engage stakeholders and contributors, and enable change. Program (managers) operate in "gray" environments and deal with powerful political forces and greater pluralism.

Beyond the tangible deliverables, a program's content encompasses the changes to be made to processes, behaviors, attitudes, or ways of working that are required to initiate and sustain beneficial change. Program management incorporates concepts and techniques for linking enabling outputs to the desired (strategic) benefits, determining the sequence of the work (projects), the size and pace of the tranches (related set of projects and activities) intended to create a step change in capability. Preparing the organization or members of society to receive and use the capability, managing the transition process, and facilitating benefits realization are core parts of the work. Developing novel approaches and knowledge, skills, and competence can be an intrinsic part of a program's work. Scope is left open as far as possible, and decisions taken as late as possible to create (real) options, flexibility, and the ability to respond to changing circumstances. The structure and content (hypothesis) of the program are intended to facilitate staged, incremental benefits realizations concurrent with capability development. Quality (fit for purpose) and performance levels are subject to review and change, typically at, but not restricted to, end of tranches, in the light of internal and external factors (e.g. competition, consumer attitudes, and/or new technology). Experience of trying to realize benefits feeds into the next tranche of capability development, thus creating in-built learning processes. The business case (particularly the investment appraisal) is a key tool for decision-making as well as securing or authorizing funding.

In some instances, the content and context of the change lend themselves to either a project or a program management approach. In other instances, in choosing to define and manage a change as a project rather than a program, a trade-off is implicitly or explicitly made between focus, control, efficiency, and effectiveness of delivery (project characteristics) and flexibility, accommodation, and staged benefits realization (program characteristics). Importantly, we argue that the management approach for the program—the coordinating framework—need not, and indeed should not, be the same as the approach for managing the constituent or component projects. In this context, project and program management approaches, concepts, and techniques are complements not substitutes.

The increasing use of programs to bring about major change offers researchers opportunities to study the phenomenon directly or as a context for extending or developing theories from other fields.

Research agenda

As Artto et al. (2008) point out, programs appear to be an integral part of research in other disciplines, such as strategy and organization theory. The opportunity is for researchers within our community to join these conversations and to establish program management, and more broadly purposeful and structured change, as a vibrant field of scholarship. We identify five areas from our own experiences and research offering a rich domain for scholarly management research that would also yield useful insights for program practitioners: organization theory, organizational change, strategic management, knowledge creation and management, leadership and competence. The above areas are neither intended to be comprehensive nor definitive, but a starting point for those interested in embarking on academic research.

Organization theory

Programs provide an organizing framework for component projects and an alternative approach for effecting change to independent projects. We argue above that projects and programs are conceptually different. Our work within organizations, though, suggests that these distinctions are frequently not recognized, not appreciated, and/or not taken into account when developing processes and governance arrangements. Senior managers are usually more familiar with projects and project management. Many expect the program manager to apply and report against the same structures, controls, disciplines, and performance metric as their project counterparts. Project and program management seem in many organizations to be regarded as (minor) variants of the same professional discipline.

The situation may be unremarkable, given the dominance of project management. The main professional bodies periodically update and codify the project management bodies of knowledge (e.g. APM 2006; PMI 2008), and promote professional qualifications. Program management has no independent professional body and, with the exception of the UK's Office of Government Commerce's publications (e.g. OGC 2007), is implicitly cast as an extension of project management. From an institutional theory perspective, one could argue that mimic (standards) and normative (professionalism and training) isomorphic pressures (DiMaggio and Powell 1983) are shaping actual practices. Such institutional factors profoundly influence organizations, making change difficult (Scott 2001).

Pellegrinelli et al. (2006), building on the earlier work of Partington, Pellegrinelli, and Young (2005) on the conceptions of program managers, explore organizational factors (structures, processes, and culture) that help or hinder the performance of program management work. Their work reveals a systematic preference amongst respondents. Those holding lower-order (broadly equivalent to project management) conceptions tend to prefer "mechanistic" systems or contexts, and those holding higher-order (broadly equivalent to program management) conceptions tend to prefer "organic" contexts (Burns and Stalker 1961). They contend that the adoption of mechanistic frameworks, structures, and processes may render program management unsuitable for many fluid and rapidly changing organizational environments.

The possibility of complementary and effective coexistence of projects and programs within organizations is thus called into question. The tension highlighted between institutional (isomorphic) pressures and the perceived need for ambidexterity (Birkinshaw and Gibson 2004; Gibson and Birkinshaw 2004) in terms of simultaneously operating loose/organic and tight/mechanistic structures for bringing about change warrants further research.

Drawing on organization theories other opportunities exist. How can the study of programs as "not-so-temporary" organizations inform our understanding of projects as temporary organizations (Packendorf 1995)? Do, and if so how do, programs facilitate the absorption, diffusion, and application of concurrent knowledge creation and deployment, especially tacit knowledge (Love, Fong, and Irani 2005; Williams 2008)? Other opportunities exist to build on the work of Lehtonen and Martinsuo (2008, 2009) on boundary spanning roles and processes, and to extend the work of Engwall (2003) and Pellegrinelli et al. (2007) by exploring how history and context shape program praxis.

Organizational change

Project management and program management are approaches often advocated and used, sometimes alongside other means such as operational planning or structural realignment, for realizing the desired (strategic) change in a rational, directive manner (Morris and Jamieson 2005; Winter and Szczepanek 2008). The "planned" approach conceptualizes change in organizations as a discrete episode (Mintzberg and Westeley

1992), initiated by senior management, or other dominant coalition, and brought about by procedural planning and execution. This conception of change echoes Kurt Lewin's three-step model of change: unfreeze—change—refreeze (Lewin 1947).

However, the translation of Lewin's model, from the study of and intervention in group dynamics where it was first developed to an organizational setting, has limitations. The organization as "ice cube" metaphor has been criticized for not reflecting the fluid nature of organizations, constantly shaped by power struggles, coalition-building, and shifting agendas and the messy, unfolding, and iterative nature of change in organizations, marked by omissions and hesitation (Kanter, Stein, and Jicks 1992; Pfeffer 1992; Huczynski and Buchanan 2001). Dawson (1994) argues that change cannot be solidified or treated as a series of linear events, but is better studied and understood from a processual lens. Lewin's model may have been useful in understanding and managing change, when organizations operated in more stable environments, but in today's world the notion of a change as a (single) step followed by an attempt to re-freeze a pattern of behavior may have less value and relevance.

More broadly, the punctuated equilibrium model (Romanelli and Tushman 1994) of a long period of evolutionary change punctuated by short periods of fundamental change has been challenged. Brown and Eisenhardt (1997) draw on complexity theory to argue that change in organizations is continuous. Weick (2000) draws on a sense-making perspective to argue that emergent change is a universal in organizations, and to propose that working with sense-making and adaptive processes within organizations may, in many circumstances, be a better approach. An alternative three-step model becomes: freeze—re-balance—un-freeze. Freezing allows members of the organization to see and examine their patterns of interactions and their assumptions. Re-balancing means reinterpreting and re-labeling their (socially constructed) organizational context and re-sequencing steps so they unfold, less hindered in the desired direction. Un-freezing allows the improvisation, learning, and adaptation to resume.

The conceptualization of real-world strategies lying in a spectrum between deliberate and emergent (Mintzberg and Waters 1985) has been transcended by the argument that organizations should combine Theory E and Theory O approaches to change (Beer and Nohria 2000). Theory E conceives change as senior management driven using structured processes and incentives aimed at maximizing economic (shareholder) value. Theory O conceives change as participative and emergent aimed at engaging stakeholders (especially employees) towards creating organizational (human) capabilities. Combining these contradictory positions is far from easy and risks ending up with the downside of both theories. Beer and Nohria (2000) offer a case example and a few guidelines on how to combine these (apparently) contradictory positions in practice, such as explicitly confronting the tensions between E and O goals; setting direction from the top and engaging people below; focusing simultaneously on the hard and soft sides of the organization; and planning for spontaneity. Managing change, especially large-scale organizational change, can however result in unpredictable outcomes, and in most instances managing change is a case of steering a course between intended strategies and unanticipated consequences (Balogun 2006).

Programs are a suitable context for studying organizational change, especially the tensions and interplay between: planned and emergent; punctuated and continuous; directive and participative. Programs are intended to straddle, and their managers address and reconcile, some of these perceived dichotomies. Program (are supposed to) have a vision, blueprint, or objectives, yet the notion of hypotheses, tranches, reviews, and revisions makes their management iterative and their nature emergent. If and how those involved in programs embrace or facilitate sense-making and sense-giving, learning and adaptation, is worthy of research. Programs (should) combine the delivery of capabilities with the human processes of development and change that enable those capabilities to be deployed and utilized beneficially.

Strategic management

The search for and understanding of competitive advantage is a key theme in strategy and strategic management research. Some have focused on the appropriateness of the relation or "fit" of the organization to its external environment and the actions adopted to reduce or avoid value eroding competition, as exemplified by Porter (1980). Others have argued that the source of competitive advantage lies within an organization (Barney 1991, 1995), embedded in the resources—tangible and intangible assets, such as patents, processes, relationships, know-how—or core competences (Prahalad and Hamel 1990). If these assets are valuable (generating economic rents in prevailing market conditions), rare, inimitable, and non-substitutable (VRIN), they represent a source of competitive advantage (Barney 1991, 1995). This latter theoretical perspective is known as the resource-base view (RBV). The RBV is a static theory, focusing on the organization's existing set of resources. Markets and business environments, though, are rarely static or even slow moving. The question then arises: How do organizations change their resource base in response to exogenous changes, or proactively as a way of shaping, and evolving favorably, their business environment(s) (Nelson and Winter 1982; Winter 2003)? The quest, after all, is for sustainable (over time) competitive advantage.

Dynamic capabilities enable an organization to change, grow, and prosper. Teece, Pisano, and Shuen (1997) frame dynamic capabilities as competencies, including tacit knowledge and practical know-how held collectively by members of the organization that enable an organization to address rapidly changing markets. Eisenhardt and Martin (2003) provide examples of dynamic capabilities as processes, such as product development routines, alliances and acquisition capabilities, resource allocation routines, and knowledge transfer and replication routines. Helfat et al. offer an inclusive and synthetic definition of a dynamic capability as: "the capacity of an organization to purposefully create, extend or modify its resource base" (2007: 4). Building on prior literature and research, they include learning, environmental scanning, opportunity identification and selection, and more broadly the insights, judgment, orchestration, coordination, and entrepreneurship of strategic managers, as intrinsic to dynamic capabilities. Project and program management fall within such a conception of dynamic capabilities. Helfat et al. differentiate between technical fitness—"how effectively a capability performs its intended function when normalized (divided) by its cost" (2007: 7), and evolutionary fitness or external fit— "how well a dynamic capability enables an organization to make a living by creating, extending or modifying its resource base" (ibid.). Organizations thus may have and deploy dynamic capabilities that (cost) effectively generate changes in the firm's resources, and so are technically fit, but the new resource base is misaligned with market or environmental requirements, and so is evolutionarily unfit. Wang and Ahmed (2007) synthesize the literature and research and describe common characteristics or components of dynamic capabilities: adaptive capability, absorptive capability, and innovative capability. Ambrosini and Bowman (2009), building on prior work on the role of dynamic capabilities in informing corporate-level strategy (Bowman and Ambrosini 2003), propose a model for understanding dynamic capabilities as part of a value creation process in the context of internal and external factors (paths and positions).

This perspective offers a lens to study program management as a dynamic capability for bringing about sustained organizational vitality. Of particular interest might be if and how programs lead to or facilitate greater evolutionary "fitness," for instance when compared to projects. Another theme might be a conceptualization of projects and programs in terms of the (possible) trade-off between evolutionary and technical fit. The research opportunities are great since more research is needed to explore and develop the conceptualization of dynamic capabilities (Wang and Ahmed 2007; Ambrosini and Bowman 2009).

Leadership

The organizational world, whether private or public sector, is shifting from formal hierarchies and management through orderly command and control processes to loosely coupled networks of different interests held in partial and fragile alignment through mutual learning and adaptation. Traditional notions of leadership as an individual task are being supplemented and replaced by ideas on shared, collective, or distributed leadership (Ancona et al. 2007).

Pearce and Conger define shared leadership as: "a dynamic, interactive influence process among individuals in a group...leadership is broadly distributed among a set of individuals instead of centralised in hands of a single individual" (2003: 1). Shared leadership shifts attention away from the "leader" and from the uni-directional process of "leading" that has dominated the literature over the last decades that often casts leaders as heroic individuals. Leadership is seen as a set of practices that are, can, and should be enacted by many people at all levels in an organization or society. The contribution and leadership of the many, though, is frequently lost in the telling of the story of the one. Shared leadership is essentially a social process—a fluid, multi-directional, collective activity that is embedded in the context in which it unfolds. The ideals of shared leadership are positive interactions characterized by zest, empowered action, increased self-esteem, new knowledge, desire for more connection (Fletcher and Kaufer 2003). Truly shared leadership must overcome the cultural and historical legacy of the heroic leader and the ego needs (recognition, power, control, etc.) of aspiring (solo, stereotypically masculine) leaders. Our language of leadership and our approach to promotion in organizations (covertly) favors ruthless self-advancement over trust, openness, and vulnerability. Many individuals may opt for the more tranquil, responsibility-free, and conflict-free life of followership or group membership, though the new generation of knowledge workers appear more demanding and impatient than their predecessors.

Shared leadership is the norm in many public sector contexts, sometimes despite the projected image of clear divisions of responsibility, delegated authorities, and reporting lines. In local authorities, elected councilors work alongside executive officers. In hospitals, managers work alongside clinicians and both groups interact with wider supervisory, funding, and professional bodies and internal constituencies. Such pluralistic settings are characterized by diffuse power and divergent objectives, which demand the formation of leadership constellations and collective leadership to bring about change (Denis, Lamothe, and Langley 2001). These constellations are fragile, subject to tensions from diverse influences and constituencies, and result in stuttering, sporadic change. Pluralism and its consequences can be expected increasingly to characterize private sector enterprises and programs.

Shared leadership, where no individual has ultimate responsibility or accountability, sits uneasily with the long held principle of a single point of integrative responsibility (Archibald 1976) that has underpinned most project and program management literature and research. Yet some degree of shared leadership is not a completely new concept in project and program management. Hunt and Rubin (1973) researching the relationships between the US Government (Department of Defense) and its contractors found that the clear separation of roles mandated to ensure probity in terms of procurement and governance did not exist in practice. Rather, they found blurred organizational boundaries, overlapping interests, and perceptions of a common fate, and interlocking, interdependent, or interpenetrating control and decision processes. Such circumstances, they posited, led to shared leadership models. Engwall (2003) attributed part of the relative success of one project studied to the project manager's "fuzzy way of coordinating," his humility, his trust in his colleagues, and his harmony with the prevailing norms and structures. Shared leadership may be favored by more consensual cultures, both organizational and national, where collectivism is favored over individualism (Hofstede 2001). The Office of Government Commerce's guidance on program management (OGC 2003, 2007), while still positing prescriptive roles, admits a broader, though not truly shared, leadership arrangement. The program manager (PgM) is principally responsible for the delivery of the new capability, the business change manager (BCM) is responsible for liaising and preparing the business for the change. Hierarchically above these roles are a sponsoring group which includes a senior responsible owner (SRO). Empirically these roles are not always performed, even where mandated (Pellegrinelli et al. 2007), and the self-perceived accountability of the SRO varies (Lupson 2007).

More research is called for to study actual rather than normative leadership in/of programs, to understand how stakeholder engagement and stakeholder collaboration and contributions create and facilitate shared leadership at multiple levels, and to explore how tensions are addressed, commitments and momentum secured, and fragile alliances and coalitions held together in relation to major or contested changes.

Competence

Understanding, developing, and leveraging competence in a work environment has long been an aim of managers and management researchers (Horton 2000). Competence can be defined as knowledge, skills, and personal attributes that lead to superior results or to meet defined performance standards (Boyatzis 1982). More simply, competence is being good at doing something. Insights into how, why, and under what conditions some people perform better than others, enable better job design, selection, and development of individuals. The two traditional approaches to studying competence are known as "work-oriented" and "worker-oriented,"

Work-oriented studies of competence take the work as the point of departure, identify work activities, and transform them into personal competencies. Project management bodies of knowledge published by professional bodies such as the UK Association for Project Management (APM 2006) and the Project Management Institute (PMI 2008) are examples of work-oriented competence, based on the accumulated knowledge of practitioners with some academic input. Typical of the genre, they define relevant knowledge areas, activities and processes, and (sometimes implied) performance indicators or benchmarks. Worker-oriented take the worker as the point of departure and attempt to capture a generalization of the attributes—typically knowledge, skills, and abilities—possessed by competent workers. In the project management field, Gadaken's (1994) study of the characteristics of top-performing project managers in UK and US military acquisition commands is an example of the genre.

An alternative interpretive approach called phenomenography was used by Partington, Pellegrinelli, and Young (2005), drawing on the ground-breaking work of Jorgen Sandberg (1994, 2000), to study the competence of individuals performing program roles. Phenomenography is an empirical research approach developed in the field of education research in Sweden in the 1970s (Marton 1981). It is "the empirical study of the differing ways in which people experience, perceive, apprehend, understand or conceptualize various phenomena in, and aspects of, the world around them" (Marton 1994: 4425). In other words, phenomenographic research attempts to see and distill as faithfully as possible the phenomenon of interest from the informant's perspective—in this case what individual workers conceive of as work and, through the elicitation of examples, how they conceive of it. An individual's competence is constituted by the subjective meaning that work takes on for workers in their lived experience of it. In any group of people, there are a limited number (typically between two and six) of conceptions of the same aspect of reality (Marton 1981). Conceptions can be arranged into a hierarchy of increasing complexity, in which "the different ways of experiencing the phenomenon in question can be defined as subsets of the component parts and relationships within more inclusive or complex ways of seeing the phenomenon" (Marton and Booth 1997: 125). The nested set of conceptions provides a way of evaluating performance and informing development.

The research and its resulting competence framework have been to underpin management development and assessment processes (Pellegrinelli, Partington, and Young 2003) and were later elaborated by Pellegrinelli (2008). Chen and Partington (2006) used the phenomenographic method to study the conceptions of construction project managers. Lupson (2007) also used the method to explore the conceptions of accountability held by British civil servants performing the role of Senior Responsible Owner for public sector programs in the UK.

This work can be extended to study the conceptions of individuals performing other roles related to programs (and portfolios) such as Sponsors in a commercial setting, Business Change Managers (OGC 2003, 2007), managers and staff of Project or Program Management Offices (Marsh 2001; Aubry, Hobbs, and Thuillier 2008), and other contributors or stakeholders. This work would complement and enrich other research into roles and competence (e.g. Blomquist and Mueller 2006; Crawford 2005).

IN SUMMARY

Our aim in this chapter has been to identify opportunities for research and scholarship in relation to programs and program management. We have sought to highlight the developments in the field and the various debates and perspectives, and to establish a platform for future research by offering our synthesis of the principal characteristics of programs and program management.

The research opportunities outlined above are not fully researched proposals, but a springboard for further inquiry, analysis, and development. Other theories and perspectives may prove fruitful for scholars wishing to add to our knowledge and to inform practice.

We hope that the chapter has stimulated thoughts and will inspire action.

REFERENCES

AMBROSINI, V., and BOWMAN, C. (2009). "What are dynamic capabilities and are they a useful construct in strategic management," *International Journal of Management Reviews*, 11/1: 29–49.

ANCONA, D., MALONE, T. W., ORLIKOWSKI, W. J., and SENGE, P. J. (2007). "In praise of the incomplete leader," *Harvard Business Review*, February: 92–100.

ARCHIBALD, R. D. (1976). *Managing High-Technology Programs and Projects*. New York: John Wiley and Sons.

ARTTO, K., MATINSUO, M., GEMUENDEN, H. G., and MURTOARO, J. (2008). "Foundations of program management: a bibliometric view," *International Journal of Project Management*, 27: 1–18.

ASSOCIATION FOR PROJECT MANAGEMENT (APM) (2006). *Body of Knowledge*, 5th edn. High Wycombe: APM.

AUBRY, M., HOBBS, B., and THUILLIER, D. (2008). "Organisational project management: an historical approach to the study of PMOs," *International Journal of Project Management*, 26: 38–43.

BALOGUN, J. (2006). "Managing change: steering a course between intended strategies and unanticipated consequences," *Long Range Planning*, 39: 29–49.

BARNEY, J. (1991). "Firm resources and sustained competitive advantage," *Journal of Management*, 17/1: 99–120.

——(1995). "Looking inside for competitive advantage," *Academy of Management Executive*, 9/4: 49–61.

BARTLETT, J. (2002). *Managing Programs of Business Change*, 3rd edn. Hook: Project Manager Today Publications.

BEER, M., and NOHRIA, N. (2000). "Cracking the code of change," *Harvard Business Review*, May–June: 133–41.

BIRKINSHAW, J., and GIBSON, C. (2004). "Building ambidexterity into an organization," *MIT Sloan Management Review*, 45/4: 47–55.

BLOMQUIST, T., and MUELLER, R. (2006). "Practices, roles, and responsibilities of middle managers in program and portfolio management," *Project Management Journal*, 37/1: 52–66.

BOWMAN, C., and AMBROSINI, V. (2003). "How the resource-based and the dynamic capability views of the firm inform corporate level strategy," *British Journal of Management*, 14: 289–303.

BOYATZIS, R. E. (1982). *The Competent Manager: A Model for Effective Performance*. New York: Wiley.

BROWN, S. L., and EISENHARDT, K. M. (1997). "The art of continuous change: linking complexity theory and time-paced evolution in relentlessly shifting organizations," *Administrative Science Quarterly*, March/42: 1–34.

Burns, T., and Stalker, G. M. (1961). *The Management of Innovation*. London: Tavistock.

Chen, P., and Partington, D. (2006), "Three conceptual levels of construction project management work," *International Journal of Project Management*, 24/5: 412–21.

Crawford, L. (2005). "Senior management perceptions of project management competence," *International Journal of Project Management*, 23: 7–16.

Dawson, P. (1994). *Organizational Change: A Processual Approach*. London: Paul Chapman Publishing.

Denis, J.-L., Lamothe, L., and Langley, A. (2001). "The dynamics of collective leadership and strategic change in pluralistic organizations," *Academy of Management Journal*, 44/4: 809–37.

DiMaggio, P. J., and Powell, W. W. (1983). "The iron cage revisited: institutional isomorphism and collective rationality in organizational fields," *American Sociological Review*, 48/April: 147–60.

Eisenhardt, K. M., and Martin, J. M. (2003). "Dynamic capabilities: what are they?" *Strategic Management Journal*, 21/10–11: 1105–21.

Engwall, M. (2003). "No project is an island: linking projects to history and context," *Research Policy*, 32: 789–808.

Evaristo, R., and van Fenema, P. C. (1999). "A typology of project management: emergence and evolution of new forms," *International Journal of Project Management*, 17/5: 275–81.

Ferns, D. C. (1991). "Developments in program management," *International Journal of Project Management*, 9/3: 148–56.

Fletcher, J. K., and Kaufer, K. (2003). "Shared leadership: paradox and possibility, in Pearce," in C. L. Pearce and J. A. Conger (eds.), *Shared Leadership: Reframing the Hows and Whys of Leadership*. Thousand Oaks, CA: Sage.

Flyvbjerg, B., Bruzelius, N., and Rothengatter, W. (2003). *Megaprojects and Risk: An Anatomy of Ambition*. Cambridge: Cambridge University Press.

Gadaken, D. O. C. (1994). "Project managers as leaders: competencies of top performers," Paper presented at 12th INTERNET World Congress on Project Management, Oslo.

Gaddie, S. (2003). "Enterprise program management: connecting strategic planning to project delivery," *Journal of Facilities Management*, 2/2: 177–89.

Gibson, C. B., and Birkinshaw, J. (2004). "The antecedents, consequences, and mediating role of organizational ambidexterity," *Academy of Management Journal*, 47/2: 209–26.

Gray, R. J. (1997). "Alternative approaches to program management," *International Journal of Project Management*, 15/3: 5–9.

Helfat, C. E., Finkelstein, S., Mitchell, W., Peteraf, M. A., Singh, H., Teece, D. J., and Winter, S. G. (2007). *Dynamic Capabilities: Understanding Strategic Change in Organizations*. Oxford: Blackwell Publishing.

Hodgson, D. (2002). "Disciplining the professional: the case of project management," *Journal of Management Studies*, 39/6: 803–21.

——(2004). "Project work: the legacy of bureaucratic control in the post-bureaucratic organization," *Organization*, 11/1: 81–100.

——and Cicmil, S. (2002). "The politics of standards in modern management: making 'the project' a reality," *Journal of Management Studies*, 44/3: 431–50.

Hofstede, G. (2001). *Culture's Consequences*, 2nd edn. Beverley Hills, CA: Sage.

Horton, S. (2000). "Introduction—the competency movement: its origins and impact on the public sector," *International Journal of Public Sector Management*, 13/4: 306–18.

HUCZYNSKI, A., and BUCHANAN, D. (2001). *Organizational Behaviour*, 4th edn. Harlow: FT/ Prentice Hall.

HUNT, R. G., and RUBIN, I. S. (1973). "Approaches to managerial control in interpenetrating systems: the case of government–industry relations," *Academy of Management Journal*, 16/2: 296–311.

KANTER, R. M., STEIN, B. A., and JICKS, T. D. (1992). *The Challenge of Organizational Change*. New York: Free Press.

LEHTONEN, P., and MARTINSUO, M. (2008). "Change program initiation: defining and managing the program-organization boundary," *International Journal of Project Management*, 26: 21–9.

——(2009). "Integrating the change program with the parent organization," *International Journal of Project Management*, 27: 154–65.

LEWIN, K. (1947). "Frontiers in group dynamics," in D. Cartwright (ed.), *Field Theory in Social Science*. London: Social Science Paperbacks.

LOVE, P., FONG, P. S. W., and IRANI, Z. (2005). "Introduction," in P. Love, P. S. W. Fong, and Z. Irani (eds.), *Management of Knowledge in Project Environments*. Oxford: Burlington/ Elsevier.

LUPSON, J. (2007). "A phenomenographic study of British civil servants' conceptions of accountability," Ph.D. thesis, Cranfield School of Management.

LYCETT, M., RASSAU, A., and DANSON, J. (2004). "Program management: a critical review," *International Journal of Project Management*, 22: 289–99.

MARSH, D. (2001). *The Project and Program Support Office Handbook*. Hook: Project Manager Today Publications.

MARTINSUO, M., and LEHTONEN, P. (2006). "Program and its initiation in practice: development program initiation in a public consortium," *International Journal of Project Management*, 25: 337–45.

MARTON, F. (1981). "Phenomenography: describing conceptions of the world around us," *Instructional Science*, 10: 177–200.

——(1994). "Phenomenography," in T. Husen and T. N. Postlethwaite (eds.), *The International Encyclopaedia of Education*. Oxford: Pergamon, 4424–9.

——and BOOTH, S. (1997). *Learning and Awareness*. Hillsdale, NJ: Lawrence Erlbaum Associates.

MAYLOR, H., BRADY, T., COOKE-DAVIES, T., and HODGSON, D. (2006). "From projectification to programmification," *International Journal of Project Management*, 24: 663–72.

MEIER, S. R. (2008). "Best project management and systems engineering practices in the preacquisition phase for federal intelligence and defense agencies," *Project Management Journal*, March: 59–71.

MIDLER, C. (1995). "Projectification of the firm: the Renault case," *Scandinavian Management Journal*, 11/4: 363–75.

MINTZBERG, H., and WATERS, J. A. (1985). "Of strategies, deliberate and emergent," *Strategic Management Journal*, 6: 257–72.

——and WESTELEY, F. (1992). "Cycles of organizational change," *Strategic Management Journal*, 13: 39–59.

MORRIS, P. W. G. (1994). *The Management of Projects*. London: Thomas Telford.

——(2009). "Implementing strategy through project management: the importance of the project front-end," in T. M. Williams, K. Samset, and K. J. Sunnevåg (eds.), *Making Essential Choices with Scant Information: Front-End Decision-Making in Major Projects*. Basingstoke: Palgrave Macmillan.

——and Hough, G. H. (1987). *The Anatomy of Major Projects: A Study of the Reality of Project Management.* Chichester: John Wiley and Sons.

——and Jamieson, A. (2005). "Moving from corporate strategy to project strategy," *Project Management Journal*, December: 5–18.

Murray-Webster, R., and Thiry, M. (2000). "Managing programs of projects," in J. R. Turner and S. J. Simister (eds.), *Gower Handbook of Project Management.* Aldershot: Gower, 33–46.

Nelson, R. R., and Winter, S. G. (1982). *An Evolutionary Theory of Economic Change.* Cambridge, MA: Harvard University Press.

Office of Government Commerce (OGC) (2003, 2007). *Managing Successful Programs.* London: The Stationery Office.

Packendorff, J. (1995). "Inquiring into temporary organization: new directions for project management research," *Scandinavian Management Journal*, 11: 319–33.

Partington, D., Pellegrinelli, S., and Young, M. (2005). "Attributes and levels of program management competence: an interpretive study," *International Journal of Project Management*, 23: 87–95.

Pearce, C. L., and Conger, J. A. (2003). "All those years ago: the historical underpinnings of shared leadership," in C. L. Pearce and J. A. Conger (eds.), *Shared Leadership: Reframing the Hows and Whys of Leadership.* Thousand Oaks, CA: Sage.

Pellegrinelli, S. (1997). "Program management: organising project based change," *International Journal of Project Management*, 15/3: 141–9.

——(2002). "Shaping context: the role and challenge for programs," *International Journal of Project Management*, 20: 229–33.

——(2008). *Thinking and Acting as a Great Program Manager*, Basingstoke: Palgrave Macmillan.

——and Partington, D. (2006). "Pitfalls in taking a project-based view of programs," *Proceedings of the PMI Congress 2006—Europe*, Madrid.

——and Young, M. (2003). "Understanding and assessing program management competence," *Proceedings of the PMI Congress 2003—Europe*, The Hague.

——Hemingway, C., Mohdzain, Z., Shah, M., and Stenning, V. (2006). "Helping or hindering? The effects of organisational factors on the performance of program management work," *Proceedings of the PMI Research Conference 2006*, Montreal.

——————(2007). "The importance of context in program management: an empirical review of program practices," *International Journal of Project Management*, 25: 41–55.

Pfeffer, J. (1992). *Managing with Power: Politics and Influence in Organizations.* Boston: Harvard Business School Press.

Pich, M. T., Loch, C. H., and DeMeyer, A. (2003). "On uncertainty, ambiguity, and complexity in project management," *Management Science*, 48/8: 1008–23.

Porter, M. (1980). *Competitive Strategy.* New York: Free Press.

Prahalad, C. K., and Hamel, G. (1990). "The core competence of the corporation," *Harvard Business Review*, May–June: 79–91.

Project Management Institute (2006). *The Standard for Program Management.* Newtown Square, PA: Project Management Institute.

——(2008). *PMBOK: A Guide to the Project Management Body of Knowledge*, 4th edn. Newtown Square, PA: Project Management Institute.

P2M (2008). *A Guidebook of Project and Program Management for Enterprise Innovation.* Tokyo: Project Management Professionals Certification Centre (PMCC).

Reiss, G. (1996). *Program Management Demystified*. London: E & TFN Spon.

Romanelli, E., and Tushman, M. L. (1994). "Organizational transformation as punctuated equilibrium: an empirical test," *Academy of Management Journal*, 37/5: 1141–66.

Sandberg, J. (1994). *Human Competence at Work: An Interpretative Approach*. Göteborg: Bas.

——(2000). "Understanding human competence at work: an interpretative approach," *Academy of Management Journal*, 43/1: 9–25.

Sapolsky, H. (1972). *The Polaris System Development: Bureaucratic and Programmatic Success in Government*. Cambridge, MA: Harvard University Press.

Scott, W. R. (2001). *Institutions and Organizations*, 2nd edn. Thousand Oaks, CA: Sage.

Söderlund, J., and Bredin, K. (2006). "HRM in project-intensive firms: changes and challenges," *Human Resource Management*, 45/2: 249–65.

Teece, D. J., Pisano, G., and Shuen, S. (1997). "Dynamic capabilities and strategic management," *Strategic Management Journal*, 18/7: 509–33.

Thiry, M. (2002). "Combining value and project management into an effective program management model," *International Journal of Project Management*, 20: 221–7.

——(2004). "For DAD: a program management life-cycle process," *International Journal of Project Management*, 22: 245–52.

Vereecke, A., Pandelaere, E., Deschoolmeester, D., and Stevens, M. (2003). "A classification of development programs and its consequences for program development," *International Journal of Operations and Production Management*, 23/10: 1279–90.

Wang, C. L., and Ahmed, P. K. (2007). "Dynamic capabilities: a review and research agenda," *International Journal of Management Reviews*, 9/1: 31–51.

Weick, K. E. (1995). *Sensemaking in Organizations*. Thousand Oaks, CA: Sage Publications.

——(2000). "Emergent change as a universal in organizations," in M. Beer and N. Nohria (eds.), *Breaking the Code of Change*. Boston: Harvard Business School Press.

Wheelwright, S. C., and Clark, K. B. (1992). "Creating project plans to focus product development," *Harvard Business Review*, March–April: 70–82.

Williams, D., and Parr, T. (2004). *Enterprise Program Management*. Basingstoke: Palgrave Macmillan.

Williams, T. (2005). "Assessing and moving on from the dominant project management discourse in the light of project overruns," *IEEE Transactions on Engineering Management*, 52/4: 497–508.

——(2008). "How do organisations learn from projects—and do they?" *IEEE Transactions on Engineering Management*, 55/2: 248–66.

Winter, M., and Szczepanek, T. (2008). "Projects and programs as value creation processes: a new perspective and some practical implications," *International Journal of Project Management*, 26: 95–103.

Winter, S. G. (2003). "Understanding dynamic capabilities," *Strategic Management Journal*, 24: 991–5.

CHAPTER 11

PROJECTS AND INNOVATION

INNOVATION AND PROJECTS

TIM BRADY

MIKE HOBDAY

INTRODUCTION

For many years now, economic prosperity has been driven by developments in science and technology. But, many major problems facing humanity today—such as climate change, the consequences of an ageing population, security—are not just technological but social, cultural, and political. Innovation, both technological and organizational, is increasingly recognized as fundamental to economic and social well-being. Those countries and organizations that can harness their knowledge, technological capabilities, and experience to create novelty in what they produce (whether it is in products or services) and/or how these are produced and delivered, are more likely to be successful in an increasingly competitive globalizing world. A few innovations might spring from a flash of genius, but most (especially the successful ones) are the result of purposeful activity (Drucker 1985). Innovation and change in organizations are often dependent on projects, one-time initiatives to launch new products, new processes, new ventures, and reorganizations (Shenhar and Dvir 2007). The project is usually the means by which innovation takes place. Projects are a therefore a key way of organizing innovation—and innovation is a major output of certain kinds of projects.

This chapter focuses on the historical and practical relationship between projects and innovation and the connections between the two, often separate, fields of research. First we provide a review of the historical linkages between innovation and projects/ project management, including early military projects in the 1950s and 1960s, showing how projects were used to ferment innovation outside of the conventional organizational forms, politics, and processes. Next we discuss the many ways in which the literature treats innovation, providing a clear and simple practical definition of innovation. Following this we provide a summary of different models of innovation, suggesting how the nature and function of innovation has changed over the past decades, how researchers have interpreted these changes, and how they link to the field of project management. We then attempt to illustrate the complex and changing interdependencies between projects and innovation by examining a particular class of projects, namely high technology, large-scale capital goods (or "complex product systems," CoPS) where the primary form of production has always been project based. We present recent research findings which elaborate on how innovation occurs in CoPS, through the building up of innovation capability within the organization, primarily centered on various kinds of projects. Next we show how so-called "vanguard" projects are used to generate novel combinations of products, systems, and services in CoPS; in effect, to create new markets, often with the direct involvement of the user or customer. The conclusion summarizes the main points and suggests how future research could further enhance our understanding between projects and innovation, touching on the idea of the "project-based economy" which proposes that a large proportion of economic and innovative activity is organized in the form of projects.

Historical linkages between innovation and project management research

Interest in the fields of innovation and project management has evolved in parallel over long periods and the two have been closely linked in terms of development. This section begins by briefly describing the contrasting origins of the disciplines of project management and innovation studies, pointing to emerging links between the two areas. It then points to four subsequent intellectual trajectories which have played a major part in the understanding and practice of projects and innovation: first, the "rational" mainstream project management approach; second, the literature on organizational design which provided early conceptualization of project-based organizing; third, cross-functional and cross-sectoral research on how project-based structures operate across multi-disciplinary fields; and fourth, the relatively new interdisciplinary area of "project business" which attempts to demonstrate the importance of projects to strategic business activities, including the creation of new markets.

The discipline of project management emerged between the 1930s and 1950s with its roots in the military and process engineering industries (Morris 1994: 8). It was in the cold war environment following the Second World War (the 1950s and 1960s) that we saw an expansion in military projects and a corresponding growth in interest in project management. This period saw the development and use of systems integration and project management tools for planning and control (e.g. PERT, CPM).

Innovation studies presents a somewhat different pattern of evolution. While the original work of Joseph Schumpeter—sometimes referred to as the "Godfather" of innovation studies (Tidd, Bessant, and Pavitt 2005: 7)—took place in the early twentieth century, and was first published in English in the 1930s, scholarly publications on innovation were few and far between before the 1960s (Fagerberg and Verspagen 2009). It was during the cold war that institutions like the Research and Development (RAND) Corporation were established by a US government well aware that their global dominance depended on their technological leadership, to help maintain this advantage. Many of the early publications on the economics of R&D and innovation originated within RAND and many people who became prominent in the field of innovation studies (such as Richard Nelson, Sidney Winter, Burton Klein, and Kenneth Arrow) were associated with RAND (Fagerberg and Verspagen 2009).

The study of projects and project management has broadly followed a number of intellectual trajectories. First, mainstream project management as a rational, technical, and managerial discipline emerged in the 1960s to serve a large practitioner-based community of professional project managers, their associations, and industry consultants. The epistemology of this newly articulated approach was strongly positivist, the underlying ethos being one of control (Smyth and Morris 2007). This is still very much the essence of "core" project management. Numerous textbooks and handbooks on project management offer guidance, concepts, tools, and techniques on how to execute projects on time, within budget, and to required customer specifications.

As pointed out recently by Shenhar and Dvir (2007) the standard, formal, approach to project management is based on a predictable, relatively simple, and rational model which is largely decoupled from changes in the environment or business needs. Morris (1994), Morris and Pinto (2004), Davies and Hobday (2005), Dvir and Lechler (2004), and Shenhar and Dvir (2004) show that this approach has major limitations in that it fails to account for (a) the "emergent" nature of projects where, for example, initial requirements cannot be fully specified at the outset; and (b) the fact that management works to shape the project definition to best fit stakeholders' strategies and to optimize the predicted benefits. In addition it treats all projects "as if" they were the same and fails to acknowledge the importance of context.

These limitations have both analytical and practical consequence. Analytically, the dominance of the "rational" approach leads to a failure in fully appreciating the different kinds of project models which exist across diverse industrial landscapes. Also, the role of uncertainty, learning, and informal processes are underplayed models of project management, in favor of simplistic, rule-based models. On the practical level, as Shenhar and Dvir (2007: 7) point out, projects exhibit high failure rates due to senior managers and project teams underestimating, up front, the extent of uncertainty and complexity involved in their projects and failing to adapt their management style to the situation. Lovallo and Kahneman (2003) put this underestimation down to what they call "optimism bias" in order to get projects approved. Flyvbjerg (2003), whilst acknowledging the existence of such bias, suggests that deliberate underestimation relates more to political pressures to make optimistic forecasts. As we show below, the rational approach is especially deficient in the uncertain environment of high-technology CoPS industries, where customer needs cannot be fully specified in advance and project success requires substantial "learning" among the many actors involved in production.

Second, the literature on organizational design laid important foundations for contemporary theorizing and empirical research on project-based organizing. In contrast to the hierarchical and mechanistic management structures used in functional organizations, a project brings people together in an organic, adaptive, and flatter structure—or adhocracy as Alvin Toffler (1970) called it—that is able to innovate around specific customer needs and sometimes a particular product. Burns and Stalker (1961) suggested that in stable conditions a mechanistic approach would be more suitable whereas in more changeable conditions, such as rapid technological or market change, then a more organic form of organization would be more appropriate for innovation to take place, but they did not explicitly refer to the project form. Lawrence and Lorsch (1967) noted that both types of organizational form could coexist in a single organization because of the different demands from the functional sub-environments. This idea was developed further by Tushman and O'Reilly (1996) who talked of the need for ambidextrous organizations that could cope with both evolutionary and revolutionary technological change.

Galbraith (1973) first identified the spectrum of organizational design alternatives ranging from pure functional through matrix to pure product/project-based organizational choices. Matrix organizations were developed by US aerospace manufacturers in the late 1950s as an efficient way of integrating the resources required to deliver larger numbers of projects (Lawrence and Lorsch 1967; Galbraith 1973; Davis and Lawrence 1977). Mintzberg (1983) was among the first organizational theorists to articulate the strengths of the project form in a rapidly changing business environment. Whereas functional organizations focus inwardly on increasing performance by perfecting standardized processes and outputs, project structures focus outwardly on solving specific customer problems and encouraging innovation. Mintzberg's classification of organizational forms that includes adhocracies is widely cited in more recent perspectives on project-based organizing (e.g. Hobday 2000; Gann and Salter 2000). While these early discussions about organizational form did not specifically place the project form at their center, in the 1990s we saw the emergence of what has been called the Scandinavian school of project organization (e.g. Lundin and Söderholm 1995, 1998; Kreiner 1995; Lindkvist, Söderlund, and Tell 1998; Sahlin-Andersson and Söderholm 2002; Engwall 2003) which did. This "school" was inspired by work in IRNOP (the International Research Network on Organizing by Projects), which had its inaugural conference in 1994 in Lycksele in the north of Sweden hosted by Umeå School of Business and Economics. The contributions from this school of thought provided valuable conceptual insights into projects as temporary organizations, showing how projects are embedded within the firm and wider networks.

This particular tradition does not directly address the innovation dimension. In theory, temporary organizations (e.g. project forms) can be central to innovation, allowing firms to conduct "out of the ordinary" experimental activities. However, we also know that many innovations are developed in stable, relatively permanent settings without the pressure of intense deadlines. It may well be that incremental innovations which need sustained periods of learning require the support of more permanent organizations, while temporary project organizations are best suited to radically new innovations. It is also likely that the most appropriate organizational setting differs according to function and technological and industrial context (as suggested in the next area of research).

Third, research has shown how different project-based structures are used to accomplish multi-disciplinary projects of various kinds, including research and development (R&D) and new product development projects (e.g. Freeman 1974; Allen 1977; Katz and Allen 1985; Clark and Fujimoto 1991; Iansiti 1998; Lindkvist, Söderlund, and Tell 1998; Chesbrough 2003; Cusumano and Nobeoka 1998). This tradition includes in-depth studies of particular types of major project (e.g. Morris and Hough 1987; Morris 1994; Wheelwright and Clark 1992; Bowen et al. 1994) and project activities in specific sectors (e.g. computers: Kidder 1982 and Bauer et al. 1992; North Sea oil projects: Stinchcombe and Heimer 1985; automobiles: Willman and Winch 1985; Whipp and Clark 1986; Clark and Fujimoto 1991; Midler 1993). In contrast to the mainstream project management approach, these studies show the importance of distinguishing between different types of projects and the need to proceed incrementally (cf. Klein and Meckling 1958), a practice now recommended by the many government bodies—including the UK Office of Government Computing and the UK National Audit Office (House of Commons 2004). Issues concerned with understanding better the causes of project failure have figured prominently in this area of research (Morris and Hough 1987; Miller and Lessard 2001; Flyvbjerg, Bruzelius, and Rothengatter 2003).

Fourth, since the mid 1990s, a new area of interdisciplinary study which has been referred to as "project enterprise" or "project business," which combines elements of each of the above traditions, has revealed the importance of projects to the strategic activities central to the direction of business enterprise and the creation of new markets (Artto and Wikström 2005; Davies and Hobday 2005; Prencipe, Davies, and Hobday 2003; Morris 2004; Morris and Jamieson 2004; Morris and Pinto 2004;

Shenhar and Dvir 2007; Artto and Kujala 2008). This work emphasizes the context in which projects are undertaken and how value and business benefit can be leveraged through more effective project management (Winter et al. 2006).

DEFINING INNOVATION

As with many broad concepts, the focus and definition of innovation has evolved over time. Much research focus has been placed on technological innovation, perhaps overly, as technological innovation is usually associated with organizational innovation. However, even the early work of Schumpeter recognized that innovation was not simply about new technology but encompassed products, methods of production, sources of supply, markets, and different ways of organizing. Over the years other definitions have maintained this approach. Freeman, one of the pioneers of the field, asserted that industrial innovation includes the technical, design, manufacturing, management, and commercial activities involved in the marketing of a new (or improved) product or the first commercial use of new (or improved) process or equipment (Freeman 1974). Affuah (1998) defines it as the use of new knowledge to offer a new product or service that customers want. Dodgson, Gann, and Salter (2008) define innovation as the successful commercial exploitation of new ideas which includes the scientific, technological, organizational, financial, and business activities leading to the introduction of a new (or improved) product or service.

The common elements in all these definitions are novelty and success—if there is nothing new about the product, process, way of organizing, etc. then it does not amount to an innovation. Equally, if an idea or attempt to change an industrial product or system does not generate commercial value then it cannot be defined as an innovation. The word innovation itself comes from the Latin word *innovare*—to make new. What is also clear from these definitions is that innovation is, above all, a process—the process of turning new ideas into reality and gaining value from them (Tidd and Bessant 2009: 19).

Scholars have also distinguished between distinct types of innovation. Most make a distinction between incremental and radical innovation. Marquis (1969) proposed three distinct types of innovation: (i) innovation related to complex systems (such as communication networks, weapon systems, or moon missions which take many years to develop and cost millions of dollars); (ii) innovation represented by a radical breakthrough in technology that transforms an industry (such as xerography, jet engines); (iii) nuts and bolts innovation—what he called the ordinary, everyday within-the-firm kind of technological change. Much of the research on innovation has been based on studies of the second two types—radical and incremental. It is clear from the earlier discussion that project management emerged from developments related to the first type of innovation Marquis referred to—complex systems. We shall return to a discussion on the nature of innovation in such sectors later, but first we shall briefly sketch out how the understanding of the innovation process has evolved over time and how this related to developments in project management.

Evolving models of innovation and links to project management

Since the 1950s there has been a proliferation of innovation models, many purporting to explain and/or guide the process of innovation within industrial firms, others to justify particular forms of government policy and intervention. In a seminal contribution to the field, Rothwell (1991, 1992, 1994) argued that the post-war era was characterized by successive waves of technological innovation associated with a corresponding evolution in corporate strategy. Table 11.1 summarizes Rothwell's view of the evolution of innovation models from the 1950s to the 1990s in five successive generations. Usually, a "model" of innovation is comprised of a high-level description of the processes, drivers, and actors involved in innovation. The term "generation" refers to how these models have changed in emphasis, nature, and key categories over time, often decades.

The first-generation models of innovation, so-called technology push models, were simple linear models developed in the 1950s which treated innovation as a sequential process which took place in discrete stages. The models assumed that scientific discovery preceded and "pushed" technological innovation via applied research, engineering, manufacturing, and marketing. As Rothwell (1994) argues, the model was often used to justify additional R&D spending by firms and governments as, it was held, this would lead to greater innovation and, in turn, faster economic growth. Public policies towards innovation stressed supply side interventions (e.g. R&D subsidies and credits) in support of innovation.

Rothwell (1994) argues that in the latter half of the 1960s empirical studies of innovation processes, notably Myers and Marquis (1969), began to emphasize market-led (or need pull) theories of innovation. These were again linear in nature, stressing the role of the marketplace and market research in identifying and responding to customer needs, as well as directing R&D investments towards these needs. In these models, the marketplace was the chief source of ideas for R&D and the role of R&D was to meet market demands.

Detailed empirical studies during the 1970s showed that both the above linear models (technology push and market pull) were extreme and atypical examples of industrial innovation. In particular, Mowery and Rosenberg (1978) argued that innovation was characterized by a coupling of (and interaction between) science

Table 11.1 Five generations of innovation models

First-generation technology push 1950s to mid 1960s	Simple linear sequential process. Emphasis on R&D push. The market "receives" the results of the R&D
Second-generation market pull mid 1960s to 1970s	Market (or need) pull; again a simple, linear sequential process. Emphasis is on marketing. The market is the source of ideas and provides direction to R&D. R&D has a reactive role.
Third-generation coupling models mid 1970s–1980s	Sequential model, but with feedback loops from later to earlier stages. Involves push or pull–push combinations. R&D and marketing more in balance. Emphasis is on integration at the R&D–marketing interface.
Fourth-generation integrated model early 1980s to 1990	Parallel development with integrated development teams. Strong upstream supplier linkages and partnerships. Close coupling with leading edge customers. Emphasis on integration between R&D and manufacturing (e.g. design for manufacturability). Horizontal collaboration including joint ventures and strategic partnerships
Fifth-generation systems integration and networking model post-1990	Fully integrated parallel development supported by advanced information technology. Use of expert systems and simulation modeling in R&D. Strong linkages with leading-edge customers (customer focus at the forefront of strategy). Strategic integration with primary suppliers including co-development of new products and linked CAD systems. Horizontal linkages including: joint ventures, collaborative research groupings, collaborative marketing arrangements, etc. Emphasis on corporate flexibility and speed of development (time-based strategy). Increased focus on quality and other non-price factors.

Source: Compiled from Rothwell (1991, 1992, 1994).

and technology (S&T) and the marketplace. Unlike the two previous models, the interactive model explicitly links the decision-making of firms to the S&T community and to the marketplace.

Although third-generation models were non-linear with feedback loops, Rothwell (1994) nevertheless criticized them as still being essentially sequential in nature. During the 1980s, following observations of innovation in Japanese automobile companies, integrated or parallel models began to be developed which involved significant functional overlap between departments and/or activities. These models attempted to capture the high degree of cross-functional integration within firms, as well as their external integration with activities in other companies including suppliers, customers, and, in some cases, universities and government agencies.

Fifth-generation systems integration and networking models emphasized the learning which goes on within and between firms, suggesting that innovation was generally and fundamentally a distributed networking process. These models were based on observations during the 1980s and 1990s of an increase in corporate alliances, partnerships, R&D consortia, and joint ventures of various kinds. These interpretations were extensions of fourth-generation integrated models, further emphasizing vertical relationships (e.g. strategic alliances with suppliers and customers) and with collaborating competitors. Rothwell's fifth-generation process also relied on the use of sophisticated electronic tools in order to increase the speed and efficiency of new product development across the entire network of innovation, including in-house functions, suppliers, customers, and external collaborators.

It should be noted that Rothwell did not claim that the world marched uniformly from one generation to another through time. Indeed, the five generations have as much to do with changing academic and business perceptions of innovation as with innovation itself (Hobday 2005). In reality, innovation proceeds unevenly across firms, countries, sectors, and technologies, often progressing only partially from one generation to another. The fifth generation is perhaps best seen as an aspirational model, born of the promise and vision of information and communications technology (ICT), rather than the substance of reality of either ICT or innovation. A more recent manifestation of the fifth-generation innovation model (Dodgson, Gann, and Salter 2002) refers to an intensification of the innovation process as a result of new digital technologies which were underdeveloped or unavailable when Rothwell's papers were published. The authors claim Rothwell's speculations about the increased influence of IT on the innovation process and of related technological and strategic integration have been proven correct. The fifth generation also conflates approaches based on ICT (e.g. networking and Linux, and fast computer-based prototyping) with management-led "systems integration" which centered on corporate strategy, including positioning within the value chain. There may be some merit in dividing these two "generations." However, in practice all these so-called "generations" overlap considerably and are best seen as academic interpretations and new emphases and insights, rather than the actual coherent processes at work at any given time. In summary, Rothwell provides a very useful "benchmark" for assessing the nature and progress of innovation in practice in particular sectors, firms, and technologies, through different periods of time—a guide or map for understanding the messy, complex, and changing nature of innovation alluded to earlier.

Links between innovation models and project management

While direct and substantiated links between innovation and project management are sparse and tenuous in the literature, it is highly likely that the first-generation R&D push model is closely associated with the kind of development projects referred to earlier—the weapons systems development projects such as Atlas and

Polaris. The strong positivist approach to project management is aligned with this science push version of innovation. Although there were dissenting views to this positivist approach to projects (such as Klein and Meckling's Mr Skeptic) it prevailed for many years.

As the use of projects spread from its military origins into business spheres related to product and process development more attention started to be paid to customer needs in the market pull model. However, the field of project management remained mostly internally facing and customer involvement was minimal. The second- and third-generation innovation models do not appear to have been mirrored by massive changes in approaches to project management, either in theory or in practice.

However, there were some major developments in project management practice which accompanied the type of innovation typified by the fourth-generation innovation model. The high levels of cross-functional integration and interaction captured in this model correspond to the emergence of different models of project organization including matrix management and its variations, and the emergence of different leadership requirements for project teams. Wheelwright and Clark (1992) distinguished between four basic structures: functional; lightweight project structure; heavyweight project structure; and project-based structure. In relation to the first two, project managers tended to be junior to functional managers and had no direct control over resources. In heavyweight and project-based structures project managers tended to have control over resources such as finance and personnel but functions such as marketing, finance, and production tended to be coordinated by managers across project lines.

In short, while there remained little integration between project management and innovation research fields, increasingly both groups drew from each other's research and a healthy overlap began to develop. Later on, research on innovation and CoPS began to integrate elements of both project management and innovation studies, to which we now turn.

INNOVATION IN COMPLEX PRODUCT SYSTEMS (CoPS)

CoPS can be defined as high-value, capital goods systems, networks, and infrastructural components, designed and produced by firms as one-offs or in small tailored batches to meet the requirements of large business or government customers. There are many different categories of CoPS (Hobday, Rush, and Tidd 2000). They can be categorized according to sector (e.g. aerospace, military, and transportation), function (e.g. control systems, communications, and R&D), and degree of complexity (e.g. as measured by the number of tailored components and sub-systems, design options, and amount of new knowledge required). Examples include flight simulators, aircraft engines, avionics systems, telecommunications exchanges, train engines, air traffic control units, systems for electricity grids, offshore oil equipment, baggage-handling systems, intelligent buildings, and cellular phone network equipment (see Hobday 1998 for a fuller list). This category of low-volume and highly customized business-to-business activity has always been organized on a project basis. Indeed, early innovations in the project form and project management techniques were pioneered by the US defense industry in the middle of the twentieth century (Hughes 1998). During the 1960s, such project innovations began to diffuse from the US military into the other industries (Gaddis 1959; Middleton 1967), such as telecommunications and construction, and beyond the public sector into other spheres of society (Morris 1994).

As major items of fixed capital, CoPS underpin the modern economy. They form the critical high-technology infrastructures that enable the flow of goods, services, energy, transportation, information, and knowledge in both advanced and developing economies. CoPS consist of many (often customized) interconnected elements including sub-systems and components which themselves are often highly complex, customized, and high cost. This complexity means that many diverse knowledge and skill inputs, often residing in a large number of firms, have to be integrated. The two core capabilities in CoPS are systems integration (including systems design and engineering) and project management. Unlike consumer goods, CoPS are never mass produced and life cycles extend over many years.

These characteristics mean the way innovation takes place, in projects, differs substantially from the way it occurs in mass-produced goods where much of the conventional wisdom about innovation and, indeed, business management has been derived. Perhaps one of the key features is that CoPS exhibit emergent properties during production (the design, systems engineering, and systems integration phases) and use that are unpredictable and unexpected. This means CoPS projects are often highly complex and uncertain activities. This complexity and uncertainty means that the simplistic, rational project management methods, tools, and techniques mentioned earlier are not only inappropriate in CoPS settings but can also be counterproductive in terms of efficiency and effectiveness.

Although it was recognized back in the 1960s that innovation in complex systems was different from other types of innovation, most theories and models of innovation are closely linked to the production paradigm of mass market commodity goods. Firms tend to be clearly defined, recognizable entities supplying goods to a marketplace where final consumers choose between different offerings. Utterback and Abernathy (1975) argue that products, and their associated innovation processes, tend to follow a life cycle from birth to maturity.

Drawing upon cases mostly from mass production consumer goods, the model describes three main phases of innovation: first, the "fluid phase" dominated by product innovation and characterized by competition between many small firms offering competing product designs; second, the "transitional phase" initiated by the emergence of a "dominant design" which signals a shakeout as an industry becomes dominated by a few large firms and characterized by an emphasis on process innovation and the production of standardized products in high volumes (driven by cost reduction); and third, the "maturity phase" when the rate of process innovation also declines as production learning and best practices are transmitted between firms. This pattern, assumed to be typical, is intermittently disrupted by discontinuous waves of radical or disruptive innovation, which compel firms with capabilities tied to the existing technologies to adopt the new innovations or risk being relegated to a minor role in the industry—or to be forced to exit.

However, the standard model is much less useful in understanding the innovation life cycle of CoPS, which tend to "remain" in the early fluid phase of system innovation (Miller et al. 1995). Although CoPS do mature, a phase when standardized products in high volumes for mass markets are realized does not take place as CoPS are essentially produced in one-off projects or small batches.

Put another way, innovation in CoPS cannot be analyzed or measured in terms of a movement from experimental, relatively small volumes of production to high-volume standardized production based on assembly, lean, agile, or mass customization techniques. In fact, the conventional product vs. process dichotomy is unhelpful in explaining the nature and determinants of innovation in CoPS, where the rate of system/solutions innovation is consistently high and product design and development and the "project" form of organization consistently characterize the core production activity in CoPS.

Also, in contrast to the pattern of industry shakeout predicted in the conventional model, Miller et al. (1995) use evidence from the flight simulator industry to show that CoPS industries are characterized by considerable stability at the systems integrator level across generations of technology and/or products. Bonaccorsi and Giura (2000) provide further evidence from the history of the turboprop engine industry (1948–97) of a "non-shakeout" pattern and a continuing dominance of the industry by a few leading firms, whose competitive advantage stems from systems innovation capability and experience and strong customer relationships rather than economies of scale and scope.

Each CoPS industry exhibits it own particular innovation pattern and length, phases, and duration of product life cycle. For example, in mobile communications, Davies (1997) suggests that CoPS (e.g. telecommunications infrastructure) evolve through two main phases of innovation. First, the development of a new systems "architecture" prior to the commercialization of the underlying CoPS product. In this phase, architectural designs are driven by system suppliers in collaboration with regulators, standard-making bodies, and large users. Second, after agreement on the architecture, there follows a phase of new system generation, where the rate of component and systemic innovation increases and successive new products and components are introduced, without fundamentally altering the established architectural design.

While repeatable mass production learning processes may not be relevant to the overall CoPS solution or system, there may well be scope for scale economies at the component level, where demand may be fairly high (e.g. in aircraft, telecoms, and high-technology buildings). Leading CoPS suppliers gain strategic advantage by modifying design architectures to increase the scope for using high-volume components.

At the level of system/solutions design, because of small volumes, CoPS producers tend not to have to account for high-volume production as a key design constraint (unlike, say, in the case of mass-produced goods such as cars, mobile phone handsets, or microwave ovens). Conversely, they do have to retain certain types of component design knowledge in-house to be able to outsource effectively. Therefore, CoPS design rules and decision procedures differ substantially from those followed in mass-produced, simpler goods where "design-for-mass-manufacture" is all important. Strategies for design in CoPS (e.g. modularity) have to account for the knowledge element which must remain within the solutions/systems integrator firm. Consequently, strategies towards core competencies, outsourcing, and design cannot emulate those followed in simpler goods made from standard components.

INNOVATION IN THE CoPS SETTING: THE KEY ROLE OF CAPABILITY

Following Penrose's (1959) original contribution, it is now well understood that organizational capabilities are critical to a firm's success in innovation (Chandler 1990; Grant 2002). As Richardson (1972) points out, successful firms tend to specialize in activities for which their capabilities provide a competitive advantage. A firm must develop the capabilities—i.e. the organization, knowledge, skills, and experience—required to carry out various functional activities—e.g. R&D, design, production, marketing, etc. A capability is "distinctive" or core when it provides a *unique* source of competitive advantage which is not widely available to other firms in an industry. Penrose argued that firms that have grown successfully in new areas of business have done so by establishing and maintaining "a basic position with respect to the use of certain types of resources and technology and the exploitation of certain types of markets" (Penrose 1959: 137–8).

A firm's *technology base* refers to the knowledge and skills required to perform research, development, design, and productive activities related to a specific field of technology, such as electronics, avionics, or packet-switching systems. The *market base* refers to the competence necessary to respond to the demands of different types of customers, such as understanding new client needs, cultivating customer relationships, marketing, distribution, and sales. A firm's innovation path is shaped by the dynamic interaction between its technology and market bases. Two key points of this approach are first, that the profitable expansion of the firm within its *existing technology and market base* is driven by the increasingly specialized—or product-specific   use of resources; and second, a firm's innovative capacity to mobilize and redeploy its resources to diversify into *new technology and/or market bases* is more important in its long run for its competitive survival and growth.

Our research shows that, in CoPS, a radical innovation is often a "base moving" project which fundamentally alters the underlying technological base of the business via changes in the core product or system (Davies and Hobday 2005; Davies, Brady, and Hobday 2006). For example, digital computer technology fundamentally altered the nature of flight simulators and the processes by which they were made, transforming it from an analogue electro-mechanical business to a semiconductor-based, software-driven business (Miller et al. 1995). An incremental innovation in CoPS is an innovation which results in a new product or service within the existing technological base (e.g. a new generation of digital flight simulators or aircraft engines). By contrast, an improvement (to a product or process) is a minor form of incremental innovation—for instance an improvement to an existing product or process of manufacture (e.g. an improved flight simulator, or a new logistics system which reduces cost and speeds up delivery of the flight simulator).

Suppliers of CoPS can innovate and create competitive advantage by: (1) managing projects more efficiently in an existing technology and market base; and/or (2) utilizing projects to envisage and implement strategies for diversification. This second type of project, that enables CoPS firms to enter new fields of technology and/or create and exploit new markets, is referred to as "strategic," "vanguard" (Brady and Davies 2004), or "base-moving" (Davies 2004). The latter study shows that there are three types of vanguard or base-moving projects which innovate by changing or extending the core technology or market of the firm:

1. expand into a *new technology base* to supply new products to existing customers (focus new technology);
2. diversify into a *new market base* using existing technology (focus new market);
3. expand into a *new market/business base—using new technology* to meet the requirements of new sets of customers (focus: new markets and new technology).

Strategic decisions to innovate by moving along one of these three paths usually involve taking large risks and deploying scarce resources in projects that may or may not succeed.

The strategic role of projects encountered in CoPS contrasts with much of the literature on project management which addresses projects as internally focused, routine activities, including R&D (Iansiti and Clark 1994; Iansiti 1995, 1998), new product development projects (e.g. Kusonoki, Nonaka, and Nogata 1998), and information technology projects. Product development projects are usually conducted in-house with an internal, often virtual, client. They are generally concerned with the integration of new technologies (Iansiti 1995, 1998). Such projects often utilize existing or known technologies configured to the customers' exact requirements. By contrast, in CoPS both product development and implementation are complex, interdependent project-based activities. Whereas in volume manufacturing the marketing department is responsible for articulating the needs of prospective customers, and hence the design is frozen prior to market introduction, in CoPS the customer is intimately involved in an ongoing process of design throughout the duration of major projects.

THE ROLE OF BASE-MOVING PROJECTS IN DEVELOPING FIRM CAPABILITIES

Base-moving projects enable the movement into a new technology or market base and are very different from those required to conduct operational projects in an existing base. Relying on base-moving projects, CoPS firms often go through stages of capability-building involving radical organizational change (see Davies and Brady 2000; Brady and Davies 2004). Base-moving projects include (1) top-down strategic projects led by senior management or (2) bottom-up unplanned (e.g. small-scale) projects (Davies, Brady, and Hobday 2006).

Top-down initiatives often originate in corporate divisions, starting with a strategic decision to create a major pioneering project and mobilizing large-scale resources. Projects are strategic when they enable a firm to "manipulate its future." The senior management team decides strategy (e.g. for diversification into new technology and market positions) and a strategic or project director with more seniority than normal operational projects leads the project. With this kind of project, the focus is on achieving a firm's overall business objectives.

By contrast, bottom-up projects are constantly being created and executed at operational levels, some of which are seed-bed initiatives requiring only limited resources. The rate and nature of bottom-up projects depends on the culture of the company. Some firms are keen to promote new experimental initiatives. Others are "threatened" by new projects which might destabilize existing operations. Many large firms, e.g. Du Pont, General Electric, and IBM, use internal corporate venturing (ICV) projects as bottom-up vehicles to initiate growth and diversification. Sometimes ICV projects can grow into separate new businesses (see also Frederiksen and Davies 2008). In other cases, project initiators can encounter top management resistance to proposals which go "against conventional corporate wisdom."

Several authors have built on the idea of vanguard projects, and the shifts over time from exploratory learning and exploitative learning. Söderlund and Tell (2009) have built on the concept of the vanguard project to identify four different project epochs in the long-term evolution of Asea/ABB over a fifty-year period (1950–2000). They show how the evolution of capabilities within the company was shaped by key projects which were the first of a kind opportunity. Midler and Silberzahn (2008) suggested new connections between the entrepreneurship field, organizational learning theory, the multi-project management domain, and organization theory. They extended the concept of vanguard projects in established firms who identify new market or technology opportunities by applying it to start-up firms and their search for market or technology opportunities which are not identified at the start of the project. They assert that these kinds of projects are the most innovative. In doing so, they enlarge the learning perspective from the classical *exploration to exploitation* question to the less debated question of *exploration to exploration* convergence. Lenfle (2008) examines the tension between exploration and exploitation within the context of projects. He distinguishes between two different views of projects—the first within the exploitation perspective where the role of the project is to organize convergence to a pre-defined objective within a given set of constraints (time, budget, quality) and a second where projects are a way of organizing the exploration of emerging innovation fields. According to Lenfle, in the former perspective, projects mainly exploit existing capabilities and this is in line with the instrumental view of projects taken by the PMI and also by work such as Clark and Fujimoto (1991). In the second perspective, it is impossible to define the objective ex ante and so the project becomes a highly uncertain, reflexive, probe and learn process. In this way they become a fundamental part of the search process rather than a part of the implementation process.

CONCLUSION

This chapter has explored the links between project management and innovation, revealing interesting connections between the two, usually separate, fields of research and practice. While, historically, there has been little integration between the two, recently both groups have begun to draw from each other's research and experience, producing a healthy if limited overlap. Recent research on innovation in CoPS has attempted to integrate major elements of both project management and innovation studies.

Regarding innovation studies, since the 1950s academic observers have developed various generations of innovation models which attempt to provide a representation of the main innovation processes, drivers, and actors, showing how these dimensions all relate to each other, and drawing on the many empirical studies of innovation. Rothwell's notion of five generations of innovation models attempts to show how these relationships and drivers of innovation have changed over the decades. While the models often fail to grasp the "messy reality" of innovation in practice they have been widely used within industrial firms for management purposes and by governments to justify particular forms of intervention. The starkest contrast is between the early linear models, which emphasized research and technology push activities, with the most recent demand-driven "networked" models which embrace advanced ICTs and recent corporate strategies towards systems integration.

These models, and the innovation field in general, have not really connected up well with the field of project management. While the latter has followed a number of intellectual trajectories, it is probably true to say that mainstream project management, a rational, technical and managerial discipline which emerged in the 1960s, still dominates in practice. However, research shows that the rational approach has major limitations in that it fails to account for the emergent and uncertain nature of major projects and skates over the implications of different kinds of project types which exist across the economy. It also provides a misleading and simplistic view of how problem-solving and technology development occurs in practice, and does not sufficiently understand the ways in which engineers and designers develop solutions to complex problems under conditions of uncertainty. It may well be that the very high project failure rates observed are partly a consequence of the enduring traditional approach. The latter is particularly deficient in the uncertain environment of CoPS industries where customers often cannot fully specify their needs in advance and project success requires systematic and substantially shared learning, through the phases of development and implementation.

Since the early 1990s, a new area of interdisciplinary study sometimes called "project business" has attempted to reveal the importance of projects to innovation and vice versa. This work emphasizes the environment in which projects are undertaken and reveals how particular types of projects are central to innovation. In CoPS radical innovation is often conducted within a "base-moving" project capable of fundamentally altering the underlying technological or market base of the business. Research shows that CoPS firms rely on such strategic projects and face the challenge of proceeding through stages of innovation capability building involving radical organizational change.

There are many unresolved issues at the interface between innovation and project studies. The theory of "temporary organizations" does not yet deal with innovation and it could well be that radical and incremental innovations demand different degrees of permanence in organizational structure, especially at the early stages of creation and development. In addition, we lack a sufficiently fine-grained understanding of how sectoral and technological factors shape the nature and role of projects during the innovation process. There may well be very different project structures required for different functions (e.g. R&D and product development) and sectors and for different phases of the innovation process. It could be that in the case of innovations which build largely on "what has gone on before," more permanent organizational structures are required, and project structures are best suited to radical and experimental innovations. The project form could well be detrimental to "learning from the past" which often benefits from a more traditional, departmental setting. If this is the case, it implies that there may well be a trade-off between learning on the one hand and innovation on the other, with projects favoring innovation and more permanent structures supporting learning.

Regarding future research needs, the case of high-technology CoPS industries testifies to the importance of projects in corporate evolution, renewal, and innovation as well as the process of market creation. Future research is needed to understand if, and to what extent, this "strategic" role of projects applies to other types of industry (e.g. electronics, automobiles, pharmaceuticals, and chemicals). At the macroeconomic level, it is important for the research field to understand and measure the importance of the "project economy," compared with other prevalent forms of organization—and to bring this to the attention of academics, business leaders, and policy-makers. We also need more in-depth research on the effective management of strategic projects, so that realistic models of project-innovation management can be devised and practicing managers can be supported by a new knowledge base centered on the twin dimensions of projects in innovation—and innovation in projects.

References

AFFUAH, A. (1998). *Innovation Management: Strategies, Implementation and Profits*. New York: Oxford University Press.

ALLEN, T. J. (1977). *Managing the Flow of Technology: Technology Transfer and the Dissemination of Technological Innovation within the R&D Organization*. Cambridge, MA: The MIT Press.

ARTTO, K. A., and KUJALA, J. (2008). "Project business as a research field," *International Journal of Managing Projects in Business*, 1/4: 469–97.

——and WIKSTRÖM, K. (2005). "What is project business?" *International Journal of Project Management*, 23/5: 343–53.

BAUER, R. A., COLLAR, E., TANG, V., with WIND, J., and HOUSTON, P. (1992). *The Silverlake Project: Transformation at IBM*. New York: Oxford University Press.

BONACCORSI, A., and GIURA, P. (2000). "When shakeout doesn't occur: the evolution of the turboprop engine industry," *Research Policy*, 29/7–8: 847–70.

BOWEN, H. K., CLARK, K. B., HOLLOWAY, C. A., and WHEELWRIGHT, S. C. (eds.) (1994). *The Perpetual Enterprise Machine*. New York: Oxford University Press.

BRADY, T., and DAVIES, A. (2004). "Building project capabilities: from exploratory to exploitative learning," *Organization Studies*, 26/9: 1601–21.

BURNS, T., and STALKER, G. M. (1961). *The Management of Innovation*. London: Tavistock.

CHANDLER, A. D. (1990). *Scale and Scope: The Dynamics of Industrial Capitalism*. Cambridge, MA: Bellknap Press.

CHESBROUGH, H. (2003). *Open Innovation: The New Imperative for Creating and Profiting from Technology*. Boston: Harvard Business School Press.

CLARK, K. B., and FUJIMOTO, T. (1991). *Product Development Performance*. Boston: Harvard Business School Press.

CUSUMANO, M. A., and NOBEOKA, K. (1998). *Thinking Beyond Lean: How Multi-Project Management Is Transforming Product Development at Toyota and Other Companies*. New York: The Free Press.

DAVIES, A. (1997). "The life cycle of a complex product system," *International Journal of Innovation Management*, 1/3: 229–56.

—— (2004). "Moving base into high-value integrated solutions: a value stream approach," *Industrial and Corporate Change*, 13/5: 727–56.

—— and BRADY, T. (2000). "Organisational capabilities and learning in complex product systems: towards repeatable solutions," *Research Policy*, 29: 931–53.

—— and HOBDAY, M. (2005). *The Business of Projects: Managing Innovation in Complex Products and Systems*. Cambridge: Cambridge University Press.

—— BRADY, T. and HOBDAY, M. (2006). "Charting a path towards integrated solutions," *MIT Sloan Management Review*, 47/3: 39–48.

DAVIS, S. M., and LAWRENCE, P. R. (1977). *Matrix*. Reading, MA: Addison-Wesley Publishing Co.

DODGSON, M., GANN, D., and SALTER, A. (2002). "The intensification of innovation," *International Journal of Innovation Management*, 6/1: 53–83.

—— —— —— (2008). *The Management of Technological Innovation*. Oxford: Oxford University Press.

DRUCKER, P. F. (1985). *Innovation and Entrepreneurship*. New York: HarperCollins.

DVIR, D., and LECHLER, T. (2004). "Plans are nothing, changing plans is everything: the impact of changes on project success," *Research Policy*, 33: 1–15.

ENGWALL, M. (2003). "No project is an island: linking projects to history and context," *Research Policy*, 32: 789–808.

FAGERBERG, J., and VERSPAGEN, B. (2009). "Innovation studies: the emerging structure of a new scientific field," *Research Policy*, 38: 218–33.

FLYVBJERG, B. (2003). "Delusions of success: comment on Dan Lovallo and Daniel Kahneman," *Harvard Business Review*, December: 121–2.

—— BRUZELIUS, N., and ROTHENGATTER, W. (2003). *Megaprojects and Risk: An Anatomy of Ambition*. Cambridge: Cambridge University Press.

FREDERIKSEN, L., and DAVIES, A. (2008). "Vanguards and ventures: projects as vehicles for corporate entrepreneurship," *International Journal of Project Management*, 26/5: 487–96.

FREEMAN, C. (1974). *The Economics of Industrial Innovation*. Harmondsworth: Penguin.

GADDIS, P. O. (1959). "The project manager," *Harvard Business Review*, May–June: 89–99.

GALBRAITH, J. (1973). *Designing Complex Organizations*. Reading, MA: Addison-Wesley.

GANN, D. M., and SALTER, A. (2000). "Innovation in project-based, service-enhanced firms: the construction of complex products and systems," *Research Policy*, 29: 955–72.

GRANT, R. M. (2002). *Contemporary Strategic Analysis*, 4th edn. Cambridge, MA: Blackwell Publishers Inc.

HOBDAY, M. (1998). "Product complexity, innovation and industrial organisation," *Research Policy*, 26: 689–710.

——(2000). "The project-based organisation: an ideal form for managing complex products and systems?" *Research Policy*, 29: 871–93.

——(2005). "Firm-level innovation models: perspectives on research in developed and developing countries," *Technology Analysis & Strategic Management*, 17/2: 121–46.

——RUSH, H., and TIDD, J. (2000). Editorial "Innovation in complex products and systems," *Research Policy*, 29/7–8: 793–804.

HOUSE OF COMMONS (2004). "Improving IT procurement: the impact of the Office of Government Commerce's initiatives on departments and suppliers of major IT-enabled projects," Report by the Comptroller and Auditor General, HC877 Session 2003–2004. London: The Stationery Office.

HUGHES, T. (1998). *Rescuing Prometheus*. New York: Pantheon.

IANSITI, M. (1995). "Technology integration: managing technological evolution in a complex environment," *Research Policy*, 24/2: 521–42.

——(1998). *Technology Integration: Making Critical Choices in a Dynamic World*. Boston: Harvard Business School Press.

——and CLARK, K. B. (1994). "Integration and dynamic capability: evidence from development in automobiles and mainframe computers," *Industrial and Corporate Change*, 3/3: 557–605.

KATZ, R., and ALLEN, T. (1985). "Project performance and the locus of influence in the R&D matrix," *Academy of Management Journal*, 28/1: 67–87.

KIDDER, T. (1982). *The Soul of a New Machine*. New York: Avon Books.

KLEIN, B. H., and MECKLING, W. (1958). "Application of operations research to development decisions," *Operations Research*, 6: 352–63.

KREINER, K. (1995). "In search of relevance: project management in drifting environments," *Scandinavian Journal of Management*, 11/4: 335–46.

KUSUNOKI, K., NONAKA, I., and NOGATA, A. (1998). "Organizational capabilities in product development of Japanese firms: a conceptual framework and empirical findings," *Organization Science*, 9/6: 699–718.

LAWRENCE, P. R., and LORSCH, J. W. (1967). "Differentiation and integration in complex organizations," *Administrative Science Quarterly*, 12: 1–47.

LENFLE, S. (2008). "Exploration and project management," *International Journal of Project Management*, 26/5: 469–78.

LINDKVIST, L., SÖDERLUND, J., and TELL, F. (1998). "Managing product development projects: on the significance of fountains and deadlines," *Organization Studies*, 19/6: 931–51.

LOVALLO, D., and KAHNEMAN, D. (2003). "Delusions of success: how optimism undermines executives' decisions," *Harvard Business Review*, July: 56–63.

LUNDIN, R. A., and SÖDERHOLM, A. (1995). "A theory of the temporary organization," *Scandinavian Journal of Management*, 11/4: 437–55.

—— ——(1998). "Conceptualizing a projectified society: discussion of an eco-institutional approach to a theory on temporary organizations," in R. A. Lundin and C. Midler (eds.), *Projects as Arenas for Renewal and Learning Processes*. Boston: Kluwer Academic Publishers, 13–23.

MARQUIS, D. G. (1969). "Ways of organizing projects," *Innovation*, 5/7: 26–33.

MIDDLETON, C. J. (1967). "How to set up a project organization," *Harvard Business Review*, March–April: 73–82.

MIDLER, C. (1993). *L'Auto qui n'existait pas: management des projets et transformation de l'entreprise*. Paris: Dunod.

——and SILBERZAHN, P. (2008) "Managing robust development process for high-tech start-ups through multi-project learning: the case of two European start-ups," *International Journal of Project Management*, 26/5: 479–86.

MILLER, R., and LESSARD, D. R. (2001). *The Strategic Management of Large Engineering Projects: Shaping Institutions, Risks, and Governance*. Cambridge, MA: The MIT Press.

——HOBDAY, M., LEROUGH-DEMERS, T., and OLLEROS, D. (1995). "Innovation in complex systems industries: the case of flight simulation," *Industrial and Corporate Change*, 4/2: 363–400.

MINTZBERG, H. (1983). *Structures in Fives: Designing Effective Organizations*. Englewood Cliffs, NJ: Prentice Hall.

MORRIS, P. W. G. (1994). *The Management of Projects*. London: Thomas Telford.

——(2004). "Moving from corporate strategy to project strategy: leadership in project management," in D. P. Slevin, D. I. Cleland, and J. K. Pinto (eds.), *Innovations: Project Management Research 2004*. Newton Square, PA: Project Management Institute.

——and HOUGH, G. H. (1987). *The Anatomy of Major Projects*. Chichester: John Wiley and Sons.

——and JAMIESON, H. A. (2004). *Translating Corporate Strategy into Project Strategy*. Newton Square, PA: Project Management Institute.

——and PINTO, J. K. (eds.) (2004). *The Wiley Guide to Managing Projects*. Englewood Cliffs, NJ: John Wiley and Sons.

MOWERY, D., and ROSENBERG, N. (1978). "The influence of market demand upon innovation: a critical review of some recent empirical studies," *Research Policy*, 8: 103–53.

MYERS, S., and MARQUIS, D. G. (1969). *Successful Industrial Innovations: A Study of Factors Underlying Innovation in Selected Firms*, NSF 69–17. Washington, DC: National Science Foundation.

PENROSE, E. T. (1959). *The Theory of the Growth of the Firm*. New York: Wiley.

PRENCIPE, A., DAVIES, A., and HOBDAY, M. (eds.) (2003). *The Business of Systems Integration*. Oxford: Oxford University Press.

RICHARDSON, G. B. (1972). "The organisation of industry," *Economic Journal*, September: 883–96.

ROTHWELL, R. (1991). "External networking and innovation in small and medium-sized manufacturing firms in Europe," *Technovation*, 11/2: 93–112.

——(1992). "Successful industrial innovation: critical factors for the 1990s," *R&D Management*, 22/3: 221–40.

——(1994). "Towards the fifth-generation innovation process," *International Marketing Review*, 11/1: 7–31.

SAHLIN-ANDERSSON, K., and SÖDERHOLM, A. (eds.) (2002). *Beyond Project Management: New Perspectives on the Temporary–Permanent Dilemma*. Copenhagen: Copenhagen Business School Press.

SHENHAR, A. (2004). "How projects differ, and what to do about it," in P. Morris and J. Pinto (eds.), *The Wiley Guide to Managing Projects*. New York: Wiley, 1265–86.

——(2007). *Reinventing Project Management*. Boston: Harvard Business School Press.

SMYTH, H. J., and MORRIS, P. W. G. (2007). "An epistemological evaluation of research into projects and their management: methodological issues," *International Journal of Project Management*, 25/4: 423–36.

SÖDERLUND, J., and TELL, F. (2009). "Exploring the dynamics of the P-form organization: project epochs in Asea/ABB 1950–2000," *International Journal of Project Management*, 27/2: 101–12.

STINCHCOMBE, A. L., and HEIMER, C. A. (1985). *Organization Theory and Project Management: Administering Uncertainty in Norwegian Offshore Oil.* Oxford: Oxford University Press.

TEECE, D. J., and PISANO, G. (1994). "The dynamic capabilities of firms: an introduction," *Industrial and Corporate Change,* 3: 537–56.

TIDD, J., and BESSANT, J. (2009). *Managing Innovation,* 4th edn. Chichester: John Wiley & Sons.

————and PAVITT, K. (2005). *Managing Innovation,* 3rd edn. Chichester: John Wiley & Sons.

TOFFLER, A. (1970). *Future Shock.* New York: Random House.

TUSHMAN, M. L., and O'REILLY, C. A., III (1996). "Ambidextrous organizations: managing evolutionary and revolutionary change," *California Management Review,* 38/4: 8–30.

UTTERBACK, J. M., and ABERNATHY, W. J. (1975). "A dynamic model of process and product innovation," *Omega,* 3/6: 639–56.

WHEELWRIGHT, S., and CLARK, K. B. (1992). *Revolutionizing Product Development.* New York: Free Press.

WHIPP, R., and CLARK, P. A. (1986). *Innovation and the Auto Industry: Product, Process and Work Organization.* London: Frances Pinter.

WILLMAN, P., and WINCH, G. (1985). *Innovation and Management Control: Labour Relations at BL Cars.* Cambridge: Cambridge University Press.

WINTER, M., SMITH, C., MORRIS, P. W. G., and CICMIL, S. (2006). "Directions for future research in project management: the main findings of a UK government-funded research network," *International Journal of Project Management,* 24/8: 638–49.

PART IV

....

GOVERNANCE AND CONTROL

....

CHAPTER 12

PROJECT GOVERNANCE

RALF MÜLLER

This chapter focuses on governance and its related subset project governance. The complementary perspectives of transaction cost economics (TCE), agency theory, and organizational control are taken to develop an overview of governance in organizations, which is subsequently extended into the realm of projects and their management. Research in governance theory is reviewed, starting from the organizational level and developing towards project specific governance models. Finally an attempt is made to identify the boundaries and issues of project governance, which should be of interest for the project management-focused research community.

BACKGROUND

The word governance derived from the Latin word "gubernare" meaning "to steer." Governance as a function originated from policy research in political science, but has outgrown this area substantially. Originally aimed at "steering" countries, it is nowadays also synonymous for "steering," for example, corporations, their operations, transactions, and projects.

These projects are either internal to an organization or as transactions with other organizations. The latter can take the form of dyadic buyer–seller relationships or networks of organizations with a joint project objective. No matter the complexity of this transaction, from internal projects to networked projects, agreements are made beforehand on the nature of the parties' transaction and its governance, typically in the form of contracts. These agreements must be acceptable for each of the parties, thus they must be in conformance with each party's individual corporate governance policy, otherwise they would not be signed by the responsible corporate managers. Agreements or contracts as governance structures between several organizations represent the common denominator of the individual corporate governance structures of the participating organizations. Corporate governance sets thereby the boundaries for project governance, most simply in companies' internal projects, more complex and potentially further restrained in projects with external parties. The boundaries for project governance are thereby set at the level of corporate governance. Among the large number of definitions of corporate governance, the one by the Organization for Economic Cooperation and Development (OECD 2004) is most often referred to:

Corporate governance involves a set of relationships between a company's management, its board, its shareholders and other stakeholders. Corporate governance also provides the structure through which the objectives of the company are set, and the means of attaining those objectives and monitoring performance are determined.

Governance aims for shaping the "conduct of conduct" in organizations. Using a self-regulation approach, governance steers indirectly through subtle forces (Lemke 2001). Examples are the team members in a project consisting of networked companies. Each participating company is responsible for its own resources, but jointly they are governed through the combination of agreed-upon contracts. The contracts define the forces which steer the undertaking indirectly, voiced through a representative, such as a steering committee. This committee is accountable for project results, but not responsible for the team members in the project. Through that governance provides contextual frameworks which shape, but do not necessarily determine the actions of individuals, for example, in projects (Clegg 1994; Clegg et al. 2002). Therefore "Governance is ultimately concerned with creating the conditions for ordered rule and collective action" (Stoker 1998: 155).

CORPORATE GOVERNANCE

Governance as a corporate-level subject originated from the work of Coase (1937) with his work on *The Nature of the Firm* and the subsequent antitrust research and policies in the middle of the twentieth century. It was further developed by Williamson (e.g. 1975, 1985), who developed an economic perspective of governance through his transaction cost economics (TCE). This perspective was subsequently complemented by agency theory (e.g. Jensen and Meckling 1976; Jensen 2000), which adds a structural perspective and addresses the link and information imbalance between the owner and the manager of a governed organization, thus the governed organization and its context. Subsequently organization theorists, such as Ouchi (e.g. 1980) and others, developed theories on the link between structure, governance, and the related control mechanisms in organizations, thereby providing a perspective internal to the governed organization. These three perspectives constitute the most popular theoretical base of governance (Williamson 1999a), and complement each other in a way that makes them the most relevant governance perspectives for the study of project governance. Complementarities are hereby achieved through the rationalism of the economic perspective of TCE, complemented by opportunism and human subjectivity described through agency theory. Organizational control allows for interaction between TCE and agency theory by balancing the level of governance rationality through objective (output) and subjective (behavior) controls. Together the three perspectives provide a comprehensive multidimensional view of governance.

Agency theory: the information perspective of governance

The importance of agency theory, as a contributor to organization theory, especially when coupled with complementary perspectives, was suggested by Eisenhardt (1989).

Jensen and Meckling (1976) define an agency relationship where one party, the principal, engages another, the agent, to perform some service on his or her behalf. This involves delegating some decision-making authority to the agent. If the aim of both parties is to maximize their economic position, then there is good reason to believe that the agent will not always act in the best interests of the principal. Thus agency theory explains the potential for conflict of interest that arises between the manager and owner of a firm, stemming from the fact that only owner-managed firms are effectively managed economically. Dividing ownership from management of the firm (as in the case of shareholder-owned companies) will cause inefficiencies because managers (as agents) will not act in the interest of others (their principals or owners) to the exclusion of their own preferences (Jensen and Meckling 1976; Jensen 2000).

The relationship between principal and agent is problematic because (Barney and Hesterly 1996; Jensen 2000):

- the interest of principal and agent will typically diverge if both are utility maximizers
- the principal cannot perfectly and costlessly monitor the actions of the agent
- the principal cannot perfectly and costlessly monitor and acquire the information available to or possessed by the agent.

Moe and Williamson (1995) summarize this in the two agency problems:

- The adverse selection problem: has the principal chosen the right agent?
- The moral hazard problem: will the agent always act in the best interest of the owner?

Both problems are grounded in an ex ante (adverse selection) and ex post (moral hazard) information imbalance between principal and agent.

The interests of principal and agent are realigned through contracts (and associated control structures), which yield the highest pay-off for the agent for behavior regarded as most appropriate by the principal (Bergen, Dutta, and Walker 1992). Where objectives cannot be defined precisely, behavior-based contracts dominate. Contrarily, clear objectives on the side of the principal lead to outcome-based contracts (Hendry 2002).

Four agency costs are associated with those structures and incentives (Jensen 2000):

1. the costs of creating and structuring contracts between principal and agent;
2. the monitoring expenditures by the principal;
3. the bonding expenditures by the agent;
4. the residual loss arising from the manager's self-interest, opportunistic behavior, or bounded rationality.

However, contracts, and especially contracts in complex projects, are always incomplete (Turner 2004; Williamson 1995), and an opportunity for agents to take advantage of a situation arises frequently. Multi-tasking environments, such as projects, provide opportunities for undiscovered low performance when performance is insufficiently measured (Holmstrom and Milgrom 1991). As empirically shown by Harrison and Harrel (1993), the presence of a situation of adverse selection can lead to decisions that are rational in the eyes of the agent, but irrational in the eyes of the principal. Agents may be inclined to continue projects that support their personal interests. Information imbalance with the principal enables presumably rational decisions on the continuation, even though the project should be terminated from a sponsor perspective. Examples include externally hired project managers, who are paid on time and material basis. The longer they stay in a project, the more they earn. In such cases a negative trend or a failing project are continued instead of terminated.

Underlying agency theory is the assumption of a homo economicus, that is, actors are individualistic, opportunistic, and self-serving in the sense of Jensen and Meckling (1994).

A somewhat different perspective towards the relationship between principal and his or her representative is taken by stewardship theory. Here individuals in organizations are assumed to be stewards whose behavior is ordered such that pro-organizational, collectivistic behaviors have a higher utility than individualistic, self-serving behaviors. Here a high level of identification with the organization creates a principal–steward relationship, which is mutually supportive, instead of mutually distrusting such as a principal–agent relationship. This impacts economic outcomes through differences in collaboration and control structures. Researchers in this stream define situations in which motives of managers are aligned with the objectives of their principals (Davies, Schoorman, and Donaldson 1997).

Literature tends to refer to stewardship theory only in the context of agency theory, but not vice versa. The relationship between the two varies contingent on industry sectors with the stewardship theory being a subset, and at best a complementary to the agency theory. A literature analysis of agency and stewardship theory by Cares et al. (2006) indicated widespread use and acceptance of agency theory in for-profit organizations, but lack of clearness as to its appropriateness for the non-profit sector. They suggest stewardship theory as a subset of agency theory, and potentially appropriate for organizations in the non-profit sector. A more integrative picture is provided by Sundaramurthy and Lewis (2003) who hypothesize the need for both control structures (as suggested by agency theory) and collaborative structures (as suggested by stewardship theory) simultaneously in modern enterprises. In particular they hypothesize that the continuation of an organization's history is influenced by the preference for control or collaboration. They conceptualize that successful organizations applying a control focus will remain stable within their strategy, whereas less successful organizations applying the same focus will enter into a self-reinforcing downward circle. Within a context of diversity and shareholder involvement they suggest balancing collaboration and control by encouraging trust in human capabilities, distrust in human limitations, and task-related cognitive conflict among governance actors (Sundaramurthy and Lewis 2003).

Summarizing the above paragraphs for the domain of projects suggests an agency perspective for successful projects and a balance between agency and stewardship perspective for projects starting to compromise their objectives.

The studies on agency theory addressed in this section vary in their unit of analysis. Earlier studies used either the contract between principal and agent or financial results as unit of analysis, whereas later studies included the level and nature of trust. In hindsight the former approaches defined input and output through the ex ante conditions and the ex post results, whereas the later approaches took more psychological and experience factors into account. Taken together the unit of analysis develops towards the collaboration between principal and agent.

Transaction cost economics: the economic perspective of governance

Transaction costs arise from running the economic system, which are different from production costs and can be perceived as the economic equivalent to friction in physical systems (Williamson 1985). They stem from the complexity of the relationship of actors within and among organizations and the impossibility of developing and agreeing on contracts comprehensive enough to structure the relationship in an all-comprehensive manner. TCE explains the different means to reduce these costs in different types of transaction. To do this TCE perceives an organization as a balanced network of contracts (e.g. between buyer and supplier, employee and company, etc.), where each contract constitutes the governance structure of a relationship. An organization is thereby viewed as a governance structure and the underlying unit of analysis is the transaction (Williamson 1985, 1999a).

TCE positions itself against the orthodox theories of companies as production functions (e.g. Coase 1937) or as capabilities-based routine operations (e.g. Penrose 1959), who have production and knowledge as respective units of analysis. TCE applies the transaction as the unit of analysis of choice for research, by referring to "John R. Commons' prescient statement of the economic problem: 'the ultimate unit of activity... must contain in itself the three principles of conflict, mutuality, and order. This unit is the transaction' (1932, p. 4)" (Williamson 2002: 2).

TCE is more microanalytic and adopts an economic perspective, whereas competence is more composite (focusing on routines) and is more concerned with processes (especially learning) and the lessons learned from it. However, Williamson concludes that TCE should not be the only perspective and that the lens of contracts is less of a substitute for than a complement to the orthodox lens of choice (Williamson 1999a).

"(T)ransaction occurs when a good or service is transferred between technologically separable stages" (Williamson 1999a: 1089). The three attributes of TCE are "the frequency with which transactions recur, the uncertainty (disturbances) to which transactions are subject, and the degree to which transactions are supported by transaction specific assets" (Williamson 1999a: 1089). We can assume projects to be a particular type of transaction.

Depending on the complexity of the transaction different more or less complex governance structures are needed in order to economize transaction costs. "Transaction costs are economized by assigning transactions (which differ in their attributes) to governance structures (the adaptive capacities and associated costs of which differ) in a discriminating way" (Williamson 1985: 18).

TCE proposes that firms adapt their governance structures to achieve the lowest expected transaction costs. To economize on transaction costs TCE proposes that high levels of asset specificity, uncertainty, and contract incompleteness lead to "make" decisions within an organization's hierarchy, whereas low levels lead to "buy" decisions in the market, if not hybrids of both. Each of these approaches requires different governance structures (Adler et al. 1998). Governance structures are adapted to the nature of the contract in a way that governance costs are economized at the minimum level of control structures needed for a transaction's balance of asset specificity, uncertainty, and frequency.

Even though TCE is criticized for its crudeness in the form of primitive models, underdeveloped trade-offs, severe measurement problems, and too many degrees of freedom (Williamson 1985), it is frequently used to address research issues and explain marketing phenomena. An example includes the investigation of the question of what governs the adaptability of organizations, where Williamson (1994) conceptually concluded that companies know better than the market what goes on, and their internal dispute leads them to adaptation, which is by outsiders viewed as the invisible hand (in the sense of Adam Smith). This view was recently expanded by O'Reilly and Tushman (2004) who identified that dynamic capability (the ability to reconfigure assets and existing capabilities) plus ambidexterity (the ability to simultaneously explore and exploit) allows for adaptation of firms to markets.

In an attempt to broaden its scope, TCE was applied to public enterprises, country studies, and other institutions. Results helped to identify the particular circumstances under which these institutions' transactions are performed economically, and those that need improvement (Williamson 1999b, 2003).

Trust and control: the organizational perspective of governance

Researchers in organization theory built on TCE and agency theory and complemented it by addressing questions of trust and control as critical features for organizations' governance.

A conceptual examination of the impact of trust on organizational performance showed that different relationships between governance and trust may coexist: (a) trust may enhance the impact of governance on performance, (b) governance may reduce the level of trust between exchange partners, (c) ex ante trust in projects may influence the level of governance complexity (Puranam and Vanneste 2009).

The interaction between structural (contract) and relational (trust) dimensions in the governance of organizational alliances was investigated by Faems et al. (2008). Their qualitative multiple-case study showed a process relationship between contracts and trust, where goodwill trust is a condition that determines how contracts are applied, the contracting process is an incremental learning process that is sensitive to changes in relative bargaining power of the organizations, and mutual interdependence and competence trust are crucial conditions for subsequent transactions.

Most influential for the understanding of control in organizations is the work by Ouchi, who started in 1975 with the quantitative identification of the conditions that govern the use of output control or behavior control by managers. While output control steadily increases when going up the corporate hierarchy, behavior control decreases. Behavior control is preferred by managers when the means–ends relationships between tasks are well understood, as well as in small, less hierarchical

firms. Output control is applied by managers in larger organizations with specialized departments, where simple measures of performance are needed which are
easily understandable for all employees, or in cases where legitimate evidence of
performance is asked for. Counter-intuitively the two control approaches are not
substitutes for each other (Ouchi and Maguire 1975; Ouchi 1977). Addressing the
question of whether behavior and output control pervade the organization in a
similar way, Ouchi found that behavior control diminishes through the hierarchy,
while output control stays. He concluded (1978: 189) that:

high performers are distinguished by the fact that the use of behavior control is influenced by task interdependence, which can be reasonably assumed to affect the need for
control, and it is influenced by the expertise of the manager, with more knowledgeable
managers applying more behavior control, while less knowledgeable managers apparently leave well enough alone and apply little behavior control. In low performing departments, however, those considerations are unimportant, and the use of behavior control
is tied to the manager's free time and his freedom from control from above. In such low
performers, the manager with more time on his hands and greater autonomy will apply
more behavior control, a condition which suggests the creation of feudal despots within
the organization.

The further work of Ouchi and his colleagues introduced the concept of clans and
their role in control in organizations. It showed that output and behavior measures
of control were incomplete and had to be complemented by psychological ways of
control. This concept was subsequently integrated with TCE and agency theory as
the third perspective of governance. A clan is defined as a culturally homogeneous
organization, with a shared set of values or objectives, together with beliefs about
how to coordinate the organization's effort in order to reach common objectives.
The clan socializes the organization's members to the extent that the individual's
and organization's goals merge, so that selfish behavior increasingly supports organizational goals (Ouchi and Price 1978).

In designing a control system for loosely coupled organizations, Ouchi (1979)
extended TCE using clan theory. Here TCE describes the simpler control systems in
terms of markets and bureaucracies, and clan theory extends these perspectives
through a psychological dimension:

- Markets act as the simplest control system through norms of reciprocity for social
  behavior and the price as information carrier,
- Bureaucracies act as a more complex control structure, because they require, in
  addition to the norms of reciprocity of the market, also the legitimate authority
  of leaders, plus the acceptance of hierarchy by the organizational members.
  Information is mainly carried by rules.
- Clans are the most complex control structure: they require not only norms of
  reciprocity and legitimate authority, but also social agreement on a broad range
  of values and beliefs. Information is carried through traditions within the
  organization.

Economic organization and a balance of control mechanisms is achieved through the combinations of these three approaches to control.

In projects trust and control are often referred to as two different mechanisms for sponsors to become comfortable with the information about a project. Here trust satisfies the subjective control needs, thus the feeling of comfortableness in placing the right manager into a project. Control then satisfies the rational and often quantitative control needs, thus the feeling of exercising control by measuring key metrics (Turner and Müller 2004).

The review above showed the complementary nature of the three perspectives toward governance, namely economical through TCE, human through agency theory, and organizational through trust and control. At this point the question of what the limits of governance are is indicated.

LIMITATIONS OF GOVERNANCE

The review of literature above showed that governance provides a mental framework for decision-making and behavior within a society's cultural, ethical, and moral standard. The authority exercised by governance institutions ranges from consultative only to governmental policy and law-making. Within this continuum the responsibility for action is delegated to the actor in a governed organization.

Several limitations spring from that and are valid at both the organizational and the project level. Decisions by actors are subject to interpretation of the framework within an organization's or project's context and the situation at hand, leading to a range of possible decisions and behaviors in the face of uncertainty and ambiguity of information, and the subjectivity of the interpretation of the situation and its context. Thus, governance does not anticipate actors' decisions and behavior, but sets the stage for actors to decide on it.

Despite the clear philosophical positioning of governance through Foucault's (1926–84) philosophy of neo-liberalism, the related ontological and epistemological basis of research on governance is less clearly articulated and left to the different research streams and its constituent perspectives. These streams are approached using objective, subjective, and conceptual approaches. However, suggestions on possible research epistemologies at the level of governance (not its constituent parts) are lacking. Stoker (1998) identified the idiosyncrasies of governance theory as:

- Actors are taken from within and outside the governed institution;
- Actors work in autonomous self-governing networks;
- Boundaries and responsibilities to tackle social problems are blurred;
- Power dependencies in collective actions are hidden and need to be identified;

• The capacity to get things done does not rest on the power of the governance institution to command or the use of its authority.

It shows that a variety of epistemological stances is indicated for future research, thus going beyond the current prevalence for conceptual and case studies.

Positioning TCE from a contract lens (the firm as governance structure) in relation to orthodoxy lens, as defined by Williamson (2002) (the firm as technology production system, focused on proper resource allocation), he concluded that as asset specificity and disturbance increase, partners become more dependent on each other, because failure has increasingly large consequences. Further research is indicated on the relevance of the unit of analysis, possibly integrating current viewpoints into new perspectives beyond the traditional ones of production, contract, or competence. The combined use of game theory, organization theory, and TCE could allow the development of more comprehensive models in the future. Further, contract science needs to be better understood and more dynamically applied in reality (Williamson 2002).

PROJECT GOVERNANCE

Project governance is the application of the principles of governance to projects. The aim of project governance is to ensure a consistent and predictable delivery of projects within the limitations set by corporate governance or its agreed upon subset in contracts with external partners. Governance, as it applies to portfolios, programs, projects, and project management, "coexists within the corporate governance framework. It comprises the value system, responsibilities, processes and policies that allow projects to achieve organizational objectives and foster implementation that is in the best interest of all the stakeholders, internal and external, and the corporation itself" (Müller 2009: 4).

Institutions for the governance of projects

The earlier part of this chapter introduced the principal governance tasks as setting goals, providing the means to achieve these goals, and controlling progress. This is done at every node in an organizational hierarchy. To that end, governance is executed at all layers of the organizational hierarchy or in hierarchical relationships in organizational networks, per the following.

Board of directors
The board of directors should define the objectives of the business and the role of projects in achieving these objectives. This influences decisions on, for example, the

establishment of steering groups, project sponsors, and Project Management Offices (PMOs) as governance institutions. Along with that the board of directors may decide on the possible roles and responsibilities of these institutions at, for example, stage gate reviews where decisions on project continuation, change, or suspension are made; or reviews/audits where the project and its management is assessed in order to assure appropriate project delivery within the constraints set by the project's governance institutions. Thus the board of directors determine the level of governance exercised over projects.

Steering groups and sponsors

For each project the sponsor sets up the particular governance infrastructure, which links the project with its parent company or contract. This includes the project governance processes, the means of controlling projects, and the roles, responsibilities, and approval requirements. Together with the steering group (or its functional equivalent) the sponsor should govern the project through the project manager in terms of managing the transaction (using a TCE perspective) and structuring the relationships between them and the project manager and its team (using an agency perspective), within the control framework set by them (balance of behavior versus outcome control).

Research by Crawford et al. (2008) on steering groups' work showed that they typically execute two different functions: governance and support of the project. In their governance role they appoint the project manager, set the project's constraints in terms of budget, time, success criteria, and define the goals to be achieved within these limits. Governance is executed by providing resources, controlling project milestones, deliverables, and change control, and acceptance at project completion. Advice and guidance is given to the project manager on an ad hoc basis when needed. In their support function role, steering groups facilitate preparation within the project's parent organization for the use of the project's deliverables, remove obstacles, help the project team to obtain required approvals from the parent organization, and help manage or influence project stakeholders. Depending on the particular circumstances a project may have a higher or lower need for governance or support. A higher need for governance is typically required where the project is business-critical or where there are rapidly changing markets. Higher need for support is indicated when resource bottlenecks occur or users of the project outcome resist acceptance (Crawford et al. 2008).

Project Management Offices (PMOs)

PMOs are organizational entities, resourced with project management experts. Their role in the governance of projects is often described as being tactical, strategic, or a combination thereof. The particular charter of a PMO is dependent on an organization's particular situation. Tactical PMOs typically focus on the improvement of project results through the provision of guidance to project managers in ensuring compliance with corporate project management standards. Governance is hereby achieved through behavior control, supported through training and the development of communities-of-practice. This resembles the establishment of clans, as outlined by Ouchi and Price (1978). The PMO homogenizes the community of project managers towards shared values or objectives, and the related coordination mechanisms needed to reach common objectives.

PMOs with more strategic roles engage in stewardship of portfolios of projects. They prepare the information for decisions to be taken by portfolio managers, thus contributing to the outcome control of governance.

Program and portfolio management

Where projects sit under programs, the programs and their processes and structures set the context for the governance of individual projects. In these cases, the program manager acts as the owner or sponsor of the projects in a program. He or she takes on the governance roles of sponsor or steering group as described above.

Portfolio managers govern the relative priority and the associated resourcing and visibility of projects. They may impact indirectly time and cost planning, milestone-setting and achievement, as well as delivery of project outcomes by prioritizing and providing the required resources.

GOVERNANCE FRAMEWORKS

Recent research on governance frameworks for projects can be categorized into:

1. General project governance frameworks
2. Project-specific governance models

These are described below.

General project governance frameworks

Research in the governance of projects started in the 1990s with the identification of the need for different governance approaches contingent on different attributes of projects, such as the (low or high) level of clearness of project goals and the (low or high) level of clearness in methods to achieve these goals. This identified four different governance types, which varied in methodology choice and project manager's management style in the project (Turner and Cochrane 1993).

Recently the focus moved from individual projects towards projects-in-context. Söderlund (2004), while referring to this developing trend, implied different governance structures depending on single- versus multi-project structures in single- versus multi-firm settings, spanning governance from single project management to entire project ecologies with multi-firm and multi-project dependencies.

Turner and Keegan (2001) researched the different governance structures in organizations along the dimensions of few to many projects, and of few to many customers for these projects. They identified generic governance roles for multi-project organizations, described as the Broker and Steward model, where the Broker maintains the interface with the client and acquires new business opportunities (often done by a program manager), whereas the Steward manages the resource pool for all or a subset of all projects and decides on the acceptance of new opportunities (often done by a project portfolio manager).

Research on the relationship between governance type and organizational performance showed that governance in multi-project organizations is typically implemented in one of four possible situations:

1. multi-project organizations, with isolated projects and without synergies across objectives or resources needed for these projects;
2. Program-driven organizations, seeking synergies among project objectives;
3. Portfolio-driven organizations, seeking synergies in resource and skills allocation;
4. Hybrid organizations, combining and balancing program and portfolio approaches.

Organizational-wide performance varies greatly among the four approaches. Hybrid organizations are significantly more successful than companies using one of the other three approaches to governance (Blomquist and Müller 2006). In line with other studies (e.g. Müller, Martinsuo, and Blomquist 2008) the same researchers found that differences in contextual characteristics, such as industry, geography, and market dynamics, have a moderating effect on project performance and need to be considered for the particular governance of projects and their portfolio-level aggregations. This includes perception of success, for example, importance of Key Performance Indicators or other measures of performance as they vary by geography, age, and project type. These variations need to be taken into account in designing or assessing project governance structures in national and international contexts (Müller and Turner 2007).

More recent work has looked at paradigms for project governance from the perspective of governance theory and organization theory. Four governance paradigms were identified by overlaying the shareholder versus stakeholder orientation of an organization (Clarke 2004), with its level of outcome control versus behavior control (Brown and Eisenhardt 1997; Ouchi and Maguire 1975). Table 12.1 shows the related paradigms.

In this matrix, organizations enforcing compliance with project management processes are behavior focused in their approach to control. Contrarily, organizations focusing on the fit between project deliverables and existing expectations are more outcome oriented. These organizations give more autonomy to their projects and project managers than behavior-oriented organizations. Typically, their projects are managed by dedicated project managers, who possess a wider spectrum of project management-related skills (Müller 2009).

The *Conformist* paradigm (Table 12.1) utilizes strict compliance with existing processes, rules, and policies in an attempt to ensure the lowest project costs in environments having a relatively homogeneous set of projects. The *Flexible Economist* paradigm aims for low project costs through a well-informed selection of project management methodologies which ensure economic delivery by only marginally compromising other success criteria. Well-educated and experienced project managers identify the most economic processes for a given project and save costs through professional management. These skilled, educated, flexible, and experienced project managers work on a heterogeneous portfolio of projects. The *Versatile Artist* paradigm maximizes benefits by balancing the diverse set of requirements arising from a number of different stakeholders and their particular needs and desires. Project managers are expected to develop new or tailor existing methodologies, processes, or tools to economically balance the diversity of requirements. Organizations using this governance paradigm posses a very heterogeneous set of projects in high-technology or high-risk environments. Finally, the *Agile Pragmatist* paradigm aims for maximization of technical usability, often through a time-phased approach to the development and product release of functionality over a period of time. Products developed under this paradigm grow from a core functionality, which is developed first, to ever-increasing features, which although of a lesser and lesser importance to the core functionality, enhance the product in flexibility, sophistication, and ease of use. These projects often use Agile/Scrum methods, with the sponsor prioritizing deliverables by business value over a given timeframe (Müller 2009).

Enterprises apply different governance paradigms in different parts of their organization, contingent on their idiosyncratic objectives, knowledge of the means–ends relationship of the organization's tasks, preferences of the leaders, market demands, and the level of project management maturity. The governance function can then be executed by looking at the project from a TCE perspective and trying to economize the associated administrative costs, but also looking at the project from an agency theory perspective in setting up the required structures to avoid opportunism on the

Table 12.1 Four governance paradigms

Control focus	*Shareholder Orientation*	*Stakeholder Orientation*
Outcome	Flexible Economist	Versatile Artist
Behavior	Conformist	Agile Pragmatist

Source: Müller (2009).

side of the project manager and team, and instilling appropriate control measures to ensure plan accomplishment through behavior or outcome control (or both). All these functions are performed within the limits set by the corporate governance framework and the legitimacy of actions within the social context (Müller 2009).

Project-specific governance frameworks

Other research in project governance has focused more on industry and project type, mainly with the aim of developing governance frameworks for construction, engineering, IT, and public projects. This stream of literature is dominated by work done in the construction industry. However, the studies show the variety of governance approaches appropriate for the different project types.

The appropriateness of TCE for understanding construction projects and their context was shown by Winch (1989), who suggested lifting the focus from the individual project to the level of the firm and applying TCE to the internal and external relationships of a firm within a project. Using this perspective he subsequently investigated the different transactions over the life cycle of construction projects (Winch 2001), by looking at projects as processes. He showed that the three TCE dimensions of asset specificity, uncertainty, and frequency do not pose a threat to a project when considered individually or if their relationship is static. However, once dynamics sets in the existing governance structure becomes imbalanced and adaptation is needed. In line with Stinchcombe's (1959) concepts and findings, Winch (2003) assessed the differences between mass production (e.g. automotive) and the construction industries, and found the mass production governance approach inappropriate for the construction industry. Instead, he proposed models of manufacturing derived from complex systems industries and project management.

A comprehensive description of the governance approach in building the facilities for the Sydney Olympics has been provided by Clegg et al. (2002). This ethnographic study addressed the "governmentality" of the project as a task, and compared the idiosyncratic governance practices at the Sydney Olympics with the governance practices in the construction industry more generally and the associated elements of TCE. By taking into account the temporality of projects the authors combined the theoretical perspectives of Foucault, Schutz, and Williamson to derive the limits of project governance. Their multi-level analysis identified variances in the clearness of the governance culture, depending on position in the hierarchy or in the network of firms. This showed problem areas that need to be addressed for continuous improvement of the project governance through corporate stakeholder management in a constantly changing context.

Coalition-building in the governance of construction projects was investigated by Pryke (2005) using Social Network Analysis (SNA). His study showed the appropriateness of SNA for investigating relationships in governance and identified, among others, the changing role of procurement officers in governance. Using this framework, Pryke and Pearson (2006) subsequently investigated the impact of different types of contractual incentives on the roles in governance of European construction projects. They showed that different forms of pain/gain-share contracts lead to inappropriate cluster building or centralization among firms in projects, and found that Guaranteed Maximum Price contracts are an effective means of transferring risks to the client associated with post-contract design development, by instilling a strong customer focus and high efficiency.

In their investigation on the design criteria of governance structures for large capital mega-projects Miller and Hobbs (2005) showed that these projects differ in their governance in terms of higher dynamics in governance structures than in smaller projects and more network relationships rather than binary buyer–seller relationships. Taken together, they bring forward the need for more self-organizing and flexible governance regimes to appropriately govern these types of projects. Similarly Klakegg et al. (2008) found that governance of public projects varies by national government. Their investigation of governance frameworks for large public projects showed a "top-down" versus a "bottom-up" preference in different countries. Some governments, for example Norway's, prefer top-down approaches for their public projects, which focus on project outcomes (as opposed to methodology compliance), and base their governance approach on guidelines such as those from the Association for Project Management (APM 2004), which take a corporate-wide view and define responsibilities, rather than roles. Other governments, for example the UK's, prefer bottom-up approaches using a control and compliance perspective, for example by applying governance standards developed on top of existing project management methodologies like PRINCE2 (Office of Government Commerce 2008).

In developing a framework for project management at NASA, Shenhar et al. (2005) applied the four-dimensional grid of novelty, pace, technology, and complexity to profile four types of projects. From this they developed different risk profiles for these types of projects, which then guides the selection of contracts for suppliers and other contributing organizations, thus determining the governance structure of the different types of projects.

Research on the governance of IT projects, through the lens of agency theory and related communication, showed that successful projects are linked to governance attributes of:

- The highest level of collaboration operationalized as the extent the project objectives are clear and the project manager and the steering group are interested in working together;
- A medium level of structure, measured as the level of bureaucracy imposed onto the project manager by the steering group and the clearness of the methods to be used in the project.

While clearness of objectives has long been known as being important for success in projects (e.g. Morris and Hough 1987), this study showed that governance institutions like steering groups must allow sufficient freedom for the project manager to manage day-to-day work autonomously, so that the resolving of issues to the higher-level governance structures is only done in exceptional cases (Turner and Müller 2004). This level of structure is, however, influenced by the contract type existing between the project owner and supplier, with fixed-price contracts leading to governance structures with too little structure and cost-reimbursement contracts to too rigid structures for the project manager to manage the daily business, the contract underlying the governance structure thereby becoming a risk in the project which needs to be managed through appropriate communication (Müller and Turner 2005).

Quantitative and conceptual studies on trust in the context of project governance showed a non-linear negative relationship between trust and control, thus permitting a substitution of one by the other, within limits. Here too much governance reduces trust, which impacts project results negatively (Turner and Müller 2004; Müller and Turner 2005). This is supported by Hartman (2002), who identified trust as an antecedent for project success, however with differences in meaning of trust contingent on contractor or owner role in projects. Among these two roles trust varies in its impact on satisfaction with relationships in projects and positive project outcomes (Pinto, Slevin, and English 2009).

SUMMARY OF RESEARCH ON PROJECT GOVERNANCE

The landscape of research on project governance is diverse. From day-to-day work in projects to strategic levels, such as portfolio management, strategic PMOs, or the board of directors, the level of analysis varies significantly. This is shown in Table 12.2 for some of the above-mentioned studies. The research is dominated by the TCE perspective, especially in construction projects, whereas others, like IT, are investigated using either TCE or agency theory perspectives. Some of the governance studies are more explorative and apply neither of these theories. In conclusion it can be said that a pluralism of theoretical perspectives, research methods, and levels of analysis emerges, which contributes to understanding the multidimensional phenomenon of project governance. To that end, more studies like those on project governance in the construction industry and those on governance of multi-project work are needed in different industries and locales.

Table 12.2 Examples for levels of analysis in project governance studies

Generic project governance models		Project specific governance models		
Authors	Level of analysis	Authors	Project type	Level of analysis
Blomquist and Müller (2006)	TCE, governance of multi-project organizations	Winch (1989, 2001) Clegg et al. (2002)	Construction projects	TCE, TCE and governmentality,
Müller (2009)	TCE and Agency Theory, Organizational governance paradigms	Pryke (2005) Pryke and Pearson (2006)	Construction projects	TCE, Relationships and incentives using SNA
Pinto, Slevin, and English (2009)	The role of trust in projects and their governance	Miller and Hobbs (2005)	Large capital projects	Criteria for setting up a governance regime
		Klakegg et al. (2008)	Large public projects	Governance approaches
		Shenhar et al. (2005)	NASA projects	Categorization and risk profile for selection of contracts
		Turner and Müller (2004) Müller and Turner (2005)	IT projects	Agency Theory, Collaboration and structure in project governance

Towards a research agenda for the future

The review showed a number of shortcomings of current concepts and theories. Most obvious is the use of TCE, which was developed for the context of permanent organizations, and its application to temporary and dynamic project settings. Questions arise as to the appropriateness of the underlying dimensions for the temporary context of projects and their specific governance methods like program and portfolio management. More research is needed to investigate the impact of inherent discontinuities of temporary organizations on the explanatory power of the three governance theories addressed herein. Examples may include:

- TCE's *first mover advantage* in the context of project alliances in networks of firms in competition,
- the stability of relationships as outlined in Eccles's (1981) quasifirm and its relevance for contemporary organizational structures, such as Open Source development projects.

From an agency theory perspective the assumptions of a homo economicus underlying Agency Theory (or the opposite underlying Stewardship Theory) can be questioned. Are these perspectives still relevant in the dynamics of current project contexts? Examples include Free Libre Open Source Software (FLOSS) development projects in global networks, where regulatory elements such as price and contracts (even psychological contracts) are absent in a global market and hierarchy-like control structures are used in market-like environments.

How will socio-cultural changes impact governance forms, including the changing value system of the generation following the baby-boomers, that is, those born 1983–97? While baby-boomers value fun in life, the now emerging Net-generation values what one knows and has to say and not where one comes from (Tapscott 1998). Correspondingly, are the concepts of behavior and outcome control still relevant in newer forms of organizing (e.g. in FLOSS) in light of extreme temporality and abundance of work opportunities for individuals in global networks? In other words: will the relative static concepts of today's governance theories retain their explanatory power in the near future?

One possible way of approaching this is by researching the substitution of older theories, like agency theory, with their migrated and contemporary successors, like prospect theory, which values gains and losses in decisions rather than final assets, and replaces probabilities with decision weights (Kahneman and Tversky 1979).

Notwithstanding these global challenges, the particularities of project governance need to be better understood. Examples include the impact of owners simply seeking to increase the return on their ownership rights, compared with others who are motivated for different reasons, including non-profit organizations. That leads to research questions, for example on:

- Governance differences between complex private sector-owned projects and equivalently complex public sector projects;
- Governance differences in projects with ex ante stated (multiple) aims and objectives and those which develop them over the course of the project;
- The role of the project governance function in setting and monitoring the incentives for the various project parties and their resource providers, in order to achieve project success;
- The critical differences in the project boards' composition, remit, and mode of operation that separate project governance from its equivalent in corporate governance;
- Learning from comparing the recent history of project failure to that of corporate failure for the development of a corresponding set of recommendations to improve the governance of projects.

More case studies are needed to understand these idiosyncrasies of project governance. However, time may also be ripe to move beyond the prevalent social constructivist epistemology towards more post-modernist studies to develop a more holistic understanding of the subject.

ACKNOWLEDGEMENT

The author is grateful to Andrew Edkins and his contributions to an earlier version of this chapter.

REFERENCES

ADLER, T. R., SCHERER, R. F., BARTON, S. L., and KATERBERG, R. (1998). "An empirical test of transaction cost theory: validating contract typology," *Journal of Applied Management Studies*, 7/2: 185–200.

APM (2004). *Directing Change: A Guide to Governance of Project Management*. High Wycombe: Association for Project Management.

BARNEY, J. B., and HESTERLY, W. (1996). "Organizational economics: understanding the relationship between organizations and economic analysis," in S. R. Clegg, C. Hardy, and W. R. Nord (eds.), *Handbook of Organization Studies*. London: Sage Publications, 115–47.

BERGEN, M., DUTTA, S., and WALKER, O. C. (1992). "Agency relationships in marketing: a review of the implications and applications of agency and related theories," *Journal of Marketing*, 56/3: 1.

BLOMQUIST, T., and MÜLLER, R. (2006). *Middle Managers in Program and Portfolio Management: Practice, Roles and Responsibilities*. Newton Square, PA: Project Management Institute.

BROWN, S., and EISENHARDT, K. M. (1997). "The art of continuous change: linking complexity theory and time-paced evolution in relentlessly shifting organizations," *Administrative Science Quarterly*, 42/1: 1–34.

CARES, R., DU BOIS, C., JEGERS, M., DE GIETER, S., SCHEPERS, C., and PEPERMANS, R. (2006). "Principal–agent relationships on the stewardship–agency axis," *Nonprofit Management & Leadership*, 17/1: 25–47.

CLARKE, T. (2004). "The stakeholder corporation: a business philosophy for the information age," in *Theories of Corporate Governance: The Philosophical Foundations of Corporate Governance*. London: Routledge, 189–202.

CLEGG, S. R. (1994). "Weber and Foucault: social theory for the study of organizations," *Organization*, 1/1: 149–78.

——PITSIS, T. S., RURA-POLLEY, T., and MAROSSZEKY, M. (2002). "Governmentality matters: designing an alliance culture of inter-organizational collaboration for managing projects," *Organization Studies*, 23/3: 317–37.

COASE, R. H. (1937). "The nature of the firm," *Economica*, 4/November: 386–405.

COMMONS, J. R. (1932). "The problem of correlating law, economics, and ethics," *Wisconsin Law Review*, 8/8: 3–26.

——(1983). "The structure of ownership and the theory of the firm," *Journal of Law and Economics*, 8: 3–26.

CRAWFORD, L., COOKE-DAVIES, T., HOBBS, B., LABUSCHAGNE, L., REMINGTON, K., and CHEN, P. (2008). "Governance and support in the sponsoring of projects and programs," *Project Management Journal*, 39/Supplement: S43–S55.

DAVIES, J. H., SCHOORMAN, F. D., and DONALDSON, L. (1997). "Toward a stewardship theory of management," *Academy of Management Review*, 22/1: 20–47.

ECCLES, R. G. (1981). "The quasifirm in the construction industry," *Journal of Economic Behavior & Organization*, 2: 335–57.

EISENHARDT, K. M. (1989). "Agency theory: an assessment and review," *Academy of Management Review*, 14/1: 57–74.

FAEMS, D., JANSSENS, M., MADHOK, A., and VAN LOOY, B. (2008). "Toward an integrative perspective on alliance governance: connecting contract design, trust dynamics, and contract application," *Academy of Management Journal*, 51/6: 1053–78.

HARPHAM, A., TURNER, J. R., and SIMISTER, S. J. (2000). "Political, economic, social and technical influences: PEST," in J. R. Turner and S. J. Simister (eds.), *Gower Handbook of Project Management*. Aldershot: Gower Publishing Limited, iii. 165–84.

HARRISON, P. D., and HARREL, A. (1993). "Impact of 'adverse selection' on managers' project evaluation," *Academy of Management Journal*, 36/3.

HARTMAN, F. T. (2002). "The role of trust in project management," in D. P. Slevin, D. L. Cleland, and J. K. Pinto (eds.), *The Frontiers of Project Management Research*. Newtown Square, PA: Project Management Institute, 225–35.

HENDRY, J. (2002). "The principal's other problems: honest incompetence and the specification of objectives," *Academy of Management Review*, 27/1.

HOLMSTROM, B., and MILGROM, P. (1991). "Multitask principal–agent analyses: incentive contracts, asset ownership, and job design," *Journal of Law, Economics, & Organization*, 7.

JENSEN, M. C. (2000). *A Theory of the Firm: Governance, Residual Claims, and Organizational Forms*. Cambridge, MA: Harvard University Press.

——(2001). "Value maximization, stakeholder theory, and the corporate objective function," retrieved from http://ssrn.com/paper=220671. Accessed August 14, 2009.

JENSEN, M. C. and MECKLING, W. H. (1976). "Theory of the firm: managerial behavior, agency costs, and ownership structure," *Journal of Financial Economics*, 3/4: 305–60.

—— —— (1994). "The nature of man," *Journal of Applied Corporate Finance*, 7/2: 4–19.

KAHNEMAN, D., and TVERSKY, A. (1979). "Prospect theory: an analysis of decision under risk," *Econometrica*, 47/2: 263–92.

KLAKEGG, O. J., WILLIAMS, T., MAGNUSSEN, O. M., and GLASSPOOL, H. (2008). "Governance frameworks for public project development and estimation," *Project Management Journal*, 30/Supplement: S27–S42.

LEMKE, T. (2001). "The birth of bio-politics: Michel Foucault's lecture at Collège de France on neo-liberal governmentality," *Economy and Society*, 30/2: 190–207.

MILLER, R., and HOBBS, B. (2005). "Governance regimes for large complex projects," *Project Management Journal*, 36/3: 42–50.

MOE, T. M., and WILLIAMSON, O. E. (1995). "The politics of structural choice: toward a theory of public bureaucracy," in *Organization Theory: From Chester Barnard to the Present and Beyond*. New York: Oxford University Press.

MORRIS, P. (1998). "Why project management doesn't always make business sense," *Project Management: International Project Management Journal, Finland*, 4/1: 12–16.

—— and HOUGH, G. (1987). *The Anatomy of Major Projects: A Study of the Reality of Project Management*, vol. i. Chichester: John Wiley & Sons, Ltd.

MÜLLER, R. (2009). *Project Governance*. Aldershot: Gower Publishing.

—— and TURNER, J. R. (2005). "The impact of principal–agent relationship and contract type on communication between project owner and manager," *International Journal of Project Management*, 23/5: 398–403.

—— —— (2007). "The influence of project managers on project success criteria and project success by type of project," *European Management Journal*, 25/4: 289–309.

—— MARTINSUO, M., and BLOMQUIST, T. (2008). "Project portfolio control and portfolio management in different contexts," *Project Management Journal*, 39/3: 28–42.

OECD (2004). "OECD Principles of Corporate Governance," www.oecd.org. Accessed January 10, 2005.

OFFICE OF GOVERNMENT COMMERCE (2008). "OGC governance," http://www.ogc.gov.uk. Accessed July 2, 2008.

O'REILLY, C. A., and TUSHMAN, M. L. (2004). "The ambidextrous organization," *Harvard Business Review*, 82/4: 74–81.

OUCHI, W. G. (1977). "The relationship between organisation structure and organisational control," *Administrative Science Quarterly*, 22/1: 95–113.

—— (1978). "The transmission of control through organizational hierarchy," *Academy of Management Journal*, 21/2: 173–92.

—— (1979). "A conceptual framework for the design of organizational control mechanisms," *Management Science*, 25/9: 833–48.

—— (1980). "Markets, bureaucracies and clans," *Administrative Science Quarterly*, 25: 129–41.

—— and MAGUIRE, M. A. (1975). "Organizational control: two functions," *Administrative Science Quarterly*, 20/4: 559–69.

—— and PRICE, R. L. (1978). "Hierarchies, clans, and theory Z: a new perspective on organization development," *Organizational Dynamics*, 7/2: 24–44.

PARTINGTON, D. (2000). "Implementing strategy through programmes of projects," in J. R. Turner and S. J. Simister (eds.), *Gower Handbook of Project Management*, 3rd edn. Aldershot: Gower Publishing Limited, 33–46.

PENROSE, E. (1959). *The Theory of Growth of the Firm.* New York: John Wiley.

PINTO, J. K., and SLEVIN, D. P. (1998). "Critical success factors," in J. K. Pinto (ed.), *The Project Management Institute Project Management Handbook.* San Francisco: Jossey-Bass.

——— and ENGLISH, B. (2009). "Trust in projects: an empirical assessment of owner/contractor relationships," *International Journal of Project Management,* 27/6: 638–48.

PURANAM, P., and VANNESTE, B. S. (2009). "Trust and governance: untangling a tangled web," *Academy of Management Review,* 34/1: 11–31.

PRYKE, S. D. (2005). "Towards a social network theory of project governance," *Construction Management and Economics,* 23: 927–39.

——— and PEARSON, S. (2006). "Project governance: case studies on financial incentives," *Building Research & Information,* 36/6: 534–45.

SHENHAR, A., DVIR, D., MILOSEVIC, D., MULENBURG, J., PATANAKUL, P., REILLY, R., RYAN, M., SAGE, A., SAUSER, B., SRIVANNABOON, S., STEFANOVIC, J., and THAMHAIN, H. (2005). "Toward a NASA-specific project management framework," *Engineering Management Journal,* 17/4: 8.

SÖDERLUND, J. (2004). "On the broadening scope of the research on projects: a review and a model for analysis," *International Journal of Project Management,* 22/8: 655–67.

STINCHCOMBE, A. L. (1959). "Bureaucratic and craft administration of production," *Administrative Science Quarterly,* 4: 168–87.

STOKER, G. (1998). "Governance as theory: five propositions," *International Social Science Journal,* 50/155: 17–28.

SUNDARAMURTHY, C., and LEWIS, M. (2003). "Control and collaboration: paradoxes of governance," *Academy of Management Review,* 28/3: 397–415.

TAPSCOTT, D. (1998). *Growing up Digital: The Rise of the Net Generation.* New York: McGraw-Hill.

TURNER, J. R. (2004). "Farsighted project contract management: incomplete in its entirety," *Construction Management and Economics,* 22/1: 75–83.

——— and COCHRANE, R. A. (1993). "Goals-and-methods matrix: coping with projects with ill defined goals and/or methods of achieving them," *International Journal of Project Management,* 11/2: 93–102.

——— and KEEGAN, A. (2001). "Mechanisms of governance in the project-based organization: roles of the broker and steward," *European Management Journal,* 19/3: 254–67.

——— and MÜLLER, R. (2004). "Communication and co-operation on projects between the project owner as principal and the project manager as agent," *European Management Journal,* 22/3: 327–36.

——— and SIMISTER, S. J. (2000). *Handbook of Project Management.* Aldershot: Gower Publishing Ltd.

WILLIAMSON, O. E. (1975). *Markets and Hierarchies: Analysis and Antitrust Implications.* New York: Collier Macmillan, Canada, Ltd.

———(1985). *The Economic Institutions of Capitalism.* New York: The Free Press.

———(1994). "Visible and invisible governance," *AEA Papers and Proceedings: Invisible Hand Theories,* 84/2: 323–6.

——— (1995). "Transaction cost economics and organization theory," in *Organization Theory.* New York: Oxford University Press, 207–56.

——— (1999a). "Strategy research: governance and competence perspectives," *Strategic Management Journal,* 20: 1087–108.

——— (1999b). "Public and private bureaucracies: a transaction cost economics perspective," *Journal of Law, Economics and Organization,* 15/1: 306–42.

WILLIAMSON, O. E. (2002). "The lens of contract: private ordering," *International Society for New Institutional Economics*, http://www.isnie.org/ISNIE02/Papers02/williamsonoliver.pdf. Accessed August 14, 2009.

—— (2003). "The economic analysis of institutions and organisations: in general and with respect to country studies," *OECD Economics Department Working Paper Series* (133).

WINCH, G. M. (1989). "The construction firm and the construction project: a transaction cost approach," *Construction Management and Economics*, 7/4: 331–45.

—— (2001). "Governing the project process: a conceptual framework," *Construction Management and Economics*, 19: 799–808.

—— (2003). "Models of manufacturing and the construction process: the genesis of re-engineering construction," *Building Research & Information*, 31/2: 107–18.

CHAPTER 13

OVER BUDGET, OVER TIME, OVER AND OVER AGAIN

MANAGING MAJOR PROJECTS

BENT FLYVBJERG

CHARACTERISTICS OF MAJOR PROJECTS

Ex post studies of the Channel Tunnel between France and the UK—the longest underwater rail tunnel in Europe—make shocking reading. Construction cost overrun was 80 percent in real terms using the final business case as baseline, overrun on financing costs was 140 percent, and the demand shortfall was 50 percent (Flyvbjerg, Bruzelius, and Rothengatter 2003). The actual net present value to the British economy is negative, at –17.8 billion dollars, as is the internal rate of return on the project, at –14.45 percent, leading to the inevitable conclusion that "the British Economy would have been better off had the Tunnel never been constructed" (Anguera 2006: 291).

If the Channel Tunnel were just an isolated instance of what Hall (1980) has aptly called "great planning disasters," we need not worry much. However, statistical analyses document that the tunnel is not the outlier it might seem at first sight, it's business as usual (Flyvbjerg, Holm, and Buhl 2004, 2005). In recent surveys of major projects, nine out of ten had cost overrun, cost overruns of 50 to 100 percent were common, and overruns above 100 percent were not uncommon. On the demand and benefit side, estimates were typically wrong by 20 percent to 70 percent compared with actual developments (Altshuler and Luberoff 2003; Flyvbjerg, Bruzelius, and Rothengatter 2003: 18–19; Morris and Hough 1987; Priemus, Flyvbjerg, and van Wee 2008).

Major projects and programmes generally have the following characteristics. (A major project is here defined as a project costing a hundred million dollars or more; a major programme as a suite of projects costing a billion dollars and up. Most of the chapter's conclusions apply equally to major projects and major programs. However, for ease of writing and reading, "major project" is the main term used in the text.)

- Such projects are inherently risky due to long planning horizons and complex interfaces.
- Decision-making, planning, and management are typically multi-actor processes with conflicting interests.
- Technology and designs are often non-standard.
- Often there is overcommitment to a certain project concept at an early stage, resulting in "lock-in" or "capture," leaving alternatives analysis weak or absent, and leading to escalated commitment in later stages.
- Due to the large sums of money involved, principal–agent problems are common.
- The project scope or ambition level will typically change significantly over time.
- Statistical evidence shows that such complexity and unplanned events are often unaccounted for, leaving budget and time contingencies sorely inadequate.
- As a consequence, misinformation about costs, schedules, benefits, and risks is the norm throughout project development and decision-making.
- The result is cost overruns and benefit shortfalls that undermine project viability during project implementation.

This is not to say that projects do not exist for which costs and/or benefits were on or better than the budget. The Bilbao Guggenheim Museum is an example of that rare breed of major project which is built on time, with costs on budget, and revenues higher than expected (Flyvbjerg 2005). But it is far easier to produce long lists of major projects that have failed in terms of cost overruns and benefit shortfalls than it is to produce lists of projects that have succeeded. To illustrate, as part of ongoing research on success in major project management the author and his associates are trying to establish a sample large enough to allow statistically valid answers. But so far they have failed. Why? Because success is so rare in major project management that at present it can be studied only as small-N research.

The characteristics of major projects listed above are deeply problematic, because they produce failure upon failure. Most of the time this impacts people mainly in terms of financial losses, which is bad enough for taxpayers and other investors who fund major projects. But worse, particular groups, who are often already disadvantaged, are sometimes forced to carry a disproportionate share of negative environmental and social impacts from projects that do not even deliver the promised benefits.

In what follows, the deeper causes of cost overruns and benefit shortfalls are uncovered. In addition, possible solutions to the problems are described.

Causes and root causes
of underperformance

It is useful to distinguish between "causes" and "root causes" in explaining cost overruns, benefit shortfalls, and delays in major projects. Conventionally, the following are listed as causes of project underperformance in the literature and in practice: project complexity, scope changes, technological uncertainty, demand uncertainty, unexpected geological features, and negative plurality (i.e. opposing stakeholder voices) (Flyvbjerg, Bruzelius, and Rothengatter 2003; Miller and Lessard 2000; Morris and Pinto 2004). No doubt, all of these factors at one time or another contribute to cost overruns and benefit shortfalls, but it may be argued that they are not the real, or root, cause. The root cause of underperformance is the fact that project planners tend to systematically underestimate or even ignore risks of complexity, scope changes, etc. during project development and decision-making (Flyvbjerg, Garbuio, and Lovallo 2009). Such ignorance or underestimation of risks is often called optimism, and if we accept this terminology the root cause of underperformance is optimism, whereas complexity, scope, technology, etc. are simply specific issues about which planners have been optimistic and through which optimism therefore manifests itself. Similarly, it may be argued that escalated commitment and lock in, which are also often listed as causes of underperformance, are not root causes (Staw and Ross 1978). These phenomena are so common in major projects that the risk of their occurrence should clearly be considered in sound project preparation. But, again, such risks are typically ignored or underestimated and that is the root cause of underperformance.

Below, the focus will be on root causes of underperformance and not on conventional causes. This means that a substantial part of the conventional literature is left out. Not because this literature is unimportant, but because the chapter has a different focus and is attempting to understand better what the deeper causes of underperformance are.

At the most basic level, the underlying causes of project underperformance may be grouped into three categories, each of which will be considered in turn: (1) bad luck or error; (2) optimism bias; and (3) strategic misrepresentation (Flyvbjerg,

Garbuio, and Lovallo 2009). Bad luck, or the unfortunate resolution of one of the major project uncertainties mentioned above, is the explanation typically given by management for a poor outcome (Ascher 1979; Clapham and Schwenk 1991; Ford 1985; Morris and Hough 1987). The problem with such explanations is that they do not hold up in the face of statistical tests. Explanations that account for underperformance in terms of bad luck or error have been able to survive for decades only because data on project performance has generally been of low quality, i.e. data has been disaggregated and inconsistent, because it came from small-N samples that did not allow rigorous statistical analyses. Once higher-quality data was established that could be consistently compared across projects in numbers high enough to establish statistical significance, explanations in terms of bad luck or error collapsed. Such explanations simply do not fit the data (Flyvbjerg, Holm, and Buhl 2002, 2005).

First, if underperformance were truly caused by bad luck and error, we would expect a relatively unbiased distribution of errors in performance around zero. In fact, the data show with very high statistical significance that the distribution of error is exceedingly biased with a mean statistically different from zero.

Second, if bad luck or error were main explanations of underperformance, we would expect an improvement in performance over time, since in a professional setting errors and their sources would be recognized and addressed through the refinement of data, methods, etc., much like in weather forecasting or medical science. Substantial resources have in fact been spent over several decades on improving data and methods in major project management, including in cost and benefit forecasting. Still the evidence shows that this has not led to improved performance in terms of lower cost overruns and benefit shortfalls. Bad luck or error, therefore, do not appear to explain the data. It is not so-called estimation "errors" or their causes that need explaining. It is the fact that, deliberately or not, in the vast majority of projects, risks of scope changes, high complexity, unexpected geological features, etc. are systematically underestimated during project preparation, resulting in underestimated costs and overestimated benefits.

We may agree with proponents of conventional explanations that it is, for example, impossible to predict for the individual project exactly *which* scope change, complexity, or geological problem will materialize and make costs soar. But we must maintain that it is possible to predict the risk, based on experience from previous projects, *that* some such problems will haunt a project and how this will affect costs. We must also maintain that such risk can and should be accounted for in forecasts of costs, but typically is not. Moreover, major projects are prone to what Taleb (2007) calls "black swans," i.e. extreme events with low probability and high impact, but forecasts and risk assessments rarely reflect this. For explanations in terms of bad luck or error to be credible, they would have to explain why forecasts of performance are so consistent in ignoring cost and benefit risks, including in the extreme version of black swans.

For the above reasons, explanations of underperformance in terms of bad luck or error must today be considered falsified, despite their long historical reign. We need to look elsewhere for valid explanations of underperformance. We need to look at explanations in terms of optimism bias and strategic misrepresentation.

Optimism bias

Explanations of project underperformance in terms of optimism bias and strategic misrepresentation both see the high failure rates for projects as a consequence of flawed decision-making (Flyvbjerg, Garbuio, and Lovallo 2009). According to the first explanation—optimism bias—the flaw consists in managers falling victim to what psychologists call the planning fallacy (Buehler, Griffin, and Ross 1994). In its grip, managers make decisions based on delusional optimism rather than on a rational weighting of gains, losses, and probabilities. They overestimate benefits and underestimate costs and time. They involuntarily spin scenarios of success and overlook the potential for mistakes and miscalculations. As a result, managers pursue initiatives that are unlikely to come in on budget or on time, or to ever deliver the expected returns. These biases are often the result of the inside view in planning: decision-makers have a strong tendency to consider problems as unique and thus focus on the particulars of the case at hand when generating solutions (Kahneman and Lovallo 1993). Adopting an outside view of the problem has been shown to mitigate delusion. It is applied by ignoring the specific details of the project at hand and uses a broad reference class of similar projects to forecast outcomes for the current project, as we will see below.

When in the grip of the inside view, managers focus tightly on the case at hand, by considering the plan and the obstacles to its completion, by constructing scenarios of future progress, and by extrapolating current trends (Kahneman and Tversky 1979b; Lovallo and Kahneman 2003). In other words, by using typical bottom-up decision-making techniques, they think about a problem by bringing to bear all they know about it, with special attention to its unique details. The inside view facilitates two cognitive delusions, namely the planning fallacy and anchoring.

When forecasting the outcomes of risky projects, managers often fall victim to the planning fallacy. Psychologists have defined it as the tendency to underestimate task completion times and costs, even knowing that the vast majority of similar tasks have run late or gone over budget (Lovallo and Kahneman 2003). It is a well-established bias in the experimental literature. In one set of experiments, Buehler, Griffin, and Ross (1994) assessed the accuracy of psychology students' estimates of completion times for their year-long honors thesis project.

In the experiments, the students' "realistic" predictions were overly optimistic: 70 percent took longer than the predicted time, even though the question was asked toward the end of the year. On average, students took fifty-five days to complete their thesis, which was twenty-two days longer than predicted, i.e. a time overrun of 67 percent. Similar results have been found with various types of subjects and for a wide variety of tasks such as holiday shopping, filing taxes, and other routine chores (Buehler, Griffin, and MacDonald 1997; Newby-Clark, McGregor, and Zanna 2002).

These findings are not limited to experiments. Cost and time overruns are well documented in the provision of large-scale infrastructure projects (Flyvbjerg, Holm, and Buhl 2002; Mott MacDonald 2002; National Audit Office 2003, 2005). In business, executives and entrepreneurs seem to be highly susceptible to optimism. Studies that compared the actual outcomes of capital investment projects, mergers and acquisitions, and market entries with managers' original expectations for those ventures show a strong tendency towards over-optimism (Malmendier and Tate 2003). An analysis of start-up ventures in a wide range of industries found that more than 80 percent failed to achieve their market-share target (Dune, Roberts, and Samuelson 1988).

Anchoring and adjustment is another consequence of the inside view in thinking that leads to optimistic forecasts (Tversky and Kahneman 1974). Anchoring on plans is one of the most robust biases of judgment. The first number that is considered as a possible answer to a question serves as an "anchor." Even when people know that the anchor is too high or too low, their adjustments away from it are almost always insufficient.

In the context of planning for major projects there is always a plan, which is very likely to serve as an anchor. Furthermore, the plan that is developed is almost always seen as a "realistic" best or most likely case, developed according to what the World Bank (1994: ii. 22) calls the "EGAP principle," i.e. the assumption that Everything Goes According to Plan. Executives know that events may develop beyond the best or most likely case so they generally attempt to capture unforeseen costs by building in a contingency fund that is proportional to the size of the project. However, when compared with actual cost overruns, such adjustments are clearly and significantly inadequate (Flyvbjerg, Bruzelius, and Rothengatter 2003). Furthermore, the initial estimate serves as an anchor for later stage estimates, which therefore insufficiently adjust to the reality of the project's performance.

The power of these heuristics and biases is well illustrated in a field study where the Rand Corporation examined forty-four chemical pioneer process plants, owned by 3M, Du Pont, and Texaco, among others. Actual construction costs were over twice as large as the initial estimates (Merrow, Phillips, and Meyers 1981). Furthermore, at every subsequent stage of the process, managers underestimated the cost of completing the construction of the plants. Finally, even a year after start-up about half of the plants (twenty-one) produced at less than 75 percent of their design capacity, with a quarter of the plants producing at less than 50 percent of their design capacity. Many of the plants in this latter category had their performance expectations permanently lowered.

Interestingly, however, when you ask forecasters about causes of inaccuracies in actual forecasts, they do not mention optimism bias as a main cause, whereas they will talk at length about scope changes, complexity, geology, and other unforeseen circumstances (Flyvbjerg, Holm, and Buhl 2005: 138–40). This may of course be because optimism bias is hard-wired and unconscious and thus not reflected by forecasters. After all, there is a large body of experimental evidence for the existence of optimism bias, referred to above. But the experimental data is mainly from simple, non-professional settings. This is a problem for psychological explanations, because it remains an open question whether such explanations are as general as they are presented to be, and thus to what extent they apply beyond the simple settings of the experiments from which the explanations were derived.

Optimism bias would be an important and credible explanation of underestimated costs and overestimated benefits in major project forecasting if estimates were produced by inexperienced forecasters, i.e. persons who were estimating costs and benefits for the first or second time and who were thus unknowing about the realities of major project development and were not drawing on the knowledge and skills of more experienced colleagues. Such situations may exist and may explain individual cases of inaccuracy. But given the fact that in modern society it is a defining characteristic of professional expertise that it is constantly tested—through scientific analysis, critical assessment, and peer review—in order to root out bias and error, it seems unlikely that a whole profession of forecasting experts would continue to innocently make the same mistakes decade after decade instead of learning from their actions. Learning would result in the reduction, if not elimination, of optimism bias, which would then result in estimates becoming more accurate over time.

But existing data clearly shows that this has not happened. Flyvbjerg, Holm, and Buhl (2002) show that cost underestimation in large transport infrastructure projects has been constant for seventy years. The profession of cost forecasters would indeed have to be an optimistic—and non-professional—group to keep their optimism bias throughout the seventy-year period of the study, and not learn that they were deceiving themselves and others by underestimating costs. This would account for the data, but is not a credible explanation. Therefore, on the basis of the data, one is led to reject optimism bias as a primary and singular cause of cost underestimation and benefit overestimation. Optimism bias may be part of the explanation of underperformance but does not appear to be the whole explanation.

STRATEGIC MISREPRESENTATION

The second explanatory model for project underperformance—strategic misrepresentation—accounts for flawed planning and decision-making in terms of political pressures and agency issues. Agency issues are covered in detail in Flyvbjerg, Garbuio, and Lovallo (2009). In what follows, the focus is therefore on explanations of project underperformance in terms of political and organizational pressures. Strategic misrepresentation is the second root cause of project underperformance; optimism bias was the first.

Whereas the first explanation is psychological, the second is political. According to this model, politicians, planners, or project champions deliberately and strategically overestimate benefits and underestimate costs in order to increase the likelihood that their projects, and not their competition's, gain approval and funding. This explanatory model has been set forth by Flyvbjerg, Holm, and Buhl (2002, 2005) and Wachs (1989, 1990). According to the model, actors purposely spin scenarios of success and gloss over the potential for failure. This results in managers promoting ventures that are unlikely to come in on budget or on time, or to deliver the promised benefits.

Strategic misrepresentation can be traced to political and organizational pressures, for instance competition for scarce funds or jockeying for position, and it is rational in this sense. If we now define a lie in the conventional fashion as making a statement intended to deceive others (Bok 1979: 14; Cliffe, Ramsey, and Bartlett 2000: 3), we see that deliberate misrepresentation of costs and benefits is lying, and we arrive at one of the most basic explanations of lying that exists: Lying pays off, or at least agents believe it does. Where there is political pressure there is misrepresentation and lying, according to this explanation. However, misrepresentation, lying, and failure can be moderated by measures that enhance transparency, provide accountability, and align incentives.

Explanations of underperformance in terms of strategic misrepresentation account well for the systematic underestimation of costs and overestimation of benefits found in the data. A strategic estimate of costs would be low, resulting in cost overrun, whereas a strategic estimate of benefits would be high, resulting in benefit shortfalls. A key question for explanations in terms of strategic misrepresentation is whether estimates of costs and benefits are intentionally biased to serve the interests of promoters in getting projects started. This question raises the difficult issue of lying. Questions of lying are notoriously hard to answer, because per definition a lie consists in making a statement intended to deceive others, and in order to establish whether lying has taken place, one must therefore know the intentions of actors. For legal, economic, moral, and other reasons, if promoters and managers have intentionally cooked estimates of costs and benefits to get a project started, they are unlikely to formally tell researchers or others that this is the case, because this could lead to sanctions. Despite such problems, two studies exist that succeeded in getting forecasters and managers to talk about strategic misrepresentation (Flyvbjerg and Cowi 2004; Wachs 1990).

Flyvbjerg and Cowi (2004) interviewed managers, public officials, planners, and consultants who had been involved in the development of large UK transportation infrastructure projects. In sum, their study shows that strong interests and strong incentives exist at the project approval stage to present projects as favorably as possible, that is, with benefits emphasized and costs and risks de-emphasized. Local authorities, local developers and landowners, local labor unions, local politicians, local officials, local MPs, and consultants all stand to benefit from a project that looks favorable on paper and they have little incentive to actively avoid bias in estimates of benefits, costs, and risks. National bodies, like certain parts of the Department for Transport and the Treasury who fund and oversee projects, may have an interest in more realistic appraisals, but until recently they have had little success in achieving such realism, although the situation may be changing with the initiatives to curb bias set out in HM Treasury (2003) and UK Department for Transport (2006).

Wachs (1986, 1990) found similar results for transit planning in the USA, also based on interviews that teased out the intentions of actors in order to establish whether lying took place or not. Taken together, the UK and US studies both account well for existing data on cost underestimation and benefit overestimation. Both studies falsify the notion that in situations with high political and organizational pressure the underestimation of costs and overestimation of benefits is caused by non-intentional error or optimism bias. Both studies support the view that in such situations promoters and forecasters intentionally use the following formula in order to secure approval and funding for their projects:

Underestimated costs + Overestimated benefits = Project approval

Using this formula results in an inverted Darwinism, i.e. the "survival of the unfittest." It is not the best projects that get implemented, but the projects that are artificially and misleadingly made to look best on paper. And such projects are the projects with the largest cost underestimates and benefit overestimates, other things being equal. But these are the worst, or "unfittest," projects in the sense that they are the very projects that will encounter most problems during implementation in terms of the largest cost overruns, benefit shortfalls, and risks of non-viability. They have been designed like that.

EXPLANATORY POWER OF OPTIMISM BIAS VS. STRATEGIC MISREPRESENTATION

We saw above how political and organizational pressure may influence and bias the outcome of the business case in major project management. Explanations of outcome in terms of optimism bias have their relative merit in situations where political and organizational pressures are absent or low, whereas such explanations hold less power in situations where political pressures are high. Conversely, explanations in terms of strategic misrepresentation have their relative merit where political and organizational pressures are high—this being the situation for most major projects—while they become immaterial when such pressures are not present.

Thus, rather than compete, the two types of explanation complement each other: one is strong where the other is weak, and both explanations are necessary to understand the phenomenon at hand—the pervasiveness of bias in major project management. It has been a problem until recently that optimism bias was presented as a global model, i.e. it was seen by its proponents as explaining all or most bias in human decision-making (Kahneman and Lovallo 2003). With the findings on strategic misrepresentation presented above, this view can no longer be upheld; it has been falsified in the Popperian manner. This does not mean that explanations in terms of optimism bias have no value, needless to say. It just means they are not as global as first assumed, which is a perfectly normal development for new theories as they are tried out in more and more areas. We need to combine optimism with strategic misrepresentation to get a fuller picture of what transpires in decision-making, and especially when we want to understand situations that are more complex—like major projects—than the simple experimental situations from which optimism models were developed. We also need to combine the two types of explanation when contemplating how to cure problems of bias and misrepresentation in decision-making.

Taking the outside view

When considering what project managers can do to root out bias in decisions on major projects, we need to distinguish between two fundamentally different situations: (1) project managers consider it important to get estimates of costs, benefits, and risks right, and (2) project managers do not consider it important to get estimates right, because optimistic estimates are seen as a necessary means to getting projects started. The first situation is the easier one to deal with and here better methodology will go a long way in improving project management. The second situation is more difficult, and more common for political projects as we saw above. Here changed incentives are essential in order to reward honesty and punish deception, where today's incentives often do the exact opposite.

Thus two main measures of reform are (1) better forecasting methods, and (2) improved incentive structures, with the latter being the more important, because political problems cannot be solved by technical means. Better forecasting methods are covered in this section, better incentives in the next.

If project managers genuinely consider it important to get forecasts right, it is recommended they use a new forecasting method called "reference class forecasting" to reduce inaccuracy and bias. This method was originally developed to compensate for the type of cognitive bias in human forecasting that Princeton psychologist Daniel Kahneman found in his Nobel prize-winning work on bias and uncertainty in decision-making (Kahneman 1994; Kahneman and Tversky 1979a). Reference class forecasting has proven more accurate than conventional forecasting. It was used in project management in practice for the first time in 2004 (Flyvbjerg and Cowi 2004), in 2005 the method was officially endorsed by the American Planning Association (2005), and since then it has been used by governments and private companies in the UK, the Netherlands, Denmark, Switzerland, Australia, and South Africa, among others.

For reasons of space, here only an outline of the method is presented, based mainly on Lovallo and Kahneman (2003) and Flyvbjerg (2006). Reference class forecasting consists in taking a so-called "outside view" on the particular project being forecasted. The outside view is established on the basis of information from a class of similar projects. The outside view does not try to forecast the specific uncertain events that will affect the particular project, but instead places the project in a statistical distribution of outcomes from this class of reference projects. Reference class forecasting requires the following three steps for the individual project:

1. Identification of a relevant reference class of past projects. The class must be broad enough to be statistically meaningful but narrow enough to be truly comparable with the specific project.
2. Establishing a probability distribution for the selected reference class. This requires access to credible, empirical data for a sufficient number of projects within the reference class to make statistically meaningful conclusions.
3. Compare the specific project with the reference class distribution, in order to establish the most likely outcome for the specific project.

Figure 13.1 shows what reference class forecasting does in statisticians' language. First, reference class forecasting regresses the best guess of the conventional forecast—here the project promoters' forecast, indicated by the dashed curve—toward the average of the reference class. The distribution of outcomes in the reference class is indicated by the dotted curve. Second, reference class forecasting expands the estimate of interval in the conventional forecast to the interval of the reference class.

With an example from major project management, planners in a city preparing to build a new subway would, first, establish a reference class of comparable projects. Through analyses the planners would establish that the projects included in the reference class were indeed comparable.

Second, if the planners were concerned, for example, with getting construction cost estimates right, they would then establish the distribution of outcomes for the reference class regarding the accuracy of construction cost forecasts. Figure 13.2 shows what this distribution looks like for a reference class relevant to building

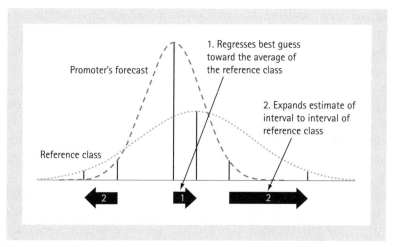

Fig. 13.1 What reference class forecasting does, in statisticians' language

subways in the UK, developed by Flyvbjerg and Cowi (2004: 23) for the UK Department for Transport.

Third, the planners would compare their subway project to the reference class distribution. This would make it clear to the planners that unless they have reason to believe they are substantially better forecasters and planners than their colleagues who did the forecasts and planning for projects in the reference class, they are likely to grossly underestimate construction costs. It is part of reference class forecasting to establish whether evidence for such reasons exists, and if it does (uncommon) to adjust the forecast for this, and if it doesn't (common) to make sure that assumed risks in the forecast are similar to actual risks in the reference class.

Finally, planners would then use this knowledge to adjust their forecasts for more realism. Figure 13.3 shows what such adjustments are for the UK situation and these adjustments are actually used by the UK Department for Transport in the manner described here to cost proposed rail projects. More specifically, Figure 13.3 shows that for a forecast of construction costs for a rail project, which has been planned in the manner that such projects are usually planned, i.e. like the projects in the reference class, this forecast would have to be adjusted upwards by 40 percent, if investors were willing to accept a risk of cost overrun of 50 percent. If investors were willing to accept a risk of overrun of only 10 percent, the uplift would have to be 68 percent. For a rail project initially estimated at, say, £4 billion, the uplifts for the 50 and 10 percent levels of risk of cost overrun would be £1.6 billion and £2.7 billion, respectively.

The capital cost of the proposed Edinburgh Tram Line 2 was estimated like this. An initial cost estimate of £320 million made by planners was adjusted for optimism bias and acceptable risk, using the probability distribution in Figure 13.2. This resulted in a new cost estimate of £400 million, including contingencies to insure against cost overruns at the 80 percent level, i.e. with a 20 percent risk of overrun. If the Scottish Parliament, who were underwriting the investment, were willing to accept a risk of overrun of 50 percent, then the cost estimate including contingencies could be lowered to £357 million. Insurance is expensive, here as elsewhere, and the marginal cost of insurance against cost overruns increases as the level of acceptable risk decreases, as seen in Figure 13.3.

The contrast between inside and outside views has been confirmed by systematic research (Gilovich, Griffin, and Kahneman 2002). The research shows that when people are asked simple questions requiring them to take an outside view, their forecasts become significantly more accurate. However, most individuals and organizations are inclined to adopt the inside view in planning major initiatives.

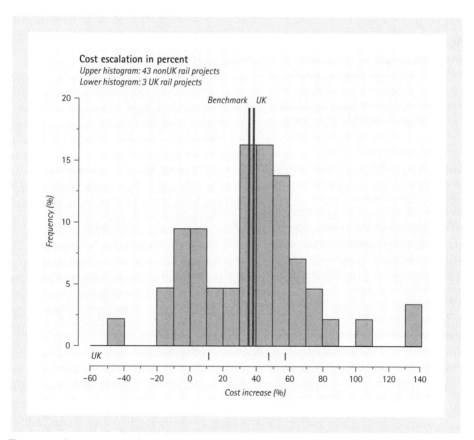

Fig. 13.2 Inaccuracy of construction cost forecasts for rail projects in reference class.

Note: Average cost increase is indicated for non-UK and UK projects, separately. Constant prices.

Source: Flyvbjerg and Cowi (2004).

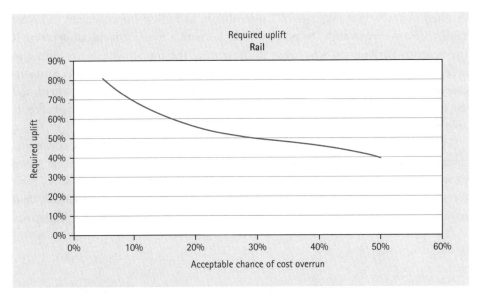

Fig. 13.3 Required adjustments to cost estimates for UK rail projects as function of the maximum acceptable level of risk for cost overrun.

Note: Constant prices.

Source: Flyvbjerg and Cowi (2004).

This is the conventional and intuitive approach. The traditional way to think about a complex project is to focus on the project itself and its details, to bring to bear what one knows about it, paying special attention to its unique or unusual features, trying to predict the events that will influence its future. The thought of going out and gathering simple statistics about related cases seldom enters a manager's mind. This is the case in general, according to Lovallo and Kahneman (2003: 61–2). And it is certainly the case for cost and benefit forecasting in large infrastructure projects. Despite the many forecasts the author and his associates have reviewed, before the Edinburgh Tram forecast, which is based on their research, they had not come across a single genuine reference class forecast of costs and benefits. Neither had Daniel Kahneman, who first conceived the idea of the reference class forecast.

While understandable, managers' preference for the inside view over the outside view is unfortunate. When both forecasting methods are applied with equal skill, the outside view is much more likely to produce a realistic estimate. That is because it bypasses cognitive and political biases such as optimism bias and strategic mis-representation and cuts directly to outcomes. In the outside view managers and forecasters are not required to make scenarios, imagine events, or gauge their own and others' levels of ability and control, so they cannot get all these things wrong. Surely the outside view, being based on historical precedent, may fail to predict extreme outcomes, that is, those that lie outside all historical precedents. But for most projects, the outside view will produce more accurate results. In contrast, a focus on inside details is the road to inaccuracy.

The comparative advantage of the outside view is most pronounced for non-routine projects, understood as projects that managers in a certain locale have never attempted before—like building an urban rail system in a city for the first time, or launching a completely new product to the market. It is in the planning of such new efforts that the biases toward optimism and strategic misrepresentation are likely to be largest. To be sure, choosing the right reference class of comparative past projects becomes more difficult when managers are forecasting initiatives for which precedents are not easily found, for instance the introduction of new and unfamiliar technologies. However, many major projects are both non-routine locally and use well-known technologies. Such projects are, therefore, particularly likely to benefit from the outside view and reference class forecasting.

Reference class forecasting is useful as a point of departure for "predict and prevent" strategies in forecasting (as opposed to "predict and provide," Owens 1995). A reference class forecast will show managers and clients where their project is heading if it performs like the projects in the reference class, which is the common situation. But such an outcome may be unacceptable to those involved. In this case, the immediate task becomes one, not only of providing contingencies for delays, cost overruns, and benefit shortfalls, but of devising a strategy that prevents these from occurring, i.e. a strategy to beat performance in the reference class, something that is difficult but not impossible to do. Pitsis et al. (2003) describe how it was done through the strategy of "future perfect thinking" for a major tunneling project that formed part of the infrastructure for the Sydney 2000 Olympics. Tunnels have a poor performance record in terms of delays and cost overruns (Flyvbjerg, Holm, and Buhl 2002), but the Sydney tunnel was built on time and almost on budget, according to Pitsis et al.

IMPROVED INCENTIVES AND ACCOUNTABILITY

In the present section we consider the situation where project managers and other influential actors do not find it important to get forecasts right and where managers, therefore, do not help to clarify and mitigate risks but, instead, generate and exacerbate them. Here project managers are part of the problem, not the solution. This situation may need some explication, because it possibly sounds to many like an unlikely state of affairs. After all, it may be agreed that project managers ought to be interested in being accurate and unbiased in their work. It is even stated in the Project Management Institute's Code of Ethics and Professional Conduct

(2006: 4, 5) that project managers should "provide accurate information in a timely manner" and they must "not engage in or condone behavior that is designed to deceive others." But there is a dark side to project management, which is remarkably underexplored in the literature (Flyvbjerg 1996).

On the dark side, project managers and planners "lie with numbers," as Wachs (1989) has aptly put it. They are busy not with getting forecasts and business cases right and following the PMI Code of Ethics but with getting projects funded and built. And accurate forecasts are often not an effective means for achieving this objective. Indeed, accurate forecasts may be counterproductive, whereas biased forecasts may be effective in competing for funds and securing the go-ahead for a project. "The most effective planner," says Wachs (1989: 477), "is sometimes the one who can cloak advocacy in the guise of scientific or technical rationality." Such advocacy would stand in direct opposition to PMI's ruling that project managers should "make decisions and take actions based on the best interests of society" (Project Management Institute 2006: 2).

Nevertheless, seemingly rational forecasts that underestimate costs and overestimate benefits have long been an established formula for project approval as we saw above. Forecasting is here mainly another kind of rent-seeking behavior, resulting in a make-believe world of misrepresentation which makes it extremely difficult to decide which projects deserve undertaking and which do not. The consequence is that too many projects proceed that should not, and that many projects don't proceed that probably should, had they not lost out to projects with "better" misrepresentation (Flyvbjerg, Holm, and Buhl 2002).

In this situation, the question is not so much what project managers can do to reduce inaccuracy and risk in forecasting, but what others can do to impose on project managers the checks and balances that would give managers the incentive to stop producing biased forecasts and begin to work according to their Code of Ethics. The challenge is to change the power relations that govern forecasting and project development. Better forecasting techniques and appeals to ethics won't do here; institutional and organizational change with a focus on transparency and accountability is necessary.

As argued in Flyvbjerg, Bruzelius, and Rothengatter (2003), two basic types of accountability define liberal democracies: (1) public sector accountability through transparency and public control, and (2) private sector accountability via competition and markets. Both types of accountability may be effective tools to curb misrepresentation in project management and to promote a culture which acknowledges and deals effectively with risk, especially where large amounts of taxpayers' money are at stake and for projects with significant social and environmental impacts, as are common for major projects. In order to achieve accountability through *transparency and public control*, the following would be required as practices embedded in the relevant institutions (the full argument for the measures may be found in Flyvbjerg, Bruzelius, and Rothengatter 2003: chapters 9–11):

- National-level government should not offer discretionary grants to local agencies for the sole purpose of building a specific type of project (aka "categorical grants"). Such grants create perverse incentives. Instead, national government should simply offer "block grants" to local governments, and let local political officials spend the funds however they choose to, but make sure that every dollar they spend on one type of project reduces their ability to fund another.
- Forecasts and business cases should be made subject to independent peer review, for instance by national audit offices.
- Forecasts should be benchmarked against comparable forecasts, for instance using reference class forecasting as described in the previous section.
- For publicly funded projects, forecasts, peer reviews, and benchmarkings should be made available for public scrutiny, including by the media.
- Public hearings, citizen juries, and the like should be organized to allow stakeholders and civil society to voice criticism and support of forecasts.
- Scientific and professional conferences should be organized where forecasters would present and defend their forecasts in the face of colleagues' scrutiny and criticism.
- Projects with inflated benefit–cost ratios should be reconsidered and stopped if recalculated costs and benefits do not warrant implementation. Projects with realistic estimates of benefits and costs should be rewarded.
- Professional and occasionally even criminal penalties should be enforced for managers and forecasters who consistently and foreseeably produce deceptive forecasts (Garett and Wachs 1996).

When the author first began suggesting, in lectures for project managers and forecasters, that deception and criminal penalties may be concepts relevant to our profession, he would get headshakes, sighs, and the occasional boo. Enron and Iraq changed that, almost overnight. Today people listen and the literature has become replete with books and articles that hammer out the links between lying, forecasting, and management. For instance, a recent book popularizing optimism bias, the planning fallacy, and strategic misrepresentation bluntly states: "Anyone who causes harm by forecasting should be treated as either a fool or a liar. Some forecasters cause more damage to society than criminals" (Taleb 2007: 163). Law-making has followed suit, most prominently with the 2002 Sarbanes–Oxley Act, which stipulates up to twenty years in prison for a knowingly false forecast intended to impede, obstruct, or influence the proper administration of affairs. There is little doubt that penalties like this influence behavior. The point is that malpractice in project management should be taken as seriously as it is in other professions, e.g. medicine and law. Failing to do this amounts to not taking the profession of project management seriously.

In order to achieve accountability in forecasting via *competition and market control*, the following would be required, again as practices that are both embedded in and enforced by the relevant institutions:

- The decision to go ahead with a major project should, where at all possible, be made contingent on the willingness of private financiers to participate without a sovereign guarantee for at least one third of the total capital needs. (A sovereign guarantee is a guarantee where government takes on the risk of paying back a loan, even if the loan was obtained in the private lending market. The lower limit of a one-third share of private risk capital for such capital to effectively influence accountability is based on practical experience (Flyvbjerg, Bruzelius, and Rothengatter 2003: 120–3).) This should be required whether projects pass the market test or not, that is, whether projects are subsidized or not or provided for social justice reasons or not.
- Forecasters and their organizations must share financial responsibility for covering cost overruns and benefit shortfalls resulting from misrepresentation and bias in forecasting.
- The participation of risk capital would not mean that government reduces control of major projects. On the contrary, it means that government can more effectively play the role it should be playing, namely as the ordinary citizen's guarantor for ensuring concerns about safety, environment, risk, and a proper use of public funds.

Whether projects are public, private, or public–private, they should be vested in one and only one project organization with a strong governance framework. The project organization may be a company or not, public or private, or a mixture. What is important is that this organization enforces accountability vis-à-vis contractors, operators, etc., and that, in turn, the directors of the organization are held accountable for any cost overruns, benefits shortfall, faulty designs, unmitigated risks, etc. that may occur during project planning, implementation, and operations.

If the institutions with responsibility for developing and building major projects would effectively implement, embed, and enforce such measures of accountability, then the misrepresentation in cost, benefit, and risk estimates, which is widespread today, might be mitigated. If this is not done, misrepresentation is likely to continue, and the allocation of funds for major projects is likely to keep on being wasteful, unethical, and sometimes even unlawful.

GLIMMERS OF HOPE

Fortunately, signs of improvement have recently appeared. The tacit consensus that deception is an acceptable business model for major project development is under attack. At a 2009 White House Fiscal Responsibility Summit, President Obama openly identified "the costly overruns, the fraud and abuse, the endless excuses" in public procurement for major projects as key problems (White House 2009). The *Washington Post* (February 24, 2009) rightly called this "a dramatic new form of discourse." Before Obama it was not *comme il faut* to talk about overruns, deception, and abuse in relation to major projects, although they were of epidemic proportions then as now, and the few who did so were ostracized. However, we cannot solve problems we cannot talk about. So talking is the first step.

A more material driver of improvement is the fact that the largest projects are now so big in relation to national economies that cost overruns, benefit shortfalls, and risks from even a single project may destabilize the finances of a whole country or region, as happened with the 2004 Olympics in Athens, where cost overruns were so large they negatively affected the credit rating of all of Greece. Similarly, when the new international airport in Hong Kong opened, computer glitches led to large revenue shortfalls that damaged Hong Kong's GNP (Flyvbjerg 2005). In the UK at the beginning of the century, cost underestimation and overrun was running rampant in so many projects in so many ministries that the reliability of national budgets suffered, leading the chancellor to order a Green Book on the problem and how to solve it (HM Treasury 2003). This move inspired other countries to follow suit. Law-makers and governments have begun to see that national fiscal distress and unreliable national budgets are too high a price to pay for the conventional way of managing major projects.

In addition, with private finance in major projects on the rise over the past fifteen to twenty years, capital funds and banks are increasingly gaining a say in the project development and management process. Private capital is no panacea for the ills in major project management, to be sure; in some cases private capital may even make things worse (Hodge and Greve 2009). But private investors place their own funds at risk, as opposed to governments who place the taxpayer's money at risk. Capital funds and banks can therefore be observed to not automatically accept at face value the forecasts of project managers and promoters. Banks typically bring in their own advisers to do independent forecasts, due diligence, and risk assessments, which is an important step in the right direction. The false assumption that one forecast or one business case (which is also a forecast) may contain the truth about a project is problematized. Instead project managers and promoters are getting used to the healthy fact that different stakeholders hold different forecasts and that forecasts are not only products of objective science and engineering but of negotiation. Why is this more healthy? Because it is more truthful about our ability to predict the future and about the risks involved.

Finally, democratic governance is generally getting stronger around the world. The Enron scandal and its successors have triggered new legislation and a war on corporate deception that is spilling over into government with the same objective: to curb financial waste and promote good governance. Although progress is slow, good governance is gaining a foothold even in major project management. The main drivers of reform come from outside the agencies and industries conventionally involved in major project management, which is good because it increases the likelihood of success.

For example, in 2003 the Treasury of the United Kingdom required, for the first time, that all ministries develop and implement procedures for major projects that will curb what the Treasury calls—with true British civility—"optimism bias." Funding will be unavailable for projects that do not take into account this bias, and methods have been developed for how to do this (HM Treasury 2003; Flyvbjerg and Cowi 2004; UK Department for Transport 2006). In the Netherlands in 2004, the Parliamentary Committee on Infrastructure Projects for the first time conducted extensive public hearings to identify measures that will limit the misinformation about large infrastructure projects given to the Parliament, public, and media (Tijdelijke Commissie Infrastructuurprojecten 2004). In Boston, the government has sued to recoup funds from contractor overcharges for the Big Dig related to cost overruns. More countries and cities are likely to follow the lead of the UK, the Netherlands, and Boston in coming years; Switzerland and Denmark are already doing so (Swiss Association of Road and Transportation Experts 2006; Danish Ministry for Transport and Energy 2006, 2008).

It's too early to tell whether the measures being implemented will ultimately be successful. It seems unlikely, however, that the forces that have triggered the measures will be reversed, and it is those forces that reform-minded groups need to support and work with in order to curb deception and waste. This is the "tension-point" where convention meets reform, power balances change, and new things are happening.

IMPLICATIONS FOR RESEARCH

If academic research is to contribute constructively and proactively to much-needed reform in major project management, we need to better understand:

- the trends that shape projects and project management, like those described above.
- strong theories of success and failure in major project management. Today too much theory in research on major project management is not intellectually robust having only weak links to leading research in economics, governance, planning, decision-making, environment, etc. Focusing on strong theory would help us bring the field forward academically. It would also allow us to develop better tools for preventing failure and replicating success.
- the importance of good data. Data on performance in major projects is generally of poor quality and is often idiosyncratic in the sense that it cannot be compared

systematically across projects and thus does not allow for statistical analyses and tests. This seriously sets back research, policy, and management. At present, the single most important thing we can do to heighten the academic level of research on major project management is to develop high-quality data that allows for systematic comparison across projects.

- the paradox that investing in and delivering major projects is a high-risk, stochastic activity, with high exposure to uncontrollable so-called "black swans"—much like investing in financial markets—but project managers and researchers widely ignore this state of affairs and thus underestimate the risks involved, still treating projects as if they exist largely in a deterministic Newtonian world of cause, effect, and control, despite all evidence to the contrary.

For someone embarking on a Ph.D. or similar research in major project management, taking these issues into account—and especially walking the extra mile for high-quality data and strong theory—would ensure a valuable contribution to the field and a comparative advantage over average research. This would benefit not only the researcher in question, but all of us, because it would raise the bar in a field that needs this to happen.

REFERENCES

ALTSHULER, A., and LUBEROFF, D. (2003). *Mega-Projects: The Changing Politics of Urban Public Investment.* Washington, DC: Brookings Institution.

AMERICAN PLANNING ASSOCIATION (2005). "JAPA Article Calls on Planners to Help End Inaccuracies in Public Project Revenue Forecasting," http://www.planning.org/newsreleases/2005/ftp040705.htm, April 7.

ANGUERA, R. (2006). "The Channel Tunnel: an ex post economic evaluation," *Transportation Research Part A*, 40: 291–315.

ASCHER, W. (1979). *Forecasting: An Appraisal for Policy-Makers and Planners.* Baltimore: The Johns Hopkins University Press.

BOK, S. (1979). *Lying: Moral Choice in Public and Private Life.* New York: Vintage.

BUEHLER, R., GRIFFIN, D., and MACDONALD, H. (1997). "The role of motivated reasoning in optimistic time predictions," *Personality and Social Psychology Bulletin*, 23/3: 238–47.

—— and ROSS, M. (1994). "Exploring the 'planning fallacy': why people underestimate their task completion times," *Journal of Personality and Social Psychology*, 67: 366–81.

CLAPHAM, S. E., and SCHWENK, C. R. (1991). "Self-serving attributions, managerial cognition, and company performance," *Strategic Management Journal*, 12/3: 219–29.

CLIFFE, L., RAMSEY, M., and BARTLETT, D. (2000). *The Politics of Lying: Implications for Democracy.* London: Macmillan.

DANISH MINISTRY FOR TRANSPORT (2006). *Aktstykke om nye budgetteringsprincipper* (Act on New Principles for Budgeting). Aktstykke no. 16, Finansudvalget, Folketinget, Copenhagen, October 24.

——(2008). "Ny anlægsbudgettering på Transportministeriets område, herunder om økonomistyringsmodel og risikohåndtering for anlægsprojekter", Copenhagen, November 18.

DUNE, T., ROBERTS, M. J., and SAMUELSON, L. (1988). "Patterns of firm entry and exit in U.S. manufacturing industries," *Rand Journal of Economics*, 19/4: 495–515.

FLYVBJERG, B. (1996). "The dark side of planning: rationality and *Realrationalität*," in S. Mandelbaum, L. Mazza, and R. Burchell (eds.), *Explorations in Planning Theory*. New Brunswick, NJ: Center for Urban Policy Research Press, 383–9.

——(1998). *Rationality and Power: Democracy in Practice*. Chicago: University of Chicago Press.

——(2005). "Design by deception: the politics of megaproject approval," *Harvard Design Magazine*, 22/Spring–Summer: 50–9.

——(2006). "From Nobel Prize to project management: getting risks right," *Project Management Journal*, 37/3: 5–15.

——BRUZELIUS, N., and ROTHENGATTER, W. (2003). *Megaprojects and Risk: An Anatomy of Ambition*. Cambridge: Cambridge University Press.

——and COWI (2004). *Procedures for Dealing with Optimism Bias in Transport Planning: Guidance Document*. London: UK Department for Transport.

——GARBUIO, M., and LOVALLO, D. (2009). "Delusion and deception in large infrastructure projects: two models for explaining and preventing executive disaster," *California Management Review*, 51/2: 170–93.

——HOLM, M. S., and BUHL, S. L. (2002). "Underestimating costs in public works projects: error or lie?" *Journal of the American Planning Association*, 68/3: 279–95.

————(2004). "What causes cost overrun in transport infrastructure projects?" *Transport Reviews*, 24/1: 3–18.

————(2005). "How (in)accurate are demand forecasts in public works projects? The case of transportation," *Journal of the American Planning Association*, 71/2: 131–46.

FORD, J. D. (1985). "The effects of causal attribution on decision makers' responses to performance downturns," *Academy of Management Review*, 10/4: 770–86.

GARETT, M., and WACHS, M. (1996). *Transportation Planning on Trial: The Clean Air Act and Travel Forecasting*. Thousand Oaks, CA: Sage.

GILOVICH, T., GRIFFIN, D., and KAHNEMAN, D. (eds.) (2002). *Heuristics and Biases: The Psychology of Intuitive Judgment*. Cambridge: Cambridge University Press.

GORDON, P., and WILSON, R. (1984). "The determinants of light-rail transit demand: an international cross-sectional comparison," *Transportation Research A*, 18A/2: 135–40.

HALL, P. (1980). *Great Planning Disasters*. Harmondsworth: Penguin.

HM TREASURY (2003). *The Green Book: Appraisal and Evaluation in Central Government, Treasury Guidance*. London: TSO.

HODGE, G. A., and GREVE, C. (2009). "PPPs: the passage of time permits a sober reflection," *Economic Affairs*, March: 33–9.

KAHNEMAN, D. (1994). "New challenges to the rationality assumption," *Journal of Institutional and Theoretical Economics*, 150: 18–36.

——and LOVALLO, D. (1993). "Timid choices and bold forecasts: a cognitive perspective on risk taking," *Management Science*, 39: 17–31.

————(2003). "Response to Bent Flyvbjerg," *Harvard Business Review*, December: 122.

——and TVERSKY, A. (1979a). "Prospect theory: an analysis of decisions under risk," *Econometrica*, 47: 313–27.

———— (1979b). "Intuitive prediction: biases and corrective procedures," in S. Makridakis and S. C. Wheelwright (eds.), *Studies in the Management Sciences: Forecasting*, vol. xii. Amsterdam: North Holland.

LOVALLO, D., and KAHNEMAN, D. (2003). "Delusions of success: how optimism undermines executives' decisions," *Harvard Business Review*, July: 56–63.

MALMENDIER, U., and TATE, G. A. (2003). "Who makes acquisitions? CEO overconfidence and market's reaction," Stanford Research Paper No. 1798.

MERROW, E. M., PHILLIPS, P. E., and MEYERS, C. W. (1981). *Understanding Cost Growth and Performance Shortfalls in Pioneer Process Plants*. Santa Monica, CA: Rand Corporation.

MILLER, R., and LESSARD, D. R. (2000). *The Strategic Management of Large Engineering Projects: Shaping Institutions, Risks, and Governance*. Cambridge, MA: MIT Press.

MORRIS, P. W. G., and HOUGH, G. H. (1987). *The Anatomy of Major Projects: A Study of the Reality of Project Management*. New York: John Wiley and Sons.

———— and PINTO, J. K. (eds.) (2004). *The Wiley Guide to Managing Projects*. Hoboken, NJ: Wiley.

MOTT MACDONALD (2002). *Review of Large Public Procurement in the UK*, study for HM Treasury. London: HM Treasury.

NATIONAL AUDIT OFFICE (2003). *PFI: Construction Performance*, report by the Comptroller and Auditor General, HC 371 Session 2002–3: February 5. London: National Audit Office.

———— (2005). *PFI: Construction Performance*, report by the Controller and Auditor General. London: HMSO.

NEWBY-CLARK, I. R., McGREGOR, I., and ZANNA, M. P. (2002). "Thinking and caring about cognitive inconsistency: when and for whom does attitudinal ambivalence feel uncomfortable?" *Journal of Personality and Social Psychology*, 82: 157–66.

OWENS, S. (1995). "From 'predict and provide' to 'predict and prevent'? Pricing and planning in transport policy," *Transport Policy*, 2/1: 43–9.

PITSIS, T. S., CLEGG, S. R., MAROSSZEKY, M., and RURA-POLLEY, T. (2003). "Constructing the Olympic dream: a future perfect strategy of project management," *Organization Science*, 14/5: 574–90.

PRIEMUS, H., FLYVBJERG, B., and VAN WEE, B. (eds.) (2008). *Decision-Making on Mega-Projects: Cost–Benefit Analysis, Planning, and Innovation*. Cheltenham: Edward Elgar.

PROJECT MANAGEMENT INSTITUTE (2006). *Code of Ethics and Professional Conduct*, http://www.pmi.org/PDF/ap_pmicodeofethics.pdf. Accessed January 22, 2009.

STAW, B. M., and ROSS, J. (1978). "Commitment to a policy decision: a multi-theoretical perspective," *Administrative Science Quarterly*, 23/1: 40–64.

SWISS ASSOCIATION OF ROAD AND TRANSPORTATION EXPERTS (2006). *Kosten-Nutzen-Analysen im Strassenverkehr*, Grundnorm 641820, valid from August 1. Zurich: Author.

TALEB, N. N. (2007). *The Black Swan: The Impact of the Highly Improbable*. London: Penguin.

TIJDELIJKE COMMISSIE INFRASTRUCTUURPROJECTEN (2004). *Grote Projecten Uitvergroot: Een Infrastructuur voor Besluitvorming*. The Hague: Tweede Kamer der Staten-Generaal.

TVERSKY, A., and KAHNEMAN, D. (1974). "Judgment under uncertainty: heuristics and biases," *Science*, 185: 1124–31.

UK DEPARTMENT FOR TRANSPORT (2006). *Changes to the Policy on Funding Major Projects*. London: Department for Transport.

WACHS, M. (1986). "Technique vs. advocacy in forecasting: a study of rail rapid transit," *Urban Resources*, 4/1: 23–30.

—— (1989). "When planners lie with numbers," *Journal of the American Planning Association*, 55/4: 476–9.

—— (1990). "Ethics and advocacy in forecasting for public policy" *Business and Professional Ethics Journal*, 9/1–2: 141–57.

WHITE HOUSE (2009). "Remarks by the President and the Vice President at opening of fiscal responsibility summit, 2-23-09," Office of the Press Secretary, February 23. http://www.whitehouse.gov/the_press_office/Remarks-by-the-President-and-the-Vice-President-at-Opening-of-Fiscal-Responsibility-Summit-2-23-09/.

WORLD BANK (1994). *World Development Report 1994: Infrastructure for Development.* Oxford: Oxford University Press.

CHAPTER 14

MANAGING RISK AND UNCERTAINTY ON PROJECTS

A COGNITIVE APPROACH

GRAHAM M. WINCH

EUNICE MAYTORENA

INTRODUCTION

The purpose of this chapter is to reconnect project risk management with its roots in psychology and economics and thereby generate a *cognitive approach* to project risk management. While there has been widespread application of the tools and techniques of project risk management, and good practice has been captured in a large number of different standards and texts, few signs of improvement are apparent in project performance. We suggest that the inappropriate use of project risk management techniques may be part of the problem rather than part of the solution here, and that we need to rethink project risk management from first principles. Starting from a presumption that project risk management is the essence of project management more generally, we will offer in this chapter a review of some of the key contributions from psychology and economics that have shaped our thinking before presenting our cognitive model of project risk managing. This model has evolved from the findings of our research into project risk identification (Maytorena et al. 2007; Winch and Maytorena 2009), and presents our first reflections on the managerial implications of that research. Space constraints have meant that we have been obliged to omit the full range of reference upon which we draw, but additional references can be found in Winch (2010).

To give the reader a sense of the direction in which we are going, we begin by defining what we mean by a cognitive approach and then provide a brief review of the state-of-the-art in project risk management so as to establish some solid ground. Next we revisit two fundamental concepts in project risk management: its conceptual basis in expected utility (EU) theory, focusing on the centrality of the rigorous elicitation of subjective probabilities for that theory; and the distinction between risk and uncertainty. We will then go on to review recent research in behavioral psychology which, we suggest, vitiates any hope that the elicitation of subjective probabilities can be a rigorous process. Influenced by research in managerial and organizational cognition (MOC) we then present our cognitive model of risk and uncertainty in projects; this attempts to combine the strengths of existing approaches to project risk management with a more subtle understanding of the behavioral and cognitive dimensions of the problem. Conclusions follow.

A COGNITIVE APPROACH DEFINED

We use the term "cognitive" to distinguish it from the rationalist and behavioralist perspectives normally used to study decision-making. Our approach is influenced by research in the area of managerial and organizational cognition (see Eden and Spender 1998). The field of MOC has taken cognitive theories, models, and relevant studies from the area of psychology and applied them to the context of management and organizational research with the aim of understanding how managers make sense of their world, how they model their reality, and how this influences behavior, with a view to improving organizational performance. Research in this area has looked at concepts such as attention, memory, mental representation, information-processing, perceptual processes, and social construction, among others.

MOC has been applied most prominently in the area of decision-making in organizations (Hodgkinson and Healey 2008). Two views of organizations are particularly influential in how decision-making has been studied in MOC research: organizations as "information-processing systems"; and organizations as "interpretation systems" (Neale et al. 2006). The former builds on Simon's (1947) bounded rationality concept, March and Simon's (1958) work theorizing organizations as information-processing systems, and Cyert and March's (1963) work on how decisions are made in organizations, as well as others in the Carnegie School tradition (Lant and Shapira 2001). From this perspective MOC acknowledges that decision-makers are limited by their information-processing capacity, information availability, accuracy, and uncertainty. The latter perspective builds on work by Weick (1979) and the concepts of "enactment" and "sense-making," where the importance of meaning continually being shaped by the social context is emphasized. From this perspective, MOC is interested in managers' mental processes of knowledge acquisition and the understanding that is gained through their daily work experience, thoughts, and sensing of their organizational context.

THE STATE OF THE ART IN PROJECT
RISK MANAGEMENT

There is now a well-developed body of literature on project risk management, which supports a number of different standards ranging across sectors and countries—see Raz and Hillson (2005) for a review. While there are differences in detail between these standards, and important debates within the literature such as on how to characterize the upside of risks, there is a high level of agreement in the state-of-the-art around three important elements. First, the risk management process is best characterized by a cyclical procedure as presented in Figure 14.1. Some procedures have different names for the phases, and others have more phases, but all share the basic principle. Second, a knowledge management tool—the risk register as shown in Figure 14.1—lies at the heart of the process which is used to assign responsibility and accountability for risks, monitor their status, and prioritize action. Third, powerful toolsets have been developed to support the cyclical process at various points, particularly in the analysis phase, and their use is often mandatory (e.g. HAZOPS) in particular situations.

Recent developments in project risk management have built on this generic approach along the following lines:

- Growing concern for the governance of projects stimulated by reforms in accounting practice has led to proposals for the formalization of accountability for the risk management process as a whole to ensure that its disciplines are being followed (OGC 2007).
- Greater emphasis is being paid to the strategic front end of projects—known as front-end loading in oil and gas—on the basis that greater investment in the clear definition of the project mission and scope will reduce risk and reap benefits in project performance (Miller and Lessard 2000).

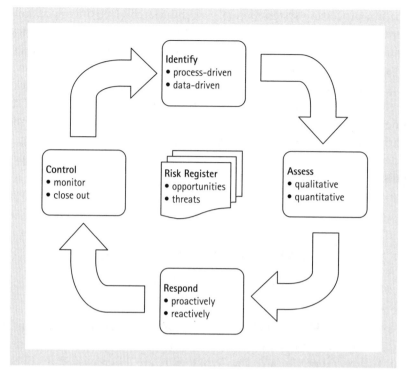

Fig. 14.1 The risk management cycle

Source: Winch (2010: fig. 13.4).

- Explicit consideration is being given to generating alternatives and giving them long enough to demonstrate their benefits or otherwise cast as either *selectionism* (Loch, DeMeyer, and Pich 2006) or formalized as real options (Gil 2009). These kinds of approach are particularly fruitful in generating opportunities by not closing down options too early.
- Systems dynamics approaches are improving our understanding of ways in which identified threats can interact to magnify each other through reinforcing loops leading to projects reaching tipping points beyond which they cannot be saved without significant external managerial intervention (Williams 2002; Lyneis and Ford 2007).

These more recent developments attest to a mature culture of research and practice in project risk management, but, we would suggest, it remains focused on tools, techniques, and processes and tends to ignore some of the important issues underlying the human dimension (Hillson and Murray-Webster 2005) of managing risk and uncertainty. The point we wish to make is well summarized in the *BP Risk Management Guidelines for Major Projects* (2005: 7)

The effective management of risk is critical to the continual improvement in project performance in individual projects and BP's overall Project Portfolio. The major challenge to a successful implementation lies primarily in the behaviors of leadership and teams rather than in processes and tools. However, a common process is important in creating alignment and rigour.

In the discussion that follows, we want to explore how the cognitive approach supports this concern for a focus on behavior and how the conceptual frame underlying the current state of the art draws attention away from an understanding of behavior due to its theoretical support for tools and techniques. At the heart of the current state-of-the-art is the expected utility (EU) paradigm. Although a rejection of EU theory as the basis for decision-making is at the heart of the Carnegie School contribution—see especially Simon (1955) and Shapira and Berndt (1997) for an application to project risk management—it remains pervasive in the fields of decision sciences and neoclassical economics which continue to shape risk management in general and project risk management in particular (Akerlof and Shiller 2009; Skidelsky 2009).

Revisiting the EU paradigm

We make no apology for reviewing the underlying economics of our topic for, as Keynes concluded the General Theory, "the ideas of economists and political philosophers, both when they are right and when they are wrong, are more powerful than is commonly understood" (1961: 383). Those who wish to understand the contributions from political philosophy—particularly from David Hume—are recommended to read Taleb (2007). The expected utility (EU) paradigm lies at the heart of much contemporary economics and decision sciences. The expected utility models in wide use today are largely derived from the work of von Neumann and Morgenstern (1944) on economic behavior complemented by the work of Savage (1954) on personal probabilities, although there are many variations on these basic models (Schoemaker 1982). The fundamental tenet of EU theory is that the rational decision-maker can clearly distinguish between two (or more) alternative courses of action by combining arithmetically the probability of an event associated with that course of action and the magnitude of the outcome (either loss or gain) resulting from that event. These outcomes can then be rank ordered so as to identify the most favorable course of action from the alternatives presented. This simple, but powerful, decision-making schema has the status of a paradigm—it is pervasive in research and advocacy of best practice on decision-making. The computer has only reinforced this trend, and it is manifested directly in project risk management in the probability/impact matrix. For its authority, it requires at least two conditions:

- Decision-makers need to be able to make the appropriate calculations, or at least to be prepared to trust the outcomes of computer-based calculations of the analysis and then to rank order transitively the options on the basis of explicit criteria.
- The distributions around the probabilities of the occurrence of a risk event, and the size of the impact should that event occur, need to be measurable.

The inability of decision-makers to make accurate inferences from probabilistic data and to rank order consistently their preferences has now been explored in countless studies—Schoemaker (1982) provides an early review, while the texts edited by researchers working in the field of "heuristics and biases" (Kahneman, Slovic, and Tversky 1982; Gilovich, Griffin, and Kahneman 2002) provide an excellent introduction to the field. However, while such research undermines the claims of the EU paradigm to accurately describe the decision-making process it does not, in itself, challenge its credibility as a normative approach (Schoemaker 1982) to how decisions ought to be made. Indeed one could argue that the whole point of the normative approach is to apply the EU paradigm properly and thereby save decision-makers from the error of their ways. However, the second criterion is more difficult to meet because it concerns epistemological issues, rather than purely analytic ones. The ability to assign a probability distribution to the outcomes and impacts is fundamental—indeed it is so fundamental that it is not always made explicit how idiosyncratic a set of decision situations the theory is based upon, and the risk of what Taleb (2007) calls the "ludic fallacy" is high. The original interest in probability and outcomes was stimulated by gamblers as an early form of action research, and the field has remained dominated by a focus on gambles such as the toss of a coin or dealing a pack of cards in order to explore its main themes (e.g. Halpern 2003). This focus has stimulated a rich line of inquiry and theoretical development, but there are a number of limitations to gambles (Huber 2007) as the basis for developing a broader perspective on project risk management. These include the following assumptions.

- The probabilistic basis of gambles is derived from repeated plays. In other words, it is from prior repeated tosses of the coin that we know that the pattern of occurrence of heads and tails is 50:50, and can, therefore, state confidently that the probability of a head on the next toss of the coin is 50 percent.
- The future is like the past. We presume that past patterns of occurrence will be repeated into the future—if they are not (e.g. a biased coin is secretly substituted for the tested one) then this is generally considered to be cheating and outside the probability calculus.
- The outcome of the event predicted probabilistically is clearly knowable. In other words, the coin lands either heads or tails, and there is not any room for argument about the outcome.

- The impact of the event is measurable and can therefore be reduced to a quantitative metric. In gambling this is a function of the wager, or the amount at stake on the toss of the coin.
- The decision-making is time-free. In other words, the lag between assessing a probability of an event, and the occurrence of that event, is trivial.

These are, of course, very demanding criteria, and decision sciences and neoclassical economics would not have developed very far if they had to be strictly adhered to. However, the reach of decision sciences has been increased greatly by the development of the concept of subjective, or personal, probability—we treat these as synonymous here.

SUBJECTIVE PROBABILITIES
AND THEIR ELICITATION

The concept of personal probability starts with a conundrum—is the 50 percent probability of a fair coin landing heads a property of the coin or the decision-maker? Clearly the coin is not making any decisions, but the (absolute) confidence of the decision-maker that there is a 50 percent chance of heads is apparently derived from empirical observations of actual events. Yet, the decision-maker is making a decision about something that does not yet exist—the orientation of the coin after the next toss—so it must be a property of the ability of individuals to mentally construct future states. Savage's (1954) contribution was to argue persuasively that these subtleties do not really matter to decision-making. He distinguishes the objectivistic view of probability associated with the British–American School of statistical science that frequencies of event are independently observable, with the subjective view, which is concerned with the extent to which a decision-maker has confidence in a particular outcome. He also identifies a third, necessary point of view where probabilities are the outcome of logical rather than empirical analysis, but does not pursue it further.

There is a crucial point to be made here. Savage argues that, from the point of view of decision-making rather than statistical inference, there is little significant difference between the objective and subjective views because the probability assessment in both cases is a property of the person and not the object—the consequences of any decision "might appropriately be called states of the person, as opposed to states of the world" (1954: 12). This insight, when married to EU theory, allows the development of a theory of decision-making based on subjective probabilities, and is fundamental to neoclassical economics. The personal perceptions of the probabilities and the utilities associated with each future state presented for a decision held by the decision-maker can, therefore, be rank ordered to form the basis of intendedly rational decision-making in the context of a normative theory.

Many texts on project risk management (e.g. Hillson 2003; Vick 2002) open by comparing "aleatory" with "epistemic" risk associated with games such as dice on the one hand and with the degrees of belief the decision-maker has in the probability of an outcome on the other. The power of Savage's insight is that there is little cognitive difference between these two types of risk—both are equally beliefs about the future. In other words even aleatory risk requires a subjective judgment that the future will be like the past. Savage provides a theoretical exploration of how decision-makers might be induced to reveal their preferences for option A over option B in terms of their expected utility by "behavioral interrogation" (1971: 783). His fundamental assumption is that given appropriate incentives to be both honest and dispassionate in specifying a personal probability then usable data will result. However, this approach presupposes that the principal problem with eliciting personal probabilities is that experts and other decision-makers know what the objective probabilities of an event are, but are poorly motivated to communicate them to others who could use the information. There is no consideration within this perspective of whether the probabilities elicited from the decision-maker bear any relation to the underlying patterns of events in the real world. The combination of subjective probabilities with expert judgment has developed into sophisticated methodologies for obtaining the data required for quantitative risk analysis along the lines proposed by Savage. A review by Spetzler and Staël von Holstein (1975) identified a number of tools for eliciting such probabilities as the "probability wheel," while Keeney and Winterfeldt (1991) advocate a fractile approach in which the expert is asked for the fractiles of the probability distribution. While there are pragmatic issues to be resolved around methods for eliciting subjective probabilities we wish to suggest here that Savage's optimism about the viability of the rigorous application of proper scoring rules is undermined by the large body of evidence from nearly four decades of research in what has become known as the "heuristics and biases" tradition.

RESEARCH IN THE HEURISTICS
AND BIASES TRADITION

The heuristics and biases approach (Gilovich, Griffin, and Kahneman 2002; Kahneman, Slovic, and Tversky 1982) takes a decision situation where the objective probability of an event is known to the experimenters and asks participants to identify the correct inference from the data. In experiment after experiment, participants make serious errors in inference. The research has identified four fundamental biases that undermine our ability to make correct inferences from data and scenarios:

- *Representativeness* captures our tendency to ignore the underlying base rate from which our sample of observations is drawn. A small sample will show more volatility than a large one according to statistical theory, yet decision-makers tend to ignore such issues.
- *Availability* captures our tendency to base our perceptions of probability upon the most recent or high-profile events in our experience, rather than the whole distribution.
- *Anchoring* is the condition where our first estimate anchors our subsequent attempts to vary our estimate in the light of new information. This phenomenon is particularly challenging for the elicitation of subjective probabilities because many such routines rely on adjustments from first approximations, and the results are highly sensitive to the routine selected.
- *Framing* effect considers that information is not perceived in isolation: we tend to interpret information based on the way it is presented and the context in which it is presented.

Although Spetzler and Staël von Holstein argue that they are taking into account the research in this tradition that was available during the 1970s we suggest that as this stream of research has matured, the claim that probability wheels and similar techniques can adequately debias experts is in serious question. Reviews of research on "debiasing" indicate that this is no trivial problem (Fischoff 1982, 2002). Multiple experiments on attempts to reduce bias in the elicitation of subjective probabilities have shown how intractable the problems are, and there is certainly no foolproof method of eliminating systematic biases in the probabilities elicited. Moreover, experts are found to be as prone to bias as the laity. Once the problem moves beyond low-impact/high-probability events the practical difficulties of debiasing start to mount, and there is a growing danger that "a debiasing procedure may be more trouble than it is worth if it increases people's faith in their judgmental abilities more than it improves the abilities themselves" (Fischoff 1982: 431).

The partial exception to this statement is the use of "calibration" or the confrontation of the decision-maker with the actual outcomes of the events predicted (Lichtenstein, Fischhoff, and Phillips 1982). This is, of course, only available with a large number of repeated elicitations of the probabilities of events with the outcomes of those events. Thus we know that the coin is true because our subjective probability of a heads of 0.5 is confirmed by repeated tosses of that same coin; if heads over a large number of tosses only turns up 0.3 times, we can recalibrate for further tosses of the coin. However, such calibration is typically unavailable for low-probability events because a very large number of outcomes would have to be plotted to allow calibration; even if the low-probability event occurs, this does not, of itself, change the prior probabilities because the occurrence could be due to chance. If the average project lasts for five years, a project manager can only work full-time on eight projects in a forty-year career, which is clearly not enough to generate any experience-based insight into the factors that actually affect project performance at a level that would satisfy the requirements of the elicitation of subjective probabilities.

A further strand of work that has developed in this tradition is on *optimism bias*, defined as unrealistic expectations about the future (Weinstein 1980). The experimental work most immediately related to project risk management focuses on the "planning fallacy" or the chronic inability to estimate task duration times (Buehler, Griffin, and Ross 2002). The researchers conclude from their experiments that the planning fallacy is a robust and pervasive phenomenon which is difficult to overcome. The later research has shown that when groups plan tasks together, the group dynamic tends to increase optimism and thereby worsen the effects of the planning fallacy. Optimism bias is becoming a widely recognized phenomenon (Flyvbjerg 2006; Kahneman and Lovallo 1993). The concept has also been picked up by HM Treasury, which now requires all budget estimates in investment appraisal to be corrected for optimism bias by prescribed factors (HM Treasury 2003, 2004). However, it can be suggested that such attempts are futile as they are likely to stimulate correcting behavior due to the risk thermostat effect (Adams 1995).

Another important aspect to consider is the concept of *illusion of control*, where a decision-maker believes, despite a lack of evidence, that an outcome can be fully controlled; this influences the perception of the probability of success (Langer 1982). In essence research has shown that an individual's intention to achieve an outcome and the motive to have personal control lead to more illusory judgments of control (Thompson 1999). In relation to risk, the awareness of the illusion of control has been noted by several authors (March and Shapira 1987; Shapira 1995; Kahneman and Lovallo 1993), but has received limited research attention. Most recently, in a study of investment traders Fenton-O'Creevy, Nicholson, and Soane (2003) showed that traders with a strong tendency to have an illusion of control performed poorly and go on to suggest that illusion of control could lead to poor risk management.

The heuristics and biases line of inquiry has developed into Behavioral Decision Theory (BDT) (Hodgkinson and Healey 2008). Bazerman (2008) is a standard text which represents this kind of approach. However, we believe that it is important to distinguish between BDT's behavioral approach, and MOC's cognitive approach which is more in line with the organizational decision-making tradition of the Carnegie School (see March and Shapira 1982 for a review). BDT's emphasis upon laboratory studies deploying an objectivist perspective on probability has tended to focus on the outcomes of individual judgment and decision-making behavior and comparing them to models of normative decision theory. MOC looks at individual processes such as information search, judgment, evaluation (see Ranyard, Crozier, and Svenson 1997)—and takes into consideration the organizational context its ambiguities, conflicts, and uncertainties. In other words, it views decision-making as a continual process, which is reflected upon, learned, and socially constructed. It is from this latter perspective that we develop our understanding of project risk and uncertainty management.

REVISITING THE CONCEPTS OF RISK AND UNCERTAINTY

Here we revisit an earlier tradition in decision-making developed during the 1920s, which was overshadowed by the EU revolution after 1945. In some ways, Savage was responding to the critiques made of the objectivist schools by writers such as Keynes (1973) and Knight (2002) who was active at Chicago around the same time as Savage. Keynes argues that a probability is a rationally held belief that a proposition is either certain, impossible, or somewhere in between those two points, where probability is the degree of rational belief in the proposition held by the decision-maker.

Keynes goes on to argue that just because a probability lies somewhere between certainty and impossibility (i.e. between 1 and 0 in terms of truth or falsity), this does not mean that it is measurable; indeed, he argues that most probabilities are not measurable, but that the concept of probability should not be restricted to only measurable propositions in the objectivist manner. Moreover, even if a rank order can be obtained, this does not mean that different propositions can be compared because their logical bases might be different: "by saying that not all probabilities are measurable, I mean that it is not possible to say of every pair of conclusions, about which we have some knowledge, that the degree of our rational belief in one bears any numerical relation to our degree of rational belief in the other" (1973: 37). Keynes goes on to distinguish the probability of a proposition being true from the *weight* of evidence to support that belief: "the weight...metaphorically measures the *sum* of the favourable and unfavourable evidence, the probability measures the *difference*" (1973: 84). Thus two comparable propositions may have equivalent net differences for and against, and hence probabilities, but one probability may be based on a much greater weight of evidence than the other. Keynes's work on probability has not generally found favor with later authorities, but, we contend, it is a fundamental contribution. Knight (2002) is perhaps best known for his distinction between uncertainty and risk, and his views are widely influential in management if not in economics and decision sciences. Knight's concern was not with probabilities and decision-making as such, but with entrepreneurship and economic growth. He develops his analysis of the role of uncertainty in decision-making, arguing that "we live only by knowing something about the future; while the problems of life, or of conduct at least, arise from the fact that we know so little" (2002: 199). Thus uncertainty is the condition of a lack of information about the future and "we do not react to past stimulus, but to the image of a future state of affairs" (2002: 201). He argues that the problem with standard accounts of probability is that they adopt Laplace's principle of indifference, which confuses the issues. He goes on to distinguish between a priori probability derived from logical relations; *statistical probability* derived from empirical observation; and *estimates* in which there is "no valid basis of any kind for classifying instances" (2002: 225). Knight goes on to insist that there is a fundamental difference between the first two types of probability and the third on account of the judgmental basis of the latter and proposes that to preserve the distinction between "the measurable uncertainty and an unmeasurable one we may use the term 'risk' to designate the former and the term 'uncertainty' for the latter," and that the tendency to use the term risk for a possible loss and uncertainty for a gain "must be gotten rid of" (2002: 233). In sum, Knight is arguing that risk is the realm of logical or quantitative analysis in decision-making, while uncertainty is the realm of judgment and intuition in entrepreneurship. There is much in common in the arguments of Keynes and Knight (Runde 1998) in their articulation of the crucial issues around measurability in probability analysis. Although Keynes did not use the word "uncertainty" in the *Treatise*, and the word "risk" only loosely and infrequently, he later adopted the term in a manner very similar to Knight as the condition where "there is no scientific basis on which to form any calculable probability whatsoever" (1937: 214). For both of these economists, the measurability—either a priori or a posteriori of the occurrence of events—is critical to their distinction between risk, where valid measurement is possible, and uncertainty where it is not. This distinction between risk and uncertainty was carried into management theory more generally through, for instance, the seminal contributions of March and Simon (1958) and Galbraith (1977). Neither Keynes nor Knight rejects the notion of subjective probabilities (LeRoy and Singell 1987), but they are clearly distinguished from the neoclassical and decision sciences traditions by their insistence that objective and subjective probabilities represent very different states of knowledge, and cannot be conflated into an expected utility calculus.

Understanding risk and uncertainty:
a cognitive approach

This all raises a rather obvious question: If we are suggesting that Savage's fundamental insight about the nature of risks should be retained, but the attempts to elicit rigorously subjective probabilities for future events are deeply flawed, where does this leave the management of risk and uncertainty on projects? We will now attempt to answer this question.

In recent years a number of writers have attempted to build on the Knight/Keynes distinction between risk and uncertainty, although these tend to be descriptive and without a clear analytical base. They also tend to be unclear whether they are taking a subjectivist or objectivist position—that is whether they see risk and uncertainty as a state of mind or a state of nature. The categorizations tend to be fourfold and have many similarities (Courtney, Kirkland, and Viguerie 1997; De Meyer, Loch, and Pich 2002; Snowden and Boone 2007; Stephens 2003). We propose here to adopt the one presented by Stephens because it has the merit of including a concept that the others do not—the deliberate hiding of information regarding threats and opportunities.

- *Risk* is the condition where inferences from historical data using analytic techniques can provide a sound basis for decision-making because it is believed with confidence that the future will be like the past and the probability of a threat or opportunity event occurring and its associated impact can be calculated from existing data. This is close to the objectivist position defended by Head (1967) against the decision scientists, but brings from Savage the notion that the relevance of the available dataset for the current decision situation remains a subjective judgment.
- The condition of *known unknowns* where possible threats and opportunities can be identified, but their impact is unclear and no reliable data is available regarding the probability of their incidence. This category encompasses the vast number of identified opportunities and threats in project risk management. Quantification of threats and opportunities is often useful, particularly if there are large numbers which need to be aggregated in some summary form for reporting purposes, or contingencies need to be assigned; the fundamental point here is that these remain judgments of those doing the analysis and have no objective status.
- The condition of *unknown unknowns* where threats and opportunities have not been identified and the cognitive state is therefore ignorance. An important issue here is whether with hindsight it can be plausibly claimed that the decision-maker *ought* to have known after the event—the condition of "predictable surprises" (Bazerman and Watkins 2004). Taleb's (2007) "black swan" concept captures high-impact unknown unknowns—i.e. unk unks with attitude.
- The condition of *unknown knowns* where threats and opportunities have been identified by others, but that information is not disclosed to the decision-maker for one reason or another. Theoretically, the category is related to Williamson's (1979) information impactedness under opportunism; practically, the Kariba Dam case (Winch 2010) shows how damaging this can be for a project.

These categorizations are defined in our framework as states of mind in line with Savage's subjectivist position—they capture beliefs about possible future states, not future states of nature themselves which are inherently unknowable. Thus we can think of any threat or opportunity as being somewhere in a continuum of certainty to impossibility (Keynes 1973)—even unknown unknowns must be possible. The more information we have about a threat or opportunity, the closer to the condition of a known known it can be placed forming an *information space* as shown in Figure 14.2—we take the term from Boisot (1995). Keynes and others (e.g. Tversky and Fox 1995) also identify the *weight* that can be given by the decision-maker to that information. However, we prefer the term *confidence*, because this formulation keeps clear the insight that confidence is a state of mind, not a state of nature. Within the area of known knowns, confidence can be used in the statistical sense (for certainty p=1; for impossibility p=0), while in the rest of the information space it is much more a matter of judgment where a threat or opportunity is placed on the certainty/impossibility continuum. Information and confidence can also be the basis for judging that few unknown knowns and unknown unknowns are possible. Confidence is distinguished from information because the information available may be available but ambiguous and therefore threats and opportunities may not be clearly identifiable. It also needs repeating here—for this is the basis of the claim that this is a cognitive model—that the information space is perceived from the point of view of the decision-maker, i.e. the project manager.

Our focus here has been strongly influenced by the Carnegie School in starting with the cognitive underpinnings of behavior in organizations. The perspective that we have developed here has taken a distinctive stance in relation to the existing literature of project risk management, which tends to be confused on a number of these issues (Perminova, Gustafsson, and Wikstrom 2008):

- We have taken a subjectivist position holding that future threats and opportunities are states of mind rather than states of nature;
- We have taken a cognitive position rather than a behavioral one, holding that the objectivism of the heuristics and biases school does not adequately address the information-processing requirements of decision-making under uncertainty;
- We have rejected the pseudo-objectivism of the decision sciences and neoclassical economics that believes that rigorously elicited subjective probabilities have the same cognitive status as objective probabilities;
- We have supported the existing process models in project risk management, but have raised important questions about the value of the analytic tools used to support those processes;
- Perhaps most importantly, we have reconnected research and practice in project risk management with theory and research in psychology and economics.

There is much research that is relevant to project risk management that we have not been able to address here due to constraints of space. For example, aspects of emotion (Slovic et al. 2004), communication (Morgan et al. 2002), and individual

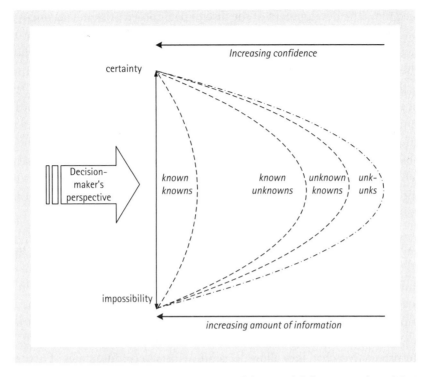

Fig. 14.2 The information space: a cognitive model for managing risk and uncertainty on projects

Source: Winch (2010: fig. 13.2).

and group differences in risk perceptions have important implications for project risk management. Breakwell (2007) provides a review of empirical research carried out on the psychology of risk highlighting the major issues associated with these topics. There is also a large body of work that can be classified as *constructivist* that has important insights for our problem—Winch and Maytorena (2009) provide a discussion. A significant body of sociological research—Lupton (1999) provides a review—also needs to be brought to bear on the issues discussed here.

CONCLUSIONS

Keynes (1961) argued that the future returns on investments in capital assets are virtually unknowable, and that it is "animal spirits" which stimulate such investments, not "cold calculation." In this stress on the entrepreneurial aspects of projects he was a lot closer to Knight than the generation of neoclassical economists who followed him. The development of the discipline of project risk management using the concepts of those later economists associated with EU theory has had the unfortunate effect of obscuring this inherent unknowability of the future and tended to give the impression that risks identified and analyzed are somehow states of nature rather than states of mind. There are, however, "no facts about the future!" David T. Hulett cited Goodpasture 2004: 27); all we can have are rationally held (Keynes 1973) perceptions of that future. In this review chapter we have attempted to develop a cognitive model of managing risk and uncertainty that takes seriously the large body of research on the behavioral aspects of risk and supports making good sense (Winch and Maytorena 2009) about the future.

Rationally held perceptions only generate a project if they are shaped into a coherent story about the future—a future perfect state (Clegg et al. 2006)—which allows the decision-makers not only to have confidence in those perceptions, but also to have faith that those perceptions synergize to a coherent whole. It is for this reason that Tim Smit, champion of the highly successful Eden Project, talks about the Tinker Bell theory of projects—projects only exist if you believe enough in them (Winch 2010). Projects are inherently uncertain adventures, and while the disciplines of project risk management can ensure that our perceptions of that uncertainty make good sense we would contend that those disciplines become counterproductive when they allow decision-makers to confuse states of nature and states of mind. Projects are fundamentally about states of mind; it is only once they are completed that they become states of nature.

Acknowledgements

The research upon which this chapter draws was financed by the EPSRC awards EP/D505461/1 and GR/R/51452/01. We are very grateful to the editors and also Dave Hillson and Steve Jewell of BP for their thoughtful comments on various drafts. A final forum to shape the argument was offered by a seminar at the School of Economics and Management, Tongji University, Shanghai.

References

ADAMS, J. (1995). *Risk*. London: UCL Press.

AKERLOF, G. A., and SHILLER, R. J. (2009). *Animal Spirits: How Human Psychology Drives the Economy, and Why it Matters for Global Capitalism*. Princeton: Princeton University Press.

BAZERMAN, M. (2008). *Judgment in Managerial Decision Making*, 7th edn. New York: John Wiley & Sons.

—— and WATKINS, M. D. (2004). *Predictable Surprises: The Disasters you Should Have Seen Coming and How to Prevent them.* Cambridge, MA: Harvard Business School Press.

BOISOT, M. (1995). *Information Space: A Framework for Learning in Organizations, Institutions and Culture.* London: Routledge.

BREAKWELL, G. M. (2007). *The Psychology of Risk.* New York: Cambridge University Press.

BUEHLER, R., GRIFFIN, D., and ROSS, M. (2002). "Inside the planning fallacy: the causes and consequences of optimistic time predictions," in T. Gilovich, D. Griffin, and D. Kahneman (eds.), *Heuristics and Biases: The Psychology of Intuitive Judgment.* Cambridge: Cambridge University Press.

CLEGG, S. R., PITSIS, T. S., MAROSSZEKY, M., and RURA-POLLEY, T. (2006). "Making the future perfect: constructing the Olympic dream," in D. Hodgson and S. Cicmil (eds.), *Making Projects Critical.* Basingstoke: Palgrave Macmillan.

COOPER, D., GREY, S., RAYMOND, G., and WALKER, P. (2005). *Managing Risk in Large Projects and Complex Procurements.* Chichester: Wiley.

COURTNEY, H., KIRKLAND, J., and VIGUERIE, P. (1997). "Strategy under uncertainty," *Harvard Business Review*, November–December: 67–79.

CYERT, R. M., and MARCH, J. G. (1963). *A Behavioral Theory of the Firm.* Englewood Cliffs, NJ: Prentice Hall.

DE MEYER, A., LOCH, C. H., and PICH, M. T. (2002). "Managing project uncertainty: from variation to chaos," *MIT Sloan Management Review*: 59–67.

EDEN, C., and SPENDER, J. C. (1998). *Managerial and Organizational Cognition: Theory, Methods and Research.* Thousand Oaks, CA: Sage.

EINHORN, H. J., and HOGARTH, R. M. (1981). "Behavioural decision theory processes of judgement and choice," *Annual Review of Psychology*, 32: 53–88.

FENTON-O'CREEVY, M., NICHOLSON, N., and SOANE, E. (2003). "Trading on illusions: unrealistic perceptions of control and trading performance," *Journal of Occupational and Organizational Psychology*, 76: 53–68.

FISCHOFF, B. (1982). "Debiasing," in D. Kahneman, P. Slovic, and A. Tversky (eds.), *Judgment under Uncertainty: Heuristics and Biases.* Cambridge: Cambridge University Press.

——(2002). "Heuristics and biases in application," in T. Gilovich, D. Griffin, and D. Kahneman (eds.), *Heuristics and Biases: The Psychology of Intuitive Judgment.* Cambridge: Cambridge University Press.

FLYVBJERG, B. (2006). "From Nobel Prize to project management: getting risks right," *Project Management Journal*, 37/3: 5–15.

GALBRAITH, J. R. (1977). *Organization Design.* Reading, MA: Addison-Wesley.

GIL, N. (2009). "Project safeguards: operationalizing option like strategic thinking in infrastructure development," *IEEE Transactions on Engineering Management* (in press).

GILOVICH, T., GRIFFIN, D., and KAHNEMAN, D. (eds.) (2002). *Heuristics and Biases: The Psychology of Intuitive Judgment.* Cambridge: Cambridge University Press.

GOODPASTURE, J. C. (2004). *Quantitative Methods in Project Management.* Boca Raton, FL: J. Ross Publishing.

HALPERN, J. Y. (2003). *Reasoning about Uncertainty.* Cambridge, MA: MIT Press.

HEAD, G. L. (1967). "An alternative to defining risk as uncertainty," *Journal of Risk and Insurance*, 2/34: 205–14.

HM Treasury (2003). *The Green Book: Appraisal and Evaluation in Central Government*. London: HM Treasury.

——(2004). *Supplementary Green Book Guidance: Optimism Bias*. London: HM Treasury.

Hillson, D. (2003). *Effective Opportunity Management for Projects: Exploiting Positive Risk*. New York: Marcel-Dekker.

——and Murray-Webster, R. (2005). *Understanding and Managing Risk Attitude*. Aldershot: Gower.

Hodgkinson, G. P., and Healey, M. P. (2008). "Cognition in organizations," *Annual Review of Psychology*, 59: 387–417.

Huber, O. (2007). "Behavior in risky decisions: focusing on risk defusing," in M. Abdellaoui, R. D. Luce, M. J. Machina, and B. Munier (eds.), *Uncertainty and Risk: Mental, Formal, Experimental Representations*. Berlin: Springer.

Kahneman, D., and Lovallo, D. (1993). "Timid choices and bold forecasts: a cognitive perspective on risk taking," *Management Science*, 39/1: 17–32.

——Slovic, P., and Tversky, A. (eds.) (1982). *Judgement under Uncertainty: Heuristics and Biases*. Cambridge: Cambridge University Press.

Keeney, R. L., and Winterfeldt, D. (1991). "Eliciting probabilities from experts in complex technical problems," *IEEE Transactions on Engineering Management*, 38/3: 191–201.

Keynes, J. M. (1937). "The general theory of employment," *Quarterly Journal of Economics*: 209–23.

——(1961). *The General Theory of Employment, Interest and Money*. London: Macmillan.

——(1973). *A Treatise on Probability: The Collected Writings of John Maynard Keynes*, viii. London: Macmillan.

Knight, F. H. (2002). *Risk, Uncertainty and Profit*. Washington, DC: Beard Books.

Langer, E. J. (1982). "The illusion of control," in D. Kahneman, P. Slovic, and A. Tversky (eds.), *Judgment under Uncertainty: Heuristics and Biases*. New York: Cambridge University Press.

Lant, T. K., and Shapira, Z. (2001). *Organizational Cognition: Computation and Interpretation*. Mahwah, NJ: Lawrence Erlbaum Associates.

LeRoy, S. F., and Singell, L. D. (1987). "Knight on risk and uncertainty," *Journal of Political Economy*, 95: 394–406.

Lichtenstein, S., Fischhoff, B., and Phillips, L. D. (1982). "Calibration of probabilities: the state of the art to 1980," in D. Kahneman, P. Slovic, and A. Tversky (eds.), *Judgment under Uncertainty: Heuristics and Biases*. New York: Cambridge University Press.

Loch, C. H., DeMeyer, A., and Pich, M. T. (2006). *Managing the Unknown: A New Approach to Managing High Uncertainty and Risk in Projects*. New York: John Wiley & Sons.

Lovallo, D., and Kahneman, D. (2003). "Delusions of success: how optimism undermines executives' decisions," *Harvard Business Review*, 81: 60–71.

Lupton, D. (1999). *Risk*. London: Routledge.

Lyneis, J. M., and Ford, D. N. (2007). "System dynamics applied to project management: a survey, assessment, and directions for future research," *System Dynamics Review*, 23: 157–89.

March, J. G., and Shapira, Z. (1987). "Managerial perspectives on risk and risk taking," *Management Science*, 33/11: 1404–19.

——and Simon, H. (1958). *Organizations*. New York: Wiley.

Maytorena, E., Winch, G. M., Freeman, J., and Kiely, T. (2007). "The influence of experience and information search styles on project risk identification performance," *IEEE Transactions on Engineering Management*, 54/2: 315–26.

MILLER, R., and LESSARD, D. R. (2000). *The Strategic Management of Large Engineering Projects*. Boston: MIT Press.

MORGAN, M. G., FISCHHOFF, B., BOSTROM, A., and ATMNAN, C. J. (2002). *Risk Communication: A Mental Model Approach*. Cambridge: Cambridge University Press.

NEALE, M. A., TENBRUNDEL, A. E., GALVIN, T., and BAZERMAN, M. H. (2006). "A decision perspective on organizations: social cognition, behavioural decision theory and the psychological links to micro and macro organizational behaviour," in S. Clegg, C. Hardy, T. B. Lawrence, and R. W. Nord (eds.), *The Sage Handbook of Organization Studies*. London: Sage.

OFFICE OF GOVERNMENT COMMERCE (OGC) (2007). *Management of Risk: Guidance for Practitioners*, 2nd edn. London: The Stationery Office.

PERMINOVA, O., GUSTAFSSON, M., and WIKSTROM, K. (2008). "Defining uncertainty in projects: a new perspective," *International Journal of Project Management*, 26/1: 73–9.

RANYARD, R., CROZIER, W. R., and SVENSON, O. (1997). *Decision Making: Cognitive Models and Explanations*. London: Routledge.

RAZ, T., and HILLSON, D. (2005). "A comparative review of risk management standards," *Risk Management*, 7/4: 53–66.

RUNDE, J. (1998). "Clarifying Frank Knight's discussion of the meaning of risk and uncertainty," *Cambridge Journal of Economics*, 22/5: 539–46.

SAVAGE, L. J. (1954). *Foundations of Statistics*. New York: John Wiley and Sons.

——(1971). "Elicitation of personal probabilities and expectations," *Journal of the American Statistical Association*, 66: 783–801.

SCHOEMAKER, J. (1982). "The expected utility model: its variants, purposes, evidence and limitations," *Journal of Economic Literature*, 20: 529–63.

SHAPIRA, Z. (1995). *Risk Taking: A Managerial Perspective*. New York: Russell Sage.

——and BERNDT, D. (1997). "Managing grand scale construction projects: a risk taking perspective," *Research in Organizational Behavior*, 19: 303–60.

SIMON, H. (1947). *Administrative Behavior*. New York: Macmillan.

——(1955). "A behavioral model of rational choice," *Quarterly Journal of Economics*, 69: 99–117.

SKIDELSKY, R. (2009). *Keynes: The Return of the Master*. London: Allen Lane.

SLOVIC, P., FINUCANE, M. L., PETERS, E., and MACGREGOR, D. G. (2004). "Risk as analysis and risk as feelings: some thoughts about affect, reason, risk and rationality," *Risk Analysis*, 24/2: 311–22.

SNOWDEN, D. J., and BOONE, M. (2007). "A leader's framework for decision making," *Harvard Business Review*, 69–76.

SPETZLER, C. S., and STAEL VON HOLSTEIN, C.-A. (1975). "Probability encoding in decision analysis," *Management Science*, 22/3: 340–58.

STEPHENS, P. (2003). "The unwitting wisdom of Rumsfeld's unknowns," *Financial Times*, March 12.

TALEB, N. N. (2007). *The Black Swan: The Impact of the Highly Improbable*. London: Penguin Books.

THOMPSON, S. C. (1999). "Illusion of control: how we overestimate our personal influence," *Current Directions in Psychological Science*, 8: 187–90.

TVERSKY, A., and FOX, C. R. (1995). "Weighing risk and uncertainty," *Psychological Review*, 102: 269–83.

VICK, S. G. (2002). *Degrees of Belief: Subjective Probability and Engineering Judgment*. Reston, VA: ASCE Press.

von Neumann, J., and Morgenstern, O. (1944). *Theory of Games and Economic Behavior.* Princeton, NJ: Princeton University Press.

Weick, K. L. (1979). *The Social Psychology of Organizing,* 2nd edn. Reading, MA: Addison-Wesley.

Weinstein, N. D. (1980). "Unrealistic optimism about future life events," *Journal of Personality and Social Psychology,* 39: 806–20.

Williams, T. (2002). *Modelling Complex Projects.* Chichester: Wiley.

Williamson, O. E. (1979). "Transaction cost economics: the governance of contractual relations," *Journal of Law and Economics,* 22: 223–61.

Winch, G. M. (2010). *Managing Construction Projects: An Information Processing Approach,* 2nd edn. Oxford: Wiley-Blackwell.

——and Maytorena, E. (2009). "Making good sense: assessing the quality of risky decision making," *Organization Studies,* 30/2–3: 181–203.

CHAPTER 15

INFORMATION MANAGEMENT AND THE MANAGEMENT OF PROJECTS

JENNIFER WHYTE

RAYMOND LEVITT

INTRODUCTION

Information management has played a central, but under-recognized, role in the history of project management. Since the mid twentieth century the need to manage and share large amounts of unique technical and management information across fragmented supply chains has spurred the development of information technology for use on projects. For example, new equipment was developed for the 1950s US military project SAGE (Semi-Automated Ground Environment), which aimed to automate detection, tracking, and interception of aircraft. This included: "a high-speed electronic digital processing machine" (Redmond and Smith 2000) at each radar site and a central computer to process data from these sites. The histories of information management, digital technologies, and project management have been intertwined ever since.

In this chapter we argue that emerging digital technologies are enabling new forms of project management in project-based industries. The 1960s project management approach originated in the mature project-based industries of petrochemicals, military, advanced manufacturing, pharmaceuticals, buildings, and infrastructure. This approach, which we term "Project Management 1.0" (PM 1.0), evolved to manage small numbers of large, complex projects in business and regulatory environments that were relatively stable by today's standards. It involves detailed up-front planning, using multiple layers of hierarchical work breakdown structures. It then manages these projects by tracking and eliminating variance from plans. The approach is alive and well in some of those same industries, and has been greatly enhanced by widespread use of digital technologies for planning, visualization, communication, procurement, logistics, and other functions. However, there are important ways in which the use of information technology begins to challenge this traditional project management approach.

In many of today's most dynamic industries—consumer electronics, telecommunications, biotechnology, software development, medical devices—companies and governments are launching large numbers of smaller projects in technological, business, and regulatory environments that are even more dynamic and less predictable than those faced by construction, petrochemicals, pharmaceuticals, and military contracting. For these industries, any detailed plan, no matter how well thought out, becomes obsolete within weeks or months. Sticking to the original plan produces technological marvels that are business white elephants, like Motorola's ill-fated Iridium project. In these industries, a new more agile approach to managing projects, which Levitt et al. (2008) call "Project Management 2.0" (PM 2.0), is rapidly gaining traction. This radically decentralized and reactive approach to project management breaks the mold of the 1960s approaches to project planning and suggests alternative approaches to project delivery in more dynamic and turbulent environments. It shifts the focus away from tracking and eliminating variances from fixed and long-lived "baseline" project plans, to monitoring, integrating, and analyzing information on real-time and predicted performance, and replanning continuously bottom up, rather than top down, as the project and its environment change. It is an "Agile" approach to project management (Schwaber 2004) that has been most widely deployed to date for software development, and that exploits information technology in completely new ways.

We see new approaches having an impact on the management of projects across these dynamic new industries, and also in contexts where the scale, complexity, and multi-vocal nature of projects challenges traditional approaches to information management and the management of projects. In the following section we clarify definitions and approaches, before considering the changing practices of information management on projects in the third section. We then discuss recent and ongoing research on knowledge practices, organization design, and strategy in the fourth section, considering how it may provide starting points for better practical understanding. The conclusions in the fifth section summarize our arguments and set out issues and directions for future research.

DEFINITIONS AND APPROACHES

Information management activities, applications, and systems

The term "information management" is used in this chapter to refer to the activities involved in shaping the flow, not of physical materials, but of data, information, and knowledge. On modern projects, much of this flow is digitally enabled and supported. Today, major projects involve complex and interrelated sets of information management activities and their associated applications and systems including:

- *Storage and retrieval systems are used to archive data.* A major project may involve a centralized data repository to archive hundreds of thousands of documents or large product models that record who took each design decision; specify the product or service to be delivered; track work in progress; and support approvals and quality assurance processes. These databases have different permission settings for project teams, management, and others within the project and for external parties such as clients and regulators. Their set-up and maintenance is a significant organizational task, and there is substantial interest in and emphasis on standards, classifications, and protocols for data storage and transfer.

- *Digital models and prototypes are developed by engineers and are used throughout the project.* There is an ongoing effort to develop structured processes and protocols for the shared use of digital models and prototypes across project stakeholders; and throughout the life cycle of a project. The use of these models is changing work on projects by making available and integrating different types of information, such as that from Geographic Information Systems (GIS) and Computer Aided Design (CAD), from the early stages of projects; and with the increasing use of intelligent 3D and 4D (three spatial dimensions plus time) models. Though the benefits of an integrated dataset are widely championed and claimed, such shared development, checking, and use of information is not straightforwardly achieved on projects.

- *Automated search facilities.* These allow textual and geometric datasets to be analyzed, connections to be made across datasets, and exceptions to be located. Such techniques are widespread in many contexts, e.g. police cases, tumor and airline baggage screening, 3D interference checking between structural and mechanical systems (e.g. between beams or columns and air conditioning ducts in buildings and industrial plants). However in some project-based industries there are debates about the value of some automated search processes that are particularly costly and time consuming. Examples here include high-throughput screening in pharmaceuticals and 4D reservoir scanning in oil and gas.

- *Simulation programs.* Simulations are often run to understand the performance of models. Algorithms may be used to combine data from multiple sources, for example by choosing a best fit from millions of pre-computed simulations using real-time data about current operations. There is an increasing integration of models and simulations.

- *Communications technologies.* In addition to shared access to centralized data sources, communication happens through text, voice, and video communications technologies using networked, mobile, and visual devices that connect project managers and engineers. Advances in this area are allowing a radical redistribution of work across offices and continents.

Information management and project stakeholders

The use of digital technologies overlays and transforms physical information management practices. They are not used only in management planning but have become pervasive in the interactions between stakeholders at all stages on projects, with an increasing emphasis on a life-cycle approach to data management. On many projects a model forms the core of a wider set of information sources for each of the stakeholders, where:

- *Clients* are manipulating information through technical and financial simulations, using the internet, email, automated search, and knowledge management systems in developing the business case. As the project is implemented they are interacting with the design through visualizations of plant or building models and simulations of production, access, egress, etc.
- *Engineers and technical managers* use a variety of scanning and monitoring technologies along with digital models for the early stages of planning, estimating, and enhanced stakeholder communication. Through later stages, their work involves using a wide range of performance data; standards; schedules; computer-aided design; organization and work process simulations; interference checking; lessons learnt databases; project databases; extranets; email; mobile technologies; and online communities of practice for knowledge-sharing within firms and across project supply chains.
- *Suppliers* draw on data provided by the engineering designers and rely on information management technologies such as automated material quotes; engineer-to-order designs; quotes for custom systems or equipment; digital purchasing; and logistics tracking.
- *Facility managers* are using digital as-built facility models; distributed control systems for heating ventilation and air conditioning (HVAC) systems or factories, facilities management databases that support warranty management, calculation of allowable depreciation for different sub-systems, etc.; archives of design drawings.
- *Regulators* are using information management technologies, such as Wikis for environmental impact assessments and public input. Singapore has pioneered the automated code-checking of total building information models.

Taken together these technologies provide a digital infrastructure for the delivery of projects. They have major consequences for the flow of data, information, and knowledge and hence the organization of work on projects. Researchers have claimed that they are changing the fabric of organization (Zammuto et al. 2007) and "intensifying" innovation processes (Dodgson, Gann, and Salter 2002, 2005). As they add information, digital infrastructures add to the complexity and inter-connectedness of organizational and economic units making them more difficult to analyze and understand.

For example, the availability of digitally mediated information changes the con-texts within which projects operate and the kinds of situations managers face. Activist groups are organizing using technologies such as the internet, email, blogs, social networking sites, and mobile communications, especially text messaging. An example of this is the one-woman campaign to save feral cats from the London 2012 Olympic site that generated substantial media interest and 12,000 online signatures and thus regained access to the construction site. Altogether 187 were taken away and re-homed by the associated charity. This power of the media makes the project delivery process multi-vocal, with the delivery team using internal and external communications as part of the process of project delivery. While these activist activ-ities have usually been seen as outside of project management or as something that project managers need to control, there is also an opportunity to see how such activities could inform better decision-making across projects.

Our focus on information management practices

Managers on projects spend significant energy defining processes. However, to understand the impact of these new forms of information management in projects, our approach in this chapter is to focus on their *practices*. There are two main reasons for this focus. First, from the existing literatures on project management, we know more about the promise of digital technologies in projects than about their practical application and use. Technology, in its broader sense—the fascination with and uncertainty of technology and the challenges of design management—is a common factor in project failure (Morris and Hough 1987). By considering the project as "an organizational entity that has to be managed successfully" (Morris, this volume, Chapter 1), we consider how information management is actually achieved on projects and we draw on a wider literature from strategic management of informa-tion systems and organization science to understand these observed practices.

Second, a focus on practice draws attention to the challenges practitioners face, but also underlines the magnitude of the ongoing changes in information manage-ment on projects and draws attention to how processes are developed around new information management technologies. In our own work, we have observed how digitally enabled information practices are changing project delivery within firms—for example observing how R&D teams seek to develop and use new visual optimization software in the large corporations that operate oil and gas assets; and how the introduction of new tools for coordination has changed practices across firms involved in major construction and civil engineering projects, such as London's Heathrow Terminal 5, 2012 Olympics, and London Underground. In the next section we look at the changes in practices across the last fifty years.

CHANGING PRACTICES OF INFORMATION MANAGEMENT

Waves of technology use: automation and information management

Different waves of technology use have automated, and then added information to, management processes (Zuboff 1988). The images of project contexts in Figure 15.1 illustrate sweeping changes in the nature of the technologies in leading use, where the processing power of computational devices; and the dominance of graphic interfaces to data in the workspace have increased substantially. Such changes have had a significant and broad impact, though at any given time there is a wide diversity in the digital methods used for information management across the range of projects in different industries and locations.

Major projects in the military, oil and gas, and automotive industries have invested heavily in using and developing digital methods for collating, managing, and displaying information over the last fifty years (NRC 1999). The computer hardware and software industries are themselves by-products of research on new digital techniques for information management, the development of which was motivated by efforts to manage large, complex projects. IBM's involvement in the early SAGE project, mentioned in the introduction to this chapter, enabled it to take a dominant role in the new computer industry (Redmond and Smith 2000). The ongoing research and development (R & D) project "Project Whirlwind" at MIT contributed to this SAGE project (Redmond and Smith 2000). IBM's involvement in developing the AN/FSQ-7 computer for use in the SAGE project enabled it to take a dominant position in the new industry, as Redmond and Smith (2000) also note.

Table 15.1 gives an overview of hardware and software technologies in use on large civilian projects and the associated new capabilities over the past six decades. (Military projects did play a major role in technology development, but because of the tight secrecy surrounding some of this work, technologies were often re-invented or took decades to diffuse into wider project practices.) During this period the cost of processing power has fallen dramatically: information

(a)

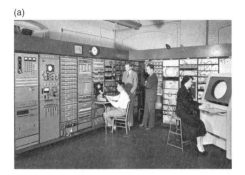

(b)

1950s Whirlwind console room, which was used in project SAGE

2000s NASA's "'Team X'" digital mission design environment adapted to "'Integrated Concurrent Engineering'" (ICE) of construction projects at CIFE

Fig. 15.1 Images of project work using digital technologies

Note: The first image is courtesy of the Mitre Corporation. The second is Courtesy of Arto Kivinierni and the Centre for Integrated Facility Engineering (CIFE). In relation to the second, see Chachere, Kunz, and Levitt (2004) for a description of both the NASA and Center for Integrated Facility Engineering (CIFE) implementations of digitally enabled Integrated Concurrent Engineering (ICE).

technologies that required investment in significant R&D projects as recently as thirty years ago are now widely available commercially at prices that put them within the reach of individuals as well as their firms. (This dramatic reduction in the cost of information processing and storage capability changes the organizational level at which purchases must be approved. Feeny and Willcocks (1998) price the processing power that cost $10,000,000 in 1975 (and was hence an institutional purchase) at under $1,000,000 in 1985 (a departmental purchase); at under $100,000 in 1995 (a grant purchase) and as under $10,000 in 2005 (a personal purchase).) On more recent projects, the access to computing has become more personal, with individuals using multiple devices. Different waves of technology have and do influence approaches to information management on projects; however the difficulty for managers is how and when to step on a wave particularly in large complex projects that have a long gestation period. Below we describe information management practices from the 1960s onwards that focus on tracking and eliminating variance from plans, and then discuss today's changing focus of project management, both in large complex projects and in projects within dynamic environments.

Application of computers to baseline planning

The computer industry that supported the management of projects in the 1950s and 1960s was rudimentary compared with current capabilities. In the early 1960s a group of civil engineering researchers began developing a computer-automated

Table 15.1 Time-line of technologies and techniques in use on major projects

	1950s	1960s	1970s	1980s	1990s	2000s
Hardware	Mainframe batch computing e.g. Whirlwind	High-end real-time e.g. DAC–1; PERT	Bitmapped screens; computer graphics	First personal computers	Laptops, internet, and first mobile computing	Mobile computing, sensors, electronic paper
Software	Automated engineering analysis tools e.g. STRUDL	Database Management Systems; e.g. ICES, IDMS	Standards, protocols and processes, e.g. IDEF0; CMM	PC-based CAD and project management; simulation; internet	Automated digital search; expert systems; project extranets	Visual decision-making tools; shared workspaces
New Capabilities	Automate analysis	Automate scheduling, accounting; share data	Text processing; widespread engineering automation; sharing of information	Diffusion of computers to smaller firms and individuals; knowledge formalization	Share information and knowledge across teams and firms	Agile, decentralized development methods using centralized data storage and applications

structural analysis package for IBM mainframes called the *Structural Design Language (STRUDL)* (Logcher and Sturman 1966). This evolved over the next decade into a series of automated analysis packages for everything from surveying to groundwater flow modeling to critical path scheduling in the Integrated Civil Engineering System (ICES) (Roos 1965; Fenves 1967). By 1964, General Motors had developed "DAC-1," a system for automotive design that was based on an IBM computer. Lockheed Georgia started development of a similar system for airplane design (Anon. 1986). In each of these cases the system was largely bespoke and custom designed. It was a stand-alone system with no clear division between hardware, operating systems, and software; a team of operators and significant bespoke development.

Project managers rapidly recognized the potential for computers to analyze multiple options to predict and compare their outcomes and pick the best option. When IBM brought out its 360 series of mainframe computers in 1965, it made commercially available a generic computer and graphics terminal. It was on such computers that the early project management and scheduling techniques, such as CPM and PERT, were developed. These approaches to project management planning, which we term PM 1.0, have dominated since then, with increasing sophistication around tracking and eliminating variance from fixed baseline plans.

Through the 1970s and 1980s, the further commoditization of software and development of standards and protocols revealed new challenges for project management and also developed new techniques, including standards such as SADT/IDEFO; and processes and management tools such as the capability maturity model (CMM).

The trajectory of this 1960s approach to information management on projects was further developed with advances in hardware and software. A significant change was heralded by a desktop package for project management, "Microsoft Project," which was launched on the Windows operating system in 1990, following others that evolved in the late 1980s. This commoditized a range of techniques for project management such as Gantt charts and critical path method analyses that had been developed over the previous three decades and moved them into the hands of millions of mainstream users. It enabled individuals or teams to develop plans, allocate resources, track progress, and manage budgets and workloads relatively easily using modern project management techniques.

Changing focus of information management in large projects

The question "Yes, but how will we ever keep track of such a large project?" motivated Berners-Lee as he hypothesized about non-hierarchical linked information systems as a way of managing information at CERN (Berners-Lee 1989). This work provided the basis for the internet and has led to a new trajectory with a fundamentally different approach to information management on projects from the 1990s onwards. It is the interconnectivity of such new linked information systems that enables them to support bottom-up as well as top-down decision-making.

Over time, as projects have been able to collate and use larger datasets, they have encountered a number of practical challenges. These include:

1. Developing standardized protocols and procedures for archiving and sharing data. Kang and Paulson (1998) return to this perennial theme in their discussion of classification systems for consistent information management on projects. The development of such standards remains a significant focus of attention in industry.
2. Work-flows, checks, and releases of information, so that data is owned by individual workers, others feel a responsibility to check this data and have the competence to ensure its validity, and that it is released to the appropriate people at the appropriate time;
3. Permissions and data security, where there is a need to get more sophisticated at not only sharing data, but also maintaining confidential information and systems within projects and project networks; and
4. Managing intellectual property; information asymmetries, and the power within a project and in the wider institutionalized environment that impacts on the project work where data may be hosted by one of the parties involved.
5. Archiving and reuse of data through the life cycle of an asset which may require the maintenance of datasets for many decades, often longer than the life of the hardware and software systems and the data representation standards with which they were developed.

Significant work has been done to address these challenges by developing processes within the PM 1.0 mold. The work on standards, procedures, and process protocols (Cooper et al. 2005) fits in this mold of project management and will continue to play an important role on large projects. However there is a new interest in monitoring, integrating, and analyzing information on real-time performance. The rise in mega-projects is made possible by advanced data-processing technologies; however the extended timescales, multiple stakeholders, and uncertainty around these projects makes it important to continually make sense of data so as to have long-term plans. There are increasingly attempts to implement more lean and agile PM 2.0 approaches in these contexts overlaying formal hierarchical structures of project management with more rapid and informal interactions and exchanges of information.

In rapid environments, the developments in software projects mentioned in the introduction have led to a set of techniques described as agile (Schwaber and Beedle 2002; Schwaber 2004). Here ideas from lean production are implemented with a stronger focus on the dynamics of social interactions. The emphasis on using high technology has also brought a need for richer face-to-face interaction. In addition, the internet, mobile computing, and shared workspaces have enabled radical decentralization of decision-making to skilled workers who understand the high-level goals and trade-offs of the project in which they are working. This combination of shared vision, decentralized decision-making, and more specialist–specialist interaction have created a form of agile project management in which data and applications become more centralized as decision-making becomes more decentralized.

In Salesforce.com, a Californian firm that sells software as an online service, the large code body of their software as a service application was broken down into relatively independent modules, each of which was assigned to a scrum team for ongoing development. Instead of releasing major software upgrades to its "on demand" that is now used by millions of customers once every twelve to sixteen months, the scrum teams have released smaller upgrades right on schedule every four months since the process was introduced.

Each team includes coders, testers, user interaction designers, and—critically—a product management representative. This allows each team to decide exactly how much scope it will include in its next release. More frequent releases eliminate a great deal of the pressure on development teams from sales and marketing to complete all of the scope planned for a given release. Each team has daily fifteen-minute "stand-up" meetings in which team members discuss their progress, challenges, and blockages, and reallocate priorities and work assignments dynamically among team members. Team leaders are responsible for eliminating blockages and for coordinating interfaces with other modules in a weekly "scrum of scrum" meeting with leaders of other module teams.

So, instead of holding scope constant and letting cost and schedule slip, this approach holds release dates constant, and allows scope to be readjusted as needed and resources to be adjusted dynamically within each team. Within a four-month release cycle the team will integrate and test its code at the end of each of four one-month scrums. Thus there are no unpleasant surprises at the end with integration problems.

More generally, these lean and agile approaches have led to reconsideration of how information dependencies should be organized, leading to a range of pull-down scheduling (Tommelein 1998); and task-optimization techniques (Sacks, Esquenazi, and Goldin 2007). Techniques such as "last-planner" have shown an ability to reorganize and streamline workflows by improving reliability. Using the last-planner tools, teams come together to discuss workflow every week and to commit to delivery on items. Such intensive focus on efficiency has been questioned in more critical studies, for example in the work of Green and May (2005), where the focus on client value at the expense of employee working conditions is discussed. However, with the increasing availability of digital information, there are increasing demands to recombine this in various ways and to make it available for wider scrutiny, monitoring, and improving workflows.

Digital technologies, such as 4D scheduling software, have been developed in parallel but are strongly related to these wider aims to improve the industrial efficiency of industries such as construction (Koo and Fischer 2000; Hartman and Fischer 2007). 3D and 4D models create more intuitive and interlinked interfaces into the vast datasets that are created, shifting attention away from managing the flow of paper documents to integrated data management systems that include geometric and semantic data in the model. Although this may suggest a more chaotic form of information management—with the sharing of models during design and construction rather than the release of drawings for approval—their effective use requires substantial discipline. A key aspect of this is the project life-cycle management approach to information management, with requirements tracked through the whole process.

Understanding information
management practices

This overview of developments has so far described the limitations of the 1960s approach to project management through tracking and eliminating variance from fixed baseline plans because of its inability to deal with the information needs of very large complex projects and dynamic project contexts. We believe it is the responsibility of the researcher to reflect on and interrogate the nature and consequences of the changes in information management practices. To show how this might be done, we discuss three literatures that mobilize very different research perspectives and methods in such an investigation. These are the literatures around:

1. Knowledge practices—which looks at how knowledge work is done in organizational settings. With roots in sociology, this work is often based on ethnographic studies of ongoing practices designed to uncover the messy reality of knowledge work as it is experienced by the practitioners involved. It provides insights into the shared nature of knowledge work on projects, how it is situated involving people and the objects they interact with, and the way that it unfolds over time.
2. Organization design and information—drawing on work in administrative science, researchers have simulated decision-making processes to look at the instrumental role information plays in project work, with an interest in exception-handling and modes of coordination. They have also looked at the symbolic role that information plays in organizations, and the challenges faced in situations of uncertainty.
3. Strategy, contracts, and e-procurement—informed by economics, this work has highlighted the effect of digital technologies on the cost of obtaining information for different project activities. By focusing on transaction costs or the use of resources, this literature draws attention to strategic questions, such as the

governance of projects through markets and hierarchies and the interactions between projects, firms, and software suppliers.

These literatures emphasize different practical and theoretical questions about information and the management of projects. Explaining practice is a concern in all three literatures, but the interest in the actual practices on real-life projects is most salient from the first perspective, to which we now turn.

Knowledge practices in organizations

The management of knowledge, rather than information, has been the focus of much of the recent literature in the sociology of organizations. Styhre (2009: 27), for example, notes that managing knowledge is not solely about handling information but it is a matter of socialization, part of a situated knowledge practice. Hence this literature would put a strong emphasis on the socialization processes and shared knowledge work that is being developed in examples such as the Salesforce.com case.

A great deal has been written about the distinction between data, information, and knowledge. From a "knowledge management" perspective (e.g. Ackoff 1989), *data* describes a set of assertions of facts that are true in the world, e.g. a catalogue may describe the dimensions and other properties of a set of standardized structural steel members. Data in a specific context becomes *information*. The choice of a wide flange 30 cm beam to span between grid points A-13 and A-14 on the second floor of the Birj Dubai Tower is information that others in the project can use to guide their decisions; the engineer who selected this particular beam for use in the building location used *knowledge*—both explicit textbook knowledge, and more tacit experience-based knowledge—to make this choice. The traditional systems perspective on knowledge management then also sees understanding and wisdom and further advanced categories on a spectrum.

This newer literature on knowledge practices instead sees knowledge as both cognitive and perceptual, anchoring competence in experience (Styhre 2009: 107). The use of new forms of information management changes the way that professionals know things. Styhre writes about the gaze as an institutionalized mode of seeing in a particular social formation. Prasad (2005) points to forms of professional vision that are inextricably linked with new digital visualization technologies. Other authors point to the way knowledge becomes represented in practices (e.g. Taxén and Lilliesköld 2008; Whyte et al. 2008). The social act of remembering in organizations has been explored through work on project memory (e.g. Weiser and Morrison 1998; Cacciatori 2008), which discusses project information in five discrete classes: projects, users, events, meetings, and documents.

Despite the virtual nature of digital information, this perspective is committed to observing the material nature of practices. Knowledge work is coordinated and developed by people who interact with objects (Star 1989; Carlile 2002; Levina and Vaast 2005;

Ewenstein and Whyte 2009) as well as each other. When the objects used in knowledge work involve computers, screens, and virtual images, researchers have described them as "technologies of representation" (Boland, Lyytinen, and Yoo 2007) or "transformational technologies" (Leonardi and Bailey 2008) to indicate both their role in local knowledge work and their availability in the practices of remote project participants.

This literature highlights the multiple interpretations of new technology, for example describing a case where the adoption of intranet technology as a vehicle for encouraging organization-wide knowledge-sharing actually helped to reinforce the existing functional and national boundaries (Newell, Scarbrough, and Swan 2001). Much of this work is informed by sociology of technology, and particularly the actor-network approaches (Harty 2005). Hartmann and Levitt (2010) draw on actor-network approaches when they describe how information technologies are inherently malleable, and are thus adapted in practice by teams learning to use them. They show that IT champions must be realistic about potential savings and learning costs in promoting innovative technologies. Yet these multiple interpretations do not detract from the material nature of information management practices, of which we are reminded most starkly in recent work on climate change. Not only will projects need to collect and analyze more data about the resources they use, but they will also take into consideration the energy used in sustaining their digital infrastructure for knowledge practices (Berkhout and Hertin 2004; Haigh and Griffiths 2008).

A focus on knowledge practices also draws attention to the temporal nature of project work. The uptake and use of digital technologies disrupts existing practices, creating alternative dynamics. Theoretical interest in the dynamic nature of relationships between technologies and organizations (Orlikowski and Yates 2002) recognizes that sequencing and pacing of work practices has important consequences for efficiency and for the quality of outputs (Perlow 1999; Perlow, Okhuysen, and Repenning 2002). Such work identifies different waves of innovation brought about by technologies of representation (Boland, Lyytinen, and Yoo 2007) and draws attention to the vicious and virtuous circles associated with managing knowledge (Garud and Kumaraswamy 1995). Counter-intuitive findings show fast decision-makers using more not less information (Eisenhardt 1989). In a project-based context, fast decision-making in co-located, cross-disciplinary teams allows for radical transformations of conceptual design processes, with significant time savings and enhanced decision quality (Chachere, Kunz, and Levitt 2004).

Organization design and information

To consider how information management affects the design of project organizations, Levitt and his colleagues (Jin and Levitt 1996; Levitt et al. 1999) use Galbraith's information-processing view of the organization to analyze the quality of problem resolution, information, and exception-handling in non-routine project work. For

Galbraith (1973, 1974, 1977) organization designs are an attempt to predict and balance the number of information-handling exceptions that will be generated by a set of interdependent tasks that need to be performed with an organization's capacity to process them. Uncertainty requires a greater amount of information to be processed by decision-makers; and to be managed through slack resources, self-contained tasks, vertical integration, and the formalization of lateral relationships via matrix structures. Practical benefits of applying this approach are that it allows more conscious decisions to be made about the design of the organization taking into account the information-processing capabilities and exceptions.

In building on this approach, Levitt et al. (1999) seek to move away from simple tool-based solutions to project management by developing a simulation model for designing project organizations, seeing process quality as contingent on an organization's work process; hierarchy, personnel makeup, environment, and IT tools. Traditional project management tools model only direct work. The "Virtual Design Team" (VDT) approach and tools developed by Levitt and his colleagues (Levitt et al. 1999) also model exception-handling and coordination as "hidden work" that must be carried out by project teams to complete a project successfully. Including hidden work helps to highlight where concurrency, uncertainty, and complex technologies will overwhelm parts of the organization with supervision and coordination work. VDT models and simulates the baseline project work plan being executed by the organization to predict information bottlenecks, and their resulting delays, cost overruns, and impacts on quality. The graphical user interface then allows a user rapidly to simulate management interventions designed to mitigate these information bottlenecks by modifying key attributes of *team structure* (reporting relationships; centralization; formalization; and matrix strength), *work processes* (activity concurrency; flexibility; complexity; and uncertainty), and *actors* (skill-set; application experience; team experience; and goal incongruence). The commercial version of this software, called SimVision™, has been used in the petrochemical, semiconductor, aerospace, and consumer product industries to design project organizations since the late 1990s.

New forms of information management also imply a renegotiation of modes of coordination and control within projects. This returns attention to classic themes of organization science around the differentiation and integration of work (Thompson 1967). Organizations may simultaneously use a number of different modes of coordination (Van de Ven, Delbecq, and Koenig 1976; McBride 2008). Critical management researchers characterize projects as dominated by bureaucratic modes of control with instrumental and rationalist beliefs in comprehensive planning and tight management control (Hodgson 2004). The literature is not consistent, however: Stinchcombe (1959) described the predominance of "craft" rather than "bureaucratic" modes of administration in complex project-based industries like construction. More recently, Bechky (2006) described coordination being achieved through professional norms and social interactions, rather than through prescriptive routines, in projects in the film industry. The changing focus of information management that we observe on large projects and in dynamic environments suggests that as information technologies make the systematic storage of data easier there is also a renewed attention on the informal mechanisms.

It is clear that technologies change the locus and nature of decision-making. However we concur with Kärreman and Alvesson (2004) that there is not a simple transition from bureaucratic to cultural-ideological modes of control but rather an interweaving of different overlaid forms of coordination and control. Some of the work draws on Mintzberg's categories of coordination through direct supervision; mutual adjustment; work processes; skills and knowledge; outputs performance; and ideology norms. These have been applied to projects by van Donka and Molloy (2008) and the role of computer-integrated technologies in changing these has also been discussed (Smith et al. 1992).

The vast quantity of data that is now available has shifted the focus from the collection and storage of data to its interpretation in time-constrained operation. The comprehensive and automated search of aggregated data (for example in high through-put screening in pharmaceuticals or in 4D reservoir modeling in oil and gas) can provide optimal solutions in theory, but in practice it may hide ambiguities in the data that would act as triggers for human sense-making or it can take too long for it to be useful in decision-making. In leading teams, the focus of technology use has shifted away from this, towards visualizing and sharing data for enhancing project awareness to support real-time decisions by skilled professionals working in a decentralized and self-synchronizing "Power-to-the-Edge" manner (Alberts and Hayes 2003) within the dynamic decision-making environments of projects. Other theorists, such as Dossick and Neff (2008), are also drawing attention to the way managers and leaders have to bridge between tightly coupled technological solutions and loosely coupled organizational structures in contexts such as construction. This work highlights the new dilemma of local computation but shared information resources: integrated information management systems only become effective when new ways of working are developed that enable people to use them in their decentralized work.

Information technologies also enable new work arrangements across firms; and projects increasingly involve collaborations between networks of organizations, with simultaneous work across the boundaries of different offices and firms (Sinha and Van de Ven 2005). Taylor (2007) draws attention to the antecedents of 3D on construction projects, articulating how the work allocation, interdependence, and current technology provide preconditions; how the alignment of the innovation to project network and firm interests affects the ease of implementation; and how the relational stability, interests, boundary permeability, and presence of an agent for change affect acceptance of new technologies by firms and, hence, their rates of diffusion.

Institutionalized practices draw attention to and prioritize certain information, and are always concerned with legitimization as well as efficiency. Clarke (1999) notes how plans continue to be made by organizations even when the uncertainty is such that these documents are "fantasy documents" because many of the key assumptions written into the plans are so uncertain. This has an impact on information management as often the systems that are put in place serve a dual role of legitimizing action as well as managing the information required to conduct the action. Systems that look inefficient from an information management perspective may serve important legitimization functions.

Strategy, contracts, and e-procurement

March and Simon (1958) described organizations as cooperative systems that rely on high levels of information-processing in decision-making. The economics and strategy literatures suggest that improved tools for information management will also have macroeconomic consequences for how industries are organized. Drawing on transaction cost economics, electronic markets theory argues that if all other variables remain constant, the introduction of more powerful and effective IT will lead to more use of markets than hierarchies for economic transactions—i.e. technology will de-layer and supply chains will fragment, as they have recently done for products like personal computers and mobile telephones (Malone 1987).

The case of the B2 "Stealth" bomber project is used by Argyres (1999) to investigate how information technology is used to coordinate within and between firms on a project. He explains how the four firms worked almost entirely digitally, using a common-access database to manage information about part design; and simulations for structural analysis. Argyres uses transaction cost theory to argue that these systems made information-processing less costly and reduced the potential for contractual hold-ups hence making governance more efficient. He argues they allow for vertical disintegration and decentralized decision-making by reducing monitoring costs.

This trend has been further reinforced by the ability of the internet to impose reverse auctions on upstream suppliers in the supply chain. This has shifted considerable power to end-users and system integrators who are close to end-users since they can force everybody upstream of them to submit competitive bids for many aspects of the work. Organizations that acted as intermediaries in the past, like employment agencies that brokered skilled labor, travel agents that supplied travel services, regional distributors for doors, windows, plumbing fixtures, etc., are being rapidly disintermediated by the internet, together with standard XML protocols for specifying a growing variety of products and services unambiguously so they can be auctioned.

Although it had been predicted that the introduction of IT would increase the number of suppliers on projects, as it reduces transaction costs, this has not always happened in practice (Banker, Kalvenes, and Patterson 2006). One explanation is that although the cost of monitoring each term in a contract is reduced, buyers simply include more terms in the contract. An alternative explanation of the limits to outsourcing in project-based industries is provided by Taylor and Levitt (2007).

They argue that an unintended side-effect of IT-driven industry fragmentation is a lock-in of current product architectures, which then hinders efforts at systemic innovation for the entire industry.

Information asymmetries have always been of interest to strategy scholars. The use of an electronic marketplace for procurement makes it easier for purchasers to standardize procedures and to compare different suppliers (Sanders and Premus 2002). Firms have a motivation to maintain goodwill in the supplier community and employ a global competitive electronic marketplace for procurement (Standing, Stockdale, and Love 2007). In understanding the effects of information technology, Bharadwaj (2000) draws attention to a hybridization between arm's-length and embedded markets, where work is done to obtain the best global suppliers through an electronic marketplace, while also fostering local links through face-to-face contacts and intensive off-line interaction.

ISSUES AND DIRECTIONS FOR RESEARCH

What of the future of information management on projects? We think this is likely to extend both the highly routinized and structured digital datasets, which are heavily inter-linked, and alongside these extend the more seemingly chaotic and informal mechanisms that are used to gain the trust of other participants and manage errors in ongoing operations. We see technologies that overlay digital data in physical environments being used to prioritize and draw managers' attention to key information. At the same time we see the digitizing of parts of the physical environment through scanning and monitoring technologies has the potential to make 3D information available in the early stages of projects.

Hence, we see the main long-term research challenge as being around creating robust and responsive systems that enable real-time interaction and information management in dynamic and complex projects. The academic literatures on knowledge practices, organization design, strategy, contracts, and e-procurement provide starting points for research into this changing landscape of practices but are only a beginning. New approaches to information management imply different forms of governance, for example, both for the project and for the project-based firm. Building on our review of the literatures in this chapter, three areas stand out as particularly important.

The first is new conceptual tools for PM 2.0, such as new forms of visualization to filter information, to focus attention on relevant features of datasets and to bring relevant stakeholders into the decision-making process. Work in this area could build on the wider literature on knowledge practices. As the choice of communication media becomes greater, managers need to be able to work in the periods between the exchange of various asynchronous text (e.g. email); voice and video communications which vary in the richness of information they convey (Daft, Lengel, and Trevino 1987). New research is needed to understand how information management can support the management of projects in such data-rich environments.

The second is new strategies for using and developing appropriate software for information management on projects. The cross-industry nature of the software that is used in business processes poses particular dilemmas (Whyte 2010). There is a need for new work to understand lock-in to technological solutions and how their development affects ongoing work. Globalization of particular software solutions has been discussed (Pollock, Williams, and D'Adderio 2007). In this work scholars of management of projects could usefully draw on the traditions of research on organization design and strategy. There are questions about how generic tools get developed, and how these get used within the local practices of different sectors, projects, and cultures.

The third is "integrated project delivery." There is a small but growing body of research on integrated project delivery for large, technically complex construction projects such as airports or hospitals. Under this form of contracting, the client, engineer, and main contractor sign a three-party agreement—sometimes also including key specialty contractors—in which all will have their costs reimbursed and will share in a project-level incentive pool based on project outcomes. Many ideas from lean construction have been adopted on such projects together with the innovative contract form, and new information technologies such as 4D CAD are often being used in various ways to support identification and coordination of interdependencies between participants. The transaction cost economics literature in economics argues for relational contracting when asset specificity and uncertainty are both high, and the parties expect to interact with each other over multiple projects, so that the shadow of future interactions can temper counterparties' incentives to pursue short-term gains through opportunistic behavior. In contrast, sociologists approach relational contracting from the point of view of promoting social exchange and shared identity (Henisz and Levitt, 2010). And information technologists argue for the benefits of visual simulations that can promote shared awareness of problems and facilitate their resolution. We suggest that research is sorely needed to integrate economic and sociological perspectives on relational contracting with insights from research on information and knowledge sharing, so that we can collectively enhance our understanding of the way in which all of these forces will play out to shape the practices and outcomes of future projects.

The changes in information management on projects present a vast area of potential research for scholars with interests in project-based industries, management, information technologies, and organization. To date, too little sustained empirical research has been done in this field. Information management is of significant concern to managers on projects, both in dynamic industries—consumer electronics, telecommunications, biotechnology, software development, medical devices—and in the increasingly large-scale complex and multi-vocal projects in industries such as construction. It is a challenge that has become global, changing the geographic reach of organizations (Sapsed et al. 2005) and encompassing many stakeholders beyond the traditional project team. Research in this area has the potential to provide insight that can inform the leadership of the next generation of projects. As we argue in this chapter, we see the leading edge of practice breaking the mold of the 1960s approach to project management, shifting the focus away from tracking and eliminating variances from fixed and long-lived "baseline" project plans, to monitoring, integrating, and analyzing information on real-time and predicted performance, and re-planning continuously bottom up, rather than top down, as the project and its environment change. This throws practitioners into a world where information overload is a constant danger. There are significant opportunities for scholars to have a profound impact on practice improving decision-making by providing the frameworks, tools, and concepts for this new mode of information management on projects.

ACKNOWLEDGEMENTS

The first author gratefully acknowledges the support of the Engineering and Physical Sciences Research Council (EPSRC) and Economic and Social Sciences Research Council (ESRC) through an Advanced Institute of Management (AIM) Fellowship on "Management Practices and Project-Based Design Environments" (grant RES-331–27–0076); The second author gratefully acknowledges the support of the Stanford Center for Integrated Facility Engineering (CIFE) and the Collaboratory for Research on Global Projects (CRGP) at Stanford University.

REFERENCES

ACKOFF, R. L. (1989). "From data to wisdom," *Journal of Applied Systems Analysis*, 16: 3–9.

ALBERTS, D. S., and HAYES, R. E. (2003). *Power to the Edge: Command…Control…in the Information Age*. CCRP Publication Series.

ANON. (1986). "Toward a machine with interactive skills," in *Understanding Computers: Computer Images*. New York: Time-Life Books.

ARGYRES, N. S. (1999). "The impact of information technology on coordination: evidence from the B-2 'Stealth' bomber," *Organization Science*, 10/2: 162–79.

BANKER, R. D., KALVENES, J., and PATTERSON, R. A. (2006). "Information technology, contract completeness, and buyer–supplier relationships," *Information Systems Research*, 17/2: 180–93.

BECHKY, B. A. (2006). "Gaffers, gofers, and grips: role-based coordination in temporary organizations," *Organization Science*, 17/1: 3–21.

BERKHOUT, F., and HERTIN, J. (2004). "De-materialising and re-materialising: digital technologies and the environment," *Futures*, 36: 903–20.

BERNERS-LEE, T. (1989). *Information Management: A Proposal*, CERN from http://www.w3.org/History/1989/proposal.html.

BHARADWAJ, A. S. (2000). "A resource-based perspective on information technology capability and firm performance: an empirical investigation," *MIS Quarterly* 24/1: 169–96.

BOLAND, R. J., LYYTINEN, K., and YOO, Y. (2007). "Wakes of innovation in project networks: the case of digital 3–D representations in architecture, engineering, and construction," *Organization Science*, 18/4: 631–47.

CACCIATORI, E. (2008). "Memory objects in project environments: storing, retrieving and adapting learning in project-based firms," *Research Policy*, 37/9: 1591–601.

CARLILE, P. R. (2002). "A pragmatic view of knowledge and boundaries: boundary objects in new product development," *Organization Science*, 13/4: 442–55.

CHACHERE, J., KUNZ, J. C., and LEVITT, R. (2004). "Can you accelerate your project using extreme collaboration? A model based analysis," *2004 International Symposium on Collaborative Technologies and Systems*, San Diego, CA, 139–45.

CLARKE, L. (1999). *Mission Improbable: Using Fantasy Documents to Tame Disaster*. Chicago: University of Chicago Press.

COOPER, R., AOUAD, G., LEE, A., WU, S., FLEMING, A., and KAGIOGLOU, M. (2005). *Process Management in Design and Construction*. Oxford: Blackwell Publishing.

DAFT, R. L., LENGEL, R. H., and TREVINO, L. K. (1987). "Message equivocality, media selection, and manager performance: implications for information systems," *MIS Quarterly*: 355–66.

DODGSON, M., GANN, D. M., and SALTER, A. J. (2002). "Intensification of innovation," *International Journal of Innovation Management*, 6/1: 53–84.

————(2005). *Think, Play, Do*. Oxford: Oxford University Press.

DOSSICK, C. S., and NEFF, G. (2008). *How Leadership Overcomes Organizational Divisions in BIM Enabled Commercial Construction*. LEAD, Stanford Sierra.

EISENHARDT, K. M. (1989). "Making fast strategic decisions in high-velocity environments," *Academy of Management Journal*, 32/3: 543–76.

EWENSTEIN, B., and WHYTE, J. (2009). "Knowledge practices in design: the role of visual representations as 'epistemic objects'," *Organization Studies*, 30/1: 7–30.

FEENY, D. F., and WILLCOCKS, L. P. (1998). "Core IS capabilities for exploiting information technology," *Sloan Management Review*, 39/3: 9–21.

FENVES, S. J. (1967). *Computer Methods in Civil Engineering*. Englewood Cliffs, NJ: Prentice-Hall.

GALBRAITH, J. R. (1973). *Designing Complex Organization*. Reading, MA: Addison-Wesley.

——(1974). "Organization design: an information processing view," *Interfaces*, 4: 28–36.

——(1977). *Organization Design*. Reading, MA: Addison-Wesley.

GARUD, R., and KUMARASWAMY, A. (1995). "Vicious and virtuous circles in the management of knowledge: the case of InfoSys technologies," *MIS Quarterly*, 29/1: 9–33.

GREEN, S. D., and MAY, S. C. (2005). "Lean construction: arenas of enactment, models of diffusion and the meaning of 'leanness'," *Building Research and Information*, 33/6: 498–511.

HAIGH, N., and GRIFFITHS, A. (2008). "The environmental sustainability of information systems: considering the impact of operational strategies and practices," *International Journal of Technology Management*, 43/1–3: 48–63.

HARTMAN, T., and FISCHER, M. (2007). "3D/4D model supported visual knowledge distribution," *Building Research and Information*, 35/1: 70–80.

——and LEVITT, R. E. (2010). "Understanding and managing 3D/4D model implementations at the project team level," *ASCE Journal of Construction Engineering and Management*.

HARTY, C. (2005). "Innovation in construction: a sociology of technology approach," *Building Research and Information*, 33/6: 512–22.

HENISZ, W., and LEVITT, R. (2010). "Regulative, normative and cognitive institutional support for relational contracting in civil infrastructure projects," *Collaboratory for Research on Global Projects Working Paper 55*. Stanford, California.

HODGSON, D. (2004). "Project work: the legacy of bureaucratic control in the post-bureaucratic organization," *Organization*, 11/1: 81–100.

JIN, Y., and LEVITT, R. E. (1996). "The virtual design team: a computational model of project organizations," *Journal of Computational and Mathematical Organization Theory*, 2/3: 171–95.

KALLINIKOS, J. (2005). "The order of technology: complexity and control in a connected world," *Information and Organization*, 15/3: 185–202.

KANG, L. S., and PAULSON, B. C. (1998). "Information management to integrate cost and schedule for civil engineering projects," *Journal of Construction Engineering and Management*, 124/5: 381.

KÄRREMAN, D., and ALVESSON, M. (2004). "Cages in tandem: management control, social identity, and identification in a knowledge-intensive firm," *Organization*, 11/1: 149–75.

KOO, B., and FISCHER, M. (2000). "Feasibility study of 4D CAD in commercial construction," *Journal of Construction Engineering and Management*, 126/4: 251–60.

LEONARDI, P. M., and BAILEY, D. E. (2008). "Transformational technologies and the creation of new work practices: making implicit knowledge explicit in task-based offshoring," *MIS Quarterly*, 32/2: 411–36.

LEVINA, N., and VAAST, E. (2005). "The emergence of boundary spanning competence in practice: implications for the implementation and use of information systems," *MIS Quarterly*, 29/2: 335–63.

LEVITT, R. E., FRY, C., GREENE, S., and KAFTAN, C. (2008). "Salesforce.com: the development dilemma," Collaboratory for Research on Global Projects Case Study Archive, http://crgp.stanford.edu.

——THOMSEN, J., CHRISTIANSEN, T. R., KUNZ, J. C., YAN, J., and NASS, C. (1999). "Simulating project work processes and organizations: toward a micro-contingency theory of organization design," *Management Science*, 45/11: 1479–95.

LOGCHER, R. D., and STURMAN, G. M. (1966). "STRUDL: a computer system for structural design," *Journal of the Structures Division, ASCE*, 92: ST6.

McBRIDE, T. (2008). "The mechanisms of project management of software development," *Journal of Systems and Software*, 81/12: 2386–95.

MALONE, T. W. (1987). "Modeling coordination in organizations and markets," *Management Science*, 33/10: 1317–32.

MARCH, J. G., and SIMON, H. A. (1958). *Organizations*. New York: Wiley.

MORRIS, P. W. G., and HOUGH, G. H. (1987). *The Anatomy of Major Projects*. Chichester: John Wiley & Sons.

NEWELL, S., SCARBROUGH, H., and SWAN, J. (2001). "From global knowledge management to internal electronic fences: contradictory outcomes of intranet development," *British Journal of Management*, 12/2: 97–111.

NRC (1999). *Funding a Revolution: Government Support for Computing Research.* Washington, DC: National Academy Press.

ORLIKOWSKI, W. J., and YATES, J. (2002). "It's about time: temporal structuring in organizations," *Organization Science*, 13/6: 684–701.

PERLOW, L. (1999). "The time famine: toward a sociology of work time," *Administrative Science Quarterly*, 44/1: 57–81.

——OKHUYSEN, G. A., and REPENNING, N. P. (2002). "The speed trap: exploring the relationship between decision making and temporal context," *Academy of Management Journal*, 45/5: 931–55.

POLLOCK, N., WILLIAMS, R., and D'ADDERIO, L. (2007). "Global software and its provenance: generification work in the production of organizational software packages," *Social Studies of Science*, 37/2: 254–80.

PRASAD, A. (2005). "Making images/making bodies: visibility and disciplining through magnetic resonance imaging (MRI)," *Science Technology and Values*, 30/2: 291–316.

REDMOND, K. C., and SMITH, T. M. (2000). *From Whirlwind to MITRE: The R&D Story of the SAGE Air Defense Computer.* Cambridge, MA: MIT Press.

ROOS, D. (1965). "An integrated computer system for engineering problem solving," *AFIPS Joint Computer Conference*, 423–33.

SACKS, R., ESQUENAZI, A., and GOLDIN, M. (2007). "LEAPCON: simulation of lean construction of high-rise apartment buildings," *Journal of Construction Engineering and Management*, 133/7: 529–39.

SANDERS, N. R., and PREMUS, R. (2002). "IT applications in supply chain organizations: a link between competitive priorities and organizational benefits," *Journal of Business Logistics*, 23/1: 65–83.

SAPSED, J., GANN, D., MARSHALL, N., and SALTER, A. (2005). "From here to eternity? The practice of knowledge transfer in dispersed and co-located project organizations," *European Planning Studies*, 13/6: 831–51.

SCHWABER, K. (2004). *Agile Project Management with Scrum.* Redmond, WA: Microsoft Press.

——and BEEDLE, M. (2002). *Agile Software Development with Scrum.* Englewood Cliffs, NJ: Prentice Hall.

SINHA, K. K., and VAN DE VEN, A. (2005). "Designing work within and between organizations," *Organization Science*, 16/4: 389–408.

SMITH, S., TRANFIELD, D., BESSANT, J., LEVY, P., and LEY, C. (1992). "Organization design for the factory of the future," *International Studies of Management and Organization*, 22/4: 61–8.

STANDING, C., STOCKDALE, R., and LOVE, P. (2007). "Hybrid buyer–supplier relationships in global electronic markets," *Information and Organization*, 17/2: 89–109.

STAR, S. L. (1989). "The structure of ill-structured solutions: boundary objects and heterogeneous distributed problem solving," in M. Huhs and L. Gasser, *Readings in Distributed Artificial Intelligence 3.* Menlo Park, CA: Morgan Kaufmann, 37–54.

STINCHCOMBE, A. L. (1959). "Bureaucratic and craft administration of production: a comparative study," *Administrative Science Quarterly*, 4/2: 168–87.

STYHRE, A. (2009). *Managing Knowledge in the Construction Industry.* London: Spon Press.

TAXÉN, L., and LILLIESKÖLD, J. (2008). "Images as action instruments in complex projects," *International Journal of Project Management*, 26/5: 527–36.

TAYLOR, J. E. (2007). "Antecedents of successful three-dimensional computer-aided design implementation in design and construction networks," *Journal of Construction Engineering and Management*, 133/12: 993–1002.

TAYLOR, J. R., and LEVITT, R. E. (2007). "Innovation alignment and project network dynamics: an integrative model for change," *Project Management Journal*, 38/3: 22–35.

THOMPSON, J. D. (1967). *Organizations in Action: Social Science Bases of Administration*. New York: McGraw-Hill.

TOMMELEIN, I. D. (1998). "Pull-driven scheduling for pipe-spool installation: simulation of lean construction technique," *Journal of Construction Engineering and Management*, 124/4: 279.

VAN DE VEN, A. H., DELBECQ, A. L., and KOENIG, R., JR. (1976). "Determinants of coordination modes within organizations," *American Sociological Review*, 41/2: 322–38.

VAN DONKA, D. P., and MOLLOY, E. (2008). "From organising as projects to projects as organisations," *International Journal of Project Management*, 26/2: 129–37.

WEISER, M., and MORRISON, J. (1998). "Project memory: information management for project teams," *Journal of Management Information Systems*, 14/4: 149–66.

WHYTE, J. (2010). "Taking time to understand: articulating relationships between technologies and organizations," *Research in the Sociology of Organizations*, 29: 217–36.

——EWENSTEIN, B., HALES, M., and TIDD, J. (2008). "Visualizing knowledge in project-based work," *Long Range Planning*, 41/1: 74–92.

ZAMMUTO, R. F., GRIFFITH, T. L., MAJCHRZAK, A., DOUGHERTY, D., and FARAJ, S. (2007). "Information technology and the changing fabric of organization," *Organization Science*, 18/5: 749–62.

ZUBOFF, S. (1988). *In the Age of the Smart Machine: The Future of Work and Power*. New York: Basic Books.

PART V

CONTRACTING AND RELATIONSHIPS

CHAPTER 16

SHAPING PROJECTS, BUILDING NETWORKS

BERNARD COVA

ROBERT SALLE

INTRODUCTION

When Hurricane Katrina ravaged the US Gulf Coast in August 2005, Bechtel—the largest engineering company in the United States (and reputed to be one of the premier project management companies in the world)—helped to launch the Gulf Rebuild: Education, Advancement, and Training programme, an initiative aimed at providing up to 20,000 workers with the skills needed to rebuild the Gulf Coast. Under the leadership of Riley Bechtel, Group Chairman and CEO, federal and state government agencies, labor organizations, owner contractors, industry associations, and local community colleges teamed up to develop this huge training programme. Indeed, for Bechtel, project-shaping is a major activity that can transpire at any point in a project—from the preparation to the implementation phases—and including all kinds of project (re)configurations. By so doing, Bechtel distances itself considerably from responsive contractors whose only involvement is during the competitive bidding phase, i.e. it constitutes a proactive contractor.

Whether the contractor is developing a reactive or proactive approach, it will be engaging in what is commonly known as project-marketing, which should be understood here as a marketing approach specifically adapted to companies selling projects to order, for the particular purpose of reducing failure rates during customer consultation response phases. Project-marketing's key characteristic is its connection to discontinuity in project business (Hadjikhani 1996). This connection is the basis for a dual approach to project-marketing (Cova and Hoskins 1997) involving a deterministic approach based on the anticipation of (and subsequent adaptation to) the project's characteristics, along with a constructivist approach based on project-shaping.

The present chapter develops project management's marketing dimension. It does not deal with instances of so-called "internal" project-marketing, conceived and carried out within a company, but focuses solely on "external" project-marketing, comprised of contractors working on their customers' behalf. This includes projects in areas such as defense, construction, engineering, telecommunications, aerospace, shipbuilding, etc., mainly involving large-scale or infrastructure projects. The purpose of this chapter is not to summarize the entire "external" project-marketing approach but to concentrate on those constructivist aspects that speak to current project management issues. Morris (1994) has identified three key points explaining project successes and failures:

- The importance of managing projects' front-end and definition stages;
- The pivotal role of the owner (or sponsor);
- The need to manage project externalities in a certain way.

The project-shaping approach to project-marketing positions a company's action at the very front-end definition stage of a project and even beyond. It revolves around the management of project externalities represented by all interconnected actors.

The chapter contains four sections. The first explains the theoretical foundations of project-marketing. The second introduces the main characteristics of project-marketing and describes their scheduling effects. The third details shaping practices at each project stage. The fourth portrays a well-organized project-marketing approach as a network-building process.

PROJECT-MARKETING THEORIES

This section presents project-marketing theory's emergence and development by positioning it in relation to four theoretical backgrounds that have all contributed— each with its own limitations—to the construction of said theory. First, we introduce the field of B2B marketing, one based on inter-organizational exchanges, some of which result from project purchases and sales. Secondly, we introduce the field of competitive bidding strategies, a traditional benchmark in project business. Thirdly, there is the theory of markets as networks, one capable of accounting for the complexity of relational interactions among actors in project business. Lastly, there are recent developments in the field of co-creation, notably ones clarifying the approaches comprising project-shaping. We introduce each of these trends by showing their contribution to project-marketing.

Business-to-business marketing

Project-marketing finds its origins in the field of business-to-business (B2B) marketing, of which it is a subfield. B2B marketing emerged in the 1970s under the pressure of the IMP Group (Industrial Marketing and Purchasing Group) and was structured according to four key characteristics of business markets (Hakansson 1982):

• The first characteristic is relative to the transactions which are episodes within an ongoing supplier–customer relationship. As a consequence, B2B marketing emphasizes the duration and intensity of the relationship—a relationship which is close, complex, and long-term oriented;
• The second characteristic relates to the manner in which the role of the customer is conceptualized. The customer is active in the interaction with the supplier;
• The third characteristic refers to market characteristics and structure. In the B2B perspective, markets are concentrated and stability dominates. The density of the supplier–customer interaction is such that it limits change and often leads firms to invest resources in maintaining and developing relationships instead of opening new accounts;
• Finally, B2B scholars (Hakansson 1982) argue that the relevant unit of analysis in marketing is the supplier–customer interaction over time. It is therefore not relevant to adopt the point of view of a sole actor: the supplier or the customer.

Thus, by putting the supplier–customer interaction at the heart of its theoretical view, B2B marketing confirms a logic of continuity in the supplier–customer relationship, the latter depending on the frequency of transactions. In other words, the greater the frequency of transactions between a supplier and a customer, the stronger the relationship between the two players will become and lead to a high level of interdependence (Ford 1982).

If this relational view proves to be relevant for transactions concerning flow products (semi-products or components used for example in manufacturing industry), it could be questioned when the transaction frequency is weak and the object of the exchange is complex. Some investigations have been carried out on the marketing of these complex objects or transactions. The concept of system selling was introduced by Mattsson (1973) then taken up by a number of European authors (Backhaus and Weiber 1987; Bonnacorsi, Pammoli, and Tani 1996; Günter 1988), and North Americans (Dunn and Thomas 1986; Hannaford 1976; Page and Siemplenski 1983). Mattsson (1973) referred to the selling of a combination of hardware products and software (including problem solutions, services, etc.) that together form an integrated system able to carry out a total function or set of functions in the buying organization. In the same spirit, the concept of package deal negotiation was introduced by Ghauri (Ghauri and Johanson 1979; Ghauri 1983). Ghauri (1983) was interested in negotiations involving parties from different environments, e.g. transactions and relations at an international level between developed and developing countries. Transactions concerning complex objects like projects and even turnkey projects (Ghauri 1986) are included under the package deal label. It is from these initial bases that project-marketing emerged as a subfield of B2B marketing at the beginning of the 1990s. More recently, a research trend has updated system selling by mobilizing the notion of system integration (Helander and Möller 2007) or of solution integration (Davies, Brady, and Hobday 2007).

Beyond competitive bidding

Project-marketing has been conceptualized as a relational approach in B2B which clashed with the traditional competitive bidding strategies (Friedman 1956; Rothkopf and Stark 1979) which focus on the awarding of the project given a certain price strategy. Aware of the evolution of project-selling firms, research in marketing has escaped the trap of the bidding process by apprehending and understanding what is happening before and after the call for bidding (Boughton 1987). The meaning of the word project in a marketing perspective has thus sought to distance itself from being just a technical object: a project for marketing is a complex transaction concerning a package of products, services, and works, designed specially to complete a specific asset for a purchaser within a certain period of time (Cova and Holstius 1993) such as a building, a turnkey factory, an electric power station, an arms system, a limited series of landing gear, and the setting up of a complex management service for electrical distribution. Project-marketing researchers thereby ended with the omnipresent winning technical proposals in traditional bidding strategies.

The theory of project-marketing was thereby founded in the 1990s (Cova and Salle 2008; Skaates and Tikkanen 2003) on the representation of the project as a complex transaction. From what has been acquired in project-marketing, the following should be retained:

- The characterization of the activities of project-marketing through the D-U-C model (Mandjak and Veres 1998) who positioned the discontinuity (D), the uniqueness (U), and the complexity (C) of each project as specific dimensions of project activities. It is particularly the notion of discontinuity of project activities (Hadjikhani 1996) which appears central in project-marketing. The first goal of project-marketing is to contend with this economic discontinuity which places the contractor in a fragile position and to recreate continuity, notably the socio-economic continuity, with a significant number of clients and actors through the network of relations;
- The major role of non-business actors in the success or failure of the project contractor (Skaates, Tikkanen, and Lindblom 2002). Project markets are, in fact,

characterized by the intervention of numerous business actors, but also non-business actors (Hadjikhani and Thilenius 2005) such as the international money lenders (Welch 2005), throughout the whole project timeframe. This therefore means that in each market it is necessary to clearly identify its actors, their inter-relations, their roles, and their influences and to position the contractor among these actors (Cova, Mazet, and Salle 1996);

- A twin-track model marketing approach of project-selling firms (Cova and Hoskins 1997). The contractor confronted with the complexity of projects and of the project activity can consider this complexity as a fact and can adapt to this complexity by preparing himself as well as possible (referred to as the determinist approach). Or, on the contrary, he can consider reducing this complexity and the incertitude that bears on him by becoming an actor in the construction of the project and in the project environment (referred to as the constructivist approach);

- The key success factors of project-marketing activities (Cova and Holstius 1993). The factors favoring the success of firms selling projects are numerous. They can however be grouped into three large categories: the structural efficacy notably including the capacity to make special financial arrangements and to develop local presence; entrepreneurial culture, particularly, risk management; the adequacy of personnel, especially their ability to develop relations and to set up strategic or opportunistic cooperation (Huemer 2004). More particularly, the notion of references has been brought to the fore (Salminen and Möller 2004) as a key success element in project-marketing approaches.

Markets as networks

To be able to take on the actors, their interrelations, their roles, and their influences and to position the contractor among these actors, project-marketing researchers moved from a vision of the market made up of contractors and clients in order to adopt a vision of the market as a network of actors connected to each other. Once again, we owe this theorization to the IMP Group. For the IMP Group (Hakansson and Snehota 1989), no company is likened to an island. Every firm is linked to other firms or organizations belonging to the same network; the actors of the industry, the clients, suppliers, etc. (Mattsson 1985). It is also connected with, from outside the industry, the other suppliers of the same clients, consultants, standards committees, chambers of commerce, etc.

Similarly to B2B marketing in general, project-marketing has become increasingly relational in nature, with a growing focus on social and political phenomena. Many project stakeholders or interveners (Cleland 1988) are members of local networks and contribute in some cases to a local socio-economic system in which the project only appears in the guise of a disturbance, i.e. an event or episode subsumed within all of the relationships that exist between various actors in the system. In other words, the basic unit of study for project-marketing researchers is the territorial network, also known as the milieu (Cova, Mazet, and Salle 1996). Project-marketing researchers focus on a firm's relational investment in a milieu. A network logic is paramount in this approach, one where exchanges are more social than technical-economic in nature insofar as business actors are not the only ones concerned. A similar network logic can be found in a number of project management studies (Hellgren and Stjernberg 1995; Havila and Salmi 2009) that are grounded in the project network concept and whose purpose is to counter-balance overly technical visions of project management.

Co-creation

Project-marketing scholars concentrate on the interaction processes of the different stakeholders involved, be they business actors or non-business actors. The mechanisms of value co-creation revealed by the Service Dominant Logic (Vargo and Lusch 2004) prove to be relevant contributions to the subject. S-D logic moves the orientation of marketing from a "market to" philosophy where clients are promoted to, targeted, and captured, to a "market with" philosophy where the client and network actors are collaborators in the entire marketing process (Lusch and Vargo 2006). For Grönroos (2006: 324) "suppliers only create the resources or means to make it possible for clients to create value for themselves. In this sense at least, when contractors and clients interact, they are engaged in co-creation of value."

Adopting this co-creation view, project-marketing scholars consider that throughout the project process, the different actors interact in one way or another to shape a project. According to Miller and Lessard (2000, 2001), project-shaping is an activity which takes place throughout the project and involves many reconfigurations of the project. In their IMEC study on large engineering projects (LEP), they show that successful projects are not selected but shaped, e.g. sponsors embark on shaping efforts to influence risk drivers ranging from project-related issues to broader governance. Thus, the seeds of success of a project are planted early and nurtured over the course of the period. As projects are very often both unique and complex, prior definition of the entire project is impossible. These projects therefore give rise to a long process of co-creation in which the different actors participate to a greater or lesser extent. This process enables the production of value for all these actors who ensure that their preoccupations and ideas are taken into consideration. This idea of co-creation applies throughout the process and in every type of decision, including the definition of the project and its specifications. Instead of project activities being subservient to requirement specifications transmitted through the bid to tender procedure, the dominant idea of project-marketing is co-creation of the demand through the contractor and other actors. This requires acting as early as possible.

Project-marketing is a relational approach to the offering of projects which focuses on building and mobilizing networks in order to shape projects in a way which is favorable for a contractor. In this way project-marketing follows the recent evolutions of project management towards project generation (Söderlund 2005) and the development of requirements instead of requirement realization.

Project-marketing characteristics

Morris (1994) emphasizes some key project success points. In particular he points out the importance of managing the front-end definition stages of a project. The companies that are not involved early enough in this phase come up against difficulties during the completion phase. This phase is therefore of prime importance for the contractor. However, the existence of a buying procedure by invitation to tender usually places the contractor in an unfavorable reactive position—he reacts to stimuli sent by the client by invitation to tender—and in a position of submission—he is submitted to the rules of the terms and conditions stipulated in the invitation to tender. Consequently, the contractor sells projects upon demand and at the client's request. This states that he is not involved in the definition stages of the project. However, most professionals agree that replying to a consultation just as the company discovers a project at the very moment the invitation to tender is published leads to a very high failure rate. May we also emphasize that from the client's point of view, practice of this nature presupposes the ability to define the project specifications in full, a task that is virtually impossible for complex projects. The observation of project-marketing practices (Cova, Ghauri, and Salle 2002) reveals a different reality where the contractors more or less shape projects by interacting with the client as early as possible. These shaping approaches that we will look at in more detail in the third part are based on a collection of project market characteristics.

Three project market characteristics that are linked together can be taken into account: uniqueness, complexity, and discontinuity. Uniqueness means that each transaction with a given client is special: what is sold, how it is financed, the actors involved on the contractor side as well as the client side...everything or a part changes each time. As a result, the possibility of an exact reproduction is relatively limited. Complexity is often the rule and it goes beyond just technical complexity: complexity of financial arrangements, decision processes taking into account all the contributors involved (politicians, administrations, the general public, contracting authorities...). We talked earlier about the business discontinuity in contractor–client relationships that depends on the frequency of transactions between a given contractor and a given client. Generally, given the nature of what is being sold (a project), a given client's frequency of purchase is weak. It is therefore quite difficult to perpetuate a long-term relationship as we saw in the case of flow products. Confronted with the uniqueness and the complexity of each project as well as with the commercial discontinuity of relations with the clients, contractors find themselves in the situation of a high degree of uncertainty in relation to the scope of the market and in relation to the rules of business. As a result, project-marketing strategy is designed with the aim of reducing uncertainty so it can be better controlled (Slater 1990; Tikkanen 1998).

Two levers to reduce uncertainty are brought into operation in project-marketing: the relational lever and the functional lever. A set of resources is mobilized for each lever and enables companies to develop favorable competitive positioning. The relational position is the result of relational investments such as contacts with actors in the milieu, with participants from the client's buying decision center involved in the project, contacts not directly related to the project, contacts involved in other projects, etc. The more favorable the relational position, the greater the capacity to pick up the existence of a project well upstream and to co-create the project with a client. The functional position is the result of functional investments such as a specific endeavor to adapt the contractor's technical, financial, and human skills to the targeted market and to a search for complementary partners capable of working together on a project. Thus, the functional position is all the more favorable because the company has internal or external resources (through the offer partners) that it can in the end mobilize on one project or another.

In project-marketing, it is necessary a priori for a company to have a strong relational position that facilitates access to the client and to the client network and a favorable functional position which enables it to interact with the client and to win the project (Jansson 1989). Here it is important to note that usually a contractor cannot compensate a weak functional position by a strong relational position. Partnerships between contractors within a project consortium are often driven by the need to improve relational or functional positions. A company can improve its functional position through its own development including its general tender policy and/or by the interaction of permanent or ad hoc partners with other companies. Similarly, the same company can also improve its relational position. In this way, the positioning in relation to the project network, the alliances, the choice of an agent, contacts with process providers, and relevant contacts in political environments are means of improving both functional position and relational position.

The joint development of functional and relational positions in project-marketing is carried out according to a temporal logic of resource mobilization depending on an extended project temporality:

• independent of any project; the project does not yet exist for the contractor but in a desire to anticipate projects (detection and/or creation), the contractor takes a number of actions in this out-of-project phase, a preliminary stage in his marketing approach;

- project generation; the contractor has identified a project and chooses whether or not to invest resources in the development of an offer and in contacts;
- tender preparation; the project officially exists in the form of a market consultation by the client (invitation to tender), calling for an offer by the contractor;
- project completion; the project is under completion and the contractor has to manage a long succession of different episodes which can include maintenance and other support activities.

Four project-shaping practices

Project-marketing is mainly centered on the possibility of shaping demand and projects throughout the project temporality with emphasis on early stages. By using the frame of the four phases of the project temporality, it is possible to identify four shaping practices (Table 16.1). These four practices can be mobilized by a contractor either quite independently or with each one following on from the other. Each one of these practices contributes towards the strengthening of the contractor's functional and relational positions thereby maximizing its performance on the project.

Macro-shaping

When there are no projects in sight at the clients in the market segment targeted by the contractor (phase independent of any project), this requires the contractor to shape the competitive arena in conjunction with other potential participants as market-makers. At this stage, the contractor tries to develop a relational position in the milieu, i.e. the segment viewed as a network of actors. Such a position is made up of relations between business and non-business actors, who are potential stakeholders in pending projects. The contractor develops its functional position through the

Table 16.1 Project–shaping practices

Form of Shaping	Phase of Project Temporality	Ability to Shape the Project	Output of Project Shaping
Macro-Shaping	Independent of any project	Strong	Creation of the demand and the project
Joint Shaping	Project generation	Average	Specification of the project
Micro-Shaping	Tender preparation	Weak	Definition of fine points of the project
Marginal Shaping	Project implementation	Very weak	Amendment of details of the project

framing of its client value proposition, i.e. its core offering plus possible external contributions from partners belonging to the milieu and/or to the contractor's network. In this phase the ideal type of action is called macro-shaping: the aim is to create the demand and the project. The contractor sets the project up and therefore is the leader of the game and its rules. In the milieu, the contractor detects and analyses a project opportunity that could correspond to a requirement that is not yet formulated. In this way he is able to position himself ahead of the potential demand and construct the client's demand and sometimes even construct the client. This approach therefore consists of creating the project by proposing a study and a project dealing with the problem that the client has not yet clearly formulated. The contractor creates the concept of the project, carries out the feasibility study, settles the financing, and identifies, for example, the actors who constitute a mixed commercial company (type BOOT, Built Owned Operated Transferred) that will become his client. In certain companies all this creative approach is entrusted to the marketing function, the tasks of which are summed up in the following: "the upstream marketing role is firstly to listen to the client, to understand his culture, to help him, to incite him to think X (the name of the company). Then compatibilities have to be matched and incompatibilities have to be limited. Our role can be broken down into three points; to understand the client and open our minds to his wishes, to accompany him when a possible issue has been identified and to play the role of internal service provider to help project operators." Other companies set up approaches called "pseudo-projects," i.e. a way of setting the client's preferences by presenting him with a virtual offer (in the sense that it does not really exist) as being a base on which he can project his requirements and wishes. This offer exists only on paper (or nowadays even better, as a virtual artifact); it incorporates a pseudo-product as a technical solution (for example a type of convention center), a pseudo-contract (a set of conditions and financial simulations), and a pseudo-network of partners on the offer (network offer) which will be put into play only if the client reacts to the stimulus. This pseudo-project is the result of the contractor's learning process experienced in previous projects.

Joint shaping

When a project emerges (phase project generation), the contractor tries to adapt to the specific characteristics of the demand like influencing it in a way that is advantageous to it. In this phase, the contractor tries to secure its relational position in the network of actors around the pending project (i.e. the project network) and to develop its functional position by re-focusing its internal and external offer on the client issues in the project (i.e. project offering). In this phase the ideal type of action is called joint shaping. The approach seeks to define the specifications of the project in conjunction with the client. If the contractor is the driving force behind the project, it will enter an active phase of interaction with the client and the client's network. If the contractor is not the driving force in the development of the project and the client has personally developed his project, there can be peripheral development on less rigid parts of the project.

Micro-shaping

When the project purchasing process is launched by the client (phase tender preparation), the contractor tries to mobilize all its relations in the network of actors inside and around the buyer (i.e. the buying network) and to make a functional proposition. In this phase the ideal type of action is called micro-shaping. The aim is to clearly set out certain details of the project. If the contractor is not the driving force in the development of the project, it tries to break the established rules in order to enable the development of new rules of the game. In this case, the contractor finds itself confronted with the terms and conditions set up autonomously by the client or under the influence of a competitor or another participant. According to the degree of the client's openness to the interaction with the contractor, i.e. its capacity to accept possible modifications to the terms and conditions, the contractor could make the client's demand evolve (Cova, Salle, and Vincent 2000).

Marginal shaping

When the project has been attributed (phase project completion), the contractor coordinates the group of actors concerned in the completion of the project (i.e. the implementation network) to successfully ensure control over costs, quality, and deadlines. In this phase the ideal type of action is called marginal shaping. The aim is to draw up creative value-added proposals regarding specific aspects of the project under completion. However, the contractor can also make use of his established position to change the project in a direction that suits him without distorting the aim of the project.

Today, efficient contractors in the project market are more and more those able to shape the client problem and its solution by very early close collaboration with him as opposed to those who content themselves with responding to the requirement expressed by the client in the terms and conditions. Nevertheless, it's important to note that a large part of project business is still awarded through traditional calls for tender.

PROJECT-SHAPING THROUGH NETWORK-BUILDING

In project-marketing, shaping practices are based essentially on the building of network positions. In fact, project-marketing is typically rooted on a network approach in which the contractor recruits and enrolls actors (Mouzas and Naudé 2007) to shape the project. According to the type of shaping covered earlier (macro/joint/

micro/marginal shaping), the network mobilization process will be more or less developed. At every step of the process, questions arise regarding the co-creation of value (Table 16.2).

Identification of the actors around the client

How can contractors ensure that their understanding of the client network actors' vision is correct? What network horizon should the contractor choose (Anderson, Hakansson, and Johanson 1994)? Does one part of the network always remain hidden? Should the contractor favor one type of actor (business or non-business)? Is the network position concept Mattsson (1985) developed relevant in this case? Are there no hybrid actors that belong to both the client and supply networks?

The process of getting to know and analyzing a client network can benefit from the general outline of the method that Johanson and Mattsson (1988) suggested. This outline encompasses the following questions. (1) Who are the actors in the client network: business and non-business actors? What are the important relationships between these actors and the client? (2) What are the relative positions of these actors in the client network? What are their roles? What possibilities do these actors around the client offer the contractor regarding access to the client? This analysis leads to the definition of the key actors in the client network. (3) What are the contractor–actor relationships in the client network? (4) What incentives would one offer the actors to mobilize in support of the contractor's breakthrough to the client? (5) What methods can one employ to mobilize in support of the contractor's breakthrough to the client?

In addition, contractors should not only care about the visible network—the socio-economic actors (e.g. the client, engineering company, bank, and other institutions)—contractually involved in the buying process, but also about the

Table 16.2 A five-step process of project-shaping through network mobilization

STEPS	KEYPOINTS
1 Identification of the actors in the client network	• Representing the client network
	• Identifying visible and hidden actors
2 Targeting actors in the client network	• Setting up a basis for selection of the actors
3 Identification of the mobilizing factors of targeted actors	• Identifying what is at stake for each actor
4 Setting up an approach of the actors targeted in the client network	• Using a direct or indirect (third party) access to the targeted actor
5 Setting up a value co-creation approach with each client network actor	• Integrating resources from the supply network

Source: Cova and Salle (2008: 276).

hidden network—the socio-economic actors (e.g. the citizens, local associations, international organizations such as Greenpeace, opponents, etc.)—that could enter the buying process on a non-contractual basis. Solution contractors who do not grasp this phenomenon and who only network visible actors may find themselves in the position of having only managed half of the network (Sahlin-Andersson 1992). This is where the approach becomes difficult, as the contractor has to enter the network to learn more about the invisible actors. Consequently, it is difficult for contractors to plan this type of network approach in full. Contractors therefore have to be reactive and know how to evolve by considering events as they occur.

Targeting in the client network

How can the contractor choose the client network actors with whom to interact? How can one avoid turning to actors who are isolated and without relationships, which is the traditional way of approaching influencers and stakeholders? What should the basis for selection be: the actor's importance in the decision-making process, which is the reason for approaching stakeholders in project management (Loosemore 2006), or a fit/matching process between the contractor and the actor? How can one integrate the relationship between actors into the selection process? How can one integrate the relationship between some of these actors and some supply network actors into the selection process?

Identification of the mobilizing factors of targeted actors

How can one identify the aim of the potential value creation between the targeted actors and the contractor? Can one base the value creation drivers on the risks associated with any organizational buying behavior? Should the contractor consider each actor's stakes more strategically? Recognition of actors' stakes refers to the process of identifying the factors that allow the mobilization of certain of these targeted actors. This process involves several levels: first, the overall corporate level of the actor concerned, thereafter the functional level of a specific entity or department within this actor, and, finally, the individual level of a particular person within the actor.

The method that could be used on the actors in the client network is similar to that used in solution selling (Bosworth 1995). This method involves detecting what isn't going well with an actor and what the actor is as yet unable to identify or face up to—a latent problem. There is a latent problem when, from their perspective and building on their experience, contractors observe a situation in the actor's organization that is inefficient or could lead to a potential problem. This situation is the result of the contractor's analysis, but of which the actor is still unaware. The contractor's dissatisfaction statement thus indicates that the actor is facing a problem. Generally, the actor does not know how to approach the poorly formulated problem.

Setting up an approach to the actors targeted in the client network

How can the contractor contact the actors in the client network when he has not yet started any value creation work with the client? On what does the contractor's legitimacy to interact with these actors build? Should the contractor use a third party to make contact with these actors? What grounds can the contractor use to make the initial contact with an actor who has neither asked for anything nor expressed a need?

Setting up a value creation approach with each client network actor

What level and form of investment can the contractor reasonably mobilize in creating value with these actors? How can the contractor guarantee that the investment will not be a total loss or, worse, an advantage for a competitor? How can the contractor hand back power to these actors in their relationship with the client? What types of skills should the contractor promote regarding the targeted actors? How does the solution generated create value for all the parties involved? How can the contractor define the relevant content of the integrated solution and, especially, of the service dimension? How can the contractor define the appropriate degree of integration and bundling of its offer?

RESEARCH ISSUES FOR THE FUTURE

The entire approach described in this chapter encourages the contractor into going upstream in order to act at the very front-end definition stages of a project. However, a number of scholars today underline the importance of downstream logic. In fact a move can be seen towards downstream logic (Oliva and Kallenberg 2003) in which the contractor is heavily involved in maintenance and management activities of operations once the project is finished. This evolution is reflected in the development of integrated solutions (Davies, Brady, and Hobday 2007) and full service contracts (Stremersch, Wuyts, and Frambach 2001). At this point, a fifth phase can be introduced into the project-marketing process: the exploitation phase after project completion. The introduction of this new phase questions the shaping practices described earlier: what type of shaping will there be in this fifth phase? What coherence will there be with the shaping practices in the other phases? What impact will the characteristics of companies have on the type of shaping? In fact we notice that the contractors are not involved in the same way in this fifth phase: some companies concentrate on service contracts established at the start through work covering maintenance, repair, and upgrading while others are engaged in exploitation which is the case for PPP and PFI projects or in the perspective of full service contracts. The replies to these questions outline an initial direction for future research.

Nonetheless, recent developments in companies in terms of shaping strategies initiated very much upstream in project temporality question researchers on the development of profiles and missions of players involved in these actions. In fact shaping actions switch the players from a techno-economic dominant logic to a socio-economic dominant logic in which managing networks is particularly important. The skills required are no longer those found in the traditional engineering field. Project managers and other managers who are involved in the project can no longer rely on engineering science to take action in that period of uncertainty when no project has yet been formalized. How are their roles and related programmes going to evolve if project-shaping develops? How are these roles going to interact with those of the key account managers whose task is precisely that of taking action at the clients very much upstream? What sort of structure should the marketing and sales operations have? What type of interface should these operations have with the technical operations introduced for shaping activities? From a more structural aspect, how can the reasoning applied to a short- or medium-term project be combined with the reasoning applied to a client's medium- and long-term view? All of this forms a second line of logical research for the future.

These lines of research could take advantage of the ANT (Actor Network Theory) developed by Callon (1999). In this theory, society is seen as constituted through a recursive process of inter-definition. Actors are not pre-determined but are effects of the social process. Thus society is performed more than given and framing is the iterative process put into play by an *actant* (Callon 1999) in order to achieve a certain order. To succeed in framing the *actant* must enroll others and create new entities by inscription and mobilization. We believe that there is some untapped potential for ANT in understanding the shaping of projects and building of networks.

Conclusion

For contractors seeking better success rates, project-marketing has become a crucial approach, one grounded in all of the research work that has been conducted over the past twenty years in areas like B2B marketing and project management itself. The focus here is the importance of project-shaping practices, meaning activities that take place throughout a project—from generation to implementation—and which normally lead to a host of (re)configurations. By using the four phases of a project's timeframe as a general setting (Table 16.1), it becomes possible to identify four shaping practices: macro; joint; micro; and marginal shaping. These practices highlight the importance of building networks.

It remains that the foundations for success are laid at the very beginning of the project. Early events, which are often independent of any project phase, usually have a significant influence on other phases. This is why the chapter pursues the afore-mentioned line of reasoning, as formulated by several authors in the project management community (Pinto and Rouhiainen 2001; Söderlund 2005) who consider that normative techniques and methods used for project management "have shown their usefulness in situations with well defined ends. However, most projects include phases and projects where these techniques and routines do not apply. Projects are also processes of organising where ends and means are continually redefined in the interactions of actors" (Hellgren and Stjernberg 1995: 378).

All in all, project-marketing approaches combine several organizational processes in an attempt to:

- Distance themselves from a purely transactional reasoning imposed by project operations by injecting continuity into relations with clients and key stakeholders;
- Avoid reasoning solely in terms of real-time adaptations to customers' terms and conditions through the development of forecasting capabilities;
- Avoid reasoning solely on the basis of submissions to project specification by co-creating projects featuring greater or lesser customer involvement;
- Find a suitable way of mobilizing and integrating the internal and external resources that help to structure the project.

References

ANDERSON, J. C., HAKANSSON, H., and JOHANSON, J. (1994). "Dyadic business relationships within a business network context," *Journal of Marketing*, 58/4: 1–15.

BACKHAUS, K., and WEIBER, R. (1987). "Systemtechnologien-Herausforderung des Investitionsgütermarketing," *Harvard Manager*, 9/4: 70–80.

BONNACORSI, A., PAMMOLI, F., and TANI, S. (1996). "The changing boundaries of system companies," *International Business Review*, 5/6: 539–60.

BOSWORTH, M. T. (1995). *Solution Selling: Creating Buyers in Difficult Selling Markets*. New York: McGraw-Hill.

BOUGHTON, P. (1987). "The competitive bidding process: beyond probability models," *Industrial Marketing Management*, 16/2: 87–94.

CALLON, M. (1999). "ANT: the market test," in J. Hassard and J. Law (eds.), *Actor-Network Theory and After*. Oxford: Blackwell, 181–95.

CLELAND, D. I. (1988). "Project stakeholder management," in D. I. Cleland and W. R. King (eds.), *Project Management Handbook*, 2nd edn. New York: Van Nostrand Reinhold, 275–301.

Cova, B., and Holstius, K. (1993). "How to create competitive advantage in project business," *Journal of Marketing Management*, 9/2: 105–21.

——and Hoskins, S. (1997). "A twin track networking approach to project marketing," *European Management Journal*, 15/5: 546–56.

——and Salle, R. (2008). "Marketing solutions in accordance with the S-D logic: co-creating value with customer network actors," *Industrial Marketing Management*, 37/3: 270–7.

——Mazet, F., and Salle, R. (1996). "Milieu as a pertinent unit of analysis in project marketing," *International Business Review*, 5/6: 647–64.

——Salle, R. and Vincent, R. (2000). "To bid or not to bid: screening of the Whorcop project," *European Management Journal*, 18/5: 551–60.

——Ghauri, P. N., and Salle, R. (2002). *Project Marketing: Beyond Competitive Bidding*. Chichester: John Wiley.

Davies, A., Brady, T., and Hobday, M. (2007). "Organizing for solutions: systems seller vs. systems integrator," *Industrial Marketing Management*, 36/2: 183–93.

Dunn, D. T., and Thomas, C. A. (1986). "Strategy for system sellers: a grid approach," *Journal of Personal Selling & Sales Management*, 6/August: 1–10.

Ford, D. (1982). "The development of buyer–seller relationships in industrial markets," in H. Hakansson (ed.), *International Marketing and Purchasing of Industrial Goods: An Interaction Approach*. Chichester: John Wiley & Sons, 288–303.

Friedman, L. (1956). "A competitive bidding strategy," *Operations Research*, 4/February: 104–12.

Ghauri, P. N. (1983). *Negotiating International Package Deals: Swedish Firms and Developing Countries*. Stockholm: Almqvist & Wiksell.

——(1986). "International business negotiations: a turn-key project," *Service Industries Journal*, 6/1: 74–89.

——and Johanson, J. (1979). "International package deal negotiations: the role of the atmosphere," *Organisation Marknad Och Samhälle*, Special Issue on Buyer–Seller Relationships International Markets, 16/5: 355–64.

Grönroos, C. (2006). "Adopting a service logic for marketing," *Marketing Theory*, 6/3: 317–34.

Günter, B. (1988). "Systemdenken und Systemgeschäft in Marketing," *Marktforschung & Management*, 32/4: 106–10.

Hadjikhani, A. (1996). "Project marketing and the management of discontinuity," *International Business Review*, 5/3: 319–36.

——and Thilenius, P. (2005). *Non Business Actors in a Business Network*. Amsterdam: Elsevier.

Hakansson, H. (1982). *Industrial Marketing and Purchasing of Industrial Goods: An Interaction Approach*. Chichester: John Wiley.

——and Snehota, I. (1989). "No business is an island," *Scandinavian Journal of Management*, 5/3: 187–200.

Hannaford, W. (1976). "Systems selling: problems and benefits for buyers and sellers," *Industrial Marketing Management*, 5/2: 139–45.

Havila, V., and Salmi, A. (2009). *Managing Project Ending*. Oxford: Routledge.

Hellander, A., and Möller, K. (2007). "System supplier's customer strategy," *Industrial Marketing Management*, 36/6: 719–30.

Hellgren, B., and Stjernberg, T. (1995). "Design and implementation in major investments: a project network approach," *Scandinavian Journal of Management*, 11/4: 377–94.

HUEMER, L. (2004). "Activating trust: the redefinition of roles and relationships in an international construction project," *International Marketing Review*, 21/2: 187–201.

JANSSON, H. (1989). "Marketing to projects in South-East Asia," in S. Cavusgil (ed.), *Advances in International Marketing*. Greenwich, CT: JAI Press, iii. 259–76.

JOHANSON, J., and MATTSSON, L. G. (1988). "Internationalisation in industrial systems: a network approach," in N. Hood and J. E. Vahlne (eds.), *Strategies in Global Competition*. London: Croom Helm, 287–314.

LOOSEMORE, M. (2006). "Managing project risks," in S. Pryke and M. Smyth (eds.), *The Management of Complex Projects: A Relationship Approach*. Oxford: Blackwell, 187–204.

LUSCH, R. F., and VARGO, S. L. (2006). "Service-dominant logic: reactions, reflections and refinements," *Marketing Theory*, 6/3: 281–8.

MANDJAK, T., and VERES, Z. (1998). "The D-U-C model and the stages of the project marketing process," in A. Halinen and N. Nummela (eds.), *14th IMP Annual Conference Proceedings*. Turku: Turku School of Economics and Business Administration, iii. 471–90.

MATTSSON, L. G. (1973). "System selling as a strategy on industrial markets," *Industrial Marketing Management*, 2/3: 107–19.

—— (1985). "An application of a network approach to marketing: defending and changing positions," in N. Dholakia and J. Arndt (eds.), *Changing the Course of Marketing: Alternative Paradigms for Widening Marketing Theory*. Greenwich, CT: JAI Press, 263–88.

MILLER, R., and LESSARD, D. R. (2000). *The Strategic Management of Large Engineering Projects: Shaping Institutions, Risks, and Governance*. Cambridge, MA: MIT Press.

————(2001). "Understanding and managing risks in large engineering projects," *International Journal of Project Management*, 19/8: 437–43.

MORRIS, P. W. G. (1994). *The Management of Projects*. London: Thomas Telford.

MOUZAS, S., and NAUDÉ, P. (2007). "Network mobilizer," *Journal of Business & Industrial Marketing*, 22/1: 62–71.

OLIVA, R., and KALLENBERG, R. (2003). "Managing the transition from products to services," *International Journal of Service Industry Management*, 14/2: 160–72.

PAGE, A., and SIEMPLENSKI, M. (1983). "Product systems marketing," *Industrial Marketing Management*, 12/2: 89–99.

PINTO, J. K., and ROUHIAINEN, P. K. (2001). *Building Customer-Based Project Organizations*. New York: John Wiley.

ROTHKOPF, H., and STARK, R. M. (1979). "Competitive bidding: a comprehensive bibliography," *Operations Research*, 27/2: 365–90.

SAHLIN-ANDERSSON, K. (1992). "The social construction of projects: a case study of organizing an extraordinary building project—the Stockholm Globe Arena," *Scandinavian Housing and Planning Research*, 9/1: 65–78.

SALMINEN, R. T., and MÖLLER, K. (2004). "Using references in industrial bidding: a decision model analysis," *Journal of Marketing Management*, 20/1–2: 133–55.

SKAATES, M. A., and TIKKANEN, H. (2003). "International project marketing: an introduction to the INPM approach," *International Journal of Project Management*, 21/7: 503–10.

————and LINDBLOM, J. (2002). "Relationships and project marketing success," *Journal of Business & Industrial Marketing*, 17/5: 389–406.

SLATER, S. P. (1990). "Strategic marketing variables under conditions of competitive bidding," *Strategic Management Journal*, 11: 309–17.

SÖDERLUND, J. (2005). "Developing project competence: empirical regularities in competitive project operations," *International Journal of Innovation Management*, 9/4: 451–80.

STREMERSCH, S., WUYTS, S., and FRAMBACH, R. T. (2001). "The purchasing of full-service contracts," *Industrial Marketing Management*, 30/1: 1–12.

TIKKANEN, H. (1998). "Research on international project marketing," in H. Tikkanen (ed.), *Marketing and International Business-Essays in Honor of Professor Karin Holstius on her 65th Birthday*. Turku: Turku School of Economics, 261–85.

VARGO, S. L., and LUSCH, R. F. (2004). "Evolving to a new dominant logic for marketing," *Journal of Marketing*, 68/1: 1–18.

WELCH, C. (2005). "Multilateral organisations and international project marketing," *International Business Review*, 14/3: 289–305.

CHAPTER 17

INNOVATING THE PRACTICE OF NORMATIVE CONTROL IN PROJECT MANAGEMENT CONTRACTUAL RELATIONS

STEWART CLEGG

KJERSTI BJØRKENG

TYRONE PITSIS

> My idea of an alliance, the contract is signed and placed in the top draw and you forget you ever had it...the glue, what keeps an alliance together is its people, its culture...I think a lot of people just don't get that.
>
> (Alliance Leadership Team Member, March 25, 2009)

The above quote prefigures a transformation in how we believe major projects will be governed in the not too distant future. Once upon a time it would have been unheard of to contemplate a multi-million dollar project that was not based on black letter legal contracts and instead relied on "soft" governance processes, such as culture and human relations. Such projects are extremely rare, but over the last ten years we have been fortunate enough to study closely at least two major projects that place human relations rather than legal contracts at the forefront of what they do and how they do it. In this chapter we will discuss the latest project and present findings from longitudinal ethnographic research of what we refer to as a mega-project alliance. For five years we followed the leadership team of a large Australian Alliance Program made up of several private organizations and a large public sector client. We focus on the Alliance Leadership Team (ALT) and the way they narrate the differences between their ways of working in the alliance from ways of managing construction under traditional design and construct contracts. We present four themes of difference: the relations between the contracting parties; the handling of variations and incidents; the negotiating of monetary apportionment; and innovation and idea work. These are essential themes with which the ALT narrates their practice as distinctive and surprising in terms of conventional project management.

In the chapter we begin by considering the institution of contract and approaches to it. We follow this with an analysis of an institutional innovation, the development of alliancing as a specific form of contract premised on a far more normative mode of control than the disciplinary mechanisms of surveillance which have tradition-ally been seen as more typically associated with conventional contracts. A new way of managing projects is evolving, as we report in this chapter. We consider some of its advantages as well as some of its disadvantages.

THE INSTITUTION OF CONTRACT

Contract has a very specific institutional role to play in contemporary society; in contrast to earlier types of social organization based on mechanical solidarity that demanded a high degree of regimentation, modern types of organization rest on organic solidarity obtained through the functional interdependence of autonomous individuals. In modern societies, social solidarity is dependent upon the individual autonomy of conduct and one of the principal ways in which this is specified is through contractual relations. Now, there is something about the reliance on project contracts that is both perplexing and irrational. The assumption is that contracts provide the glue of good project governance and relations, that they are a "good" and effective control mechanism, reducing risk for project actors. While the latter aim, of risk reduction, dominates traditional ideas about contracts it actually reduces the likelihood of achieving good project governance.

Contracts might seem to be straightforward, a set of agreements captured in more or less precise notations and inscription, cross-referenced from one section to another, supported by considerable additional matter: consultant's reports, draw-ings, and much technical detail. It might seem as if the job of construction is then "merely" to turn this "blueprint" into a building. In some conceptions the "merely" is glossed as a purely technical exercise. It is, however, a complex, indeterminate and highly indexical process of interpretation, instantiation, decoding, and general negotiation of meaning around a set of texts that are rarely all in accord, transparent or decisive pointers for action. Contracts are material objects that have their meaning embedded in organizations and constituted by diverse and often conflicting disciplinary practices: engineers and architects, for instance, can read a document and see it in entirely different terms. Moreover they are constantly being interpreted in a flow of events whereby the here and now interpretation is always capable of reinterpreting something decided back there and then or that will be a matter for issue—or perhaps, erroneously thought to be a matter for non-issue at some time in the future. In construction, contractural documents become a point of condensation and concentration of diverse professional and practical discourses; they are capable of shifting interpretations by different actors and by the same actors at different times; the import they carry qua documents can change as they are enacted into concrete materializations, and they are always interpreted in a broader political economy context. They will be interpreted differently if the economy is booming or heading for a bust; what might be problematic in the one condition— such as securing a contribution to profit or ensuring a steady supply of appropriately skilled labour—may well be unproblematic in the other context.

To a significant degree, economic theories dominate ideas about contracts, and underpin the legal framework. While there are many strategic approaches to contract we will restrict discussion to the dominant approaches of transaction cost economics and resource dependency. (There are of course many variations to such themes, including agency theory, economic rents, and the relational view, for example.) Generally, large-scale projects are constituted by black letter legal contracts that are representative of an implicit climate of mistrust: operating with the anticipation that people will "screw" the project in order to maximize their own self-interests and profits; as such contractors wrote contracts as watertight as possible. Such contractual arrangements require governance mechanisms that involve high degrees of surveillance of work to check that it is completed in accord with the contract (Lundin and Söderholm 1998; Charue-Duboc and Midler 1998). Such contractual and governance systems created a culture that focused attention on what goes wrong and the resultant punishment rather than what is going right and on the resultant reward and recognition. A situation is produced by such mechanisms of control where it is in the interests of resourceful project managers to ensure that sufficient things go wrong whose responsibility can be attached to the client organization that a financial punishment can be extracted from that organization to the benefit of the contractors' organization. Although it may not be a strong part of the formal curriculum of project management it is a key part of informal workplace learning. Moreover, in the psychology of learning and on motivation it is well established that punishment and the threat of punishments restricts behavior and learning, rather than promoting learning and hence creativity and innovation (Glasser 1985). This is not surprising in the case of project management where profit can sometimes be assured only by exploiting the situation.

While contracts as an object of analysis are not unknown in organization and management theory they have tended to be seen in rather specific and privileged terms. Contracts are seen to be entered into between free agents operating in markets where the conditions allow; where the conditions do not allow then agents are obliged to accept the economically inferior option of arranging their affairs through hierarchies rather than markets. Much of the organizations literature looks at how contracts are translated into practice—through transactions, for instance (see transaction cost economics—TCE—in the work of Williamson 1975). In management and organization theory most scholars would be familiar with transaction cost economics (also known as the contract approach to economic organizations) as a field that has developed thinking about contractual relationships, around the themes of markets and hierarchies (e.g. Williamson 1979, 1985, 1991), where the rhetoric implies that contracts should minimize transaction costs. Here contracts are seen as basic building blocks of the social order, in a move that goes back at least as far as Hobbes (1651). Hobbes's contractual solution to the problem of social order, that authoritative images of the social order are encapsulated in the notion of an implicit "contract," is still routinely practiced in at least one arena of organizational life—large-scale project organization.

Williamson (e.g. 2002a, 2002b, 2003) argues that the contract perspective on economic organizations is a "microanalytic construction...more amenable to the lessons of organization theory" than the orthodox economic view of the firm in terms of a production function (2003: 917). The contract approach describes the firm as a mode of organization conceived as a governance structure, which needs to be examined in relation to other possible modes of governance, e.g. markets and hybrids, which all have different governance attributes.

Major characteristics of contracts from this economic point of view are (1) their incompleteness due to the bounded rationality of individuals, (2) the openness of contracts for defection due to the self-interestedness of individuals, and (3) the need of mechanisms and adaptive properties in contracts in order to minimize the possibility of opportunism (Williamson 1985, 1991, 2003). Such mechanisms have to enable the realignment and restore the efficiency of contracts in the case of unanticipated disturbances (Williamson 1991).

The unit of analysis from the contract perspective is the transaction. Therefore, TCE concentrates on discrete contracts in which "no relation exists between the parties apart from the simple exchange of goods" (MacNeil 1980: 10). Transactions are specified by three elements: asset specificity, frequency, and uncertainty. Because of bounded rationality and uncertainty, all complex contracts are unavoidably incomplete and require some ex post adaptation. Thus, TCE turns its attention to the ex post stage of contracts, which is in contrast to the principal agent theory (or agency theory, which is another economic theory that deals with contracts) that

focuses entirely on the ex ante incentive alignment of contracts and rules for efficient risk-bearing (Williamson 2000).

The requirements for an ex post adaptation differ, however, between different
forms of transaction. Williamson regards three main types of transactions and,
respectively, three governance forms—market, hierarchy, and hybrid. In the case of
markets, the classical contract law applies, which emphasizes formal rules, formal
documents, and self-liquidating transactions and aims for "complete presentation"
(Williamson 1979). (Presentation means to "make or render present in place or
time; to cause to be perceived or realized at present" (Macneil 1974: 863 cited in
Williamson 1979: 236; see also Macneil 1980).) Hybrids, in contrast, need to be supported by more flexible neoclassical contract law, characterized by the autonomy of
the contracting parties, their higher interdependency than in the case of markets,
the incompleteness of contracts, and by elastic contracting mechanisms (Williamson
1991). The adaptability of neoclassical contracts is, however, restricted. When disturbances become highly consequential, adaptation becomes costly and time consuming because the autonomous ownership status of the parties poses growing
incentives that will create defects in the contract's execution (Williamson 1991).
Williamson proposes that in such cases the internal organization, hierarchy, quali-
fies as the more elastic and adaptive mode of organization. It relies on a "forbear-
ance contract law," i.e. an internal adaptation can be achieved through fiat without
the need to consult, complete, or revise inter-firm agreements (Williamson 1979).

The main implication of the above arguments is that the most important function of contracts from a TCE point of view is to prevent opportunistic behavior as
much as possible and to provide flexible mechanisms that allow the adjustment of
the contract to changing conditions. In other words, the main function of contracts
is to ensure minimum transaction cost and as such, the efficiency of the transaction.
(This is in line with the argument that firms and hybrids exist in order to minimize
transaction costs.) Such contracts involve only a small part of the personality of the
involved individuals, they are limited in scope, the involved communications are
linguistic and formal, and the satisfactions derived are limited to the accomplishment of the narrow economic exchange. It is assumed that no future cooperation
will take place (Macneil 1980).

Contract theories in organization analysis are littered with an inherent uneasiness
about trust (e.g. Granovetter 1985, 1992). Often they ignore the fact that every contract is necessarily partially relational as it involves relations other than a discrete
exchange (Macneil 1980). Sociologists argue that the contract perspective on organizations conceived in largely instrumental terms is very restricted as there are organization forms with a distinct ethic or value orientation on the part of the exchange
partners (Podolny and Page 1998), implying trust (Granovetter 1985, 1992) and reciprocity (Powell 1990). "Continuing economic relations become overlaid with social
content that, apart from economic self-interest, carries strong expectations of trust
and abstention from opportunism" (Granovetter 1992: 42). These authors argue,

therefore, that especially network forms of organizations (called hybrids in TCE) should not be viewed primarily from an economic contract point of view.

As with TCE, resource-based views draw on an economic perspective of contract at the organizational level of analysis. In resource dependency theory, organizations seek to avoid becoming over-dependent on other organizations, yet at the same time seek to exploit situations where organizations are dependent upon them. One of the ways that organizations respond to their resource contexts is by adaptation. Adaptive strategies are attempts to mitigate resource dependencies through actions such as the use of long-term contracts. Again, the emphasis is on the contract as a stable instrument of control rather than something whose sense is negotiated. There has been a lengthy sociological interest in the non-contractual elements of contract stretching back at least to Durkheim, which serves as a useful correction to the overly rationalist and somewhat utilitarian views that TCE offers. Durkheim argued against the utilitarians of his day, notably Herbert Spencer, noting that it is not possible to derive society from the propensity of individuals to trade and barter in order to maximize their own happiness. In the terms of Granovetter's (1985) sociology of contract, social relations are embedded not in the utility of the various opportunities to truck and trade that produce them but in the social relations that individuals enjoy. These are built slowly over time and involve the development of trust rather than just the calculation of utilities—even though the relations might start at that point. When people make a contract then they must have a prior commitment to the meaning of a contract in its own right as well as an ongoing commitment to the ways in which the contract may shape and form their social relations in future. These two aspects—the prior collective commitment to the non-contractual element of contracts and the projection of this commitment into trust relations that will govern future perfect relations through the contract—constitutes the framework of normative control.

Contract has a very specific institutional role to play in contemporary society; in contrast to earlier types of social organization based on mechanical solidarity that demanded a high degree of regimentation, modern types of organization rest on organic solidarity obtained through the functional interdependence of autonomous individuals. In modern societies, social solidarity is dependent upon the individual autonomy of conduct and one of the principal ways in which this is specified is through contractual relations. Now, this is a very different interpretation of contract from that which is most often encountered:

To law professors, "contract" is a body of doctrine delineating how transacting parties can make agreements that the legal system will treat as binding. To economists, contracts are agreements that impose tangible costs in exchange for tangible benefits, regardless of whether these agreements enjoy legal recognition. To business lawyers, contracts are written instruments formalizing agreements that their clients believe themselves to have made—as well as addressing remote contingencies that their clients should have considered but probably overlooked. To trial lawyers, contracts are pieces of evidence, either to be invoked as proof of agreements willingly made, or to be dismissed as ambiguous, inequitable or unreflective of actual events. To lay people, contracts are simply pieces of paper that one signs in the course of commerce, often with an uneasy sense of finality, but rarely with a comprehensive understanding of the relevant scholarly doctrines, economic exchanges, contingent claims, or evidentiary implications. (Suchman 2003: 91)

All of these perspectives take a somewhat non-indexical and immaterial view of contracts—that is to say they do not situate them as substantive phenomena, as social artifacts, whose meaning is constituted in the ebb and flow of discursive encounters, but rather as things whose essence may be occluded but is, nonetheless, in principle, knowable and fixable with finality. To say that a contract is a social artifact is not simply to make the observation that it is material, comprising marks on paper, or patterns of words on a screen. It is to observe that contracts are the product of work grounded in the experiences of those who write them; they are often embedded in organizations that have a considerable degree of experience with contracts as material objects. Not only are contracts material objects but they are also practical technologies—that is, they are means of getting things done. Contracts, especially as they become more complex, always present the possibility of being indexical (Clegg 1975), of carrying much more meaning than they might appear to bear when viewed out of context. In the contexts of their use the meaning of contracts is always a matter of interpretation constituted in a temporal flow, by structurally differentiated actors, in different spatial locations. As Suchman (2003: 92) puts it, "contract regimes are at once both technical systems and communities of discourse." As such, contract regimes have a reciprocal relationship with the contexts in which they are born and embedded; experience with the contract changes both the organizations in whom their initiation is embedded and those in which their use is situated. By the same token, contracts, much as any artifact, "are themselves capable of affecting these environments, both culturally and economically" (Suchman 2003: 92).

For critical commentators on construction sites as organizations, contracts have been seen to play a specific role in power relations. Contractual surveillance involves complex practices of power (Clegg 1975, 1989, 1995, 2000; Hardy and Clegg 1996: 375; Clegg et al. 2006). Critical organization theory has emphasized how contracts enable individuals to be subjected to close surveillance and control (Dandekker 1990; Marks 2000; Sewell and Wilkinson 1992; Knights and Vurdubakis 1993; Sewell 1998), as well as being the subjects of disciplinary practices (Covaleski et al. 1998) and forms of language (Oakes, Townley, and Cooper 1998) that can dominate them (Clegg 1975). Typically, in construction projects, control on site is exercised through as tight a surveillance of contractors and employees as is possible in often spatially disaggregated spheres of action, with the contract usually being used as an indexical grid for what organizational self-interest suggests practice should be expected to be. We want to report on empirical materials that run counterfactually against the common view of the construction site as a setting for detailed panoptical and indexical power.

Theoretically, there are at least four approaches to the analysis of contracts identified by Suchman (2003: 93): these are contract as doctrine; contract as relation, contract as artifacts; and contract as indexical documents. The relational approach has provided the raw material for a number of significant theoretical studies, including Uzzi (1996) and Granovetter (1985), whose main empirically oriented points are that exchange agreements are generally incomplete, emergent, and thus time and context dependent, as well as governed by informal norms that are largely noncontractual. These insights fit well with the more empirically oriented research that has been undertaken by researchers such as Clegg (1975), for whom temporal and contextual dependency and emergence is captured by the ethnomethodological terms of "indexicality" (Garfinkel 1967): from this perspective contracts for major construction projects are a classical case of indexical documents whose meaning is only ever enacted in context.

A contract is both a noun and a verb, and it refers to something artifactual: it can refer both to the object that represents a voluntary agreement between two or more parties projecting some type of exchange into the future, as well as the process by which such agreement is defined and interpreted, as well as how it may be reinterpreted in specific contexts. The essential elements are that there is an exchange relationship as well as interpretive contexts in which the contract's sense is reflexively embedded. The contract has to be enacted, made sense of. Different sense will be made by parties with different interests in the interpretation of the contractual particulars—which, with supporting documents, can be very detailed and provide lots of opportunity for interpretive ability where non-conformance issues arise between different elements. In this way various indexical accounts will be generated, each indexing some particular rather than another, some of which, in certain contexts, such as a court of law, will prove to be more binding obligations.

In the contracts as indexical documents approach what the contract means is always subject to interpretation and is never a matter of black letter law; interpretation is always contextually and temporally dependent, and in these contexts of interpretation, how the contract is interpreted always indexes the changing political relevancies of the agents engaged in the interpretation of the contract.

The epitome of indexical construction industry practice is the competitively tendered "hard money contract." Although competitively tendered hard money contracts are almost always preferred by audit committees, it is a preference that displays a certain naivety. What is not significant is the cost of a contract at the outset but at the conclusion—and it can reasonably be expected that there will be a significant variance between these figures. When agents contract competitively they do so to offer the lowest price estimate for completing a particular project. In such cases, as is well known by industry insiders, the contract is merely an opportunity for subsequent negotiation and bargaining about its interpretation, designed either to try and protect the integrity of the contractual agreements entered into, on the clients' side, or to disturb them mightily through the successful negotiation of variation orders in relation to the original contract, on the contracting agencies' side. Thus, in this perspective, the analysis shades into the contract as artifact approach: the artifact that is the contract is seen as something whose reality—its meaning—is never understandable in itself. It cannot be seen merely in the words and drawings in various documents but has to be seen in the uses to which those words and drawings are put.

The contract conceived as an indexical document approach makes a number of assumptions about the nature of the contractual setting. It assumes a competitive context for interpretation rather than a collaborative one; a context where agents will assume oppositional and conflictual states vis-à-vis the other agents' interpretations almost as a matter of course. The reason is evident: how the contract is interpreted after the formal document has been agreed and signed can have a significant effect on the profitability of the work associated with that contract. Indeed, some contracts will be entered into which, if they were strictly observed with respect to their terms, would almost certainly not make a contribution to profit. What was important was securing the contract, at whatever price, in order to make a contribution to covering fixed costs, in the anticipation of the agents engaged in contractual negotiation being able to exploit the essential indexicality of the contract to drive up the number of variations, and thus charge a premium from which profit will be secured.

Alliancing as an approach to contract

In recent years there has been increasing recourse to more innovative models of contract in construction. These models are a long way from traditional competitive hard money contracts and much closer to the form of contracting studied elsewhere as relational-based alliancing contracts (Clegg et al. 2002; Pitsis et al. 2003). In this chapter alliancing is the object of discussion as a relatively new contractual form of control (it had been used in the oil industry since the early 1990s); it is one in which control shifts from being something that is externally imposed on the actors in an arena in an attempt to achieve compliance with the contract as an a priori of organizational behavior—which, experience suggests, is often an activity doomed to disappointment (Clegg 1975)—to something that the actors impose on themselves. In doing so they build a collective commitment to the non-contractual element of contracts, a commitment that they project into trust relations that they use to govern themselves, the contract, and the project organization, through a framework of normative control. To explicate the argument we draw on a specific case study of the form of contract known as "alliancing."

We define alliancing as the coming together of two or more organizations to share risks and rewards, pool resources, provide and share expertise and knowledge in order to complete a project (Pitsis, Kornberger, and Clegg 2004). In the case referred to in this chapter, we are focusing on an alliance mega-project, a mega-project being a large-scale, complex, and costly project usually delivered as a public–private partnership (van Marrewijk et al. 2008). In alliancing, as we shall see, rather than the contract being used to police the emergence of actualities in a punitive mode, the alliance becomes an arena in which the contracting parties learn to regard each other's actions and engagements critically but constructively: the alliance functions as a synoptical power mechanism in which each watches the other for cues as to the normativization of conduct.

Alliances are often used as a strategic tool to gain efficiency and flexibility when rapid change is required (Westley and Vredenburg 1991: 66) because they can establish "[a] process through which parties who see different aspects of a problem can constructively explore their differences and search for solutions that go beyond their own limited vision of what is possible." Typically, inter-organizational collaboration is established by the lead organization to spread risk and responsibility, as well as to pool resources (Josserand and Pitsis 2007; Clegg 2005; Pitsis, Kornberger, and Clegg 2004; Pitsis et al. 2003; Clegg et al. 2002), both of which were the case in the Alliance Program we researched.

A CASE OF ALLIANCING

We explore material drawn from research into a large Australian Alliance Program. This Alliance Program is a public–private partnership with an estimated duration of eight years and an AUD$383 million target cost. The alliance consists of five organizations: the public sector client and four large international engineering and consultant companies, each with their designated field of expertise. These five organizations all contributed personnel, experience, contacts, and ideas to the contracted construction processes. Initially the alliance was designed to last for five projects; together they have however operated as a unique organizational entity and collaboratively landed additional projects. The Alliance Leadership Team consists of top management team members from each of the parent companies involved. These team members all have decision-making power on behalf of their companies. The Alliance Leadership Team is the formal decision-making organ of the Alliance. It is the work of this group that we have followed since their inception in 2002.

We used a number of rich ethnographic tools in collecting empirical material for this research. The main source of empirical material is participatory observation. From 2002 up to and including May 2007 one or more researchers sat in on and observed all the Leadership Team's monthly meetings, and we have been engaged in further but less intensive research with the project subsequently. In addition, a range of informal meetings and discussions with Alliance Leadership members prior to and after the scheduled meetings occurred; also we have conducted three workshops with the Leadership Team, in which ongoing findings have been presented and discussed. We have also conducted twenty-four semi-structured interviews of between one and two hours' length. Follow-up email interviews have also been performed with the Leadership Team members.

The majority of the interviews were performed by two researchers, in order to provide a better basis for critical reflection in the interpretive phases of the research. The researchers also visited all the current and past construction schemes in conjunction with the Alliance Leadership Team meetings. The researchers made all their field notes from these formal and informal meetings available to each other. In addition, large samples of secondary data, such as the initial program contract, financial reports, managerial reports, official media and alliance documents, and policy documents were collected. Archival material, such as documents tracing the evolution of (formal) vision, mission, values and commitments, the key performance indicators (KPIs) and key responsibility areas (KRAs), as well as the bimonthly reports from the AMT to the ALT (on all program developments such as economy, design, construction, environment, safety, community communication), were also studied.

The alliance has achieved exemplary results, even when compared to almost all other projects conducted by each of the parent organizations. On a number of schemes they have come in under budget, under schedule, and have contributed significant innovations both in managerial practices, but also in work methods and approaches. For much of the time, the alliance operated under conditions of great uncertainty and ambiguity and complexities; not only in terms of engineering, geotechnical specifications, difficult geographic terrain, and a significant shortage of talent due to engineering expertise being in high demand in the mining industry elsewhere in Australia due to a booming world economy but also in terms of the political dimensions of uncertain funding from government, the uncertainty of approval of future projects, and the initially self-inflicted and extremely complex and over-designed set of key performance indicators.

THE ANALYSIS

Our original research inquiry was into how learning occurred across the different schemes in the alliance program; however, through the process of analyzing the empirical material collaboration practices that to us were marked by a difference from traditional design and construct projects were impossible to overlook. We are only ever able to observe practices against the background of our own expectations. In this particular case, this was the background of what the interviewees as well as the researchers both took to be "normal" construction management. In the interviews we were frequently told that this project "is not like ordinary construction projects," a phrase that was often used when explaining the work practices of the Alliance Leadership team (for more detail on the Alliance Leadership Team practice see Bjørkeng, Clegg, and Pitsis 2009).

The material presented in this chapter grew out of a narrative analysis (Riessman 2002) of our empirical material. We attended to narratives differentiating the alliance practice from traditional design and construct practices. This includes the narratives presented in interviews and narratives told and retold in real-time retrospective sense-making processes (Weick 1995) in Alliance Leadership Team meetings as well as prospective future perfect stories guiding action (Pitsis et al. 2003). In addition, the researchers' own narratives of competitive control in traditional construction practice, as well as known theoretical contributions in this field, have guided our attention to the particular narratives of deviation presented here.

The most salient narratives of deviations from more traditional design and construct contracts were told in terms of, first, the relations between the contracting parties; second, the handling of variations and incidents; third, the negotiating of monetary apportionment and innovation; and fourth, the idea work performed. The new modes of control practiced in and by this alliance leadership we have labeled synoptical control, contrasting this with the more traditional panoptical control.

In the following we will explore examples of each of these deviations and discuss the patterns of collaborative (project) control that rise from these. The emergent practice of synoptical control consists of ALT members looking at the other ALT members in order to affirm their conformance of approach in the ways in which they conceive of appropriate project practice (see Clegg and Baumeler forthcoming). In Mathiesen's (1997) terms, they are engaged in observing these significant others as exemplars with the intention of emulating them. Instead of policing the boundaries of autonomy the maintenance of patterned behavior is now less subject to external management and more an act of "choice." By contrast, panoptical control is premised on policing the project and using the contract as a major mechanism for doing so. Relations on the site are premised on extensive surveillance of laborers, contractors, and sub-contractors. What is done is premised on what is represented as having to be done in the contractual documentation.

If, in competitively tendered contracts, politics are oriented towards seeking to impose a particular disciplinary reading of the contractual documents, such as the architects over the project managers, the engineering sub-contractors over the project managers, and so on, policing the contract and the site to ensure conformance, under alliancing the politics shift from being largely disciplinary, inter-organizational, and contestable to a more positive mode. What is crucial to alliancing and its delivery is the power of the norm "and the particular way in which knowledge that revolves around the virtual—instead of actual facts—is produced" (Macmillan 2009: 158). These virtual facts are produced through key performance indicators which create "a field of objects on which power will be able to intervene in order to control production" (Macmillan 2009: 158). Key performance indicators construct

Table 17.1 Contrasting modes of control

Observations from the Mega-alliance	Explanatory construct: Synoptical control	Traditional theories and practices: Panoptical control
Relation between the contracting parties	**"Autopoietic ideal we"**	**Loosely connected self-interested actors**
• The managers constantly refer to a common "we"	• Authoring a shared indexicality	• Distinct organizations contracted to collaborate through a construction process
• It is hard to distinguish who represents which company	• Creating a collective we acting on behalf of the alliance not the individual partners	• Projects last as long as the contract
• The ALT (re)creates tasks and relations for as long as possible, because they can do so	• The alliance has developed a contextual rationality in which the collaboration is reason in itself to continue collaborative work	• Relations between actors are subject to contractual surveillance and disciplinary control
Handling variations and incidents:	**Collective relief and enacting benevolence:**	**Blame game:**
• Failure is toned down	• Letting go of the idea that everything can be controlled and thus explained	• Using contract to renegotiate terms governing relations
• Explanations are given in terms of a "deus ex machina"	• Actors are relieved of the necessity for retrospective causal analysis	• Distributing blame and costs through formal mechanisms
• Causes are often undetermined, responsibilities are shared, and consequently there is no allocation of costs/ blame	• The propensity to learn from mistakes is minimized	• Mistakes are costly; variations are resolved through open conflict and, if necessary, lawyers
• Unanticipated costs are not fought but collectively accepted	• Cost control is potentially compromised by goodwill	• Exploiting additional costs in the project is the dominant mode of project management rationality
Innovation and idea work:	**Open source innovation:**	**Protected IP:**
• Co-created and background IP encouraged between partners but potential competitors excluded from access to knowledge	• Shared encouragement of open innovation	• Protectionism and tight control of background IP

specific forms of knowledge as a strategic ideal: if performance on a project always accorded with the strategic ideal the project would always rate 100 percent on any performance indicator. Rarely will this be the case, however. The point of the performance norms is to create virtual objects around which reality can be related normatively, in terms of the distribution of outcomes according to measures that can be represented in terms of means and standard distributions around the virtual norm. What the key performance indicators do is to construct a series of virtual realities represented in the norms that actually are recorded around those measures constructed. The measures construct the environment of the project, one in which community, safety, or environment, as well as costs and schedule, can be talked into being. They take on a life independent of the project through their projection and measurement of behavior in accord with these projections. The point is not to make behaviors accord with some pre-established norm, such as those that might be specified in a quantity survey, but to start from the given state of affairs in the project as seen through the key performance indicators. These constitute the norms as the average of the performance measured. Such a politics of power does not require exhaustive and continuous control of the particulars of the project in its minute execution. On the contrary, all that is required is the registering of an actual range of performances, its inspection in terms of the norms established, and the communication of these norms to those whose performance is being regulated so that they may maintain the targets or try harder, as the case may be. Aligning the final project averages with a "risk and reward" scheme in which all parties to the contract are implicated does the rest: there is an evident self-interest in registering outstanding performances across the board. To ensure that this is the case the specific key performance indicators are made non-negotiable with each other: each establishes its own norm and it is only outstanding performance across all norms that will generate rewards. The regulation of behavior is thus achieved by normativization.

"Autopoietic Ideal We"

In the Alliance Leadership Team practice we find the discourse and practice of a well-developed collaborating collective. Most notably the ALT is recognized by a strong collective voice unheard of in traditional contracts. In addition the ALT works not just because the contract and its completion binds their work together but because they seem to enjoy the fact that they are collaborating, and continue to do so simply because they can. We have labeled this mode of work the "Autopoietic Ideal We," and we will next present some examples of this way of collaborating.

In a late stage of observation of the ALT meetings, a new Alliance Leadership Team (ALT) participant, from one of the contracted engineering companies, was

introduced to the group. The alliance procedures were discussed and the ALT's decision-making mode was reiterated—that all decisions should be unanimous. The
new ALT participant challenged the "decision" that no decisions should be made
unless they were made unanimously. The rest of the participants looked at him in a
stunned way, clearly indicating that this was an awkward question, almost blasphe-
mous. Here was a clear example of clash of practices and the response by the ALT
was fascinating and remarkable. In response to such a "naive" observation regarding
unanimity, one of the ALT members said: "This is what alliancing is! That's part of
alliancing." The "stranger" to the alliance's practice asked: "Don't you mean consensus? [rather than unanimity]," only to have someone else say: "We may discuss it till
we find consensus, but we have no decisions at the [ALT] unless they are unanimous!" The stranger looked utterly stunned. All the others nodded in agreement
with the experienced team member.

Such an emphasis on unanimity certainly does not find a parallel in the normal
design and construct contract that the stranger, the new ALT participant, was used
to. More importantly nor does it seem to us to find a parallel in any traditional
organizational leadership team: consensus perhaps, but not total unanimity. One of
the key phenomenologically agreed contours of sense-making of the ALT seems to
be that they should govern democratically, by unanimous decision. Interestingly,
without any intellectual knowledge of Habermas's (1972) "ideal speech situation" or
Rawls's (1971) "original position," the leadership team seemingly strove to achieve
something close to these models. The common building block in this and other
events was the repeated reference (in speech and other acts) to the alliance "we,"
That this was the case should not be too surprising, considering that the Alliance
Leadership Team defined itself as negotiating such a collective "we" on behalf of a
set of independent organizations. What is surprising though, and contributes to our
interpretation of the "ideal we" as (part of) the collective practicing of the Alliance
Leadership Team, is that it was not possible to discern which organizations the alliance members came from, and more importantly on whose behalf they were talking
and whom they were representing.

The reality of the Alliance Leadership Team is thoroughly assumed by its long-
standing members. The ALT members seem to be always talking on behalf of the
Leadership Team. Interestingly, one of the researchers joined the project in the later
stages of the alliance and it was literally impossible for her to distinguish between
members of the parent companies of the different members of the Leadership Team.
Indeed, two separate consulting firms that worked with the alliance on different aspects
of the project, during informal discussion that we had with them relayed the same
observations to us; one consultant said, "I can't tell who is with what company".

In addition, there is a remarkably continuous narrative in the instantiations of
the ALT's "we" characterized by the relative lack of antagonist voices in the ALT
meetings. The content that constitutes this particular "we" seems to be authored as
ideal, flawless. The practice of identification, the narrating of identity found in

their forecasting and rationalizing of their practices, all seem to be reified in an idealizing manner. While the events retailed above can be said to construct and be constructed by the conception of an "ideal we," at the same time, the "ideal we" could not exist without "the other" that defines it as such. The other is constructed by the ALT members when they are accounting for and contrasting their ALT practice with other construction projects of which they have been or are a part, and also by us, the researchers, with the contrast in practice and with theory, stunning in its difference.

We suggest that these practitioners are authoring a collective "we" as they are performing arrays of activities that are simultaneously identifying them with, and distinguishing them from, "the other," and that the particular variation of authoring collectivity (Carlsen 2006; Carlsen and Pitsis 2009) that we find in the ALT is repeated as an ideal "we." While the identity of the other, opposition to which constitutes the "we," is not immediately clear, any other project constructed on normal design-and-construct lines can be seen to fall into this category. Such an interpretation presents itself by constant individual projection of the here-and-now in an alliance as necessarily differing from the background of a traditional design-and-construct project, where the construction management practice's identity is interpreted through the idea of "the irresponsible other," and through discussions on how to distribute costs that occur due to construction variations. Such contrasting work was performed both explicitly and implicitly by the ALT members and by other interviewees.

Another remarkable feature of this "ideal we" is the autopoietic character of the collaboration. Initially the Alliance Program contract was designed to guide the collaboration through five mega-projects. At present the Alliance Program has taken on seven mega-projects, and the ALT is continuously discussing how the alliance can attain more collaborative work and is actively pursuing such opportunities. What is particularly interesting is that the ALT members spend more time on these alliancing projects than on equivalent size and larger design-and-construct projects; the direct monetary profit is less with respect to labor invested; the risk is relatively large, and the reward structure unclear. Interestingly, there is no immediately present narrating of reasons for continuing the collaboration; it seems to be a taken-for-granted datum that the program is the best advertisement for the collaboration. Only when pushed on the issue do the participants provide stories cast in terms of the collective effort that has been put in to obtain the level of collaboration that the ALT is now experiencing, as well as stressing the potential benefits from continuing collaboration. "It takes time to get the trust, the relations and the ease of collaboration that is necessary to get the alliance going; finally we can really reap rewards." We suggest that the ALT is authoring a shared indexicality rather than one that is combative and conflictual. Creating a collective we, acting on behalf of the alliance, not the collaborating parties, the alliance has developed a contextual rationality in which the collaboration is a reason in itself to continue collaborative work. There is a sense in which the opportunities for more positive and less dog-eat-dog relations in the project become an enjoyable end in themselves rather than merely a means to the ends of making money, completing projects, and fulfilling contracts.

In the Alliance Leadership Team practice we find a well-developed discourse and practice of a collaborating collective. Most notably the ALT is recognizable by its strong collective voice, one almost unheard of in more traditional contracts. In addition the ALT works as if it is not the contract, and time-limited projects, that bind their work together; rather it sometimes seems as if they are collaborating, and continue to do so, simply because they can. We have labeled this mode of work the Autopoietic Ideal We, and will present some examples of this way of collaborating.

COLLECTIVE RELIEF AND ENACTING
BENEVOLENCE

In the work of the ALT we see that reported incidents, failures, and potential variations are toned down. Traditional design and construct projects are always disposed to a "blame game" in which there are amendments of contracts, distribution of blame and costs, and negotiations of payments for additional tasks. By contrast, the ALT provides explanations constructed in terms of a "deus ex machina." The causes of failure often remain undetermined, are often explained as indeterminable, because responsibility is shared so that there is no consequent distribution of costs/blame. We suggest that letting go of the idea that everything can be controlled—thus must be explained—gives relief with respect to the necessity of retrospective causal analysis. However, it may also lead to the loss of potentially strong learning situations.

Let us provide you with a narrative that occurred around establishing the truth in relation to a potentially costly incident. The construction projects of the Alliance Program are geographically dispersed across Sydney in some of the most rugged and environmentally sensitive terrain of the Sydney basin and hinterland. Some schemes are over 120 kilometers away from the Alliance Program headquarters, which is situated in the Central Business District of Sydney. All the projects in the Alliance Program cannot help but be highly intrusive for the local communities in which they are performed.

Five days before one of the Leadership Team meetings the expected breakthrough from the boring of a new waste-water tunnel into existing water lines occurred. The expected breakthrough saw some unexpected events unfold. In Sydney, in some areas, water from waste-water lines is sent into a cleaning system and becomes part of the city's drinking water. Potential contamination of drinking water is thus a serious issue. In Sydney water has recently been a critically scarce resource with the city undergoing a formally declared drought for several years in a row, with the main dam's holding capacity being down at less than 30 percent at the time this event occurred. Two days after the breakthrough, it was noticed that the downstream washbasins into which drinking water was discharging were discolored. As the ALT meeting commenced, tests were taken from the basin, the waterlines, as well as the newly bored tunnel, in order to investigate where the source of contamination occurred. Due to the proximity in time, and the location of the breakthrough point in relation to the washbasins, the breakthrough was evaluated as the cause of the contamination.

One important question remained, however: how did this contamination happen? Especially given that in order to prevent contamination in the first place the bore hole had been flushed seven times, well beyond expected industry standards. The ALT discussed the investigation of the incident, and three potential explanations were brought to bear. First, given the density of the sandstone, the clay in the bore hole might have been different from that assumed, and thus the calculations on the amount of cleaning wrong. As samples of the clay consistent with the calculations were taken this explanation was dismissed. It was then suggested that the bottom of the hole might not have been flushed well enough, even though it was done beyond industry standards. The suggestion was made that samples of clean water that came up from the bore hole prior to the breakthrough did not include samples from the very end of the bore hole, an explanation that was not dismissed. It was also suggested that the flow of the breakthrough itself had such force that it cleaned the waterlines downstream. In other words: prior to the breakthrough the waterlines were very dirty and thus the contamination could not be blamed on the alliance's work, and consequently not on the Leadership Team, because it was an existing contamination that had been flushed by the breakthrough water. Several doubts were raised about this explanation, the most important being that any big storm produces the same amount of flushing as the breakthrough would produce—if this flush was enough to clean the lines, they would already have been clean. Of the three theories, the third became the official "history" of the events unfolding, despite the fact that all discussion seemed to be in favor of the second explanation, rather than the third.

One could argue that any contracting collaboration would try to minimize their responsibility in the face of environmental contamination. However, two of the participants in the ALT are managers from the Public Service Provider that is also the Alliance Program contractor, which will be left with this responsibility regardless of any explanation favored by the ALT. In a competitive design-and-construct contract, a management meeting discussing contingencies on a large construction site would be charged by one question: Who is going to pay for this mistake? When such an event occurs, expectations are that sides will be taken, positions assumed, antagonisms expressed, and responsibilities promoted and denied. Not in this Leadership Team.

During the particular meeting above none of the participants' involvement in the discourse strayed far from the narrative accounts of the other members: "We cleaned it better than industry standards," "we really did everything right," "we have excellent environmental ratings"; "we properly cleaned those water pipes." There is an insistence on the competence of the alliance, a translation and interpretation of events unfolding so that they fit the authoring collective. The shared reward system could to some extent explain this repeated practice. However, the Public Service Provider was also a contractor and stood to lose, economically and in terms of public relations, from the story of the event unfolding. Indeed, for the Public Service Provider, contamination would have major ramifications because, several years earlier, but still etched in most people's memories, a Sydney-wide water contamination of giardia and cryptosporidium occurred. For a week households had to boil all water that was to be used for drinking, cooking, and cleaning dishes. Politically, another contamination of any sort would be very serious for the client.

One of the main *raisons d'être* for establishing the ALT as an organizational super-structure over the seven projects was to instigate learning possibilities in and between these projects, a goal that we saw as being potentially thwarted by the unfolding of the "ideal we." The unanticipated consequence of the *ideal we*, when it is interrupted by such events as above, may be an inability to learn from those events. One may say that the "ideal we" functions as such a strong central value system that its reproduction as such in and through the ALT makes registering the meaning of untoward events as learning opportunities difficult (see Clegg et al. 2002). It seems as if the collective interpretation of events makes them fit the shared understanding of themselves as competent (yes, even ideal) practitioners, as opposed to negotiating what it takes for practitioners to act competently.

As we thought about what it was that the ALT did that most frequently departed from traditional construction processes, we recognized that the ALT's relative lack of conflict was a breach with a more or less unspoken norm of construction practices. There was conflict, and sometimes quite serious conflict, but what was different was that the parties would work through the conflict without the need to resort to costly and damaging legal solutions. Alliances such as this are generally held to have many fewer variations because they are formed around a trust-based, psychological contract that reflects that planning and design is based on uncertainty and that much of the construction process will involve improvisation and adaptation to constant surprises. In traditional construction projects, where the contract is based on price, variations are made in order to maximize profit by extending the gap between quoted and actual costs (Pitsis, Kornberger, and Clegg 2004; Pitsis et al. 2003). In many ways what we see in the ALT is what in the behavioral science literature is referred to as "group-think." In this case such group-think functioned to escalate commitment to the "ideal we" (Clegg, Kornberger, and Pitsis 2008; Pitsis et al. 2003; Clegg et al. 2002) rather than registering that a problematic situation had occurred (Dewey 1934). The accepted account offered as an interpretation of the contamination of the water lines did nothing to prevent the same events from occurring again. Despite the changes in alliance configuration, despite a change of participants in the Leadership Team, despite the proclaimed learning goals, the of antagonistic voices being raised about critical issues was a repeated phenomenon in the ALT meetings; however, it is appropriate to ask how this course of action affects the totality of the project compared with a traditional contract of competitive control: Would a blame game lead to any more learning?

In traditional design-and-construct projects, monetary apportionment is settled through contract, and negotiated through variations and amendments to contract. If necessary disagreements are solved through open conflict, and regulated by contract and legal battles. In the ALT, however, we have observed how the monetary apportionments are the subject of continuous negotiation, these negotiations are based on an idea of earnings as explicitly uneven: the contractual parties are to get paid "as if" their employees were invoicing in a normal design-and-construct project and any additional rewards and costs are distributed amongst the parties as the projects concludes. The "as if" clause makes the contract inherently unclear, as it implies that the contract conditions change as the individual participants change their internal reward structures.

Given that alliances are trust-based psychological contracts, decisions, such as variations, are often taken at face value. There are, however, events one would expect to challenge these conditions. We will present one such event as an example of consistent practicing, reasoning, and sense-making in the ALT. As the ALT was going through the deviances between budget and cost structure, Private Company B informed the ALT that they had sent an invoice for bonuses to their employees. In the initial alliance contract it was agreed that employee bonuses that were paid based on the different companies' overall, non-alliance-related performance should not be part of the cost structure. The alliance was to be invoiced for work performed by members of all organizations and all expenses would be covered. The claim from Private Company B was backdated and concerned three years of bonuses. If the payment had been accrued it would not have been a cost to the Alliance Program but if it is paid on the invoice tendered it will be a cost and will be charged to the alliance. The potential cost to the alliance is large and will affect the overall Alliance Program performance.

In the first meeting at which this topic was discussed, no decision was taken. The ALT's concern was whether the specific type of bonuses of Private Company B should be considered as bonuses or real costs. The issue was referred to financial expertise to provide the ALT with advice. The financial advisers informed the ALT that, given the cost structure in Private Company B and the history of the invoicing, it would be equally justifiable to accept the invoice as to not accept it. The topic was on the ALT agenda for several months without being discussed, and when a decision was made, the item was not discussed but simply raised as an inquiry that "maybe we should pay that invoice from Private Company B?" The suggestion received confirmative nods around the table. Private Company B coincidentally did not feature in this particular ALT meeting where the invoice was affirmed.

een this action and that which one would expect from tradi-
l panoptically controlled projects is stunning, as is the differ-
l theory. Cost control is central to profitability in more
:tion contracts and the modes of rationality that we find in
:nted to the dominance of profit as an icon. While we do not
rganizing and strategizing that bear the blueprint of modern-
1965; Chandler 1962; Porter 1980, 1990, 1996), and would see
ing into a stream of thought that can be characterized as more
reflexive and critical (Mintzberg 1987; Pettigrew 1979, 1985; Pettigrew and Whipp
1991), we nevertheless expected the management team to make strategic decisions
strategically, and more importantly, seeing the participants came from a range of
organizations, with different stakes, we did expect decisions of monetary apportionment to be made in favor of the alliance, or at least in favor of the majority of
stakeholders. After all, strategic management is increasingly understood as *the* task
of the top management team, and has achieved a status that is almost talismanic in
importance (e.g. Clegg, Carter, and Kornberger 2004; Carter, Clegg, and Kornberger
2008), but in the ALT this was not the case.

OPEN SOURCE INNOVATION

When several organizations come together they do so with different organizational
cultures, values, intentions, knowledge, skills, and capabilities. These differences are
especially pronounced in public–private partnerships where the conflict and tensions between public value and private value are inherent. While one could predict
with validity that these organizational differences can be the source of potential
conflict, it is just as valid to argue that these organizational differences can lead to
significant innovations not only in terms of the intended outcomes (i.e. products,
services, infrastructure), but also in terms of organization and management innovation by way of innovations in systems, processes, and practices organizational
wide (Mol and Birkinshaw 2008; Bjørkeng, Clegg, and Pitsis 2009).

Traditional contracts are underpinned by a strong protectionism. Often organizations are clear about the protection of their background intellectual property (IP),
and while value created within projects is often shared, its use and application typically lie with the most powerful parties, who benefit most from innovations generated in projects. Indeed, more powerful organizations also have the best legal advice
and legal teams working on IP agreements. In the alliance, all project-related innovation was shared between the partner organizations. One innovation co-created by
the alliance but now used by many of the parent organizations was the use of infra-
red pipe location devices. Typically, sub-contractors on projects are responsible for

locating pipes prior to the start of digging and drilling work. On most sites what is concealed beneath the ground is not always known. Indicative maps are often wrong and incomplete; pipes laid by other services are often found where they are not expected. Whatever pipes may be present vary in size, length, and material and are often very difficult to locate. On the alliance there were occasions where pipes were damaged or destroyed, thus causing potential problems in meeting targets for all of schedule, cost, community, and the ecology. To get round the problem of incomplete knowledge of existing pipe works the alliance modified a radar device that was almost foolproof in locating pipe works and thus eliminating costly damage and destruction. As indicated by the program manager, "this is an innovation created by us, for us, and anyone can use it…there are many examples of our innovations like the pressure pumping system" (July 13, 2009). Other innovations included trenchless drilling technologies that meant no disruption to roads and streets, as well as developing a world best practice in reducing the creation of extremely dangerous dust particles during construction works, just to name a few innovations.

Work practices and processes were also innovated as a result of the alliance. The most telling sign of innovation in work practices was discovered serendipitously when Tyrone was chatting informally with three staff members during a break in a post-execution review workshop in which Tyrone and Stewart participated. One staff member was from the public organization and two were from the private partners. All three claimed that they had found their learning on the alliance had been unparalleled (two staff members were quite junior, but one was more senior), and one claimed that "I do things very differently now," and then she said, "I don't think I'll be able to go back to what I used to do," a sentiment with which the other two staff members vigorously agreed. Such statements are not unique to this alliance as we have heard identical sentiments on other alliance projects (Pitsis et al. 2003; Clegg et al. 2002). Innovation in practice occurs as actors engage in work that is uncertain, risky, and demanding yet conducted in close collaboration with talented, knowledgeable, and able colleagues whose experiences of different practices, processes, and cultures extends what individuals bring to the project. Indeed, the newness of relations cannot be underestimated in creating positive work experience, as illustrated by one employee: "I suppose it's that I work closely with people I don't usually get to see, and you work on problems with an attitude of not thinking 'oh look we can't do that because of this and that,' but more 'how can we get this done.'"

The alliance provides an innovative way for private industry to meet its corporate social responsibility (both as a legal requirement and also in a marketing sense), and it enabled the public organization to operate in more efficient and streamlined ways that bypassed its historically bureaucratically heavy approach (see Bjørkeng, Clegg, and Pitsis, 2009; Carlsen and Pitsis 2009). Where there is innovation in practice there is also resistance, however. The "openness" to innovation of the alliance was not always experienced as positive within the client organization's more traditional bureaucratic enclaves. Indeed, for many within the client organization the alliance represented an "opportunity for private industry to write its own checks." The core innovations developed in the alliance were seen by some within the client organization but outside the ALT as having been actually already developed by the client organization, with the implication being that the private sector partners were innovation free-riders. More importantly, despite all the innovations in practice and process, despite meeting and exceeding all the key performance indicators on some of the largest projects, the alliance continues to face stiff opposition, even at the highest levels of the client organization. The question is: Alliances are innovative and they innovate, but do these innovations matter?

There is a fundamental challenge for alliance partnerships that no contract—be it economic, legal, or even relational—can adequately handle and it concerns the question of perceived value. Perceptions, experiences, expectations, and assumptions concerning alliances remain contested spaces because the *ideal we* that the alliance generates does not control external perceptions of the alliance.

The perceived value of innovation is constituted by the eye of the beholder. The value of organizational innovation in an alliance has to be externally legitimized by the embedding organizations; hence, a key organizational and managerial innovation required in alliance contract relations is the ability and capability to define, determine, drive, and disseminate the value of the project-related innovations beyond the boundaries of the alliance. That is, if the innovative value created is not deemed as necessary by the organizations in which the alliance partners are embedded then no amount of innovation beyond the explicitly stated and agreed upon project objectives will be valued. In the public–private partnerships described in this chapter, the ability to create and innovate value that "matters" was crucial for securing future projects. The problem is in knowing what matters and what does not matter to the client. While this is a simple question it is one that is extremely difficult to answer because the alliance's rhetoric about what matters does not necessarily match the reality of what matters for the home organizations. Organizations involved in alliance projects have an opportunity to be highly innovative, but if the innovations are not what the client organization believes that it needs or values, should the alliance cease trying to create such innovations? The trick is to know what matters to the client and demonstrating its achievement.

THE CLOSE-OUT

Projects, especially those that are predominately relationally rather than legally contractual, can promote positive, innovative, and generative outcomes for both individuals and organizations (see Carlsen and Pitsis 2009, 2008). A traditional design-and-construct contract is almost inimical to innovation by definition—because innovation means variation. While traditional contracts seek to use the panoptical basis associated with design and construct to cancel variation explicitly, implicitly they create considerable innovativeness in how to interpret and read contractual documents so that their interpretation is to the advantage of organizational self-interest. Of course, with all contracting actors engaged in these kinds of zero-sum power games the reality of much project experience is psychologically wearing, emotionally tense, and organizationally expensive. Hence, it is not surprising that the ALT, in its *ideal we*, sees such value in doing things in the ways that they have developed and that the members are so committed to these ways of managing. The orientation of the ALT is towards normativization of conduct rather than its disciplinization through the mechanism of the contract, its indexical exploitation, and associated systems of surveillance. The risk in such a collective orientation to normative behavior is that the collective become so wrapped up in the emotional value of the approach that the practical value to external agencies and partners is neglected. Especially this will be the case where what is being pioneered and innovated seems to fly in the face of the dominant institutional logics of the age, those icons of competition and cost control that are wrapped up in the competitively tendered contract. It is important to realize that the ALT is an experiment in becoming. While some elements of its work were quite traditionally panoptical in power terms where they were exercising oversight of the project implementation and seeking to ensure that its practice met the expectations that they held for it, there was a sense in which they were also innovating a new mode of power relations where they sought not so much to govern subordinate others as themselves and the other selves that formed the ALT. New forms of governmentality were being forged (Clegg et al. 2002). We said much earlier in the chapter that the ALT have been engaged in observing themselves as significant exemplars making innovative "choices." But acts of choice have to be rationalized externally. At the time of writing the biggest challenge that the alliance faces is that of establishing that its new disciplines of power both deliver value and that the value established is clearly understood outside the collective by key stakeholders.

ACKNOWLEDGEMENTS

We would like to acknowledge the kind sponsorship of the Australian Research Council through the ARC Linkage Project grant (project number LP0348816). We also acknowledge the contribution and involvement of our industry partners; their openness and honesty throughout the research project have been an exemplary basis for research collaboration.

REFERENCES

ALTHUSSER, L. (1969). *For Marx.* London: Allen Lane.

ANSOFF, H. I. (1965). *Corporate Strategy.* Harmondsworth: Penguin.

ANTONACOPOULOU, E. (2007). "Practice," in S. R. Clegg and J. R. Bailey, *The Sage International Encyclopaedia of Organization Studies.* Thousand Oaks, CA: Sage.

BARNES, B. (2001). "Practices as collective action," in T. R. Schatzki, K. Knorr Cetina, and E. Von Savigny (eds.), *The Practice Turn in Contemporary Theory.* London: Routledge.

BJØRKENG, K. (2000). *Dualism: A Metaphysical Necessity or a Conceivable Impossibility?* Oslo: UiO Press.

——CLEGG, S. R., and PITSIS, T. (2009). "Becoming a practice," *Management Learning,* 40: 145–59.

BLACKMORE, S. J. (1999). *The Meme Machine.* Oxford: Oxford University Press.

BOROFSKY, R. (1994). "On the knowledge and knowing of cultural activities," in R. Borofsky (ed.), *Assessing Cultural Anthropology.* New York: McGraw Hill Inc.

BOWKER, G., and STAR, S. L. (1999). *Sorting Things Out: Classification and its Consequences.* Cambridge, MA: MIT Press.

BRUNSSON, N. (2002). *The Organization of Hypocrisy: Talk, Decisions and Actions in Organizations.* Stockholm: Abstrakt forlag AS.

CARLSEN, A. (2006). "Organizational becoming as dialogic imagination of practice: the case of the indomitable Gauls," *Organization Science,* 17/1: 132–49.

——and PITSIS, T. S. (2008). "Projects for life: the narrative of positive organizational change," in S. R. Clegg and C. L. Cooper (eds.), *The Sage Handbook of Organizational Behavior.* Thousand Oaks, CA: Sage.

————(2009). "Experiencing hope in organizational life," in *Exploring Positive Identities and Organizations: Building a Theoretical and Research Foundation.* New York: Psychology Press.

CARTER, C., CLEGG, S. R., and KORNBERGER, M. (2008). *A Very Short, Fairly Interesting and Reasonably Cheap Book about Studying Strategy.* London: Sage.

CHANDLER, A. D. (1962). *Strategy and Structure. Chapters in the History of the American Industrial Enterprise.* Cambridge, MA: MIT Press.

CHARUE-DUBOC, F., and MIDLER, C. (1998). "Beyond advanced project management: renewing engineering practices and organizations," in R. A. Lundin and C. Midler (eds.), *Projects as Arenas for Renewal and Learning Processes.* Boston: Kluwer.

CLEGG, S. R. (1975). *Power, Rule and Domination.* London: Routledge and Kegan Paul.

——(1989). *Frameworks of Power.* London: Sage.

——(1995). "Weber and Foucault: social theory for the study of organizations," *Organization,* 1/1: 149–78.

——(2000). "Power and authority: resistance and legitimacy," in H. Goverde, P. G. Cerny, M. Haugaard, and H. Lentner (eds.), *Power in Contemporary Politics: Theories, Practice, Globalizations.* London: Sage, 77–92.

——(2005). "Talking construction into being," Inaugural Address at the Vrije Universiteit of Amsterdam, September 15.

——and BAUMLER, C. (forthcoming). "From iron cages to liquid modernity in organisation analysis," *Organization Studies.*

——Carter, C., and Kornberger, M. (2004). "Get up, I feel like being a strategy machine," *European Management Review*, 1/1: 21–8.

——Courpasson, D., and Phillips, N. (2006). *Power and Organizations*. Thousand Oaks, CA: Sage Foundations of Organization Science.

——Kornberger, M., and Pitsis, T. (2008). *Managing and Organizations*, 2nd edn. London: Sage.

—— —— ——(in press). *Managing and Organizations: An Introduction to Theory and Practice*, 3rd edn. London: Sage.

——Pitsis, T. S., Rura-Polley, T., and Marosszeky, M. (2002). "Governmentality matters: designing an alliance culture of inter-organizational collaboration for managing projects," *Organization Studies*, 23/3: 317–37.

Covaleski, M. A., Dirsmith, M. W., Heian, J. B., and Samuel, S. (1998). "The calculated and the avowed: techniques of discipline and struggle over identity in six big public accounting firms," *Administrative Science Quarterly*, 43/2: 293–327.

Dandekker, C. (1990). *Surveillance, Power and Modernity: Bureaucracy and Discipline from 1700 to the Present Day*. Cambridge: Cambridge University Press.

Dewey, J. (1934). *Art as Experience*. New York: The Berkeley Publishing Group.

Engstrom, Y., Puonti, A., and Seppanen, L. (2003). "Spatial and temporal expansion of the object as a challenge for reorganizing work," in D. Nicolini, S. Gherardi, and D. Yanow (eds.), *Knowing in Organizations: A Practice-Based Approach*. London: M. E. Sharpe.

Festinger, L. (1957). *A Theory of Cognitive Dissonance*. Stanford, CA: Stanford University Press.

Garfinkel, H. (1967). *Studies in Ethnomethodology*. Englewood Cliffs, NJ: Prentice Hall.

Gherardi, S. (1999). "Learning as problem-driven or learning in the face of mystery?," *Organization Studies*, 20/1: 101–23.

——and Nicolini, D. (2003). "To transfer is to transform: the circulation of safety knowledge," in D. Nicolini, S. Gherardi, and D. Yanow (eds.), *Knowing in Organizations: A Practice-Based Approach*. London: M. E. Sharpe.

Glasser, W. (1985). *Control Theory*. New York: HarperCollins.

Gomez, M.-L., Bouty, I., and Drucker-Godard, C. (2003). "Developing knowing in practice, behind the scene of haute cuisine," in D. Nicolini, S. Gherardi, and D. Yanow (eds.), *Knowing in Organizations: A Practice-Based Approach*. London: M. E. Sharpe.

Granovetter, M. (1985). "Economic action and social structure: the problem of embeddedness," *American Journal of Sociology*, 91/3: 481–510.

——(1992). "Problems of explanation in economic sociology," in N. Nohria and R. G. Eccles, *Networks and Organizations*. Boston: Harvard Business School Press.

Habermas, J. (1972). *Knowledge and Human Interests*. London: Heinemann.

Hardy, C., and Clegg, S. R. (1996). "Some dare call it power," in S. Clegg, C. Hardy, and W. Nord (eds.), *Handbook of Organization Studies*. London: Sage, 622–41.

Hobbes, T. (1651). *Leviathan*, ed. A. D. Lindsay. New York: Dutton, 1914.

Josserand, E., and Pitsis, T. S. (2007). "Inter-organizational collaborations and relationships," in S. R. Clegg and J. Bailey (eds.), *The International Encyclopaedia of Organization Studies*. New York: Sage.

Knights, D., and Vurdubakis, T. (1993) "Power, resistance and all that," in J. M. Jermier, D. Knights, and W. R. Nord (eds.) *Resistance and Power in Organizations*. London: Routledge, 167–98.

KORNBERGER, M., CLEGG, S. R., and RHODES, C. (2005). "Learning/becoming/organizing," *Organization*, 12/2: 147–67.

LAVE, J., and WENGER, E. (1991). *Situated Learning: Legitimate Peripheral Participation.* Cambridge: Cambridge University Press.

LUNDIN, R. A., and SÖDERHOLM, A. (1998). "Conceptualizing a projectified society: discussion of an eco-institutional approach to a theory on temporary organizations," in R. A. Lundin and C. Midler (eds.), *Projects as Arenas for Renewal and Learning Processes.*Boston: Kluwer Academic Publishers, 13–24.

MACMILLAN, A. (2009). "Foucault and the examination: a reading of 'Truth and judicial forms'," *Journal of Power*, 2/1: 155–72.

MACNEIL, I. R. (1980). *The New Social Contract: An Inquiry into Modern Contractual Relations.* New Haven: Yale University Press.

MACNEIL, J. (1974). "The many futures of contracts," *Southern California Law Review*, 47/3: 691–816.

MARKS, J. (2000). "Foucault, Franks, Gauls: il faut défendre la société: the 1976 lectures at the Collège de France," *Theory, Culture and Society*, 17/5: 127–47.

MATHIESEN, T.(1997). "The viewer society: Michel Foucault's panopticon revisited," *Theoretical Criminology*, 1: 215–34.

MINTZBERG, H. (1987). "The strategy concept I: Five Ps for strategy, and Strategy concept II: Another look at why organizations need strategies," *California Management Review*, 30/1: 11–32.

MOL, M., and BIRKINSHAW, J. (2008). *Giant Steps in Management: Innovations That Change the Way You Work.* Harlow: Pearson.

MUNRO, R. (2008). "Actor network theory," in S. R. Clegg and M. Haugaard (eds.), *Handbook of Power.* London: Sage (forthcoming).

NICOLINI, D., GHERARDI, S., and YANOW, D. (2003). "Introduction: toward a practice based view of knowing and learning in organizations," in D. Nicolini, S. Gherardi, and D. Yanow (eds.), *Knowing in Organizations: A Practice-Based Approach.* London: M. E. Sharpe.

OAKES, L. S., TOWNLEY, B., and COOPER, D. J. (1998). "Business planning as pedagogy: language and control in a changing institutional field," *Administrative Science Quarterly*, 43: 257–92.

PETTIGREW, A. M. (1979). "On studying organizational culture," *Administrative Science Quarterly*, 24: 570–81.

——(1985). *The Awakening Giant: Continuity and Change at ICI.* Oxford: Blackwell.

——and WHIPP, R. (1991). *Managing Change for Competitive Success.* Oxford: Blackwell.

PITSIS, T. S., KORNBERGER, M., and CLEGG, S. R. (2004). "The art of managing relationships in inter-organizational collaboration," *Management*, 7/3: 47–67.

——CLEGG, S. R., MAROSSZEKY, M., and RURA-POLLEY, T. (2003). "Constructing the Olympic dream: a future perfect strategy of project management," *Organization Science*, 14/5: 574–90.

PODOLNY, J. M., and PAGE, K. L. (1998). "Network forms of organization," *Annual Review of Sociology*, 24: 101–16.

PORTER, M. E. (1980). *Competitive Positioning.* New York: The Free Press.

——(1990). *The Competitive Advantage of Nations.* New York: Free Press.

——(1996). "What Is Strategy?" *Harvard Business Review*, November–December.

POWELL, W. W. (1990). "Neither market nor hierarchy: network forms of organization," *Research in Organizational Behavior*, 12: 295–336.

RAWLS, J. (1971). *A Theory of Justice.* Cambridge, MA: Harvard University Press.

Riessman, C. K. (2002). "Narrative analysis," in A. M. Huberman and M. B. Miles (eds.), *The Qualitative Researcher's Companion*. Thousand Oaks, CA: Sage Publications, 217–70.

Schatzki, T. R. (2001). "Introduction: practice theory," in T. R. Schatzki, K. Knorr Cetina, and E. Von Savigny (eds.), *The Practice Turn in Contemporary Theory*. London: Routledge.

Schütz, A. (1967). *The Phenomenology of the Social World*, trans. G. Walsh and F. Lehnert. Evanston, IL: Northwestern University Press.

Sewell, G. (1998). "The discipline of teams: the control of team-based industrial work through electronic and peer surveillance," *Administrative Science Quarterly*, 43/2: 397–428.

——and Wilkinson, B. (1992). "Someone to watch over me: surveillance, discipline, and the just in time labour process," *Sociology*, 26/2: 271–89.

Suchman, L. (2003). "Organization alignment: the case of bridge building," in D. Nicolini, S. Gherardi, and D. Yanow (eds.), *Knowing in Organizations: A Practice-Based Approach*. London: M. E. Sharpe.

Tsoukas, H., and Chia, R. (2002). "On organizational becoming: rethinking organizational change," *Organization Science*, 13/5: 567–82.

Uzzi, B. (1996). "The sources and consequences of embeddedness for the economic performance of organizations: the network effect," *American Sociological Review*, 61/9: 674–98.

van Marrewijk, A., Clegg, S. R., Pitsis, T., and Veenswijk, M. (2008). "Managing public–private megaprojects: paradoxes, complexity and project design," *International Journal of Project Management*, 26: 591–600.

Weeks, J. (2004). *Unpopular Culture: The Ritual of Complaint in a British Bank*. Chicago: University of Chicago Press.

Weick, K. E. (1995). *Sensemaking*. Thousand Oaks, CA: Sage.

Wenger, E. (1998). *Communities of Practice: Learning, Meaning, and Identity*. Cambridge: Cambridge University Press.

Westley, F., and Vredenburg, H. (1991). "Strategic bridging: the collaboration between environmentalists and business in the marketing of green products," *Journal of Applied Behavioral Science*, 27/1: 65–90.

Williamson, O. E. (1975). *Markets and Hierarchies: Analysis and Antitrust Implications: A Study in the Economics of Internal Organization*. New York: Free Press.

——(1979). "Transaction cost economics: the governance of contractual relations," *Journal of Law and Economics*, 22/October: 233–61.

——(1985). *The Economic Institutions of Capitalism*. New York: Free Press.

——(1991). "Comparative economic organizations: the analysis of discrete structural alternatives," *Administrative Science Quarterly*, 36/June: 269–96.

——(2000). "The new institutional economics: taking stock, looking ahead," *Journal of Economic Literature*, 38/3: 595–613.

——(2002a). "The lens of contract: private ordering," *American Economic Review*, 92/May: 438–43.

——(2002b). "The theory of the firm as governance structure: from choice to contract," *Journal of Economic Perspective*, 16/Summer: 171–95.

——(2003)."Examining economic organization through the lens of contract," *Industrial and Corporate Change*, 12/4: 917–42.

Wittgenstein, L. (1953). *Philosophical Investigations*. Oxford: Blackwell.

Yanow, D. (2003). "Seeing organizational learning, a 'cultural' view," in D. Nicolini, S. Gherardi, and D. Yanow (eds.), *Knowing in Organizations: A Practice-Based Approach*. London: M. E. Sharpe.

CHAPTER 18

TRUST IN RELATIONAL CONTRACTING AND AS A CRITICAL ORGANIZATIONAL ATTRIBUTE

NUNO GIL

JEFFREY PINTO

HEDLEY SMYTH

INTRODUCTION

IN recent years, a considerable interest in and literature regarding relational contracting and trust have emerged in the project management field. Though there are distinct and important differences in the nature of these two phenomena, their central premises underscore an important movement in re-evaluating inter-organizational relationships (partnering, for example) that are so prevalent in modern projects. The motivations for undertaking such partnerships are varied and not within the milieu of this chapter; nevertheless, as the nature of relational contracting continues to be explored by a wide variety of project organizations, it would be helpful to understand the dynamics of inter-firm collaboration and its corollary focus, trust, particularly as a project governance mechanism and within project partnering arrangements.

A large and growing literature has pointed to the importance of trust as a critical component of project stakeholder management and as a facilitator of successful project outcomes (cf. Kadefors 2004). Trust here is defined as "a disposition or attitude concerning the willingness to rely upon the actions of another party, under circumstances of contractual and social obligations, with the potential for collaboration" (Edkins and Smyth 2006: 84). As a result, there exists a conviction that other parties will behave in line with a reasonable range of expectations, which are iteratively assessed so vulnerability is small at any time. This adds some nuance to Rousseau et al.'s (1998: 395)definition of trust as the willingness to be vulnerable, i.e. "the psychological state comprising the intention to accept vulnerability based upon positive expectation of the intentions or behaviors of another." (Distrust results when actual behavior falls outside a reasonable range of expectations.)

Underlying the research and theorizing that have emerged on trust is the notion that the management of inter-firm relationships in projects can recognize the value in relationship-building, eschewing the traditional contractual relationships which seek to identify and formalize the full spectrum of contracted services and obligations so as to act as a safety net in the face of distrust. This is not to argue that contracts are inherently wrong, though they may indeed sometimes contribute to project process inefficiencies through too-strict codification or application. A clear advantage of promoting trust and positive relationships in project partnerships lies in their desirability as an alternative to the transaction costs of monitoring and controlling, thereby making working relationships more efficient (see Chapter 17 by Clegg et al., this volume).

There is a critical challenge with this trust-based perspective, however, as it seeks to reorient the historical, Western, inter-organizational business paradigm away from the standard, contract-laden obligatory relationships toward one—relational contracting—that is, arguably, while more positively focused, naive. Essentially, the challenge is: How can we better understand the nature of project partnerships as a function of relational contracting and trust and, given this understanding, what are the manners in which we can thus work to improve project inter-firm relationships? Does the effort to build trust-based relationships offer project organizations competitive or operating advantages? In a business context, practitioners will be wary of any calls for dispensing with contract rigor as a means to promote trust. But the existence of a contract should also not rule out opportunity for two parties engaged in a contractual relationship to develop mutual trust. Hypothetically, each party can continuously assess how the other behaves relative to the contract. Evidence of trustworthiness that may surface over project time can then provide a basis to build expectations about the other party's behavior which can be played against the unfolding reality in an iterative fashion. The key, of course, lies in understanding the advantages that mutually accrue from strengthening inter-firm relationships and seeking a level of trust that allows for such enhanced relationships.

This chapter addresses these issues from both theory and practice viewpoints. Trust, as a larger perspective, and relational contracting, as a practical phenomenon, are critical concepts within project-based organizations. Nowhere are these issues more relevant than in the architecture-engineering-construction industry, which has seen long-term adversarial relationships on the part of its multiple contractors, sub-contractors, customers, and other stakeholders. As a result, our goal is to develop the role of trust as a critical organizational attribute and explore how one practical operationalization of trust (relational contracting) can play a crucial role in reorienting often contentious stakeholder relationships.

We seek to first establish a better understanding of relational contracting through the examination of a recent large-scale project: the design and construction of Terminal 5 (T5) at Heathrow Airport in London, which was promoted as a highly successful project venture. Each first-tier consultant and contractor in this project entered into a unique contractual relationship with the private developer and project client, British Airports Authority (BAA). The case will show that, first, writing a contract that is genuinely relational (as framed by the theory) is not a trivial task; second, implementing a relational contract is not conflict free, but involves instead mutual adaptation and adjustment by all parties involved; and third, relational contracting as a one-size-fits-all commercial strategy can be interpreted as an overkill for the case of simple transactions that are also part of a large engineering project. Not recognizing this seems to detrimentally affect the perceived effectiveness of the contract, which in turn can undermine the sustainability of a relational contracting strategy over a capital program time.

We then build on these insights to elaborate on some of the key research questions that a study of trust in inter-firm project relationships offers. We discuss as to whether that trust can emerge, not simply as a happy coincidence of the project or as a function of an adopted relational contract, but as a result of demonstrated and repeated interactions and behaviors among members of different organizations. Trust requires a reasonable definitional and actual understanding between parties (e.g. "What are we trusting you to do? How are we trusting you to act?") that is critical to our understanding of the phenomenon at hand. These issues become critical to formulating a series of research questions that highlight the importance of inter-organizational relationship development. To build the argument, we draw on conceptual differences between a traditional view of self-interested trust as opposed to socially oriented trust—the latter an outward focus which can proceed by managing the risk of misplaced trust through self-reflection and relationship assessment. Specifically, we argue there is opportunity for organizations involved in project joint ventures to move beyond Rousseau et al.'s (1998) "calculus-based trust" (predicated on self-interest or economic incentives) to behavior that genuinely promotes positive and long-lasting relationships of business value.

On relational contracting, inter-firm collaboration, and mutual trust

Contract theory

Contract theory builds upon the assumption in Western legal philosophy that formal contracts are essential to mediate the relationship between firms. Contracts concern cooperative social behavior where parties are willing and able to work with others (Macneil 1980). They represent obligations to perform specified actions in the future. The more potential hazards the parties involved associate to those actions, the more they deem contracts necessary (Macneil 1987). The theory also acknowledges that contracts are formulated both by the parties engaged in an economic exchange, as well as by society and law. All contracts have relational elements since all economic exchanges happen in a relational context (Macneil 2001), therefore an element of trust is foundational to fair exchange (Smyth, Gustafsson, and Ganskau 2010; Gustafsson et al. 2010).

At one end of the spectrum are the discrete, complete classical contracts (Macneil 1987). They are expected to detail the job roles and responsibilities, specify procedures for monitoring performance and penalties for non-conformance, and determine outcomes or outputs to be delivered (Poppo and Zenger 2002). Transaction cost theory argues that they suit short-term transactions involving limited personal interaction. Conceptually, complete contracts require minimal or foundational trust and invoke high confidence levels, where confidence is considered a probability statement (Smyth 2008).

At the other end are "relational" or "intertwined" contracts in the sense that personal relations become heavily intertwined with the economic exchange (Macneil 1987; cf. Eccles 1981). The conceptualization of relational contracts draws on social systems and tenets that are thought to induce collaboration, for example the employer–employee contract or agreements between subsidiaries in a vertically integrated company (Williamson 1985). Relational contracting is therefore akin to a domestic market (cf. Campbell 1995). It presumes that the parties are willing to discard adversarial forms of contracting for others that nurture cooperative, long-term relationships, and mutual dependence; it is also conceived as emphasizing governance by trust over price and authority. In this way, relational contracts, whether informally agreed as forms of intent through partnering or in written form through supply chain alliances, are designed to induce trust. Indeed, theory argues relational contracts suit long-term repeated transactions allowing adjustments over time. Technically, relational contracts build upon the notion of a contract as a flexible framework for yielding rules, involving open-ended and sometimes vague provisions, some of which may be of dubious enforceability (Llewellyn 1931). Conceptually, not only is trust an important factor of governance in relational contracts, but there is also greater reliance upon trust due to incompleteness.

Large engineering projects are a context particularly fit to explore how relational contracts work, and the extent to which they induce inter-firm collaborative work and trust. In these projects, many of the contracts between the client and the different suppliers have to be necessarily incomplete because the project requirements are characterized by uncertainty and ambiguity, exacerbated by long project timescales. Further, the fragmentation of the supply chain is prone to cause problems in information flow and decision-making, miscommunication between design and construction parties, and difficulties in planning and control (Stinchombe and Heimer 1985).

The following section examines the particular motivations underpinning the use of a relational contract in the T5 project, the extent to which the T5 agreement sought to embody this notion, and how it played out at implementation.

The case of the T5 agreement: a quasi-realization of a relational contract?

At the genesis of the T5 project, the £4.2bn (2005 prices) expansion of Heathrow Airport was conceived as an attempt to emulate Japanese-style partnerships in large engineering projects, traceable to the internationally influential *Rethinking Construction* report (1998), the study commissioned by the UK government and coordinated by Sir John Egan, CEO of BAA at the time and a former CEO of Jaguar, the automobile manufacturing company. This report had exhorted clients to replace short-term competitive tendering of suppliers with long-term partnerships, sustained through trust, performance measurement, and incentives for continuous improvement. The recommendations built upon studies about collaborative relationships between Toyota and its suppliers. These argued mutual trust was an outcome of the reliability demonstrated over repeated market interactions and of the shared knowledge that the parties need one another (Womack, Jones, and Roos 1990; Wheelwright and Clark, 1992). The recommendations were also influenced by studies on Western corporations such as Chrysler suggesting these practices were transferable and not culture-bound (Liker et al. 1996).

This section of the chapter builds on in-depth fieldwork conducted between 2004 and 2007, funded by a research council—see Gil (2009)for details. Our analysis focuses on a salient proposition tested in the T5 project—that the T5 agreement could enable cooperative behavior between BAA and the first-tier suppliers (architectural practices, engineering consultants, contractors, and manufacturers). The contract was putatively framed as relational by BAA, and assumed as such in recent discussions (Gil 2009).

After submitting the outline planning application in 1993, BAA was granted planning consent in 2001. Schematic design and implementation (i.e. detailed design, manufacturing, construction) started right after, and T5 opened in March 2008. This accomplished the first milestone of a broader capital program for Heathrow Airport, which included opening a second satellite in T5 around 2012, and replacing the terminals 1 and 2 with a new terminal around 2015.

Two notions were at the core of BAA strategy for the capital program: one, improve the efficiency of the suppliers; and two, create value for the customers. But to accomplish these goals in the T5 project was not trivial because some premises informing its conceptual design were no longer valid when schematic design started in 2002. BAA also understood that the airline and airport industries were volatile businesses, and the main T5 customers and users (e.g., British Airways, BAA retail, Home Office) were likely to request business-critical changes as the project unfolded:

The idea of building £4bn worth of infrastructure over 4 or 5 years and not having to rework and go around the loop a couple of times is nonsensical. Therefore, we've to manage change and minimize it in the best way. We won't be able to get it right the first time. Change is a fact of life. (T5 Project Lawyer)

BAA was not alone in believing that high client–supplier collaboration and flexibility to respond to change could only be enabled through a relational form of contract. Standard forms of contract had started to emerge encouraging clients to adopt a relational approach. The New Engineering and Construction contract (2005), for example, was first published in 1993, introducing the notions of "trust," "working together," and "cooperation in planning." And in 1995, BP received an "Innovation in Industry" award for its relational contracting strategy— "Alliancing"—on the Andrew facilities alliance project (Knott 1996). Still, comprehensive studies were lacking as to whether these contracts could lead to superior outcomes in large engineering projects.

The T5 agreement contractual terms and conditions

BAA deemed that a relational contracting strategy was fundamental for encouraging the T5 suppliers to achieve "exceptional" performance. Hence, the T5 agreement—the "absolute bedrock of getting the relationships right" in BAA terms—aimed at creating incentives for "positive problem-solving behaviors that would not allow things to go wrong in the first place." Its ethos was about creating an environment where "attitudes and roles bedeviled with concern about exposure to risk, unbalanced focus on capital cost, lowest costs, and layers of practices that inhibit change are unacceptable" (T5 Handbook). This was explained by the T5 lawyer:

We cannot load suppliers with risk, drive prices down, and complain this is costing us more than we thought. It's fundamentally dishonest and economically illiterate. Our approach is: we can drive prices down by removing inherent waste and allowing suppliers to have a decent return just like us.

The T5 agreement called for integrated teams to focus upon cause rather than mitigate problems (BAA T5 fact sheet, cited in Potts 2008) and for suppliers to reduce production costs while remaining flexible to accommodate design changes. The principle for remunerating the suppliers was reimbursable cost of time and materials plus an agreed profit margin. The T5 contract manager explained the rationale:

> The fact that we're paying people by the hour allows us to be pretty flexible in using resources, and changing and moving things quickly around…We'll give suppliers a level of profit for the tasks we can see ahead of us, but suppliers won't be taking any of the risks of inefficiency or overspend. Suppliers may not make their best returns here, but they aren't making any losses.

The T5 suppliers were expected to demonstrate to BAA that the costs had been properly incurred. BAA reserved unfettered rights to carry out reviews to audit supplier accounts, staff and labor payrolls, purchase ledger systems, volume discounts, retrospective rebates, early payment discounts, and cash flow statements. Three contractual details were, however, built in the T5 commercial policy that affected the profit mark-up made by the suppliers (Gil 2008):

1. *Ring-fenced profit.* The commercial policy spelled out that the T5 suppliers' profit was ring fenced as an agreed lump sum against an agreed estimate of resources for a defined scope of work. Suppliers could increase their profit margin percentage by delivering their work at a cost less than the estimate. Conversely, the profit margin could shrink if the estimate of resources was too optimistic relative to the actual work needed to deliver the defined scope of work.

2. *Incentive plan.* BAA agreed to share benefits of "exceptional performance" with the suppliers. The benefits were calculated as the difference between the baseline target cost and the actual cost of work. Target costs were agreed with the suppliers involved in the T5 design and implementation. The targets were meant to reflect benchmarks, yardsticks, and norms free of allowances and contingencies for inherent construction risks.

3. *Compensating for change.* BAA set two main categories for design change requests, one of which impacted the profit margin of the supplier. Changes that BAA described as "design evolution" meant that, in the view of the T5 agreement, they did not alter the design scope. Thus, BAA did not amend the ring-fenced profit in response to design evolution—while suppliers were reimbursed for the actual costs incurred with work stemming from design evolution, their profit margin was reduced. Conversely, BAA considered as "exceptional" all the events and issues changing the project scope. In these circumstances, BAA would amend the ring-fenced profit not to affect the supplier's aim: profit margin. Conversations

between BAA and the suppliers preceded the categorization of an event as design evolution or scope change.

ANALYSIS

While the BAA administrators insisted that "there was no better deal on the market" than the T5 agreement, the research fieldwork repeatedly uncovered tensions associated with the implementation of the strategy. The findings revealed that occasional inadequate management of these tensions could hinder supplier cooperation, in essence defeating the purpose of the contract. BAA respondents tended to frame the difficulties as a cultural issue: "our biggest challenge is educating and working with suppliers and getting them to see the vision," argued a project director. And indeed, studies of efforts to align the systems and cultures of the buyers and suppliers for facilitating coordination and generating relational rents highlight the long time and commitment involved whenever total cultural and organizational changes are required (Dyer and Nobeoka 2000). But, the fieldwork also revealed two important challenges in implementing effectively the T5 agreement.

First, some terms and conditions as they were worded in the commercial policy that integrated the T5 agreement moved the contract away from a relational contracting ethos towards a more classical contracting regime. The mechanisms to ring-fence the profit and to set target costs, for example, were largely a reconfiguration of price governance. They required suppliers to trust both their own ability to estimate costs, as well as BAA's willingness to agree to realistic targets. Any emergent confidence relied upon the accuracy and fairness of the benchmarks, yardsticks, and norms in that context. And the mechanism to compensate for change required suppliers to trust that BAA would behave in a reasonable way when negotiating at the borderline between design evolution and change of scope; and that market power would not be used to impose unreasonable outcomes. Similarly, BAA required suppliers to behave reasonably and realistically in negotiations, thus not being opportunistic or adversarial. Thus, it seems more accurate to position the T5 agreement relative to theory in economics and law as somewhat of a hybrid: it was unarguably relational in intent and objectives, but it integrated in its commercial policy terms and conditions that were characteristic of (neo-)classical contracts.

And second, the actual way through which BAA implemented the T5 agreement, including both its relational ethos and its commercial policy, affected the capability of the contract to encourage inter-firm cooperative work: "It's very easy to write the words, to sell the concept, but how to actually make it work is really tough," confided a project director. In-depth analysis unearthed five critical factors that affected its effectiveness at implementation (Gil 2009):

1. *Suppliers are keen to reap reputation benefits*

Reputation is an integral part of a relational contract. Reputation partly embodies trust derived from past behavior and performance. Interestingly, the findings of the study reveal that the capability of the T5 agreement to encourage cooperative work was limited whenever the suppliers were indifferent as to whether they wished to reap reputational benefits from project participation or not. Some T5 suppliers were strategically interested in establishing a presence in the world of airport projects. For this group, a good reputation was important. Others wanted to grow their domestic business. The participation in the T5 project could be a springboard for success, and a good reputation was equally important. But, for other firms, the T5 project work represented a small fraction of their annual turnover with limited strategic importance. For these suppliers, reputation was not reliant on the performance on the T5 project, suggesting perhaps that relationship reputation "travels a short distance." Trust and confidence generally were not therefore important for the wider market.

2. *Suppliers have flexibility in their production processes*

A core motivation underpinning the adoption of a relational contract is encouraging project suppliers to be flexible to accommodate client-driven requests to change the design or the construction sequences. The findings suggest, however, that the effectiveness of the T5 agreement in this regard was limited by the degree of flexibility in the production processes of the suppliers. The engineering design and architectural consultants were inherently flexible to accommodate change. And commercial tensions rarely emerged when BAA requested it (Gil 2009). Conversely, some suppliers of manufactured components disliked the notion of design evolution. Unlike the autonomy exhibited by the site teams of consultants relative to the head offices, the site teams for some manufacturers needed to coordinate their plans with the production schedules for their factories. Because the factories invariably served a number of projects at any time, the site managers were under pressure to commit to specific production slots months in advance to optimize the utilization of the fixed assets. The supplier staff believed it would be hard to recoup the full cost of disrupting production due to a change request since it would be difficult to distinguish the costs attributable to the client intervention from normal costs associated with production.

The fieldwork also suggested that the resistance to change exhibited by a few suppliers was partly due to the way BAA ring-fenced the profit. Hence, late changes reduced the chances for suppliers to make the originally agreed profit margin unless BAA adjusted the maximum lump sum to compensate for the additional work. But BAA did not do so unless it considered that the change altered the scope, given that the contract assumed that suppliers were flexible to accommodate change associated with design evolution.

Over time, BAA realized that the T5 agreement would not automatically eliminate commercial tensions with the suppliers. Confidence in the T5 agreement meeting expectations in this respect waned. Some adversarial behavior surfaced. BAA staff needed to understand how to interpret and manage emergent issues, while suppliers' staff needed to stay attuned to the relational principles when searching and negotiating solutions for adverse situations. Although trust and confidence played an important part, price emerged as important and influenced the inter-firm relationships.

3. *Client and suppliers choose the right people for the jobs*

The findings revealed that the limited financial risk borne by the T5 suppliers did not suffice to temper the ambitions of some suppliers' staff for making higher returns. Evidence suggests that this misalignment of expectations could drive two responses deleterious to working cooperatively. Occasionally, the supplier administrators agreed to the T5 deal but found it hard to assign to the project the most competent managers, being unimpressed by what BAA termed "decent profit." Rather, the latter preferred to work for fixed-price projects gained through competitive bidding offering greater rewards for leveraging their skills in getting the work done efficiently. Alternatively, suppliers could assign competent individuals to the project but they could fail to grasp the ethos of the T5 agreement if they had been accustomed to working in adversarial environments. In both cases "behaving opportunistically with guile" reverted to price-based negotiations with the consequence of eroding trust and confidence beyond the contested issues and tasks.

The findings show that relational contracting does not automatically induce trust. It is left to individuals to take responsibility, but not all individuals fit a cooperative environment. Clients and suppliers both need to ensure staff fit and support a relational culture. They should replace staff that cannot acquire the mindset required. It would also be naive to expect induction workshops on relational contracts to quickly change behaviors, especially, as we argue later, if inter-firm trust is not embedded as a core competency in the firm.

4. *Client learns to contract in response to supplier feedback*

Writing a contract is an incremental and local process, seldom very far-sighted, that occurs over a long period of time (Mayer and Argyres 2004). This requires organizations to align the knowledge of the different groups (with respect to the different types of contract terms) with the writing of the different types of contractual provisions. As a result, project clients are unlikely to get the commercial details right at the first attempt. Rather, ex post capabilities to interpret and adapt the contract are crucial to the project over time. The value of learning was conspicuous, for example, in the process that BAA and the suppliers went through to implement the principle of rewarding suppliers for performing exceptionally well. The idea was to allow the suppliers to reap monetary rewards when they executed the work at a cost below the target cost. But the extent to which this incentive actually worked depended as to whether it met two major concerns of the suppliers. The first pertained to whether BAA planned to distribute the incentives shortly after the date when the suppliers had completed their work; and the second pertained to whether the suppliers perceived the cost targets to be realistic. Through trial and error, BAA and the suppliers jointly reworked the incentive scheme until they had figured out a mutually acceptable scheme. This involved both trust and confidence between parties, and appeared to have been effective.

5. *Client aligns practices to control and improve performance with supplier capabilities*

BAA decided to use the T5 agreement regardless of the size of the first-tier suppliers, but the implementation of some details turned out to be challenging with the smallest first-tier suppliers. Project participation was unarguably important for these firms—"these projects don't come along every day!" explained one director. Yet, small suppliers seldom had adequate organizational structures and procedures in place for addressing the demand for detailed performance reports and cost data. In T5, the BAA construction director termed the set of practices institutionalized for "never letting suppliers feel entirely comfortable in a reimbursable environment" as "vigilant trust." He deemed it necessary to scrutinize how suppliers were planning the work and incurring costs, as well as continuously exploring ways to meet targets and improve performance. Yet, the smaller firms were often unable to meet the expectations of BAA in this regard. BAA also found it difficult, at the project onset, to persuade some consultants to cooperate with the demands for information because the latter seemed less attuned to a culture of monitoring performance and continuous improvement than contractors. The lack of cooperation frustrated BAA, which was incurring expenses in employing staff to monitor costs and ensure best value for money. Small firms found the transaction costs too demanding and some consultants found the accountability challenging to professional conduct.

Discussion on the T5 agreement:
intent and practice

This study yields three main insights. First, the findings suggest the contract was not as relational as BAA and many others commentators assumed, using an employer–employee contract as the archetypal comparator. Trust and confidence were indeed present, but some elements were reconfigurations of price and power drivers. Still, this quasi-relational contract strategy used in the T5 agreement enabled cooperative behavior between project client and suppliers. Specifically, the T5 agreement provided BAA flexibility and transparency in using resources to accommodate volatility in project requirements. This, in turn, enabled many project-based production practices aimed at improving process reliability (Gil 2009), suggesting an almost symbiotic relationship between the contract and project management practice. Overall, the implementation of the T5 agreement was effective whenever client and supplier staff fitted a relational environment, and managed to interpret the contract sensibly.

Second, high-levels of inter-firm collaboration were not enough to dissuade BAA from monitoring and controlling the performance of suppliers, what BAA termed "vigilant trust." This is not unusual since while social safeguards, such as trust, reputation, and continuity, help to manage under uncertainty, they can prove insufficient to dissuade opportunistic behavior when there is high ambiguity about available courses of action, variables, and cause–effect relationships (Daft and Lengel 1986; Carson, Madhok, and Wu 2006). Ambiguity increases the possibility of opportunism with reduced risks of being uncovered, especially at the level of the individual. Implementing "vigilant trust" is not trivial, however. At T5, mutual trust and confidence were stifled due to a failure to adjust the practices associated with vigilant trust to the capabilities of smaller suppliers and to the professional codes of conduct of some consultants. Arguably, this is when higher trust levels could be most beneficial. Yet, they may be beyond the bounds of a quasi-relational contract such as the T5 agreement and, we conjecture, of relational contracting more generally.

Third, the findings suggest that by positioning the implementation of the T5 agreement at one extreme—"one size fits to all" first-tier suppliers—BAA undermined the sustainability of this quasi-relational contracting strategy over the capital program. With credit to the T5 agreement, T5 opened on time and reportedly on budget on 27 March 2008 as announced years in advance. But the successes of design and construction were not attributed to the contract by some top management. Many argued instead that the inclusive application of the agreement had failed to create enough commercial tension with the suppliers, thereby occasioning a "lazy" budget and program for the T5 project, as well as complacency from some suppliers. We conjecture this perception was factored in BAA's announcement in January 2008 that it would put out to competitive tender forthcoming capital projects.

Of course, it remains unclear whether BAA would have dropped its relational contracting strategy had the world economy not entered into recession in 2008— shortly after BAA had been bought in a highly leveraged bid. The new top management team may have seen an opportunity to get better deals (reduced capital costs) through competitive tendering since the order books of the suppliers suddenly became less full; that is, commercial conditions shifted firmly to a buyers' market. And, hypothetically, BAA may succeed in freezing project designs early on so as to require less flexibility from suppliers. We are mindful, however, that airport projects serve the volatile and fast-moving airline industry, which makes some late change requests inevitable. This, in turn, makes it likely that wasteful tensions, lack of collaboration, and increased inter-firm distrust will surface if BAA insists in using fixed-price contract in capital projects under conditions of uncertainty.

Interestingly, BAA's decision is not unique. BP, for example, also abandoned a similar relational contracting strategy after it employed it in the Andrew project, partly due to problems arising in follow-on projects (ETAP) but largely due to a new less sympathetic culture brought in by Amoco which BP had just acquired. In both cases, a decision to use a relational contract across the board seems to have triggered two responses: one arguing that this strategy is an important element of the delivery of large engineering projects, and another arguing that it is an expensive way of achieving these objectives. The question of how fixed-price and reimbursable contracts can be effectively combined in the overall project contracting strategy as a function of the nature of the transactions, suppliers' capabilities, economic cycle, and institutional context clearly merits further exploration.

TRUST AS A CRITICAL ATTRIBUTE

From a trust perspective, while the T5 agreement was conceptually inducing trusting behavior from suppliers, the primary objective for BAA appeared to be the generation of confidence, especially around price-based governance. This concurs with the criticism that "calculative trust" from transaction cost theory (Williamson 1993; cf. Luhmann 1988) is closer to the concept of confidence derived from probabilities rather than the sense or conviction embodied in the concept of trust (Edkins and Smyth 2006; Smyth 2008; Gustafsson et al. 2010). It also sets the ground for a broader discussion of the role of trust as a critical organizational attribute.

The empirical findings from T5 have shown both the advantages and limitations of trust generation through the implementation of a governing agreement, a putative relational contract. They illustrate the complexity and challenges of attempting to develop trust-based relationships, particularly as difficulties and organizational impediments continue to operate in the face of "best laid plans." The findings also imply that trust required for relational contracting can be supported from organizationally generated trust. This poses an interesting research question: under what circumstances and in what manner can firms choose to explore trust as a core attribute as opposed to opting to revert to adversarial ways in the long tradition of inter-firm relationships? In the following section, we address this question from the point of view of the future research issues it presents, including how trust can (or even whether it should) be employed as a competitive tool.

To develop trust at a deeper level, trust needs to be encouraged through the culture of a firm and through its systems and procedures. Ultimately and through continued commitment, trust becomes a critical attribute embedded and spread in the firm (e.g. Prahalad and Hamel 1990) which can be mobilized across projects for value and co-value creation (Prahalad and Ramaswamy 2004). This seems also to be the logical path for project clients and suppliers claiming they are serious about non-adversarial relations. From a supplier perspective in particular, research shows, on the basis of financial evidence from over 300 projects, that trust-based relationships can have positive financial benefits for an organization's suppliers and projects can become a source of both repeat business and increased profitability (Gustafsson et al. 2010).

The sources of trust

The focus for trust is twofold within the project business environment—individuals and organizations. People have dispositions to trust and organizations have histories concerning trust. Personal history and the choices made about how to interpret past events effect willingness to trust or defensiveness towards others. This is largely psychological and is tied into our sense of security and identity. Organizational history gives rise to a culture, systems, and procedures that create path dependencies along two lines:

1. The capacity to mobilize trust within the organization and then into the market;
2. The reputation individuals and organizations have in the market for trustworthiness, which is partly a reflection of their history, which informs the other parties about trustworthiness.

In examining the trust relationships evidenced by the T5 case and its use of relational contracting, one model that sheds light on the concept is the notion of trust as a series of progressive steps, as suggested by Lewicki and Bunker (1996). In their conceptualization, trust emerges through a series of steps and is based, at each step in the longitudinal relationship, on alternative mindsets. Thus, at a first-stage level of trust, Lewicki and Bunker posited that firms engage in "*deterrence-based trust*," which is largely cognitive, thus is really about evidence of confidence, which may be informed by underlying trust derived from intuitive and habitual assessment of the other party. Deterrence-based confidence may point towards parties that can be trusted to keep their word in order to avoid sanctions for violation. The implied underlying trust suggests that organizations' primary motivation for developing the relationship is to avoid, or deter, the retribution that would occur should they violate their word. Traditional contracting, with its terms and conditions, including sanctions, offers an example of the type of deterrence that firms wish to avoid and so are motivated to build relationships with other parties to keep similar agreed-to conditions.

Relational contracting, as we have noted, is intended to move beyond this sense of negative reinforcement of behavior into a more cooperative and mutually dependent form. Lewicki and Bunker's next level, "*knowledge-based trust*," is also largely cognitive and based in practice on evidence, which gives confidence in the relationship, that is, predicated on the idea that parties know each other sufficiently well that their behavior toward each other is, to some degree, predictable. Indeed, the notion of relational contracting implies the desire to employ governance by transactional "trust" which is closer to confidence in practice, necessitating knowledge of other parties—and more: the willingness of these parties to make their genuine concerns and motives explicit.

Finally, the highest level of trust that can be reached is "*identification-based trust*," which can be largely intuitive and thus be genuinely grounded in trust rather than confidence. It is present when one party has fully internalized the other's preferences and acts in ways to demonstrate appreciation of the other's viewpoint. The model is useful precisely because it recognizes that confidence and trust are emergent phenomena and must be developed over time. Relational contracting is a mechanism for the promotion of relationships based upon "calculative trust" or confidence, as it effectively codifies this alternative form of governance, but it must be understood as a means of preparing the soil. There may be underlying trust to support the emergence of confidence as there is a clear link between the two, yet this is not an automatic cause–effect and confidence can emerge from other factors other than trust, for example timely information. Confidence from trust and other sources acts back in ways that can help develop (further) trust in the relationships. Subsequent behaviors and attitudes need to evolve over the course of the longer-term relationship as parties become more comfortable with each other and move to this identification-based trust.

Trust, then, can be nurtured (Baier 1994) and strategies and tactics served by cultures, systems, and procedures can be employed to create trust. This condition is apparent not only between organizations (the focus of this chapter) but also must be understood as a corporate initiative within the firm. Put another way, trust as an attribute can occur between firms as an offshoot of a compelling commitment within the organization to alter culture, reward systems, and operating philosophies to promote this trust and confidence. Where there are personal and organizational dispositions to trust, then parties reach back into the personal and organizational history to inform the present circumstances. The further back they reach, the further they will tend to form expectations of being able to trust others into the future. Thus, the source of the propensity to trust is based upon past experience and organizational capability, which is perceived by others in the market as reputation or goodwill—part of the social capital of the firm or project organization (Gustafsson et al. 2010).

This potential formation of trust is depicted in the first stage of the sequence shown in Figure 18.1, covering personal, corporate, and project disposition to trust from the supplier standpoint. The client looks upon this disposition and makes a highly intuitive assessment of their collective trustworthiness. The intuitive assess-

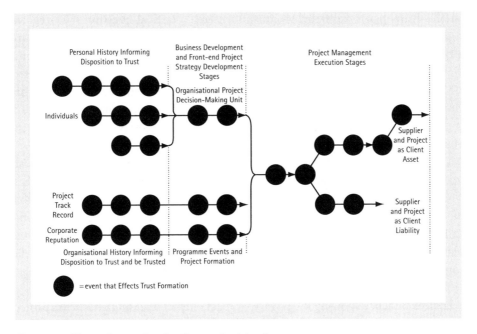

Fig. 18.1 Trust formation in the project business

Source: Adopted and developed from figure 5 in Smyth et al. (2010) and figure 7 in Gustafsson et al. (2010)

ment of the individuals will also draw upon cognition of organizational project track record and corporate reputation on organizational behavior. Where there is some evidence of trustworthiness in these early stages of the relationship life cycle, cognition and confidence come to the fore, and trust has potential to grow to new levels.

Mobilizing socially oriented trust in the management of projects

The front-end stages of projects are important for setting the behavioral and relationship scene for the specific project execution stages, as shown in the final sequence in Figure 18.1. Corporate investment in creating the right conditions for trust to prevail provides the means to build up trust at the front end and subsequently to carry it over to the project execution stage, providing there is continuity and consistency of services. Personnel continuity is important, sometimes provided through key account management and through a relay team approach with effective handovers (McDonald, Millman, and Rogers 1997; Kempeners and van der Hart 1999). Nevertheless, the above begs a critical question with regards to the emergence of trust as both a critical organizational attribute and (assumedly) competitive advantage. That is, what does the experience with relational contracting and T5 suggest for the utility of organizational trust and what are some of the critical questions that must be addressed on this basis? Put another way, before advocating a normative model of trust development, it is important to consider some critical and, to a degree, unanswered questions regarding the trust attribute.

The circumstances of relational contracting in T5 offer some extremely interesting points of departure for the examination of inter-organizational trust, how it evolves, and its stability. As we noted, a common theme from the T5 history was that relational contracting does not automatically induce mutual trust; indeed, the actions and attitudes of the principal parties need to be reinforced and evaluated relative to the principles articulated in the contract. Thus, addressing trust and relational contracting together, some interesting questions are:

1. Is there evidence showing the positive impact of trust-building on a firm's project management operations and ultimately, its bottom line?

   Trust-building can be addressed from a normative viewpoint; i.e. building trust within and between organizations is a positive development that improves the operations and culture/job satisfaction in an organization while facilitating positive exchanges between organizations. Certainly this viewpoint is an attractive one; nevertheless it needs critical examination in that, while one could argue that trust is a useful end unto itself, it would be much more meaningful if we could show that it also offers competitive advantage in the marketplace. Put another way: it is important to develop a body of evidence that firms committed to nurturing trust-based relationships are more successful, suffer less from transaction costs, and create a stronger and more enduring "supplier–organization–customer" supply chain than organizations that continue to employ aggressive, restrictive, and punitive contracts. In short, there needs to be a meeting of the normative and descriptive viewpoints on the long-term advantages of trust as an organizational attribute.

   Interestingly, preliminary studies are beginning to develop just such a body of data as to the efficacy and profitability of the investment in trust as a critical organizational attribute. Indeed, exploratory empirical studies on multiple international projects suggest that value derived from projects grows where socially oriented trust is high and profitability of the supplier also grows where trust is high, highlighting the value of trust to the project business enterprise (Smyth, Gustafsson, and Ganskau 2010; Gustafsson et al. 2010). More rigorous empirical studies are nonetheless necessary to offer scholars and project executives compelling evidence of the bottom-line benefits that can emerge from promoting trust-based relationships.

2. How do project-based trust relationships actually evolve in practice?

What are the conditions that allow for trust to emerge and, once introduced into inter-firm project relationships, are there recognizable stages in the development and evolution of trust? Previous theorists such as Rousseau et al. (1998)and Lewicki and Bunker (1996) argue for an evolution of relationships based on alternative motivations (fear of sanctions, self-interest, knowledge of each other, etc.). Cases such as T5 can be used as instruments to empirically test these alternative theories. A further question along these lines is to determine the degree to which these states of trust and confidence are "maintained"; that is, how resilient is trust and confidence in general and under certain circumstances, particularly in the face of potentially violating behavior? As these authors and others argue that trust and confidence are not monolithic states, but in fact, the compendium of multiple interactions and "levels," it merits investigating the degree to which trust and confidence endure (or slide into misplaced trust and confidence), confounding behavior on the part of corporate partners. When, in the T5 case, partners to the relational contract began violating its precepts, was stronger pressure felt to reinforce the relationship or simply to retreat into standard antagonist relationships?

3. What does the T5 story suggest for the development of trust as a key attribute?

Clearly, relational contracting created a positive atmosphere conducive to confidence emerging and some trust being nurtured. This leads to the question of how critical relational contracting or some other form of "soil preparation" is to the creation of inter-firm trust. Logic would suggest that there must be some conditions met in order to support and encourage confidence and trust to develop; thus, one is led to ask: Is (formal or informal) relational contracting a necessary yet insufficient prerequisite for the development of trust? In the T5 story, this appears to be the case—this is not to argue that trust is always dependent upon first employing relational contracts, nor is it to deny the successes of T5. Nevertheless, it seems fundamental to address the nature of trust conditions as they apply to inter-firm project settings. The T5 story also shows the strength of confidence distilled, a significant portion of which is thought to have arisen from the underlying trust in the relationships, yet the link articulating the two remains tacit to date in terms of cause and effect.

4. What is the relationship between intra-firm trust development and inter-firm trust behaviors?

By definition, for trust to develop as an organizational core attribute, it must first be encouraged internally before we can reasonably expect organizational members to employ it in inter-firm settings. Creating a culture of trust requires a significant commitment on the part of executives and employees alike, as rewards systems, operating procedures, and even structural elements within the organization require mutual adaptation. The larger question is how do firms develop trust-based working relationships by balancing cultural aspects (e.g. harnessing individuals taking responsibility for developing trusting relationships), systems integration to improve consistency of service provision (e.g. at the corporate–project interface), and procedures (e.g. behavioral codes of conduct) in ways that work for their existing organization and are valued in their markets?

CONCLUSION

This chapter has argued that one of the critical elements in effective stakeholder management requires a commitment to relationship-building within the context of inter-firm project development. Standard, traditional approaches that emphasize contract management bring with them a host of related transaction costs that can both impede the performance of the project and codify organizational relationships so rigidly that the greater good (i.e. project development) can actually suffer as parties seek to enforce their rights relative to other parties. The alternative, to develop a relational contracting philosophy predicated on trust and confidence, is an attractive one yet one that is also fraught with its own concerns. As President Ronald Reagan was commonly quoted in his dealings with then Soviet leader Gorbachev, "Trust, but verify," which invokes the link yet highlights the conceptual and practical tension between trust and confidence.

Earlier in this chapter, we observed that the quasi-relational contracting employed in T5 may be thought in many ways to represent "confidence creation" perhaps more than "trust creation," Yet, the critical point to observe is that trust, as an operating philosophy, rarely emerges *ex nihilo* into an organization's set of standard practices. And this seems to be true whether the focus is self-interested trust seeking win-win situations, or socially oriented trust with a greater outward focus. Mutual trust often evolves iteratively through stages, edging up levels as organizations gain confidence in the behaviors and motivations of their partners as well as recognizing the positive results for their joint project ventures and acting accordingly.

There are a number of fruitful avenues for future research that are suggested from this study of relational contracting, trust, and confidence, for example:

- How should a relational contract be articulated in projects, in regards to their architecture and to the exact wording of any commercial terms and conditions? And how should clients and suppliers go about implementing a relational contract so as to behave congruently with the intended ethos, and sustain the strategy over time?
- Research into the direct relationship between transaction costs and the development and promotion of trust and confidence: transaction cost economics theory suggests

that economic self-interest should be apparent in inter-organizational relationships; however, as trust expands, we would expect that the costs associated with maintaining the relationship with a partner would drop commensurately. Future research could evaluate the relationship dynamics predicted between transaction cost economics theory, trust, and confidence.

- Trust is often viewed as an antecedent variable in the nature of relationship development between firms; yet, because trust is usually viewed as a psychological state, it would be interesting to identify some of the contextual issues that influence the development of trust: What variables motivate the emergence of trust itself?
- The direct linkage between trust and relational contracting needs further explication. Does relational contracting require mutual trust, and if so, is mutuality encouraged based upon equity (leverage) or equality (fairness)?
- To what extent can trust be developed and managed in the firm as both a cost-effective and a valuable asset to be taken into the project market to the benefit of all parties?
- We posit that developing inter-firm trust as a core attribute can help project-based firms achieve superior performance. This proposition warrants rigorous further empirical testing.

The explicit nature of the interrelationship of these constructs is an important avenue for future research and theory-building. Relational contracting and trust are important elements affecting the management of projects. The better we can understand and formulate policies for effective management of inter-firm relationships, the greater the likelihood will be for developing win-win for project-based firms.

REFERENCES

BAA T5 fact sheet (1996). *The Key Stages of Terminal 5*,www.baa.com/t5. Accessed July 1996.

BAIDEN, B. K., PRICE, A. D. F., and DAINTY, A. R. J. (2006). "The extent of team integration within construction projects," *International Journal of Project Management*, 24: 13–23.

BAIER, A. C. (1994). *Moral Prejudices: Essays on Ethics*. Cambridge, MA: Harvard Business Press.

BECHKY, B. A. (2006). "Gaffers, gofers, and grips: role-based coordination in temporary organizations," *Organization Science*, 17/1: 3–21.

BENNETT, J., and JAYES, S. (1995). *Trusting the Team*. Reading: Reading Construction Forum, Centre for Strategic Studies in Construction, University of Reading.

CAMPBELL, N. (1995). *An Interaction Approach to Organisation Buying Behaviour: Relationship Marketing for Competitive Advantage*. Oxford: Butterworth-Heinemann.

CARSON, S. J., MADHOK, A., and WU, T. (2006). "Uncertainty, opportunism, and governance: the effects of volatility and ambiguity on formal and relational contracting," *Academy of Management Journal*, 49/5: 1058–77.

CLARK, M. S. (1978). "Reactions to a request for a benefit in communal and exchange relationships," *Dissertation Abstracts International*, 38/10-B: 5089–90.

DAFT, R. L., and LENGEL, R. H. (1986). "Information richness: a new approach to managerial behaviour and organization design," in B. M. Staw and L. L. Cummings (eds.), *Research in Organizational Behavior*. Greenwich, CT: JAI, 91–233.

DOUGLAS, M. (1999). "Four cultures: the evolution of parsimonious model," *GeoJournal*, 47: 411–15.

DYER, J. H., and NOBEOKA, K. (2000). "Creating and managing a high-performance knowledge-sharing network: the Toyota case," *Strategic Management Journal*, 21: 345–67.

ECCLES, R. G. (1981). "The quasifirm in the construction industry," *Journal of Economic Behavior & Organization*, 2: 335–57.

EDKINS, A. J., and SMYTH, H. J. (2006). "Contractual management in PPP projects: evaluation of legal versus relational contracting for service delivery," *ASCE Journal of Professional Issues in Engineering Education and Practice*, 132/1: 82–93.

GIL, N. (2008). "BAA: The T5 project agreement (A)," ECCH Ref. 308–308–1.

——(2009). "Developing project client–supplier cooperative relationships: how much to expect from relational contracts?," *California Management Review*, Winter: 144–69.

GUMMESSON, E. (2001). *Total Relationship Marketing*. Oxford: Butterworth-Heinemann.

GUSTAFSSON, M., SMYTH, H. J., GANSKAU, E., and ARHIPPAINEN, T. (2010). "Managing trust: bridging strategic and operational issues for project business," *International Journal of Managing Projects in Business* (forthcoming).

KADEFORS, A. (2004). "Trust in project relationships: inside the black box," *International Journal of Project Management*, 22: 175–82.

KEMPENERS, M., and VAN DER HART, H. W. (1999). "Designing account management organizations," *Journal of Business and Industrial Marketing*, 14/4: 310–27.

KNOTT, T. (1996). *No Business as Usual. An Extraordinary North Sea Result*. The British Petroleum Company, plc.

KURTZBERG, T., and MEDVEC, V. H. (1999). "Can we negotiate and still be friends?," *Negotiation Journal*, 15/4: 355–62.

LEWICKI, R. J., and BUNKER, B. B. (1996). "Developing and maintaining trust in work relationships," in R. M. Kramer and T. R. Tyler (eds.), *Trust in Organizations: Frontiers of Theory and Research*. London: Sage Publications, 114–39.

LIKER, J. K., KAMATH, R. R., WASTI, S. N., and NAGAMACHI, M. (1996). "Supplier involvement in automotive component design: are there really large US Japan differences?," *Research Policy*, 25: 59–89.

LLEWELLYN, K. N. (1931). "What price contract? An essay in perspective," *Yale Law Journal*, 40: 704–51.

LUHMANN, N. (1988). "Familiarity, confidence, trust: problems and alternatives," in D. Gambetta (ed.), *Trust: Making and Breaking Cooperative Relations*. Oxford: Basil Blackwell.

LYONS, B., and MEHTA, J. (1997). "Contracts, opportunism and trust: self-interest and social orientation," *Cambridge Journal of Economics*, 21: 239–57.

McDONALD, M., MILLMAN, T., and ROGERS, B. (1997). "Key account management: theory, practice and challenges," *Journal of Marketing Management*, 13: 737–57.

MACNEIL, I. R. (1980). *The New Social Contract: An Inquiry into Modern Contractual Relations*. New Haven: Yale University Press.

——(1987). "Barriers to the idea of relational contracts," in F. Nicklish (ed.), *The Complex Long-Term Contract*. Heidelberg: C. F. Muller Juristischer Verlag, 31–44.

——(2001). *The Relational Theory of Contract: Selected Works of Ian Macneil*, ed. David Campbell. London: Sweet & Maxwell.

MAYER, K. J., and ARGYRES, N. S. (2004). "Learning to contract: evidence from the personal computer industry," *Organization Science*, 15/4: 394–410.

MEYERSON, D., WEICK, K. E., and KRAMER, R. M. (1996). "Swift trust and temporary groups," in R. M. Kramer and T. R. Tyler (eds.), *Trust in Organizations: Frontiers of Theory and Research*. Thousand Oaks, CA: Sage.

NEC3 (2005). *New Engineering and Construction Contract*. London: Thomas Telford Ltd.

POPPO, L., and ZENGER, T. (2002). "Do formal contracts and relational governance function as substitutes or complements?" *Strategic Management Journal*, 23: 707–25.

POTTS, K. (2008). "Change in the quantity surveying profession: Heathrow Terminal 5 case study," in H. J. Smyth and S. D. Pryke (eds.), *Collaborative Relationships in Construction: Developing Frameworks and Networks*. Oxford: Wiley-Blackwell, 42–58.

PRAHALAD, C. K., and HAMEL, G. (1990). "The core competence of the corporation," *Harvard Business Review*, May–June: 79 91.

—— and RAMASWAMY, V. (2004). "Co-creating experiences: the next practice in value creation," *Journal of Interactive Marketing*, 18/3: 5–14.

PRYKE, S. D., and SMYTH, H. J. (2006). "Scoping a relationship approach to the management of projects," in *Management of Complex Projects: A Relationship Approach*. Oxford: Blackwell, 21–46.

REICHHELD, F. F. (1996). *The Loyalty Effect*. Boston: Harvard Business School Press.

RETHINKING CONSTRUCTION (1998). *The Report of the Construction Task Force*. London: Department of Trade and Industry.

ROUSSEAU, D. M., SITKIN, B., BURT, R. S., and CAMERER, C. (1998). "Not so different after all: a cross-discipline view of trust," *Academy of Management Review*, 23: 393–404.

SAKO, M. (1992). *Prices, Quality and Trust: Inter-Firm Relations in Britain and Japan*. New York: Cambridge University Press.

SCHÖN, D. A. (1983). *The Reflective Practitioner: How Professionals Think in Action*, Basic Books.

SKITMORE, M., and SMYTH, H. J. (2007). "Pricing construction work: a marketing viewpoint," *Construction Management and Economics*, 25: 619–30.

SMYTH, H. J. (2008). "Developing trust," in H. J. Smyth and S. D. Pryke (eds.), *Collaborative Relationships in Construction: Developing Frameworks and Networks*. Oxford: Wiley-Blackwell, 129–60.

—— GUSTAFSSON, M., and GANSKAU, E. (2010). "The value of trust in project business," *International Journal of Project Management*, Special Edition for EURAM, 28: 117–29.

STINCHCOMBE, A. L., and HEIMER, C. A. (1985). *Organization Theory and Project Management*. Oslo: Norwegian University Press.

STORBACKA, K., STRANDVIK, T., and GRÖNROOS, C. (1994). "Managing customer relationships for profit: the dynamics of relationship quality," *International Journal of Service Industry Management*, 5/5: 21–38.

SWAN, W., WOOD, G., and MCDERMOTT, P. (2001). *Trust in Construction: Achieving Cultural Change*, http://www.scpm.salford.ac.uk/trust/publications.htm.

WHEELWRIGHT, S. C., and CLARK, K. (1992). "Creating project plans to focus product development," *Harvard Business Review*, 70/2: 70–82.

WILLIAMSON, O. E. (1985). *The Economic Institutions of Capitalism*. New York: Free Press.

——(1993). "Calculativeness, trust, and economic organization," *Journal of Law and Economics*, 36/April: 453–86.

WOMACK, J. P., JONES, D. T., and ROOS, D. (1990). *The Machine that Changed the World*. New York: Harper Perennial.

PART VI

ORGANIZING
AND LEARNING

CHAPTER 19

KNOWLEDGE INTEGRATION IN PRODUCT DEVELOPMENT PROJECTS

A CONTINGENCY FRAMEWORK

LARS LINDKVIST

INTRODUCTION

Projects typically rely on a division of labor, where many of those involved represent a specialist knowledge area or have long-term experience. Reaping the benefits of such specialization would presuppose some kind of knowledge integration, referring generally to processes wherein individual or organizational knowledge bases are being used collaboratively to accomplish a specific task or goal. The existence of significant diversity of knowledge bases in such settings should provide fertile soil for creativity and innovation (Sydow, Lindkvist, and DeFillippi 2004; Scarbrough et al. 2004; DeFillippi, Arthur, and Lindsay 2006). The downside of diversity, however, is that it may also render the process of knowledge integration difficult. For example, Dougherty (1992) proposed that those belonging to different knowledge domains may actually live in different "thought worlds," and not only know different things but interpret the same things differently. Thus, although members from different "occupational cultures" may have a common interest in a successful performance, they tend to "value different sets of criteria for system design and promising modi-fications," as discussed by Von Meier (1999: 101). Hence, while it is desirable for project development teams to comprise a substantial diversity of knowledge bases this would also give rise to a demanding challenge of integrating them.

There seem to be basically two different ways of managing this problematic—one which relies on the principle of promoting "knowledge base similarity," and a second one that favors the principle of promoting "well-connectedness of knowledge bases." Below, I start by outlining these approaches and argue that the latter one, which is associated with the idea of understanding projects as "know-ledge-collectivities" (Lindkvist 2005), provides a fruitful point of departure for thinking about knowledge integration in many project settings. Second, I intro-duce a contingency framework to show how this general approach would cover a variety of knowledge integration modes and project management contexts. Third, I illustrate part of this contingency framework empirically using excerpts from two case studies taken from the literature, a mobile telephone project and a drug development project. Fourth, I specifically address the project manage-ment features and propose that traditional concerns regarding project goals, the view of deviations, etc. should be seen as being intertwined with the issue of knowledge integration. Finally, I suggest that continued research efforts should be devoted to advancing our ability to match a set of congruent knowledge inte-gration and project management features to the demands of specific project contexts.

APPROACHING KNOWLEDGE INTEGRATION

Focusing on "knowledge base similarity"

Considering the frequency of reports on how misunderstandings and conflicts tend to occur when project members belong to different functional units or represent dif-ferent disciplines, it is unsurprising to find that many propose "knowledge-sharing" and "knowledge transfer" as recipes that would facilitate collaborative effort. Carlile (2004), for example, underlines that the development of a common knowledge base is a vital precondition for people to be able to share, assess, and integrate their domain-specific knowledge, Bechky (2003) discusses how the co-creation of a com-mon ground mitigates communication impasses and misunderstandings, and Huang and Newell (2003: 167) propose that knowledge integration is achieved by "con-structing, articulating and redefining shared beliefs." Some other authors advocat-ing the importance of common knowledge focus primarily on how project teams may achieve tacit knowledge homogeneity. Nonaka, Toyama, and Konno suggest that practicing together is a prime recipe for arriving at such commonality in cross-functional project teams:

tacit knowledge can be acquired only through shared experience, such as spending time together or living in the same environment. (2000: 9)

According to Nonaka (1994: 19), such processes of tacit-knowledge-sharing may even proceed silently: "One important point to note is that an individual can acquire tacit knowledge without language." This view closely parallels the communities-of-practice notion (Wenger 1998), with its emphasis on the importance of socialization to bring about tacit knowledge transfer and a shared knowledge base among project members.

Such dispositional knowledge is not only revealed in practice. It is also created out of practice. That is, know-how is to a great extent the product of experience and the tacit insights experience provides. (Brown and Duguid 1998: 95)

As a result, members of a community-of-practice tend to know approximately the same things, experience things alike, and have a common worldview, etc. By practicing together, they acquire the embodied ability to behave as community members. Such practices would be well suited for "replicating and preserving existing knowledge" in the context of craft/task-based activity, as argued by Amin and Roberts (2008: 359). Moreover, for such a socially and cognitively dense group to emerge, an extended period of time where those involved can work together without much turnover of staff and in relative isolation would seem to be beneficial. Empirical examples of CoPs provided in the literature including butchers, midwives (Lave and Wenger, 1991), photocopier repair technicians (Orr 1990), flute makers (Cook and Yanow 1996), technicians (Barley 1996), and medical claims processing (Wenger 1998) suggest settings where such preconditions might well prevail.

Hence, the community-of-practice notion refers to "tightly knit" (Brown and Duguid 1998) groups that have been practicing together long enough to rely on the integrative power of a strong basis of communal knowledge. Yet, while this would appear to be difficult to achieve in many project settings, we can conceive of project contexts where such community-like features might be prominent. For example, basing her opinion on a case study of a new car development project, Bragd (2002: 147) reports that the "project team was clearly a community of practice." Similarly, Bresnen et al. (2003: 165) state that the processes of project-based learning observed in their case study within the construction industry "emphasize the value and importance of adopting a community-based approach." In conclusion, the development of such a socially and cognitively tight and community-like project group would be an option, in situations where a sizeable amount of communal knowledge is imperative for people to integrate the diverse knowledge bases involved.

Focusing on "well-connectedness of knowledge bases"

Efforts towards knowledge-sharing may often facilitate processes of knowledge integration. While certainly some common ground is called for (see Grant 1996; Carlile 2004), heavy investments in making individual knowledge bases similar can, however, be prohibitively costly and time consuming, and even counteract the mere rationale of cross-functional effort. Effective knowledge integration, Grant (1996) argues, should instead be approached as a matter of selecting a mode of interaction that minimizes interpersonal knowledge transfer—while recognizing the nature of those contingencies that prevail. Thus, where minimal interdependencies, limited complexity, and uncertainty prevail, the use of cheap mechanisms such as rules, roles, and routines may suffice, whereas severe "team interdependencies" (Van de Ven, Delbecq, and Hoenig 1976) will call for expensive and communication-intensive mechanisms, such as "group problem solving and decision making" (Grant 1996: 114). In a similar vein, Kellogg, Orlikowski, and Yates (2006) argue that it is difficult to arrive at common knowledge in contexts characterized by uncertainty and rapid change. Efforts at establishing a "common ground" (Bechky 2003) or "common knowledge" (Carlile 2004) may be less effective in such dynamic contexts, which should instead be conceived of as "trading zones" (Galison 1997), where common rules of communication and exchange, rather than the content of a common knowledge base, benefit concerted action.

Moreover, as illustrated in a case study of an R&D unit (Lindkvist 2004), projects tend to promote an action orientation among team members and an inclination to solve problems "here and now," whereby people have to react immediately to the actions of others and emerging contingencies. In solving their problems, people then approach each other, probing their ideas, hoping to get feedback about their strengths and weaknesses, and in that way use each other as parties in a co-evolution of new knowledge. In relation to this, Cross and Sproull (2004) point out that within relatively short-term projects, problem-solving is directed towards acquiring or creating "actionable knowledge," i.e. knowledge that leads to immediate progress on a current assignment. Hence, in particular when the problems encountered are ill defined and time is scarce, people tend to turn to each other for help, for advice, for a new angle on their conjectures, etc.

This makes it important that members know "who knows what" in a "transactive memory" fashion (Wegner, Erber, and Raymond 1991), using each other as external memories, facilitating knowing where to start the search process when problems arise within projects. Knowledge, held by project members or by "outside" people, is then activated and exchanged, in a spontaneous manner, at the point of time it is needed. Firms relying on such a largely informal "network memory" infrastructure thus tend to let knowledge "stay in place" and encourage people to learn how to search for relevant knowledge which resides in individuals or other media (Lindkvist 2008).

In conclusion, project teams, where members must or prefer to collaborate on the basis of distributed knowledge and a limited basis of communal knowledge, are not likely to operate as communities-of-practice. The connotations of intimacy, endurance, and enculturation processes associated with the "community" notion would seem to be less fitting in such project contexts. Unlike communities-of-practice, projects are typically time limited, focus on a specific task, rely on identities formed outside the project, and lack a shared negotiated perspective and practice, as summarized by Sense (2003). Instead, as proposed by Lindkvist (2005), they may be designated as "knowledge-collectivities." Within such a view of project teams, knowledge integration is instead seen as a matter of taking advantage of knowledge complementarities, guided by the principle of "well-connectedness of knowledge bases" (2005: 1215). Below, I extend this general approach to knowledge integration in projects into a more fine-grained exposition, and identify four different knowledge-collectivity contexts. Two of them will then be illustrated empirically.

A CONTINGENCY FRAMEWORK

Although we may think of projects as knowledge collectivities, this does not mean that all projects are seen as being alike. Hence, in order to illustrate variety within such a conception I will use an adapted version of a contingency model introduced by Lindkvist, Söderlund, and Tell (1998). The model relies on a two-dimensional reasoning. One dimension distinguishes between development processes of a "systemic" character and those that are "analyzable." Systemic processes then refer to situations where, due to severe and unforeseeable interdependencies, etc., the relevant work activities and causal relations and sequences between them are hard to specify a priori. Analyzable processes, accordingly, refer to situations where such a priori specifications are relatively easy to establish. Generally, this dimension mirrors Perrow's (1970) division of technologies into analyzable versus non-analyzable ones and the decomposable/non-decomposable dichotomy in Simon (1973).

The other dimension builds on the exploitation/exploration distinction in March (1991) and the closely related discussion of "error detection" and "error diagnostics" in Levinthal and March (1993). Generally, we would then expect error detection to be a common problematic in projects related to exploitation, while error diagnostics would be a feature of projects aiming at the exploration of new possibilities (March 1991). In error detection situations, a limited degree of new knowledge generation is required in order to handle each individual error. A primary problematic is instead to achieve a global or system-wide search for errors.

Exploration and error diagnostics, on the other hand, indicate project contexts involving more fundamental problem-solving. This dimension thus differentiates project contexts that imply less novelty from those where deep or specialized knowledge generation is required.

Taking the four cells seriatim, we first have a "scheduling" logic, where the analyzability of processes combined with a need for error detection should turn the project very much into an optimization endeavor. In such a programmable context project activities may be grouped into a complete "work-breakdown structure" with well-established standards in terms of time, cost, functionality, etc. Errors or deviations from these standards are thus easily found, interpreted, and corrected with little need for interaction and discussion whatsoever.

If sub-processes are reasonably analyzable, a "separating" logic will be an option. By decoupling or separating units, complexity is reduced, and a deep penetration of specific knowledge areas is favored. Cutting off or strictly regulating a sub-unit's relations to other units here allows for a concentrated effort at solving a difficult and clearly bounded problematic. Furthermore, due to the condition of analyzability, it is assumed that it will be possible to put together the outcomes provided by the different specialized work groups, in a way that is straightforward and uncomplicated. Although vital knowledge is distributed among such modular units, this implies that the issue of overall knowledge integration is rather easily taken care of.

In the third cell, identifying a "coupling" logic, error detection is more complicated due to the systemic context, associated with the emergence of many unforeseeable errors. Frequent interaction and communication between the various sub-groups, or members of a project, would then be a fitting recipe for knowledge integration. Using the terminology of Orton and Weick (1990), coupling signifies

	Type of complexity	
	Analyzable	Systemic
Exploitation	Scheduling	Coupling
Exploration	Separating	Semi-coupling

Degree of novelty

Fig. 19.1 A typology of project logics

Source: Adapted from Lindkvist, Söderlund, and Tell (1998).

the need for a high degree of responsiveness. This logic would thus favor system-wide error detection, and involve new knowledge generation to a limited extent. Below, I will use the Telecom case to illustrate and detail its operation.

The fourth cell identifies projects adhering to a "semi-coupling" logic. Here, the knowledge integration process becomes problematic not only due to a multitude of complex interdependencies (as in the coupling context), but also because highly specialized knowledge bases are involved (as in the separating context). This calls for a logic that simultaneously allows for coupling and separation or, in the words of Orton and Weick (1990), for both responsiveness and distinctiveness. Such a process may be expected to generate variety and creativity. However, since most new ideas tend to be bad ideas (Levinthal and March 1993), there are many risks and potential errors involved, and one has to look for "strategic errors" that indicate that the whole project is moving in a wrong direction or dealing with unsolvable problems. As discussed in Sitkin (1996), too rapid action/feedback/adjustment cycles may lead to "groupthink" (Janis 1972), "escalating commitment to a failing course of action" (Staw and Ross 1987), and other kinds of myopia. Hence, in such a context, fast learning would have its liabilities (March 1991), and a fairly "slow" learning process should be preferred. The Pharma case will be used to illustrate this logic.

THE TELECOM CASE

Ericsson is one of the leading suppliers of mobile telephone systems around the world. During the late 1980s it was heavily occupied in developing such systems based on the digital standard for Europe (GSM) and the American market. Due to the resource demands of these investments, as late as 1990, Ericsson had kept a low profile on the Japanese market. To be able to defend its dominant position within this high-technology industry, it was now considered to be of strategic importance to get a contract with one of the newly established operators in Japan.

In late December 1991 Ericsson wrote a letter of intent together with Tokyo Digital Phone. In the contract negotiations, the representatives of the Japanese customer made it clear that they wanted the system, including switches and radio base stations, installed and ready for commercial operation in Tokyo on 1 April 1994, or else the customer would consider another supplier. This was a win or lose contract, and one where a successful project was expected to lead to many business transactions in the future. But it was a challenging task Ericsson was facing, as it meant that it had to develop the system in twelve months, on half the time compared to the development of GSM, and the division managers remarked that it appeared to be a "mission impossible."

Hence, the project's deadline was very definitive and unambiguous and the project leaders made it very clear that a strict discipline and focus on the final deadline and the milestones was a necessity.

If we said that it was to be ready by Friday, we did not accept anything else. If it did not work we hunted down the person responsible for the delivery no matter where he was. You have to get people to understand that next week is too late. Trying hard is not enough. It is only success that counts—nothing else. (Project Leader)

To be able to meet the deadline, competence gained during development projects for the European and American markets had to be used. The division manager also underlined that he wanted people who had learned from the mistakes of earlier projects. All this led to a thorough examination of competence in and around the organization in order to decide which units should be engaged in developing and producing the new system.

We did not get stuck in a lot of organizational muddle. Instead we said clearly; let's use as much as possible of what we have, let's take as many short cuts as possible, let's re-use as many people as possible. (Marketing Director)

Moreover, to reach the goal in time it was also deemed necessary to carry out many of the activities simultaneously which put strong demands on frequent interaction and communication among projects members with different knowledge bases, and who belong to different functional units. While the responsibility for many project activities and sub-parts of the product was clearly allocated to separate functional teams, the relations between the parts and the teams could not be specified in advance. What kinds of problems would emerge during the process of developing and integrating the pieces could not be anticipated. Moreover, it seemed that failures would be both frequent and unavoidable.

It is just as important to realize that it will not work at once. What you need is the courage to fail, and never give up. (Project Leader)

One of the main problems that the two project leaders had to deal with was the trade-off between functionality and time. It was of great importance to have a system of radio base stations that was operative on the prescribed date, so to reach that goal, reductions in the level of the functionality of various parts had to be considered. A constant dialogue about what was "good enough" was thus needed. Generally, the emphasis on deadlines and milestones triggered such re-evaluations of optimal versus necessary functionality. Furthermore, a variety of tests and other controls could be used to indicate global progress achieved so far. One method of doing this was called "practicing the processes," as illustrated by the set-up of a "quality demonstration" of a radio base station.

We ordered a radio base station from the warehouse. Everybody thought that it was destined for shipment to Japan. However, we arranged a quality demonstration in Stockholm and invited top management, quality managers, designers, etc. When we did this demonstration, it turned out that the product did not work. There were all kinds of problems, such as mechanical problems, packaging problems, things were missing, and that created enormous attention. I think this was the first time that the designers had seen a complete radio base station. (Project Leader)

All this required arenas where information could flow swiftly between project members from different functional units and a variety of such forums for problem-solving were introduced and, in some periods of the project, they were used on a daily basis.

for us in the project management team it was a matter of organizing the information flow to create a fast and flexible project. For example, we used video and telephone conferences, project newsletters and short meetings were often held daily. Moreover, the systems emergency ward was a forum where trouble reports were dealt with. In this forum we had some of the most competent Ericsson people within this area. We could therefore respond very quickly and make fast decisions. (Project Leader)

Comment. With reference to the contingency model, the Telecom project would qualify as a case of "systemic complexity," displaying an integration problematic, where dealing with a great many unforeseeable errors constitutes a basic challenge. In this case, the mere number and interdependencies of activities and knowledge bases was no doubt a basic cause of complexity. Turning to the other model dimension, this case would be characterized as a matter of "exploitation." The reuse of competence was a much sought-after feature and resolving the "interface" errors that arose only occasionally involved extended ventures into unfamiliar knowledge terrains. Nor was there any sign of efforts aimed at facilitating work by engaging in knowledge-sharing or knowledge transfer activities. Thus, such a project would be a case of inter-functional knowledge integration, primarily honoring the virtue of responsiveness. As hypothesized by Levinthal and March (1993), a tightly coupled model would seem to have efficiency properties when system-wide error detection rather than error diagnosis is the main issue. Furthermore, in such contexts, "fast learning" and frequency of feedback cycles would then characterize the process of knowledge integration.

THE PHARMA CASE

Developing new pharmaceuticals is a time-consuming process. Development times of up to ten years are not unusual and only a few of the projects that are started actually lead to a commercially viable medicine. Drug development projects are usually divided into phases that represent quite different challenges, and the focus in this chapter is on the first phase, the so-called pre-clinical phase. In simple terms, the aim of pre-clinical development is that, from a basic idea about a possible way to attack a specific illness, substances are created that in a laboratory environment prove to be effective, and which generate so few side-effects that it is possible to begin to test the effects of these substances in clinical trials, i.e. on people. After having passed all the tests for effect and side-effects, the substance that constitutes the final result of a pre-clinical project, many of which last for four to six years, is called the Candidate Drug (CD). The research is carried out in projects of an interdisciplinary nature involving a range of specialists such as chemists, pharmacologists, biochemists, and molecular biologists. Typically, a project leader is in charge of a project management group composed of some four to seven group leaders of the different scientific disciplines.

A central characteristic of this field of work is the high level of uncertainty. Periods of progress are mixed with periods of standing still or of retrogression. Setbacks happen all the time. Sometimes they can be foreseen and the feeling that things can go wrong can have slowly grown stronger as the work has progressed, while sometimes they come suddenly. You are trying to control "nature" and do things that other people have not done or succeeded with. To succeed, it is not enough to have access to resources, a high level of competence, good teamwork, a creative climate, and unique basic ideas, if what you are trying to do is impossible. Many also point to the importance of luck and scientific intuition. You should do as well as you can, dare to fail, be prepared for constant setbacks, and not take them personally.

You also need luck. It is in fact the case that you improve something little by little so that it gets a little better and a little better, a little better, a little better, and then you hit a brick wall. It just doesn't work. And then you have to take it a bit in small steps in some way as it were, and how you do that is a matter of intuition and luck. (Group Leader)

To a great extent, such projects involve basic research and the members who belong to the scientific core can be seen as "researchers in industry" (Marcson 1960; Pelz and Andrews 1976). In such a context, the reuse of competence cannot be widely relied upon, and there is often not much in the literature that is useful as his group begins its work:

This is basic research....So what really starts and what drives the development of [the name of a disease that takes a long time to develop] is really unknown. But that is something you have to live with if your ambition is to make original medicines...so you have to just live with the fact that all that research area is unknown. (Group Leader)

Much of the development work was carried out within highly specialized sub-units and their laboratories, e.g. in the pharmacological department and the chemistry department. Considering the depth of knowledge required for work in each of them would no doubt imply that investing in inter-departmental knowledge-sharing and knowledge transfer would be prohibitively costly. Success in such a project is highly dependent on the quality of the knowledge work done in these distributed specialist departments. Apart from informal discussions, progress meetings were frequently held in these discipline-based groups. Expectations as to what outcomes could be expected in the near future were built from the progress made between these meetings. On the basis of these expectations, groups and individuals compared what was achieved and reflected over deviations. Sometimes, these deviations were easy to interpret, basically confirming previous hunches and ideas, while at other times, they rather increased ambiguity and called for deep and extensive discussion. The project's own dynamics, as well as unexpected events, made it important to continuously create meaning from the results that were generated. As argued by one of the group leaders, the possibility for sharing ideas and "thinking together" in both intra- and interdepartmental settings was a major stimulus for imagination and knowledge creation.

It is when you share your thoughts with others that ideas are evaluated and you get the scientific analysis and processing that is stimulating. The analyses that take place in the project group and the feeling that your ideas are considered valuable there and that my opinions have an impact there is tremendously stimulating. It is there that creativity and self-esteem are very present.

However, to assess on a continuous basis whether or not progress had been made was problematic. The CD, as a comprehensive goal for the project, was not of much help here. Sometimes, deadlines could be set and evaluations made when these were reached, but more often "the feeling that a project is moving along" was seen as a better indication of progress. As stated by one of the interviewees, the extensive use of sub-goals helped to create a feeling of momentum, that you had "made it to the next milking stool" and that you were (slowly) moving forwards. Yet, it was hardly possible to clearly relate these sub-goals to the project's end goal. Here, project leaders here did their best to provide a comprehensive "picture" out of this fragmented goal structure, and this would then serve as a backdrop for evaluating progress for the project in its entirety.

Comment. With reference to the contingency model, the Pharma case too warrants the designation "systemic complexity," considering the profound uncertainty inherent in such development work. Furthermore, it clearly represents an "exploration" context, recognizing the high degree of novelty involved in such work, which makes the reuse of competence difficult. Here, much work was carried out in the different departments, which indicates the importance of honoring distinctiveness. Yet, as evidenced by the presence of various regular meetings and the appreciation attached to opportunities to "think together," responsiveness was also an important ingredient. Hence, this project would be a case of interdisciplinary knowledge integration, guided by the idea of semi-coupling. Here, working with sub-goal formulation and recurrent collective reflection was a means of finding its rhythm, and seeing how various contributions and ideas would fit together as the project was moving forward. While feedback was constantly looked for, its use generally reflected the wisdom of "slow learning."

A PROJECT MANAGEMENT COMPARISON

As shown above, the process of knowledge integration differed substantially between the two contexts, broadly mirroring the difference between a coupling and a semi-coupling logic. Yet, while this discussion mainly featured the general issue of knowledge integration, it should also be seen as inseparably intertwined with some basic project management concerns. Hence, I will focus below specifically on the classical project management issues of the role of goals and the view of deviations, in the two contexts.

On goals and deviations in the Telecom case

In the Telecom case, the project goal was very clear with regard to the time of delivery and what kind of operative functionality the system should have. Everything happening throughout the project had to be aligned with the goal set. In a sense, such a project could be carried out in a kind of backward tracking manner, where activities undertaken could be measured against their contribution to the final goal. Working from the desired output and figuring out how this could be achieved is a typical feature of a technology development context (Nightingale 2004). Here, the strong goals became a means of motivation and a standard against which the project's global progress could be measured. The risk of encountering major setbacks or suddenly realizing that you were moving fast, but in the wrong direction, was hardly something those involved would fear. With reasonable precision it was possible to assess what had been achieved, what was left to do, and how much could be done before the deadline date. These assessments also facilitated trade-off decisions between technical perfection and "good enough" quality—and if needed, more resources could be put in to improve quality or speed up the process.

Keeping the deadline made it necessary to have a well-functioning system-wide error-detection process. Errors or deviations tended to turn up at the functional interfaces and many different ways of identifying and resolving all these not-wanted-errors were used, such as the systems emergency ward, daily stand-up meetings, etc. Moreover, prototyping such as with the "radio base demonstration," where the actual product acted like some kind of boundary object (Carlile 2004) for identifying which parts did not fit together, was sometimes an option. In these collective arenas, problems could be identified and who should deal with them decided. During these encounters, not much specialist knowledge was turned into communal knowledge. It was rather the case that people from different functional units were engaged in a collective effort at finding errors or deviations, and deciding what problem-solving efforts were needed to "weed" them out.

On goals and deviations in the Pharma case

In the Pharma case, the Candidate Drug goal was seen to be far too distant and too uncertain to be effective in guiding and regulating the project process. Instead, pressure and ways of structuring work had to come from within the project itself. This project was largely a matter of scientific work, which as stated by Nightingale (2004: 1271), typically starts from the particulars, exploring the "*unknown* result from a *known* set of starting conditions." Here, trial-and-error experimenting was conducted as a way of weeding out errors, but, even more important, as a way to "weed-in" novel ideas (Dougherty 2007). In particular, if severe setbacks were encountered, and there was great ambiguity as to what should be done next, trial-and-error experimenting was seen as a fitting means of searching for clues. Such processes could result in deviations from what was expected or produce results that were completely unimaginable. Yet, in any case they would produce vital "raw material" for thinking. Focusing on unexpected findings would promote heuristics such as "if the finding is unexpected, then set a goal of discovering the causes of the unexpected finding" (Dunbar 1997: 478). Thus, deviations were something that was seen as positive and something that could nourish the process of searching for clues when project members met and discussed their problems. As expressed by one of the interviewees, such "thinking together" was a highly appreciated way for people to probe their ideas and make them proliferate.

Yet, as we have seen, it was not possible to subject the integration of results from the various departments to a comprehensive plan or schedule. Instead, it was very much an emergent process in which the specialized departments were continually aligning and integrating their findings locally and sequentially in a kind of a "trading zone" (Galison 1997; Kellogg, Orlikowski, and Yates 2006), where people had to interact on a limited basis of shared knowledge. While project managers did their best to assess and provide pictures and images of global progress, this was without doubt an endeavor which called for individuals mastering a broad knowledge base and having good intuitions based on experience. As setbacks can happen suddenly and late in the process, it is difficult to know if you are moving in the right direction, or to assess how much is left to be done. Moreover, there is little space here for making a trade-off between optimal and "good enough" quality in the face of time left to deadline. Getting acceptance for a new CD is a very demanding process, and one in which perfection is needed and where few or no side-effects are tolerated. Finally, while there is some space for speeding up the process by providing more resources for screening and other laboratory processes, the correlation between resources invested and time to completion will generally tend to be weak, and even zero if what is wanted is denied by Mother Nature.

Concluding discussion

In a knowledge collectivity, the process of knowledge integration is seen as being guided by the principle of "well-connectedness of knowledge bases." Moreover, if we use the contingency model, we may identify variation within such a conception. To account in part for such variation, we have shown how connectivity was played out in a telecom and a pharmaceutical project. These illustrations were chosen to show how knowledge collectivities may operate in actual practice in two widely different contexts, a typical engineering or technology development project and a science-based development project. Below, I consider the cases seriatim and conclude with a summarizing table.

Knowledge integration features

The two project contexts were similar in several respects. In both cases, the knowledge integration process relied basically on co-applying the different knowledge bases without making any specific efforts aimed at increasing the communal knowledge base through knowledge-sharing and transfer initiatives, as is suggested by the recipe for promoting "knowledge base similarity." They were also similar in that both cases qualified as being associated with "systemic complexity," turning knowledge integration into an emergent process, wherein decisions and choices had to be made sequentially, without a grand plan, as the projects' trajectories enfolded. They differed, however, with regard to the "degree of novelty" dimension of the contingency model.

Generally, it would seem that the Telecom case is informative about how knowledge integration processes may be managed in an exploitation project. In such a project it should be possible to build to a significant extent on a well-established technology base. Yet, as members co-apply their diverse knowledge bases in such product development projects, many unforeseeable and hard to detect interface problems will emerge and have to be managed creatively and swiftly. Mirroring the need for frequent vertical and horizontal interaction and communication in such a context would make responsiveness a virtue within a knowledge integration logic of "coupling." Progress in such a limited uncertainty context would benefit from a short feedback cycle system and a "fast learning" mode being applied.

Contrary to this, the Pharma case would display an exploration context, where little reusable competence is available, calling for a heavy engagement with profound error diagnostics and new knowledge generation. Here, both distinctiveness and responsiveness would be important, signifying that sub-units and project members need to work, both separately, in order to penetrate deeply into their specialist areas and, at times, need to attend a variety of meetings and arenas that allow for "thinking together" and making a collective search for clues. In such a context, the interpretation of findings and deviations would tend to be highly ambiguous, and constitute input within a semi-coupling logic of knowledge integration, operating according to a more long-linked and "slow learning" mode.

Project management features

Starting with the "goal issue," the guiding power of the overall project goal can obviously be very different. As shown in the Telecom case, the goal could exert a strong influence throughout the project, affecting what to do and considerations regarding how much could still be done in the face of the approaching deadline. In this case, the "assessment of global progress" became a reasonable possibility. The frequent use of a multitude of different test activities not only indicated quite well what interface error existed, but also gave a good indication of progress so far, what compromises were necessary, etc. Similarly, mirroring the limited uncertainty in this kind of project, decisions to supply more resources would seem to have a good chance of benefiting operations and ensuring that goals were reached in time.

The Pharma case illustrated a contrasting context where the project goal was of little use in moving the project forward. It was seen as too distant, was often extended, and people knew that most projects would actually fail to find a viable CD. Here, progress tended to originate in the achievements of sub-units, the integration of which was notoriously difficult. A project enjoying success over a lengthy period could suddenly face severe setbacks or hit a "brick wall." Hence, "assessment of global progress" was associated with much uncertainty. In this case, there was also little room for "good enough" thinking and compromise, as CDs are submitted to tough tests by the drug-regulating authorities. Moreover, putting in more resources in order to improve the quality of the knowledge creation process or to reach goals faster would be a recipe and an investment with a highly uncertain outcome.

Turning specifically to the "deviation" issue, it is of course logical that a project focusing on exploitation will differ from one focusing on exploration. In the Telecom project, a main issue was to arrange for a global error detection process, in which errors were both rather easily interpreted and dealt with. While such errors or deviations could sometimes be informative of new interesting ways of working, most of the time they were something that should be "weeded out." In the Pharma case, weeding out errors was certainly important, but in addition, deviations were intentionally sought after, as a way of providing raw material for thinking and discussion, for finding new clues, ideas, and explanations in the face of some perplexing ambiguities.

In project management literature, the role of goals, control, deviations, and timing considerations is among the most frequently and extensively discussed subject areas. The terminology used then is often quite different from the one associated with knowledge integration as featured above. Yet, I like to think that both discourses are needed and that using them simultaneously should be a fruitful endeavor. Building inductively from the above case analyses, I suggest below a generalizing summary table of how the two facets of project organization may "go together" in an exploitation and exploration context. This table illustrates the general idea of thinking about the basic knowledge integration and project management problematic as two sides of the same coin, as two sides that are both compatible and complementary. The presentation of this table, it is hoped, may inspire its further elaboration and use in a great variety of other project practices.

WHERE TO NEXT?

The issue of knowledge integration has attracted a rapidly growing interest in recent years, with most articles published within the last five to ten years. While the somewhat earlier passion for knowledge management issues was an important antecedent, it was probably the seminal article by Grant (1996) which provided

Table 19.1 Some important dimensions on which the two contexts tend to differ

	Exploitation	Exploration
Knowledge Integration features		
• Knowledge integration approach	Coupling	Semi-coupling
• Knowledge base relations	Responsiveness	Responsiveness and distinctiveness
• Learning cycle	Fast learning	Slow learning
Project Management features		
• Guiding power of goals	Strong	Weak
• Global progress assessment	Possible	Problematic
• Effect of additional resources	Positive	No clear relation
• Role of deviations	Locate errors	Further reflection

the main inspiration for this specific field of inquiry. As in the case of Grant, subsequent works rely strongly on the works on activity integration by Lawrence and Lorsch (1967), Thompson (1967), Perrow (1970), and Simon (1973) on activity integration. Most of them also use, and sometimes modify, the same basic contingency variables (uncertainty, complexity, novelty, and interdependence) in accounting for the additional intricacies associated with the integration of highly specialized knowledge, tacit knowledge, etc. As would be expected in this quite juvenile research area, there are few substantial studies and little agreement on how to define and measure contingency variables and integration mechanisms. Furthermore, as noticed by Carlile and Rebentisch, it seems that the frameworks suggested so far are somewhat biased towards understanding relatively simple tasks.

This knowledge integration challenge becomes more problematic when we realize that current frameworks of knowledge transfer and integration do not apply with equal explanatory power to both simple and complex knowledge integration tasks. (2003: 1182)

Furthermore, although some kind of contingency reasoning is often present, the literature on knowledge integration still tends to promote an overly strong image of such contexts as being similar. Actually, a similar concern has long been acknowledged in the project management literature. As stated by Shenhar (2001) in his well-known advocacy thesis "one size does not fit all projects," much project management literature still conveys the idea that all projects are similar and can be handled using generic measures. As shown by a later comprehensive overview (Sauser, Reilly, and Shenhar 2009), while there are quite a few project management contingency frameworks available, in most of these, the set of contingency variables used relies heavily on the ones suggested in connection with activity integration. Furthermore, these authors state in conclusion that, still, the current state of project management practice has not adopted an explicit, well-accepted way to identify project uniqueness and select an appropriate management style.

With the general aim of proposing a continued effort at "integrating" the knowledge integration and project management fields of inquiry, I have in this chapter relied mainly on the convincing power of example. Choosing two very different project contexts would then be a good idea. Acknowledging the alleged "simplicity" bias in the knowledge integration literature, and the fact that most studies in the project management literature focus on "engineering" projects, my choice was to introduce variety by also including a "science-based" project. Finally, this chapter advocates that the linking of knowledge integration and project management would benefit from contingency modeling. In my view, such models should honor the idea of including a few variables which may explain much, rather than the idea of explaining little with many. If successful, the generation of simple, powerful contingency models will not only advance academic knowledge but also function as useful conceptual tools for analysis in practice.

NOTES

The Telecom illustration is an excerpt from a comprehensive study within Ericsson, by Lindkvist, Söderlund, and Tell (1998), built on thirty interviews with division management, functional line managers, and project leaders/members. The Pharma illustration comprises typical project features taken from a study of four pre-clinical development projects in two large internationally operating pharmaceutical firms, reported in Vik and Lindkvist (2001), and built on forty-seven interviews with project leaders/members and research directors.

REFERENCES

AMIN, A., and ROBERTS, J. (2008). "Knowing in action: beyond communities of practice," *Research Policy*, 37: 353–69.

BARLEY, S. (1996). "Technicians in the workplace: ethnographic evidence for bringing work into organizational studies," *Administrative Science Quarterly*, 41: 404–41.

BECHKY, B. (2003). "Sharing meaning across occupational communities: the transformation of understanding on the production floor," *Organization Science*, 14: 312–30.

BRAGD, A. (2002). "Knowing management: an ethnographic study of tinkering with a new car," Ph.D. thesis, School of Economics and Commercial Law at Gothenburg University, Gothenburg.

BRESNEN, M., EDELMAN, L., NEWELL, S., SCARBROUGH, H., and SWAN, J. (2003). "Social practices and the management of knowledge in project environments," *Journal of Project Management*, 21: 157–65.

BROWN, J. S., and DUGUID, P. (1998). "Organizing knowledge," *California Management Review*, 40: 90–111.

CARLILE, P. R. (2004). "Transferring, translating and transforming: an integrative framework for managing knowledge across boundaries," *Organization Science*, 15/5: 555–68.

——and REBENTISCH, E. S. (2003). "Into the black box: the knowledge transformation cycle," *Management Science*, 49/9: 1180–95.

COOK, S. D., and YANOW, D. (1996). "Culture and organizational learning," in M. D. Cohen and L. S. Sproull (eds.), *Organisational Learning*. Thousand Oaks, CA: Sage.

CROSS, R., and SPROULL, L. (2004). "More than an answer: information relationships for actionable knowledge," *Organization Science*, 15/4: 446–62.

DeFILLIPPI, R. J., ARTHUR, M. B., and LINDSAY, V. J. (2006). *Knowledge at Work: Creating Collaboration in the Global Economy*. Oxford: Blackwell Press.

DOUGHERTY, D. (1992). "Interpretative barriers to successful product innovation in large firms," *Organization Science*, 3: 179–202.

——(2007). "Trapped in the 20th century: why models of organizational learning, knowledge and capabilities do not fit bio-pharmaceuticals, and what to do about that," *Management Learning*, 38/3: 265–70.

DUNBAR, K. (1997). "How scientists think: on-line creativity and conceptual change in science," in T. B. Ward, S. M. Smith, and J. Vaid (eds.), *Creative Thought: An Investigation of Conceptual Structures and Processes*. American Psychological Association.

GALISON, P. (1997). *Image and Logic: A Material Culture of Microphysics*. Chicago: University of Chicago Press.

GRANT, R. M. (1996). "Toward a knowledge-based theory of the firm," *Strategic Management Journal*, 17/Winter Special Issue: 109–22.

HUANG, J., and NEWELL, S. (2003). "Knowledge integration processes and dynamics in the context of cross-functional projects," *International Journal of Project Management*, 21/3: 167–76.

JANIS, I. L. (1972). *Victims of Groupthink: A Psychological Study of Foreign Policy Decisions and Fiascoes*. Boston: Houghton Mifflin.

KELLOGG, K. C., ORLIKOWSKI, W. J., and YATES, J. (2006). "Life in the trading zone: structuring coordination across boundaries in postbureucratic organizations," *Organization Science*, 17/1: 22–44.

LAVE, J., and WENGER, E. (1991). *Situated Learning: Legitimate Peripheral Participation*. New York: Cambridge University Press.

LAWRENCE, P. R., and LORSCH, J. W. (1967). *Organization and Environment: Managing Differentiation and Integration*. Boston: Division of Research Graduate School of Business Administration Harvard University.

LEVINTHAL, D. A., and MARCH, J. G. (1993). "The myopia of learning," *Strategic Management Journal*, 14/Winter Special Issue: 95–112.

LINDKVIST, L. (2004). "Governing project-based firms: promoting market-like processes within hierarchies," *Journal of Management and Governance*, 8: 3–25.

—— (2005). "Knowledge communities and knowledge collectivities: a typology of knowledge work in groups," *Journal of Management Studies*, 42/6: 1189–210.

—— (2008). "Project organization: exploring its adaptation properties," *International Journal of Project Management*, 13: 13–20.

—— SÖDERLUND, J., and TELL, F. (1998). "Managing product development projects: on the significance of fountains and deadlines," *Organization Studies*, 19: 931–51.

MARCH, J. G. (1991). "Exploration and exploitation in organizational learning," *Organization Science*, 2/1: 71–87.

MARCSON, S. (1960). *The Scientist in American Industry: Some Organizational Determinants in Manpower Utilization*. Princeton: Princeton University Press.

NIGHTINGALE, P. (2004). "Technological capabilities, invisible infrastructure and the unsocial construction of predictability: the overlooked fixed costs of useful research," *Research Policy*, 33: 1259–84.

NONAKA, I. (1994). "A dynamic theory of organizational knowledge creation," *Organization Science*, 5/1: 14–37.

—— TOYAMA, R., and KONNO, N. (2000). "SECI, *Ba* and leadership: a unified model of dynamic knowledge creation," *Long Range Planning*, 33: 5–34.

ORR, J. (1990). "Sharing knowledge, celebrating identity: war stories and community memory in a service community," in D. S. Middleton and D. Edwards (eds.), *Collective Remembering: Memory in Society*. Beverly Hills, CA: Sage.

ORTON, D. J., and WEICK, K. E. (1990). "Loosely coupled systems: a reconceptualization," *Academy of Management Review*, 15/2: 203–23.

PELZ, D. C., and ANDREWS, F. M. (1976). *Scientists in Organizations: Productive Climate for Research and Development*. Ann Arbor: University of Michigan Press.

PERROW, C. (1970). *Organizational Analysis: A Sociological Review*. Belmont, CA: Wadsworth.

SAUSER, B. J., REILLY, R. R., and SHENHAR, A. J. (2009). "Why projects fail? How contingency theory can provide new insights: a comparative analysis of NASA's Mars Climate Orbiter loss," *International Journal of Project Management* (article in press).

SCARBROUGH, H., SWAN, J., LAURENT, S., BRESNEN, M., EDELMAN, L. F., and NEWELL, S. (2004). "Project-based learning and the role of learning boundaries," *Organization Studies*, 25/9: 1579–600.

SENSE, A. J. (2003). "Learning generators: project teams re-conceptualized," *Project Management Journal*, September: 4–12.

SHENHAR, A. J. (2001). "One size does not fit all projects: exploring classical contingency domains," *Management Science*, 47/3: 394–414.

SIMON, H. A. (1973). "The organization of complex systems," in H. H. Pattee (ed.), *Hierarchy Theory: The Challenge of Complex Systems*. New York: George Braziller, 3–27.

SITKIN, S. B. (1996). "Learning through failure: the strategy of small losses," in M. D. Cohen and L. S. Sproull (eds.), *Organizational Learning*. Thousand Oaks, CA: Sage, 541–77.

STAW, B. M., and ROSS, J. (1987). "Behavior in escalation situations: antecedents, prototypes, and solutions," in B. M. Staw and L. L. Cummings (eds.), *Research in Organizational Behavior*. Greenwich: JAI Press, 9: 39–78.

SYDOW, J., LINDKVIST, L., and DEFILLIPPI, R. (2004). "Project-based organizations, embeddedness and repositories of knowledge: editorial," *Organization Studies*, 25: 1475–89.

THOMPSON, J. D. (1967). *Organizations in Action, Social Science Basis of Administrative Theory*. New York: McGraw-Hill.

VAN DE VEN, A. H., DELBECQ, A. L., and HOENIG, R. (1976). "Determinants of coordination modes within organizations," *American Sociological Review*, 41: 322–38.

VIK, M., and LINDKVIST, L. (2001). "Styrning av prekliniska utvecklingsprojekt," in C. Berggren and L. Lindkvist (eds.), *Projekt: Organisation för målorientering och lärande*. Lund: Studentlitteratur.

VON MEIER, A. (1999). "Occupational cultures as a challenge to technological innovation," *IEEE Transactions on Engineering Management*, 46/1: 101–14.

WEGNER, D. M., ERBER, R., and RAYMOND, P. (1991). "Transactive memory in close relationships," *Journal of Personality and Social Psychology*, 61: 923–9.

WENGER, E. (1998). *Communities of Practice*. Cambridge: Cambridge University Press.

CHAPTER 20

LEADERSHIP AND TEAMWORK IN DISPERSED PROJECTS

MARTIN HOEGL

MIRIAM MUETHEL

HANS GEORG GEMUENDEN

INTRODUCTION

Geographically dispersed, or virtual, project teams are increasingly used to engage specialized knowledge at different locations. This is particularly true for complex and dynamic projects (Gibson and Gibbs 2006), such as product development (e.g. a new software solution) and process development (e.g. a new manufacturing or distribution system). In such contexts, companies seek to leverage superior knowledge residing at different locations (e.g. technical knowledge, local market knowledge) through direct collaboration, partly relying on computer-mediated communication. Likewise, companies are staffing projects with individuals at different sites to capture favorable labor costs.

However, extant literature indicates that it may prove highly difficult to capitalize on such potential benefits. For instance, critical team processes, e.g. teamwork quality (Hoegl and Gemuenden 2001), such as open sharing of information and task coordination, tend to suffer as teams become increasingly virtual (Hoegl and Proserpio 2004a). Moreover, recent research indicates that while high-quality teamwork is harder to achieve in virtual projects, it is even more relevant in such settings (Siebdrat, Hoegl, and Ernst 2009). In other words, while teamwork quality has repeatedly been established as a key success factor for project teams (Hoegl and Gemuenden 2001; Hoegl, Weinkauf, and Gemuenden 2004), this performance effect becomes stronger as projects are increasingly virtual (Hoegl, Ernst, and Proserpio 2007). Moreover, studies from the 1970s to now have consistently shown that even low levels of geographic dispersion (or virtuality), such as being dispersed across two floors of the same building, matter significantly to the collaborative processes and the performance of projects (Allen 1971; Siebdrat, Hoegl, and Ernst 2009). As such, most project teams are likely to experience some degree of virtuality, utilizing computer-mediated communication (e.g. email) alongside face-to-face communication during their project work. While this chapter focuses on dispersed teams, we note that our discussions pertain also to project teams that experience only temporary or small degrees of dispersion (and would therefore regularly be labeled "co-located project teams"). By analogy, our discussions also apply to multi-team projects (Hoegl, Weinkauf, and Gemuenden 2004), where sub-project teams may be largely co-located, but the entire project may be fairly dispersed, or virtual.

Virtuality, in turn, has been specified as a multidimensional construct. Such virtual project teams may cross several boundaries, including geography, time, and organizations, using telecommunication and information technologies to accomplish a common task. Specifically, their work and task context can include four key characteristics; geographical dispersion, electronic dependence, national diversity, and task uncertainty. Each of these characteristics poses challenges to the performance of dispersed teams. Complex and dynamic tasks place high demands on ensuring efficient and effective task processes (Uhl-Bien, Marion, and McKelvey 2007). At the same time, the contextual characteristics of geographic dispersion, national diversity, and electronically mediated communication are often seen as inhibitors of team performance (Gibson and Gibbs 2006).

Leadership is a key driver of project performance, particularly in virtual projects (Carte, Chidambaram, and Becker 2006; Martins, Gilson, and Maynard 2004). Leadership in teams can generally be defined as influencing the attitudes and behaviors of individuals and the interaction within and between groups for the purpose of achieving goals (Bass 1990). However, traditional vertical leadership (from the formal project leader) is challenged by dispersion, as the feasibility of the leader exerting direct influence on the team diminishes due to fewer opportunities for direct and immediate communication with the team members (Avolio, Kahai, and Dodge 2001). As such, leadership behaviors like information search and structuring, information use in problem-solving, trust-building, as well as coaching and facilitating, become more difficult to perform as team members are physically remote and culturally diverse, the task being uncertain, and communication largely electronically mediated (Gibson and Gibbs 2006). Thus, specific leadership behaviors addressing the virtual context are needed. For the remainder of this chapter, we use the terms dispersed project and virtual project interchangeably.

A review of the leadership literature offers at least three ways of addressing the challenges of dispersed projects. First, leader-centered leadership approaches such as e-leadership (leadership approach focusing on the changing roles of vertical leaders in virtual projects, e.g. how to handle virtual team meetings) focus on ways to strengthen the potential influence of the vertical leader (i.e. the formal project leader) through the use of communication technology (Avolio, Kahai, and Dodge 2001). Second, self-leadership approaches focus on a shift of leadership distribution from the vertical leader to the individuals themselves (Self-Leadership; Manz 1986) or to the team as a whole (Team Self-Leadership; Neck, Stewart, and Manz 1996). Third, shared leadership, as proposed by Pearce and Conger (2003), describes simultaneous, ongoing mutual influence processes within the team (Houghton, Neck, and Manz 2003), characterized by the "serial emergence" of informal as well as formal leaders.

Given the specific challenges of dispersed projects (as highlighted above), we will build on shared leadership to focus on team members as an additional source of leadership behavior in dispersed teams, while also acknowledging the opportunities provided by advanced communication technology facilitating leadership at a distance (Avolio, Kahai, and Dodge 2001). The rather recent concept of shared leadership has been studied in the context of new venture top management teams (Ensley, Hmieleski, and Pearce 2006), sales teams (Perry and Pearce 1999), hospital emergency room staff (Klein et al. 2006), and change management teams (Pearce and Sims 2002). As such, we conceptualize how team-shared leadership can be particularly effective in the context of dispersed project teams, given the challenges of geographical dispersion, electronic dependence, diversity, and task uncertainty. Moreover, we extend this concept by specifying the contributions of the vertical leader to the effectiveness of team-shared leadership in dispersed projects.

The remainder of this chapter starts with a more detailed discussion of the four characteristics of the work and task context of dispersed project teams, specifically highlighting the leadership challenges stemming from these characteristics. We then discuss how shared leadership in dispersed project teams drives their teamwork quality, arguing that shared leadership helps overcome the challenges of geographic dispersion, national diversity, electronic dependence, and task uncertainty.

LEADERSHIP CHALLENGES OF
VIRTUAL PROJECT TEAMS

Teams can generally be defined as social systems of a small number of people, which are embedded in organizations (context), whose members perceive themselves as such and are perceived as members by others (identity), and who collaborate on a common task (teamwork) (Hackman 1987; Hoegl and Gemuenden 2001). Project teams are a subset of teams with a pre-defined lifespan, bounded by project start and end dates. Much prior research on dispersed project teams has typically regarded geographical dispersion as a definitional feature of such teams (Montoya-Weiss, Massey, and Song 2001), with a number of studies comparing virtual teams to *co-located* teams, the latter of which were implicitly assumed to be fully co-located (McDonough, Kahn, and Barczaka 2001). More recent investigations, however, have focused on the *degree* to which team members are in geographical proximity (or dispersion) (Hoegl, Ernst, and Proserpio 2007) and have extended scholarly attention to related (continuous) characteristics of dispersed teams. As already alluded to in the introduction, the work and task context of dispersed (or virtual) teams has more comprehensively been described along four key characteristics (Gibson and Gibbs 2006), including geographical dispersion, electronic dependence, national diversity, and task uncertainty. Each of these characteristics poses leadership challenges, which we will discuss below. It is worth noting again, however, that research indicates that even very low degrees of dispersion (e.g. within the same building or the same site) are likely to have significant effects on teamwork and project success.

Geographical dispersion hints at the physical and temporal distance of the team members, varying between the same place and global distribution. Recent research has distinguished several dimensions of geographic dispersion, including spatial (e.g. mileage), temporal (e.g. time zones), and configurational (e.g. imbalance of membership across sites) characteristics (O'Leary and Cummings 2007). As O'Leary and Cummings (2007) highlight, these dimensions have previously been identified as performance inhibitors of dispersed teams, with spatial dispersion reducing spontaneous communication, temporal dispersion diminishing real-time problem-solving, and configurational dispersion decreasing awareness of team members' work status, while increasing conflicts between sub-groups at different sites.

Although physical dispersion does not necessarily influence the use of communication technologies (highly dispersed teams can also travel and fairly co-located teams mostly communicate via email or telephone), it is often assumed that more geographically distributed teams are also higher in *electronic dependence* (Kirkman et al. 2004). Dispersed teams relying more on technology have been found to experience communication problems in terms of failure to communicate contextual information, failure to communicate information evenly, differences in salience of information to individuals, differences in speed and access to information, and interpretation in the meaning of salience (Kankanhalli, Tan, and Kwok-Kee 2006). These communication problems contribute to misunderstandings and task conflict in these teams. Moreover, as social influence can better be exerted face-to-face than electronically, project leadership functions (such as providing direction and feedback, coaching team members, collecting and distributing information, etc.) are difficult to enact in the same quality as in co-located settings. As such, even if full use is made of advanced communication technology, limited media richness (Johnson and Lederer 2005) and limited social presence (Kock 2004) hinder the exertion of influence. Likewise, increasing travel activities in the project to achieve more face-to-face interaction regularly come with significant budgetary implications and time lost to travel.

Another characteristic often assumed to coincide with geographical dispersion is *national diversity* (Maznevski and Chudoba 2000). The more a team is nationally diverse, the more it is faced with national and linguistic differences among members as well as differences along broader cultural dimensions such as individualism and assertiveness. Culture is a set of values which serve as a filter for one's perception of the surrounding environment, guiding behavior and social interaction. Teams with high national diversity demonstrate divergent preferences for social interaction norms, which can create difficulties in executing processes related to task integration, such as coordination. For project leadership, facing cultural distances of the team members (above and beyond physical ones) and differing expectations on effective leadership behavior poses critical challenges of exerting social influence.

Independent of the team's degree of geographic dispersion, *task uncertainty*, coming along with dynamic and complex tasks such as product and process development, poses a strong need for direct collaboration among team members (Baba et al. 2004). For instance, developing a comprehensive software solution for a global logistics network, the overall task cannot be entirely separated into work packages to be carried out independently by individual team members or sub-teams. Instead, to accomplish the task, at least several of the team members have to collaborate to contribute to the team task. Moreover, high task complexity is reflected in interrelated and sometimes even conflicting subtasks, multiple alternatives with multiple attributes, uncertain alternatives or outcomes, information (over-)load, diversity and rate of change, information interrelationships, and constraints that need to be satisfied. Prior research indicates that such task characteristics drive the need for close integration of team members, further intensifying the leadership challenges of ensuring the necessary high level of information exchange and task coordination despite geographic and cultural distances, and largely depending on electronic means of communication.

In sum, task uncertainty places high demands on project leadership to ensure efficient and effective task processes. At the same time, the contextual characteristics of geographic dispersion and national diversity provide disabling factors, making it difficult to exert the necessary social influence across geographic and cultural distances (Derosa et al. 2004). Even though advanced use of the latest information and communication technology may partly mitigate this effect, we conclude, based on related prior research, that geographic dispersion, national diversity, electronic dependence, and task uncertainty pose critical leadership challenges. We now turn to the shared leadership concept and discuss its specific relevance given these particular characteristics of dispersed project teams.

Team members as an additional source of leadership

For our discussion, we take the shared leadership concept as formulated by Pearce and Conger (2003) as our point of departure. Shared leadership is defined as "a dynamic, interactive influence process among individuals in work groups in which the objective is to lead one another to the achievement of group goals" (Pearce and Conger 2003: 286). As such, shared leadership delineates a collective team process through which individual team members share in performing behaviors and roles of the traditional leader (Pearce and Conger 2003). It entails a simultaneous, on going shared leadership process within the team to maximize the potential of the team as a whole (Houghton, Neck, and Manz 2003).

In the following, we detail how team-shared leadership in dispersed project teams supports the performance-relevant team processes described in the teamwork quality construct (Hoegl and Gemuenden 2001), making specific reference to their critical work context characteristics.

Team-shared leadership and teamwork quality

Leadership has been shown to be an important driver of team processes (Burke et al. 2006). Consequently, we show below that team-shared leadership is positively related to teamwork quality (Hoegl and Gemuenden 2001) in virtual projects. We also describe critical functions of the vertical (i.e. formal or hierarchical) project leader enabling team-shared leadership (i.e. initiating structure, monitoring project progress, solving team conflict, and empowerment).

To capture the complex nature of team members working together, Hoegl and Gemuenden (2001) conceptualized and empirically validated teamwork quality as a higher-order construct with six facets, i.e. communication, coordination, balance of member contributions, mutual support, effort, and cohesion. The teamwork quality construct and measures have later been validated in empirical studies by Easley, Devaraj, and Crant (2003) as well as Hoegl, Weinkauf, and Gemuenden (2004). The underlying proposition of this latent construct is that highly collaborative teams display behaviors related to all six teamwork quality facets. In teams with high teamwork quality, team members openly communicate relevant information, coordinate their activities, ensure that all team members can contribute their knowledge to their full potential, mutually support each other in team discussion and individual task work, establish and maintain work norms of high effort, and foster an adequate level of team cohesion where team members maintain the group. The following discussion of the relationship between team-shared leadership and teamwork in dispersed project teams relates to the teamwork quality construct and its six facets.

Communication. Team-shared leadership behaviors are initiated by the individual team members with the aim to increase not only their own performance but the performance of the team as a whole. When approaching other team members with this aim, the individual decides on whether to interact face-to-face or via computer-mediated communication. Research has shown that there is a communication media fit between the level of decision processes and the richness of media (Hertel, Geister, and Konradt 2005). Maznevski and Chudoba (2000) found that communication technologies with low media richness (such as email) are better used for gathering information, while communication technologies with medium levels of media richness are better used for solving problems, and face-to-face contact for generating ideas and making comprehensive decisions. However, communication patterns in teams are less a function of the media fit than of the norms, practices, and social conditions surrounding the media use (Desanctis and Monge 1999). Considering that in dispersed project teams (as a temporary organization) team members regularly come from different departments (intra-organizational collaboration) or even different companies (inter-organizational collaboration), they are likely to demonstrate differing communication patterns. Yet, when entering into processes of shared leadership with other team members, the individual starts a learning process of how (in the sense of "by which communication media") to approach other team members (Martins, Gilson, and Maynard 2004). As team members engaging in shared leadership are motivated to identify action needs and influence other team members in the interest of project performance, they cognitively evaluate alternative modes of communication and employ them in order to maximize reciprocity (Rogers and Lea 2005). That is, team members engaging in shared leadership deliberately select, implement, and refine their communication strategy. Team-shared leadership therefore fosters active management of geographical distance (when to have face-to-face meetings), and continuous reflection not only on the task, but also on the communication strategy. Challenging team members to argue pro or contra a proposal, team-shared leadership also leads to a higher quality of information exchange and subsequently better knowledge integration (Okhuysen and Eisenhardt 2002).

Coordination. Team-shared leadership increases task coordination within teams. Continuous monitoring and analyzing task strategies and interdependencies (e.g. how do current changes in my area affect others?) enhances efficiency as it largely preempts the need for later rework. Interdependence, i.e. the outcomes are based on a combination of parties' efforts, is considered a defining characteristic of social exchange (Cropanzano and Mitchell 2005). A recent study documents that under conditions of high speed, uncertainty, and rapid change, team members can achieve a high degree of coordination by making their work visible to others while simultaneously observing others' work progress (Kellogg, Orlikowski, and Yates 2006). In such a task context, and with team members physically dispersed, team task reflection inherent in team-shared leadership (West 1996) will help uncover any emerging gaps or overlaps between individual work packages, with team members seeking out and negotiating technical interfaces between their contributions (Hoegl, Weinkauf, and Gemuenden 2004). Monitoring and influencing originates from various (ideally all) team members residing at different locations and having different information bases. As team members expand effort to keep track of the overall project and team members' individual contributions, they are in a position to quickly react to any changes. This is particularly important given the complex and dynamic tasks and the dispersed nature of the teams (e.g. setting obstacles for everyone to be aware of current developments). As such, team-shared leadership leads to increased flexibility and adaptability of dispersed teams. Virtual teams' decisions regarding work strategies (or necessary adaptations to it) can be made more quickly and more accurately given a more current and broader information basis provided by team-shared leadership.

Balance of team member contributions. By anticipating information and action needs and initiating appropriate action, team members make explicit use of their knowledge and skills (West 1996). Continuous interaction stemming from shared leadership behaviors fosters the development of shared codes and language, facilitating both access to information and integration of exchanged knowledge (Collins and Smith 2006). Furthermore, team-shared leadership strengthens the relational ties between the team members, which are positively related to the transfer of useful knowledge. Such relational ties encompass on the one hand the willingness of the team to share ideas and feedback. On the other hand, they comprise the readiness of the team to receive information and recognition from other team members (Seers 1989) in the interest of overall team performance. Considering virtual teams' physical dispersion and often national diversity, such relationship-building among the team members becomes particularly crucial for teamwork quality. As such, team-shared leadership is likely to foster every team member's full involvement and integration into the project, what Hoegl and Gemuenden (2001) call balance of team member contributions.

Mutual support and effort. Moreover, team-shared leadership behaviors demonstrate consideration for others' contributions as well as for the entire project. As such, team-shared leadership creates an atmosphere of interest for each other aimed at improving the performance of the entire team, along with every member's contribution (Tjosvold 1995). As the team members are often from different departments, they are continuously challenged by tasks other than the common project that call for their effort. The consideration of other's contributions within the project team helps re-focus everyone on the overall project objectives, and thus motivates the team members to mobilize all their effort (Hackman 1987). As such, team-shared leadership helps explain dispersed team members' levels of engagement and their mutual support, as their interest in other team members' contributions and subsequent advice-giving are central elements in team-shared leadership.

Cohesion. Particularly in intercultural environments, members of virtual project teams are faced with different behavioral expectations, critically challenging the team's level of cohesion (Siebdrat, Hoegl, and Ernst 2009). In these settings, shared norms of cooperative behavior become an important factor. The GLOBE study revealed several attributes which are universally related to effective leaders, such as being trustworthy, just, and honest, having foresight and planning ahead, being positive, dynamic, encouraging, motivating, and building confidence, being communicative, informed, a coordinator, and a team integrator (Javidan et al. 2006). Shared leadership encompasses related behaviors. Proactively approaching other team members or the team as a whole demonstrates dynamic and encouraging behaviors. Furthermore, the interest in the team performance instead of pure individual performance integrates the team and coordinates team action. As initiative is taken when an individual identifies action needs for other team members or the dispersed project team as a whole, shared leadership also demonstrates foresight and planning ahead. Finally, shared leadership comprises mutual influence between peers (Pearce and Conger 2003), with individuals relying on their persuasive power as they cannot force the other team members to follow their advice or adhere to their request. Hence, team members have to demonstrate not only their technical competence, but also their trustworthiness when striving for social influence. In sum, shared leadership behaviors are closely related to universally accepted leadership behaviors and therefore address the challenges to team cohesion in dispersed projects.

Flexible vertical leadership

The vertical leader (i.e. the formal hierarchical project leader) plays an important part in initiating and supporting team-shared leadership. As team-shared leadership is based on participative decision-making, the team members depend on the vertical leader sharing decision authority (Houghton, Neck, and Manz 2003). On the other hand, when the team is not able to solve conflicts and reach project goals, project leader's authority is needed to support conflict resolution and to draw attention to the achievement of project results. Hence, the project leaders have an important role in initiating and supporting social exchange in terms of team-shared leadership by flexibly adapting their leadership behaviors (Klein et al. 2006).

Building on empirical research of effective leadership in virtual teams (Kayworth and Leidner 2001), we conclude that such flexible vertical leadership (by the formal project leader) supports team-shared leadership through (1) initiating structure, (2) empowering the team, (3) monitoring project progress and providing feedback with regard to project accomplishment, as well as (4) solving team task conflict.

Project leaders initiate and support such activities as participative assignments of tasks (Burke et al. 2006) as well as mapping and communicating technical interdependencies between team members. Team events initiated by the project leader at the start of a project (ideally in a face-to-face kickoff meeting) offer the team the possibility to share information and to openly discuss goals, processes, and procedures. Content clarification (elucidating projects' scopes and requirements, gathering supportive background information, and creating work documents) and process information (laying out work plans and associated timetables) enable the team to anticipate information, action needs of others (West 1996) and facilitate social exchange processes.

As team-shared leadership targets "a dynamic, interactive influence process among individuals in work groups in which the objective is to lead one another to the achievement of group goals" (Pearce and Conger 2003: 286), the project leader needs to empower the virtual project team. Empowerment embraces coaching, monitoring, and feedback behaviors (Hackman and Wageman 2005) along with those behaviors indicative of participative, facilitative, and consultative leadership styles (Burke et al. 2006).

Another task of the project leader is to solve task (content and goals), relational (interpersonal relationships), and procedural (how the work gets done) conflicts (Jehn 1997). Should there be team conflict, the project leader fosters cooperative team conflict-solving, serving as a mediator, i.e. guiding the process but allowing disputants control over the outcome, helping them engage in perspective-taking, guiding them toward a realistic settlement, and helping to improve the relationship between them (Jameson 2001). Only if a consensus team decision seems not possible, or the consensus does not sufficiently reflect organizational or project goals, does the project leader make authoritarian decisions.

We use the term *flexible* vertical leadership to indicate that the project leader generally engages in team empowerment but also takes over an active leadership role (Klein et al. 2006) when perceiving the team as not being able to reach schedule, budget, or product quality expectations on its own (or when team members ask the vertical leader to do so having the impression that the team will not meet the expectations). Therefore, the behavioral expectations on the project leaders are at least partly contradictory (Denison, Hooijberg, and Quinn 1995). While participative decision-making depends on empowerment and delegation of authority, initiation of structure or problem-solving behaviors might include autocratic leadership behaviors. According to Denison et al. (1995), effective leaders must have the social perceptiveness and behavioral flexibility "to react to paradox, contradiction, and complexity in their environments."

DISCUSSION

Theoretical implications

Leadership has been shown to be a critical driver of team processes. Recent publications in leading international journals indicate the current interest of the scientific community in (1) context-specific team leadership approaches (Klein et al. 2006), (2) leadership substitution (Howell et al. 1990), (3) more attention on levels of analysis (Hunt and Ropo 1995), and (4) on behavioral complexity (Kayworth and Leidner 2001). The discussion in this chapter both integrates with and challenges these aspects in several ways.

Context-specific team leadership approaches. First, we contribute to context-specific approaches of leadership, which recently have been demanded by several authors (Uhl-Bien, Marion, and McKelvey 2007) as our discussion of team-shared leadership relates to processes of team collaboration in virtual projects, highlighting how team-shared leadership affects performance-relevant elements of the team collaborative process (Hoegl, Weinkauf, and Gemuenden 2004).

Leadership substitution. In line with approaches to leadership substitution (Howell et al. 1990), we draw attention toward the integration of team members as an additional source for leadership. However, we do not propose the substitution of the vertical leader, arguing that the vertical leader remains critical to the team's collaborative processes. Instead, we integrate with research on team leadership, such as team self-leadership (Neck, Stewart, and Manz 1996), collective leadership (Hiller, Day, and Vance 2006), and shared leadership (Pearce and Conger 2003), and point to the potential of team members performing leadership behaviors.

Levels of analysis. However, in contrast to prior work on shared leadership (Houghton, Neck, and Manz 2003; Pearce and Conger 2003), we do not regard shared leadership primarily as a collective team process. We emphasize that it is the individual team member who initiates team-shared leadership, which, in turn, involves other team members. Team-shared leadership behaviors are primarily driven by the team members' interests in ensuring team-level goal achievement, i.e. that the overall team output meets expectations regarding quality, cost, and time.

Behavioral complexity. Building on the empirical analysis of Kayworth and Leidner (2001), who discovered that highly effective virtual team leaders empower the team and at the same time assert their authority without being perceived as overbearing or inflexible, we point to the behavioral complexity of vertical leadership in dispersed teams. With the term *flexible* vertical leadership we address related issues of contradiction and paradox (Denison, Hooijberg, and Quinn 1995). Moreover, defining criteria of when the vertical leader should take over the active leadership role and when to support team solutions, we relate to the theoretical conceptualization of dynamic delegation (i.e. shifts in the active leadership role) by Klein et al. (2006).

Social exchange theory. We tie in with Seers and colleagues (Seers, Keller, and Wilkerson 2003), arguing that social exchange between peers positively influences team performance. However, while these authors focus on teamwork-related social exchanges, such as coordination of individual contributions to the team task, we emphasize the importance of an exchange of active influence in terms of shared leadership. As such, we demonstrate that the context can also influence the operationalization of exchange norms.

Project management. Recent work on project management points to emotional (Geoghegan and Dulewicz 2008), authentic (Toor and Ofori 2008), and ethical behaviors (Lee 2009) as being relevant to successful project leaders. With shared leadership particularly relying on the positive relationship between the project members, our chapter also contributes to this trend of regarding "soft facts as the real hard facts."

Project management usually aims at subdividing tasks into subtasks and to assign responsibility for them to different project members according to their expertise. Despite such a top-down task-structuring approach, successful dispersed projects also depend on a bottom-up integrating mechanism that allows for the alignment of interdependent subtasks. Shared leadership mechanisms are likely to provide such a function.

FURTHER RESEARCH

The concept of team-shared leadership in dispersed project teams, as outlined in this chapter, provides a basis for necessary further conceptual and empirical work. Surely an interesting perspective for such future research on leadership and teamwork in dispersed projects pertains to how shared leadership unfolds over time. Based on prior longitudinal research on leadership in project teams (Hoegl and Weinkauf 2005) it seems likely that intense shared leadership may be more critical in early project phases (with higher levels of perceived task uncertainty and complexity) rather than later stages. Such longitudinal analyses would also allow study of how shared leadership and teamwork quality develop and interact over time.

Beyond this general call for a more dynamic analysis of leadership and teamwork processes, we see antecedent and contextual conditions for shared leadership in dispersed project teams as particularly necessary further extensions of extant research. Furthermore, future work on the intersection of project management as an organizational routine and shared leadership as a flexible coordination mechanism might offer additional insights into how highly structured projects can keep their flexibility in complex and dynamic environments. These ideas are briefly sketched below, turning first to contextual and antecedent conditions at various levels of analysis.

Organizational-level antecedents of shared leadership may include organizational culture. For example, organizational culture as conceptualized by Hurley and Hult (1998) comprises, among other elements, innovativeness (e.g. seeking new ideas), participative decision-making (e.g. decisions based on open discussion), and power-sharing (e.g. atmosphere of cooperation). These organizational factors might positively influence the likelihood of shared leadership.

Possible project- and team-level antecedents may include shared mental models (Carson, Tesluk, and Marrone 2007) and team commitment to shared goals. Shared mental models comprise an organized understanding or mental representation of knowledge of or beliefs about key elements of the team's relevant environment that are shared by its members. Team commitment to shared goals refers to the team's belief in the shared goals and its willingness to exert effort in respect of the team task. These properties are, in turn, likely to be positive for shared leadership in dispersed teams. Moreover, it is quite likely that the type of project a team pursues influences the effects that shared leadership has on teamwork quality. For instance, highly volatile and unpredictable tasks (such as the development of a new-to-the-world product) may pose extreme challenges for team members to perform shared leadership effectively and efficiently in a dispersed setting. By contrast, more predictable project tasks, such as a specific adaptation of an existing IT system, may lend themselves more to dispersed settings, with shared leadership being more beneficial in such cases. Moreover, fluidity (or flexibility) of project team membership (from stable to rapidly changing membership) may well have an influence on both shared leadership and teamwork quality. Such and other possible contingencies are important to investigate, in order to better understand the boundary conditions for successful shared leadership in dispersed project teams.

Moreover, at the individual level, antecedents most probably include self-leadership skills (Bligh, Pearce, and Kohles 2006) and social skills (Cox, Pearce, and Perry 2003). Self-leadership comprises behavioral and cognitive strategies through which the individual influences himself or herself to achieve the self-direction and self-motivation needed to perform, such as self-regulation, self-control, and self-management (Houghton, Neck, and Manz 2003). Social skills enable team members to resolve conflicts (e.g. to recognize the type and source of conflict, employ interactive win-win negotiation strategies), to collaborate in problem-solving (e.g. to identify situations in which participation is appropriate and utilize a proper degree of participation), and to communicate effectively (e.g. to understand communication networks, communicate openly and supportively, use active listening). Moreover, it is important to note that all team members, rather than just the team leader, need to possess sufficient skills in these critical areas to facilitate shared leadership. This, in turn, implies that organizations need to invest in the leadership and social skills development of not only dedicated leadership staff, but everyone involved in dispersed projects.

With regard to the intersection of project management and shared leadership, we suggest further research to explore the mechanisms of standardization (i.e. routinized use of project management tools) and shared leadership as a flexible adaptation process. To a certain degree, high levels of structuring might negatively influence the project team's capability to flexibly adapt to complex and dynamic environments. Shared leadership, the proactive engagement of all team members to take over responsibility for task achievement, might be a valuable mechanism to prevent highly standardized project teams from potential inadaptability.

The most persuasive demand for additional research on team-shared leadership, however, derives from the practical relevance of dispersed projects. Companies are rapidly increasing their use of dispersed teams (McDonough, Kahn, and Barczaka 2001; Vaccaro, Veloso, and Brusoni 2009) and many find it difficult to reap their potential. While our discussions in this chapter focused primarily on dispersed project teams, highlighting their specific leadership challenges, it is obvious that such challenges are also common in a wide array of other contexts and industry sectors. As such, we expect that our ideas on shared leadership and teamwork quality pertain also to large construction projects with changing memberships and varying degrees of dispersion as well as to global organizational change projects with high levels of national diversity.

REFERENCES

ALLEN, T. J. (1971). "Communication networks in RandD laboratories," *R&D Management*, 1: 14–21.

AVOLIO, B. J., KAHAI, S. S., and DODGE, G. E. (2001). "E-leadership: implications for theory, research, and practice," *Leadership Quarterly*, 11/4: 615–68.

BABA, M. L., GLUESING, J., RATNER, H., and WAGNER, K. H. (2004). "The contexts of knowing: natural history of a globally distributed team," *Journal of Organizational Behavior*, 25/5: 547.

BASS, B. (1990). *Bass and Stogdill's Handbook of Leadership*. New York: Free Press.

BLIGH, M. C., PEARCE, C. L., and KOHLES, J. C. (2006). "The importance of self- and shared leadership in team based knowledge work," *Journal of Managerial Psychology*, 21/4: 296.

BURKE, C. S., STAGL, K. C., KLEIN, C., GOODWIN, G. F., SALAS, E., and HALPIN, S. M. (2006). "What type of leadership behaviors are functional in teams? A meta-analysis," *Leadership Quarterly*, 17: 288–307.

CARSON, J. B., TESLUK, P. E., and MARRONE, J. A. (2007). "Shared leadership in teams: an investigation of antecedent conditions and performance," *Academy of Management Journal*, 50/5: 1217–34.

CARTE, T., CHIDAMBARAM, L., and BECKER, A. (2006). "Emergent leadership in self-managed virtual teams," *Group Decision and Negotiation*, 15/4: 323.

COLLINS, C. J., and SMITH, K. G. (2006). "Knowledge exchange and combination: the role of human resource practices in the performance of high-technology firms," *Academy of Management Journal*, 49/3: 544.

COX, J. F., PEARCE, C. L., and PERRY, M. L. (2003). "Toward a model of shared leadership and distributed influence in the innovation process: how shared leadership can enhance new product development team dynamics and effectiveness," in C. L. Pearce and J. A. Conger (eds.), *Shared Leadership: Reframing the Hows and Whys of Leadership*. Thousand Oaks, CA: Sage Publications, 48–76.

CROPANZANO, R., and MITCHELL, M. S. (2005). "Social exchange theory: an interdisciplinary review," *Journal of Management*, 31/6: 874–900.

DENISON, D. R., HOOIJBERG, R., and QUINN, R. E. (1995). "Paradox and performance: toward a theory of behavioral complexity in managerial leadership," *Organization Science*, 6/5: 524.

DEROSA, D. M., HANTULA, D. A., KOCK, N., and D'ARCY, J. (2004). "Trust and leadership in virtual teamwork: a media naturalness perspective," *Human Resource Management*, 43/2–3: 219.

DESANCTIS, G., and MONGE, P. (1999). "Introduction to the special issue: communication processes for virtual organizations," *Organization Science*, 10/6: 693.

EASLEY, R. F., DEVARAJ, S., and CRANT, M. (2003). "Relating collaborative technology use to teamwork quality and performance: an empirical analysis," *Journal of Management Information Systems*, 19/4: 247–68.

ENSLEY, M. D., HMIELESKI, K. M., and PEARCE, C. L. (2006). "The importance of vertical and shared leadership within new venture top management teams: implications for the performance of startups," *Leadership Quarterly*, 17: 217–31.

——PEARSON, A., and PEARCE, C. L. (2003). "Top management team process, shared leadership, and new venture performance: a theoretical model and research agenda," *Human Resource Management Review*, 13/2: 329.

GEOGHEGAN, L., and DULEWICZ, V. (2008). "Do project managers' leadership competencies contribute to project success?," *Project Management Journal*, 39/4: 58–67.

GIBSON, C. B., and GIBBS, J. L. (2006). "Unpacking the concept of virtuality: the effects of geographic dispersion, electronic dependence, dynamic structure, and national diversity on team innovation," *Administrative Science Quarterly*, 51/3: 451.

HACKMAN, J. R. (1987). "The design of work teams," in J. W. Lorsch (ed.), *Handbook of Organizational Behavior*. Englewood Cliffs, NJ: Prentice-Hall, 315–42.

——and WAGEMAN, R. (2005). "A theory of team coaching," *Academy of Management Review*, 30/2: 269–87.

HERTEL, G., GEISTER, S., and KONRADT, U. (2005). "Managing virtual teams: a review of current empirical research," *Human Resource Management Review*, 15/1: 69.

HILLER, N. J., DAY, D. V., and VANCE, R. J. (2006). "Collective enactment of leadership roles and team effectiveness: a field study," *Leadership Quarterly*, 17/4: 387.

HOEGL, M., and GEMUENDEN, H. G. (2001). "Teamwork quality and the success of innovative projects: a theoretical concept and empirical evidence," *Organization Science*, 12/4: 435–49.

——and PROSERPIO, L. (2004a). "Team member proximity and teamwork in innovative projects," *Research Policy*, 33/8: 1153–65.

————(2004b). "Team member proximity and teamwork in innovative projects," *Research Policy*, 33: 1153–65.

———— and WEINKAUF, K. (2005). "Managing task interdependencies in multi-team projects: a longitudinal study," *Journal of Management Studies*, 42/6: 1287–308.

———————— and GEMUENDEN, H. G. (2004). "Interteam coordination, project commitment, and teamwork in multiteam RandD projects: a longitudinal study," *Organization Science*, 15/1: 38–55.

————ERNST, H., and PROSERPIO, L. (2007). "How teamwork matters more as team member dispersion increases," *Journal of Product Innovation Management*, 24/1: 156–65.

HOUGHTON, J. D., NECK, C. P., and MANZ, C. C. (2003). "Self-leadership and superleadership," in C. L. Pearce and J. A. Conger (eds.), *Shared Leadership: Reframing the Hows and Whys of Leadership*. Thousand Oaks, CA: Sage Publication, 123–40.

HOWELL, J. P., BOWEN, D. E., DORFMAN, P. W., KERR, S., and PODSAKOFF, P. M. (1990). "Substitutes for leadership: effective alternatives to ineffective leadership," *Organizational Dynamics*.

HUNT, J. G., and ROPO, A. (1995). "Multi-level leadership: grounded theory and mainstream theory applied to the case of general motors," *Leadership Quarterly*, 6/3: 379–412.

HURLEY, R. F., and HULT, G. T. M. (1998). "Innovation, market orientation, and organizational learning: an integration and empirical examination," *Journal of Marketing*, 62/3: 42–54.

JAMESON, J. K. (2001). "Employee perceptions of the availability and use of interest-based, right-based, and power-based conflict management strategies," *Conflict Resolution Quarterly*, 19/2: 163–96.

JAVIDAN, M., DORFMAN, P. W., DE LUQUE, M. S., and HOUSE, R. J. (2006). "In the eye of the beholder: cross cultural lessons in leadership from project GLOBE," *Academy of Management Perspectives*, 20/1: 67–90.

JEHN, K. A. (1997). "A qualitative analysis of conflict types and dimensions in organizational groups," *Administrative Science Quarterly*, 42/3: 530–57.

JOHNSON, A. M., and LEDERER, A. L. (2005). "The effect of communication frequency and channel richness on the convergence between chief executive and chief information officers," *Journal of Management Information Systems*, 22/2: 227.

KANKANHALLI, A., TAN, B. C. Y., and KWOK-KEE, W. E. I. (2006). "Conflict and performance in global virtual teams," *Journal of Management Information Systems*, 23/3: 237.

KAYWORTH, T. R., and LEIDNER, D. E. (2001). "Leadership effectiveness in global virtual teams," *Journal of Management Information Systems*, 18/3: 7.

KELLOGG, K. C., ORLIKOWSKI, W. J., and YATES, J. (2006). "Life in the trading zone: structuring coordination across boundaries in postbureaucratic organizations," *Organization Science*, 17/1: 22–44.

KIRKMAN, B. L., ROSEN, B., TESLUK, P. E., and GIBSON, C. B. (2004). "The impact of team empowerment on virtual team performance: the moderating role of face-to-face interaction," *Academy of Management Journal*, 47/2: 175.

KLEIN, K. J., ZIEGERT, J. C., KNIGHT, A. P., and YAN, X. (2006). "Dynamic delegation: shared, hierarchical, and deindividualized leadership in extreme action teams," *Administrative Science Quarterly*, 51/4: 590.

KOCK, N. (2004). "The psychobiological model: towards a new theory of computer-mediated communication based on Darwinian evolution," *Organization Science*, 15/3: 327.

LEE, M. R. (2009). "E-ethical leadership for virtual project teams," *International Journal of Project Management*, 27/5: 456–63.

McDonough, E. F., Kahn, K. B., and Barczaka, G. (2001). "An investigation of the use of global, virtual, and colocated new product development teams," *Journal of Product Innovation Management*, 18: 110–20.

Manz, C. C. (1986). "Self-leadership: toward an expanded theory of self-influence processes in organizations," *Academy of Management Review*, 11/3: 585–600.

Martins, L. L., Gilson, L. L., and Maynard, M. T. (2004). "Virtual teams: what do we know and where do we go from here?," *Journal of Management*, 30/6: 805.

Maznevski, M. L., and Chudoba, K. M. (2000). "Bridging space over time: global virtual team dynamics and effectiveness," *Organization Science*, 11/5: 473.

Montoya-Weiss, M. M., Massey, A. P., and Song, M. (2001). "Getting it together: temporal coordination and conflict management in global virtual teams," *Academy of Management Journal*, 44/6: 1251–62.

Neck, C. P., Stewart, G. L., and Manz, C. C. (1996). "Self-leaders within self-leading teams: toward an optimal equilibrium," *Advances in Interdisciplinary Studies of Work Teams*, 3: 43–65.

Okhuysen, G. A., and Eisenhardt, K. M. (2002). "Integrating knowledge in groups: how formal interventions enable flexibility," *Organization Science*, 13/4: 370–86.

O'Leary, M. B., and Cummings, J. N. (2007). "The spatial, temporal, and configurational characteristics of geographic dispersion in teams," *MIS Quarterly*, 31/3: 433–52.

Pearce, C. L., and Conger, J. A. (2003). *Shared Leadership: Reframing the Hows and Whys of Leadership*. Thousand Oaks, CA: Sage Publications.

——and Sims, H. P. (2002). "Vertical versus shared leadership as predictors of the effectiveness of change management teams: an examination of aversive, directive, transactional, transformational, and empowering leader behaviors," *Group Dynamics*, 6/2: 172.

Perry, M. L., and Pearce, C. L. (1999). "Who's leading the selling teams? Vertical versus shared leadership in team selling," *AMA Winter Educators Conference Proceedings*, 10: 169.

Rogers, P., and Lea, M. (2005). "Social presence in distributed group environments: the role of social identity," *Behaviour and Information Technology*, 24/2: 151–8.

Seers, A. (1989). "Team-member exchange quality: a new construct for role-making research," *Organizational Behavior and Human Decision Process*, 43: 118–35.

——Keller, T., and Wilkerson, J. M. (2003). "Can team members share leadership? Foundations in research and theory," in C. L. Pearce and J. A. Conger (eds.), *Shared Leadership: Reframing the Hows and Whys of Leadership*. Thousand Oaks, CA: Sage Publications, 77–101.

Siebdrat, F., Hoegl, M., and Ernst, H. (2009). "How to manage virtual teams," *MIT Sloan Management Review*, 50/4: 63–8.

Tjosvold, D. (1995). "Cooperation theory, constructive controversy, and effectiveness: learning from crisis," in R. A. Guzzo and E. A. A. Salas (eds.), *Team Effectiveness and Decision Making in Organizations*. San Francisco: Jossey-Bass, 79–112.

Toor, S.-u.-R., and Ofori, G. (2008). "Leadership for future construction industry: agenda for authentic leadership," *International Journal of Project Management*, 26/6: 620–30.

Uhl-Bien, M., Marion, R., and McKelvey, B. (2007). "Complexity leadership theory: shifting leadership from the industrial age to the knowledge era," *Leadership Quarterly*, 18/4: 298–318.

Vaccaro, A., Veloso, F., and Brusoni, S. (2009). "The impact of virtual technologies on knowledge-based processes: an empirical study," *Research Policy*, 38/8: 1278–87.

West, M. A. (1996). "Reflexity and work group effectiveness: a conceptual integration," in M. A. West (ed.), *Handbook of Work Group Psychology*. London: Wiley, 555–79.

CHAPTER 21

PROJECTS-AS-PRACTICE

NEW APPROACH, NEW INSIGHTS

MARKUS HÄLLGREN

ANDERS SÖDERHOLM

INTRODUCTION

The realization of a project involves many tasks, such as ensuring sufficient funds, preparing plans, writing reports, and meeting with contractors and steering committees. The amount of work can place a significant amount of stress on the people involved, which can lead to burn-out, family problems, or simply long hours at work. The everyday work of project members, including managers, engineers, steering committee members, project contractors, and clients, deserves serious attention but has not been the subject of a great deal of research to date.

Research on projects can be roughly divided into two main streams. The first is a traditional and somewhat structural stream in which the focus is on best practice and the development of tools and models. The second stream is more process oriented and is primarily empirical, with a descriptive focus. Whereas the first, or traditional, stream focuses on methods, organizational form, routine, and leadership styles, the second, or process, stream emphasizes change, social processes, and organizational and business development. Because it takes an interest in why and how certain series of events evolve the way they do, the process approach comes closer to understanding human behavior. However, both streams are typically based on assumptions of practice, the practice itself is too often taken for granted, and the basis of the assumptions is obscured in details. The result of this is that the role of people and their actions in accomplishing the project—the full dynamic—is not properly laid out and understood.

The prime focus of this chapter is projects-as-practice based in the social sciences, and it suggests that the situated practice side of a social phenomenon is also important as a basis of study for understanding what is done. While the study is empirical, it focuses on the actions and actors involved in building or organizing environments, rather than simply looking at aggregated social processes or structures. With this approach, projects are seen as the sum of the actions of the people involved, which emphasizes both how people involved in projects act and how their typical workdays are structured. This may shed light on areas such as the importance of project management practice for strategic organizational change (Balogun 2007) or the improvisation that is necessary for project execution (Lindahl 2003). Drawing on what has been called the "practice turn" in social sciences (Schatzki, Knorr Cetina, and Von Savigny 2001), this chapter addresses the projects-as-practice approach with the purpose of presenting an overview of the approach and its benefits for a deeper understanding of projects.

Positioning projects-as-practice

Recent practice research has been addressed as a distinct phenomenon in relation to other areas of research (Schatzki, Knorr Cetina, and Von Savigny 2001; Reckwitz 2002), including product development (Orlikowsk, 2002), strategy (Balogun 2007), and, more recently, projects (e.g. Bechky 2006; Blomquist et al. 2010). The purpose of projects-as-practice is not to replace existing research on projects, which takes either the traditional, structural approach or the more human-oriented process approach. By sharing some features from both approaches, this chapter will differentiate the process and practice approaches (for the differences from the traditional approach, please refer, for example, to Cimil and Hodgson 2006).

The process approach focuses on human activities over time. As a result, it pays greater attention to the complexities of organizing (Cicmil and Hodgson 2006: 10) and views projects as continuous developments, emphasizing the longitudinal in the past, the present, and the future. The process approach is generally considered to have emerged in Scandinavia in the mid 1990s. The Scandinavian School of project management is often synonymous with the process approach. One important contribution came from Kreiner (1995), who analyzed how environments could drift over time and create new contingencies for a project, while project processes could have difficulty adapting to the new environment. A similar observation, albeit one that comes mainly from a project internal perspective, was made by Lundin and Söderholm (1995), who discussed the different action orientations at various stages of the project process. Midler (1995) took yet another process approach, observing how a particular R&D endeavor changed its processes. A more recent contribution is that of Brady and Davies (2004), who discussed phases of learning (a "vanguard project" phase, a "project-to-project" phase, and a "project-to-organization" phase), which occur when a firm moves into a new market/technology.

A process approach makes the findings contextually dependent and socially sensitive. Although both the traditional and process approaches have made valuable contributions in terms of developing tools and attending to social considerations, they both lack the ability to explain the situated activities of human beings, which suggests that the process approach does not incorporate the implications of actions in its final conclusions. Some process studies are more structural, investigating the process from a top-down perspective. Others are closer to the practice approach and oriented towards understanding situated activities. Process approaches with an interest in specific situations come close to investigating the same phenomena as projects-as-practice but in a slightly different way that leads them in a somewhat different direction. One example would be Alsakini, Wikström, and Kiiras's (2004) study of how planning is affected by deviations. That study provided few details of situated activities and practice and, therefore, did not provide any clues to how things are managed.

Projects-as-practice grew from a critique of how previous approaches treated project activities as something that organizations applied normatively, regardless of their contexts and less as situated activities accomplished in a social setting. This is not to say that previous approaches were wrong, just that they were different. Prior to examining the practice approach in detail, some important differences between the process and practice approaches need to be considered in order to avoid confusion (see Table 21.1).

- A practice approach focuses upon the activities and the practice, per se, and their meaning in a specific social setting. A process approach, on the other hand, focuses on how the activities flow and the development over time (specifically, how the project evolves). When activities are the point of departure for analysis there is a minor overlap between the two. The difference lies mainly in the purpose of the study. In a practice approach the activities are seen as both a part of the origin, and a consequence, of the practice. Here the understanding of the practice, of which activities are an essential part, is the final outcome of the study. In a process approach on the other hand the activities are the means for understanding the process. In this case the understanding of the process is the final outcome.
- A practice approach treats the project as the constantly renegotiated sum of the activities of the individuals involved, whereas a process approach tends to treat a project as something that the organization has. Treating the project as the property of the organization with certain content (tools, methods, etc.) assumes that people will behave in a certain fashion. Potential shortcomings of a process approach include inability to understand processes that does not follow a defined model.

- The practice approach is concerned with how practice comes about, whereas the process approach is more interested in change over time than in development. From a practice approach, for example, the way in which the project manager visualizes the concurrent engineering practice in the project plan's Gantt chart is of more interest than how the concurrent engineering shapes the project processes. From a practice approach, these activities, performed while sitting in front of the computer screen, are important for gaining an understanding of subsequent practice. The value of this approach is that the development of the Gantt chart, for example, helps explain the subsequent organization of the project team and their activities. In a broader sense, the processes do not explain what people do and, therefore, do not explain the assumptions that form the basis of the processes.
- A practice approach tends to call for more intimate situated investigations through participant observations studies, whereas a process approach often examines the focal object from an organizational point of view and through case studies and interviews. The practice approach, therefore, tends to examine the phenomenon under study more closely, placing less emphasis on the case and more on the activities, which provides additional details to the process concepts.
- The practice approach assumes that what people do, in its mundane, routine micro-details, has an impact on how the task is achieved. The practice approach therefore deals with "the nitty gritty work of practitioners" (Whittington 1996: 732). A process approach, on the other hand, cannot provide this understanding because it lacks details and interest in the social setting in which the practice was executed; it is therefore more of a longitudinal top-down perspective. When the details of what is happening are understood from the practice-based, bottom-up perspective, it provides a second perspective for an understanding of processes, the use of tools, and the impact of structures.
- Consequently, differing research questions may be posed from the two approaches. An example of a research question from a practice approach could be "How is the project execution reflected in the practice of developing the Gantt chart in a construction project?" A research question from a process approach could be "What are the milestones in the concurrent engineering process?"

From these different understandings, several researchers have come to focus on the mundane details of work (e.g. Blackburn 2002; Bragd 2002; Lindahl 2003; Engwall and Westling 2004; Sapsed and Salter 2004; Hellström and Wikström 2005; Karrbom-Gustafsson 2006; Bechky 2006; Simon 2006; Cicmil et al. 2006; Jarzabkowski and Fenton 2006; Whittington et al. 2006, Molloy and Whittington 2006; Balogun 2007; Hällgren 2009; Hällgren and Wilson 2007; Söderholm 2008; Berggren, Järkvik, and Söderlund 2008; Jerbrant 2009). This focus, which has been termed "projects-as-practice," and which the studies above can be seen as examples of, indicates a sincere interest in the workings of a project. It also involves paying

Table 21.1 Comparison: practice approach and process approach

	PRACTICE APPROACH	PROCESS APPROACH
The role of activities	The activities and their meaning in a specific social setting, explain how the practice comes about	The activities and how they flow, and their general development over time, explain the function of the processes
Relation to the empirical setting	Viewed as the constantly renegotiated sum of people's practice	Viewed as behaving according to a certain pattern
Point of interest	Emphasis is on how a particular part of the project is achieved through micro-level practice	Emphasis is on how things change on an organizational level
Type of investigation	Traditionally rely on participant observations	Traditionally rely on interviews
Research perspective	The understanding is constructed from a bottom-up perspective of the organization	The understanding is constructed with a top-down longitudinal perspective on the organization
Example of research question	How is the project execution reflected in the practice of developing the Gantt chart in a construction project?	What are the milestones in the concurrent engineering process?
Examples of studies	Bechky (2006); Whittington et al. (2006); Hällgren and Wilson (2007)	Lundin and Söderholm (1995); Midler (1995); Brady and Davies (2004)

attention to "the situated doing of the individual human beings (micro) and to the different socially defined practices (macro) that the individuals are drawing upon in these doings" (Jarzabkowski, Balogun, and Seidl 2007: 7). The focus is therefore on the inseparable relationship between the micro (human beings and their actions) and the macro (the social and structural forces of society) (Whittington 2006: 614). It is crucial to acknowledge that it is not a case of either praxis or practices (discussed in detail later) but the simultaneous combination of the two, which puts emphasis on the "site" in which a certain practice occurs. The concept of "site" should not be confused with, for example, a construction site. As Schatzki (2003) explained, the term goes beyond the physical place. In order to avoid confusion, Schatzki's concept is written with quotation marks as "site":

Site ontologies contend that social life, by which I mean human coexistence, is inherently tied to a type of context in which it occurs. The contexts involved, sites, are contexts of which some of what exists or occurs within them are inherently parts. Site ontologies maintain that social phenomena can only be analyzed by examining the sites where human coexistence transpires. (Schatzki 2003: 175–6)

Therefore, a practice approach would emphasize how the practice is located and created in the site. However, a site is not only a physical place where a bundle of praxis occurs, but also a social and institutional context for actions or projects. A situation is, in itself, a continuously negotiated part of situated activities and social practices, the emphasis of which is not on the situation but the praxis (the situated doings), practices (the norms, values, routines, and rules that are drawn upon when acting), and on the ones that act, the practitioners. These three concepts are tied together in episodes of practice, such as a meeting or a project (Hendry and Seidl 2003). In order to explain practice it is necessary to look out for episodes and the meeting between the three concepts of praxis, practices, and practitioners.

CORE CONCEPTS FOR UNDERSTANDING PROJECTS-AS-PRACTICE

Praxis

Praxis is the situated doings of an individual. Therefore, it is not seen as an activity that occurs in isolation without any context, but rather as a part of a whole, the "site," to which the praxis is related. In a product development project, therefore, praxis would typically involve the creation of the project plan, debriefings to steering committees, and, in its simplicity, the creation of PowerPoint slides for a presentation. Praxis may be informal or formal, or more or less peripheral in relation to the object of study, that is, the project (Whittington 2006: 619). From a practice approach, no activity is too small to deserve attention; an email sent in anger, for example, could change the course of the events in a project. When a situated activity is related to the object, for example, a hired consultant's phone call to a colleague regarding a project in which he or she is involved, it may involve situated actions that are worthy of interest. Praxis is, therefore, the work that "gets the job done," implying that it is not necessarily following the plan or rules but rather utilizing tools and methods in order to finish the task.

There are several studies that describe how "the job gets done," including Nilsson (2008), who studied the work (praxis) of a project manager. His analysis showed how the praxis relates to the practices (focusing primarily on the knowledge areas in the PMBoK). A similar study is Hällgren and Wilson's (2008) study of the management of deviations in projects. In their study of diesel power plants they found that project managers typically assembled ad hoc response teams whenever it was deemed necessary in order to come to terms with a certain deviation. A typical feature of these studies is that they maintained the detail of the work without making assumptions about how the work should be done. The studies described in detail how the work got done, the situations in which the response teams were called together, and what practices triggered those situations. The lesson is that project work is seldom just about tools; rather it is constant small changes in the activities that keep naturally unstable projects stable.

Practices

Practices are the norms, values, rules, and policies that are drawn upon when executing a project (Whittington 2006: 620). Practices are routinized behavior that is embodied in different layers of the human existence and the resources with which the job gets done. This includes knowledge of how to use a tool such as Microsoft Project or how to get a contractor to work extra hard. Praxis is governed by practices and practices are constructed out of praxis. When a person acts in a certain way, they do so based on their preconceptions about the situation. The person will draw upon previous knowledge in order to make sense of the situation, and these new experiences will influence future behavior.

While much practice research focuses on the micro level of practices, practices are not limited to the micro level: they exist on both a meso and a macro level (Whittington 2006: 620). However, the levels cannot necessarily be separated in ways other than theoretically, as they all tie together and influence the behavior of the practitioner. Micro-level practices are those routines that describe how the works get done, such as meetings. Meso-level practices describe organizational or sub-organizational practices, such as how a certain project model is utilized. Macro-level practices are those extra-organizational practices that govern the general behavior of a firm. These can be fads and trends in the industry or regulations that specify omission rates or quality assurance, for example.

There are plenty of examples of practices at all levels. On a micro level, Söderholm (2008) showed how unexpected events are managed in four different contexts. He found that the managers either took innovative action, applying detachment strategies from other project activities, setting up intensive meeting schedules or negotiated project conditions. On a meso level, Hellström and Wikström (2005) showed how competition in the distributed power industry has created a concurrent and modularized way of organizing and executing projects. On a macro level, the standards influence what can be expected from a project manager. On a macro level, Sapsed and Salter (2004) demonstrated the role of project management tools as boundary objects for knowledge-sharing among distributed teams.

Practitioners

Practitioners are the people who interpret and execute the praxis and practices. Put simply, "practitioners are those who do the work of making, shaping and executing [projects]" (Whittington 2006: 619). Managers have traditionally been the focus of studies of practitioners in both management and project management, but a project practitioner could also be anyone involved in the making, shaping, and execution of the project, such as consultants, steering committee members, contractors, line managers. However, the roles and practices of these examples are far less researched and understood.

Gaddis (1959) argued that the project manager's task is to be "the man between," although he did not describe in detail what that entails. Simon (2006) studied computer game development project managers and found that their days were quite fragmented. In his study of the software industry, Nilsson (2008) also found that project managers' days were highly fragmented because of their relations with different levels, activities, and issues in the organization. Nilsson connected this understanding to the use of formal project management tools and routines and how those formal practices may or may not be related to everyday activities. Another important contribution to understanding the work of a project manager, this time from a knowledge perspective, was made by Bragd (2002), who studied how a car is developed. Bragd followed a project manager closely through meetings and everyday challenges and was able to show how a car emerges and takes shape.

Without practitioners there would be no way to identify praxis or practices; this means that practitioners are typically one of the obvious analytical units from the perspective of the practice approach. There remains a lot to learn about the activities of project managers (Crawford et al. 2006) and other practitioners related to projects.

UNDERSTANDING PRACTICE: A POWER PLANT EXAMPLE

Practice is where the words and actions of the participants meet and integrate. The praxis is inseparable from the practices that govern activities and, together, they form the practice of project management (cf. Reckwitz 2002: 249). For example, a practice might include having knowledge about how to produce an acceptable Gantt chart or conduct discussions with a contractor. A practice approach unveils other aspects of an empirical situation, compared to other project management research approaches, simply because different questions are asked when practice is considered first.

Instead of evaluating, describing, or developing tools used in projects, a projects-as-practice research question would analyze how people relate to the tools available, how they interpret and embed tools in a context of different practitioners and with parallel tools. A recent study looked at the project deliveries of a major power solutions provider (Hällgren 2009) and one practice used to facilitate project progress was meetings. In addition to being a rational part of the project management tool box, meetings were also a sense-making activity and an opportunity to gain support for various considerations on how to proceed. Meetings were considered important in many cases when project progress was disturbed by deviations in the project activities. A meeting practice with negotiations and sense-making activities helped getting the project back on track and made it possible to rearrange project activities, negotiate new agreements within existing contracts, and streamline the understanding of what had happened and needed to be done. Meetings were followed by intensive periods of activities that were novel in terms of not having been expected or described in plans but still highly relevant for the execution of the project. This is an understanding that is not commonly offered from a longitudinal process approach.

When observations were aggregated it became evident that a substantial part of the project management team's activities actually focused on solving short-term problems or ensuring that project progress was secured despite constant deviations from the original plans. On this basis, a renewed understanding of the project challenges could be designed. It includes an understanding of how traditional project management tools could be used to enhance understanding, facilitate negotiations, and create mutual sense-making in the project.

In somewhat more abstract fashion, the past, present, and future melt together into a shared sense-giving episode during the meeting (cf. Hendry and Seidl 2003). The practice is co-created and shared among the participants, which allows them to stay in business together. The situatedness of the actions has thus occurred within meetings and been constructed, taking into account past knowledge and future expectations of the involved practitioners. This, in essence, is how practice emerges.

The meeting activities themselves are part of a broader set of events and activities. For example, there were developments prior to the meeting that made the project manager increasingly worried and angry. Situated activities prior to the required meeting involved numerous emails, threats, and other conversations. Examining the practice prior to the meeting makes it possible to understand the meeting itself differently; more importantly, the meeting can be seen as the culmination of an issue rather than the issue itself.

By putting the meeting into context but also maintaining the focus on deviations and how they occur throughout a project, the practice of meetings is seen as one of several ways to manage deviations. Other ways include reports for management or informal discussions with contractors, project report meetings, or accepting deficiencies in order to create goodwill. The common denominator is that these practices link to one another in the management of deviations. The practices are not necessarily described in formal means but instead are developed by iteration. The purpose of the practice is to manage the deviation by isolating the deviating situation, managing the deviation separately from other activities within the project and continuously relating the activities associated with the deviation to the plan until the deviation is resolved. In order to achieve the isolation the situation must be collectively accepted as problematic, uncertain, and thereby ensuring the right to do something different than the original plan. This places demands on project members to convince their counterparts that something must be done. Thus, by advocating uncertainty, the project team achieves isolation through the deviation. If this is drawn to its natural conclusion, it allows the project to continue since other activities in the project remain unaffected.

The isolation of deviations is achieved through the project members' practice. Through this practice projects can be understood as somewhere where uncertainty and management thereof is natural. This management of uncertainty is both key to understanding what is happening and key to keeping the project on track. The actions of the practitioners can be seen as part of a general "site" that creates and molds the project (Schatzki 2003). In analytical terms, praxis, practices, and practitioners combined in the study to deliver an understanding of the interrelatedness of the concepts and to show how they impact project management activities and progress. This understanding is created differently than other approaches in that it does not assume that uncertainty is inherently bad and it is not managed through conventional actions. Instead, the understanding is based on specific situated activities that are formed by the "site" of which it is a part.

The above is only an illustration of how a projects-as-practice approach can move research on projects into new paths, asking novel questions and providing analysis from a different, but still useful, angle. The next section will discuss some contributions and major challenges facing projects-as-practice research.

CHALLENGES AND CONTRIBUTIONS OF THE PROJECTS-AS-PRACTICE APPROACH

Two key challenges need to be considered. First, projects-as-practice, as defined here, searches for valuable insights based on research into micro-activities. Such observations must be connected or embedded in larger patterns of individuals, groups, organizations and even society. Defining and analyzing the embeddedness of a practice is a "pattern challenge." Secondly, the research must always be of importance for an audience out of the immediate vicinity of the researcher or empirical instances; this is a "relevance challenge."

Of course, these challenges are not restricted to a practice approach, per se. However, overcoming them is particularly important for proving and improving the usefulness of a projects-as-practice approach for the project management knowledge domain.

Pattern challenge

The pattern challenge is how to move from observations of particular issues to more general conclusions (Smyth and Morris 2007). It is evident that a single set of observations carries limited explanations of what it takes to manage a project. One way to create patterns is to define what kind of situation is being observed and to see more general issues that are dealt with in a specific situation with a beginning and end. This would be an episode of project practice in which praxis, practices, and practitioners meet (Hendry and Seidl 2003: 180). Analyzing the brief empirical example of meetings (presented above) would be quite uninteresting unless meeting practices could be claimed to be an important part of general project management activities. The practice is lifted to a more general issue of accomplishing projects by emphasizing that meetings are held in and are a part of a social context. It is also possible to connect activities of a certain period to both past experiences and future expectations in order to identify a more general pattern. For an understanding of what is occurring in projects, beyond assumptions of the activities, it is important to pay attention to the local praxis of those involved in projects.

A second way to create patterns is to analyze what different situations have in common, and practitioners often do this by developing a joint understanding of events. Before the meeting described above, the project manager had held extensive discussions with people at the company level regarding how the problematic situation could be resolved. Certain interpretations, or conceptualizations, of the problem were then presented to the logistics representatives at the meeting (in addition to what they had received in the form of emails and phone calls). As the meeting progressed the participants came to share a similar, although not identical, view of the problem, which allowed them to discuss the issues. This allowed the meeting to contribute to sense-making among the practitioners and thus to the framing of joint interpretations, expectations, and activity patterns.

A third way to meet the pattern challenge is to examine the interconnectedness between praxis, practices, and practitioners. Being part of the same "site" (Schatzki 2003), which consists of episodes of practice (Hendry and Seidl 2003), inevitably forces praxis, practices, and practitioners to become parts of each other. Jarzabkowski, Balogun, and Seidl (2007) suggested that a study does not necessarily need to focus on all three but that the aspects that receive less focus will unavoidably be a part of the study and therefore need some representation. One example of this is how the project manager carefully prepared the meeting by engaging a number of people, ensuring line management support and also discussing issues with all parties prior to the meeting, including the supplier. At the same time, project management plans were examined and estimates were considered regarding the consequences for the overall project in terms of money and time. The actions involved the engagement of practitioners, displayed company praxis, and relied on practices applied in situations of this kind. This suggests that meetings are a way to investigate organization-specific practices as well as project management praxis.

A fourth issue to consider is that praxis is not ad hoc. Actions are driven by mechanisms that are part of the company's formal routines and procedures but also part of general bodies of knowledge (Whittington 2006), in this case for project management. For instance, Hodgson (2004) found that projects were heavily dependent on traditional bureaucratic principles, as opposed to the de-bureaucratization, flexibility, and freedom that contemporary management literature often attaches to project management. Project management tools such as earned value, status reports, Critical Path methods, and Gantt charts provide ample opportunities for bureaucracy. Tools and techniques influence what is done and how it is done. Project management activities such as meetings can therefore be used as episodes to be analyzed in order to understand how tools are used, for what purposes, and with which frequency or intensity. The challenge is to understand that what appears as a random and ad hoc activity when observed can in fact be deeply founded in routines and procedures, and what happens is part of changing or stabilizing certain behavior. One implication of this is that bringing in a consultant may very well change not only the course of events but also the way in which future projects are executed. This would be one reason why consultants are often brought in to facilitate change.

Relevance challenge

The relevance challenge focuses on the usefulness or implications of research carried out for a domain of knowledge. Schatzki (2003) discusses "sites" as social phenomena of which, for example, a project is a part. The "site" thus goes beyond the physical space in which the project is executed. Understanding the "site" is a core challenge for researchers, regardless of whether they take the traditional approach or a process-oriented approach. The difference is that the "site" is formally recognized as something larger than the physical context, not just as where the tools are applied (as in the first case) or where the process occurs (in the latter case). As noted above, the "site" is where praxis, practices, and practitioners are intertwined. Researching practice therefore involves research and an understanding of a specific "site" in which a certain practice takes place. An important part of the research agenda is to define the "site" and identify its particular characteristics in order to understand its influence and contributions to and from the general.

The challenge is to define the "site" for which the empirical observations, such as meetings, are of interest, in this case project organizations. As described above, meetings are part of an engineering culture, a corporate setting, and a customer relation. In the absence of an established link between empirical observations or empirical instances and the "site," there is a chance that research will be too abstract and reduced to a set of observations. However, it is not sufficient to simply establish the link. The consequences should also be investigated and analyzed in order to understand the development of a certain practice.

It can be difficult to avoid jumping to conclusions on how to define a "site," This is also the stage at which conflicts may arise between a projects-as-practice approach and the other approaches that are more on the generalizability side of studies. For example, it could go wrong if the Project Management Body of Knowledge (PMBoK), or another similar model of project management tasks and issues, is used as a description or list of the available research issues. Furthermore, based on a projects-as-practice approach, it may be difficult to research empirical issues topic by topic according to PMBoK definitions, especially since empirical issues and theoretical definitions rarely correspond exactly.

From this angle, textbook versions of projects are "espoused theories" (Argyris 1976) that have distinct value as models to be used by practitioners deciding what to do, how to do it, and in what order. However, they are not valid models as starting points for defining the "site" for the research. That said, as long as these practices (PMBoK and the like) are recognized for what they are, they can be important and influential tools that can contribute to successful projects. Instead, relevance needs to be sought when defining the "site" of the "theories in use," to follow up on Argyris's concepts. A practice approach does not assume that routines (or bodies of knowledge) are followed; instead the focus is on what happens in terms of, for example, phone calls, emails, meetings, discussions, social relations, and status reports within a "site."

A "site" therefore provides the context for the research. Because the "site" is dependent and provides an understanding of the empirical situation and how it is organized, it must be defined and understood with reference to a research problem and a theoretical angle. "Site" definitions may therefore have to evolve as the research is carried out in case the empirical environment turns out to be different from what was expected. In theoretical terms, "site" definitions can rely on any one, or a combination, of the core concepts and, consequently, can focus on the practitioner, the praxis in action, or the practices used. Having said that, independent of the strategy used to define the "site," the desired result is a context for the research that makes the analysis relevant for theory development and/or management practice.

It is important to understand that a "site" is not a single-level concept. Praxis is applicable and affects at least three empirical levels: micro (the individual), meso (the group, the project, the company), and macro (the society). It can also affect various analytical layers, such as historical, social, cultural, and institutional layers. Turning to the example again, the interpretation could be done on a micro level (for example, the silence of some individuals), the meso level (on the company's meeting traditions), and the macro level (on how contractors are usually retained for reasons of convenience and for the comfort of joint routines). Several different interpretations become possible, with equal and rightful explanatory power on different levels. The multitude of possible analyses is another way of emphasizing the need to define the "site" and the analytical ambitions of academics, as well as defining what empirical instances to research. Data can be impossible to understand without an understanding of what it constitutes and what it is a part of.

Contributions

The contribution of the practice approach is quite intuitive to the practitioner, with an explicit focus on everyday activities and "how things are done around here." It speaks to the practitioner in that it is "descriptions of what really goes on." The practice approach is a search for the micro activities, the often mundane, dull details of the tasks that make up most of the working lives of practitioners. In doing this, projects-as-practice contributes to an understanding of those details that are typically forgotten and/or considered too insignificant to deserve attention and explanatory value. For example, "how things are done" allows the practitioner to know which short cuts are allowed and which ones are off limits. This allows the projects-as-practice approach to reveal secrets and practices that go beyond common sense and, on the surface, a visible understanding of project work. Projects-as-practice therefore contributes with complementary and contradictory analyses that can trigger change in organizations and allow a practitioner to reflect upon his or her practice. Although not applicable to all contexts, these short cuts are a natural part of the minor activities that fill a working day. The projects-as-practice approach can make a significant contribution to research in terms of how patterns are shaped and how details can explain how projects come about. This is shown, for example, in the work by Bechky (2006) on how roles are created in and from the practices on a movie set and the crucial role this plays in the movie's production. The shift from a film to another kind of project is not great, especially given that the same phenomenon is found in general organizational research. Bechky therefore moves beyond the specific context and provides insights into how ordinary projects function. Balogun (2007), on the other hand, found that project management practice was inherently an important part of strategic firm restructuring. She concluded that the practice through which the restructuring occurred contributed to significant changes in sense-making and how the changes were perceived.

An important contribution comes when an analysis of practice can be aggregated into a more comprehensive understanding of projects or certain aspects of projects. An example of this would be when studies on project planning, project meetings, or project deviation reach conclusions regarding the general management of projects, general project organization conclusions, or discussions on general project management activities. A project-as-practice approach can therefore contribute to a comprehensive understanding of projects as a general management and organization phenomenon. An example of a study that goes this "extra mile" is Engwall and Westling's (2004) study of moments of peripety in product development projects. Their analysis provides insights into how projects were organized to identify solutions to standstills and subsequently finalize the projects.

CONCLUDING REMARKS

The projects-as-practice approach is different from the top-down and process past–present–future approaches that are traditionally used in project management and project organization research. Instead of investigating the efficiency of project management tools or defining best practice, a projects-as-practice approach focuses on how projects are carried out in a social and institutional context under the influence of different praxis (situated activities), practices (norms, values, and routines that are drawn upon when acting), and practitioners (the ones doing the praxis). Essentially, projects-as-practice is interested in activities that comprise the project work and it focuses on organizing rather than organization, on becoming rather than being, on theories in use rather than espoused theories, and on social and institutional embeddedness rather than tool or organization efficiency or effectiveness (cf. Blomquist et al. 2010). This chapter has argued that, from a project-as-practice approach, empirical data is categorized and analyzed not based on established bodies of knowledge but with the purpose of building patterns (and thus models and theories) of relevant project management research.

Following from the need to understand the "site," the research questions, aims, and methodologies that are suitable for studying projects from a practice approach may appear limited to "how" questions and qualitative research in general (and participant observations in particular). Such an assumption is not correct, however.

A practice approach does require a certain sensitivity to situated activities but this can be achieved through a variety of data-gathering techniques such as interviews, observations, field diaries, or surveys. As always, the methodology depends on the questions that are asked.

While the presented and discussed concepts are guides for facilitating an understanding of empirical data, they are also intended to design empirical research. The concepts do not provide an immediate understanding of project management unless they are related to data and, furthermore, used to aggregate the analysis to a more general discussion of patterns of practice in relevant "sites." Consequently, the projects-as-practice approach's contributions to project management are most valuable when conclusions are discussed in terms of pattern and relevance.

Finally, it is worthwhile outlining some research options that would be valuable for developing the practice approach further and for making a comprehensive contribution to the project management field and practice. Many areas deserve future investigation, including the focus on different contexts, both traditional ones such as construction or software projects and also community projects, expedition projects, or movie projects. Other areas of study include detailed accounts of entire projects, from start to finish, and further elaboration on the differences from other approaches. Above all, however, three particular areas could benefit from further development.

1. *Good or bad practice.* Practice can be either good or bad if it is related to areas like project goals, profitability, or the well-being of people. Nothing has been said so far about the relationship between practice and various outcomes of the practice studied. Such a relationship could be established and made a focus of research as well. Research on good versus bad practice needs to be founded on a conscious choice of the variable to be used for defining good or bad. Profitability could be chosen as an example, and a selection of cases within the same corporate or industry setting could be made based on their track record in terms of profitability. A projects-as-practice study would add valuable knowledge as to how poor or excellent profitability has been achieved in terms of the patterns that can be derived from the project practice.

2. *Adding to the best practice agenda.* An important issue to remember is that a projects-as-practice study can be limited to certain aspects of the practice, as was indicated in the discussion on patterns earlier in this chapter. Issues to focus on could be defined, for example, based on the need for inspiration for best practice. Research projects could single out a specific type of praxis or practice in order to determine differences between different "sites" that could, for example, represent different sizes of projects, different types of clients, different industries, or different companies. One example would be a focus on the practice associated with deviations (as mentioned earlier in this text), but other areas such as planning, teamwork, risk assessment, or project formation practice would be equally interesting. A second step could be to take the knowledge gained to redefine and refine

best practice. The benefit would be that data used for best practice development would have been collected and analyzed with the use of a more comprehensive understanding of the practice that best practice is meant to guide.

3. *Projects-as-practice "sites" and episodes.* Core concepts in a project-as-practice research approach have been discussed in this chapter. Some parts of the research approach would benefit from further theoretical elaboration in order to make the approach more coherent. The "site" concept is elaborated upon by Schatzki (2003), among others, with an emphasis on the importance of site ontologies. However, defining the "site" is also an empirical and research design issue since such definitions will have a profound impact on the data that can and will be collected. The "site" is also of importance for analysis since it determines how the interpretation and analysis of data can be aggregated. It would be beneficial for the projects-as-practice approach to discuss and elaborate this further. A study in which a research question is tested against different "site" definitions would be one approach for reaching a better understanding of the "site" concept and the impact of site ontologies. Episodes are another important concept that deserve attention. Episodes are sequences of practice that are tied to each other in one way or another (Hendry and Seidl 2003). However, how they should be defined is a strategic question for each research effort since the definition is dependent on the research focus. An episode is different in a study of project planning than it is in a study of project termination. Another question to determine is whether an episode should be mainly defined from data, that is, a question for empirical research, or if it is a theoretical concept to be defined as one of the data selection and research design decisions. These issues could be further researched in order to improve the projects-as-practice approach.

References

ALSAKINI, W., WIKSTRÖM, K., and KIIRAS, J. (2004). "Proactive schedule management of industrial turnkey projects in developing countries," *International Journal of Project Management*, 22/1: 75–85.

ARGYRIS, C. (1976). "Single-loop and double-loop models in research on decision making," *Administrative Science Quarterly*, 21/3: 363–75.

BALOGUN, J. (2007). "The practice of organizational restructuring: from design to reality," *European Management Journal*, 25/2: 81–91.

BECHKY, B. A. (2006). "Gaffers, gofers, and grips: role-based coordination in temporary organizations," *Organization Science*, 17/1: 3–21.

BERGGREN, C., JÄRKVIK, J., and SÖDERLUND, J. (2008). "Lagomizing, organic integration, and systems emergency wards: innovative practices in managing complex systems development projects," *Project Management Journal*, 39/1: 111–22.

BLACKBURN, S. (2002). "The project manager and the project-network," *International Journal of Project Management*, 20/3: 199–204.

BLOMQUIST, T., HÄLLGREN, M., NILSSON, A., and SÖDERHOLM, A. (2010). "Project as practice: making project research matter," *Project Management Journal*, accepted for publication.

BRADY, T., and DAVIES, A. (2004). "Building project capabilities: from exploratory to exploitative learning," *Organization Studies*, 25/9, Special Issue on "Project-Based Organizations, Embeddedness and Repositories of Knowledge": 1601–22.

BRAGD, A. (2002). "Knowing management: an ethnographic study of tinkering with a new car," Ph.D. thesis, School of Economics and Commercial Law at Gothenburg University, Gothenburg.

BROWN, J. S., and DUGUID, P. (1991). "Organizational learning and communities-of-practice: toward a unified view of working, learning and innovation," *Organization Science*, 2/1: 40–57.

CICMIL, S., and HODGSON, D. (2006). "Making projects critical: an introduction," in S. Cicmil and D. Hodgson (eds.), *Making Projects Critical*. New York: Palgrave Macmillan.

——WILLIAMS, T., THOMAS, J., and HODGSON, D. (2006). "Rethinking project management: researching the actuality of projects," *International Journal of Project Management*, 24/8: 675–86.

CRAWFORD, L., MORRIS, P., THOMAS, J., and WINTER, M. (2006). "Practitioner development: from trained technicians to reflective practitioners," *International Journal of Project Management*, 24/8: 722–33.

ENGWALL, M., and WESTLING, G. (2004). "Peripety in an R&D drama: capturing a turnaround in project dynamics," *Organization Studies*, 25/9: 1557–78.

GADDIS, P. O. (1959). "The project manager," *Harvard Business Review*, 27/3: 89–97.

HÄLLGREN, M. (2009). "Avvikelsens mekanismer: Observationer av projekt i praktiken" ["The mechanisms of deviations: observations of projects in practice"], Ph.D. thesis, Umeå University, Umeå.

——and WILSON, T. (2007). "Mini muddling: learning from project plan deviations," *Journal of Workplace Learning*, 19/2: 92–107.

————(2008). "The nature and management of crises in construction projects: projects-as-practice observations," *International Journal of Project Management*, 26/8: 830–8.

HELLSTRÖM, M., and WIKSTRÖM, K. (2005). "Project business concepts based on modularity-improved manoeuvrability through unstable structures," *International Journal of Project Management*, 23/5: 392–7.

HENDRY, J., and SEIDL, D. (2003). "The structure and significance of strategic episodes: social systems theory and the routine practices of strategic change," *Journal of Management Studies*, 40/1: 175–97.

HODGSON, D. E. (2004). "Project work: the legacy of bureaucratic control in the post-bureaucratic organization," *Organization*, 11/1: 81–100.

JARZABKOWSKI, P., BALOGUN, J., and SEIDL, D. (2007). "Strategizing: the challenges of a practice perspective," *Human Relations*, 60/1: 5–27.

——and FENTON, E. (2006). "Strategizing and organizing in pluralistic contexts," *Long Range Planning*, 39/6: 631–48.

JERBRANT, A. (2009). "Organisering av projektbaserade företag: Ledning, styrning och genomförande av projektbaserad industriell verksamhet" ["Organizing of project based companies: management and execution of project based industrial activity"], Ph.D. thesis, Royal Institute of Technology, Stockholm.

Karrbom-Gustafsson, T. (2006). "Det tillfälliga praktik: om möten och småprat som organiserande mekanismer i anläggningsprojekt" ["The practice of the temporary: about meetings and small talk as organizing mechanisms in project-based industrial business"], Ph.D. thesis, Royal Institute of Technology, Stockholm.

Kreiner, K. (1995). "In search of relevance: project management in drifting environments," *Scandinavian Journal of Management*, 11/4: 335–46.

Lindahl, M. (2003). "Produktion till varje pris: om planering och improvisation i anläggningsprojekt" ["Production to any price: about planning and improvisation in construction projects"], Ph.D. thesis, The Department of Industrial Management, Royal Institute of Technology, Stockholm.

Lundin, R. A., and Söderholm, A. (1995). "A theory of the temporary organization," *Scandinavian Journal of Management*, 11/4: 437–55.

Midler, C. (1995). "'Projectification' of the firm: the Renault case," *Scandinavian Journal of Management*, 11/4: 363–75.

Molloy, E., and Whittington, R. (2006). "Reorganisation projects and five uncertainties," in S. Cicmil and D. Hodgson (eds.), *Making Projects Critical*. New York: Palgrave Macmillan.

Nilsson, A. (2008). "Projektledning i Praktiken: Observationer av projektledares arbete i korta project" ["Project management in practice: observations of the work of project managers in short-duration projects"], Ph.D. thesis, Umeå University, Umeå.

Orlikowski, W. J. (2002). "Knowing in practice: enacting a collective capability in distributive organizing," *Organization Science*, 13/3: 249–73.

Reckwitz, A. (2002). "Toward a theory of social practices: a development in culturalist theorizing," *European Journal of Social Theory*, 5/2: 243–63.

Sapsed, J., and Salter, A. (2004). "Postcards from the edge: local communities, global programs and boundary objects," *Organization Studies*, 25/9: 1515–34.

Schatzki, T. R. (2003). "A new societist social ontology," *Philosophy of the Social Sciences*, 33/2: 174–202.

——Knorr Cetina, K., and Von Savigny, E. (2001). *The Practice Turn in Contemporary Theory*. New York: Routledge.

Simon, L. (2006). "Managing creative projects: an empirical synthesis of activities," *International Journal of Project Management*, 24/2: 116–26.

Smyth, H. J., and Morris, P. W. G. (2007). "An epistemological evaluation of research into projects and their management: methodological issues," *International Journal of Project Management*, 25/4: 423–36.

Söderholm, A. (2008). "Project management of unexpected events," *International Journal of Project Management*, 26/1: 80–6.

Whittington, R. (1996). "Strategy as practice," *Long Range Planning*, 29/5: 731–5.

——(2006). "Completing the practice turn in strategy research," *Organization Studies*, 27/5: 613–34.

——Molloy, E., Mayer, M., and Smith, A. (2006). "Practice of strategising/organising: broadening strategy work and skills," *Long Range Planning*, 39/6: 615–29.

Author Index

....

Notes: Page numbers in **bold** indicate chapter extents, and those in *italics* indicate illustrations and diagrams.

SUBJECT INDEX

Notes: Page numbers in **bold** indicate chapter extents, and those in *italics* indicate illustrations and diagrams.